C0-AVX-649

International Dimensions of Monetary Policy

A National Bureau
of Economic Research
Conference Report

International Dimensions of Monetary Policy

Edited by **Jordi Galí and Mark Gertler**

The University of Chicago Press

Chicago and London

Jordi Galí is professor of economics at the Universitat Pompeu Fabra and a research associate of the National Bureau of Economic Research. Mark Gertler is the Henry and Lucy Moses Professor of Economics at New York University and a research associate of the National Bureau of Economic Research.

The University of Chicago Press, Chicago 60637
The University of Chicago Press, Ltd., London

Printed in the United States of America

18 17 16 15 14 13 12 11 10 09 1 2 3 4 5
ISBN-13: 978-0-226-27886-5 (cloth)
ISBN-10: 0-226-27886-7 (cloth)

Library of Congress Cataloging-in-Publication Data

International dimensions of monetary policy / edited by Jordi Galí and Mark Gertler.
p. cm.—(National Bureau of Economic Research conference report)
Papers from a conference held June 2007 in Spain.
Includes bibliographical references and index.
ISBN-13: 978-0-226-27886-5 (alk. paper)
ISBN-10: 0-226-27886-7 (alk. paper)
1. Monetary policy—Congresses. 2. Globalization—Congresses. 3. International finance—Congresses. I. Galí, Jordi, 1961– II. Gertler, Mark. III. Series: National Bureau of Economic Research conference report.
HG230.3.I576 2010
339.5′4—dc22

2009014293

⊗ The paper used in this publication meets the minimum requirements of the American National Standard for Information Sciences—Permanence of Paper for Printed Library Materials, ANSI Z39.48-1992.

Relation of the Directors to the Work and Publications of the National Bureau of Economic Research

1. The object of the NBER is to ascertain and present to the economics profession, and to the public more generally, important economic facts and their interpretation in a scientific manner without policy recommendations. The Board of Directors is charged with the responsibility of ensuring that the work of the NBER is carried on in strict conformity with this object.

2. The President shall establish an internal review process to ensure that book manuscripts proposed for publication DO NOT contain policy recommendations. This shall apply both to the proceedings of conferences and to manuscripts by a single author or by one or more co-authors but shall not apply to authors of comments at NBER conferences who are not NBER affiliates.

3. No book manuscript reporting research shall be published by the NBER until the President has sent to each member of the Board a notice that a manuscript is recommended for publication and that in the President's opinion it is suitable for publication in accordance with the above principles of the NBER. Such notification will include a table of contents and an abstract or summary of the manuscript's content, a list of contributors if applicable, and a response form for use by Directors who desire a copy of the manuscript for review. Each manuscript shall contain a summary drawing attention to the nature and treatment of the problem studied and the main conclusions reached.

4. No volume shall be published until forty-five days have elapsed from the above notification of intention to publish it. During this period a copy shall be sent to any Director requesting it, and if any Director objects to publication on the grounds that the manuscript contains policy recommendations, the objection will be presented to the author(s) or editor(s). In case of dispute, all members of the Board shall be notified, and the President shall appoint an ad hoc committee of the Board to decide the matter; thirty days additional shall be granted for this purpose.

5. The President shall present annually to the Board a report describing the internal manuscript review process, any objections made by Directors before publication or by anyone after publication, any disputes about such matters, and how they were handled.

6. Publications of the NBER issued for informational purposes concerning the work of the Bureau, or issued to inform the public of the activities at the Bureau, including but not limited to the NBER Digest and Reporter, shall be consistent with the object stated in paragraph 1. They shall contain a specific disclaimer noting that they have not passed through the review procedures required in this resolution. The Executive Committee of the Board is charged with the review of all such publications from time to time.

7. NBER working papers and manuscripts distributed on the Bureau's web site are not deemed to be publications for the purpose of this resolution, but they shall be consistent with the object stated in paragraph 1. Working papers shall contain a specific disclaimer noting that they have not passed through the review procedures required in this resolution. The NBER's web site shall contain a similar disclaimer. The President shall establish an internal review process to ensure that the working papers and the web site do not contain policy recommendations, and shall report annually to the Board on this process and any concerns raised in connection with it.

8. Unless otherwise determined by the Board or exempted by the terms of paragraphs 6 and 7, a copy of this resolution shall be printed in each NBER publication as described in paragraph 2 above.

Contents

Introduction

Jordi Galí and Mark Gertler

For much of the postwar period the Federal Reserve conducted monetary policy as if it were a closed economy. This strategy was warranted since international factors did not seem to have much of an effect on U.S. economic performance and they were certainly not central to the policy debate. Globalization, however, is changing this. A combination of a reduction in trading costs, technological developments, and greater integration of goods and capital markets around the globe has tightened the link between national economies. As a result, one would expect international factors to play a growing role in shaping the performance of the U.S. economy. The global nature of the financial and economic crisis that began in the summer of 2007, and the efforts, led by the G20 countries, to coordinate the policy responses, is clear proof of the high degree of interconnectedness among economies, rich and poor.

The implications of this continuing evolution toward globalization for the conduct of monetary policy is a new and important question. The purpose of the volume is to bring together fresh research to address this issue. It contains the ten papers (along with the discussions, speeches, and panelists' remarks) that were presented at the NBER Conference "International Dimensions of Monetary Policy," which was held June 11 through 13, 2007 in the Hostal de la Gavina, located in the catalan village of S'Agaró. The papers presented at the conference and published in the present volume cover what we think are some of the main areas of concern. The broad goal is to provide a starting point for subsequent work on this fresh and exciting topic.

Jordi Galí is a professor of economics at the Universitat Pompeu Fabra and a research associate of the National Bureau of Economic Research. Mark Gertler is the Henry and Lucy Moses Professor of Economics at New York University, and a research associate of the National Bureau of Economic Research.

The chapters have been organized into three parts. The first part, titled "Baseline Models for International Monetary Policy Analysis," contains three chapters that discuss some of the challenges facing open economy extensions of the workhorse monetary model as well as some key implications of those extensions, relative to their closed economy counterparts. The second part, titled "Extending the Baseline Models to Address Policy Issues," develops the baseline open economy model in specific dimensions in order to address the policy implications of three particular issues of interest; namely, current account deficits, dollarization, and imperfect pass-through. The third part, "Empirical Issues in International Monetary Policy Analysis," includes four chapters that provide empirical evidence on four different areas of interest pertaining to the international dimension of monetary policy: the macroeconomic effects of oil price shocks, the role of global factors in shaping the effectiveness of monetary policy, differences between Fed and European Central Bank (ECB) policies, and the impact of globalization on inflation dynamics. In the remainder of this introduction we briefly summarize each of the contributions to the present volume and at the end try to draw some general conclusions.

Baseline Models for International Monetary Policy Analysis

Much of the research on monetary policy and its design conducted over the past decade has relied on closed economy models. That was also a feature of the early estimated medium-scale dynamic stochastic general equilibrium (DSGE) models.[1] Three of the papers presented at the conference examined the implications of introducing open economy elements in otherwise standard optimizing monetary models with nominal rigidities.

The potentially negative effects of globalization on the ability of national central banks to control inflation and output within its own boundaries has become a subject of great controversy in recent years, especially in policy circles. In "Globalization and Monetary Control," this volume's opening chapter, Michael Woodford brings economic theory to bear on this subject. Using a simple two-country version of the new-Keynesian model, Woodford studies three different channels through which globalization is often argued to limit the effectiveness of national monetary policies. Such popular arguments can be summarized as follows. First, highly integrated financial markets may hamper a central bank's ability to influence real interest rates and hence, aggregate demand. Second, the same phenomenon may make it harder for a central bank to control domestic nominal interest rates through changes in the domestic money supply, especially if foreign and domestic currency are viewed as partial substitutes. Finally, domestic inflation may

1. See, for example, Christiano, Eichenbaum, and Evans (2005), and Smets and Wouters (2003, 2007).

have become less responsive to domestic output and more responsive to measures of global slack; this would limit a central bank's effective control of domestic inflation, even if it were to succeed in steering domestic aggregate demand and output at will. Woodford scrutinizes each of these hypotheses under the lens of modern monetary theory, finding little or no support for any of them. Even in the limiting case of an economy of negligible size, with access to complete international financial markets and an arbitrarily large share of foreign goods in the consumption basket of its residents, Woodford's analysis shows how the central bank can still influence decisively domestic economic outcomes and, in particular, can still hold a firm grip on domestic inflation. Furthermore, he shows how the effects of global factors on domestic variables often have the opposite sign from that associated with common views of proponents of a dominant role for those factors. In the final analysis, Woodford's contribution suggests that globalization can be no excuse not to hold central banks accountable for the inflation performance of their respective economies.

In chapter 2 Christopher Erceg, Christopher Gust, and David López-Salido, all of them economists at the Federal Reserve Board, analyze the extent to which openness to trade may influence the economy's response to *domestic* shocks. Their analysis is conducted in terms of two models: a medium-scale two-country model used at the Federal Reserve Board for policy simulations (known as SIGMA), and a two-country version of the Erceg-Henderson-Levin (2000) model. While the former can be viewed as a more realistic model, the latter is more analytically tractable, which helps shed some light on the mechanisms underlying some of the findings. The authors examine the effects of three domestic shocks in each of the models: a permanent decline in the inflation target, a persistent increase in government spending, and a persistent technology shock. For each model and shock they compare the impulse responses of different variables under three different calibrations of the economy's degree of trade openness. For plausible values of the elasticity of substitution between domestic and foreign goods, the chapter's findings point to a small impact of openness on the response of domestic inflation and output to the aforementioned shocks. On the other hand, openness is shown to have a larger impact on the composition of aggregate demand, and on the wedge between consumer price index (CPI) and domestic inflation, in response to the same shocks. A corollary of the chapter's findings is that any substantial differences observed in the volatility and persistence of output and domestic inflation between highly open and relatively closed (but otherwise similar) economies will hardly be attributable to differences in the propagation mechanisms of domestic shocks, but rather must be the consequence of their differential response to shocks in the rest of the world.

Chapter 3 by Gunter Coenen, Giovanni Lombardo, Frank Smets, and Roland Straub (hereafter CLSS), titled "International Transmission and

Monetary Policy Cooperation," revisits a classic theme of international macroeconomics: the gains from policy cooperation in the presence of policy spillovers across countries. In line with other chapters in this volume, CLSS adopt a calibrated two-region DSGE model with nominal rigidities as a framework for their analysis, with which they provide a quantitative evaluation of those cooperation gains. More specifically, they use a version of the New Area-Wide Model (NAWM) developed at the ECB, calibrated to match a number of features of the U.S. and euro area economies. In the context of that model they derive and analyze the properties of the equilibrium under two alternative regimes. Under the cooperative regime, the two central banks implement the policies that jointly maximize a weighted average of the welfare of U.S. and euro area representative consumers. In contrast, under the noncooperative regime each central bank chooses the allocation that maximizes the welfare of its country's representative household, while taking as given the path of the money supply in the other country. A measure of the gains from cooperation can be derived by comparing the welfare of each country under the two regimes. For realistic calibrations of the degree of openness of the U.S. and euro area economies, CLSS find that the eventual gains from cooperation are very small, amounting to less than one-tenth of a percent of steady-state consumption. Furthermore, their analysis shows that such gains are largely the result of the different responses under the two regimes to markup shocks. The latter are the shocks that appear to generate the strongest trade-offs for the policymaker, and hence the greater incentive to export some of its costs to the foreign country. The finding of small welfare gain from cooperation appears to be robust to alternative calibrations of a number of parameters. Only when the openness parameter is assumed to take an unrealistically large value (implying import shares for both areas of about 30 percent) do the gains from cooperation attain values close to 1 percent of consumption. Finally, the findings of CLSS suggest that if simple, self-oriented interest rate rules are pursued by the Fed and the ECB, the losses relative to the full cooperation case will be limited to about one-tenth of steady state consumption.

Extending the Baseline Models to Address Policy Issues

The second block of chapters in the volume address three specific policy issues, using extensions of the baseline model developed with that purpose in mind. The issues addressed include the role and implications for monetary policy of the unwinding of current account balances, the specific challenges facing monetary policy in emerging economies, and the consequences of imperfect exchange rate pass-through for monetary policy design.

A striking feature of global economy has been the emergence of significant imbalances in saving and investment across countries, highlighted by the large and persistent U.S. current account deficit. For two basic reasons, the current imbalances may be relevant for monetary policy. First, as Obstfeld and Rogoff (2006) argue, adjustment of the U.S. current account may involve a substantial depreciation of the dollar. To the extent they are correct, the depreciation will fuel short-run inflationary pressures. Second, even if unlikely, there is the potential for a rapid reversal of the current account, which could have disruptive effects on real economic activity. In chapter 4, Andrea Ferrero, Mark Gertler, and Lars Svensson examine the implications of current account adjustment for monetary policy. In order to study the role of global imbalances, the authors develop a two-country monetary DSGE model with nominal rigidities and incomplete international financial markets. The framework is initialized to match the recent U.S. account deficit as well as its overall indebtedness with respect to the rest of the world. The authors then consider two different adjustment scenarios. The first is a "slow burn" scenario where the adjustment of the current account deficit plays out smoothly and slowly over time. The second is a "fast burn" scenario, where a sudden shift in expectations of relative productivity growth rates leads to a rapid reversal of the home country's current account. Overall, the authors find that good monetary management can significantly mitigate any pain from current account adjustment. A policy that works well under either the slow or fast burn scenarios is domestic inflation targeting. By contrast, attempts to peg the exchange under the fast burn can lead to considerable damage to the economy. On the other hand, CPI inflation targeting is relatively harmful under full exchange rate pass-through, but not so much when the latter is partial.

Most of the chapters in this volume examine the implications of increased openness for monetary policy in the context of industrialized economies. In Chapter 5, Nicoletta Batini, Paul Levine, and Joseph Pearlman consider the ramifications for emerging market economies. As the authors note, for the question at hand there are several aspects that distinguish those economies. First, they typically have less developed financial markets; second, foreign liabilities are generally denominated in foreign currency; and third, foreign currency is often used in some domestic transactions. The authors integrate those features into an open economy monetary DSGE model with nominal rigidities, of the type used elsewhere in the volume. They first confirm the conventional wisdom that the combination of financial market frictions and foreign currency denominated debt enhances the vulnerability of the economy to disturbances. They find, however, that attempting to peg the exchange rate only serves to create more instability, as it leads to movements in interest rates that, in combination with financial factors, only serve to raise the variability of real output. This finding is consistent with Stanley Fischer's observation in the wake of the emerging market crises in Southeast Asia in the late 1990s, that the economies that suffered greater disruptions were those that had fixed exchange rate regimes in place. Targeting CPI inflation (as opposed to domestic inflation) is also rejected by the authors as a desirable strategy, given that it implicitly requires that the nominal exchange rate be (partly) stabilized. At the same time, the authors show that a simple Taylor rule under flexible exchange rates may be problematic due to the lower bound on the nominal interest rate. They then derive an optimal policy in light of this constraint. The policy allows the exchange rate to float but takes into account that the nominal interest rate cannot be negative. Finally, the authors show that the fact that foreign currency may be used for domestic transactions may not pose a significant problem, so long as the country maintains control over its short-term nominal interest rate.

To the extent it encourages greater economic intergration, globalization raises the sensitivity of inflation to movements in exchange rates. Going forward, it is important for central banks interested in maintaining price stability to understand this mechanism and the implications it may have for optimal monetary policy. Developing this understanding is the objective of chapter 6, a contribution to this volume by Giancarlo Corsetti, Luca Dedola, and Sylvain Leduc. The authors begin with the observation that the evidence from industrialized economies suggests that pass-through of exchange rate movements into import prices is imperfect. They then develop a model of imperfect pass-through that is based on a combination of nominal rigidities—importers set prices on a staggered basis—and endogenous destination-specific markup adjustment. The authors then integrate this model of imperfect pass-through into a complete monetary DSGE model with nominal rigidities, in order to study the implications for optimal monetary policy. The authors find that in this kind of environment it is optimal for the central bank to stabilize different components of the CPI, though this policy does not exactly correspond to either targeting of headline inflation or domestic inflation. Furthermore, they show that the optimal policy does not necessarily imply that the real exchange rate should be less volatile than the terms of trade; whether that is the case or not depends on a number of characteristics of the economies involved.

Empirical Issues in International Monetary Policy Analysis

The last papers presented at the conference dealt with four empirical issues: the macroeconomic effects of oil price shocks, the role of global factors in shaping the effectiveness of monetary policy, differences between Fed and ECB policies, and the impact of globalization on inflation dynamics.

In chapter 7, authors Olivier J. Blanchard and Jordi Galí start out by documenting the large output losses and the rises in inflation rates that accompanied the two oil shocks of the 1970s in most industrialized countries, and show the absence of analogous effects in the recent period, even though the rise in oil prices has been of a similar magnitude. Using a Value at Risk (VAR) to identify exogenous oil price shocks, the authors show that the latter can only account for a relatively small part of the stagflationary episodes of the 1970s, suggesting that shocks other than oil but coinciding in time with the latter should also be held responsible for the dismal macroeconomic performance of that period. Interestingly, however, the authors' estimates also point to a much more muted impact of an oil price shock of a given size on both prices and quantities in the period after the mid-1980s, thus suggesting the presence of some structural changes in the economy that might be needed to explain those differences. In the second part of the chapter, Blanchard and Galí put forward three alternative explanations for the dampening effects of oil price shocks: a smaller share of oil in production and consumption, more flexible labor markets, and an enhanced credibility of monetary policy. Using an extension of the new-Keynesian model that incorporates exogenous variations in the price of imported oil, and that is calibrated to the U.S. economy, they evaluate the likely quantitative significance of those three hypothesis, concluding that they all seem to have played a role in explaining the smaller fluctuations in output and inflation resulting from oil price movements.

In chapter 8, Jean Boivin and Marc P. Giannoni develop a Factor-Augmented VAR in order to shed light on the role played by international factors in U.S. economic fluctuations and in the transmission mechanism of U.S. monetary policy. Their approach starts by identifying and estimating a small number of domestic and foreign latent factors that are common to a large set of U.S. and non-U.S. variables. They subsequently model those factors (which include, by construction, the Federal Funds rate) by means of a standard VAR. Overall, Boivin and Giannoni's analysis uncovers a small role for international factors in accounting for fluctuations in U.S. variables. That role appears to have changed over time for some variables, but not always in the upward direction that popular accounts of the impact of the process of globalization on domestic economic performance might suggest. That evidence of a limited role for international factors carries over to measures of the U.S. economy's response to an identified exogenous monetary policy shock: estimates of that response are shown to be largely independent of whether feedback effects from the estimated global factors are allowed for or not, with little evidence found of any changes over time in the significance of those effects.

Within the industrialized world, the two major central banks are the Federal Reserve and the European Central Bank. In chapter 9, Harald Uhlig examines how each central bank has performed in recent years with the aim of understanding the similarities and differences. Uhlig is motivated by the observation that the paths of both interest rates and real output in the two economies have been rather different over the years. As Uhlig notes, it is useful to understand the sources of the differences. In principle they could reflect (a) differences in policy; (b) differences in structure (e.g., flexible versus rigid labor markets, bank versus open market finance, etc.); or (c) differences in the nature of the shocks. To get at the issue, Uhlig estimates a small-scale monetary DSGE model for each country that is flexible enough to allow for differences in policy, structure, and shocks. His principal finding is that the sluggish behavior of the euro area economy relative to the United States primarily reflects differences in shocks. The monetary policy rules of each central bank were not that dissimilar. Rather, the relative U.S. productivity boom and differences in exogenous wage demands across the two regions appears to account for most of the differences in economic behavior. Both central banks appear to agree on the basic template for feedback monetary policy responses.

There has been much speculation among central bankers about how globalization might affect a central bank's ability to stabilize inflation. Indeed, a recent Bank for International Settlements (BIS) study by Borio and Filardo (2006) suggests that globalization may have raised the sacrifice ratio; that is, the percentage reduction in output required to reduce steady state inflation. In chapter 10, Argia Sbordone systematically addresses how globalization may have influenced the short-run Phillips curve trade-off between inflation and output. She begins by developing a Phillips curve relation that stems from optimization-based price setting at the individual firm level. Within this setting firms adjust prices on a staggered basis. How much they adjust depends on the degree of market competition. Sbordone then interprets globalization as inducing a rise in competition through the increase in the number of goods varieties available. She then proceeds to show explicitly how the degree of competition influences the relation between inflation and movements in real marginal cost. The weaker this relation, the more difficult it is to stabilize inflation without incurring undesirable output losses. In general, the chapter shows that the impact of increased competition from globalization has an ambiguous effect on the short-run trade-off between inflation and real activity, though for large changes in the number of goods varieties the sensitivity of inflation to changes in real marginal costs declines, thus flattening the slope of the Phillips curve through this mechanism. Yet Sbordone argues that there is no evidence to presume that the United States is already subject to that negative relationship.

Finally, the conference benefited from a set of interesting speeches by Lucas Papademos and John Taylor, and also a fascinating panel discussion by Donald L. Kohn of the Federal Reserve Board, Rakesh Mohan of the Reserve Bank of India, and José Viñals of the Bank of Spain. We include these in section 4.

Lessons

Despite the diversity of topics and approaches, many of the chapters in the present volume appear to converge in some of their conclusions, in general terms if not in the details. At the risk of oversimplification, one could argue that a common thread of the chapters presented is that, even though rising globalization may have large effects on the allocation of resources and welfare, its impact on short-run fluctuations and stabilization policies is likely to be muted. This is reflected in the following findings:

1. Globalization is unlikely to hamper the ability of central banks to affect output, employment, and inflation, a prediction that seems to be borne by the evidence.

2. The economy's response to domestic shocks is not substantially affected by a rise in trade openness, at least of the magnitude observed in industrialized economies over the past two decades.

3. The size of the policy spillovers that result from the current degree of interconnectedness between economies like the United States and the euro area is not large enough to imply large welfare gains from monetary policy coordination.

4. Globalization does not seem to have significantly affected key U.S. economy's structural relations, including the slope of the Phillips curve.

5. Even in highly open economies, central banks should be advised to pursue policies that focus on stabilization of domestic prices. Pegging the exchange rate or partially stabilizing it through the back door of CPI inflation targeting are not advisable strategies. Only in the presence of a limited pass-through may there be a case for some version of CPI inflation targeting.

6. Improvements in credibility, together with greater flexibility in labor markets, have made it possible for monetary policy to achieve better outcomes in the face of global shocks, like the rise in oil prices. Furthermore, the policy rules of major central banks, like the ECB and the Fed, seem to have converged to a great extent.

Finally, as organizers of the conference and editors of this volume, we want to thank all the authors, discussants, and panelists for the high quality of their contributions. Special thanks goes to Martin Feldstein, who not only proposed the topic, but was the driving force in making the conference come together. We also thank Brett Maranjian from the NBER and Eulàlia Ribas from the Centre de Recerca en Economia Internacional (CREI) for their logistical support, and Helena Fitz-Patrick for her role in putting the volume together. Finally, we want to express our gratitude to the Smith Richardson Foundation for its generous financial support.

References

Borio, C., and A. Filardo. 2006. Globalization and inflation: New cross-country evidence on the global determinants of domestic inflation. Bank for International Settlements (BIS) Working Paper no. 227.

Christiano, L. J., M. Eichenbaum, and C. L. Evans. 2005. Nominal rigidities and the dynamic effects of a shock to monetary policy. *Journal of Political Economy* 113 (1): 1–45.

Erceg, C. J., D. W. Henderson, and A. T. Levin. 2000. Optimal monetary policy with staggered wage and price contracts. *Journal of Monetary Economics* 46 (2): 281–314.

Smets, F., and R. Wouters. 2003. An estimated dynamic stochastic general equilibrium model of the Euro area. *Journal of the European Economic Association* 1 (5): 1123–75.

Smets, F., and R. Wouters. 2007. Shocks and frictions in U.S. business cycles: A Bayesian DSGE approach. *American Economic Review* 97 (3): 586–606.

Obstfeld, M., and K. Rogoff. 2006. The unsustainable U.S. current account position revisited. In *G7 current account imbalances: Sustainability and adjustment,* ed. Richard Clarida, 339–76. Chicago: University of Chicago Press.

I

Baseline Models for International Monetary Policy Analysis

1

Globalization and Monetary Control

Michael Woodford

Concern has recently been expressed in a variety of quarters that the problems facing central banks may be substantially complicated by the increasing globalization of goods markets, factor markets, and financial markets in recent years. Some of the more alarmist views suggest that the very ability of national central banks to materially influence the dynamics of inflation in their countries through monetary policy actions may be undermined by globalization. According to such accounts, the recently observed low and stable inflation in many parts of the world should be attributed mainly to favorable (and likely transient) global developments rather than to the sound policies of central banks in those parts of the world; and rather than congratulating themselves on how skilled they have become at the conduct of monetary stabilization policy, central bankers should instead live in dread of the day when the implacable global market forces instead turn against them, making a return of inflation all but inevitable.

In this chapter I consider a variety of reasons why globalization might be expected to weaken the control of national central banks over inflation within their borders. These correspond to three distinct aspects of the transmission mechanism for monetary policy: the link between central-bank actions and overnight nominal interest rates (in a conventional 3-equation

Michael Woodford is the John Bates Clark Professor of Political Economy at Columbia University and a research associate of the National Bureau of Economic Research.

Prepared for the NBER conference on International Dimensions of Monetary Policy, Girona, Spain, June 11–13, 2007. I would like to thank Pierpaolo Benigno, Pierre-Olivier Gourinchas, David Romer, Argia Sbordone, and Lars Svensson for helpful discussions and comments on earlier drafts, Luminita Stevens for research assistance, and the (U.S.) National Science Foundation for research support through a grant to the National Bureau of Economic Research.

model, the extent to which it is possible for central bank policy to shift the "LM curve"); the link between real interest rates and the balance between saving and investment in the economy (described by the "IS curve"); and the link between variations in domestic real activity and inflation (described by the "AS curve").

On the one hand, it might be thought that in a globalized world, it is "global liquidity" that should determine world interest rates rather than the supply of liquidity by a single central bank (especially a small one); thus, one might fear that a small central bank will no longer have any instrument with which to shift the LM curve. Alternatively, it might be thought that changes in the balance between investment and saving in one country should matter little for the common world level of real interest rates, so that the "IS curve" should become perfectly horizontal even if the LM curve could be shifted. It might then be feared that loss of control over domestic real interest rates would eliminate any leverage of domestic monetary policy over domestic spending or inflation. Or as still another possibility, it might be thought that inflation should cease to depend on economic slack in one country alone (especially a small one), but rather upon "global slack." In this case the AS curve would become horizontal, implying that even if domestic monetary policy can be effectively used to control domestic aggregate demand, this might not allow any control over domestic inflation.

I take up each of these possibilities by discussing the effects of openness (of goods markets, of factor markets, and of financial markets) on each of these three parts of a "new Keynesian" model of the monetary transmission mechanism. I first consider each argument in the context of a canonical open economy monetary model (following the exposition by Clarida, Galí, and Gertler [2002]), and show that openness need not have any of the kinds of effects that I have just proposed. In each case, I also consider possible variants of the standard model in which the effects of globalization might be more extreme. These cases are not always intended to be regarded as especially realistic, but are taken up in an effort to determine if there are conditions under which the fear of globalization would be justified. Yet I find it difficult to construct scenarios under which globalization would interfere in any substantial way with the ability of domestic monetary policy to maintain control over the dynamics of domestic inflation.

It is true that in a globalized economy, foreign developments will be among the sources of economic disturbances to which it will be appropriate for a central bank to respond in order for it to achieve its stabilization goals. But there is little reason to fear that the capacity of national central banks to stabilize domestic inflation—without having to rely upon coordinated action with other central banks—will be weakened by increasing openness of national economies. Thus it will continue to be appropriate to hold national central banks responsible for domestic inflation outcomes, and confidence regarding the future outlook for inflation remains justified in the case of national central banks that have demonstrated vigilance in controlling inflation thus far.

1.1 International Financial Integration and the Scope for National Monetary Policies

I shall first consider the implications of the international integration of financial markets for the monetary transmission mechanism. I consider this issue first because there can be little doubt that financial markets are already, to an important extent, global markets. The volume of cross-border financial claims of all sorts has grown explosively over the past quarter century, and real interest rates in different countries have been observed to be more strongly correlated as well (Kose et al. 2006).

It is sometimes argued that increased integration of international financial markets should imply that interest rates in each country will come to be determined largely by world conditions rather than domestic conditions. It is then feared that as a result, domestic monetary policy will come to have little leverage over domestic interest rates. Rogoff (2006) suggests that this is already occurring, and argues that even large central banks like the Fed are able to affect financial markets as much as they do only thanks to the fact that many other central banks tend to *follow* their policy decisions. That is, Rogoff argues that even though "individual central banks' monetary policies matter less in a globalized world," this "does not imply that central banks have less influence over real interest rates *collectively*" (272–73). To the extent that this is true, it would seem to imply a substantial reduction in the ability of national central banks to use domestic monetary policy as an instrument of stabilization policy. It might be thought to present a strong argument for explicit agreements among central banks for the coordination of policy, and perhaps even for global monetary union. One might expect that especially in the case of a small country (that can have only a correspondingly small effect on the global balance between investment and savings) domestic monetary policy should cease to be useful for controlling aggregate domestic expenditure or domestic inflation.

In this section of the chapter, I consider whether such inferences are valid by analyzing the connection between real interest rates and aggregate demand in a two-country model with fully integrated international financial markets. Here I focus solely on the way in which equilibrium real interest rates must be consistent with the relation that exists between the economy's time path of output on the one hand and the private sector's preferences over alternative time paths of consumption on the other—the structural relations that correspond to the "IS curve" of a canonical closed-economy model. I defer until the following section the question of how globalization might affect the central bank's ability to influence domestic interest rates owing to changes in the demand for central-bank liabilities. For the moment, I shall take it for granted that a central bank is able to shift the "LM curve," and ask how that affects the aggregate demand curve; that is, the equilibrium relation between domestic inflation and real expenditure.

1.1.1 Interest-Rate Policy and Aggregate Demand in a Two-Country Model

I first consider the "aggregate demand block" of a canonical two-country new-Keynesian model, as expounded for example in Clarida, Galí, and Gertler (2002) (hereafter CGG).[1] I consider first the case of complete international financial integration, so that there is even complete international risk sharing. Moreover, following CGG, I suppose that households in both countries consume the same basket of internationally traded goods. This extreme case has the implication that there is clearly a single real interest rate that is relevant to the intertemporal substitution decisions of households in both countries—the intertemporal relative price of the composite consumption good that is consumed in both countries. This allows me to consider the implications of the equalization of real interest rates across borders in the case where the strongest possible result of this kind obtains.

Let us assume that each of two countries are made up of infinite-lived households, and that each household (in either country) has identical preferences over intertemporal consumption streams. Specifically, following CGG, let us assume that each household ranks consumption streams according to a utility function of the form[2]

$$E_0 \sum_{t=0}^{\infty} \beta^t u(C_t), \tag{1.1}$$

where $0 < \beta < 1$ is a discount factor,

$$u(C) = \frac{C^{1-\sigma^{-1}}}{1-\sigma^{-1}}, \tag{1.2}$$

is the period utility flow from consumption (where $\sigma > 0$ is the constant intertemporal elasticity of substitution of consumer expenditure), and C_t is an index of the household's consumption of both domestically-produced and foreign-produced goods. In particular, CGG assume that

$$C_t = C_{Ht}^{1-\gamma} C_{Ft}^{\gamma}, \tag{1.3}$$

where C_{Ht} represents an index of the household's purchases of goods produced in the "home" country and C_{Ft} an index of purchases of goods pro-

1. Models with a similar structure have been extensively used in the recent literature on the analysis of monetary policy for open economies; see, for example, Svensson (2000), Benigno and Benigno (2001, 2005, 2006), or Gali and Monacelli (2005).

2. Here I specify only the way in which utility depends on consumption expenditure. The disutility of working and the liquidity services provided by money balances are assumed to contribute terms to the utility function that are additively separable from the terms included in (1.1); these extensions are discussed in sections 1.2 and 1.3.

duced in the "foreign" country. Thus, there is assumed to be a unit elasticity of substitution between the two categories of goods, and $0 < \gamma < 1$ indicates the expenditure share of the foreign country's goods in the consumption basket of households in either country. By considering the determination of aggregate demand in country H in the limit as γ approaches 1, we can consider the consequences of globalization for a country that is small relative to world markets.

It is important to note that here an H subscript refers to purchases of goods produced in country H, by households in either country, and not purchases of goods produced in one's own country; thus, a large value of γ means that country H supplies most of the goods consumed worldwide, not that few imported goods are consumed in either country. Regardless of the value of γ, the model describes a world with full integration of goods markets, in the sense that an identical basket of goods (all of which are traded on world markets) is consumed in both countries. I shall use variables without stars to denote the purchases of the representative household in country H, and the corresponding starred variables to denote the purchases of these same goods by the representative household in country F. Because preferences are the same in both countries, one has, for example, the relation $C_t^* = C_{Ht}^{*1-\gamma} C_{Ft}^{*\gamma}$.

Given preferences (1.3), intratemporal optimization implies that households in the home country allocate expenditure across domestic and foreign goods according to the relations

$$P_{Ht} C_{Ht} = (1 - \gamma) P_t C_t, \tag{1.4}$$

$$P_{Ft} C_{Ft} = \gamma P_t C_t. \tag{1.5}$$

Here P_{Ht} is an index of the prices charged in country H for domestic goods (specifically, the price of a unit of the composite good, the quantity of which is measured by C_{Ht}, in units of currency H), P_{Ft} is a corresponding index of the prices charged in country H for foreign goods, and

$$P_t = k^{-1} P_{Ht}^{1-\gamma} P_{Ft}^{\gamma}, \tag{1.6}$$

where $k \equiv (1 - \gamma)^{1-\gamma} \gamma^{\gamma}$, is an index of the price of all consumer goods (including imported goods). Corresponding relations (for example, $P_{Ft}^* C_{Ft}^* = \gamma P_t^* C_t^*$) hold for consumer expenditure in the foreign country, where the starred prices indicate price indices for the same baskets of goods in country F (and in terms of the foreign currency).

The existence of complete financial markets implies the existence of a uniquely defined stochastic discount factor $Q_{t,T}$ that defines the present value in period t (in units of the domestic currency) of random income in period $T > t$ (also in units of the domestic currency). Optimal allocation of consumption expenditure over time and across states then implies that

$$\beta \left(\frac{C_T}{C_t} \right)^{-\sigma^{-1}} = Q_{t,T} \frac{P_T}{P_t} \tag{1.7}$$

for each possible state of the world at date T. Let i_t be the one-period riskless nominal interest rate in terms of the domestic currency; given (1.7), consistency of this rate with the stochastic discount factor (that is, the absence of financial arbitrage opportunities) requires that

$$(1.8) \qquad (1 + i_t)^{-1} = \beta E_t\left[\left(\frac{C_{t+1}}{C_t}\right)^{-\sigma^{-1}} \frac{P_t}{P_{t+1}}\right].$$

This is the key equilibrium relation between the short-term nominal interest rate i_t controlled by the central bank of country H and aggregate expenditure in that country.[3] The riskless one-period real rate of return r_t in country H must satisfy a corresponding relation

$$(1.9) \qquad (1 + r_t)^{-1} = \beta E_t\left[\left(\frac{C_{t+1}}{C_t}\right)^{-\sigma^{-1}}\right].$$

Finally, relations of exactly the same form relate the intertemporal consumption allocation in the foreign country to asset prices there; equations corresponding to (1.7), (1.8), and (1.9) each hold, with each variable replaced by a corresponding starred variable.

The relations stated thus far would hold equally in the case of two closed-economy models, one for each country. (In that case of course, one would have to assume that both H goods and F goods are produced in each country.) Clarida, Galí, and Gertler further assume that each good is sold in a world market, and that the law of one price holds. Hence, one must have

$$P_{Ht} = \varepsilon_t P^*_{Ht},$$

$$P_{Ft} = \varepsilon_t P^*_{Ft},$$

and as a consequence

$$(1.10) \qquad P_t = \varepsilon_t P^*_t$$

as well, where ε_t is the nominal exchange rate in period t. (Note that [1.10] depends not only on the validity of the law of one price, but also on the existence of identical consumption baskets in the two countries.) Similarly, complete international financial integration (frictionless cross-border trade in all financial assets) implies the relation

$$(1.11) \qquad Q_{t,T} = \frac{\varepsilon_t}{\varepsilon_T} Q^*_{t,T}$$

between the stochastic discount factors (and hence asset prices) in the two countries.

Conditions (1.10) and (1.11) together imply that

3. The means by which it is possible for the central bank to control this interest rate are discussed in the following section.

$$Q_{t,T}\frac{P_T}{P_t} = Q^*_{t,T}\frac{P^*_T}{P^*_t}, \tag{1.12}$$

that is, the stochastic discount factors for *real* income streams must be identical in the two countries, and hence that

$$r_t = r^*_t. \tag{1.13}$$

Thus, real interest rates must be equalized in the two countries. In (1.13) the equality of short-term real rates is stated, but in fact, since the real stochastic discount factors are identical, the entire real term structure must be identical in the two countries. This is true regardless of the monetary policies pursued by the two national central banks.

However, this result does *not* depend on the hypothesis of complete international financial integration. In fact, under the preference specification assumed by CGG, an identical result would hold under the hypothesis of complete financial autarchy. Let us suppose that there is a mass $1 - \gamma$ of households in country H and a mass γ in country F, so that income per household is the same in both countries (when expressed in units of the same currency). Under the assumption of financial autarchy, trade must be balanced each period so that

$$(1 - \gamma)P_{Ft}C_{Ft} = \gamma\varepsilon_t P^*_{Ht}C^*_{Ht}.$$

Because expenditure is allocated to the two classes of goods in the shares indicated by (1.4) and (1.5), and the corresponding relations for households in country F, this implies that

$$P_t C_t = \varepsilon_t P^*_t C^*_t.$$

It would then follow from (1.10) that $C_t = C^*_t$ each period. This in turn implies (given [1.7] and the corresponding relation for country F) that (1.12) must hold, and hence that the term structure of real interest rates must be the same in each country.

Thus we find that the same allocation of resources and system of asset prices represents an equilibrium under either the assumption of costless cross-border trade in financial assets or the assumption of no trade at all.[4] Because these prices and quantities achieve asset-price equalization with zero exchange of financial assets, it follows that they would also represent an equilibrium under *any* assumption about costs of asset trade or incompleteness of international financial markets.[5] Hence, in this model, increased financial openness *has no consequences whatsoever* for asset-price determination or aggregate demand under any monetary policies. Of course this irrel-

4. This equivalence in a model with a unit elasticity of substitution between home and foreign goods was first pointed out by Cole and Obstfeld (1991).

5. Here I assume that we start from an initial condition with zero net cross-border financial claims, as would necessarily be true in the case of financial autarchy.

evance result is a fairly special one; in particular, it is not exactly true except in the case of preferences of the precise form (1.3); that is, a unit elasticity of substitution between domestic and foreign goods, and identical preferences in the two countries. But the fact that complete irrelevance is possible (and does not even require an "extreme" preference specification) indicates that the effects of financial globalization need not be large.

It is also important to note that real interest-rate equalization does not imply that domestic monetary policy has no effect on domestic aggregate demand, even in the case of a country that is small relative to global markets (country H in the case in which γ is near 1). Let us derive the "aggregate demand block" of our two-country model (a generalization of the "AD curve" of a static, single-country textbook model), by combining the equilibrium relations between interest rates, real activity, and prices implied by intertemporal optimization and goods market clearing (corresponding to the "IS curve" of the textbook model) with those implied by the monetary policies of the two central banks (corresponding to the "LM curve").

First, note that world demand for the composite world consumption good

$$C_t^w \equiv (1-\gamma)C_t + \gamma C_t^* \tag{1.14}$$

must equal the supply of the composite world good, so that

$$C_t^w = kY_t^{1-\gamma}Y_t^{*\gamma}, \tag{1.15}$$

where Y_t and Y_t^* are per capita aggregate production of the domestic and foreign composite goods, respectively. Next, note that (1.12) together with (1.7) implies that the consumption growth factor C_T/C_t (for any state at any date $T > t$) is the same for households in both countries. Hence, world demand for the composite world good must grow at that same rate as well, so that one must also have

$$\beta\left(\frac{C_T^w}{C_t^w}\right)^{-\sigma^{-1}} = Q_{t,T}\frac{P_T}{P_t} = Q_{t,T}^*\frac{P_T^*}{P_t^*}.$$

Substituting (1.15), we then have

$$Q_{t,T}\frac{P_T}{P_t} = Q_{t,T}^*\frac{P_T^*}{P_t^*} = \beta\left(\frac{Y_t}{Y_T}\right)^{\sigma^{-1}(1-\gamma)}\left(\frac{Y_t^*}{Y_T^*}\right)^{\sigma^{-1}\gamma}. \tag{1.16}$$

Given these stochastic discount factors, the two nominal interest rates must satisfy

$$(1+i_t)^{-1} = \beta E_t\left[\left(\frac{Y_t}{Y_{t+1}}\right)^{\sigma^{-1}(1-\gamma)}\left(\frac{Y_t^*}{Y_{t+1}^*}\right)^{\sigma^{-1}\gamma}\frac{P_t}{P_{t+1}}\right] \tag{1.17}$$

and

$$(1+i_t^*)^{-1} = \beta E_t\left[\left(\frac{Y_t}{Y_{t+1}}\right)^{\sigma^{-1}(1-\gamma)}\left(\frac{Y_t^*}{Y_{t+1}^*}\right)^{\sigma^{-1}\gamma}\frac{P_t^*}{P_{t+1}^*}\right]. \tag{1.18}$$

Relations (1.17) and (1.18) are a pair of "IS equations" relating interest rates to output (real aggregate demand for each of the two countries' products) and to expected inflation, generalizing the "intertemporal IS relation"[6] of a closed-economy new Keynesian model.

To complete the "aggregate demand block" of the model, we must adjoin to these equations a pair of equations representing the monetary policies of the two central banks. For example, monetary policy might be specified by a pair of "Taylor rules,"

$$1 + i_t = \bar{I}_t\left(\frac{P_t}{P_{t-1}}\right)^{\phi_\pi} Y_t^{\phi_y}, \tag{1.19}$$

$$1 + i_t^* = \bar{I}_t^*\left(\frac{P_t^*}{P_{t-1}^*}\right)^{\phi_\pi^*} Y_t^{*\phi_y^*}, \tag{1.20}$$

where $\bar{I}_t$ and $\bar{I}_t^*$ are two state-dependent factors that may represent time-variation in the inflation target, a desire to respond to departures of output from a time-varying measure of potential, a time-varying conception of the "neutral" rate of interest, or a random control error in the implementation of the central bank's interest-rate target, among other possibilities. (For purposes of our analysis it matters only that the processes $\{\bar{I}_t, \bar{I}_t^*\}$ be exogenously specified, rather than depending on the evolution of any endogenous variables.) Then (1.17) through (1.20) represent a system of four equations per period to determine the evolution of the four nominal variables $\{P_t, P_t^*, i_t, i_t^*\}$, given the evolution of the real quantities $\{Y_t, Y_t^*\}$. They thus represent a two-country (and dynamic) version of the "AD equation" of a textbook macro model. Together with a model of aggregate supply (discussed in section 1.3), they allow one to understand the endogenous determination of both output and inflation in the two countries.

The question that we wish to address is, to what extent are the monetary policies of the two countries—here represented in particular by the evolution over time of the intercept terms $\bar{I}_t$ and $\bar{I}_t^*$—able to exert independent influence over aggregate demand (and hence the general level of prices) in each country? To examine the way in which the various endogenous variables are jointly determined, it is as usual convenient to log-linearize the system of equilibrium relations around some steady-state equilibrium values of the variables. The steady state that we shall consider is one in which there is a common steady-state level of output in each country, $Y_t = Y_t^* = \bar{Y} > 0$, and zero inflation in each country; it follows that in each country the steady-state nominal interest rate is equal to $i_t = i_t^* = \beta^{-1} - 1 > 0$. The monetary policy specification is consistent with this if in the steady state, $\bar{I} = \beta^{-1}\bar{Y}^{-\phi_y}$ and $\bar{I}^* = \beta^{-1}\bar{Y}^{-\phi_y^*}$. The log-linear approximations to the two "IS equations" (1.17) and (1.18) are given by

6. See, for example, equation (1.1) of Woodford (2003, chapter 4).

$$(1.21)\quad (1-\gamma)\hat{Y}_t + \gamma\hat{Y}^*_t = E_t[(1-\gamma)\hat{Y}_{t+1} + \gamma\hat{Y}^*_{t+1}] - \sigma(\hat{\imath}_t - E_t\pi_{t+1}),$$

$$(1.22)\quad (1-\gamma)\hat{Y}_t + \gamma\hat{Y}^*_t = E_t[(1-\gamma)\hat{Y}_{t+1} + \gamma\hat{Y}^*_{t+1}] - \sigma(\hat{\imath}^*_t - E_t\pi^*_{t+1}),$$

while the log-linear approximations to the two monetary policy rules (which here replace the "LM equations" that would be appropriate if, as in many textbook expositions, we were to specify monetary policy by a fixed money supply[7]) are given by

$$(1.23)\quad \hat{\imath}_t = \bar{\imath}_t + \phi_\pi \pi_t + \phi_y \hat{Y}_t,$$

$$(1.24)\quad \hat{\imath}^*_t = \bar{\imath}^*_t + \phi^*_\pi \pi^*_t + \phi^*_y \hat{Y}^*_t.$$

Here I use the notation $\hat{Y}_t \equiv \log(Y_t/\bar{Y})$, $\pi_t \equiv \log(P_t/P_{t-1})$, $\hat{\imath}_t \equiv \log(1 + i_t/1 + \bar{\imath})$, $\bar{\imath}_t \equiv \log(\bar{I}_t/\bar{I})$, and correspondingly for the starred variables.

The system of equations (1.21) through (1.24) can be simplified by using (1.23) and (1.24) to substitute for $\hat{\imath}_t$ and $\hat{\imath}^*_t$ in the other two equations. Under the assumption that $\phi_\pi, \phi^*_\pi > 0$, the resulting system can be written in the form

$$(1.25)\quad \begin{bmatrix} \pi_t \\ \pi^*_t \end{bmatrix} = A \begin{bmatrix} E_t\pi_{t+1} \\ E_t\pi^*_{t+1} \end{bmatrix} - B_0 \begin{bmatrix} \hat{Y}_t \\ \hat{Y}^*_t \end{bmatrix} + B_1 \begin{bmatrix} E_t\hat{Y}_{t+1} \\ E_t\hat{Y}^*_{t+1} \end{bmatrix} - A \begin{bmatrix} \bar{\imath}_t \\ \bar{\imath}^*_t \end{bmatrix}.$$

Here

$$A \equiv \begin{bmatrix} \phi_\pi^{-1} & 0 \\ 0 & \phi_\pi^{*-1} \end{bmatrix},$$

and B_0, B_1 are two matrices of coefficients, all of which are positive in the case that $\phi_y, \phi^*_y \geq 0$. In the case that $\phi_\pi, \phi^*_\pi > 1$ (as recommended by Taylor [1999]), we observe that

$$\lim_{n\to\infty} A^n = 0,$$

and the system (1.25) can be "solved forward" to yield a unique bounded solution for the two inflation rates in the case of any bounded processes $\{\hat{Y}_t, \hat{Y}^*_t, \bar{\imath}_t, \bar{\imath}^*_t\}$, given by

$$(1.26)\quad \begin{bmatrix} \pi_t \\ \pi^*_t \end{bmatrix} = -B_0 \begin{bmatrix} \hat{Y}_t \\ \hat{Y}^*_t \end{bmatrix} + \sum_{j=0}^{\infty} A^j(B_1 - AB_0) \begin{bmatrix} E_t\hat{Y}_{t+j+1} \\ E_t\hat{Y}^*_{t+j+1} \end{bmatrix} - \sum_{j=0}^{\infty} A^{j+1} \begin{bmatrix} E_t\bar{\imath}_{t+j} \\ E_t\bar{\imath}^*_{t+j} \end{bmatrix}.$$

This generalizes the result obtained for a closed-economy model in the case of a Taylor rule with $\phi_\pi > 1$.[8]

7. The addition of "LM equations" of this conventional sort to the model is discussed in section 1.2.

8. See, for example, equation (2.7) of Woodford (2003, chapter 2). The discussion there is of inflation determination in a flexible-price model where $\{\hat{Y}_t\}$ is exogenously given, but the same calculation can be viewed as deriving a dynamic "AD relation" for a sticky-price model.

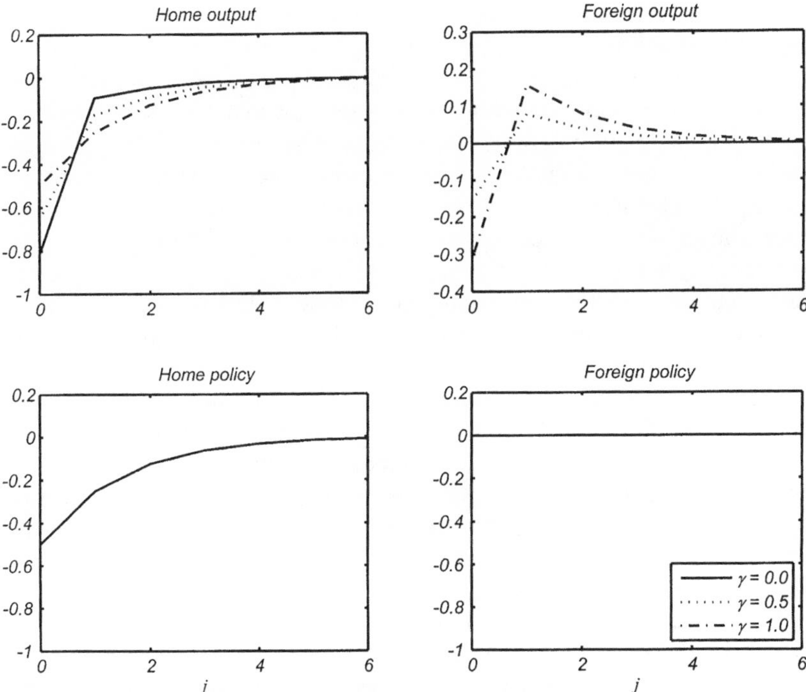

Fig. 1.1 Coefficients of the dynamic AD relation (1.27), for alternative degrees of openness

The solution obtained for home-country inflation can be written in the form

$$(1.27) \qquad \pi_t = \sum_{j=0}^{\infty}(\psi_{1,j}E_t\hat{Y}_{t+j} + \psi_{2,j}E_t\hat{Y}^*_{t+j} + \psi_{3,j}E_t\bar{\imath}_{t+j} + \psi_{4,j}E_t\bar{\imath}^*_{t+j}).$$

The coefficients $\{\psi_{i,j}\}$ for successive horizons j are plotted (for each of the values $i = 1, 2, 3, 4$) in the four panels of figure 1.1. In these numerical illustrations, I assume coefficients $\phi_\pi = 2$, $\phi_y = 1$ for the Taylor rule in each country,[9] a value $\sigma = 6.37$ for the intertemporal elasticity of substitution,[10] and a period length of one quarter. The coefficients of the solution are plotted for each

9. In the notation of the chapter, where π_t is a one-period inflation rate and $\hat{\imath}_t$ a one-period interest rate, then the values used are actually $\phi_\pi = 2$, $\phi_y = 0.25$. The values quoted in the text are the equivalent coefficients of a Taylor rule written in terms of an annualized interest rate and an annualized inflation rate, as in Taylor (1999), where a rule with these coefficients is argued to be relatively similar to Fed policy under Alan Greenspan.

10. This is the value estimated for the U.S. economy by Rotemberg and Woodford (1997). Here and elsewhere, the parameter values used in the numerical illustrations are such that in the case of a closed economy (the $\gamma = 0$ case in figure 1.1), the model coincides with the baseline parameter values used in the numerical analysis of the basic new-Keynesian model in Woodford (2003, chapter 4).

of three possible values of γ: $\gamma = 0$, the closed economy limit; $\gamma = 0.5$, the case of two countries of equal size; and $\gamma = 1$, the small open economy limit.

The solution (1.26) can be viewed as describing a pair of dynamic "AD relations" for the two open economies, in each of which there is a downward-sloping static relation between the inflation rate and output, or aggregate real expenditure on that country's products. (The observation about the slope follows from the fact that the elements of B_0 are positive. In the numerical examples, it is illustrated by the negative values for $\psi_{1,0}$ shown in the upper left panel of figure 1.1.) Here we are especially interested in the question of how changes in each country's monetary policy affect the location of the AD curve in that country, and hence the inflation rate that would result in the case of a given level of real activity.

Let us first consider the effect of the anticipated time path of the intercept $\{\bar{\imath}_t\}$ on inflation in the home country, taking as given the magnitude of the response coefficients ϕ_π, ϕ_y, and also leaving fixed the specification of monetary policy in the other country. These effects are indicated by the coefficients $\{\psi_{3,j}\}$ plotted in the lower left panel of figure 1.1. A first important observation is that it is *possible* to shift the central-bank reaction function arbitrarily in one country, without violating any requirement for the existence of equilibrium—thus no market forces prevent a central bank from having an independent monetary policy, even in the case of complete financial integration. (We see this from the fact that we have been able to solve the system [1.25] under an arbitrary perturbation of the path $\{\bar{\imath}_t\}$.)

Moreover, tightening policy in the home country (increasing $\bar{\imath}_t$, or being expected to increase it in a later period) shifts the AD relation for that country, so as to imply a lower inflation rate π_t for any expected paths of real activity in the two countries. (This is indicated by the negative coefficients in the lower left panel of the figure.) Thus it continues to be possible to use monetary policy to control nominal expenditure and inflation, even in a fully globalized economy. Indeed, the coefficients indicating the effect of current or expected future tightenings of policy on current inflation are *identical* to those that would apply in the case of a closed economy, and are independent of the size of the home economy relative to the world economy (i.e., are independent of the value of γ). Thus, even in the case of a very small open economy, monetary policy does not cease to be effective for domestic inflation control as a result of globalization.

The solution (1.26) can also be used to examine the degree to which there are monetary policy "spillovers" as a result of openness, at least to the extent that these are thought to operate through effects of foreign monetary policy on aggregate demand. While the system solution (1.26) might make it appear that inflation in each country depends on the monetary policies of both, this is not true (for given paths of output in the two countries). Because the matrix A is diagonal, the solution for π_t is independent of the expected path of $\{\bar{\imath}^*_{t+j}\}$, and π^*_t is similarly independent of the expected path of $\{\bar{\imath}_{t+j}\}$. (This is shown by the zero coefficients at all horizons in the lower right panel of figure 1.1.) One can similarly show that the values of the coefficients ϕ^*_π, ϕ^*_y affect only the solution for π^*_t, and not the solution for π_t.

The implication is that foreign monetary policy cannot affect inflation determination in the home country, except to the extent that this occurs through effects of foreign monetary policy on foreign output. (In the case of completely flexible wages and prices, so that monetary policy would have little effect on real activity, there would be no possibility of "spillovers" from expansionary foreign monetary policy to domestic inflation, assuming the home central bank follows a Taylor rule of the form [1.19].) And even the cross-border effects that are possible when monetary policy affects real activity are not necessarily of the kind often assumed in popular discussions of the implications of "excess global liquidity." To the extent that expansionary monetary policy in the rest of the world makes foreign output temporarily high, the equilibrium real rate of return consistent with a given path of output in the home country is *lowered* (as indicated by [1.21]). This makes a given Taylor rule for the home central bank *more contractionary*, as shown by the negative coefficient $\psi_{2,0}$ in the upper right panel of figure 1.1: if one is to avoid disinflation and/or reduced aggregate demand, it is necessary to lower $\bar{\imath}_t$ in accordance with the reduction in the equilibrium real rate of return associated with trend output.[11]

It might seem surprising that an independent domestic monetary policy can exert the same effect on domestic inflation as in a closed economy, despite the fact that (at least in the case of a sufficiently small open economy) there is no possibility of a nonnegligible affect of domestic monetary policy on the common world real interest rate. But this should not really be a surprise. It is commonly understood in the case of closed economy monetary models that even in the case of fully flexible wages and prices—so that neither output nor equilibrium real interest rates can be affected by monetary policy—it remains possible for monetary policy to determine the general level of prices. This means that monetary policy can shift the AD relation even when it cannot change the equilibrium real rate of interest.[12] And the classic Mundell-Fleming analysis concludes that monetary policy should be *more* effective, rather than less, in the case of international capital mobility, even though this is assumed to imply the existence of a common world interest rate; the fact that a monetary expansion cannot lower interest rates simply ensures

11. These remarks apply to the case in which expansionary foreign monetary policy makes foreign output *currently* high relative to its expected future level. The anticipation of a foreign monetary expansion in the *future* would instead be currently *inflationary* in the home country; for this would imply that foreign output should be higher in the future than it is now, making the equilibrium real rate of return higher rather than lower.

12. For an analysis of inflation determination in such a model when monetary policy is specified by a Taylor rule, see Woodford (2003, chapter 2).

that all of the adjustment that results in a larger quantity of money being voluntarily held must involve increases in output or prices rather than lower interest rates. A similar conclusion obtains if the change in monetary policy is modeled as a shift in an interest-rate reaction function rather than a change in the money supply: both are simply reasons for the LM curve to shift.

1.1.2 Exchange-Rate Determination

One way to understand how monetary policy continues to be effective even in the globalized economy is by considering the consequences of domestic monetary policy for the exchange rate, and the implications of exchange rate changes for inflation. A log-linear approximation to (1.11) implies that any equilibrium (in which departures from the steady state are sufficiently small) must satisfy the uncovered interest rate parity condition,

$$\hat{\imath}_t - \hat{\imath}_t^* = E_t(e_{t+1} - e_t), \tag{1.28}$$

where $e_t \equiv \log \varepsilon_t$. The implications of this relation for the equilibrium exchange rate are most easily derived in the case that we assume common reaction-function coefficients for the two central banks ($\phi_\pi^* = \phi_\pi$, $\phi_y^* = \phi_y$), while allowing the intercepts $\bar{\imath}_t$, $\bar{\imath}_t^*$ to follow different paths. In this case the monetary policy specifications (1.19) and (1.20) imply that

$$\hat{\imath}_t - \hat{\imath}_t^* = (\bar{\imath}_t - \bar{\imath}_t^*) + \phi_\pi(z_t - z_{t-1}) + \phi_y(\hat{Y}_t - \hat{Y}_t^*), \tag{1.29}$$

introducing the notation $z_t \equiv \log(P_t/P_t^*)$ for the differential in the absolute level of prices between the two countries. Then using the fact that (1.10) implies that $z_t = e_t$ to substitute for z_t in (1.29), and using this relation to substitute for the interest rate differential in (1.28), we obtain a difference equation of the form

$$E_t\Delta e_{t+1} = (\bar{\imath}_t - \bar{\imath}_t^*) + \phi_\pi\Delta e_t + \phi_y(\hat{Y}_t - \hat{Y}_t^*), \tag{1.30}$$

for the rate of exchange rate depreciation.

Under the assumption that $\phi_\pi > 1$, this has a unique bounded solution for the depreciation rate,

$$\Delta e_t = \sum_{j=0}^{\infty} \phi_\pi^{-(j+1)}[E_t(\bar{\imath}_{t+j}^* - \bar{\imath}_{t+j}) + \phi_y E_t(\hat{Y}_{t+j}^* - \hat{Y}_{t+j})]. \tag{1.31}$$

This shows how the exchange rate must depreciate as a result either of an increase in the relative tightness of foreign monetary policy or of an increase in relative foreign output. The law of one price implies that changes in the exchange rate must correspond directly to differences in the inflation rates of the two countries, so that[13]

13. This solution is consistent, of course, with (1.26), derived earlier under more general assumptions; in fact, it is simply the difference between the first and second lines of (1.26). The alternative derivation is intended simply to provide additional insight into the economic mechanisms reflected by this solution.

(1.32) $$\pi_t - \pi_t^* = \Delta z_t = \sum_{j=0}^{\infty} \phi_\pi^{-(j+1)}[E_t(\bar{\imath}_{t+j}^* - \bar{\imath}_{t+j}) + \phi_y E_t(\hat{Y}_{t+j}^* - \hat{Y}_{t+j})].$$

Equation (1.32) shows how a change in the monetary policy of one central bank, not perfectly matched by a corresponding change in the policy of the other central bank, must create a difference in the inflation rates of the two countries. The result here only identifies the equilibrium inflation differential for a *given* output differential, but in the case that $\phi_y = 0$, the output differential is irrelevant, and the equation directly tells us what the inflation differential must be. Moreover, the coefficients in this relation do not involve γ. It follows that even the central bank of a very small country must be able to substantially affect domestic inflation by changing its policy; for it can change the inflation differential, and (at least in the case of a very small country) this must not be because it changes the inflation rate in the rest of world but not at home.

The argument just given implies not only that the central bank must be able to shift the aggregate demand curve, but more specifically that it must be able to *control the inflation rate,* regardless of the nature of aggregate supply (for example, no matter how sticky prices or wages may be). It is the flexibility of the prices of imports in terms of the domestic currency in this model (implied by the assumption of producer-currency pricing) that allows for such a strong conclusion. Indeed, Svensson (2000) argues that achievement of a central bank's consumer price index (CPI) inflation target is possible over a shorter horizon in the case that the economy is substantially open, under the assumption (as in the CGG model) that there is relatively immediate pass-through of exchange-rate changes to the prices of imported goods.[14]

1.1.3 Determination of the Domestic Price Index

In the previous discussion, I have assumed that the central bank is interested in controlling the evolution of a broad consumer price index, including the prices of imported consumer goods, and so have derived an "aggregate demand" relation that relates this price index to the volume of real activity in an open economy. This assumption is consistent with the kind of official inflation target that inflation-targeting central banks in small open economies typically aim at. However, one might also be interested in the ability of monetary policy to control the rate of growth of a *domestic price index,* in which one considers only the prices of goods produced in that country. This is certainly of analytical interest in isolating the various channels through which monetary policy can affect inflation, even if one's stabilization objective is assumed to involve only CPI inflation.[15]

14. Svensson calls this "the direct exchange-rate channel" for the transmission of monetary policy.

15. See, for example, the discussion in Svensson (2000).

But it is also arguable that a central bank should concern itself with stabilization of domestic prices rather than a consumer price index. Suppose, for example, that one takes the goal of monetary policy to be to eliminate the distortions resulting from nominal rigidities, by bringing about the allocation of resources that would occur in the case of fully-flexible wages and prices. In a model of the kind considered by CGG (with flexible wages and producer-currency pricing), this will be achieved if the monetary policies of the two central banks bring about an equilibrium in which the domestic price index is completely stabilized in each country. Import prices will instead vary in response to (asymmetric) shocks to real "fundamentals" in such an equilibrium, since the relative prices of the goods produced in the two countries would vary in the case of flexible wages and prices. Hence it might be deemed reasonable to hold each central bank responsible for stabilizing the domestic price index in its country, while allowing import prices to vary.

Here I consider the effects of monetary policy on domestic inflation in a globalized economy in order to clarify that the effects on inflation discussed in the previous section do not result purely from what Svensson calls the "direct exchange-rate channel." I show that one can also derive an aggregate-demand equation that relates the *domestic* price index to domestic output, and indeed it might seem more reasonable to call this "the aggregate demand curve," since it is the product of these two quantities that represents aggregate expenditure on domestic products.

Under the preferences previously assumed, consumer optimization implies a simple connection between the equilibrium terms of trade and the composition of world output. The law of one price implies that the relative price of home and foreign goods is the same in both countries, and consequently (1.4) and (1.5) imply that households choose the same ratio of foreign goods to home goods in both countries. Market-clearing requires that this common ratio equal the relative supplies of the two types of goods; hence the equilibrium terms of trade must satisfy[16]

$$S_t \equiv \frac{P_{Ft}}{P_{Ht}} = \frac{Y_t}{Y_t^*}. \tag{1.33}$$

The definition of the consumption price index P_t then implies that

$$\frac{P_{Ht}}{P_t} = kS_t^{-\gamma} = kY_t^{-\gamma}Y_t^{*\gamma}, \tag{1.34}$$

$$\frac{P_{Ft}}{P_t} = kS_t^{1-\gamma} = kY_t^{1-\gamma}Y_t^{*\gamma-1}. \tag{1.35}$$

We now have a solution for equilibrium relative prices, given output in the two countries. Combining this with our previous solution for consumer price

16. Note that Y_t is output *per capita* in the home country, and similarly with Y_t^*; hence the relative supply of the two composite goods is equal to $(1-\gamma)Y_t/\gamma Y_t^*$.

inflation given output, we can obtain a solution for domestic price inflation in each country, given the two countries' levels of output. If we define the domestic inflation rates in each country as $\pi_{Ht} \equiv \Delta \log P_{Ht}$, $\pi^*_{Ft} \equiv \Delta \log P^*_{Ft}$,[17] then relations (1.34) and (1.35) imply that

$$\pi_{Ht} = \pi_t + \gamma(\Delta\hat{Y}^*_t - \Delta\hat{Y}_t), \tag{1.36}$$

$$\pi^*_{Ft} = \pi^*_t + (1 - \gamma)(\Delta\hat{Y}_t - \Delta\hat{Y}^*_t). \tag{1.37}$$

If we then substitute the previous solution (1.26) for the consumer price inflation rates in these expressions, we obtain solutions for π_{Ht} and π^*_{Ft} as functions of the paths of output in the two countries and the two monetary policies, under the assumption that monetary policy is described by two rules of the form (1.19) and (1.20). Our conclusions about the magnitude of the effect on home country inflation of a change in home country monetary policy remain exactly the same as before, since (as long as we are controlling for the paths of output in the two countries) there is no additional effect on the terms of trade.

If, however, the central bank is concerned with stabilization of domestic inflation rather than consumer price inflation, it may be of more interest to consider the consequences of monetary policy rules that respond to domestic inflation rather than to CPI inflation as assumed in (1.19) and (1.20). Suppose, then, that we replace (1.19) by a policy of the form

$$1 + i_t = \bar{I}_t\left(\frac{P_{Ht}}{P_{Ht-1}}\right)^{\phi_\pi} Y_t^{\phi_y}, \tag{1.38}$$

and similarly for the foreign central bank. In this case, we can no longer simply use the solution (1.26) for the CPI inflation rates, but must instead repeat the derivation using the alternative monetary policy rules.

Rewriting (1.21) and (1.22) in terms of domestic inflation rates, by using (1.36) and (1.37) to substitute for the CPI inflation rates, we obtain

$$(1 + \theta)\hat{Y}_t - \theta\hat{Y}^*_t = E_t[(1 + \theta)\hat{Y}_{t+1} - \theta\hat{Y}^*_{t+1}] - \sigma(\hat{\imath}_t - E_t\pi_{Ht+1}), \tag{1.39}$$

$$(1 + \theta^*)\hat{Y}^*_t - \theta^*\hat{Y}_t = E_t[(1 + \theta^*)\hat{Y}^*_{t+1} - \theta^*\hat{Y}_{t+1}] - \sigma(\hat{\imath}^*_t - E_t\pi^*_{Ft+1}), \tag{1.40}$$

where

$$\theta \equiv \gamma(\sigma - 1), \quad \theta^* \equiv (1 - \gamma)(\sigma - 1).$$

Combining these with the log-linearized central-bank reaction functions,

$$\hat{\imath}_t = \bar{\imath}_t + \phi_\pi\pi_{Ht} + \phi_y\hat{Y}_t, \tag{1.41}$$

$$\hat{\imath}^*_t = \bar{\imath}^*_t + \phi^*_\pi\pi^*_{Ft} + \phi^*_y\hat{Y}^*_t, \tag{1.42}$$

17. Clarida, Galí, and Gertler simply call the domestic inflation rates π_t and π_t^*, respectively; thus their notation encourages an emphasis on domestic inflation stabilization.

we then have a system of four equations per period to solve for the paths of $\{\pi_{Ht}, \pi^*_{Ft}, \hat{\imath}_t, \hat{\imath}^*_t\}$, given the paths of $\{\hat{Y}_t, \hat{Y}^*_t, \bar{\imath}_t, \bar{\imath}^*_t\}$. Once one has a solution to these equations, the evolution of the CPI inflation rates in the two countries is then given by equations (1.36) and (1.37).

The system of equations (1.39) through (1.42) can again be reduced to a pair of equations for the two domestic inflation rates, and this system can again be written in the form

$$(1.43)\quad \begin{bmatrix} \pi_{Ht} \\ \pi^*_{Ft} \end{bmatrix} = A \begin{bmatrix} E_t\pi_{Ht+1} \\ E_t\pi^*_{Ft+1} \end{bmatrix} - \tilde{B}_0 \begin{bmatrix} \hat{Y}_t \\ \hat{Y}^*_t \end{bmatrix} + \tilde{B}_1 \begin{bmatrix} E_t\hat{Y}_{t+1} \\ E_t\hat{Y}^*_{t+1} \end{bmatrix} - A \begin{bmatrix} \bar{\imath}_t \\ \bar{\imath}^*_t \end{bmatrix},$$

where the matrix A is the same as in (1.25), but the matrices $\tilde{B}_0$, $\tilde{B}_1$ are different. Again the system has a unique bounded solution in the case that $\phi_\pi, \phi^*_\pi > 1$, and again it is of the form (1.26), making the appropriate substitutions. Because the diagonal elements of $\tilde{B}_0$ are again necessarily positive, this solution again defines a downward-sloping AD curve for each country; but now each AD curve relates the price index for that country's products to a corresponding index of the quantity sold of those products. The AD relation for the home country can again be written in the form (1.27), except that this is now an equation for domestic inflation rather than CPI inflation; the numerical values of the coefficients (under the same parameter values as before) are now shown in figure 1.2.[18]

We again find that there is scope for independent variation in the monetary policies of the two central banks, and that either central bank can shift the AD curve for its country (and hence the domestic inflation rate associated with given paths of real activity in the two countries) by varying its policy. In fact, because the matrix A is the same as in the previous section, we find exactly the same coefficients as before for the quantitative effects of current or expected future changes in $\bar{\imath}_{t+j}$ on the domestic rate of inflation. And once again, we find that any spillovers from foreign monetary policy on aggregate demand in the home country must be due to the effects of foreign monetary policy on foreign output. However, the sign and likely magnitude of any spillovers are now more ambiguous, as negative terms have been added to the off-diagonal elements of $\tilde{B}_0$ and $\tilde{B}_1$ that tend to reduce the size of these elements, and can even reverse their sign.[19]

When we expressed the AD curve as a relation between P_t and Y_t, the effect of higher foreign output was clearly contractionary, because higher equilibrium consumption of foreign output by domestic households implies a lower marginal utility of income for any given level of domestic output

18. Note that while I again assume that $\phi_\pi = 2$, the coefficient has a different meaning, as it now indicates the response to variations in *domestic* inflation only.

19. For the parameter values used in the numerical example shown in figure 1.2, the sign of the effect of foreign monetary stimulus on home inflation is reversed, as shown in the upper right panel.

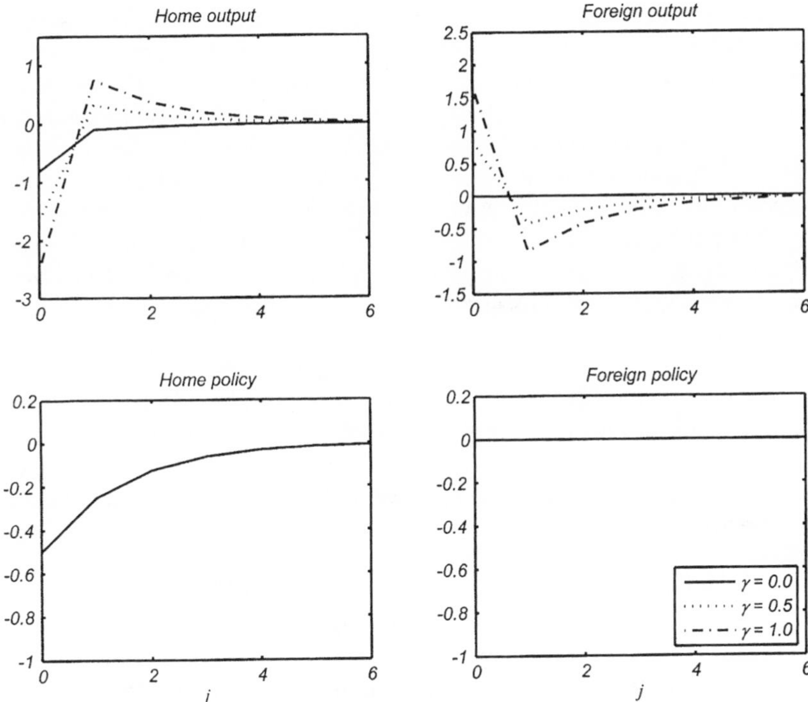

Fig. 1.2 Coefficients of the dynamic AD relation in terms of domestic inflation, for alternative degrees of openness

(and hence domestic consumption of domestic output), just as if there had been a reduction in domestic households' impatience to consume. But now we must also take into account the fact that higher foreign output implies an improvement of the home country's terms of trade (for any given level of home output), and hence a higher value of P_{Ht} relative to P_t; this additional effect tends to shift the AD curve in terms of P_{Ht} and Y_t outward, offsetting the other effect. In fact, if $\sigma = 1$ (the case of log utility of consumption), the two effects exactly cancel, and both $\tilde{B}_0$ and $\tilde{B}_1$ are diagonal matrices. In this case, the solution (1.26) implies that the location of the home-country AD curve depends only on home monetary policy and the expected future path of home output (and likewise for the foreign-country AD curve); thus there are *no* international monetary policy spillovers in the AD block of the model.[20]

This last result is a fairly special one. In fact, it is not obvious that $\sigma = 1$

20. This result is obtained by CGG, who express the model structural relations entirely in terms of domestic inflation. They find a similar decoupling of the structural equations for the two countries in the aggregate-supply block of the model in the case that $\sigma = 1$, as discussed in section 1.3.

should be regarded as a realistic calibration of the model. While the assumption of log utility of consumption is fairly common in real business-cycle models, it is important to note that this is a specification of the intertemporal elasticity of substitution of *nondurable consumer expenditure* only, in a model in which investment spending is separately modeled (and specified to be much more substitutable over time). In a model in which all private expenditure is modeled as if it were consumer expenditure (i.e., we abstract from any effects of private spending on the evolution of productive capacity), more realistic conclusions are obtained if we specify preferences over the time path of such "consumption" with an intertemporal elasticity of substitution well above one.[21] In this case, the terms-of-trade effect of higher foreign output is quantitatively more important than the implied reduction of the marginal utility of income (which is proportional to σ^{-1}), so there will be a nonzero net effect on home aggregate demand that is *expansionary*. (This is illustrated in the upper right panel of figure 1.2.) Nonetheless, the fact that the two effects have opposite signs means that we may have less reason to expect such spillovers to be quantitatively significant if we are concerned with an AD relation specified in terms of the domestic price index.

It should also be recalled that even if $\sigma = 1$, while it is then possible to choose a Taylor rule that should completely stabilize domestic inflation without requiring any response to foreign variables, this does not mean that one can stabilize *CPI inflation* without responding to foreign variables. Thus, the "decoupling" of the aggregate demand curves that occurs in this case would not really imply that a central bank has no need to monitor foreign developments, except under a particular view of its stabilization objectives.

We can also derive an AD relation between the consumer price index and domestic output, as in section 1.1.1, even if we assume that monetary policy responds to domestic inflation only. Equation (1.36) together with our solution of the form (1.27) for π_{Ht} allow us to derive a relation of the form

$$\pi_t = \sum_{j=0}^{\infty}(\psi_{1,j}E_t\hat{Y}_{t+j} + \psi_{2,j}E_t\hat{Y}^*_{t+j} + \psi_{3,j}E_t\bar{\imath}_{t+j} + \psi_{4,j}E_t\bar{\imath}^*_{t+j}) - \gamma \log S_{t-1}$$

for CPI inflation. (Here the lagged terms of trade matter for CPI inflation determination, contrary to what we previously found in equation [1.27], because we now assume that the domestic policy rule involves the lagged *domestic* price index, whereas the CPI inflation rate is defined relative to the lagged *consumer* price index.) The coefficient $\psi_{2,0}$ is *more negative* than in the case of the solution for domestic inflation, by an amount that is greater the more open is the economy, owing to the effect of higher foreign output on the terms of trade. Figure 1.3 plots the coefficients for the same numerical examples as in figure 1.2; one observes that the sign of the coefficient $\psi_{2,0}$ is

21. See Woodford (2003, 242–43, 362–63) for further discussion of the proper interpretation of this parameter in a basic new-Keynesian model of the monetary transmission mechanism.

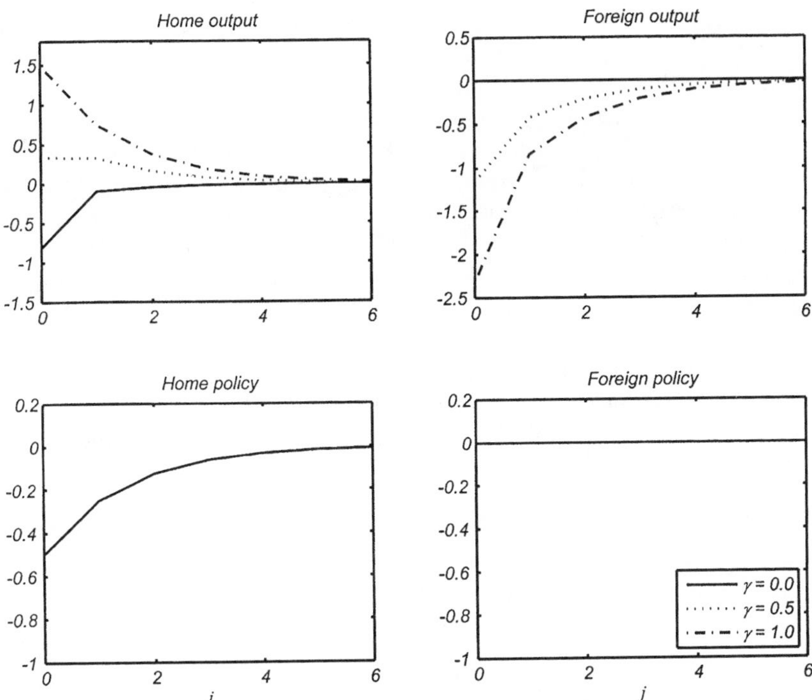

Fig. 1.3 Coefficients of the dynamic AD relation in terms of CPI inflation, when the policy rule is (1.38)

reversed. Thus one finds, once again, that (for these parameter values) stimulative foreign monetary policy will have a contractionary effect on aggregate demand in the home country; indeed, the effect is even stronger than in the model of section 1.1.1.

1.1.4 Consequences of Local-Currency Pricing

The argument previously given for the ability of domestic monetary policy to control the domestic inflation rate depends, as explained at the end of section 1.1.1, on a supposition that exchange rate changes automatically imply changes in the prices charged for the same goods in the two different countries. But it is often observed that exchange rate changes are not immediately "passed through" to import prices in this way. If imported goods instead have sticky prices in terms of the currency of the country where they are sold—so that the law of one price need not hold, in the short run—does the argument given for the effectiveness of monetary policy in controlling domestic inflation still hold?

To examine this question, I present a variant of the model of "local-currency pricing" proposed by Betts and Devereux (2000), in which, however, price changes are staggered after the fashion proposed by Calvo (just as in CGG).[22] I shall assume the same preferences as in CGG (and the previous section), so that once again households in the two countries consume the same goods and have identical preferences.

Certain equilibrium conditions of the CGG model that did not depend on the law of one price continue to hold in the model with local-currency pricing. Intertemporal optimization by households continues to imply that (1.8) must hold, and likewise the corresponding equation for the starred variables. Log-linearizing these equilibrium relations, we obtain

$$\hat{C}_t = E_t\hat{C}_{t+1} - \sigma(\hat{\imath}_t - E_t\pi_{t+1}),$$

and a corresponding equation for the starred variables. Taking a weighted average of this equation (multiplied by $1 - \gamma$) and the corresponding equation for the starred variables (multiplied by γ), we obtain the additional implication that

$$\hat{C}^w_t = E_t\hat{C}^w_{t+1} - \sigma(\hat{\imath}^w_t - E_t\pi^w_{t+1}), \tag{1.44}$$

using the notation $\hat{C}^w_t \equiv \log(C^w_t/k\overline{Y}) = (1-\gamma)\hat{C}_t + \gamma\hat{C}^*_t$, $\hat{\imath}^w_t \equiv (1-\gamma)\hat{\imath}_t + \gamma\hat{\imath}^*_t$, and $\pi^w_t \equiv (1-\gamma)\pi_t + \gamma\pi^*_t$. Moreover, clearing of the goods markets requires (to a first-order approximation[23]) that

$$\hat{C}^w_t = \hat{Y}^w_t,$$

where $\hat{Y}^w_t \equiv (1-\gamma)\hat{Y}_t + \gamma\hat{Y}^*_t$. Using this to substitute for $\hat{C}^w_t$ in (1.44), we obtain

$$\hat{Y}^w_t = E_t\hat{Y}^w_{t+1} - \sigma(\hat{\imath}^w_t - E_t\pi^w_{t+1}). \tag{1.45}$$

Note that (1.45) is just a weighted average of the two conditions (1.21) and (1.22) derived for the model with producer-currency pricing (PCP). In fact, all of the implications of the system (1.21) and (1.22) are contained in the pair of conditions consisting of (1.45) and the condition

$$\hat{\imath}_t - \hat{\imath}^*_t = E_t\pi_{t+1} - E_t\pi^*_{t+1}, \tag{1.46}$$

obtained by subtracting (1.22) from (1.21). In order to complete our analysis of the aggregate demand block of the model, we must find the relation corresponding to (1.46) for the model with local-currency pricing (LCP).

Another condition derived earlier that continues to hold in the LCP model is (1.11), and again this implies the uncovered interest-parity relation (1.28) when log-linearized. In the model with producer-currency pricing, the result that $z_t = e_t$ together with (1.28) implies the condition (1.46). With local-

22. The model is essentially a simplified version of the one presented in Benigno (2004).

23. Aggregate supply of the composite world good need not equal aggregate demand for it, if the composition of the consumption bundles of households in the two countries are not identical. But even in that case, the discrepancy is of second order in the amplitude of departures from the steady-state allocation.

currency pricing, instead, (1.28) still holds, but z_t need not equal e_t, so that this derivation is no longer possible.

The relation between the relative absolute price levels in the two countries and the exchange rate will instead depend on what we assume about price adjustment. With local-currency pricing, there are four different price-setting problems to consider: for each of the two types of goods (goods produced in the home country and goods produced in the foreign country), prices are set in terms of both the home currency and the foreign currency. Each supplier chooses two prices, and the decisions are independent, in the sense that the price charged in one currency does not constrain the price that can be charged in the other.[24] The two prices for any given good are the prices charged to buyers in the two different countries; there is assumed to be no opportunity for cross-border arbitrage by households. Producers can instead sell the same goods in either country, so that a common marginal cost of supplying additional goods is relevant to their pricing decision in each country. Here I furthermore assume Calvo-style staggered price setting (as in the model of CGG), and more specifically that there is a common fraction $0 < \alpha < 1$ of prices of each of the four types that remain fixed from one period to the next.[25]

Under this form of price setting (discussed further in section 1.3), the index of home goods prices in units of the home currency (which are the prices charged for these goods in the home country) evolves in accordance with a relation of the form

$$\pi_{Ht} = \xi(\mu + \log MC_t - \log P_{Ht}) + \beta E_t \pi_{Ht+1}, \tag{1.47}$$

where MC_t is the nominal marginal cost (in units of the home currency) of supplying additional home goods (a geometric average across the different producers of home goods), $\mu > 0$ is the log of the desired markup of price over marginal cost (reflecting the market power of the monopolistically competitive suppliers), and $\xi > 0$ is a coefficient (defined in section 1.3) that is smaller the less frequently prices are reconsidered. The producers of home goods face a similar problem in choosing the prices that they charge for their goods in the foreign country, and in this case the marginal cost of supplying additional home goods in units of the foreign currency is MC_t/ε_t. As a result, the evolution of π^*_{Ht} satisfies a corresponding equilibrium relation

$$\pi^*_{Ht} = \xi(\mu + \log MC_t - e_t - \log P^*_{Ht}) + \beta E_t \pi^*_{Ht+1}. \tag{1.48}$$

One then observes that subtraction of (1.48) from (1.47) implies that

24. Similar conclusions would obtain if we were to assume that the producers sell to separate retailers in the two countries, each of which sets the retail price in its market. What is crucial is the assumption that each retailer has a monopoly over sales of the good in a particular country.

25. It does not matter whether we assume that a given firm reconsiders its prices in both countries at the same time, or at random dates that arrive independently in the two cases.

(1.49) $$\Delta z_{Ht} = \xi(e_t - z_{Ht}) + \beta E_t \Delta z_{Ht+1},$$

where $z_{Ht} \equiv \log(P_{Ht}/P^*_{Ht})$ is the differential price of home goods in the two countries. This can alternatively be written as

$$E_t[A(L)z_{Ht+1}] + \xi e_t = 0,$$

where

(1.50) $$A(L) \equiv \beta - (1 + \beta + \xi)L + L^2.$$

We can alternatively write

$$A(L) = \beta(1 - \mu_1 L)(1 - \mu_2 L) = -\mu_1^{-1}(1 - \mu_1 L)(1 - \beta\mu_1 L^{-1})L,$$

where $0 < \mu_1 < 1 < \mu_2$ are the two roots of the characteristic equation

$$\mu^2 A(\mu^{-1}) = 0.$$

It follows that given a difference-stationary process for $\{e_t\}$, there is a unique difference-stationary process for $\{z_{Ht}\}$ consistent with (1.49), given by

(1.51) $$z_{Ht} = \mu_1 z_{Ht-1} + (1 - \mu_1)(1 - \beta\mu_1)\sum_{j=0}^{\infty}(\beta\mu_1)^j E_t e_{t+j}.$$

Similar calculations are possible in the case of the prices set by the producers of foreign goods in the two countries, as a result of which one concludes that the differential price of foreign goods in the two countries, $z_{Ft} \equiv \log(P_{Ft}/P^*_{Ft})$, satisfies *exactly the same* difference equation (1.49). (While the marginal cost of producing foreign goods need not be the same as that of producing home goods, what matters for this calculation is that the *ratio* of the marginal costs of supplying goods in the two countries is in each case given by the exchange rate.) Hence, z_{Ft} must also be given by (1.51). It follows that $z_{Ft} = z_{Ht} = z_t$ at all times. The overall price differential between the two countries, z_t, therefore satisfies a difference equation of the form

(1.52) $$\Delta z_t = \xi(e_t - z_t) + \beta E_t \Delta z_{t+1},$$

the solution to which is given by

(1.53) $$z_t = \mu_1 z_{t-1} + (1 - \mu_1)(1 - \beta\mu_1)\sum_{j=0}^{\infty}(\beta\mu_1)^j E_t e_{t+j}.$$

Equation (1.53) indicates that the path of z_t (and hence of the inflation differential between the two countries) is completely determined by the path of the exchange rate, just as in the PCP model; this solution replaces the simpler relation $z_t = e_t$ that held under the earlier assumption. Note that (1.53) implies that z_t is a two-sided moving average of past and expected future values of the log exchange rate. The moving average smooths the exchange rate over a longer time window the closer μ_1 is to 1, or alternatively, the smaller is ξ (which is to say, the larger is α). In the limit as $\alpha \to 0$, so that prices are completely flexible, the solution (1.53) reduces simply to $z_t = e_t$.

The complete aggregate-demand block[26] of the model with local-currency pricing then consists of equations (1.19) and (1.20) specifying the monetary policies of the two central banks, and equations (1.28), (1.45), and (1.52) that result from private optimization. Among these equilibrium conditions, all except the last also apply to the model with producer-currency pricing. The PCP model replaces (1.52) with the relation $z_t = e_t$, which is just the limiting case of (1.52) when $\alpha \to 0$. Hence the aggregate-demand relations of the PCP model correspond to the case $\alpha = 0$ of the aggregate-demand relations of the LCP model; under the PCP assumption, however, unlike the LCP model, the aggregate-demand relations are the same regardless of the degree of stickiness of prices.

A pair of aggregate-demand relations parallel to (1.26) in the case of the PCP can also be derived here. As long as the response coefficients of the policy rules satisfy certain inequalities,[27] it is possible to uniquely solve the system of equations consisting of (1.19) and (1.20), (1.28), (1.45), and (1.52) for bounded processes $\{\pi_t, \pi_t^*, \hat{\imath}_t, \hat{\imath}_t^*, e_t - z_t\}$, given any bounded processes $\{\hat{Y}_t, \hat{Y}_t^*, \bar{\imath}_t, \bar{\imath}_t^*\}$. (And once again the solution is purely forward-looking, in the sense that each of the five endogenous variables depends only on current and expected future values of the four forcing variables.) Again we find that existence of equilibrium places no (local) restrictions on the way in which monetary policy may be independently varied in the two countries, and again we find that adjustment of monetary policy in one country alone can alter the path of inflation in that country (for any given paths of real activity in the two countries).

The effects of monetary policy on inflation (or on the location of the AD curve) can be stated more explicitly in the special case in which $\phi_\pi = \phi_\pi^*$ and $\phi_y = \phi_y^*$. In this case, (1.19) and (1.20) again imply (1.29), and this can again be used to substitute for the interest-rate differential in (1.28), yielding

$$E_t \Delta e_{t+1} = (\bar{\imath}_t - \bar{\imath}_t^*) + \phi_\pi \Delta z_t + \phi_y(\hat{Y}_t - \hat{Y}_t^*). \tag{1.54}$$

However, we can no longer use the requirement that $z_t = e_t$ to transform (1.54) into (1.30). Instead we must solve the system consisting of (1.52) and (1.54) for the paths of e_t and z_t.

26. It might not seem right to call equation (1.52) part of the "aggregate-demand block" of the model, as it depends on one's model of price-setting behavior, and on the value of the parameter α. However, it is independent of the evolution of marginal cost, and so can be derived without discussing the specification of the production technology, preferences regarding labor supply, or the degree of integration of factor markets. It is also clear that (1.52) plays the same role in the LCP model as the requirement that $z_t = e_t$ in the PCP model, and we did use that relation in deriving the AD equations for the earlier model, despite the fact that it follows from an assumption about the pricing of goods. Finally, we do clearly require (1.52) in order to be able to derive the AD relations for the LCP model.

27. As in section 1.1.1, these involve only the inflation-response coefficient ϕ_π, ϕ_π^*, and once again it is necessary for a unique solution that $\phi_\pi, \phi_\pi^* > 1$.

This pair of equations can be written in the form

$$\begin{bmatrix} \Delta z_t \\ e_t - z_t \end{bmatrix} = A \begin{bmatrix} E_t \Delta z_{t+1} \\ E_t(e_{t+1} - z_{t+1}) \end{bmatrix} + a[\bar{\imath}_t^* - \bar{\imath}_t + \phi_y(\hat{Y}_t^* - \hat{Y}_t)],$$

where

$$A \equiv (1 + \phi_\pi \xi)^{-1} \begin{bmatrix} \xi & 1 \\ 1 & -\phi_\pi \end{bmatrix}$$

and a is the second column of A. One can show that A has both eigenvalues inside the unit circle if and only if $\phi_\pi > 1$; under this assumption, there is a unique bounded solution given by

$$\begin{bmatrix} \Delta z_t \\ e_t - z_t \end{bmatrix} = \sum_{j=0}^{\infty} A^j a E_t[\bar{\imath}_{t+j}^* - \bar{\imath}_{t+j} + \phi_y(\hat{Y}_{t+j}^* - \hat{Y}_{t+j})]. \tag{1.55}$$

The first line of (1.55) generalizes our previous solution (1.32) for the inflation differential;[28] while it is algebraically more complex, we again obtain a solution for the inflation differential as a function of the expected future paths of exactly the same variables as before. Once again, we find that a change in monetary policy in one country that is not matched by an equivalent change in the other country's policy necessarily changes the inflation differential between the two countries, for any given paths of output in the two countries. Moreover, in the case that $\phi_y = 0$, one can determine the effect on the inflation differential *independently* of what one may assume about aggregate supply. It is also noteworthy that while the size of the effect of a change in monetary policy on the inflation differential depends on the degree of inflation sensitivity (ϕ_π) of the central banks' reaction functions and the degree of price flexibility (ξ), it does *not* depend on the relative size of the countries (i.e., on γ).

We can complete the derivation of the AD relations for the two countries in this symmetric case, by using (1.19) and (1.20) to substitute for the interest rates in (1.45), yielding a difference equation for the world average inflation rate,

$$\pi_t^w = \phi_\pi^{-1}[E_t \pi_{t+1}^w + \sigma^{-1} E_t \hat{Y}_{t+1}^w - (\sigma^{-1} + \phi_y)\hat{Y}_t^w - \bar{\imath}_t^w]. \tag{1.56}$$

This relation can then be "solved forward" to yield[29]

$$\begin{aligned} \pi_t^w = {} & -\phi_\pi^{-1}(\sigma^{-1} + \phi_y)\hat{Y}_t^w \\ & + \sum_{j=0}^{\infty} \phi_\pi^{-(j+1)} E_t\{[\sigma^{-1} - \phi_\pi^{-1}(\sigma^{-1} + \phi_y)]\hat{Y}_{t+j+1}^w - \bar{\imath}_{t+j}^w\} \end{aligned} \tag{1.57}$$

28. Note that the first line of (1.55) reduces precisely to (1.32) in the limit as $\xi \to \infty$.

29. The necessary and sufficient condition for a unique bounded solution is again that $\phi_\pi > 1$. Under this assumption, the infinite sum is well-defined and bounded in the case of bounded forcing processes.

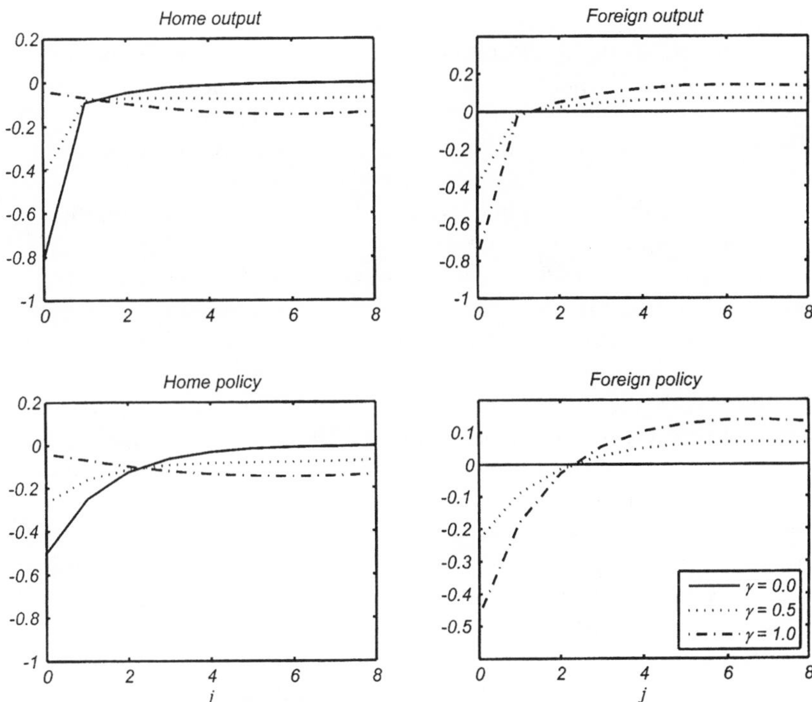

Fig. 1.4 Coefficients of the dynamic AD relation (1.27) for the model with local-currency pricing

Since both π_t and π_t^* can be expressed as linear combinations of the world average inflation rate π_t^w and the inflation differential Δz_t, the pair of equations (1.55) and (1.57) completely characterize the AD relations for the two countries.

The AD relation for the home country can again be written in the form (1.27), just as in the case of the PCP model. Figure 1.4 illustrates the numerical coefficients in the case of the same parameter values as before, and assuming in addition that $\xi = 0.04$.[30] Again the coefficients are shown for three different possible values of γ. When $\gamma = 0$ (the closed-economy limit), the LCP model is indistinguishable from the PCP model (as there are no import prices), but for $\gamma > 0$ the two models are no longer equivalent.

Note that in the limiting case of a very small country (the home country in the case that $\gamma \to 1$), domestic monetary policy is no longer able to have any influence on the predicted path of π_t^w given the expected evolution of world

30. This value as well corresponds to the magnitude of this coefficient in the empirical model of Rotemberg and Woodford (1997); see also Woodford (2003, chapter 5).

output. (Indeed, in this limiting case, π_t^w depends only on foreign output and foreign monetary policy.) But even so, (1.55) implies that the sensitivity of the inflation differential to domestic monetary policy is exactly as great as it would be for a larger country. Hence domestic inflation is still affected by domestic monetary policy, and to a nontrivial extent, as is illustrated by the coefficients in the upper left panel of figure 1.4.

It is true that in the LCP model, the slow (and smoothed) pass-through of exchange rate changes to import prices reduces the size of the immediate effect on domestic inflation of a transitory change in domestic monetary policy, relative to what occurs in the PCP model. However, this does not mean that it is harder for monetary policy to affect inflation than would be the case in a closed economy in which prices are sticky for a similar length of time. While the coefficient $\psi_{1,0}$ becomes quite small in the small open economy case, the coefficients $\psi_{1,j}$, indicating the effects of anticipated *future* domestic monetary policy on current inflation, no longer die out quickly as the horizon j increases. This means that a *persistent* shift in the central bank's policy reaction function can have a substantial immediate effect. The crucial difference is that in this model it becomes more important for interest rates to be adjusted in a relatively *inertial* way in order to have a substantial impact on aggregate demand.

In fact, a sufficiently persistent shift in policy (that is understood by the private sector) still affects inflation to the same extent as in the LCP model. For example, it follows from (1.55) that a permanent unit increase in the intercept $\bar{\imath}_t$ (corresponding to a reduction in the implicit domestic inflation target of size $[\phi_\pi - 1]^{-1}$) lowers the inflation differential immediately and permanently by the amount of the reduction in the implicit inflation target, which is the same prediction as is implied by (1.32). In the case that the home country is very small, this is also the size of the immediate, permanent reduction in domestic inflation; thus the same size effect on inflation is predicted as in the case of a closed economy.

In the example shown in figure 1.4, prices are relatively sticky,[31] as shown by the small value of ξ. This makes the equilibrium dynamics under the LCP model quite different from those of the PCP model. In figure 1.5, the coefficients of the dynamic AD relation are instead computed under the assumption that $\xi = 0.4$, implying a short-run aggregate-supply curve that is ten times as steep. In this case, the difference with figure 1.1 is less dramatic. As the value of ξ is increased still further, the coefficients for each of the values of γ all approach those shown in figure 1.1.

31. By this I mean that the rate of adjustment of price indices to changing aggregate conditions is relatively slow. This is not due solely to the value assumed for α, but also to the fact that the parameter values used by Rotemberg and Woodford imply substantial "real rigidities." See Woodford (2003, chapter 3) for further discussion.

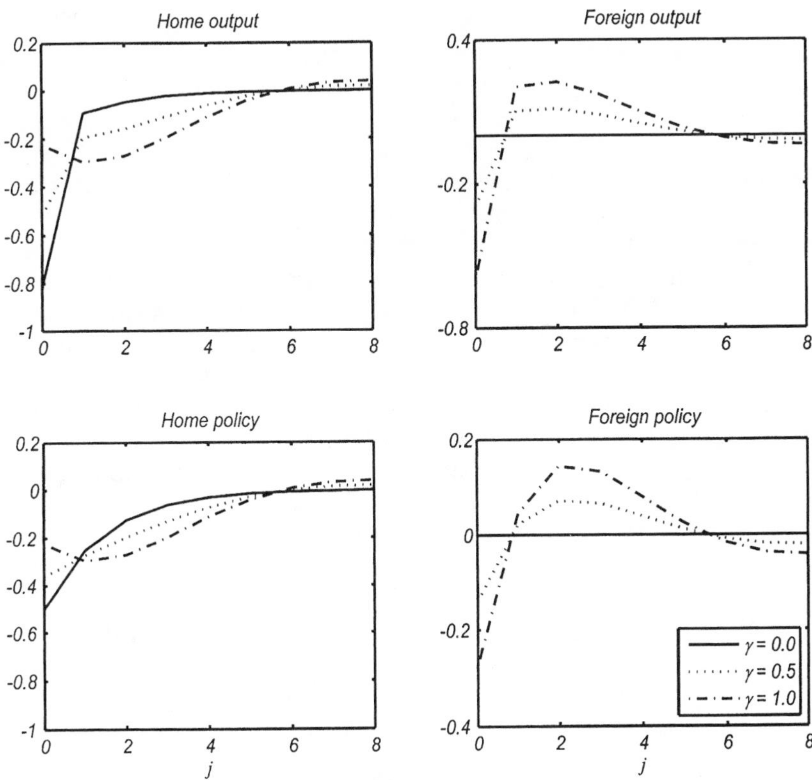

Fig. 1.5 Coefficients of the dynamic AD relation for the LCP model with $\xi = 0.4$

1.2 "Global Liquidity" and the Instruments of Monetary Policy

Another way in which globalization is sometimes supposed to reduce the significance of individual national monetary policies is by making the aggregate supply of "liquidity" by the world's central banks (rather than that supplied by a given country's central bank alone) the variable that determines the degree of stimulus to aggregate demand (and hence inflationary pressure) in that country as well as abroad. Market analysts in financial institutions have spoken a great deal recently of "global liquidity" as a factor that has supposedly been responsible for asset-price booms worldwide, and it is often proposed that this factor can be measured by growth in some aggregate of the money supplies in different currencies (e.g., Global Research, 2007), following the lead of European Central Bank (ECB) researchers such as Sousa and Zaghini (2004, 2006) and Rüffer and Stracca (2006). To the extent that such a view is correct in a globally integrated world economy, one might expect that it should mean a reduced ability of national central banks to control national inflation rates, especially in the case of small countries that supply a correspondingly small proportion of "global liquidity."

As noted in the previous section, in an open economy there are channels through which foreign monetary policy developments (among other foreign factors) will generally affect the level of domestic aggregate demand, for any given stance of domestic monetary policy. It may even be the case, though it need not be, that the effect of domestic interest-rate policy on domestic aggregate demand is smaller in the case of a small open economy than it would be for a large economy (or a closed economy). But as explained in the previous section, even in the case of full integration and the limiting case of a very small economy, the effect of domestic monetary policy on domestic demand does not become negligible, and thus the idea that only some global aggregate of liquidity creation by central banks is relevant is clearly mistaken. Moreover, monetary stimulus abroad may contract demand for domestic output, owing to the terms-of-trade effect of the depreciation of the foreign currency; in such a case, while foreign monetary policy is relevant to domestic conditions, the sign of the effect is the opposite of the one suggested by loose talk about "global liquidity."

The analysis in the previous section, however, took for granted the existence of an instrument through which a central bank can control the level of short-term nominal interest rates in terms of its currency, as long as the possibility exists of a savings-investment equilibrium at a different level of interest rates; thus it was assumed that policy can be represented by a Taylor rule, without asking how a central bank is able to implement its operating target for the nominal interest rate. It is often supposed that central-bank control over nominal interest rates depends on the central bank's role as a monopoly supplier of financial claims ("base money") that are uniquely liquid. Might integration of financial markets erode this monopoly power, so that the liquidity premium associated with base money in any country comes to depend on the global supply of liquid assets, rather than the supply by that country's central bank alone? And if so, would this mean that central banks (at least, small central banks) would lose the capacity to control nominal interest rates within their borders?

In order to consider this possibility, I first discuss the instruments through which a central bank's operating target for a domestic short-term nominal interest rate can be implemented in an open economy, relying upon a conventional model of money demand, in which it is assumed that only the liabilities of a given country's central bank are useful for facilitating transactions (and so supply liquidity services) in that country. I then consider the extent to which the conclusions would be changed if globalization were to imply that the liquidity services provided by the liabilities of a given central bank were available equally to households in all countries.

1.2.1 Money Demand and Monetary Policy Implementation in a Two-Country Model

We can introduce liquidity services from holdings of base money by supposing that the utility of households in the home economy is of the form

$$E_0 \sum_{t=0}^{\infty} \beta^t \left[u(C_t) + w\left(\frac{M_t}{P_t}\right)\right], \tag{2.1}$$

where $u(C)$ is again defined by (1.2) and (1.3), M_t indicates home-currency money balances, and

$$w(m) \equiv \lambda \frac{m^{1-\sigma_m^{-1}}}{1-\sigma_m^{-1}}$$

for some $\sigma_m > 0$. Because of the additive separability of the utility function between consumption and liquidity services, the conclusions of section 1.1 are not changed by the addition of the new term; this will only affect the demand for money balances (not treated earlier).

Base money is assumed to be a one-period liability of the central bank that promises a riskless nominal return (in units of the domestic currency) of i_t^m between periods t and $t+1$; the rate i_t^m is an administered rate (rather than market-determined), and the choice of it is an additional potential instrument of policy for the central bank. (Under some regimes, like that of the United States at present, $i_t^m = 0$ at all times; but this is a choice rather than a logical necessity.[32]) The flow budget constraint of a household is then of the form[33]

$$P_tC_t + M_t + E_t[Q_{t,t+1}A_{t+1}] \leq (1 + i_{t-1}^m)M_{t-1} + A_t + P_tY_t - T_t,$$

where A_t denotes the state-contingent nominal value (in units of the home currency) of the household's portfolio of nonmonetary financial claims carried into period t and T_t represents net nominal tax collections by the home government. Here it is assumed that (in order for there to exist no arbitrage opportunities) all nonmonetary financial assets are priced using the common stochastic discount factor $Q_{t,t+1}$ (so that any portfolio with state-contingent payoff A_{t+1} in period $t+1$ must cost $E_t[Q_{t,t+1}A_{t+1}]$ in period t), while money is not because of its additional service flow. Under the assumption of complete financial markets, we need not describe any specific nonmonetary financial

32. See Woodford (2001) and Woodford (2003, chapter 1) for discussion of other countries where interest is paid on central-bank balances, and where variation in the administered deposit rate in accordance with changes in the central bank's interest rate target plays an important role in the implementation of policy.

33. See the text explaining equations (1.2) and (1.3) of Woodford (2003, chapter 2) for further discussion. The flow budget constraint here is of exactly the same form as in a closed economy model, as purchases of foreign goods are included as part of the aggregate C_t and the prices of imported goods are included as part of the price index P_t.

assets, and can suppose that households directly choose the state-contingent future payoffs that they prefer.[34]

One can alternatively write the flow budget constraint in the form[35]

$$P_tC_t + \Delta_tM_t + E_t[Q_{t,t+1}W_{t+1}] \leq W_t + P_tY_t - T_t, \tag{2.2}$$

where $W_t \equiv (1 + i^m_{t-1})M_{t-1} + A_t$ is the total value of nominal financial wealth at the beginning of period t, and

$$\Delta_t \equiv \frac{i_t - i^m_t}{1 + i_t}$$

is the *interest-rate differential* between equally riskless, equally short-maturity *nonmonetary* nominal assets (assumed not to yield any "liquidity services") and money. (In the familiar textbook case of zero interest on money balances, Δ_t is simply a monotonic transformation of the nominal interest rate i_t.) It is evident from (2.2) that the differential Δ_t measures the opportunity cost of holding part of one's wealth in monetary form. Consequently household optimization requires that

$$\frac{w'(M_t/P_t)}{u'(C_t)} = \Delta_t \tag{2.3}$$

each period.

We can solve (2.3) for desired real money balances, obtaining

$$\frac{M_t}{P_t} = L(C_t, \Delta_t) \equiv \lambda^{\sigma_m}\frac{C_t^{\sigma_m/\sigma}}{\Delta_t^{\sigma_m}}.$$

Substituting (1.15), we obtain

$$\frac{M_t}{P_t} = \lambda^{\sigma_m}k^{\sigma_m/\sigma}\frac{Y_t^{(1-\gamma)\sigma_m/\sigma}Y_t^{*\gamma\sigma_m/\sigma}}{\Delta_t^{\sigma_m}} \tag{2.4}$$

as an open economy generalization of the "LM equation" of a canonical closed economy model. Similar equations hold for the foreign country; in particular, we obtain the equilibrium relation

$$\frac{M_t^*}{P_t^*} = \lambda^{\sigma_m}k^{\sigma_m/\sigma}\frac{Y_t^{(1-\gamma)\sigma_m/\sigma}Y_t^{*\gamma\sigma_m/\sigma}}{\Delta_t^{*\sigma_m}}, \tag{2.5}$$

where M_t^* represents holdings of foreign-currency money balances per foreign household, and Δ_t^* is the corresponding differential between the

34. Our conclusions about money demand in this section do not depend on the assumption of complete markets; the first-order condition (2.3) derived following for optimal money holdings would also be obtained for an economy with no financial assets other than money and a one-period riskless nominal claim earning the interest rate i_t.

35. Again, see the discussion of equation (1.7) in Woodford (2003, chapter 2) for explanation.

foreign-currency nominal interest rate i_t^* and the interest rate i_t^{m*} paid by the foreign central bank.

If we represent the monetary policy of each central bank by a path for the monetary base (rather than a Taylor rule), as is often done in models of exchange rate determination, then the aggregate-demand block of the model (with producer-currency pricing) consists of equations (1.17) and (1.18) and (2.4) and (2.5): two equations for each country (an "IS equation" and an "LM equation"), that jointly suffice to determine the paths of $\{P_t, P_t^*, i_t, i_t^*\}$, given paths for $\{Y_t, Y_t^*\}$ and the policy variables $\{M_t, M_t^*, i_t^m, i_t^{m*}\}$. Alternatively, if we suppose that policy is specified in each country by a Taylor rule, and adjustments of the monetary base (through open-market purchases of securities) are simply used to *implement* the prescriptions of the Taylor rule, then equations (1.17) and (1.18) and (1.19) and (1.20) determine the relations between prices, interest rates, and real activity as before; but equations (2.4) and (2.5) must now also hold, and determine the adjustments of the monetary base and/or the interest paid on base money that are required in order to implement the policies.

Local equilibrium determination can again be studied by log-linearizing equations (2.4) and (2.5), yielding

$$\log M_t - \log P_t = \eta_y \hat{Y}_t + \eta_y^* \hat{Y}_t^* - \eta_i(\hat{\imath}_t - \hat{\imath}_t^m), \tag{2.6}$$

$$\log M_t^* - \log P_t^* = \eta_y \hat{Y}_t + \eta_y^* \hat{Y}_t^* - \eta_i(\hat{\imath}_t^* - \hat{\imath}_t^{m*}), \tag{2.7}$$

where

$$\eta_y \equiv (1-\gamma)\frac{\sigma_m}{\sigma}, \quad \eta_y^* \equiv \gamma\frac{\sigma_m}{\sigma}, \quad \eta_i \equiv \left(\frac{1-\bar{\Delta}}{\bar{\Delta}}\right)\sigma_m.$$

Here I have log-linearized around a zero-inflation steady state in which the rate of interest on money is assumed to satisfy

$$0 \leq \bar{\imath}^m < \beta^{-1} - 1,$$

as is necessary for the existence of such a steady state;

$$\bar{\Delta} \equiv 1 - \beta(1 + \bar{\imath}^m) > 0$$

is the implied steady-state interest differential; and

$$\hat{\imath}_t^m \equiv \log\left(\frac{1 + i_t^m}{1 + \bar{\imath}^m}\right)$$

is defined analogously with the previous definition of $\hat{\imath}_t$.[36]

36. The method and notation follow the treatment of a closed economy model in Woodford (2003, chapter 2, section 3.3). Note that I have also chosen units (as is possible without loss of generality) in which the steady-state level of real money balances is equal to 1 in each country, so that I can drop the constant that would otherwise appear in each of the equations (2.6) and (2.7).

One observes that to this order of approximation, the allowance for two distinct instruments of monetary policy (variations in the base and variations in the rate of interest paid on the base) is redundant. This follows from the fact that it is only the quantity $\log M_t - \eta_i \hat{\imath}_t^m$ that matters in equation (2.6). This means that any policy aim that can be achieved by varying the interest rate paid on money can alternatively be achieved through an appropriate adjustment of the monetary base.[37] In the case of the very conventional assumption made here about the nature of the demand for liquidity, no underestimation of the scope for an independent national monetary policy results from stipulating that $i_t^m = 0$ at all times, as is typically assumed in textbook treatments. One can then represent the monetary policies of the two countries simply in terms of the paths of the two countries' monetary bases; that is, the supply of "liquidity" by the two central banks.

We see that openness results in the "LM equations" of the two economies' being interrelated, just as was true (in general) of their "IS equations" in section 1.1. To what extent does it make sense, though, to say that in a globalized economy, the supply of "global liquidity" should be an important determinant of equilibrium in each individual country? Suppose that we derive AD relations for each of the two countries, taking as given the paths of money for the two countries. We can do this by using each country's IS relation to eliminate the nominal interest rate from its LM relation. We obtain a difference equation for the price level of the form

$$(1 + \eta_i)\log P_t - \eta_i E_t \log P_{t+1} = \log M_t - \eta_i \hat{\imath}_t^m - (\eta_y + \eta_i \sigma^{-1})\hat{Y}_t^w + \eta_i \sigma^{-1} E_t \hat{Y}_{t+1}^w,$$

which can be solved forward to yield

$$\log P_t = \sum_{j=0}^{\infty}(1 - \alpha)\alpha^j E_t[\log M_{t+j} - \eta_i \hat{\imath}_{t+j}^m] - [(1 - \alpha)\eta_y + \alpha\sigma^{-1}]\hat{Y}_t^w - \sum_{j=1}^{\infty}(1 - \alpha)\alpha^j[\eta_y - \sigma^{-1}]E_t \hat{Y}_{t+j}^w \tag{2.8}$$

for the equilibrium domestic price level corresponding to any expected paths of domestic and foreign output, where

$$\alpha \equiv \frac{\eta_i}{1 + \eta_i} < 1.$$

(A similar equation holds for the foreign price level.)

We see that, conditioning on the paths of real activity in the two countries,

37. Of course, there could nonetheless be practical advantages to the use of one technique over the other. For example, calculating the interest-rate effect of a given size change in the rate of interest paid on base money is much more straightforward than guessing the size of open-market operation required to achieve the same effect, especially in the presence of disturbances to the money-demand relation, not modeled in the simple treatment here.

the price level in a given country depends only on current and expected future monetary policy in *that country alone,* and not on "global liquidity" at all. (This is the same conclusion as we reached in section 1.1, when monetary policy was instead specified by a Taylor rule for each country.) Thus to the extent that monetary policy spillovers exist between countries, they do not occur through the aggregate demand side of the model, as the notion of "global liquidity" would suggest. And if we specify the supply side of the model in such a way that output is unaffected by monetary policy (for example, by assuming flexible wages and prices), it will follow that inflation in one country will be completely independent of monetary policy in the other country, no matter how small the country in question may be.

If, instead, we assume the existence of nominal rigidities that allow monetary policy to affect real activity, foreign monetary policy will affect inflation determination in the home country (assuming again that home country monetary policy is specified by a given path for the monetary base). However, the spillovers that exist will not be of the sort suggested by the theory of "global liquidity." We observe from (2.6) that a change in the level of foreign economic activity will shift the home country LM curve, for a given home money supply. But (since $\eta_y^* > 0$) expansionary policy in the foreign country, which raises Y^*, will have the same effect as a *contractionary* monetary shock in the home country. This is because higher foreign output increases demand for the home currency at any given level of domestic output. Such an effect is the *opposite* of the effect that the "global liquidity" thesis would suggest.

1.2.2 Consequences of Currency Substitution

Some may suppose that the model presented previously fails to find a role for "global liquidity" because of the conventional assumption that households in a given country obtain liquidity services only by holding the money issued by their own central bank (on the grounds that only this asset has a special role as a means of payment within those borders). What if globalization also means global competition among media for executing payments? There is little evidence that this is already an important phenomenon at present, but one might conjecture that it could happen in the future as a result of the same sorts of improvements in communications technology (and relaxation of regulations) that have already led to great increases in the degree of integration of financial markets. To the extent that this were to occur, would some global liquidity aggregate, rather than the money supplied by the local central bank, become a primary determinant of aggregate demand in all countries? And if so, would this mean a loss of control over domestic inflation by central banks, unless they arrange an appropriate worldwide coordination of their policies?

To clarify ideas, I shall proceed directly to the most extreme hypothetical, of a world in which each of the two central banks' currencies supply liquidity services *of exactly the same kind* to households in either country. Would only "global liquidity" matter in that case? One possible case of this kind is that in which households in each country have the same utility function,

$$E_0 \sum_{t=0}^{\infty} \beta^t \left[u(C_t) + \delta w\left(\frac{M_{Ht}}{P_t}\right) + \delta^* w\left(\frac{M_{Ft}}{P_t^*}\right) \right], \tag{2.9}$$

for some weights $\delta, \delta^* > 0$, where $w(m)$ is the same function as before. Here C_t is the household's purchases of the world consumption aggregate, M_{Ht} is its holdings of the home currency, and M_{Ft} its holdings of the foreign currency. (This notation applies to the choices of a household in the home country. A foreign household has an identical utility function, but its choice variables are starred.) The liquidity services obtained from money balances depend on the purchasing power of those balances, in units of the world good (which is what the household cares about purchasing). Because the law of one price holds (in the PCP version of the model), the relevant measure of real balances for households in either country is obtained by deflating home-currency balances by P_t and deflating foreign-currency balances by P_t^*.

In this case, households in each country choose to hold positive balances of both currencies, and the demand for the home currency by households in either country is of the form (2.4), with λ replaced by the appropriate multiplicative factor. Total world demand for the home currency will then equal supply if and only if

$$\begin{aligned}(1-\gamma)M_t &= (1-\gamma)M_{Ht} + \gamma M_{Ht}^* \\ &= (1-\gamma)\delta^{\sigma_m} L(C_t, \Delta_t)P_t + \gamma\delta^{\sigma_m} L(C_t^*, \Delta_t)P_t \\ &= (1-\gamma)\tilde{\lambda}^{\sigma_m} k^{\sigma_m/\sigma} \frac{Y_t^{(1-\gamma)\sigma_m/\sigma} Y_t^{*\gamma\sigma_m/\sigma}}{\Delta_t^{\sigma_m}} P_t,\end{aligned}$$

where $\tilde{\lambda} \equiv \delta\lambda/(1-\gamma)^{\sigma_m^{-1}}$. This is an equilibrium relation of *exactly the same form* as (2.4), except that λ is replaced by $\tilde{\lambda}$. The two equations are identical, even in scale, if $\delta = (1-\gamma)^{\sigma_m^{-1}}$; but even if not, they have the same form (2.6) when log-linearized. The condition for supply of the foreign currency to equal world demand for it similarly leads to an equilibrium condition of exactly the same form as (2.5). Hence the form of the two "LM equations" is *exactly the same* in this variant of the model, with exactly the same implications for the ability of a central bank to control domestic aggregate demand through the instruments of monetary policy.

Thus, the fact that independent variation in the supply of one currency influences the corresponding price level in the way indicated in (2.8) is not at all dependent on assuming that the advantages flowing from holding a particular liquid asset are only available in one country. The only assumption that is essential is the assumption that the two currencies are not *perfect substitutes* as means of facilitating transactions in either country. (Preferences

[2.9] imply that the elasticity of substitution between the two types of cash balances in the provision of liquidity services is only σ_m.)

A still more extreme assumption would be to suppose that the two kinds of money are instead perfect substitutes in liquidity provision. One might instead assume that households in each country have preferences of the form

$$E_0 \sum_{t=0}^{\infty} \beta^t \left[u(C_t) + w\left(\frac{M_{Ht}}{P_t} + \frac{M_{Ft}}{P_t^*} \right) \right], \tag{2.10}$$

where $w(m)$ is the same function as before. In this case, one would no longer be able to derive separate demand functions for the two currencies. All households will instead choose to hold only the currency with the lower opportunity cost; if positive quantities of both are supplied, equilibrium is only possible if

$$\Delta_t = \Delta_t^*. \tag{2.11}$$

There will then be a well-behaved demand function for the sum of the two types of real balances, and a corresponding equilibrium condition

$$(1-\gamma)\frac{M_t}{P_t} + \gamma \frac{M_t^*}{P_t^*} = \lambda^{\sigma_m} k^{\sigma_m/\sigma} \frac{Y_t^{(1-\gamma)\sigma_m/\sigma} Y_t^{*\gamma\sigma_m/\sigma}}{\Delta_t^{\sigma_m}}. \tag{2.12}$$

The pair of equilibrium conditions (2.11) and (2.12) would replace the conditions (2.4) and (2.5) in the aggregate demand block of a model with perfect currency substitutability.

In this case, it really would be true that only "global liquidity" matters for aggregate demand determination; that is, the money supply of neither country would matter, except through its contribution to aggregate global real balances, defined by the left-hand side of (2.12). In the case of a small country, the monetary base of which would make only a negligible contribution to global real balances, variations in the monetary base would have essentially no effect on aggregate demand there or elsewhere, and so would be irrelevant to domestic inflation determination.

Nonetheless, it would not follow that a small country would be unable to use an independent monetary policy to control domestic inflation. The reason is that in this case the additional instrument of policy, the possibility of varying the interest rate paid on money, would no longer be redundant. Condition (2.11), which can alternatively be written

$$\frac{1+i_t}{1+i_t^*} = \frac{1+i_t^m}{1+i_t^{m*}},$$

implies that the nominal interest-rate differential between the two countries (for nonmonetary riskless assets) must be directly determined by the differential between the interest rates paid on money by the two central banks. This means that independent variation in the rate paid on money in a small country can influence aggregate nominal expenditure in that country, whether or not it is accompanied by changes in the monetary base. Thus, in a world in which the liabilities of different central banks came to be close substitutes for one another in facilitating transactions worldwide, it would become essential to use variations in the (administratively determined) interest yield on base money as the means through which central-bank operating targets for domestic short-term nominal interest rates are implemented.[38]

As a simple example of how inflation control would be possible using this instrument, consider a small open economy (i.e., one for which γ is essentially equal to 1), so that monetary policy decisions of the small country can have no effect on the evolution of foreign variables such as P_t^*, Y_t^*, i_t^*, or i_t^{m*}. It follows from (2.12) that the small country's policy will be unable to affect the value of Δ_t either. Nonetheless, the small country's central bank can set the interest rate i_t^m on the domestic monetary base as it pleases. Suppose that it sets it in accordance with a reaction function of the form

$$\hat{\imath}_t^m = \bar{\imath}_t + \phi_\pi \pi_t,$$

where $\bar{\imath}_t$ is an exogenous process with respect to the evolution of domestic variables, but may depend on the evolution of foreign variables.

Then subtracting (1.22) from (1.21), and using the log-linearized version of (2.11) to replace the interest-rate differential $\hat{\imath}_t - \hat{\imath}_t^*$ by $\hat{\imath}_t^m - \hat{\imath}_t^{m*}$, we obtain the equilibrium relation

$$\hat{\imath}_t^m - \hat{\imath}_t^{m*} = E_t(\pi_{t+1} - \pi_{t+1}^*).$$

Substituting the reaction function for $\hat{\imath}_t^m$, we find that in equilibrium, the domestic inflation process must satisfy

$$\phi_\pi \pi_t = E_t \pi_{t+1} + (\hat{\imath}_t^{m*} - E_t \pi_{t+1}^* - \bar{\imath}_t).$$

In the case that $\phi_\pi > 1$, this has a unique bounded solution,

$$\pi_t = \sum_{j=0}^{\infty} \phi_\pi^{-(j+1)} E_t(\hat{\imath}_{t+j}^{m*} - \pi_{t+j+1}^* - \bar{\imath}_{t+j}). \tag{2.13}$$

This shows that variations in the rate of interest paid on the monetary base can still be effectively used to control the domestic rate of inflation, even under the assumption that the liabilities of different central banks are equally useful as sources of liquidity in all parts of the world. It is true that in such a world, foreign developments would matter for inflation determina-

38. This is already a crucial element in monetary policy implementation in countries with "channel systems" like Canada, Australia, and New Zealand, and their success indicates that it would remain entirely feasible to conduct a national interest rate policy without any ability to alter the spread between the returns on nonmonetary assets and base money. See discussion in Woodford (2001) of the related issue of monetary policy implementation in a world where central banks have to compete with private suppliers of transactions media.

tion in the small country, and the interest paid on money would have to be adjusted so as to offset those developments, in order for a stable inflation rate to be maintained in the small country. But even so, it is not true that the central bank's main problem would be offsetting the inflationary impact of variations in "global liquidity." One sees from (2.13) that what the central bank actually needs to offset is variations in *the real rate of return on money balances* in the rest of the world. Moreover, it is *increases* rather than decreases in the real return on money elsewhere in the world that would be inflationary in the small country, if not offset by a corresponding increase in the interest paid on money in the small country.

Of course, "dollarization" does imply reduced efficacy of domestic monetary policy in a small open economy in one respect, if it means not only that the foreign currency can be used a means of payment (and so supplies liquidity services), but also that prices of domestic goods are quoted in, and sticky in, the foreign currency rather than the domestic currency. In that case, it would remain true that domestic monetary policy should be able to stabilize the purchasing power of the domestic currency, but this would no longer imply an ability to *eliminate the distortions due to price stickiness* in the domestic economy.[39] Indeed, if few domestic goods continue to be priced in terms of the domestic currency, then the stability or otherwise of the value of that currency would cease to have any real consequences, and cease to have any welfare consequences—domestic monetary policy would indeed be irrelevant. But this is hardly an inevitable result of globalization, even under the assumption that eventually multiple currencies might come to be widely accepted as means of payment in a given location. When one observes prices being fixed in a currency other than the local currency, this is typically because the purchasing power of the local currency is expected to be less stable than that of the foreign currency; a central bank that stabilizes a domestic price index in terms of its own currency has little reason to fear that domestic prices will cease to be fixed in that currency, even if the costs of transacting in foreign currencies are reduced.

1.3 "Global Slack" and Inflation Determination

Thus far I have discussed only the aggregate demand block of an open economy macroeconomic model, asking how monetary policy affects the equilibrium inflation rate that would be associated with any given path for real activity. This has meant leaving aside the question of the extent to which a given effect of national monetary policy on the aggregate demand relation should result in a different rate of inflation as opposed to a different level of real activity. If we are willing to assume that the level of real activity in each country should be determined by factors such as technology and

39. This has been stressed by David Romer, in a comment on an earlier draft.

preferences, quite independently of monetary policy in either country (as real business cycle theories assert), then the analysis previously given would already offer a complete answer to the question of how monetary policy affects inflation in a globalized economy. But in the presence of nominal rigidities this will not be true, and we need to consider the "aggregate supply block" of the model as well in order to determine the effects of monetary policy on *either* output or inflation.

The question of how globalization should affect aggregate supply relations—the connection that should exist between inflation and real activity as a result of the way that the incentives that firms have to change their prices vary depending on the degree of utilization of productive capacity—is of considerable interest in its own right. It is sometimes argued that increased international trade in goods and services should make inflation in any country more a function of "global slack"—the balance that exists between worldwide productive capacity and world demand—than of the balance between demand and capacity in that country alone. Economists at the Bank for International Settlements (BIS) in particular (Borio and Filardo 2007) have argued that in a globalized economy, domestic slack alone should matter less than global slack as a determinant of domestic inflation, and have suggested that there is evidence that this is already true to some extent. (See, however, Ihrig et al. [2007] for a contrary view of the empirical evidence.)

To the extent that this thesis is correct, one might expect it to pose a threat to central bank control of domestic inflation, even granting our previous conclusions about the continued influence of national monetary policy over aggregate demand. In particular, one might suppose that even if domestic monetary policy can affect aggregate demand for domestic output, if the domestic output gap ceases to be a significant determinant of inflation, a national central bank will cease to have much ability to influence the domestic inflation rate, which will instead depend primarily on the international factors that determine "global slack." Thus, one might expect national monetary policy to become ineffective in controlling inflation, especially in the case of a small country that can contribute little to either world demand or world productive capacity. Our conclusions about the continued significance of national monetary policy for aggregate demand would presumably then imply that monetary policy should have an even greater effect on real activity in a globalized economy—but this would be little comfort to those concerned about inflation risk.

Indeed, under the "global slack" hypothesis, the efficacy of domestic monetary policy in affecting the level of real activity, without any notable effect on domestic inflation, might be expected to lead to monetary policies in each country with joint consequences for global slack that are more inflationary than any country would like. Even if one were to grant that central banks should still be able to control inflation, one might fear that they will have less incentive to do so if they perceive themselves to face a flatter Phillips-curve trade-off between domestic output expansion and domestic inflation. (This is presumably the reason for the concern of Borio and Filardo that a "more elastic" economy will encourage a loss of monetary discipline.)

In this section, I consider the degree of concern that should be given to threats of this kind by analyzing the consequences of openness in goods and factor markets for aggregate-supply relations in a model with nominal rigidities. I give particular attention to the consequences of openness for the slope of the Phillips curve trade-off, and also to the degree to which it is true that domestic inflation should be determined by "global slack" as opposed to (or in addition to) a domestic output gap. I begin by reviewing the answers to these questions in the canonical two-country model of CGG, and then consider some variations on that model that might be expected to increase the importance of "global slack."

1.3.1 Aggregate Supply In a Two-Country Model

A variety of arguments have been given for the view that world economic activity, rather than domestic activity alone, should be important for inflation determination in a globalized economy. Bernanke (2007) interprets the global slack hypothesis as a simple observation that if domestic products are sold in global markets, global income (rather than domestic income alone) will become an important determinant of the demand for those products and hence, of the incentives that domestic producers have to raise their prices. Note that under this interpretation it is still the domestic output gap (the balance between the demand for domestic products and domestic productive capacity) that determines domestic inflation, rather than any concept of global slack; but global income affects domestic inflation insofar as it may be an important determinant—perhaps even the main determinant—of domestic aggregate demand.

This mechanism is one that we have already considered in the analysis of aggregate demand in section 1.1. In the model of consumer demand in a globalized economy presented there, the demand for any given product does indeed depend on world income rather than domestic income, since households in both countries are assumed to allocate their expenditure across different goods in precisely the same proportions. (This is obviously an extreme assumption that gives the greatest possible weight to the consideration raised by Bernanke.) But this obviously has no consequences for the slope of the Phillips curve, and as already shown in the earlier discussion, it does not imply any reduction in the effectiveness of domestic monetary policy in controlling domestic inflation. The effects of monetary policy on domestic inflation do not decline in the case that γ is made large, even though this means that nearly all of the demand for domestic products is foreign demand.

Another argument that similarly does not depend on any denial of the link between the domestic output gap and domestic inflation (here understood to be the rate of increase of the prices of domestically produced goods), is to observe that in a globalized economy, a larger part of the consumption basket in the domestic economy will consist of imported goods. Even if domestic inflation depends solely on the domestic output gap, a broader measure of CPI inflation will also depend on the rate of growth of import prices. A naive argument might suggest that just as domestic inflation depends on the domestic output gap, the rate of growth of the prices of foreign goods should depend on the foreign output gap (which would therefore also matter for domestic CPI inflation, and would arguably be the main thing that should matter in the case of a small country that consumes mainly foreign goods). This would be incorrect, as it neglects the effects of exchange rate changes. Nonetheless, CPI inflation should depend on changes in the terms of trade in addition to the determinants of domestic inflation, and the equilibrium terms of trade should depend on foreign output (though not the foreign output gap).

But the main argument of proponents of the global slack hypothesis seems to be that in a globalized economy, the domestic output gap ceases to be the sole determinant of the incentive that domestic firms have to raise their prices. There are a variety of reasons why the simple relation between real marginal cost (more precisely, the ratio of the marginal cost of domestic production to the price of domestic products, and hence the incentive of domestic firms to change their prices) and the domestic output gap that holds in a closed economy model will generally not hold in an open economy model. Even in the simple model of CGG, where the only variable factor is labor and there is no international mobility of labor, real wage demands should not depend solely on domestic production. This is because of the way in which the representative household's marginal utility of income (in units of domestic goods) depends both on the quantity consumed of foreign as well as domestic goods and on the terms of trade. These factors result in the presence, in general, of foreign-output terms in the domestic aggregate-supply equation of a canonical two-country model.

Here I present a basic model that essentially recapitulates the results of CGG before turning to an alternative model that incorporates an additional reason for world economic activity to matter. The demand side of the model is the one already explained in section 1.1.1. The home economy consists of a continuum (of length $1 - \gamma$) of households, indexed by h. Each of these seeks to maximize[40]

$$E_0 \sum_{t=0}^{\infty} \beta^t [u(C_t) - v(H_t; \overline{H}_t)], \tag{3.1}$$

40. Here I again abstract from the liquidity services that may be provided by money balances, as in section 1.1. Adding additional terms to the utility function, as in (2.1), would make no difference for the issues addressed in this section.

where the utility from consumption $u(C)$ is again defined by (1.2) and (1.3), H_t is hours worked, $\overline{H}_t$ is an exogenous preference shock,[41] and the disutility of working is assumed to be of the form

$$v(H; \overline{H}) = \frac{1}{1+\nu}\left(\frac{H}{\overline{H}}\right)^{1+\nu}$$

for some $\nu \geq 0$. For now I shall assume, like CGG, that firms hire labor only from households in their own country.

Assuming for simplicity a competitive spot market for labor, the preferences (3.1) imply that in each period, the labor supply of each household is given by

$$H_t = \overline{H}_t\left(\frac{W_t}{P_t C_t^{\sigma^{-1}}}\right)^{\nu^{-1}}, \tag{3.2}$$

where W_t is home country nominal wage. We can alternatively invert this relation to write the real wage as a function of per capita labor demand, obtaining

$$\frac{W_t}{P_t} = C_t^{\sigma^{-1}}\left(\frac{H_t}{\overline{H}_t}\right)^{\nu}. \tag{3.3}$$

In each country, there is assumed to be a continuum of length 1 of differentiated goods produced; thus C_{Ht} is a Dixit-Stiglitz constant elasticity of substitution (CES) aggregate of the quantities consumed of the continuum of goods produced in the home country (and similarly for C_{Ft}). It follows as usual that optimal allocation of expenditure across goods implies a per capita demand for each good given by

$$y_t(i) = Y_t\left(\frac{p_t(i)}{P_{Ht}}\right)^{-\theta}, \tag{3.4}$$

where Y_t is the per capita demand for the composite home good (as in section 1.1), $p_t(i)$ is the price of individual home good i, P_{Ht} is the Dixit-Stiglitz index of home goods prices

$$P_{Ht}^{1-\theta} \equiv \int_0^1 p_t(i)^{1-\theta} di \tag{3.5}$$

41. The preference shock $\overline{H}_t$ is introduced in order to allow for a country-specific labor supply shock. Clarida, Galí, and Gertler allow for one, but in their model it is interpreted as exogenous variation in a "wage markup," due to variation in the elasticity of substitution between the different types of labor supplied by monopolistically competitive households, rather than a preference shock. The assumption of a preference shock here is more conventional, and in addition the assumption here of perfect substitutability of the labor supplied by different households facilitates the discussion of the consequences of globalization of the labor market in the next section. The difference between the two types of labor-supply shocks would be important in an analysis of optimal stabilization policy, but that is not the concern of this chapter.

already introduced in section 1.1, and $\theta > 1$ is the elasticity of substitution among these goods.

Let us suppose further that the producer of each differentiated good i has a production function of the form

$$y_t(i) = A_t h_t(i)^{1/\phi}, \tag{3.6}$$

where A_t is a productivity factor common to all of the firms in the same country, $h_t(i)$ is the labor input hired by firm i, and $\phi \geq 1$. Here I generalize the specification of CGG to allow for the possibility of diminishing returns to the labor input; the case $\phi > 1$ can be interpreted as a technology with constant returns to scale in capital and labor, but with the capital stock of each firm fixed, as discussed in Woodford (2003, chapter 3). It follows that the labor demanded by each firm will equal

$$h_t(i) = \left(\frac{y_t(i)}{A_t}\right)^{\phi} = \left(\frac{Y_t}{A_t}\right)^{\phi}\left(\frac{p_t(i)}{P_{Ht}}\right)^{-\theta\phi},$$

using the demand curve (3.4) to express the firm's sales as a function of its price. Similarly, the aggregate demand for labor in the home country will equal

$$H_t = \int_0^1 h_t(i)di = \left(\frac{Y_t}{A_t}\right)^{\phi}\delta_t, \tag{3.7}$$

where

$$\delta_t \equiv \int_0^1 \left(\frac{p_t(i)}{P_{Ht}}\right)^{-\theta\phi} di \geq 1$$

is a measure of the dispersion of home goods prices (achieving its minimum value of 1 if and only if all home goods have identical prices).

The producer of each differentiated good is assumed to adjust the price of the goods only at random intervals, as in the model of staggered pricing introduced by Calvo (1983). Let us suppose that a fraction $0 < \alpha < 1$ of the producers leave the prices of their goods unchanged each period; those that revise their prices in period t each choose a new price $p_t(i)$ to maximize

$$E_t \sum_{T=t}^{\infty} \alpha^{T-t} Q_{t,T}[p_t(i)y_T(i) - C(y_T(i); W_T, A_T)],$$

where

$$C_t(y_t(i); W_t, A_t) \equiv W_t\left(\frac{y_t(i)}{A_t}\right)^{\phi}$$

is the (nominal) cost of producing quantity $y_t(i)$, subject to the constraint that the firm's sales will be given by (3.4) in each period. (Here the firm treats the evolution of the variables $\{Y_t, P_t, W_t\}$ as independent of its own pricing decision, because it is small compared to the overall markets for domestic goods and labor.) The optimal price $p_t(i)$ that is chosen then satisfies a first-order condition of the form

$$E_t \sum_{T=t}^{\infty} \alpha^{T-t} Q_{t,T} y_T(i)[p_t(i) - \tilde{\mu} MC_T(i)] = 0, \tag{3.8}$$

where $MC_t(i)$ is the (nominal) marginal cost of production by firm i in period t, and $\tilde{\mu} \equiv \theta/(\theta - 1) > 1$ is each firm's desired markup of price over marginal cost. Thus, the price that is chosen is $\tilde{\mu}$ times a weighted average of the marginal cost that is anticipated at each of the future dates at which the currently chosen price may still apply.

Finally, substitution of (3.3) for the wage in the cost function, and (3.7) for the demand for labor in the resulting expression, allows us to derive an expression of the form

$$MC_t(i) = MC_t \left(\frac{y_t(i)}{Y_t} \right)^{\omega_p} \tag{3.9}$$

for the marginal cost of production of firm i, where

$$MC_t = \phi P_t \frac{Y_t^{\omega} C_t^{\sigma^{-1}}}{A_t^{1+\omega} \overline{H}_t^{\nu}} \delta_t^{\nu} \tag{3.10}$$

is a geometric average of the marginal costs of all home firms, and I define the new coefficients[42]

$$\omega \equiv (1 + \nu)\phi - 1 \geq \omega_p \equiv \phi - 1 \geq 0.$$

In the case of a closed economy model, one would furthermore equate C_t with Y_t, so that (3.10) would imply an elasticity of average real marginal cost with respect to output of $\omega + \sigma^{-1}$, as in Woodford (2003, chapter 3). In the open economy model of CGG, instead, C_t must equal the right-hand side of (1.15).[43] Using this relation to substitute for C_t in (3.10), one obtains the alternative expression

$$MC_t = \phi k^{\sigma^{-1}} P_t \frac{Y_t^{\omega+\sigma^{-1}(1-\gamma)} Y_t^{*\sigma^{-1}\gamma}}{A_t^{1+\omega} \overline{H}_t^{\nu}} \delta_t^{\nu}.$$

(Note that this reduces to the closed economy marginal cost function in the case that $\gamma = 0$.) We can instead write marginal cost purely as a function of

42. Here the notation follows Woodford (2003, chapter 3), where these coefficients are defined in the case of more general utility and production functions. The first inequality is strict unless $\nu = 0$ (no increasing marginal disutility of work), and the second inequality is strict unless $\phi = 1$ (no diminishing returns to labor).

43. Here I assume that $C_t = C_t^* = C_t^w$. It has already been shown in section 1.1.1 that the ratio C_t/C_t^* must be constant over time, as the growth rate of consumption must always be the same in both countries. If one assumes an appropriate initial wealth distribution (i.e., zero initial net foreign assets for each country), the constant ratio is equal to 1, so that one must have $C_t = C_t^* = C_t^w$. Even without this assumption, C_t would always be a fixed proportion of C_t^w, so that the asserted conclusion about the marginal cost function would still hold, up to a multiplicative constant.

domestic goods prices and real variables by using (1.34) to substitute for P_t in the previous expression, yielding

$$(3.11) \qquad MC_t = \frac{\phi}{k^{1-\sigma^{-1}}} P_{Ht} \frac{Y_t^{\omega+\sigma^{-1}+\gamma(1-\sigma^{-1})} Y_t^{*\gamma(\sigma^{-1}-1)}}{A_t^{1+\omega} \bar{H}_t^{\nu}} \delta_t^{\nu}.$$

Substituting (3.9) for $MC_t(i)$ in (3.8), and using (3.4) to substitute for the relative output of firm i, one obtains an alternative expression for the first-order condition for optimal price setting,

$$(3.12) \qquad E_t \sum_{T=t}^{\infty} \alpha^{T-t} Q_{t,T} Y_T P_{HT}^{\theta} [p_t^{\dagger(1+\omega_p\theta)} - \tilde{\mu} MC_T P_{HT}^{\omega_p\theta}] = 0.$$

Here I have introduced the notation $p_t^{\dagger}$ for the optimal price for a firm that reconsiders its price at date t—the quantity called $p_t(i)$ in 3.8—as we see that condition (3.8) is the same for all firms i that reconsider their prices at that date, and we may assume that they all choose the same price. It then follows from the definition (3.5) that the domestic price index evolves according to a law of motion

$$(3.13) \qquad P_{Ht}^{1-\theta} = \alpha P_{Ht-1}^{1-\theta} + (1-\alpha) p_t^{\dagger(1-\theta)},$$

and similarly from the definition of δ_t that the price-dispersion measure evolves according to a law of motion

$$(3.14) \qquad \delta_t = \left(\frac{P_{Ht}}{P_{Ht-1}}\right)^{\theta\phi} \left[\alpha\delta_{t-1} + (1-\alpha)\left(\frac{p_t^{\dagger}}{P_{Ht-1}}\right)^{-\theta\phi}\right].$$

We can further reduce the set of endogenous variables referred to in these equations if we replace $Q_{t,T}$ in (3.12) by

$$(3.15) \qquad Q_{t,T} = \beta\left(\frac{Y_t}{Y_T}\right)^{\sigma^{-1}+\gamma(1-\sigma^{-1})} \left(\frac{Y_t^*}{Y_T^*}\right)^{\gamma(\sigma^{-1}-1)} \frac{P_{Ht}}{P_{HT}}.$$

This follows from (1.16), using (1.34) to substitute for the consumer price indexes.

The aggregate-supply block of equations for the home economy then consists of the equations (3.11) through (3.14).[44] These equations jointly determine the paths of the domestic variables $\{MC_t, p_t^{\dagger}, P_{Ht}, \delta_t\}$ consistent with optimal price-setting by each of the domestic firms, given assumed paths for the levels of real activity $\{Y_t, Y_t^*\}$ and initial conditions $P_{H,-1}, \delta_{-1}$. The implied path of the consumer price index is then given by

$$(3.16) \qquad P_t = k^{-1} P_{Ht} Y_t^{\gamma} Y_t^{*-\gamma},$$

which is implied by (1.34). Alternatively, we may think of the aggregate-supply relations as determining the paths of the variables $\{Y_t, MC_t, p_t^{\dagger}, \delta_t\}$ for given paths of $\{P_{Ht}\}$ (or $\{P_t\}$) and foreign real activity.

44. Here it should be understood that $Q_{t,T}$ has been substituted out in (3.12), using (3.15).

Here I have written the aggregate-supply equations for the home country; but a set of equations of the same form applies to the foreign country. For example, (3.10) also holds when all variables (both endogenous and exogenous) are replaced by the corresponding starred variables.[45] Substitutions similar to the ones above then lead to

$$(3.17) \qquad MC_t^* = \frac{\phi}{k^{1-\sigma^{-1}}} P_{Ft}^* \frac{Y_t^{*\omega+\sigma^{-1}+(1-\gamma)(1-\sigma^{-1})} Y_t^{(1-\gamma)(\sigma^{-1}-1)}}{A_t^{*1+\omega} \overline{H}_t^{*\nu}} \delta_t^{*\nu}$$

as a relation corresponding to (3.11) for producers in the foreign country. Equations corresponding to (3.12) through (3.14) for the foreign country are similarly straightforward to derive.[46] The complete set of eight equations (four for each country) constitutes the "aggregate supply block" of the two-country model. These equations determine the evolution of domestic prices (and hence the indexes P_{Ht} and P_{Ft}^*) in both countries, and the consumer price indexes P_t and P_t^* as well, given the paths of real activity in both countries. Alternatively, they can be viewed as determining the evolution of real activity in both countries given the paths of the general level of prices (specified by either a domestic price index or a consumer price index) in both countries.

We observe that even in this model with full integration of goods markets (not only are all final goods traded, but the same consumption basket is consumed in all parts of the world), foreign variables do not affect the aggregate-supply relations for a given country, except in one respect. This is the relation (3.11) between real activity and the marginal cost of domestic production. Marginal cost depends on foreign production as well as domestic production because the wage demanded by domestic households depends not only on the marginal disutility of labor (which depends only on domestic production, under the present assumption of no international trade in factors of production), but also on the marginal utility of additional income (in units of the domestic currency). The marginal utility of domestic-currency income depends on foreign variables for two reasons. For a given level of domestic production (and hence of consumption of home-produced goods), a higher level of foreign output will mean a higher level of consumption of foreign goods, hence a higher level of consumption of the world composite good, and a *lower* marginal utility of consumption, or marginal utility of income in units of the world composite good. At the same time, a higher level of foreign output will mean an appreciation of the home country's terms of trade, and hence a *higher* marginal of utility of income in units of domestic goods relative to the marginal utility of income in units of the world good.

Since the two effects have opposite signs, there is a tendency for them

45. Here I allow the technology shock and labor supply shock to be different in the two countries.

46. In each case, one obtains the corresponding equation for the foreign country by adding stars to all variables, replacing *H*s by *F*s, and replacing γ by $1 - \gamma$ in each place where it occurs.

to cancel one another. In fact, in the case that $\sigma = 1$ exactly (log utility of consumption), the two effects completely cancel, and we observe that (3.11) does not involve any foreign variables. (Similarly, in this case [3.17] does not involve any home-country variables.) In this case, the aggregate-supply trade-off between P_{Ht} and Y_t takes exactly the same form as in a closed economy: no foreign variables shift this trade-off, and the slope of the trade-off (as well as its sensitivity to domestic shocks or to shifts in expectations) is independent of the degree of openness γ, since the value of γ affects none of the equations in the aggregate-supply block in this case. Since we have noted in section 1.1.2 that in this case the aggregate-demand relation between P_{Ht} and Y_t is also unaffected by foreign variables, or by the economy's degree of openness (as long as domestic monetary policy is of the form [1.41]), it follows that in this special case we obtain a complete theory of the determination of domestic inflation, output, and interest rates that is *independent of the economy's degree of openness.*[47]

In general, of course, the two effects need not cancel altogether. The most empirically realistic case, however, is that in which $\sigma > 1$, as discussed in section 1.1.2. In this case, the terms-of-trade effect is stronger than the marginal-utility-of-consumption effect, and on net, an increase in foreign output *reduces* the marginal cost of domestic production. While this makes foreign economic activity relevant to the determination of (supply-side) inflationary pressures in the home country, the sign of the effect is not the one predicted by the "global slack" thesis. Not only is it not *only* world activity that matters for domestic inflationary pressure, but foreign activity has an effect with the *opposite sign* of the effect of domestic activity. And rather than implying a reduced slope of the aggregate-supply curve as a consequence of increased openness, this channel implies that greater openness should *increase* the slope of the aggregate-supply relation between domestic inflation and domestic output.

In order to see directly the implications of the previous equations for the aggregate-supply relation, it is useful to log-linearize them, as with the aggregate-demand block of the model in section 1.1. Following CGG (and the literature on the closed economy "new-Keynesian Phillips curve"), I shall log-linearize them around an allocation with zero inflation and zero price dispersion in both countries, as well as constant preferences and technology (identical in the two countries). As in the closed economy model,[48] log-linearization of (3.12) and (3.13) leads to the equation[49]

47. Benigno and Benigno (2005) generalize this result to the case in which the elasticity of substitution between home and foreign goods in the preferences of households is not necessarily equal to 1, as assumed here and in CGG. In their more general model, domestic inflation and output are determined independently of foreign variables in the case that the intertemporal elasticity of substitution σ is equal to the elasticity of substitution between home and foreign goods.

48. See Woodford (2003, chapter 3) for details of the derivation.

49. Note that this is just the equation (1.47) already anticipated in section 1.1.3. The derivation of this equation is the same in the case of a model with local-currency pricing, though the relation between marginal cost and output is different.

(3.18) $$\pi_{Ht} = \xi(\mu + \log MC_t - \log P_{Ht}) + \beta E_t \pi_{Ht+1}$$

for the evolution of the domestic price index, where $\mu \equiv \log \tilde{\mu}$ and

$$\xi \equiv \frac{(1-\alpha)(1-\alpha\beta)}{\alpha(1+\omega_p\theta)} > 0.$$

Substituting (3.11) for MC_t in (3.18), we obtain

(3.19) $$\pi_{Ht} = \kappa_H \hat{Y}_t + \kappa_F \hat{Y}^*_t + \beta E_t \pi_{Ht+1} - \xi \omega q_t$$

as an open economy generalization of the new-Keynesian Phillips curve. Here $\hat{Y}_t$ and $\hat{Y}^*_t$ are log deviations from a steady-state level of output as in section 1.1, and the steady-state output level $\overline{Y}$ is now defined by the relation[50]

$$\overline{Y}^{\omega+\sigma^{-1}} = \frac{k^{1-\sigma^{-1}}}{\phi\tilde{\mu}} A^{1+\omega} \overline{H}^{\nu},$$

where A, $\overline{H}$ are the common steady-state values of the technology and preference factors in the two countries. The exogenous disturbance term q_t indicates the percentage change in domestic output that is required to maintain the marginal disutility of supplying output at its steady-state level;[51] it is defined as

$$\omega q_t \equiv (1+\omega)a_t + \nu \bar{h}_t,$$

where $a_t \equiv \log(A_t/A)$, $\bar{h}_t \equiv \log(\overline{H}_t/\overline{H})$. Note that in this simple model (without government purchases or variation in impatience to consume, for example), q_t is also proportional to the log deviation of the equilibrium level of output in a closed economy model with flexible wages and prices, or the "natural rate" of output defined in Woodford (2003, chapter 4); it follows from the formulas given there that in the present model,

$$\omega q_t = \kappa \hat{Y}^n_t,$$

where $\kappa \equiv \xi(\omega + \sigma^{-1})$ is the slope of the closed economy AS curve. Finally, it follows directly from (3.11) that the two output elasticities in the open economy AS relation are given by

$$\kappa_H = \xi[\omega + \sigma^{-1} + \gamma(1-\sigma^{-1})],$$
$$\kappa_F = -\xi\gamma(1-\sigma^{-1}).$$

For the foreign country, we similarly obtain

(3.20) $$\pi^*_{Ft} = \kappa^*_H \hat{Y}_t + \kappa^*_F \hat{Y}^*_t + \beta E_t \pi^*_{Ft+1} - \xi \omega q^*_t,$$

50. One can easily show that $Y_t = Y^*_t = \overline{Y}$ is the condition under which one will have both $\tilde{\mu} MC_t = P_{Ht}$ and $\tilde{\mu} MC^*_t = P^*_{Ft}$, as is required for a steady state with zero inflation in both countries.

51. Here again I follow the notation used in Woodford (2003, chapter 4) for the closed economy model.

where

$$\kappa_H^* = -\xi(1-\gamma)(1-\sigma^{-1}),$$
$$\kappa_F^* = \xi[\omega + \sigma^{-1} + (1-\gamma)(1-\sigma^{-1})],$$

and q_t^* is the corresponding compound of the foreign technology and preference shocks. Equations (3.19) and (3.20) then represent the aggregate supply block of the log-linearized model. Together, they suffice to determine the paths of $\{\pi_{Ht}, \pi_{Ft}^*\}$ given the paths of $\{Y_t, Y_t^*\}$, or vice versa. The CPI inflation rates are also determined if we adjoin the relations

$$(3.21)\quad \pi_t = \pi_{Ht} + \gamma(\Delta\hat{Y}_t - \Delta\hat{Y}_t^*), \quad \pi_t^* = \pi_{Ft}^* + (1-\gamma)(\Delta\hat{Y}_t^* - \Delta\hat{Y}_t)$$

implied by (3.16) and the corresponding relation for the foreign index.

In the case that the monetary policies of the two central banks are given by equations of the form (1.19) and (1.20), then, as shown in section 1.1.1, the log-linearized AD block of the model consists of equations (1.21) through (1.24). If we combine these with the log-linearized AS block consisting of equations (3.19) through (3.21), we have a system of eight equations per period to determine the eight endogenous variables $\{\pi_t, \pi_{Ht}, \hat{Y}_t, \hat{\imath}_t, \pi_t^*, \pi_{Ft}^*, \hat{Y}_t^*, \hat{\imath}_t^*\}$ each period. In the case that the response coefficients of the two policy rules satisfy certain inequalities, this system has a determinate equilibrium, and when it does, we are able to solve for each of the eight endogenous variables as a function of current and expected future values of the forcing variables $\{\bar{\imath}_t, \bar{\imath}_t^*, q_t, q_t^*\}$, and the lagged relative output $\hat{Y}_{t-1}^r \equiv \hat{Y}_{t-1} - \hat{Y}_{t-1}^*$.[52] For example, the solution for equilibrium consumer price inflation in the home country will be of the form

$$(3.22)\quad \pi_t = \sum_{j=0}^{\infty}[\psi_{1,j}E_t\bar{\imath}_{t+j} + \psi_{2,j}E_t\bar{\imath}_{t+j}^* + \psi_{3,j}E_t\hat{Y}_{t+j}^n + \psi_{4,j}E_t\hat{Y}_{t+j}^{n*}] + \delta\hat{Y}_{t-1}^r.$$

To what extent do our results imply that globalization should be expected to change the nature of the aggregate-supply relation in each country? One should note first of all that, once again, *financial* globalization has no effect whatsoever in this model. As discussed in section 1.1, under the preferences assumed here, the equilibrium relation between consumption in each country (and each country's stochastic discount factor) and the world pattern of production is *the same* whether we assume financial autarchy, complete international risk-sharing, or any kind of incomplete markets or costly international trade in financial assets. Hence the derivation of the previous aggregate-supply relations is unaffected by which of these we assume.[53]

52. Note that this is the only lagged state variable that appears in any of the eight structural equations; it appears in (3.21).

53. This contrasts with the result of Razin and Yuen (2002). These authors do not assume the same preferences as are assumed here (they instead assume the same elasticity of substitution $\theta > 1$ between home and foreign goods as exists among individual home goods or among individual foreign goods), but this is not the main reason for the differing conclusion. Razin

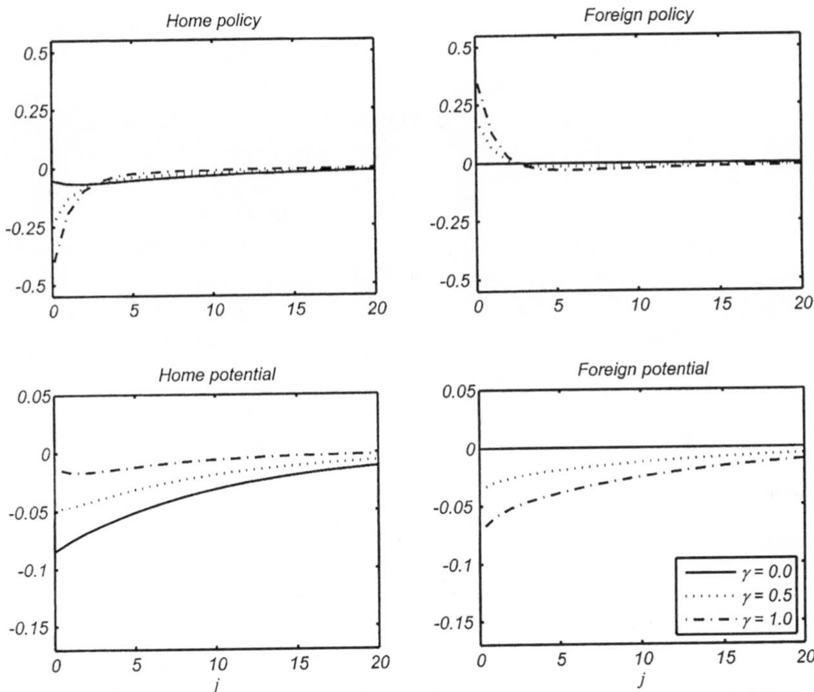

Fig. 1.6 Coefficients of the solution (3.22) for inflation, for alternative degrees of openness

What about the effects of an increase in the degree of integration of goods markets, here modeled by an increase in γ? Figure 1.6 illustrates the numerical values of the four sequences of coefficients $\{\psi_{k,j}\}$ in (3.22) in the case of policy rules for each country in which $\phi_\pi = 2$, $\phi_y = 1$, as also assumed in figure 1.1, with values for the other structural parameters

and Yuen note that under financial autarchy, consumption each period must fluctuate with domestic income, and assume as a consequence that $\hat{C}_t = \hat{Y}_t$, whereas $\hat{C}_t = \hat{C}_t^*$ (as here) in the case of financial integration. They therefore conclude that domestic consumption (and correspondingly the marginal utility of income of domestic households) will be less sensitive to variations in domestic output in the case of financial integration, making domestic real wage demands less sensitive to domestic output in that case, and hence the slope of the Phillips curve smaller. But their argument neglects the effect of terms-of-trade changes, which vary with the relative output of the two countries in such a way as to make the number of units of *the consumption basket* that can be purchased with the income from domestic production vary less than does domestic output. In the case of a unit elasticity of substitution between home and foreign goods, as assumed here, the terms-of-trade effect completely *eliminates* any difference between the effects of variations in Y_t on consumption in the two countries, even under financial autarchy. Under the preferences assumed by Razin and Yuen, the terms-of-trade effect would be smaller, but will still reduce the degree to which financial integration affects the slope of the Phillips curve, relative to what they find.

again taken from the closed economy model of Rotemberg and Woodford (1997).[54] Once again the figure compares the solutions obtained for three different values of γ. We observe that even in the case of completely integrated goods markets and financial markets, individual national monetary policies still have a substantial effect on the rate of CPI inflation in that country. Indeed, the upper left panel of figure 1.6 shows that the immediate effect on inflation of a relatively transitory shift in monetary policy is (at least in the calibrated example) even *larger* in the case of a highly open economy than in the case of an otherwise similar closed economy. Hence, whatever other validity there may be to the "global slack" thesis, openness does not reduce the ability of a central bank to influence the local rate of inflation.

1.3.2 Global Economic Activity and Inflation

Nonetheless, our previous results do show that the aggregate supply block of our model, like the aggregate demand block, is affected by the degree of openness of the economy. Equations (3.19) and (3.20) each indicate that in general the other country's level of economic activity is relevant to the determination of a given country's domestic inflation rate. To what extent do they support the view that "global slack" becomes an important determinant of inflation in each country as a result of economic integration?

It is true that for analytical purposes, it may be convenient to solve a model of this kind by first solving for the implied dynamics of "global" endogenous variables, and then solving for national departures from the world averages taking the solution for the world averages as given. Note that (3.21) implies that the world average inflation rate π_t^w (defined as in [1.44]) can also be written as a world average of *domestic* inflation rates,

$$\pi_t^w = (1 - \gamma)\pi_{Ht} + \gamma\pi_{Ft}^*.$$

It then follows that we can take a weighted average of (3.19) and (3.20) and obtain

$$\pi_t^w = \kappa(\hat{Y}_t^w - \hat{Y}_t^{nw}) + \beta E_t \pi_{t+1}^w \tag{3.23}$$

as a "global Phillips curve" relation. Here $\hat{Y}_t^w$ is the world average level of output (defined as in [1.45]), and $\hat{Y}_t^{nw}$ is a corresponding average of the *closed economy* "natural rates of output" for the two economies.

Thus, one can argue that "global inflation" is determined by a "global output gap" in this model. In the case that the Taylor rule coefficients are the same in both countries, the aggregate-demand block of the model also allows us to derive relation (1.56) between world inflation and world output that does not involve any nation-specific variables. Equations (1.56) and

54. In addition to the parameter values used in the previous numerical illustrations, I now also assume that $\kappa = 0.0236$.

(3.23) then jointly determine the evolution of the world variables $\{\pi_t^w, \hat{Y}_t^w\}$ given the paths of the world disturbances $\{\bar{\imath}_t^w, \hat{Y}_t^{nw}\}$.[55]

In the case of identical Taylor rule coefficients in the two countries, it is also possible to solve independently for the evolution of the *inflation differential* Δz_t between the two countries. From (3.21) it follows that

$$\Delta z_t = \pi_{Ht} - \pi_{Ft}^* + (\Delta Y_t - \Delta Y_t^*).$$

Then subtracting (3.20) from (3.19) yields a relation of the form

$$\Delta z_t = \beta E_t \Delta z_{t+1} - E_t[C(L)(\hat{Y}_{t+1} - \hat{Y}_{t+1}^*)] - \xi\omega(q_t - q_t^*) \tag{3.24}$$

between the evolution of the inflation differential and the evolution of the output differential, where

$$C(L) \equiv L^2 - [1 + \beta + \kappa + \xi(1 - \sigma^{-1})]L + \beta.$$

These two variables are also linked by the demand-side equilibrium relation

$$E_t \Delta z_{t+1} = (\bar{\imath}_t - \bar{\imath}_t^*) + \phi_\pi \Delta z_t + \phi_y(\hat{Y}_t - \hat{Y}_t^*), \tag{3.25}$$

which follows from (1.30), when we recall that $e_t = z_t$ in this model. Conditions (3.24) and (3.25) form a system of two equations per period to solve for the evolution of the inflation differential and the output differential, given the paths of the exogenous disturbance $\{q_t - q_t^*\}$ and the policy differential $\{\bar{\imath}_t - \bar{\imath}_t^*\}$. Combining the solution for world inflation with the solution for the inflation differential then yields a solution for inflation in either country; for example,

$$\pi_t = \pi_t^w + \gamma\Delta z_t. \tag{3.26}$$

Figure 1.7 illustrates the character of the solution for these two components of inflation, in the case of the same parameter values as are assumed in figure 1.6. The two lines in each panel indicate the way in which world inflation and relative inflation respectively depend on the current and expected future values of the four forcing variables. To be precise, each panel decomposes the response of CPI inflation to one of the forcing variables shown in figure 1.6 for the case $\gamma = 0.5$ into two parts, corresponding to the two terms in (3.26): the effect of the forcing variable on world inflation (the solid line in each panel) and the effect on γ times relative inflation (the dash-dotted line). (If we were to compute a similar decomposition of the inflation responses for any other values of γ than 0.5, the two components would be proportional to those shown in figure 1.7, but scaled by factors that depend

55. This pair of equations has a determinate solution if and only if the Taylor rule coefficients satisfy the "Taylor Principle" (Woodford 2003, Proposition 4.3), just as in a closed economy model. The solutions obtained for the evolution of world inflation and world output are also exactly the same functions of the world disturbances as in the closed economy model.

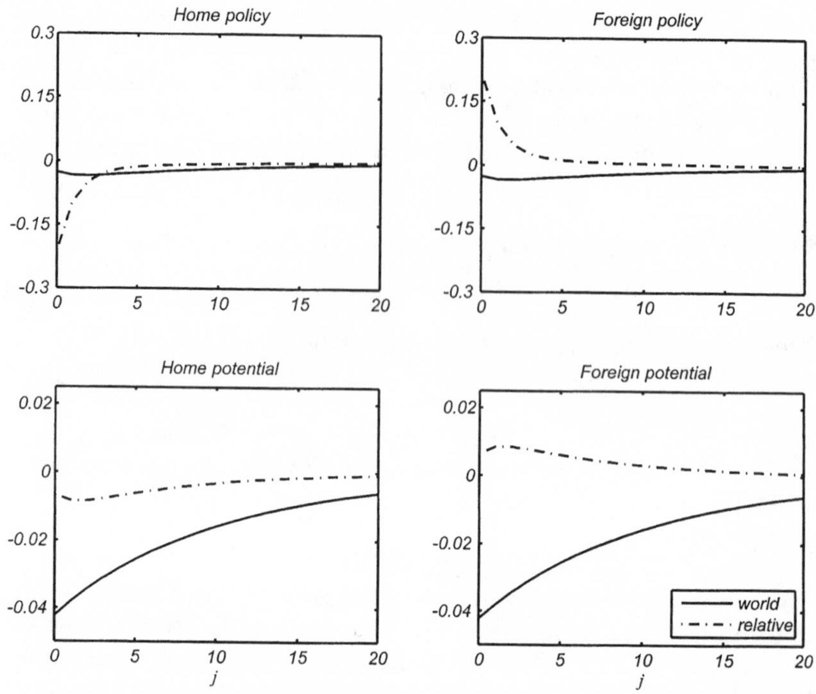

Fig. 1.7 Decomposition of the solution for home-country inflation into solutions for world inflation and relative inflation, shown for the case $\gamma = 0.5$

on γ.) Note that world inflation is affected to precisely the same extent by the forcing variables for each of the countries, while relative inflation is affected by the two countries' forcing variables to the same extent but with the opposite sign.

While this approach to expressing the solution of the complete model has some convenient features, one should not conclude that the "global output gap" is accordingly a crucial determinant of inflation in each country. Our observation about the possibility of writing a "global Phillips curve" relation (3.23) would be equally true in the case of complete *autarchy,* given our assumption of identical parameter values for the two countries (and our use of a log-linear approximation). This might be a useful observation if one were interested in modeling the average world rate of inflation rather than inflation in a single country, but it would not imply any necessity or even convenience of using the concept of the "global output gap" to explain inflation in one country.

Even in the case of two open economies, in the case that $\sigma = 1$, we observe that $\kappa_F = \kappa_H^* = 0$, so that the aggregate-supply relation connects domestic inflation in either country with economic activity in that country alone, as noted by CGG. As shown in section 1.1.2, the aggregate-demand relations for each economy also connect domestic inflation with domestic output alone in that case, if we assume that monetary policy in each country responds only to the domestic inflation rate. In this case, it is possible to solve equations (1.39), (1.41), and (3.19) for the evolution of the domestic endogenous variables $\{\pi_{Ht}, \hat{Y}_t\}$, given the paths of the domestic endogenous variables $\{\bar{\imath}_t, \hat{Y}_t^n\}$, without any reference to either disturbances or policy in the foreign country. The solution obtained is the same as the one that would be obtained by solving for world average inflation and the inflation differential and summing them; but the latter, more roundabout method conceals the fact that foreign variables actually play no role in determining domestic inflation.

In the more realistic case in which $\sigma > 1$ and monetary policy responds to consumer price inflation rather than to domestic inflation alone, the structural equations for the two countries no longer perfectly decouple. Nonetheless, it remains the case that the mere fact that "global slack" determines the evolution of world inflation through (3.23) does not mean that it will be the main determinant of inflation in individual countries. The upper two panels of figure 1.7 (which relate to a case in which $\sigma > 1$ and monetary policy in each country responds to CPI inflation) show that the effects of each country's monetary policy on *relative* inflation swamp the effects on *world* inflation that are mediated by changes in the world output gap $\hat{Y}_t^w - \hat{Y}_t^{nw}$. Hence the global slack thesis is quite misleading as a guide to understanding the effects of monetary policy on an open economy.

Moreover, in the case in which $\sigma > 1$, we observe that κ_F is *negative,* and thus opposite in sign to κ_H, contrary to what the "global slack" thesis would suggest.[56] Moreover, κ_H is *larger* than the value $\kappa = \xi(\omega + \sigma^{-1})$ that would be obtained in the case of a closed economy, and by more so the greater the degree of openness. We similarly find that $\kappa_H^* < 0$ and that κ_F^* is larger than the closed economy value. Hence the supposition on the basis of the global slack thesis that the Phillips curve trade-off between domestic inflation and domestic real activity should be *flatter* in a more open economy is not borne out.

In the previous paragraph I have considered only the nature of the Phillips curve trade-off between domestic inflation and domestic activity. If instead we are interested in the relation between CPI inflation and domestic output, then foreign activity affects this relationship even in the case that $\sigma = 1$, owing to its consequences for the terms of trade. However, the effects of foreign activity on the domestic aggregate-supply relation are again not of the kind suggested by the global slack thesis. The aggregate-supply curve in this case is of the form

$$\log P_t = (\kappa_H + \gamma)\hat{Y}_t + (\kappa_F - \gamma)\hat{Y}_t^*,$$

56. The effect of foreign output is in fact found often to be negative by Ihrig et al. (2007).

neglecting the terms corresponding to lagged values, disturbances, and expectations. In this case we have a further reason for openness to *increase* the (positive) slope of the AS curve (i.e., the sensitivity to domestic output), and also for openness to make the effects of foreign output on domestic inflation *more negative;* namely, the way in which both domestic and foreign output affect the terms of trade. Thus, to the extent that this model represents the effects of increased international integration of goods markets, there is no reason whatsoever to expect that globalization should reduce the sensitivity of domestic inflation to domestic activity.

The global slack thesis is misleading in another respect as well. It suggests that inflationary pressure at home should depend not just on foreign economy, but on foreign activity *relative to potential.* This suggests that domestic monetary policy may need to be conditioned on changes in foreign potential output. This is one of the main reasons why Dallas Fed President Richard Fisher (2006) argues that globalized markets will make the conduct of monetary policy more difficult. "How can we calculate an 'output gap,'" he asks, "without knowing the present capacity of, say, the Chinese and Indian economies? How can we fashion a Phillips curve without imputing the behavioral patterns of foreign labor pools?" But according to the previously developed model, the Phillips curve for an open economy does not involve foreign potential output or foreign labor supply behavior; the exogenous disturbance term q_t involves only *domestic* technology and preferences regarding labor supply.[57]

In fact, foreign developments affect domestic inflation in this model *solely* through their effects on the terms of trade. The aggregate-supply relation (3.19) can alternatively be written in the form

$$\pi_{Ht} = \kappa(\hat{Y}_t - \hat{Y}_t^n) - \kappa_F \log S_t + \beta E_t \pi_{Ht+1}, \quad (3.27)$$

where κ is the closed economy Phillips curve slope, $\hat{Y}_t^n$ is the closed economy "natural rate of output" (i.e., the equilibrium level of output in a closed economy model with flexible prices, which depends only on domestic technology and preferences), and S_t indicates the terms of trade. The domestic aggregate-demand block (consisting of equations [1.39] and [1.41]) can similarly be written entirely in terms of domestic variables and the terms of trade; hence one can solve for the equilibrium paths $\{\pi_{Ht}, \hat{Y}_t\}$ purely as a function of domestic real fundamentals, domestic monetary policy, and

57. This is somewhat hidden in the way that the national AS relations are written in Benigno and Benigno (2005). Domestic inflation is written as being determined by a domestic output gap and a terms-of-trade gap, with the "natural" levels of both domestic output and the terms of trade being functions in turn of both q_t and q_t^*. Nonetheless, the domestic aggregate-supply equation actually involves only q_t and not q_t^*, as written here. Benigno and Benigno choose to write the AS relation in terms of their more complicated "gap" variables because of the role of those variables in their expression for the welfare-based stabilization objective; writing the AS equations in terms of the same variables facilitates their characterization of optimal policy.

the path of the terms of trade.[58] The implied path of CPI inflation, given a path for domestic inflation, also depends only on the terms of trade. Thus, while it is true that a policy aimed at stabilizing domestic inflation, CPI inflation, and/or domestic economic activity will need in general to monitor developments with regard to the terms of trade, it will not require a judgment about foreign potential output, except to the extent that views about foreign fundamentals may help one to form a more accurate forecast of the future evolution of the terms of trade. Thus, the information requirements for using a Phillips curve model in the conduct of policy in an open economy are not as daunting as Fisher makes them sound.

Of course, the fact that foreign potential output does not enter the home country's AS relation does not make it irrelevant to equilibrium determination in the home country, as shown by the lower right panel of figure 1.6. This is because foreign potential output certainly *does* matter for the foreign AS relation, and hence for the determination of foreign output, inflation, and interest rates, which variables affect the home-economy AD and AS relations. Nonetheless, while figure 1.6 indicates that variations in the foreign natural rate of output are of considerable consequence (when γ is large), if one wishes to attribute inflation variations in the home economy to their various ultimate causes, it does not imply that a policymaker in the home country must concern herself with the estimation of foreign potential. In order to correctly understand the structural trade-offs facing the home economy, it suffices that one is able to forecast the evolution of foreign output, inflation, and interest rates; this is especially true in the case of a small economy, which cannot expect its own decisions to have any great effect on the determination of output, inflation, or interest rates elsewhere.

1.3.3 Consequences of Global Factor Markets

The previous section shows that there is no role for "global slack" as a determinant of supply-side inflationary pressure in an open economy model where both final goods markets and financial markets are fully integrated, but factor markets are still nation-specific (or perhaps even more segmented). Proponents of the global slack thesis, however, are perhaps concerned with the consequences of global trade in *factors of production* as well. This could mean international integration of labor markets (as emphasized by those who assert that globalization has recently held down real wage demands in countries like the United States), or alternatively that internationally traded commodities or imported intermediate goods are important inputs in the domestic production technology, along with labor.

Because both the hypothesis of a global labor market and that of globally traded inputs of other kinds have similar consequences for the way the aggregate-supply relation will come to depend on domestic and foreign real

58. Even the terms of trade are only relevant to the extent that σ is not equal to 1.

activity, I shall here treat explicitly only the case of a global labor market. I shall also proceed immediately to the extreme case that is most favorable to the global slack thesis. This is the case in which there is only a single kind of homogeneous labor used in production in either country, and a competitive global market for the sale of that labor, so that households in one country can equally easily sell labor to firms in either country. I shall furthermore assume in this section that $\phi = 1$, so that there is no additional fixed (and hence immobile) factor of production, and the marginal cost of production (in units of the world good) will depend *only* on the price of labor in the global market. In such a case, the marginal cost of production is necessarily identical worldwide, regardless of the relative levels of economic activity in the two countries.

The existence of a single global market for labor requires that

$$\frac{W_t}{P_t} = \frac{W_t^*}{P_t^*}, \tag{3.28}$$

so that there is a common world price of labor in units of the world good. Labor supply in each country is still given by a function of the form (3.2), where the real wage is the common world real wage, and the labor employed in each country is still given by (3.7). Hence, clearing of the world labor market requires that

$$\left(\frac{W_t}{P_t C_t^{\sigma^{-1}}}\right)^{\nu-1} = (1-\gamma)\frac{Y_t}{A_t}\delta_t + \gamma\frac{Y_t^*}{A_t^*}\delta_t^*. \tag{3.29}$$

(Here I have used [3.28] and the fact that $C_t = C_t^*$ to simplify the left-hand side expression for the world demand for labor.) Equations (3.28) and (3.29) replace the two labor-market clearing conditions (one for each country) in the model with national labor markets that are obtained for each country by equating the right-hand sides of (3.2) and (3.7).

Equation (3.29) can be solved for the world real wage as a function of real activity in the two countries. (Recall that one can use [1.15] to substitute for C_t.) Dividing the real wage by the productivity factor A_t (because we are now assuming a linear production function), we obtain the common marginal cost of production for each firm in the home country. One can again write marginal cost purely as a function of domestic goods prices and real variables by using (1.34) to substitute for P_t, yielding

$$MC_t = \frac{1}{k^{1-\sigma^{-1}}A_t}P_{Ht}Y_t^{\gamma+(1-\gamma)\sigma^{-1}}Y_t^{*\gamma(\sigma^{-1}-1)} \cdot \left[\frac{(1-\gamma)(Y_t/A_t)\delta_t + \gamma(Y_t^*/A_t^*)\delta_t^*}{(1-\gamma)\overline{H}_t + \gamma\overline{H}_t^*}\right]^{\nu}. \tag{3.30}$$

This condition replaces (3.11) in the case of national labor markets.

The corresponding equation for the marginal cost of production in the foreign country is given by

$$MC_t^* = \frac{1}{k^{1-\sigma^{-1}}A_t^*}P_{Ft}^* Y_t^{(1-\gamma)(\sigma^{-1}-1)} Y_t^{*(1-\gamma)+\gamma\sigma^{-1}} \cdot \left[\frac{(1-\gamma)(Y_t/A_t)\delta_t + \gamma(Y_t^*/A_t^*)\delta_t^*}{(1-\gamma)\overline{H}_t + \gamma\overline{H}_t^*}\right]^{\nu}. \tag{3.31}$$

Note that even when we assume that there is a single world price for the unique factor of production (and a linear production function), it does not follow that real marginal cost must be the same in the two countries, if we measure real marginal cost in units of the composite domestic good (which is the concept of real marginal cost that measures the incentive for domestic price increases). Instead, MC_t^*/P_{Ft}^*, differs from MC_t/P_{Ht}, not only because of the (exogenous) productivity differential between the two countries, but also because of the *terms of trade.* The latter factor depends on the relative output of the two countries, and so can be affected by national monetary policies.

Log-linearizing (3.30) and substituting into (3.18), we obtain an open economy new-Keynesian Phillips curve for the home economy, given by

$$\pi_{Ht} = \kappa(\hat{Y}_t^w - \hat{Y}_t^{nw}) + \xi\gamma(\hat{Y}_t - \hat{Y}_t^*) + \beta E_t\pi_{Ht+1} - \xi\gamma(a_t - a_t^*). \tag{3.32}$$

The corresponding aggregate-supply relation for the foreign economy is given by

$$\pi_{Ft}^* = \kappa(\hat{Y}_t^w - \hat{Y}_t^{nw}) - \xi(1-\gamma)(\hat{Y}_t - \hat{Y}_t^*) + \beta E_t\pi_{Ft+1}^* + \xi(1-\gamma)(a_t - a_t^*). \tag{3.33}$$

Here, $\hat{Y}_t^w$ is the same measure of world average output as in (3.23).

Here we find a role for the "global output gap" in determining the evolution of domestic inflation in each country. Nonetheless, even in this most extreme case—when the marginal cost of production in either country depends *solely* on the common world price of a globally traded factor (apart from an exogenous country-specific productivity factor)—it does not follow that domestic monetary policy can exert no influence over the dynamics of domestic inflation, even in the case of a very small country.

One observes that in the model with a global labor market, the equilibrium solution for home-country inflation is again of the form (3.22). Figure 1.8 plots the coefficients of this solution, in the same format as in figure 1.6, for an economy that is parameterized in the same way as in the earlier figure, except that there is now assumed to be a global labor market.[59] Figure 1.8 is

59. The same value of κ is assumed as in figures 1.6 and 1.7, even though, if we were instead to fix the assumed parameters of the utility function, the assumption here is that $\phi = 1$ would imply a different value of κ than the one in the Rotemberg-Woodford model, which involves diminishing returns to labor.

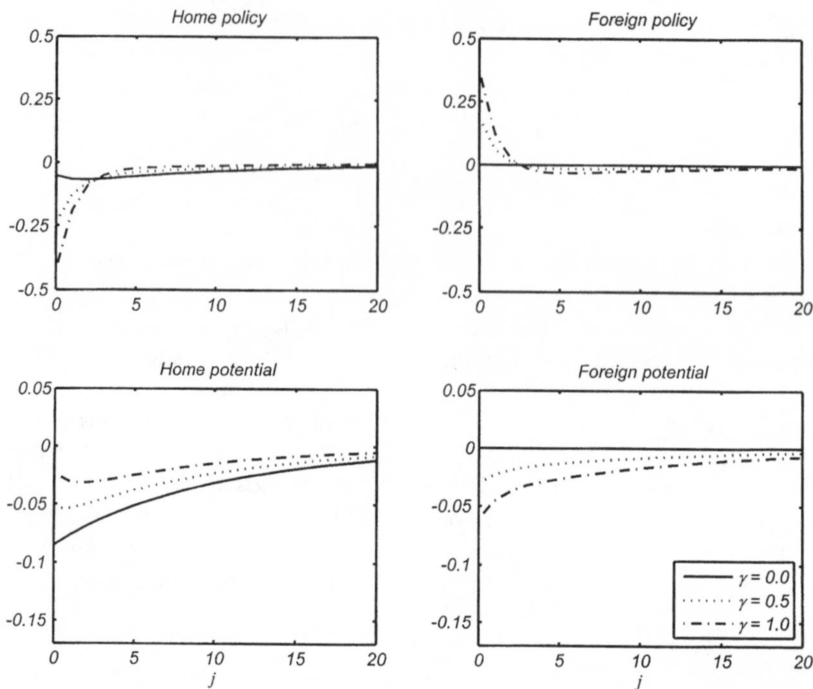

Fig. 1.8 Coefficients of the solution (3.22) for inflation, with a global labor market

quite similar to figure 1.6; the existence of a global market for all factors of production does not to any notable extent diminish the effect of domestic monetary policy on home-country inflation.

Once again, the key to understanding the effects of domestic monetary policy on inflation in a small open economy is provided by a consideration of the relations that determine *relative* inflation. If we subtract (3.33) from (3.32), we obtain

$$\Delta z_t = \beta E_t \Delta z_{t+1} - E_t[A(L)(\hat{Y}_{t+1} - \hat{Y}^*_{t+1})] - \xi(a_t - a^*_t), \tag{3.34}$$

where $A(L)$ is again the lag polynomial defined in (1.50). Note that this relation does *not* require the inflation differential to be zero, or even to evolve exogenously in a way determined purely by the evolution of the productivity differential. It also allows for variations in the inflation differential to the extent that there are variations in the relative output of the two countries (owing to a terms-of-trade effect), and the relative output levels depend on the monetary policies of the two countries. In the case that the Taylor rule coefficients are the same in both countries, equation (3.25) again applies, and equations (3.25) and (3.34) form a system of two equations per period to solve for the evolution of the inflation differential and the output

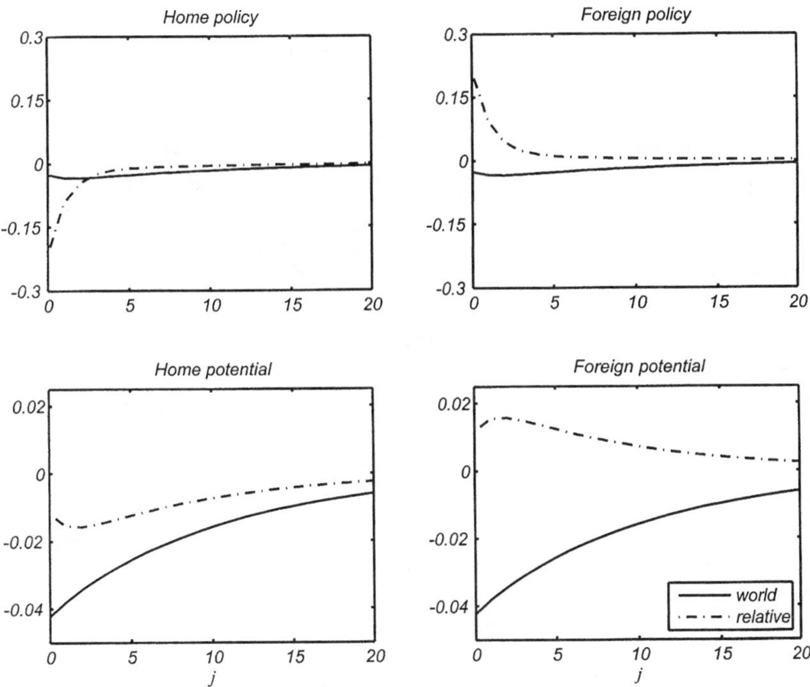

Fig. 1.9 Decomposition of the solution for home-country inflation into solutions for world inflation and relative inflation, in the case of a global labor market

differential, given the paths of the productivity differential $\{a_t - a_t^*\}$ and the policy differential $\{\bar{\imath}_t - \bar{\imath}_t^*\}$.

In the case of a very small country, monetary policy in the home country can have no noticeable effect on the world average inflation rate. But because domestic monetary policy can still affect the inflation differential, it can still affect the domestic inflation rate. (Note that none of the coefficients in either [3.25] or [3.34] depend on γ, so the effects of policy on the inflation differential obtained by solving these equations remains of the same size even if γ approaches 1.) Figure 1.9 shows how this effect accounts for the results plotted in figure 1.8 by decomposing the effects shown in figure 1.8 for the case $\gamma = 0.5$ into effects on world inflation and on relative inflation, respectively, using the same format as in figure 1.7. Even in the case that $\gamma = 0.5$, we observe that the effects of the national monetary policies on relative inflation dominate the effects on world inflation (at least at the short horizons where the effects of policy are largest); since the component of the total effect that results from the effect on relative inflation grows in proportion to γ, the result would be even more dramatic in the case of a larger value of γ (i.e., a smaller open economy).

Nor is it necessarily true, even in the extreme case considered in this section, that global integration of markets reduces the slope of the Phillips curve trade-off between domestic inflation and domestic output. One observes that in (3.32), the elasticity of domestic inflation with respect to domestic output is equal to $\tilde{\kappa}_H \equiv \kappa(1-\gamma) + \xi\gamma$. This is smaller than the elasticity κ_H obtained for the open economy model with national factor markets (for the same value of γ and all other parameters). However, it is not necessarily smaller than the Phillips curve slope κ that would obtain in the case of a closed economy. One finds that $\tilde{\kappa}_H < \kappa$ if and only if $\nu + \sigma^{-1} > 1$, which need not be true. For example, it is not true under the calibration adopted by Rotemberg and Woodford (1997) for the U.S. economy (where $\nu + \sigma^{-1} = 0.3$). I have already argued that it is realistic to assume that $\sigma^{-1} < 1$; thus one will have $\tilde{\kappa}_H > \kappa$ for any small enough value of ν, which is to say, in the case of sufficiently elastic labor supply.[60]

Thus, even in the extreme case of a world market for all factors of production, common interpretations of the "global slack" thesis would be valid to only a rather limited extent. While foreign economic activity affects the Phillips curve trade-off between domestic inflation and domestic activity in such a model, the sign of the effect of foreign output on domestic inflation can easily be *negative,* the opposite of what the global slack thesis would suggest. (Note that $\tilde{\kappa}_F = \gamma[\kappa - \xi] < 0$ if $\omega + \sigma^{-1} < 1$.) Similarly, even if global integration means integration of factor markets as well as final goods markets and financial markets, the slope of the Phillips curve trade-off can easily be *increased* by integration rather than being decreased. And certainly global integration of markets does not imply that domestic inflationary pressure ceases to depend on domestic economic activity, so that it ceases to be possible for domestic monetary policy to influence the evolution of domestic inflation. Even in this most extreme case, it remains possible to use monetary policy to stabilize inflation, and this can be done by a national central bank of even a small country, without requiring coordination with other central banks.

1.4 Conclusion

All of the previously made arguments reach a similar conclusion: it is difficult to think of plausible economic mechanisms through which globalization should impair in any substantial way the ability of central banks to control domestic inflation through national monetary policy. I have considered the consequences of potential increases in international integration of three

60. In a closed-economy model like that of Rotemberg and Woodford, $\nu + \sigma^{-1}$ measures the elasticity of the real wage with respect to an increase in output that is due to a purely monetary disturbance (i.e., that is not associated with a change in either preferences or technology). Thus if real wages rise less than in proportion to output, one may conclude that $\nu + \sigma^{-1} < 1$. Typical estimates suggest that this is realistic; for example, the Vector Autoregression (VAR) study of Christiano, Eichenbaum, and Evans (1996) indicates a real wage response about one-fourth the size of the output response.

distinct types—financial integration (including international risk-sharing), goods market integration (including reduction in the share of home goods in a country's consumption basket), and factor market integration—and I have considered the implications of these changes for three distinct links in the transmission mechanism for monetary policy: the relation between interest rates and the intertemporal allocation of expenditure, the means by which central bank actions affect money-market interest rates, and the Phillips curve relation between real activity and inflation. It has proven difficult to think of cases under which increased openness should lead either to a reduced effect of domestic monetary policy on domestic aggregate demand or to any substantial reduction of the effects of domestic economic activity on domestic inflation, even when I have considered relatively extreme theoretical possibilities that go far beyond the degree of international integration that has yet been observed on any of these dimensions.

This does not mean that the degree of openness of an economy is of no significance for the conduct of monetary policy. As shown previously, changes in the degree of goods market integration, represented by variation in the coefficient γ of preferences, affect the quantitative specification of both the aggregate-demand and aggregate-supply blocks of the simple models of the monetary transmission mechanism considered here; and there would be additional quantitative effects of other types of potential changes that have not been taken up here.[61] Furthermore, openness, to the degree that it is significant, forces central bankers to confront a variety of practical issues that would not be present in the case of a closed economy, such as the question whether to stabilize an index of domestic prices only, or an index of the prices of all goods consumed in the domestic economy. And to the extent that the degree of international integration is thought to be changing especially rapidly at present or in the near future, this makes the issue of change over time in the correct quantitative specification of the structural models used in a central bank a more pressing one to consider.

Nonetheless, globalization, even if expected to be rapid, does not seem to justify quite the degree of alarm that some commentators would urge upon central banks. When Richard Fisher (2006) declares that "the old models simply no longer apply in our globalized, interconnected and expanded economy," one might imagine that a radical reconceptualization of the determinants of inflation is needed, but I see no reason to expect this. Increased international trade in financial assets, consumer goods, and factors of production should lead to quantitative changes in the magnitudes of

61. For example, the theoretical analysis in this chapter deals only with the case in which consumption baskets are identical in all parts of the world, which represents an extreme assumption of integration in one respect; in the case of "home bias" in countries' consumption baskets, the structural relations would be somewhat different. I have also considered only the case of a unit elasticity of substitution between home and foreign goods, in which case financial integration has no consequences for either the aggregate demand or aggregate supply block of the model; but with an elasticity of substitution not exactly equal to one, there would be some quantitative effects (though no radical qualitative changes) of alternative degrees of international financial integration.

various key response elasticities relevant to the transmission mechanism for monetary policy, but should not require fundamental reconsideration of the framework of monetary policy analysis. For example, it does not seem that notions such as "global liquidity" or "global slack" are particularly helpful in thinking about the main determinants of inflation, even in the case of a very highly integrated world economy.

Above all, there is little reason to expect that globalization should eliminate, or even substantially weaken, the influence of domestic monetary policy over domestic inflation. Whatever the pace of globalization and however great its eventual extent may be, it should remain possible for a central bank with a consistent strategy directed to the achievement of a clearly formulated inflation target to achieve that goal, without any need for coordination of policy with other central banks. Hence, it remains appropriate for central banks to be assigned responsibility for stabilizing a suitably chosen index of domestic prices—despite continuing changes in the real economy—whether domestic or foreign in origin.

References

Benigno, G. 2004. Real exchange rate persistence and monetary policy rules. *Journal of Monetary Economics* 51 (3): 473–502.

Benigno, G., and P. Benigno. 2001. Monetary policy rules and the exchange rate. Center for Economic and Policy Research (CEPR) Discussion Paper no. 2807, May.

———. 2005. Implementing international monetary cooperation through inflation targeting. London School of Economics. Unpublished Manuscript, October.

———. 2006. Designing targeting rules for international monetary policy cooperation. *Journal of Monetary Economics* 53 (3): 473–506.

Bernanke, B. S. 2007. Globalization and monetary policy. Speech at the Fourth Economic Summit, Stanford Institute for Economic Policy Research. 2 March, Stanford, California.

Betts, C., and M. B. Devereux. 2000. Exchange rate dynamics in a model of pricing-to-market. *Journal of International Economics* 50 (1): 215–44.

Borio, C., and A. Filardo. 2007. Globalisation and inflation: New cross-country evidence on the global determinants of domestic inflation. Bank for International Settlements. Working Paper, March.

Calvo, G. 1983. Staggered prices in a utility-maximizing framework. *Journal of Monetary Economics* 12 (3): 383–98.

Christiano, L., M. Eichenbaum, and C. Evans. 1996. The effects of monetary policy shocks: Evidence from the flow of funds. *Review of Economics and Statistics* 78 (1): 16–34.

Cole, H. L., and M. Obstfeld. 1991. Commodity trade and international risk sharing: How much do financial markets matter? *Journal of Monetary Economics* 28 (1): 3–24.

Clarida, R., J. Gali, and M. Gertler. 2002. A simple framework for international monetary policy analysis. *Journal of Monetary Economics* 49 (2): 879–904.

Fisher, R. W. 2006. Coping with globalization's impact on monetary policy. Panel Discussion, Allied Social Science Association meetings. Available at: http://www.dallasfed.org/news/speeches/fisher/2006/fs060106.html. 6 January, Boston, Massachusetts.

Galí, J., and T. Monacelli. 2005. Monetary policy and exchange rate volatility in a small open economy. *Review of Economic Studies* 72 (3): 707–34.

HypoVereinsbank (HVB) Group Global Markets Research. 2007. Rolling in money. *Friday Notes,* UniCredit Group, March 2.

Ihrig, J., S. B. Kamin, D. Lindner, and J. Marquez. 2007. Some simple tests of the globalization and inflation hypothesis. Federal Reserve Board. Working Paper, April.

Kose, A., E. Prasad, K. Rogoff, and S.-J. Wei. 2006. Financial globalization: A reappraisal. IMF Working Paper no. 06/189. Washington, DC: International Monetary Fund, August.

Razin, A., and C.-W. Yuen. 2002. The "new Keynesian" Phillips curve: Closed economy versus open economy. *Economics Letters* 75 (1): 1–9.

Rogoff, K. S. 2006. Impact of globalization on monetary policy. In *Monetary policy and uncertainty: Adapting to a changing economy,* Federal Reserve Bank of Kansas City. Kansas City: Federal Reserve Bank of Kansas City.

Rotemberg, J. J., and M. Woodford. 1997. An optimization-based econometric framework for the evaluation of monetary policy. *NBER Macroeconomics Annual* 12:297–346.

Rüffer, R., and L. Stracca. 2006. What is global excess liquidity, and does it matter? ECB Working Paper no. 696. European Central Bank, November.

Sousa, J. M., and A. Zaghini. 2004. Monetary policy shocks in the euro area and global liquidity spillovers. ECB Working Paper no. 309. European Central Bank, February.

———. 2006. Global monetary policy shocks in the G5: A SVAR approach. CFS Working Paper no. 2006/30. Center for Financial Studies, December.

Svensson, L. E. O. 2000. Open-economy inflation targeting. *Journal of International Economics* 50 (1): 155–83.

Taylor, J. B. 1999. A historical analysis of monetary policy rules. In *Monetary policy rules,* ed. J. B. Taylor, 319–48. Chicago: University of Chicago Press.

Woodford, M. 2001. Monetary policy in the information economy. In *Economic policy for the information economy,* ed. Federal Reserve Bank of Kansas City, A. Greenspan, 297–370. Kansas City: Federal Reserve Bank of Kansas City.

———. 2003. *Interest and prices: Foundations of a theory of monetary policy.* Princeton, NJ: Princeton University Press.

Comment David Romer

This is an excellent chapter. The issue it addresses—whether globalization has the potential to reduce or even eliminate the ability of a domestic central bank to influence domestic economic developments—is already

David Romer is the Herman Royer Professor of Political Economy at the University of California, Berkeley, and a research associate of the National Bureau of Economic Research.

being debated, and is likely to become increasingly important as economic integration continues. Most previous analyses of this issue by both non-economists (e.g., Fisher 2006) and economists (e.g., Ball 2006; Rogoff 2006) have been relatively informal. This chapter's formal analysis is a significant step forward. The chapter's organization around the IS, LM, and AS relationships (and its clear separation of the issues involving each of those relationships) is sensible and insightful. The comprehensive discussion of a wide range of ways that globalization might affect the central bank's ability to influence the economy is very valuable, and the focus on extreme cases is a powerful way of clarifying the issues and of identifying problems with many earlier analyses. Finally, I agree with virtually all of Woodford's conclusions.

In my comments, I want to focus on one narrow area where I disagree with Woodford's conclusions, and where it appears that globalization does have the potential to significantly reduce the central bank's ability to influence the economy. In section 1.2.2 of his chapter, as part of his analysis of possible effects of globalization on the LM curve, Woodford discusses the possibility of multiple currencies circulating in a country. He concludes that unless the currencies are perfect substitutes, this development would not affect the domestic central bank's ability to control inflation. This seems counterintuitive. If many prices are not being quoted in units of domestic currency and many transactions are not being carried out using domestic currency, one would think the central bank's ability to affect how rapidly prices are rising would be reduced.

The reason Woodford reaches his conclusion is simple: he focuses on the central bank's ability to influence the price level *measured in units of domestic currency*. Because the central bank can control the value of domestic currency even in a highly globalized economy, it can continue to control this measure of inflation. But while there may be reasons to be interested in inflation measured this way, one might also be interested in inflation measured as an appropriate weighted average of the change in each price in units of whatever currency in which it is quoted. Because the central bank does not determine the values of foreign currencies, it is not clear it can control this measure of inflation in a highly globalized economy.

I therefore want to discuss how the circulation of multiple currencies affects the central bank's ability to influence this measure of inflation. The main thing I will do is present and analyze a simple model of this issue. At the end, I will briefly discuss the question of which measure of inflation is likely to be more important to the central bank. To preview, I find that if globalization really does proceed that far, central banks' ability to achieve their objectives may be substantially constrained. I also find that the constraint is asymmetric: the circulation of multiple currencies limits a central bank's ability to achieve higher inflation than other countries much more than it limits its ability to achieve lower inflation. As a result, whether the constraint is good or bad depends largely on the reliability of central banks. To the extent they are prone to follow high-inflation policies when they should not, the constraint is potentially valuable. But to the extent they sometimes wish to achieve higher inflation than other countries for legitimate reasons, the constraint is harmful.

Assumptions

I am interested in the central bank's ability to control the average level of inflation. I therefore focus on the steady state of a flexible price model. The model is set in discrete time. Each period, households consume a continuum of differentiated goods. There is no international trade, so all goods that households consume are produced domestically, and domestic producers do not sell abroad.

Households' consumption preferences are described by the usual constant intertemporal elasticity of substitution form over time, and the usual constant elasticity of substitution (CES) form at a point in time. That is:

$$(1)\qquad U = \sum_{t=0}^{\infty} e^{-\rho t} u(C_t),$$

$$u(C_t) = \frac{C_t^{(\sigma-1)/\sigma}}{(\sigma-1)/\sigma}, \quad \sigma > 0,$$

$$C_t = \left[\int_{i=0}^{1} C_t(i)^{(\theta-1)/\theta} \right]^{\theta/(\theta-1)}, \quad \theta > 1,$$

where $C_t(i)$ is the household's consumption of good i in period t. The real interest rate is exogenous, constant, and equal to households' rate of time preference: $r = \rho$.

Money enters the model because households face a cash-in-advance constraint on purchases of goods. There are two currencies in the economy, "pesos" and "dollars." Pesos are issued by the domestic central bank, while dollars are not. I therefore treat the rate of peso inflation (i.e., the rate at which prices quoted in pesos rise) as a choice variable of the central bank, and the rate of dollar inflation as exogenous. I denote the two inflation rates by π^P and $\pi^\$$, respectively. Because I focus on steady states, both are constant.

Each producer can post its price and accept payment in either pesos or dollars. To buy from a given producer, a household must hold the needed amount of the relevant currency one period in advance. If we let F denote the fraction of prices that are quoted in pesos, then the average rate at which prices are rising in this economy—which is the inflation measure I will focus on—is:

$$(2)\qquad \pi = F\pi^P + (1 - F)\pi^\$.$$

We can rewrite this as

$$\pi = \pi^{\$} + F\Delta, \tag{3}$$

where Δ is the inflation differential, $\pi^{P} - \pi^{\$}$.

All firms produce using the same constant returns to scale technology. There are no cash-in-advance constraints for payments to factors of production, and factor payments and firm revenues can be used immediately in foreign exchange and asset markets. Thus in any period, all producers have the same marginal cost.

A key assumption is that each producer faces a cost of conducting business in dollars rather than pesos. This cost is heterogeneous across producers, and it may be negative. It is easiest to think of it as a direct utility cost. A highly patriotic producer may be very reluctant to do business in dollars; another producer may prefer to use dollars all else equal; and so on.

We will see that when peso inflation is greater relative to dollar inflation, the demand for goods priced in pesos relative to the demand for goods priced in dollars is lower. The heterogeneous cost of using dollars therefore causes the fraction of firms that price in pesos to be a decreasing function of the inflation differential. That is,

$$F = F(\Delta),\ F'(\cdot) \leq 0. \tag{4}$$

Currency Competition, Inflation, and Distortions

With a cash-in-advance constraint, the effective price of a good to households depends on the inflation rate. With two currencies with differing inflation rates, the result is a distortion of households' choices toward goods sold in the lower inflation currency.

To see how the distortion operates, let P_t^P and $P_t^{\$}$ be the prices charged by the producer of a representative "peso good" and the producer of a representative "dollar good" in period t. If a household decides to buy one unit less of a peso good in period t, it needs P_t^P fewer pesos in period $t-1$. It can use those pesos to purchase P_t^P/ε_{t-1} dollars in period $t-1$, where ε is the exchange rate (i.e., the price of dollars in pesos), and then use those dollars to buy $P_t^P/(\varepsilon_{t-1}P_t^{\$})$ units of a dollar good in period t. Because the producers of peso goods and dollar goods face the same marginal cost and the same elasticity of demand (and since they face no cash-in-advance constraint), they charge the same price. That is, P_t^P and $P_t^{\$}$ are related by

$$P_t^P = \varepsilon_t P_t^{\$}. \tag{5}$$

Thus for households, the price of a peso good relative to a dollar good is $\varepsilon_t/\varepsilon_{(t-1)}$. And since (5) holds each period, $\varepsilon_t/\varepsilon_{(t-1)}$ is determined by the difference in the inflation rates.[1]

1. Inflation rates are measured as changes in log prices.

$$\frac{\varepsilon_t}{\varepsilon_{t-1}} = e^{\Delta}. \tag{6}$$

Given the CES assumption about households' preferences, this implies that the representative household's consumptions of a generic peso good and a generic dollar good are related by

$$\frac{C_t^P}{C_t^\$} = e^{-\theta\Delta}. \tag{7}$$

This analysis shows that differences in inflation between the two currencies produce differences in the effective prices that households face for different goods, and thus differences in their purchases. These differences have no counterpart in the social opportunity costs of producing the goods. That is, differential inflation creates distortions.

The welfare cost of these distortions is approximately equal to a constant times the variance of (log) relative prices faced by households. With fraction F of goods priced in pesos and the remainder in dollars, this variance is

$$V = F(\Delta)[1 - F(\Delta)]\Delta^2. \tag{8}$$

It is useful to rewrite this as

$$V = [\Delta F(\Delta)]^2\left[\frac{1 - F(\Delta)}{F(\Delta)}\right]. \tag{9}$$

The distortions from different purchases of peso and dollar goods are zero if all goods are priced in dollars ($F = 0$), if all goods are priced in pesos ($F = 1$), or if the two inflation rates are the same ($\Delta = 0$). For a given Δ, they are greatest when $F = 1/2$; for a given F, they are increasing in the absolute value of Δ.

Currency Competition and Inflation Control

Recall that the measure of inflation I focus on—the average rate of increase of prices, in whatever currencies they are quoted in—is $\pi = \pi^\$ + F(\Delta)\Delta$, where Δ is the inflation differential, $\pi^P - \pi^\$$ (see [3]). One can use this expression, together with equation (9) for the variance of relative prices caused by differential inflation, to establish the following results. Throughout, I assume that strictly positive amounts of both currencies circulate (i.e., $0 < F < 1$).

Result 1. There may be an upper bound to inflation. To see this, recall that $\pi = \pi^\$ + F(\Delta)\Delta$. For $\Delta > 0$, raising Δ increases inflation by raising the Δ term, but lowers it by reducing the $F(\Delta)$ term. For many $F(\cdot)$'s, the second effect eventually dominates, so there is maximum inflation rate that can be attained. The numerical example presented later illustrates this possibility.

Result 2. Obtaining inflation different from foreign inflation introduces a distortion that is not present under a single currency. This follows from the facts that $\pi \neq \pi^{\$}$ requires $\pi^{P} \neq \pi^{\$}$ and that when $\pi^{P} \neq \pi^{\$}$ and $0 < F < 1$, $V > 0$.

Result 3. A given departure of inflation above foreign inflation involves greater distortions than the same departure of inflation below foreign inflation. To see this, consider equation (9) for V. Since $\pi = \pi^{\$} + F(\Delta)\Delta$, equal departures of inflation above and below $\pi^{\$}$ involve equal and opposite values of $F(\Delta)\Delta$, and thus the same value of $[F(\Delta)\Delta]^2$. But since $F'(\Delta) \leq 0$, $[1 - F(\Delta)]/F(\Delta)$ is greater for a positive value of Δ than for a negative value of Δ of equal magnitude.

Result 4. When inflation is above foreign inflation, if an increase in peso inflation raises overall inflation, it increases distortions. This follows immediately from (9) and the fact that $F'(\Delta) \leq 0$.

Thus, the only case where raising peso inflation further above dollar inflation could reduce distortions is when it reduces overall inflation. But the central bank would never put the economy in that situation: if the economy is at a point where $\Delta F(\Delta)$ is decreasing in Δ, then (as long as $F[\cdot]$ is smooth) there is some lower value of Δ that yields the same $\Delta F(\Delta)$, and so yields the same inflation rate with smaller distortions. Thus, result 4 says that the further inflation is increased above foreign inflation, the greater the distortions.

Result 5. When inflation is below foreign inflation, lowering inflation further can either raise or lower distortions. Lowering inflation further below foreign inflation requires increasing the magnitude of the difference between peso inflation and dollar inflation, which acts to raise distortions. But it increases the fraction of prices quoted in pesos. If most prices are already quoted in pesos, this acts to lower distortions. The numerical example shows that the overall effect can go in either direction.

Result 6. The lowest inflation rate that can be attained with a strictly positive nominal domestic interest rate is greater when foreign currency circulates than when only domestic currency is used. However, when currency competition is greater, that inflation rate is lower. The assumption that the real interest rate equals the rate of time preference, ρ, implies that the nominal interest rate on peso-denominated bonds is $i^{p} = \pi^{p} + \rho$. Thus the *peso* inflation rate must exceed $-\rho$ for i^{p} to be positive. This means that the overall inflation rate must exceed $\pi^{\$} + F(-\rho - \pi^{\$})(-\rho - \pi^{\$})$, or $-\rho + [1 - F(-\rho - \pi^{\$})](\pi^{\$} + \rho)$. Unless $F(-\rho - \pi^{\$})$ equals 1 (or $\pi^{\$} \leq \rho$, which would imply a nominal dollar interest rate of zero), this exceeds the lower bound of $-\rho$ that occurs in the absence of multiple currencies. However, the more that households use pesos when peso inflation is low (i.e., the greater is $F[-\rho - \pi^{\$}]$), the lower is the lower bound.

Finally, result 3 suggests the following.

Result 7. With multiple currencies, there is likely to be deflationary bias. Addressing this issue formally would require extending the model. To see the intuition, however, suppose there are two countries in the world, and that one prefers lower inflation than the other. Result 3 suggests that it will be less costly for the central bank that prefers low inflation to push overall inflation in its country down than for the central bank that prefers high inflation to push its overall inflation up. Thus, there is a force acting to make average inflation in the world closer to the level preferred by the low-inflation central bank than to that preferred by the high-inflation central bank.

Example

To illustrate these ideas (other than result 7), consider the case where $F(\cdot)$ is one minus a cumulative normal distribution with a mean of zero and a standard deviation of 5 percentage points. This implies that when the two inflation rates are the same, half of transactions are conducted in each currency, and that if the inflation differential is 5 percentage points, five-sixths of transactions are conducted in the lower inflation currency. Thus, it implies a high degree of substitutability between the currencies.

Figure 1C.1 plots overall inflation as a function of the inflation differential. For simplicity, I normalize dollar inflation to zero. Currency competition greatly constrains the ability of the domestic central bank to create inflation. Inflation can be raised only 0.85 percentage points above dollar inflation; this occurs when the inflation differential is 3.76 percentage points. In contrast, the presence of multiple currencies has little impact on the central bank's ability to achieve low inflation. As peso inflation falls, households

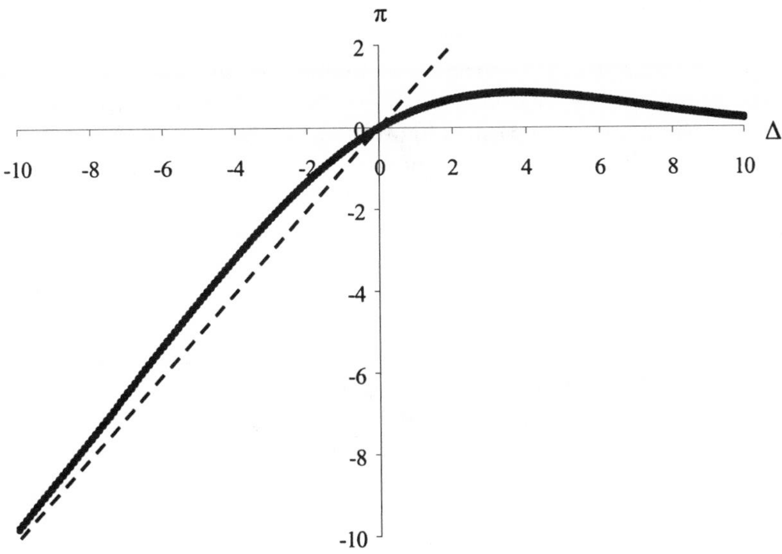

Fig. 1C.1 Overall inflation as a function of the difference between peso and dollar inflation (dollar inflation normalized to zero)

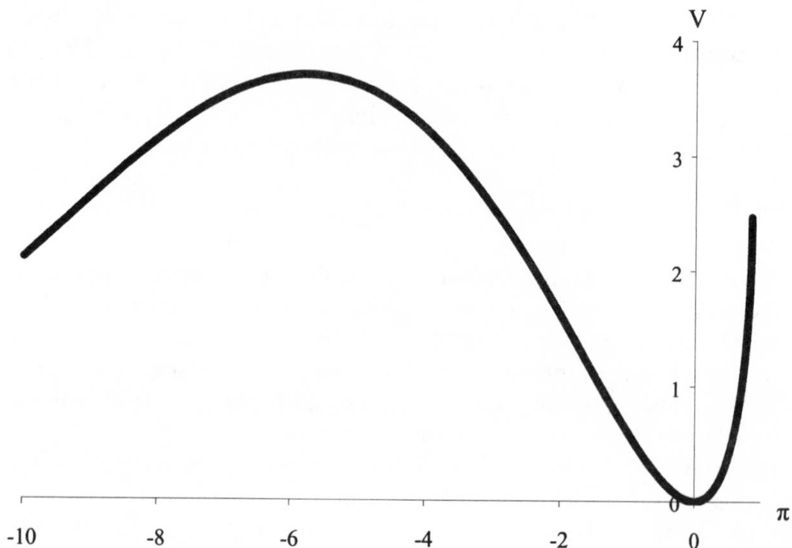

Fig. 1C.2 The variance of relative prices faced by households as a function of inflation (dollar inflation normalized to zero)

move rapidly out of dollars, and so overall inflation is determined mainly by peso inflation.[2]

Figure 1C.2 shows the variance of relative prices as a function of overall inflation (with dollar inflation again normalized to zero). For positive inflation (i.e., inflation above dollar inflation), the variance of relative prices is rising with inflation up to the maximum attainable inflation rate, as shown by result 4. For negative inflation, reductions in inflation first raise distortions (by increasing the difference in the opportunity cost to households of peso and dollar goods) and then lower them (by causing households to switch mainly into pesos).

An Extension

A natural extension of the model is to allow the fraction of prices posted in pesos and the fraction of goods purchased with pesos to differ. For example, some producers could post their prices in one currency but accept payment in either. One could model each fraction as a decreasing function

2. The figure can be reinterpreted to show the lower bound on inflation with and without currency competition. With multiple currencies (and $\pi^{\$} = 0$), overall inflation must exceed $-\rho F(-\rho)$ for i^P to be nonnegative; with only domestic currency, it must exceed $-\rho$. Thus if we measure $-\rho$ on the horizontal axis, the solid line shows the lower bound on inflation with currency competition, and the dashed line shows the lower bound without currency competition.

of the inflation differential, with the functions now no longer necessarily the same. Redoing the analysis in this more complicated case is straightforward.

An interesting special case of the extended model arises when all transactions are conducted in the lower inflation currency, but not all prices are necessarily posted in that currency. One situation where this would effectively occur is when households can trade in foreign exchange markets costlessly and instantaneously. In this case, households hold only the lower inflation currency, and buy the higher inflation currency only the instant before using it to make purchases.

In this case, inflation (the average rate at which posted prices are rising) continues to be given by $\pi = \pi^{\$} + F(\Delta)\Delta$, where $F(\Delta)$ is now the fraction of prices quoted in pesos. However, because households no longer need to hold the high-inflation currency for a period to buy goods whose prices are posted in terms of that currency, they face the same effective price for all goods. Thus, differential inflation no longer produces distortions. However, result 1—the possibility of an upper bound to inflation—still holds, as does result 6 about the lower bound to inflation.

Which Measure of Inflation Is the Central Bank Likely to Care about?

Is control of peso inflation sufficient for the central bank to attain its objectives, or will it care about dollar inflation as well? A firm answer to this question requires a full understanding of the welfare effects of inflation, which we do not have. Thus, I will merely offer some preliminary comments about various forces that may affect the central bank's views about inflation.

I see only one consideration for which control of peso inflation is likely to be sufficient: nonindexation of the tax system. If the tax system is written in nominal terms, it is presumably in terms of domestic currency. Thus, to the extent the central bank is concerned about inflation because it is concerned about the distortions arising from this nonindexation, control over peso inflation is enough to allow it to achieve its objectives. In the model I have described, the central bank continues to have control over peso inflation, although this comes with some costs if it chooses a level that differs from dollar inflation.

For other factors that influence the welfare effects of inflation, the central bank will almost certainly care about both peso and dollar inflation. One cost of inflation is that it makes money costly to hold even though it is costless to produce, and so introduces inefficiency. In the model I have described, for example, inflation makes it more costly for households to obtain goods, and so could distort their labor-leisure choices. With foreign currency circulating in the country, some of these costs are determined by foreign central banks. Thus, the domestic central bank's control over peso inflation is not enough to give it full control over these costs.

A potentially more important consideration in the central bank's choice of inflation is that inflation can grease the wheels of labor and goods markets by making the need for nominal wage and price cuts less common. For wages and prices that are quoted in terms of foreign currency, inflation in terms of the domestic currency is not relevant. Thus, this is another case where the circulation of multiple currencies restricts the central bank's ability to achieve its objectives.

Another consideration in the determination of optimal inflation is that, since nominal prices are not continually adjusted, higher inflation increases the relative price variability that arises as different prices are adjusted at different times. Again, what affects welfare is not just inflation in terms of domestic currency, but the various inflation rates in terms of the different currencies in which prices are quoted. Thus again, control of inflation in terms of domestic currency is not enough.

Inflation also affects the chances that an adverse shock will put the central bank in a position where it wants to reduce the nominal interest rate to zero. Here I am not certain what to think, but my guess is that the news is mixed. On the one hand, if globalization proceeds to the point where multiple currencies are circulating in significant quantities in a country, goods and financial markets are likely to be so integrated that domestic monetary policy will have powerful effects via exchange rates rather than interest rates. Thus, the zero lower bound on the domestic interest rate is unlikely to matter much for the central bank's responses to domestic shocks. On the other hand, with this type of economic integration and the use of multiple currencies within a country, a worldwide shock that pushed foreign nominal interest rates to zero would likely affect the domestic economy, and the level of peso inflation would not affect the chances of this occurring. Thus, it appears that control of peso inflation does not give the central bank full control over the probability that a shock will push a nominal interest rate that matters to the economy to zero.

Finally, it has been suggested that high inflation in effect directly lowers utility, essentially because seeing prices rise makes people unhappy, or that inflation can cause people to make suboptimal financial plans because they have difficulty accounting for inflation. Here the relevant inflation rate is inflation in terms of whatever units people use to think about prices and financial plans. In an economy where many prices are quoted in units of foreign currency and many transactions are carried out using foreign currency, for at least some households those units are likely to be in foreign currency.

Conclusion

I have two main conclusions. First, I want to emphasize what I said at the outset, which is that this is an excellent chapter that should become the standard reference on globalization and monetary policy.

Second, there appears to be at least one important way that globalization could severely limit a central bank's ability to achieve its goals. If globalization proceeds to the point where a significant fraction of prices are quoted in terms of foreign currency and a significant fraction of transactions are conducted in foreign currency, the central bank is likely to lose some of its influence over overall inflation, and this loss of influence is likely to matter for its ability to achieve its broader objectives.

This loss of influence is asymmetric: it is more costly for the central bank to raise inflation above foreign inflation than to lower it below, and raising it beyond some level may be impossible. Thus, the constraints that currency competition can create for central banks are not altogether bad: to the extent that some central banks' pursuit of higher inflation than their neighbors is undesirable (resulting from such factors as misguided views about the benefits of loose monetary policy, political pressures, and desires for seignorage), currency competition can impose useful discipline. But a country can also have legitimate reasons for wanting higher inflation than its neighbors. For example, its institutions or history may make nominal wage or price cuts particularly difficult, and so greasing-the-wheels considerations may make its optimal inflation rate higher than its neighbors'. My general point is that currency competition has the potential to prevent central banks from accomplishing some things they were previously able to. Whether this is good or bad depends on how well central banks were using the powers that become limited by globalization.

References

Ball, L. M. 2006. Has globalization changed inflation? NBER Working Paper no. 12687. Cambridge, MA: National Bureau of Economic Research, June.

Fisher, R. W. 2006. Coping with globalization's impact on monetary policy. Panel discussion, Allied Social Science Association Meetings. January, Boston, Massachusetts.

Rogoff, K. S. 2006. Impact of globalization on monetary policy. In *The new economic geography: Effects and policy implications,* 265–305. Kansas City: Federal Reserve Bank of Kansas City.

2 The Transmission of Domestic Shocks in Open Economies

Christopher Erceg, Christopher Gust, and
David López-Salido

2.1 Introduction

With the rapid expansion in world trade during the past two decades, policymakers have become increasingly interested in the consequences of greater trade openness for macroeconomic behavior. Considerable attention has focused on how external shocks may play a more prominent role in driving domestic fluctuations as trade linkages grow, and as developing countries such as China exert a progressively larger influence on global energy and commodity prices. Our chapter examines a different aspect of globalization that has received less scrutiny in the recent literature. In particular, we investigate whether changes in trade openness are likely to have a substantial impact on the transmission of domestic shocks.

Economists have long recognized that openness could potentially affect the responses of real activity to domestic shocks, including to monetary and fiscal policy. The Mundell (1962) and Fleming (1962) framework showed that fiscal shocks could have dramatically different effects depending on whether an economy was open or closed: in contrast to the stimulative effect of a government spending rise on output in a closed economy, the same

Christopher Erceg is an assistant director of the Division of International Finance at the Federal Reserve Board. Christopher Gust is a senior economist in the Division of International Finance at the Federal Reserve Board. David López-Salido is chief of the Monetary Studies Section in the Division of Monetary Affairs at the Federal Reserve Board.

We thank Malin Adolfson (our discussant), Jordi Galí, Mark Gertler, Steve Kamin, Donald Kohn, Andrew Levin, and John Taylor for helpful comments and suggestions, and seminar participants at the Federal Reserve Board, and at the June 2007 NBER conference "International Dimensions of Monetary Policy." We also thank Hilary Croke for excellent research assistance. The views expressed in this chapter are solely the responsibility of the authors and should not be interpreted as reflecting the views of the Board of Governors of the Federal Reserve System or of any other person associated with the Federal Reserve System.

shock had no effect on output in an open economy, as real exchange rate appreciation crowded out real net exports.

A long-standing literature has also assessed the implications of openness for the effects of domestic shocks on inflation. Perhaps most obviously, economists drew attention to the potential divergence between domestic prices and consumer prices in an open economy, reflecting the sensitivity of the latter to import prices. But important contributions in the 1970s and early 1980s also analyzed how the behavior of domestic price setting could be affected by openness. Influential work by Dornbusch (1983) linked the desired markup in a monopolistic competition framework to the real exchange rate, and showed how the markup could be expected to decline in response to real exchange rate appreciation (reflecting increased competitive pressure from abroad). In an NBER conference volume a quarter century ago, Dornbusch and Fischer (1984) used this framework to argue that changes in the slope of the Phillips curve due to increased trade openness were likely to have substantial implications for the transmission of monetary and fiscal policy. Specifically, these authors argued that monetary shocks were likely to cause domestic prices to respond more quickly due to an effective steepening of the Phillips curve.

In this chapter, we use a two-country dynamic stochastic general equilibrium (DSGE) modeling framework to revisit the question of how changes in trade openness affect the economy's responses to monetary and fiscal shocks, as well as to a representative supply shock.[1] Our analysis is heavily influenced by several important papers that compare the characteristics of optimal policy rules in closed and open economies by Clarida, Galí, and Gertler (2001, 2002), and Galí and Monacelli (2005).[2] However, the main objective of these papers was to highlight conditions under which the policy problem in closed and open economies was formally similar: under such conditions, policy prescriptions from the closed economy carried over to the open economy with suitable changes in parameters. Our chapter differs substantially insofar as its objective is to provide a quantitative assessment of the differences in the transmission channel as the trade openness of the economy varies.

We focus much of our analysis on a simple "workhorse" open economy model that extends Galí and Monacelli (2005) by incorporating nominal wage rigidities and additional shocks. Although our model allows for spillover effects between the two countries, it can be approximated by a system of dynamic equations that parallels the closed economy model of Erceg, Hen-

1. Our approach follows the seminal work of Obstfeld and Rogoff (1995) and a large subsequent literature that incorporates nominal rigidities into microfounded open economy DSGE models. See Lane (2001) for a survey.

2. There is a burgeoning literature examining optimal monetary policy in an open economy setting. Some notable examples include Benigno and Benigno (2003), Corsetti and Pesenti (2005), and Devereux and Engel (2003).

derson, and Levin (2000) in the special case in which the home country's share of world output becomes arbitrarily small. As in the Erceg, Henderson, and Levin (2000) model, the presence of nominal wage rigidities confronts the policymaker with a trade-off between stabilizing inflation and the output (or employment) gap. The parsimonious structure of our open economy model makes it easy to identify the economic channels through which openness affects aggregate demand and supply, and hence the trade-offs confronting policymakers. In fact, the differences between the closed and open economies can be attributed to effects on a single composite parameter that affects the behavioral equations in the same way as the intertemporal elasticity of substitution parameter (σ) in a closed economy model; that is, by affecting the interest elasticity of aggregate demand and the wealth effect on labor supply.[3] Given that this parameter can be expressed as a weighted average of the intertemporal elasticity of substitution and the trade price elasticity, where the weight on the latter varies directly with openness, it is straightforward to assess how changes in openness affect equilibrium responses under a wide range of calibrations.

Our analysis shows that, in principle, there could be very pronounced divergence in the effects of the domestic shocks on output and domestic inflation as trade openness increases. In particular, with both a very high trade price elasticity and Frisch elasticity of labor supply, the enhanced ability to smooth consumption in the open economy markedly alters the wealth effect of shocks on labor supply, and the slope of the household's marginal rate of substitution (MRS) schedule (tending to flatten it). These changes can have substantial effects on aggregate supply, and through their effect on marginal costs, on domestic inflation and output. Moreover, on the aggregate demand side, higher openness increases the effective interest elasticity of the economy, provided that the trade price elasticity is higher than the intertemporal elasticity of substitution in consumption. In the extreme case in which the trade price elasticity becomes infinitely high, our workhorse model in fact implies that government shocks have no effect on output, inflation, or interest rates.

However, under more empirically plausible values of the trade price elasticity, aggregate supply is not very sensitive to trade openness. The interest sensitivity of aggregate demand, or "slope" of the new-Keynesian IS curve, exhibits somewhat more variation with openness, reflecting that the trade price elasticity (of 1.5) is much higher than the intertemporal elasticity of substitution of consumption under our benchmark calibration (so that putting a larger weight on the former, as occurs with greater openness, increases the interest sensitivity of the economy). Overall, although openness does exert some effect on the responses of domestic inflation, output, and real

3. This extends the results of Galí and Monacelli (2005), who also showed that the effects of openness can be summarized in a single composite parameter.

interest rates to the inflation target change, government spending, and technology shocks we consider, the size of the changes seems quite modest given the wide range of variation in the trade share examined (from 0 to 35 percent). The main implications of openness are apparent in the composition of the expenditure response, with exports playing a larger role in a highly open economy, and in the wedge between consumer and domestic prices.

We then proceed to consider several variants of our workhorse model. First, we compare incomplete markets with the complete markets setting, and again conclude that openness exerts fairly small effects unless the trade price elasticity and Frisch elasticity of labor supply are quite high. Second, we consider endogenous capital accumulation, and find that the differences between closed and open economies are even smaller than in our workhorse model, reflecting in part that endogenous capital boosts the interest rate elasticity of domestic demand. Third, we consider a specification in which imports are used as intermediate goods; for reasonable calibrations of the import share, the results are very similar to the workhorse model. Fourth, we examine the implications of a framework that allows for both local currency pricing (as in Betts and Devereux [1996]; Devereux and Engel [2002]) and variable desired markups in the spirit of Dornbusch. We find that these mechanisms can amplify differences in the response of domestic inflation as the degree of openness varies. For example, domestic inflation falls by less in response to a positive technology shock in a highly open economy, reflecting that the associated exchange rate depreciation reduces the price competitiveness of imports (which encourages domestic producers to boost their markups). However, large differences in trade openness appear required for these effects to show through quantitatively.

A natural question is whether the alternative specifications suggested previously would affect our conclusions if they were incorporated into our model jointly rather than in isolation. We address this question by examining the responses of the SIGMA model. This is a multicountry DSGE model used at the Federal Reserve Board for policy simulations, and is well-suited to address this question insofar as it includes many of the key features of the workhorse model and the variants, as well as various real rigidities designed to improve its empirical performance (e.g., adjustment costs on imports). We consider the responses of the SIGMA model to the same underlying shocks—including to the inflation target, government spending, and technology—and essentially corroborate our main finding that the responses of domestic inflation and output are not particularly sensitive to openness.

This chapter is organized as follows. We begin by presenting the simulations of the SIGMA model in section 2.2. This approach proves helpful both as a way of highlighting our main results and for pointing out some restrictive features of the heuristic models discussed in the subsequent sections against the backdrop of this more general model (e.g., the implications of abstracting from capital accumulation in the workhorse model). Section 2.3 describes the workhorse model, and then assesses how openness affects the equilibrium under both flexible and sticky prices. Section 2.4 considers several modifications of the workhorse model. Section 2.5 concludes.

2.2 Theoretical and Empirical Motivation

In this section, we use a two-country version of the SIGMA model to illustrate how trade openness affects the propagation of three different domestic shocks, including a reduction in the central bank's target inflation rate, a rise in government spending, and a highly persistent rise in technology. In the case of the shock to the inflation target, we compare the model's implications to historical episodes of disinflation that occurred in the United States, Canada, and the United Kingdom during the early 1980s and early 1990s. Readers who wish to skip ahead to sections 2.3 and 2.4—in which we fully describe a much simpler workhorse DSGE model and some variants to investigate the same questions—may do so without loss of continuity.

2.2.1 SIGMA Simulations

The SIGMA incorporates an array of nominal and real rigidities to help the model yield plausible implications across a broad spectrum of domestic and international shocks.[4] On the aggregate demand side, it allows for habit persistence in consumption, costs of changing the level of investment, and costs of adjusting trade flows.[5] Final consumption and investment goods are produced using both domestically-produced goods and imports. International financial markets are incomplete, so that households are restricted to borrowing or lending internationally through the medium of a nonstate contingent bond. On the supply side, prices are set in staggered Calvo-style contracts in both the home and foreign market, with exporters setting their price in local currency terms, as in Betts and Devereux (1996) and Devereux and Engel (2002). The SIGMA embeds demand curves with nonconstant elasticities (NCES) that induce "strategic complementarity" in price setting (as in Kimball [1995]). In the spirit of Dornbusch (1983), this feature implies that the desired markup varies in response to real exchange rate fluctuations, creating an incentive for firms to charge different prices in home and foreign markets even under fully flexible prices. As shown by Bergin and Feenstra (2001), Gust, Leduc, and Vigfusson (2006), and Gust and Sheets (2006), it

4. An inclusive description of SIGMA is provided by Erceg, Guerrieri, and Gust (2006) for the case in which product demand is characterized by a Dixit-Stiglitz CES aggregator, implying a constant desired markup. Gust and Sheets (2006) extend the model to allow for variable desired markups, as in the version used in this chapter, though they abstract from capital accumulation and examine a smaller array of shocks.

5. Our specification of habit persistence in consumption and adjustment costs on investment follows Smets and Wouters (2003).

can account for low exchange rate pass-through to import prices. Wages are also set in staggered Calvo-style contracts.[6]

Monetary policy is assumed to follow a Taylor rule in which the nominal interest rate responds to the deviation of *domestic* inflation from the central bank's inflation target and to the output gap. Although it is more realistic empirically to specify the monetary rule as responding to consumer price inflation, such a specification implicitly assigns a higher weight to import price inflation as openness increases. This complicates the task of disentangling the effects of openness on transmission due to changes in the aggregate demand and supply blocks of the model—which is our main objective—from effects due to a higher effective weight on import price inflation in the monetary rule. Accordingly, we find it very useful for heuristic purposes to simply condition on a rule that does not vary with openness, while still providing a reasonable characterization of policy in a relatively closed economy.[7]

Government purchases are exogenous, have no direct effect on the utility of households, and are financed by lump-sum taxes. Although SIGMA allows for some fraction of households to make "rule-of-thumb" consumption decisions, we set this share to zero in what follows, so that there is effectively a single representative household in each country.

Figure 2.1 shows the effects of a 1 percentage point permanent reduction in the home country's inflation target under three different calibrations of trade openness. The solid line shows the effects under our benchmark calibration based on U.S. data, so that the ratio of imports to gross domestic product (GDP) is 12 percent. The dashed line shows an alternative in which we lower the import share to 1 percent (labeled "nearly closed"), while the dotted line shows a second alternative in which the import share is 35 percent ("high openness"), roughly consistent with the import to GDP ratio in highly open economies such Canada and the United Kingdom.[8] The horizontal axis shows quarters that have elapsed following the shock.

The effects of the reduction in the inflation target are qualitatively similar regardless of the degree of openness. The reduction in the inflation target

6. Following Christiano, Eichenbaum, and Evans (2005), SIGMA incorporates dynamic indexation of both price and wage contracts, though the latter are indexed to past aggregate wage inflation.

7. There are clearly many ways through which openness can affect the transmission of domestic shocks through the monetary policy rule. Even within the class of rules responding to consumer price inflation, the manner in which impulse responses to domestic shocks vary with openness can be quite sensitive to whether monetary policy responds to realized consumer price inflation or to a forecast of inflation. For example, a stimulative government spending shock typically causes ex post import price inflation to fall (because the real exchange rate initially appreciates), but causes expected import price inflation to rise. Although it remains interesting to explore some of these possibilities in future work, it is worth observing that the difference between consumer price inflation and domestic price inflation shows much less variation with openness in SIGMA—which has features that account for low pass-through of exchange rate changes to import prices—than in most open economy models that effectively impose full pass-through within a couple of quarters.

8. In these experiments, we vary openness by changing the share parameter in the aggregators with a nonconstant elasticity of substitution (NCES) used to produce consumption and investment from the home and foreign goods.

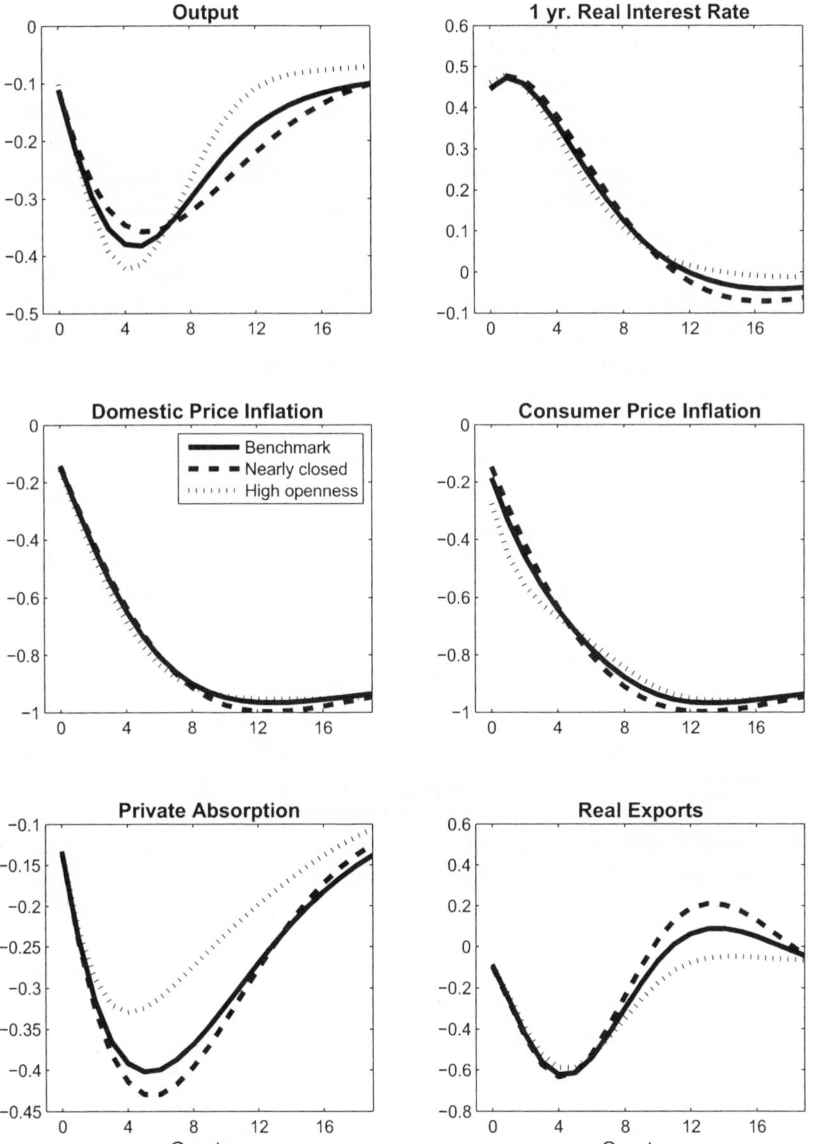

Fig. 2.1 Permanent reduction in the inflation target in SIGMA (deviation from steady state)

requires policymakers to increase interest rates, causing output to contract and the real exchange rate (not shown) to appreciate. Private absorption falls in response to the higher interest rates, and exports also decline due to the induced appreciation of the real exchange rate. Both domestic and consumer price inflation fall, and roughly converge to their new target level after two years.

Perhaps somewhat remarkably, the responses of key macro aggregates—including output, domestic price inflation, and the real interest rate—show little quantitative variation with different degrees of openness. The sacrifice ratio—which we measure as the sum of (annualized) output gaps in the twenty quarters following the start of the disinflation, divided by the change in the inflation rate of 1 percentage point—is about 1.1 under each calibration. Aside from the slightly larger initial output decline under the high openness calibration, the main differences in the responses are compositional. For the highly open economy, more of the output contraction is attributable to a fall in real net exports; in addition, given the larger share of imported goods in the consumption basket, there is a greater disparity between the response of consumer price inflation and domestic price inflation.

The similarity in the responses of output, domestic price inflation, and the real interest rate is mainly attributable to two factors. First, the interest-sensitivity of aggregate demand only rises modestly as trade openness increases. Although our benchmark calibration imposes a rather high long-run trade price elasticity of 1.5, providing a strong channel (through the uncovered interest parity condition) for real interest rates to influence exports, private absorption is also quite interest-sensitive due to the high responsiveness of investment. This can be garnered from the bottom panels of the figure: the contraction in exports in response to higher real interest rates does not markedly exceed the fall in private absorption. This helps to explain why output only shows a slightly larger contraction under a 35 percent trade share than in the case in which the trade share is only 1 percent of GDP.[9] The second factor is that desired price markups and real marginal costs do not change significantly with greater openness, so that domestic price inflation responds very similarly across the different calibrations. Overall, these results do not indicate a significant quantitative "steepening" of the Phillips curve due to greater openness in response to this particular shock.[10]

9. Given the presence of adjustment costs on the expenditure components, the interest sensitivity depends on how persistent an effect the shock has on the real interest rate. For shocks that exert more persistent effects on real interest rates, exports show a relatively higher interest sensitivity than private domestic demand, and the aggregate interest sensitivity of the economy rises more substantially with openness. For example, the interest sensitivity rises more with greater openness under an alternative model calibration that increases the duration of wage and price contracts (since the real interest rate response in that case is more persistent). Similarly, the government spending shock following has a more persistent impact on the real interest rate, with the implication that the economy becomes more interest sensitive with greater openness.

10. The limited variation in the desired markup reflects that the real interest rate shows a fairly transient rise; hence, the real exchange rate does not appreciate much. Under an alternative model calibration implying a more persistent rise in real interest rates—derived by assuming

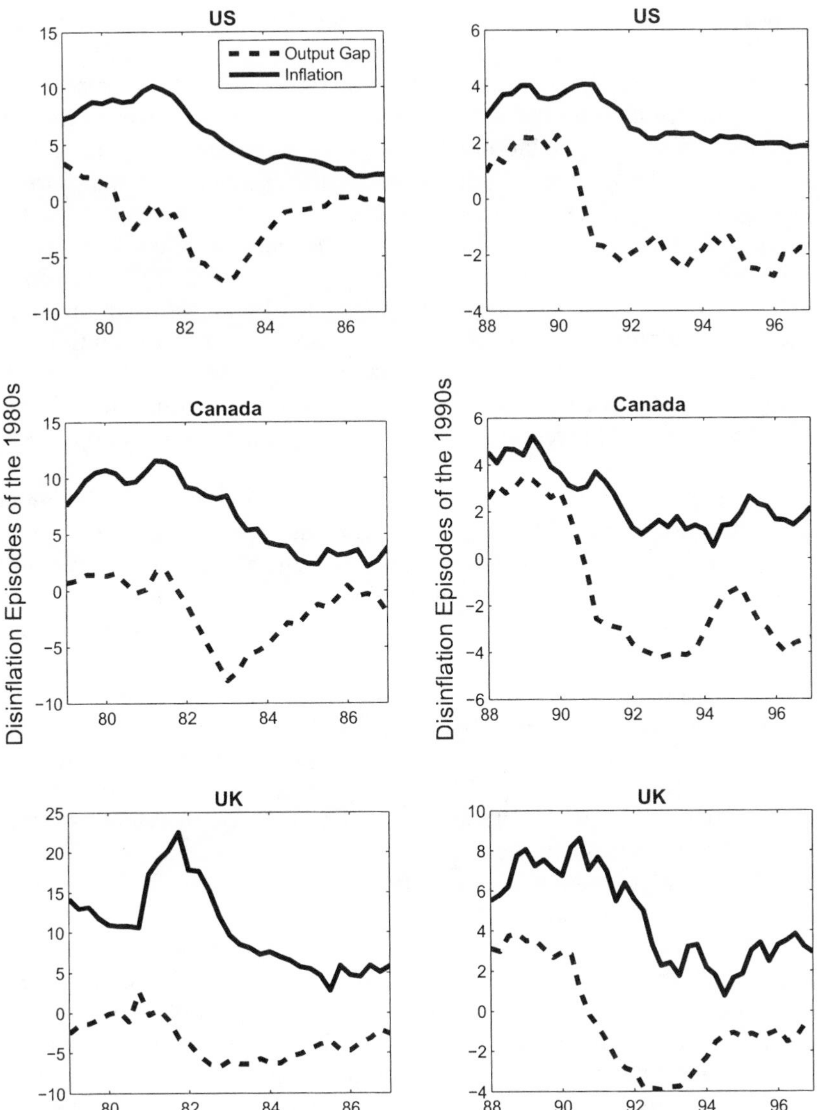

Fig. 2.2 Disinflation episodes in the United States, Canada, and the United Kingdom

Interestingly, historical episodes of disinflation in the United States, Canada, and the United Kingdom seem reasonably supportive of the model's implications. Figure 2.2 shows the evolution of inflation (measured as the

longer contract durations—desired markups, and hence, inflation show more variation with openness.

annual changes in the GDP deflator) and the output gap (as measured by the Organization for Economic Cooperation and Development [OECD]) for the United States, Canada, and the United Kingdom for two different periods of disinflation (the early 1980s and early 1990s). As seen in the left column of figure 2.2, inflation in both the United States and Canada fell from roughly 10 percent to 4 percent during the disinflations that occurred during the early 1980s, while the output gap expanded (in absolute value) by roughly 6 to 7 percent in each country. The sacrifice ratio in the United Kingdom was somewhat lower during that episode, as inflation fell by considerably more, while the output gap expanded by a similar amount. In the 1990s, the three experiences also were reasonably similar, with Canada perhaps having a somewhat higher sacrifice ratio than the United States, and the United Kingdom a slightly lower sacrifice ratio. Thus, while the evidence is somewhat noisy, the sacrifice ratio does not appear to vary with openness in a systematic way.[11]

Figure 2.3 shows the effects of an increase in government spending.[12] From a qualitative perspective, the government spending hike has similar effects on key macroeconomic variables across the alternative calibrations. The expansion in aggregate demand initially raises output and real interest rates. Some of the output rise is attributable to an increase in potential output, as a negative wealth effect on consumption induces some expansion in labor supply. Higher real interest rates and an induced appreciation of the real exchange rate eventually cause output to revert toward baseline due to a crowding out of private domestic demand and real net exports. Domestic inflation rises because of a positive output gap, and because the expansion in potential output puts additional upward pressure on marginal cost; the latter effect reflects the interplay of diminishing returns and nominal wage rigidity so that the real wage remains above the level that would prevail under flexible wage adjustment.[13]

Comparing the alternative calibrations, the magnitude of the output response declines with greater openness, though the differences do not seem dramatic given the wide variation in trade shares examined. A highly open economy can rely more heavily on a decline in real net exports to alleviate pressure on domestic resources. This cushions the wealth effect on labor supply in the more open economy, and causes potential output to rise by

11. Ball (1994) reached similar conclusions based on sacrifice ratios for a much larger set of episodes. Our approach differs insofar as we compare sacrifice ratios across countries over similar time periods (rather than pooling all episodes together) as a rough means of controlling for different levels of monetary policy credibility.

12. Government spending is modelled as an AR(1) process with an autocorrelation coefficient equal to 0.97.

13. Thus, even if the monetary rule were aggressive enough to close the output gap, the gap between the real wage and flexible price real wage would put upward pressure on marginal cost and inflation. We provide an extensive discussion of the implications of the "real wage gap" for marginal cost and inflation in section 2.3.7.

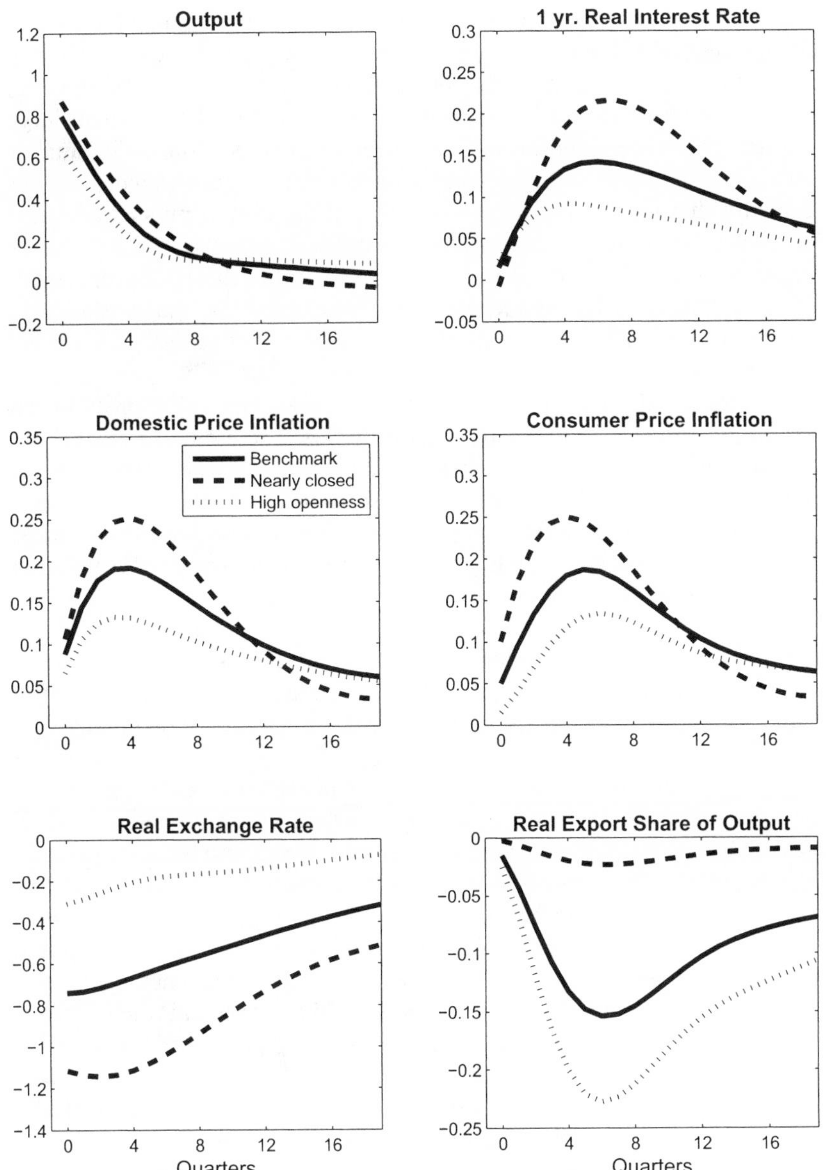

Fig. 2.3 Increase in government spending in SIGMA (deviation from steady state)

less. In addition, the output gap expands by less due to some increase in the interest-sensitivity of aggregate demand with greater openness. The responses of domestic price inflation exhibit somewhat larger variation with trade openness, with the peak inflation response only about half as large in the highly open economy as in the nearly closed economy. The smaller inflation response in the highly open economy reflects both a smaller output gap, and that the smaller expansion in potential output puts less upward pressure on marginal costs. In addition, our framework with variable markups implies that domestic producers desire to reduce their price markup in response to heighted competitive pressure from abroad (as the real exchange rate appreciates, and, as a result, import prices fall). The restraining effect on inflation is larger in a more open economy.

The composition of the expenditure response show more pronounced variation across calibrations. In a relatively closed economy, falling private absorption (especially investment) bears the burden of adjustment, while a decline in real net exports is the catalyst for adjustment in a highly open economy. Given that the fall in import prices has a larger effect on consumer prices when trade openness is high, the responses of consumer price inflation show more divergence than those of domestic inflation.

Figure 2.4 shows a persistent increase in the level of technology.[14] The effects are qualitatively similar across the three calibrations. In each case, output has a hump-shaped response peaking around five or six quarters after the shock, both domestic and consumer price inflation fall on impact, and the real exchange rate depreciates.

The fall in domestic price inflation occurs because the real wage remains persistently below the *potential* real wage, where the potential real wage is defined as the real wage that would prevail if prices and wages were completely flexible. Openness tends to mute the decline in domestic price inflation through two channels. First, it reduces the magnitude of the rise in the potential real wage. This is because the real exchange rate depreciation retards the expansion in consumption as the economy becomes more open, so that the wealth effect on labor supply is smaller. Second, the depreciation of the real exchange rate and consequent rise in import prices induce domestic producers to raise their markup, as they feel less competition from foreign producers. In a more open economy, the pricing decisions of foreign exporters becomes relatively more important to the price decisions of domestic firms; thus, the rise in import prices plays a more noticeable role in moderating the fall in domestic prices.

Finally, there are pronounced differences in the composition of the output response as openness increases, with real exports playing a more prominent role, as well as in the degree of divergence between consumer and domestic

14. The technology shock is an AR(1) process with an autocorrelation coefficient equal to 0.97.

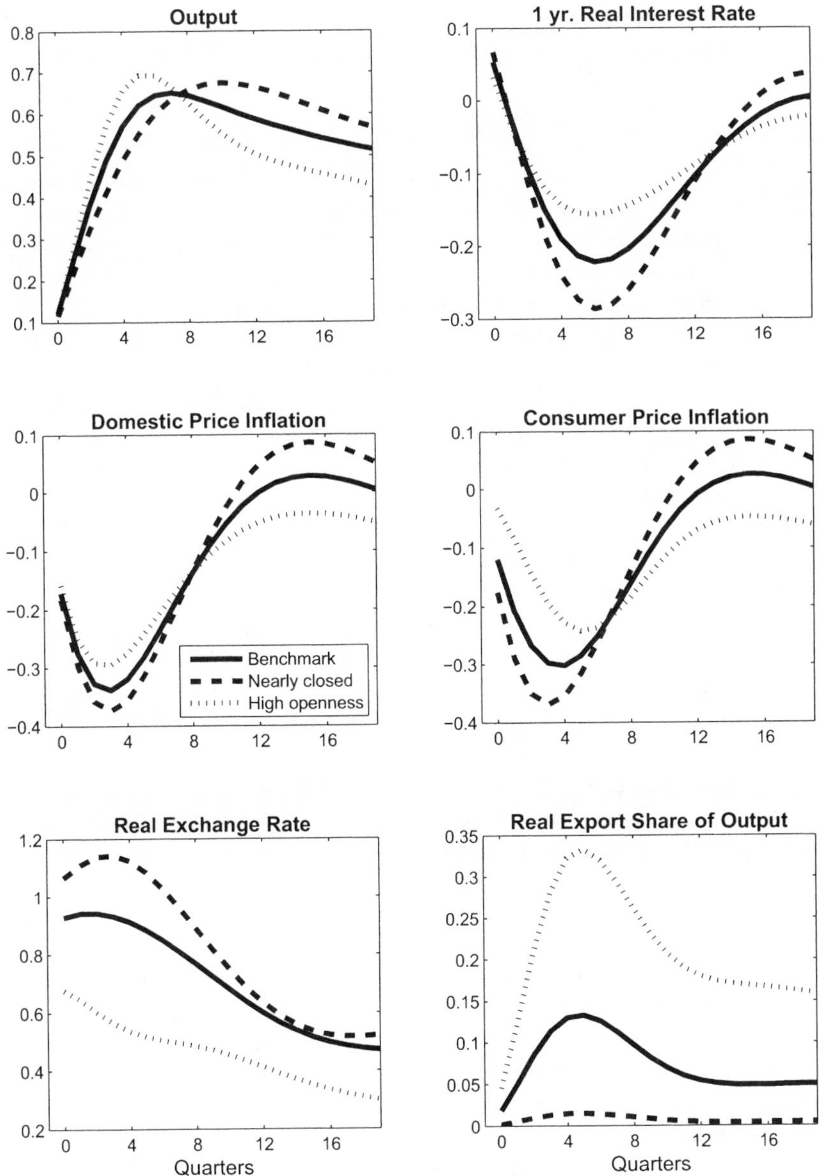

Fig. 2.4 Increase in technology in SIGMA (deviation from steady state)

price inflation. Notably, given that exchange rate depreciation pushes up import prices, consumer prices show less of a decline in the highly open economy.

2.3 The Workhorse Model

Our workhorse model builds heavily on the small open economy model of Galí and Monacelli (2005), which we extend to a two-country setting. Because these countries may differ in population size but are otherwise isomorphic, our exposition focuses on the "home" country. Each country in effect produces a single domestic output good, though we adopt a standard monopolistically competitive framework to rationalize stickiness in the aggregate price level. Households consume both the domestically-produced good and an imported good. Household preferences are assumed to be of the constant elasticity form, which allows us to analyze the implications of home bias, and a price elasticity of import demand different from unity. Finally, we generalize the Galí and Monacelli (2005) model by incorporating nominal wage rigidities.

2.3.1 Households and Wage Setting

There is a continuum of monopolistically competitive households indexed by $h \in [0, 1]$, each of which supplies a differentiated labor service to an intermediate goods-producing sector (the only producers demanding labor services in our framework). It is convenient to assume that a representative labor aggregator (or "employment agency") combines households' labor hours in the same proportions as firms would choose. Thus, the aggregator's demand for each household's labor is equal to the sum of firms' demands. The aggregate labor index L_t has the Dixit-Stiglitz form:

$$L_t = \left[\int_0^1 [\zeta N_t(h)]^{1/(1+\theta_w)} dh \right]^{1+\theta_w}, \tag{1}$$

where $\theta_w > 0$ and $N_t(h)$ is hours worked by each member of household h. The parameter ζ is the size of a household of type h. It determines the size of the home country's population, and effectively the share of world output produced by the home country in the steady state. The aggregator minimizes the cost of producing a given amount of the aggregate labor index, taking each household's wage rate $W_t(h)$ as given, and then sells units of the labor index to the production sector at their unit cost W_t:

$$W_t = \left[\int_0^1 W_t(h)^{-1/\theta_w} dh \right]^{-\theta_w}. \tag{2}$$

It is natural to interpret W_t as the aggregate wage index. The aggregator's demand for the labor services of a typical member of household h is given by

$$(3) \qquad N_t(h) = \left[\frac{W_t(h)}{W_t}\right]^{-(1+\theta_w)/\theta_w} \frac{L_t}{\zeta}.$$

The utility functional of household h is

$$(4) \qquad \mathbb{E}_t \sum_{j=0}^{\infty} \beta^j \frac{\sigma}{\sigma - 1} C_{t+j}(h)^{(\sigma-1)/\sigma} - \frac{\chi_0}{1+\chi} N_{t+j}(h)^{1+\chi},$$

where $C_t(h)$ and $N_t(h)$ denote each household's current consumption and hours of labor, respectively (which are assumed to be identical across the household's individual members). The intertemporal elasticity of substitution in consumption, σ, satisfies $\sigma > 0$, and we assume that $0 < \beta < 1$, $\chi > 0$, and $\chi_0 > 0$.

Household h faces a flow budget constraint in period t, which states that combined expenditure on goods and on the net accumulation of financial assets must equal its disposable income:

$$(5) \qquad P_{Ct}C_t(h) + \int_s \xi_{t,t+1}B_{t+1}(h) = B_t(h) + (1+\tau_w)W_t(h)N_t(h) + R_{Kt}K + \Gamma_t(h) - T_t(h)$$

(where variables have been expressed in per capita terms). We assume that household h can trade a complete set of contingent claims, with $\xi_{t,t+1}$ denoting the price of an asset that will pay one unit of domestic currency in a particular state of nature at date $t+1$, and $B_{t+1}(h)$ the quantity of claims purchased (for notational simplicity, we have suppressed all of the state indexes). Each household purchases the consumption good at a price P_{Ct}, and earns (per capita) labor income of $(1+\tau_W)W_t(h)N_t(h)$, where τ_W is an employment subsidy (designed to allow the flexible price equilibrium to be efficient). Each household also has a fixed stock of capital K, which it leases to firms at the rental rate R_{Kt}. It receives an aliquot share $\Gamma_t(h)$ of the profits of all firms, and pays lump sum taxes $T_t(h)$ to the government. In every period t, household h maximizes the utility functional (4) with respect to its consumption and holdings of contingent claims subject to its budget constraint (5), taking bond prices, the rental price of capital, and the price of the consumption bundle as given.

We assume that household wages are determined by Calvo-style staggered contracts subject to wage indexation. In particular, with probability $1-\xi_w$, each household is allowed to reoptimize its wage contract. If a household is not allowed to optimize its wage rate, it resets its wage according to $W_t(h) = \omega_{t-1}W_{t-1}(h)$, where $\omega_t = W_t/W_{t-1}$. Household h chooses the value of $W_t(h)$ to maximize its utility functional (4), yielding the following first-order condition:

$$(6) \qquad \mathbb{E}_t \sum_{j=0}^{\infty} \beta^j \xi_w^j \left[\frac{(1+\tau_w)}{(1+\theta_w)} \frac{\Lambda_{t+j}}{P_{Ct+j}} V_{wt+j} W_t(h) - \chi_0 N_{t+j}(h)^{\chi}\right] N_{t+j}(h) = 0,$$

where Λ_t is the marginal value of a unit of consumption, and $V_{wt+j} = \Pi_{h=1}^{j} \omega_{t+h-1}$. The employment subsidy τ_W is chosen to exactly offset the monopolistic distortion θ_W, so that the household's marginal rate of substitution would equal the consumption real wage in the absence of nominal wage rigidities.

2.3.2 Firms and Price Setting

Production of Domestic Intermediate Goods

There is a continuum of differentiated intermediate goods (indexed by $i \in [0, 1]$) in the home country, each of which is produced by a single monopolistically competitive firm. These differentiated goods are combined into a composite home good, Y_t, according to

$$(7) \qquad Y_t = \left[\int_0^1 Y_t(i)^{1/(1+\theta_p)} di \right]^{1+\theta_p},$$

by a representative firm (or "domestic goods aggregator") that is a perfect competitor in both output and input markets. The aggregator's demand for good i is given by:

$$(8) \qquad Y_t(i) = \left(\frac{P_{Dt}(i)}{P_{Dt}} \right)^{-(1+\theta_p)/\theta_p} Y_t,$$

where $P_{Dt}(i)$ is the price of good i and P_{Dt} is an aggregate price index given by $P_{Dt} = [\int_0^1 P_{Dt}(i)^{-1/\theta_p} di]^{-\theta_p}$.

Intermediate good i is produced by a monopolistically competitive firm, whose output $Y_t(i)$ is produced according to a Cobb-Douglas production function:

$$(9) \qquad Y_t(i) = K_t(i)^{\alpha}(Z_t L_t(i))^{1-\alpha},$$

where $\alpha > 0$ and Z_t denotes a stationary, country-specific shock to the level of technology. Intermediate goods producers face perfectly competitive factor markets for hiring capital and labor. Thus, each firm chooses $K_t(i)$ and $L_t(i)$, taking as given both the rental price of capital R_{Kt} and the aggregate wage index W_t. Within a country, both capital and labor are completely mobile; thus, the standard static first-order conditions for cost minimization imply that all firms have identical marginal cost per unit of output:

$$(10) \qquad MC_t = \left(\frac{W_t}{1-\alpha} \right)^{1-\alpha} \left(\frac{R_{Kt}}{\alpha} \right)^{\alpha}.$$

Similar to household wages, the domestic-currency prices of firms are determined according to Calvo-style staggered contracts subject to indexation. In particular, firm i faces a constant probability, $1 - \xi_p$, of being able to reoptimize its price, $P_{Dt}(i)$. If firm i cannot reoptimize its price in period t, the firm resets its price according to $P_{Dt}(i) = \pi_{t-1}P_{Dt-1}(i)$, where $\pi_t = P_{Dt}/P_{Dt-1}$. When firm i can reoptimize in period t, the firm maximizes

$$(11) \qquad \mathbb{E}_t \sum_{j=0}^{\infty} \xi_p^j \psi_{t,t+j}[(1+\tau_p)V_{Dt+j}P_{Dt}(i)Y_{t+j}(i) - MC_{t+j}Y_{t+j}(i)],$$

taking $\psi_{t,t+j}$, MC_t, τ_p, V_{Dt}, and its demand schedule as given. Here, $\psi_{t,t+j}$ is the stochastic discount factor, V_{Dt+j} is defined as $V_{Dt+j} = \Pi_{h=1}^{j}\pi_{t+h-1}$, and τ_p is a production subsidy that is calibrated to make the flexible price equilibrium efficient.[15] The first-order condition for setting $P_{Dt}(i)$ is:

$$(12) \qquad \mathbb{E}_t \sum_{j=0}^{\infty} \psi_{t,t+j}\xi_p^j \left(\frac{(1+\tau_p)V_{Dt+j}P_{Dt}(i)}{(1+\theta_p)} - MC_{t+j} \right) Y_{t+j}(i) = 0.$$

Production of Consumption Goods

Final consumption goods are produced by a perfectly competitive "consumption good distributor." The representative distributor combines purchases of the domestically-produced composite good, C_{Dt} (obtained from the domestic goods distributor), with an imported good, M_{Ct}, to produce private consumption, C_t, according to a constant elasticity of substitution (CES) production function:

$$(13) \qquad C_t = ((1-\omega_c)^{\rho_c/(1+\rho_c)} C_{Dt}^{1/(1+\rho_c)} + \omega_c^{\rho_c/(1+\rho_c)} M_{Ct}^{1/(1+\rho_c)})^{1+\rho_c},$$

We assume that the form of this CES aggregator mirrors the preferences of households over consumption of domestically produced goods and imports. Accordingly, the quasi-share parameter ω_c in equation (13) may be interpreted as determining household preferences for foreign relative to domestic goods. In the steady state, ω_c is the share of imports in the household's consumption bundle, so that the import share of the economy is determined as the product of ω_c and the (private) consumption share of GDP.

The distributor sells its final consumption good to households at price P_{Ct} and also purchases the home and foreign composite goods at their respective prices, P_{Dt} and P_{Mt}. We assume that producers of the composite domestic and foreign goods practice producer currency pricing. Accordingly, $P_{Mt} = e_t P^*_{Dt}$, where e_t is the exchange rate expressed as units of domestic currency required to purchase one unit of foreign currency and P^*_{Dt} is the price of the foreign composite good in the foreign currency (we use an asterisk to denote foreign variables). Profit maximization implies that the demand schedules for the imported and domestically produced aggregate goods are given by:

15. As discussed earlier in the household problem, we defined $\xi_{t,t+j}$ to be the price in period t of a claim that pays one dollar if the specified state occurs in period $t + j$. Thus, the corresponding element of $\psi_{t,t+j}$ equals $\xi_{t,t+j}$, divided by the probability that the specified state will occur.

$$(14)\ M_{Ct} = \omega_c \left(\frac{P_{Mt}}{P_{Ct}} \right)^{-(1+\rho_c)/\rho_c} C_t \quad \text{and} \quad C_{Dt} = (1-\omega_c) \left(\frac{P_{Dt}}{P_{Ct}} \right)^{-(1+\rho_c)/\rho_c} C_t.$$

The zero profit condition in the distribution sector implies:

$$(15)\qquad P_{Ct} = ((1-\omega_c)P_{Dt}^{1/(1+\rho_c)} + \omega_c P_{Mt}^{1/(1+\rho_c)})^{1+\rho_c}.$$

According to equation (15), in an open economy the consumer price level depends on both domestic and foreign prices, while if an economy is closed to trade (i.e., $\omega_c = 0$), consumer prices depend only on domestic prices.

2.3.3 Monetary and Fiscal Policy

We assume that the central bank follows an interest rate reaction function:

$$(16)\qquad i_t = \pi_t + \gamma_\pi(\pi_t - \pi_t^T) + \gamma_y(y_t - y_t^{pot}),$$

where the variables have been specified as the logarithmic deviation from its steady-state value. The nominal interest rate responds to the deviation of domestic price inflation from the central bank's exogenous inflation target, π_t^T, and the deviation of output from potential output (y^{pot}), where potential output is defined as the economy's level of output in the absence of sticky wages and prices.

As previously noted, openness can give rise to important differences between the domestic price level and the consumer price level. We specify a rule that responds to domestic price inflation rather than consumer price inflation in order to minimize differences between an open and closed economy that would simply be attributable to the monetary rule, rather than to differences in the underlying structure of the economy.

The government purchases some of the domestically produced good. Government purchases, G_t, are assumed to follow an exogenous, stochastic process. The government's budget is balanced every period so that lump sum taxes equal government spending plus the subsidy to firms and households.

2.3.4 Market Clearing

The home economy's aggregate resource constraint can be written as:

$$(17)\qquad Y_t = C_{Dt} + G_t + \frac{\zeta^*}{\zeta} M_{Ct}^*,$$

where the inclusion of the relative population size ζ^*/ζ reflects that all variables are expressed in per capita terms, and M_{Ct}^* denotes the purchases of the domestically produced good by foreign final consumption producers. Market clearing in the labor and capital markets implies:

$$(18)\qquad K = \int_0^1 K_t(i)di \quad \text{and} \quad L_t = \int_0^1 L_t(i)di.$$

Finally, we assume that the structure of the foreign economy is isomorphic to that of the home country.

2.3.5 Benchmark Calibration

Three key parameters that play a crucial role in influencing our results are the price elasticity of demand for traded goods, $\eta_c = (1+\rho_c)/\rho_c$; the intertemporal elasticity of substitution, σ; and the labor supply elasticity, χ. While we choose benchmark values of these parameters to be consistent with our interpretation of the evidence, it is important to note that there is wide range of values for these parameters used in the literature; thus, we also consider alternative calibrations.

For the trade price elasticity, we assume that $\rho_c = 2$, which implies $\eta_c = (1+\rho_c)/\rho_c = 1.5$. This estimate is toward the higher end of estimates derived using macroeconomic data, which are typically below unity in the short run and near unity in the long run (e.g., Hooper, Johnson, and Marquez 2000). Nevertheless, estimates of this elasticity following a tariff change are typically much higher, and we consider higher values in alternative calibrations.[16]

We choose the intertemporal elasticity of substitution to be an intermediate value between estimates derived from two separate literatures. In the micro literature, estimates of the coefficient of relative risk aversion, which correspond to the inverse of the intertemporal elasticity of substitution, suggest values in the range of 0.2 to 0.7.[17] In contrast, the business cycle literature frequently uses log utility over consumption (i.e., $\sigma = 1$) to be consistent with balanced growth. We set $\sigma = 0.5$ as a compromise between these two different perspectives.

The parameter χ corresponds to the inverse of the (Frisch) wage elasticity of labor supply. A vast amount of evidence from microdata suggests labor supply elasticities in the range of 0.05 to 0.3, though the real business cycle literature tends to use much higher values.[18] We set $\chi = 5$ for the benchmark calibration, which is at the upper end of estimates from the micro data.

We choose the remaining parameters of the model as follows. Given that the model is calibrated at a quarterly frequency, our choice of $\beta = 0.9925$ implies an annualized real interest rate of 3 percent. The government spending share of output is set to 18 percent, so $g_y = 0.18$. We set the elasticity of capital in production function $\alpha = 0.35$, and choose χ_0 so that hours worked

16. For a discussion of the macro estimates and estimates after trade liberalizations, see Ruhl (2005).

17. See, for example, Attanasio and Weber (1995), Attanasio et al. (1999), or Barsky et al. (1997).

18. MacCurdy (1981) obtained a point estimate of 0.15 for the Frisch elasticity of labor supply for men, a finding largely confirmed in the literature (e.g., Altonji [1986], Card [1994], and more recently Pencavel [2002]). For an alternative view, see Mulligan (1998). Finally, there is more uncertainty regarding the labor supply elasticity for females. For this group, Pencavel (1998) obtained a point estimate of 0.21.

are normalized to unity in steady state. For the price and wage markup parameters, we choose $\theta_p = \theta_w = 0.2$, and set the corresponding subsidies to equivalent values, $\tau_p = \tau_w = 0.2$. We choose ξ_p and ξ_w to be consistent with four quarter contracts (subject to full indexation). The parameters of the monetary policy rule are set in line with the original Taylor (1993) rule, so that $\lambda_\pi = 0.5$ and $\lambda_y = 0.125$ (corresponding to 0.5 at an annualized rate). Finally, we set the relative population size of the home economy (ζ/ζ^*) to 1/3. This value implies that the home economy corresponds to 25 percent of world output, which is roughly consistent with the U.S. share of world output.

2.3.6 The Flexible Price and Wage Equilibrium

It is useful to begin our analysis by investigating the behavior of a log-linearized version of the workhorse model under the assumption that wages and prices are fully flexible. For heuristic reasons, we conduct this analysis under the assumption that home country is a small enough fraction of world output that any spillovers to the foreign country (in particular, to interest rates and domestic demand) can be ignored. Insofar as we have verified by model simulations that spillovers from domestic shocks to the foreign sector are small even when the home country constitutes 25 percent of world output (as in our benchmark calibration), examining the model's implications under the assumption of a very small world output share yields considerable insight. Thus, our analysis here closely parallels that of Galí and Monacelli (2005), aside from modest differences arising from our inclusion of a government spending shock, and allowing for diminishing returns to labor. However, while their paper focused on the formal similarity between open and closed economy models, our goal is to explore the quantitative differences that arise as an economy becomes more open, and how these differences depend on underlying structural parameters such as trade price elasticities.

We begin by deriving a relationship between output and the domestic real interest rate, which Galí and Monacelli (2005) and Clarida, Galí, and Gertler (2002) have characterized as an open economy IS curve. Substituting the (log-linearized) production function for final consumption goods (13) into the resource constraint (17), the latter may be expressed:

$$y_t = (1 - g_y)(c_t + \omega_c(m^*_{ct} - m_{ct})) + g_y g_t, \tag{19}$$

where small letters denote the deviations of the logarithms of variables from their corresponding level, and g_y is the government share of output. The risk-sharing condition under complete markets can be used to relate private consumption to foreign consumption c^*_t and to the terms of trade τ_t:

$$c_t = c^*_t + \sigma(1 - \omega_c)\tau_t = c^*_t + \varepsilon_c \tau_t \tag{20}$$

where the parameter $\varepsilon_c = \sigma(1 - \omega_c)$ denotes the sensitivity of private consumption to the terms of trade. Using the export and import demand functions, the difference between real exports and imports $m^*_{ct} - m_{ct}$ may be expressed:

$$(21)\quad m^*_{ct} - m_{ct} = (c^*_t - c_t) + (1 + (1 - \omega_c))\eta_c\tau_t = (c^*_t - c_t) + \varepsilon_{nx}\tau_t.$$

Thus, real net exports depend on an activity term (rising as foreign consumption expands relative to domestic consumption), and on the terms of trade. Because a 1 percent deterioration of the terms of trade raises exports by an amount equal to the export price elasticity of demand η_c, while causing real imports to contract by $(1 - \omega_c)\eta_c$, the overall relative price sensitivity of net exports is captured by the composite parameter $\varepsilon_{nx} = (1 + (1 - \omega_c))\eta_c$.

Substituting these expressions into the resource constraint (19) yields:

$$(22)\qquad y_t = (1 - g_y)[(1 - \omega_c)\varepsilon_c + \omega_c\varepsilon_{nx}]\tau_t + g_y g_t + (1 - g_y)c^*_t$$

or simply:

$$(23)\qquad y_t = (1 - g_y)\sigma^{open}\tau_t + g_y g_t + (1 - g_y)c^*_t.$$

The parameter $\sigma^{open} = ((1 - \omega_c)\varepsilon_c + \omega_c\varepsilon_{nx})$ may be interpreted as either the sensitivity of private aggregate demand to the terms of trade, or the (absolute value of) the sensitivity of private aggregate demand to the long-term real rate of interest. The latter follows from the uncovered interest parity (UIP) condition:

$$(24)\qquad \tau_t = \mathbb{E}_t\tau_{t+1} + r^*_t - r_t = \mathbb{E}_t\sum_{j=0}^{\infty}(r^*_{t+j} - r_{t+j}) = (r^*_{Lt} - r_{Lt})$$

where the long-term real interest rate r_{Lt} is an infinite sum of expected short-term real interest rates (r_{t+j}). Alternatively, equation (23) can be expressed in terms of the current short-term real interest rate to yield an "open economy IS curve" of the form:

$$(25)\qquad y_t = \mathbb{E}_t y_{t+1} - (1 - g_y)\sigma^{open}(r_t - r^*_t) + g_y(g_t - \mathbb{E}_t g_{t+1}) + (1 - g_y)(c^*_t - \mathbb{E}_t c^*_{t+1}).$$

Based on the foregoing analysis, the interest sensitivity of private demand σ^{open} can be regarded as a weighted average of the interest sensitivity of consumption ε_c, and of real net exports ε_{nx}, with the interest sensitivity of the latter arising from the UIP relation, and depending on the trade price elasticity. With some algebraic manipulation, σ^{open} can be expressed alternatively as a simple weighted average of the underlying structural parameters σ (the intertemporal elasticity of substitution in consumption) and η_c (the price elasticity of both exports and imports):

$$(26)\qquad \sigma^{open} = (1 - \omega_c)^2\sigma + (1 - (1 - \omega_c)^2)\eta_c.$$

The quadratic weight $(1 - \omega_c)^2$ on σ reflects both that consumption gets an effective weight of $(1 - \omega_c)$ in private demand (as seen from equation [22]), and that the elasticity of private consumption with respect to the domestic real interest rate ($\varepsilon_c = \sigma(1 - \omega_c)$) declines linearly as the share of foreign goods rises in the domestic consumption bundle.

Equation (26) provides confirmation of the intuitively plausible argument that the interest-sensitivity of the economy should rise with openness if the trade price elasticity is high relative to the intertemporal elasticity of substitution in consumption; and conversely, if the trade price elasticity is relatively low.[19] Formally, the derivative of σ^{open} with respect to ω_c equals $2(1 - \omega_c)(\eta_c - \sigma)$, and hence rises if $\eta_c > \sigma$. Thus, even if consumption responded very little to the domestic real interest rate—implying a low interest elasticity of output in a closed economy—output could still be highly interest sensitive in an open economy if the interest rate changes generated large movements in real exports and imports (through their influence on the terms of trade).

From a quantitative perspective, the quadratic weights in (26) imply that openness can have very substantial implications for the interest sensitivity of the economy if there is a significant divergence between the intertemporal elasticity σ and the trade price elasticity η_c. This is apparent from table 2.1, which shows how the interest elasticity of aggregate demand σ^{open} varies with openness for alternative values of σ and η_c. For example, using a trade share of $\omega_c = .35$, the weight on σ in determining the interest elasticity of private demand is only 0.42 ($= [1 - .35]^2$). In this case, an open economy with $\sigma = 0.5$ and $\eta_c = 1.5$ (as in our benchmark calibration) implies $\sigma^{open} = 1.1$, or more than double the interest sensitivity of its closed economy counterpart. With an even higher trade price elasticity of 6, σ^{open} rises to 3.6, or more than seven times its closed economy counterpart. However, changes in the effective interest sensitivity of aggregate output due to openness are almost certainly much smaller than suggested by this latter computation, and probably significantly smaller than implied by our workhorse model, which ignores capital. As we show in what follows, to the extent that the disparity between the effective interest sensitivity of domestic demand and that of real trade narrows in a model with capital accumulation, the interest sensitivity of the economy shows less variation with openness.

We next turn to the determinants of employment, output, and the real

19. In closely related work, Woodford (2007) examines how the monetary transmission mechanism changes with the degree of trade openness in a sticky price model. His model specification imposes a trade price elasticity of unity, and he calibrates the intertemporal elasticity of substitution $\sigma = 6$ to proxy for the high interest rate sensitivity of investment. Accordingly, given that the intertemporal elasticity of substitution is much higher than the trade price elasticity for this choice of parameters, it is clear from equation (26) that an increase in openness lowers the interest sensitivity of the economy.

Table 2.1 **Implications of alternative calibrations under benchmark Frisch Elasticity ($\chi^{-1} = 0.2$)**

Parameters					Flexible price responses to:						
					Technology shock				Government spending shock		
ω_c	σ	η_c	σ^{open}	MRS slope	c_t^{pot}	y_t^{pot}	L_t^{pot}	ζ_t^{pot}	c_t^{pot}	y_t^{pot}	ζ_t^{pot}
0	0.25	1	0.25	12	0.6	0.49	–0.25	0.74	–0.82	0.33	–0.18
	0.5	1	0.5	9.7	0.72	0.59	–0.098	0.68	–0.98	0.2	–0.11
	1	1	1	8.7	0.79	0.65	0	0.65	–1.1	0.11	–0.058
0.12	0.25	1	0.42	10	0.36	0.56	–0.13	0.7	–0.49	0.22	–0.12
	0.25	1.5	0.53	9.6	0.3	0.59	–0.088	0.68	–0.41	0.19	–0.1
	0.25	6	1.5	8.4	0.12	0.67	0.038	0.64	–0.16	0.074	–0.04
	0.5	1	0.61	9.3	0.53	0.61	–0.064	0.67	–0.73	0.17	–0.089
	0.5	1.5	0.72	9.1	0.46	0.62	–0.039	0.66	–0.63	0.14	–0.077
	0.5	6	1.7	8.3	0.21	0.68	0.048	0.63	–0.29	0.066	–0.035
	1	1	1	8.7	0.7	0.65	0	0.65	–0.96	0.11	–0.058
	1	1.5	1.1	8.6	0.63	0.66	0.011	0.65	–0.87	0.098	–0.053
	1	6	2.1	8.2	0.35	0.69	0.061	0.63	–0.48	0.054	–0.029
0.35	0.25	1	0.68	9.2	0.18	0.62	–0.049	0.67	–0.24	0.15	–0.082
	0.25	1.5	0.96	8.7	0.13	0.65	–0.0047	0.65	–0.18	0.11	–0.061
	0.25	6	3.3	8	0.039	0.7	0.082	0.62	–0.053	0.035	–0.019
	0.5	1	0.79	9	0.32	0.63	–0.028	0.66	–0.43	0.13	–0.072
	0.5	1.5	1.1	8.6	0.24	0.65	0.0074	0.65	–0.33	0.1	–0.055
	0.5	6	3.6	8	0.075	0.7	0.084	0.62	–0.1	0.033	–0.018
	1	1	1	8.7	0.51	0.65	0	0.65	–0.7	0.11	–0.058
	1	1.5	1.3	8.5	0.41	0.67	0.025	0.64	–0.56	0.086	–0.046
	1	6	3.8	8	0.14	0.71	0.087	0.62	–0.2	0.031	–0.017

wage (which we will refer to as potential employment, potential output, and the potential real wage in the model with sticky prices). If prices are flexible, firms behave identically in setting prices and hiring factor inputs, so that there is effectively a single representative firm. The labor demand schedule is derived directly from the representative firm's optimality condition for choosing its price, which equates the marginal product of labor to the product real wage (n.b., the product real wage is expressed in units of the domestically produced good). Thus, the (inverse) labor demand schedule may be expressed:

$$(27)\qquad \zeta_t^d = mpl_t = (1-\alpha)z_t - \alpha l_t = (1-\alpha)z_t - \lambda_{mpl} l_t,$$

so that the "demand real wage" ζ_t^d varies inversely with hours worked. The parameter λ_{mpl} following the second equality is used to denote the absolute value of the slope of the labor demand (or marginal product of labor [MPL]) schedule, which is simply equal to α in this model. Clearly, both the slope of the MPL schedule and the manner in which it is affected by shocks are identical to a closed economy.

The labor supply schedule is derived from the household's optimality condition equating its marginal rate of substitution between leisure and consumption to the consumption real wage. It is convenient to express labor supply in terms of the product real wage, so that:

$$(28)\qquad \zeta_t^s = mrs_t = \chi l_t + \frac{1}{\sigma}c_t + \omega_c \tau_t,$$

where mrs_t should be interpreted as the marginal cost of working in terms of the domestically produced good. The terms of trade enters as an additional shift variable. A depreciation of the terms of trade shifts the labor supply schedule inward, because a given product real wage translates into a smaller consumption real wage.

For heuristic purposes, it is useful to derive a labor supply schedule that is expressed exclusively in terms of labor (or output) and endogenous shocks, as is familiar from the closed economy analogue; that is,

$$(29)\qquad \zeta_t^{s,closed} = \chi l_t + \frac{1}{\sigma}\frac{1}{1-g_y}((1-\alpha)(l_t + z_t) - g_y g_t).$$

This is easily accomplished by using equation (23) to solve for the terms of trade in terms of output, and also the risk-sharing condition (20) to solve for consumption in terms of output. Finally, using the production function to solve for output in terms of labor, the labor supply function may be expressed:

$$(30)\qquad \zeta_t^s = \chi l_t + \frac{1}{\sigma^{open}}\frac{1}{1-g_y}((1-\alpha)(l_t + z_t) - g_y g_{ct}) + \left[\frac{1}{\sigma} - \frac{1}{\sigma^{open}}\right]c_{Dt}^*,$$

or equivalently,

$$(31) \quad \zeta_t^s = \lambda_{mrs} l_t + \frac{1}{\sigma^{open}} \frac{1}{1 - g_y}((1 - \alpha)z_t - g_y g_t) + \left[\frac{1}{\sigma} - \frac{1}{\sigma^{open}}\right] c_{Dt}^*,$$

where the second equation (31) simply defines the parameter λ_{mrs}, the slope of the labor supply (or MRS) schedule, as $\lambda_{mrs} = \chi + (1 - \alpha)/[\sigma^{open}(1 - g_y)]$. It is clear from comparing equation (30) with its closed economy analogue (29) that openness can only alter the impact of domestic shocks on the labor market through the parameter σ^{open}. This parameter can be interpreted as determining the wealth effect on labor supply in an open economy, influencing both the slope of the labor supply schedule, and how it is affected by shocks. Given the dependence of the "primitive" labor supply schedule (28) on both consumption and the terms of trade, the wealth effect in (30) captures the effects of movements in both variables. From our earlier derivation of the open economy IS curve, σ^{open} rises relative to the intertemporal elasticity σ if the trade price elasticity η_c exceeds σ. Intuitively, a relatively high degree of substitutibility between home and foreign goods should enhance opportunities for international risk-sharing, serving to weaken the relationship between consumption and output, and hence the wealth effect on labor supply.[20]

Figure 2.5 illustrates how openness affects labor market equilibrium in response to a technology shock through changing both the slope of the labor supply schedule and the extent to which it shifts in response to the shock. The left panel shows the response in a closed economy, while the right panel shows the response in an open economy. The technology shock shifts the labor demand schedule up by 1 percent in both the closed and open economy (recalling that this schedule is the same in each). In the closed economy, the wealth effect on labor supply is determined by the parameter σ (in equation [29]), which is assumed to be less than unity. Accordingly, the wealth effect on labor supply dominates the substitution effect. In the new equilibrium at point B, hours worked decline, and the real wage rises. Turning to the open economy case, the structural parameters are assumed to imply a value of σ^{open} in equation (30) that significantly exceeds unity (as would occur with a high value of the trade price elasticity, and high degree of openness). In this case, the open economy MRS schedule shifts inward by much less (i.e., from A to E) than its closed economy counterpart (from A to D in the left panel). In addition to reducing the shift in the schedule, the smaller wealth effect implies a flatter MRS schedule. Accordingly, with the substitution effect dominating the wealth effect, labor hours expand and the real wage rises by less than in the closed economy.

20. Moreover, the terms of trade, which act as a shift variable on the primitive labor supply schedule, also varies less with domestic output.

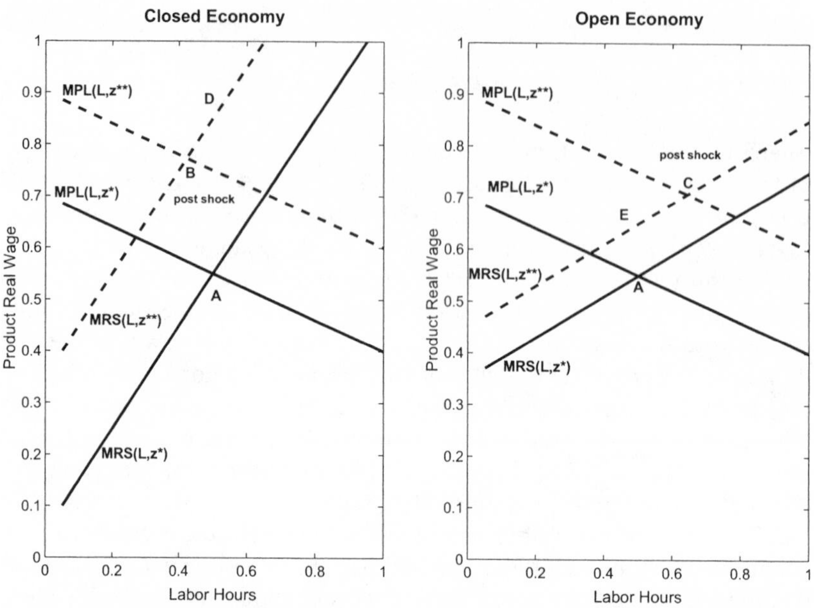

Fig. 2.5 Rise in technology: Closed vs. open labor market equilibrium under flexible prices and wages

From a quantitative perspective, openness can exert sizable macroeconomic consequences on the flexible wage and price equilibrium under calibrations in which openness markedly influences the wealth effect on labor supply, and in which the wealth effect plays a prominent role in determining the slope of the labor supply schedule. Given the open economy labor supply schedule (30), this translates into calibrations that give rise to a large wedge between σ^{open} and σ as the trade share increases, and that embed a high Frisch elasticity of labor supply $1/\chi$ (as the latter accentuates the role of the wealth effect in determining the slope of the labor supply schedule λ_{mrs}). With a very high Frisch elasticity of labor supply and trade price elasticity, wealth effects are attenuated significantly as trade openness increases (as σ^{open} rises relative to σ), flattening the labor supply schedule and making it less responsive to technology and government spending shocks. In the limit (as χ converges to zero, and η_c to infinity), the productivity shock has no impact on the equilibrium real wage, and a comparatively large impact on equilibrium output. The government spending shock has no effect on equilibrium output, employment, or the real wage (reflecting that it operates exclusively through a wealth effect, which is eliminated under this calibration). The insulation of output from fiscal policy is reminiscient of the dramatically different effects of fiscal expansion in a closed versus open economy that obtain in a traditional Mundell-Fleming style model.

However, although increased openness can have large effects in principle, it has much less dramatic implications for flexible-price employment, output, and the real wage under plausible calibrations. This is apparent from tables 2.1 (p. 111) and 2.2 (p. 116), which show how the responses of these key variables in the flexible price equilibrium vary with openness under a wide range of values of the trade price elasticity and the intertemporal elasticity of substitution in consumption (the superscript "*pot*" on each variable is used to denote "potential" responses, meaning the responses under flexible prices and wages). Table 2.1 shows responses under a Frisch elasticity of 0.2, as in our benchmark calibration, while table 2.2 considers a higher elasticity of unity. Importantly, for trade price elasticities in the empirically reasonable neighborhood of 1 to 1.5, and a Frisch elasticity of unity or below, differences between the closed and open economy responses to a technology shock are quite small, and only modestly larger in the case of a government spending shock.

2.3.7 Sticky Prices and Wages

We next turn to analyzing the model's behavior in the presence of nominal wage and price rigidities. We continue to maintain the assumption that the relative share of the home economy in world output is arbitrarily small. In this case, the log-linearized behavioral equations can be expressed in a simple form that is essentially identical to that derived in the closed economy model of Erceg, Henderson, and Levin (2000), aside from allowing for the indexation of wages and prices:

$$x_t = x_{t+1|t} - \sigma^{open}(1 - g_y)(i_t - \pi_{t+1|t} - r_t^{pot}) \tag{32}$$

$$\Delta\pi_t = \beta\Delta\pi_{t+1|t} + \kappa_p(\zeta_t - mpl_t) \tag{33}$$

$$\Delta\omega_t = \beta\Delta\omega_{t+1|t} + \kappa_w(mrs_t - \zeta_t) \tag{34}$$

$$mpl_t = \zeta_t^{pot} - \lambda_{mpl}x_{Lt} = \zeta_t^{pot} - \frac{\lambda_{mpl}}{(1-\alpha)}x_t \tag{35}$$

$$mrs_t = \zeta_t^{pot} + \lambda_{mrs}x_{Lt} = \zeta_t^{pot} + \frac{\lambda_{mrs}}{(1-\alpha)}x_t \tag{36}$$

$$\zeta_t = \zeta_{t-1} + \omega_t - \pi_t, \tag{37}$$

where x_t is the output gap (i.e., $y_t - y_t^{pot}$), x_{Lt} is the employment gap (i.e., $l_t - l_t^{pot}$), r_t^{pot} is the "potential" (or "natural") rate of interest, ζ_t^{pot} the potential real wage, and the composite parameters are defined by $\kappa_p = (1 - \xi_p)(1 - \beta\xi_p)/\xi_p$, $\kappa_w = (1 - \xi_w)(1 - \beta\xi_w)/[\xi_w(1 + \chi)(1 + \theta_w)/\theta_w]$, $\lambda_{mrs} = \chi + (1 - \alpha)/[\sigma^{open}(1 - g_y)]$, and $\lambda_{mpl} = \alpha$. The potential level of a variable is defined as the value it would assume if prices and wages were fully flexible. The model is completed with the inclusion of the monetary rule given in equation (16).[21]

21. Both for expositional simplicity, and because our focus is on domestic shocks, terms involving foreign variables are omitted from these equations.

Table 2.2 **Implications of alternative calibrations under higher Frisch elasticity ($\chi^{-1} = 1$)**

Parameters					Flexible price responses to:						
					Technology shock				Government spending shock		
ω_c	σ	η_c	σ^{open}	MRS slope	c_t^{pot}	y_t^{pot}	L_t^{pot}	ζ_t^{pot}	c_t^{pot}	y_t^{pot}	ζ_t^{pot}
0	0.25	1	0.25	5.5	0.4	0.33	–0.49	0.82	–0.42	0.66	–0.35
	0.5	1	0.5	3.5	0.6	0.49	–0.25	0.74	–0.62	0.49	–0.26
	1	1	1	2.5	0.79	0.65	0	0.65	–0.82	0.33	–0.17
0.12	0.25	1	0.42	3.9	0.29	0.45	–0.31	0.76	–0.3	0.53	–0.29
	0.25	1.5	0.53	3.4	0.25	0.5	–0.22	0.73	–0.26	0.48	–0.26
	0.25	6	1.5	2.2	0.13	0.73	0.12	0.61	–0.13	0.24	–0.13
	0.5	1	0.61	3.2	0.47	0.54	–0.17	0.71	–0.49	0.44	–0.24
	0.5	1.5	0.72	2.9	0.43	0.58	–0.11	0.69	–0.44	0.4	–0.21
	0.5	6	1.7	2.1	0.23	0.75	0.16	0.59	–0.24	0.22	–0.12
	1	1	1	2.5	0.7	0.65	0	0.65	–0.72	0.33	–0.17
	1	1.5	1.1	2.4	0.65	0.67	0.034	0.64	–0.67	0.3	–0.16
	1	6	2.1	2	0.39	0.78	0.21	0.58	–0.41	0.19	–0.1
0.35	0.25	1	0.68	3	0.16	0.56	–0.13	0.7	–0.17	0.42	–0.22
	0.25	1.5	0.96	2.6	0.13	0.64	–0.014	0.65	–0.13	0.33	–0.18
	0.25	6	3.3	1.8	0.046	0.84	0.29	0.55	–0.048	0.13	–0.068
	0.5	1	0.79	2.8	0.3	0.6	–0.081	0.68	–0.31	0.38	–0.2
	0.5	1.5	1.1	2.5	0.24	0.66	0.022	0.64	–0.25	0.31	–0.17
	0.5	6	3.6	1.8	0.091	0.85	0.3	0.54	–0.094	0.12	–0.064
	1	1	1	2.5	0.51	0.65	0	0.65	–0.53	0.33	–0.17
	1	1.5	1.3	2.3	0.43	0.7	0.078	0.62	–0.44	0.27	–0.15
	1	6	3.8	1.8	0.17	0.86	0.32	0.54	–0.18	0.11	–0.06

Equation (32) parsimoniously expresses the open economy IS curve in terms of output and real interest rate gaps. Thus, the output gap depends inversely on the deviation of the real interest rate $(i_t - \pi_{t+1|t})$ from its potential rate r_t^{pot}. The price setting equation (33) specifies the change in domestic price inflation to depend on the future expected change in inflation and real marginal cost, where the latter is the difference between the real wage and marginal product of labor. The wage setting equation (34) specifies the change in wage inflation to depend on the future expected change in wage inflation and the difference between the MRS and real wage (both in product terms). The equations determining the MPL (35) and MRS (36) can be specified to depend only on the real wage under flexible prices ζ_t^{pot}, and the employment gap (or equivalently, the output gap, since the latter is proportional). Finally, equation (37) is an identity for the evolution of the product real wage.

The log-linearized representation given by equations (32) through (37) is insightful in helping to assess how openness affects the transmission of domestic shocks under a given policy rule, and also the policymaker's trade-off frontier under certain commonly specified loss functions. In particular, equations (32) through (37) identify several channels through which openness can affect the economy. It is evident from (32) that openness can influence aggregate demand through affecting both the potential real interest rate r_t^{pot}, and the sensitivity of the output gap to a given sized real interest rate change (this sensitivity is determined by $\sigma^{open}(1 - g_y)$). The interest sensitivity of aggregate demand increases with openness if the trade price elasticity exceeds the intertemporal elasticity of substitution in consumption; conversely, the interest sensitivity decreases if the trade price elasticity is relatively low.

It is apparent that openness influences aggregate supply directly through affecting the sensitivity of the household's MRS to the employment gap; that is, the parameter λ_{mrs} in equation (36). The effects of this slope change on price setting are most pronounced in the special case of fully flexible wages. In this case, equation (36) implies that the real wage can be expressed directly in terms of the potential real wage and employment gap; that is, $\zeta_t = \zeta_t^{pot} + \lambda_{mrs} x_{Lt}$. Substituting for the real wage into the price setting equation (33), and for the MPL using (35), yields an "open economy new-Keynesian Phillips curve" similar to that derived by Clarida, Galí, and Gertler (aside from allowing for indexation):

$$(38) \qquad \Delta\pi_t = \beta\Delta\pi_{t+1|t} + \kappa_p((\lambda_{mpl} + \lambda_{mrs})x_{Lt}).$$

Given that λ_{mpl} is determined by the capital share—a small number equal to 0.35 under our benchmark calibration—the slope of the Phillips curve hinges crucially on λ_{mrs}. Under the conditions discussed previously in which openness markedly affects λ_{mrs}, it also exerts substantial effects on the Phillips curve slope. For instance, if openness significantly reduces λ_{mrs} (as occurs under a high Frisch elasticity and relatively high trade price elasticity) marginal cost and price inflation are much less responsive to the output gap in a highly open economy, so that the Phillips curve flattens. In the presence of nominal wage rigidities, however, the close linkage between the real wage and employment gap is severed, with the implication that the MRS slope has less of a direct impact on the real wage.

Openness also influences both price and wage setting through altering the response of the potential real wage ζ_t^{pot}. As discussed following equation (30), openness affects ζ_t^{pot} through influencing the size of the wealth effect on the household's MRS schedule, as well as through changing the slope of the MRS schedule. To see how ζ_t^{pot} in turn affects price setting, it is helpful to substitute equation (35) into (33) to obtain:

$$\Delta\pi_t = \beta\Delta\pi_{t+1|t} + \kappa_p(\zeta_t - \zeta_t^{pot} + \lambda_{mpl}x_{Lt}). \tag{39}$$

Thus, in the presence of sticky nominal wages, price inflation depends on the wage gap $\zeta_t - \zeta_t^{pot}$ in addition to the employment gap x_{Lt}. Even a policy that closed the employment (or output) gap would imply pressure on inflation if real wages did not immediately adjust to their potential level, implying a policymaker trade-off between stabilizing inflation and the employment gap.

Because the actual real wage adjusts sluggishly, the behavior of the wage gap depends critically on how shocks affect the potential real wage. To the extent that openness reduces variation in the ζ_t^{pot}—as under our benchmark calibration—greater openness can be expected to reduce the real wage gap associated with a zero employment gap, allowing policymakers to come closer to stabilizing both employment and inflation. But recalling tables 2.1 and 2.2, openness does not exert large quantitative effects on ζ_t^{pot} under reasonable calibrations: even with the high Frisch elasticity of unity, increased openness only has a modest effect in dampening the response of ζ_t^{pot} to real shocks.

Notwithstanding that it is helpful for economic interpretation to think of openness as operating through several channels that affect both aggregate demand supply, it bears emphasizing that the composite parameter σ^{open} provides a summary statistic for how the model economy is affected by openness. As an implication, differences between closed and open economy responses—including of nominal variables such as inflation—can only be substantial under conditions that induce a significant disparity between σ^{open} and the intertemporal substitution elasticity σ. Moreover, while such a wedge is clearly a sufficient condition for the IS curve (32) to be affected by openness, the effects of openness on the AS block still tend to be quite small under plausible calibrations of the Frisch elasticity of labor supply and trade price elasticity.

These considerations are useful in interpreting how impulse responses to the same three shocks previously considered in our SIGMA simulations depend on the openness of the economy. Figure 2.6 compares responses to a

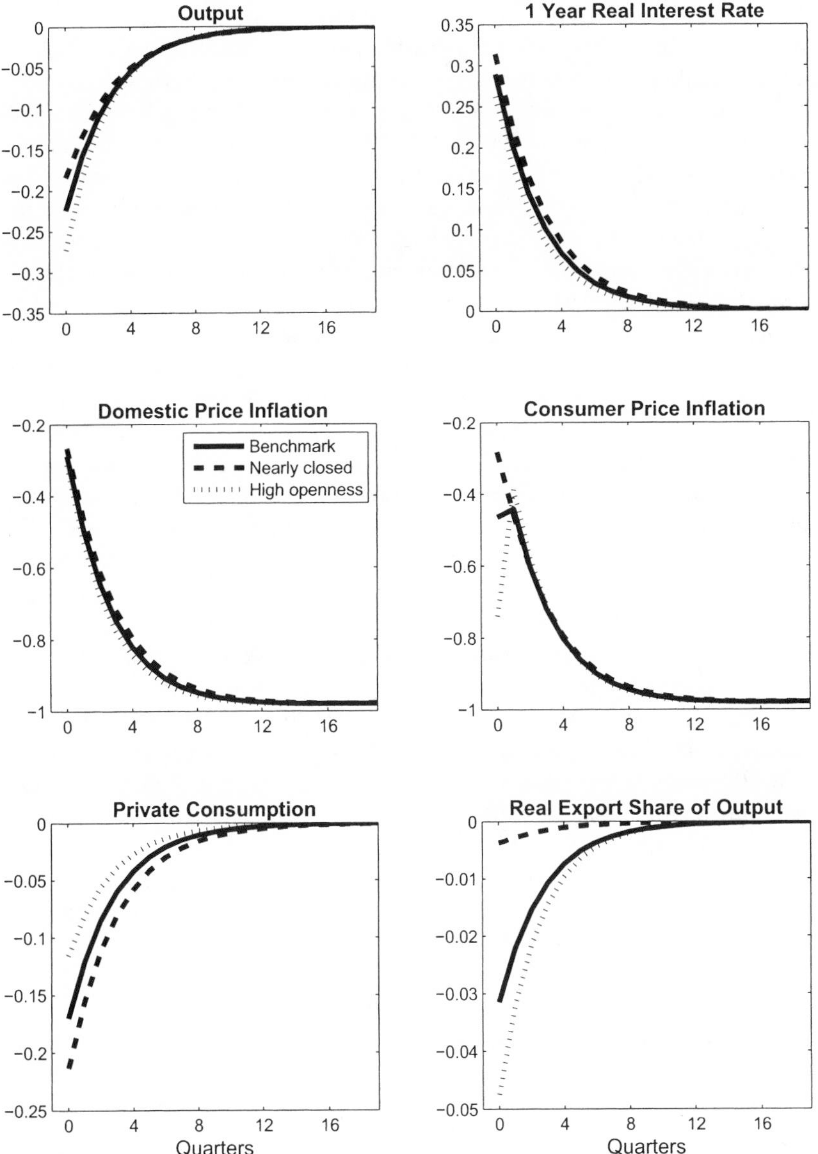

Fig. 2.6 Increase in inflation target in workhorse model (deviation from steady state)

1 percentage point decline in the inflation target under three calibrations of openness, ranging from a trade share of 1 percent of GDP under the "nearly closed" calibration, to 12 percent under our benchmark, to 35 percent under "high openness."[22] As in the SIGMA simulations examined in section 2.2, the persistence of the shock is set to 0.995, so that it is nearly a permanent shock. It is evident that output contracts by a somewhat larger amount in the highly open economy. The larger output contraction occurs because the target reduction causes a rise in real interest rates, and the interest sensitivity of output rises with greater openness in our benchmark calibration (quantitatively, the interest sensitivity $\sigma^{open}(1 - g_y)$ rises from $0.5^*(1 - .18) = 0.41$ under the "nearly closed" calibration to 0.90 in the high openness case). Price inflation also falls a bit more as openness increases, reflecting the larger output contraction; however, the low sensitivity of marginal cost to the employment gap (i.e., λ_{mpl} in equation [35] is only 0.35) accounts for the small quantitative differences in the responses.[23] Overall, given the wide differences in the trade shares, the responses of aggregate output, inflation, and the real interest rate seem quite unresponsive to openness. The main differences are that exports account for a larger share of the output contraction as openness increases (i.e., exports/GDP fall by more), and that consumer price inflation falls more abruptly in the highly open economy (as the real exchange rate appreciation exerts a larger effect given the greater share of imported goods in the household consumption bundle).

Figure 2.7 compares the effects of a rise in government spending across the three calibrations (as in section 2.2, the persistence of the shock is 0.97). The responses of output and inflation diverge noticeably with openness, with output and inflation rising much less under the high openness calibration. Because the Taylor rule keeps output close to potential (y^{pot}) under each calibration, the differences in the output responses mainly reflect that the wealth effect on labor supply is smaller in a relatively open economy (as noted in our discussion of the flexible price equilibrium).[24] Given sluggish wage adjustment, the smaller output expansion in turn reduces pressure on marginal cost in the more open economy. In terms of our discussion of (39), the real wage gap $\zeta_t - \zeta_t^{pot}$ is smaller and less persistent in a relatively

22. The simulations are derived in the two-country version of the model in which the home country constitutes 25 percent of world output. However, it makes little difference to our results if the relative size of the home country were set close to zero (even in the high openness case, we found that the sensitivity of the simulation results to the relative size of the home economy is quite small).

23. Moreover, as suggested by our prior discussion, differences in the MRS slope due to openness have little influence on the real wage response. Thus, with the potential real wage unaffected by the shock, the real wage gap in equation (39) behaves similarly irrespective of openness, so that marginal cost depends mainly on the response of the employment (or output) gap.

24. The simple dynamics in this model appear to contribute to the success of the standard Taylor rule in keeping output close to potential. This is in some contrast to the results in SIGMA (discussed in section 2.2), in which the Taylor rule induces a persistent expansion of the output gap.

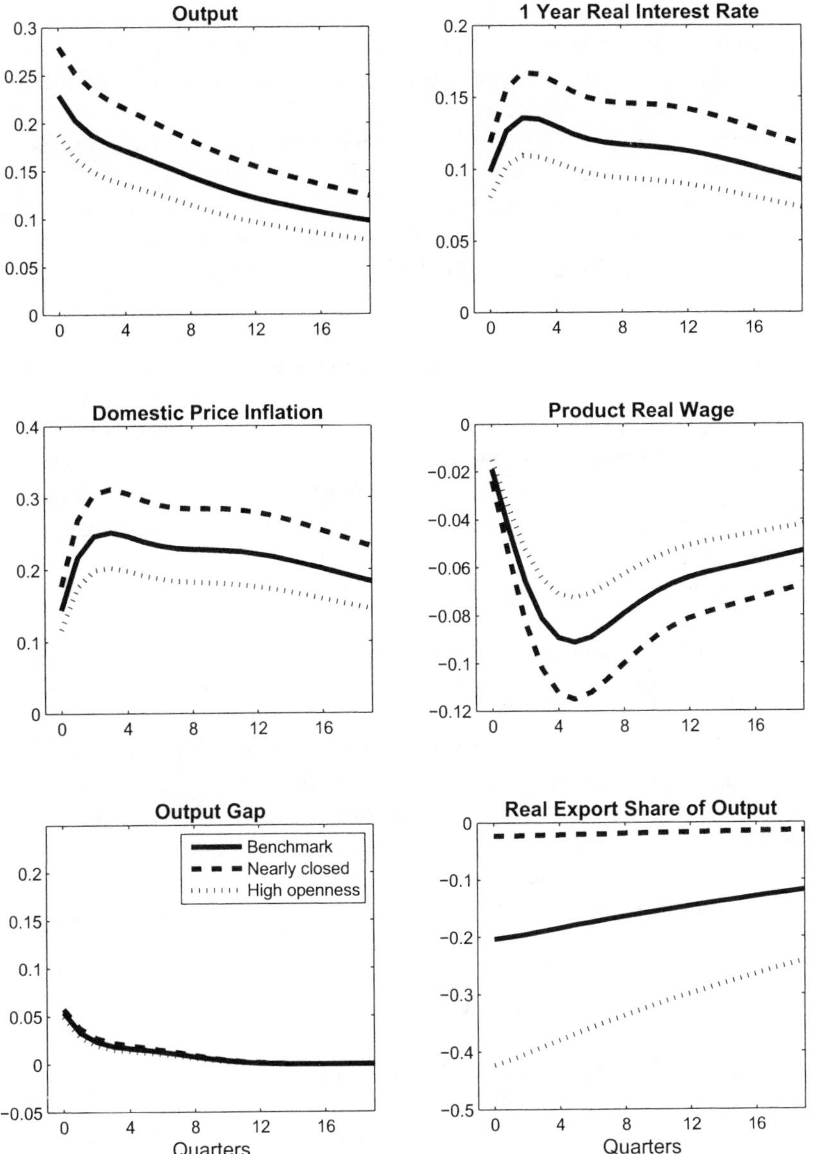

Fig. 2.7 Increase in government spending in workhorse model (deviation from steady state)

open economy (as ζ^{pot} falls by less); hence, generating weaker pressure on inflation. Finally, given both a smaller rise in inflation and a higher interest elasticity of aggregate demand in the highly open economy, the real interest rate rises by noticeably less.

Figure 2.8 compares the effects of a highly persistent rise in technology (as in section 2.2, the persistence of the shock is 0.97). The response of output is somewhat larger in the highly open calibration, while the response of the real wage is smaller. To understand this, recall from our discussion of the flexible price equilibrium that greater openness (assuming $\eta_c > \sigma$ as under our benchmark calibration) tends to damp the wealth effect of the shock on labor supply. This boosts potential output—and thus accounts for some of the larger output increase in the figure in the high openness case—while reducing the rise in the flexible price real wage. The smaller real wage gap (in absolute value) helps account for some of the less pronounced decline in inflation. In addition, as we discuss in section 2.3.8, some of the disparity in the output and inflation responses reflects that our calibrated Taylor rule with fixed response coefficients fails to account for the higher interest sensitivity of the economy as openness increases; thus, an alternative policy that kept output at potential under each calibration would imply smaller disparities in the output and inflation responses than depicted in the figure.

Overall, the salient message seems to be that even dramatic changes in the level of openness exert pretty small effects on the responses, except perhaps for the case of the government spending shock. The larger differences in the case of the government spending shock are perhaps unsurprising, given that this shock operates through a wealth effect, and that openness affects aggregate supply by altering the size of the wealth effect. Moreover, the SIGMA simulations discussed in section 2.2 indicate that some of the disparities in the responses to the fiscal shock would narrow with the inclusion of endogenous capital and adjustment costs on the expenditure components; notably, endogenous capital would reduce the pronounced disparity between the interest elasticity of private absorption and of trade flows under our benchmark calibration, so that the interest elasticity of demand would rise by less as openness increased.

We conclude this section by illustrating a case in which openness exerts extremely pronounced effects on the impulse responses of the model. In particular, figure 2.9 shows responses to the technology shock under an alternative calibration that imposes a very high trade price elasticity of 6, and a Frisch elasticity of labor supply of unity. As seen in table 2.2, the parameter σ^{open} rises from 0.5 under the "nearly closed" calibration to 3.6 in the high openness case, consistent with roughly a halving of the slope of the MRS schedule (from 3.5 to 1.8). Given that the wealth effect on labor supply diminishes rapidly with greater openness under this calibration, output exhibits a much more pronounced rise in the highly open economy. The smaller rise in the real wage in the highly open economy implies a much

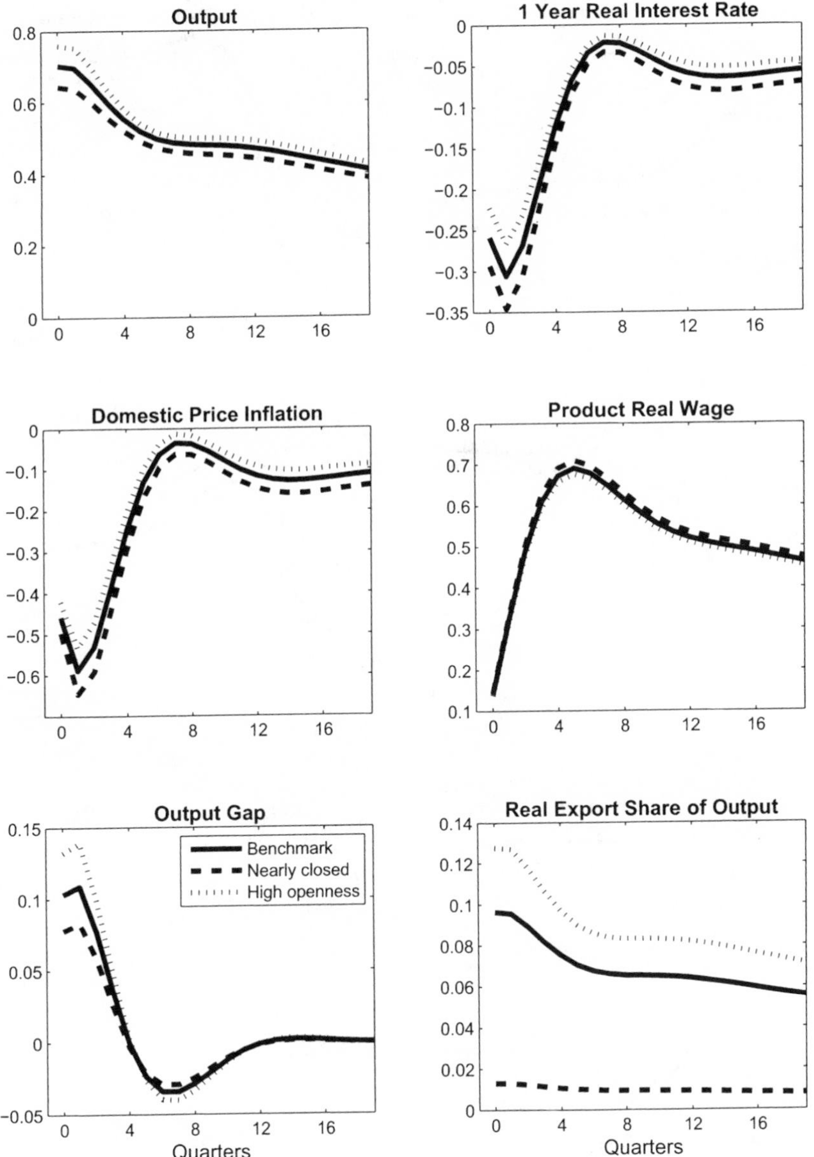

Fig. 2.8 Increase in technology in workhorse model (deviation from steady state)

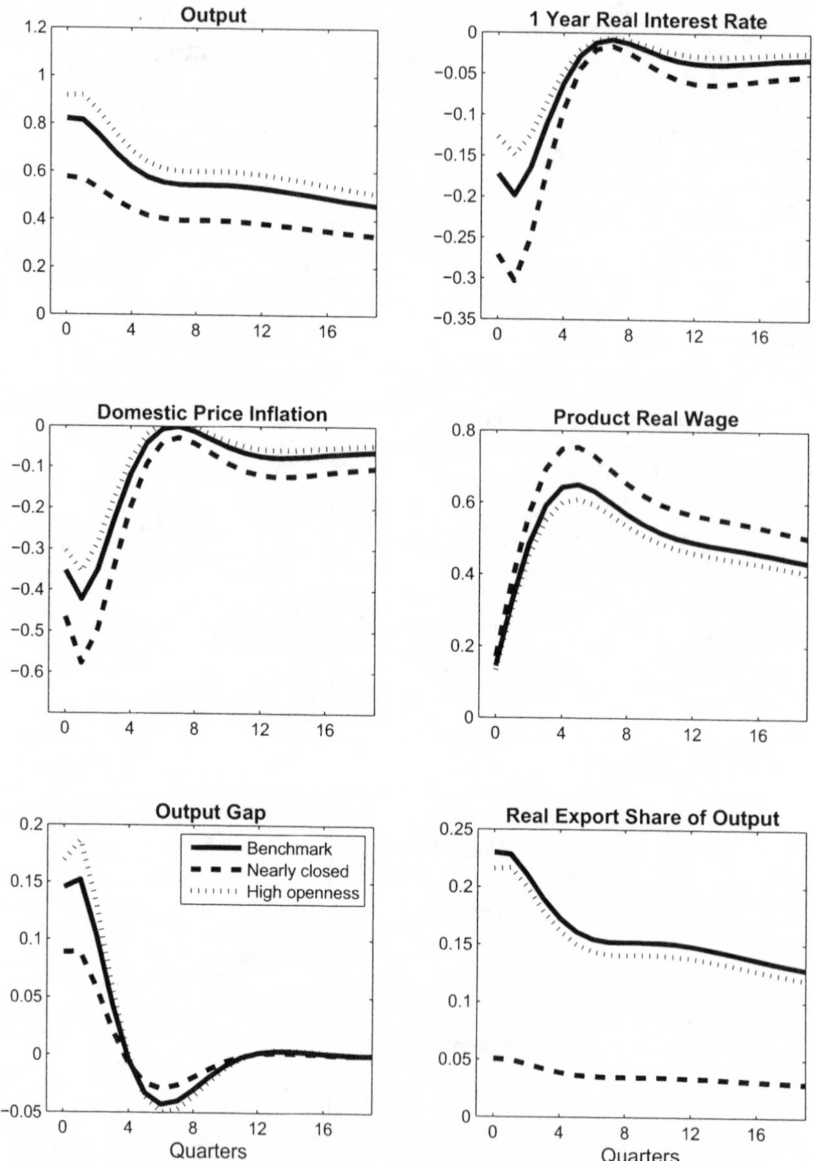

Fig. 2.9 Increase in technology in workhorse model (alternative calibration: $\eta = 6$ and $\chi^{-1} = 1$)

smaller real wage gap (in absolute value), and accounts for why inflation falls only about half as much on impact as in the closed economy. Accordingly, as suggested by the figure, a policymaker concerned about the variability of domestic price inflation and the output gap would face a markedly improved trade-off locus in the open economy. However, we emphasize that this large divergence hinges on a high Frisch elasticity of labor supply, and a fairly extreme assumption about the trade price elasticity.

2.3.8 Variance Trade-off Frontiers

A limitation of our preceding analysis that characterized policy as following a simple (Taylor-style) interest rate reaction function is that it is difficult to disentangle what components of the transmission channel change with trade openness. In particular, it is hard to ascertain whether differences are attributable to disparities in the "IS" block of the model; that is, in the interest sensitivity of the economy, or in the equations governing aggregate supply.

Toward this end, it is useful to follow Taylor (1979) in characterizing the variance trade-off frontier of the home economy. Accordingly, we assume that the monetary policy of the home country is determined by an optimal targeting rule that minimizes the following quadratic discounted loss function:

$$\mathbb{E}_t \sum_{j=0}^{\infty} \beta^j(\pi_{t+j}^2 + \lambda_x x_{t+j}^2), \tag{40}$$

where λ_x is the relative weight on the output gap. The policymaker is assumed to minimize the loss function subject to the log-linearized behavioral equations of the model, while taking as given that monetary policy in the foreign economy continues to follow a Taylor rule.[25] As in the closed economy setting of Clarida, Galí, and Gertler (1999) and Woodford (2003), the optimal policy does not depend on the model's IS curve in the special case in which the home country comprises an infinitesimal fraction of world output.

The left panel of figure 2.10 shows a policy trade-off frontier between inflation and output gap variability for the case of a technology shock. The trade-off frontier is obtained by minimizing the policymaker's loss function (40) over all possible values of λ_x subject to the log-linearized behavioral equations.[26] For visual clarity, the trade-off frontiers are shown only for the

25. The variance trade-off frontier is not very sensitive to the relative size of the home country. Hence, although we derive our results assuming that the home country constitutes 25 percent of world output, the trade-off frontiers are not markedly different in the case in which the home country share of world output is close to zero. In the latter case, the policymaker trade-off frontier can be derived by minimizing the loss function subject to the behavioral equations (32) through (37) that apply in the small open economy variant of our model.

26. Note that the vertical axis shows the standard deviation of inflation, and the horizontal axis the standard deviation of the output gap.

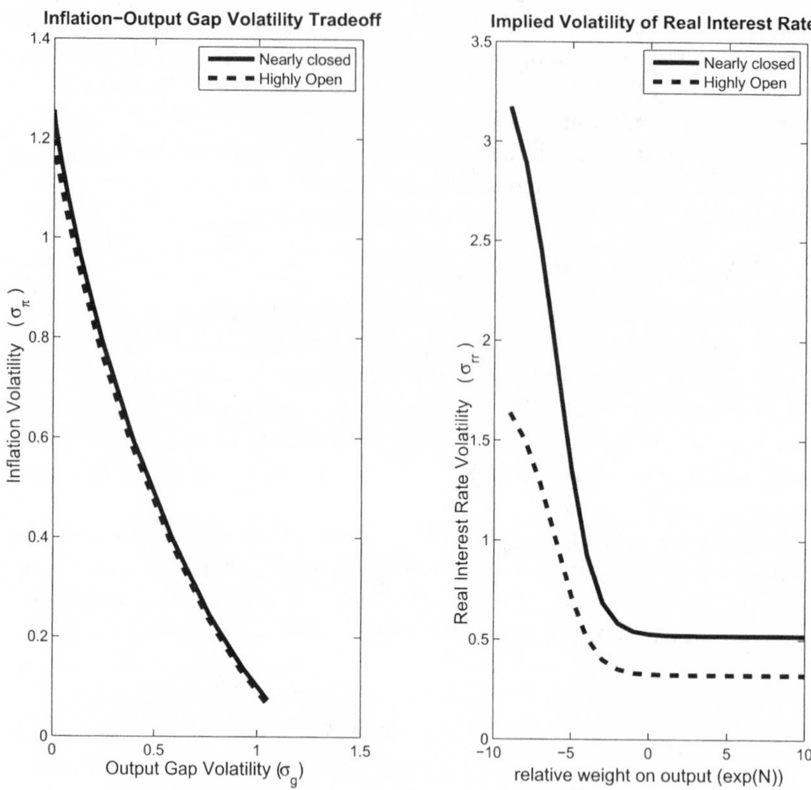

Fig. 2.10 Policy trade-off frontier for technology shock benchmark calibration

alternative calibrations of a highly open economy (in which the trade share is 35 percent), and the nearly closed case (with a trade share of 1 percent). Under either calibration, the standard deviation of inflation declines to zero as the policymaker's weight on the output gap λ_x declines to zero, while the standard deviation of the output gap declines to zero as λ_x approaches infinity.

As discussed previously, the presence of wage rigidities gives rise to a trade-off between stabilizing the output gap and inflation. However, the striking feature of the figure is that the trade-off frontiers are virtually identical, notwithstanding very pronounced differences in trade openness. This similarity reflects that the only channels through which trade openness can influence the trade-off frontier is by affecting the slope of the MRS schedule (recalling the MPL is invariant), or by affecting the potential real wage ζ_t^{pot}; as noted above, while openness affects the slope of the IS curve and potential real interest rate r_t^{pot}, this is inconsequential for a policymaker loss function such as (40) that does not explicitly depend on the interest rate. Thus, insofar as it is clear from table 2.1 that the potential real wage and slope of the MRS show little variation with openness under our benchmark calibration, it is unsurprising that the policy frontiers are nearly identical.

Although the policy trade-off frontiers are nearly identical, the right panel—which plots how interest rate volatility varies with λ_x—shows that implementation of the policy implies considerably less real interest variation in the more open economy.[27] This simply reflects that openness markedly raises the interest sensitivity of the economy, even if not the slope of the MRS schedule, and ζ_t^{pot} (as seen from table 2.1, σ^{open} rises from 0.5 in the closed economy case to 1.1 when the trade share is 35 percent). Thus, some of the relatively small differences in the transmission of the technology shock shown in figure 2.8 are in fact attributable to the aggregate demand block of the model. In particular, an optimal rule that puts a high enough weight on output gap stabilization to keep output at potential (i.e., a very large λ_x) implies output and inflation responses that are even closer than those depicted in figure 2.8.

Figure 2.11 considers how the highly open and closed economy policy frontiers shift given changes in key structural parameters that affect the slope of the MRS schedule. The upper panel shows that even adopting an extremely high value of the trade price elasticity η_c of 3 and a fairly high Frisch elasticity of labor supply of 0.5 (i.e., $\chi = 2$), is not sufficient to induce much of a disparity between the trade-off frontiers. Not surprisingly, the high trade price elasticity does drive a large wedge in the variability of the interest rate response associated with any given policy rule; that is, value of λ_x.

The policy frontiers may show considerably more variation with openness, but only under rather extreme calibrations. Thus, the middle panel shows that the open economy trade-off frontier would move further inside the (nearly) closed economy frontier in the case in which both the trade price elasticity and Frisch elasticity of labor supply were extremely high ($\eta_c = 6$, and the value of χ of .05 implies a Frisch elasticity of 20). In this case, the wealth effect dominates the behavior of the MRS slope, so that the latter flattens considerably with openness. Provided that the MPL slopes downward enough, the response of the potential real wage is damped considerably as openness increases; and because real wages are sticky, this improves the trade-off locus open to policymakers in the highly open economy. However, the manner in which the trade-off frontier varies with openness in an environment with an extremely flat MRS tends to be quite sensitive to the slope of the MPL schedule (unlike under our benchmark, in which the frontier is much less sensitive to the slope of the MPL). As illustrated by the last panel,

27. Note that figures 2.10 and 2.11 depict the relative weight on the output gap using an exponential scale, so that, for example, the tick label –5 corresponds to a weight of unity on inflation, and exp(–5) on the output gap.

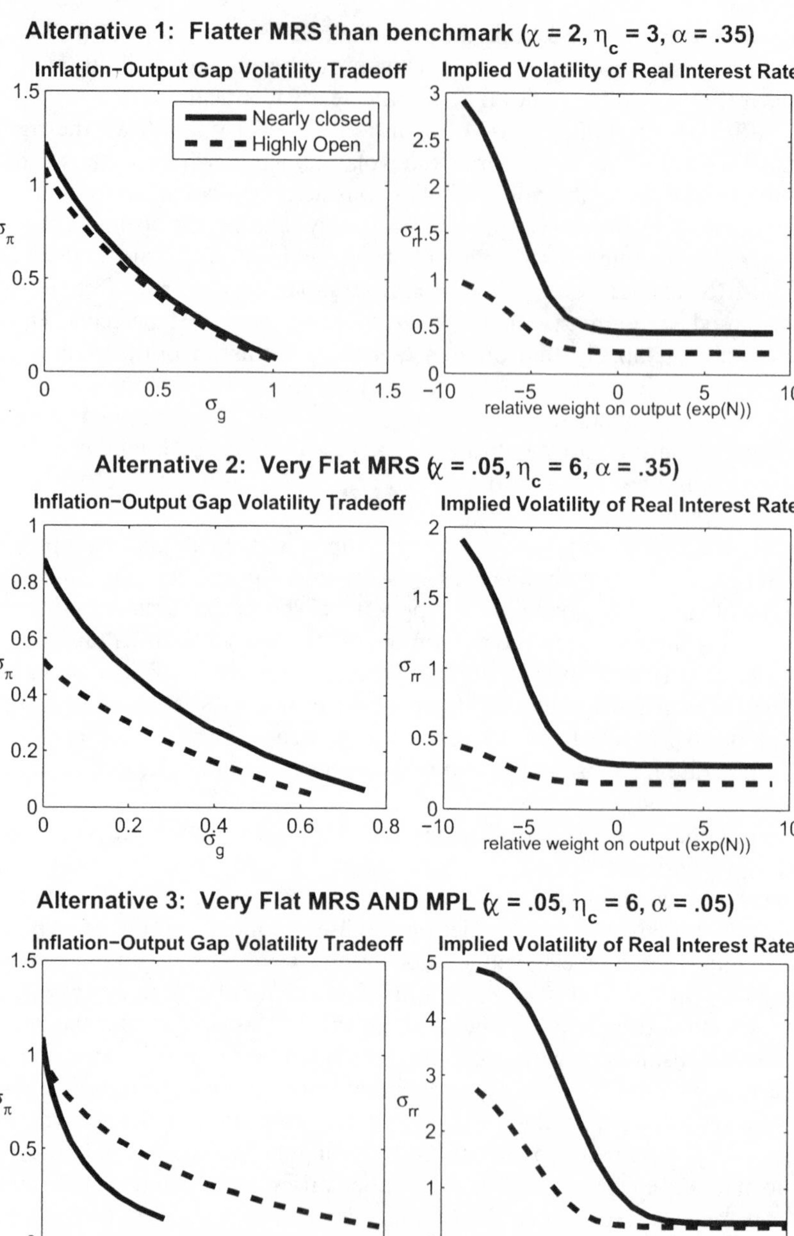

Fig. 2.11 Policy trade-off frontier for technology shock alternative calibrations

the open economy trade-off frontier actually lies well outside the closed economy frontier if the MPL slope is reduced to 0.05 in absolute value.

2.4 Alternative Model Specifications

Our workhorse model made a number of simplifying assumptions to keep the analysis tractable. We now investigate the robustness of these conclusions to several extensions of the model, including incomplete asset markets, endogenous capital accumulation, imported intermediate goods, and local currency pricing. As a prelude, it is useful to observe that in these extensions it is not possible to summarize how openness affects both the aggregate demand and supply blocks of the model in terms of effects on a single composite parameter, as in the workhorse model. Nonetheless, much of the intuition garnered from the simple model is helpful for understanding the effects of openness in these variants (e.g., openness tends to increase the interest sensitivity of aggregate demand if the trade price elasticity is high relative to that of domestic demand).[28]

2.4.1 Incomplete International Financial Markets

Our baseline model assumes that asset markets are complete both domestically and internationally. However, as this is an extreme assumption, we now consider an alternative in which households only have access to a nonstate contingent international bond.

Under this alternative, the household's budget constraint can be expressed as:

$$(41)\quad P_{Ct}C_t(h) + \int_s \xi_{Dt,t+1}B_{Dt+1}(h) + \frac{e_t P^*_{Ft} B_{Ft+1}(h)}{\phi_{Ft}(b_{Ft+1})} = W_t(h)N_t(h) + R_{Kt}K + \Gamma_t(h) - T_t(h) + B_{Dt}(h) + e_t B_{Ft}(h).$$

where $B_{Ft+1}(h)$ denotes the household's purchases of the foreign bond, P^*_{Ft} is the price of the foreign bond (in foreign currency), and $B_{Dt+1}(h)$ denotes state-contingent bonds traded among domestic households. We follow Turnovsky (1985) and assume there is an intermediation cost, $\phi_F(b_{Ft+1})$, paid by domestic households for purchases of the international bond to ensure that net foreign assets are stationary.[29] This intermediation cost depends on the ratio of economy-wide holdings of net foreign assets to nominal output (b_{Ft+1}):

$$(42)\quad \phi_F(b_{Ft+1}) = \exp\left(-\nu_F \frac{e_t P^*_{Ft} B_{Ft+1}(h)}{P_{Dt}Y_t}\right)$$

28. Each of the modifications considered in what follows are examined in isolation (i.e., taking the workhorse model as a point of departure, rather than building on previous modifications).

29. This intermediation cost is asymmetric, as foreign households do not face this cost; rather, they collect profits on the monopoly rents associated with the intermediation costs.

and rises when the home country is a net debtor. We set v_F to be very small ($v_F = 0.001$), which effectively implies that uncovered interest rate parity holds in our model.

Given this alternative financial structure, the risk-sharing condition (i.e., equation [20]) no longer holds and the domestic economy's level of net foreign assets influences model dynamics. To understand how, we begin by considering the demand side of the model. As in section 2.3, it remains possible to derive a (log-linearized) open economy IS curve of the form:

$$(43) \qquad y_t = \mathbb{E}_t y_{t+1} - (1 - g_y)\sigma^{open}\{r_t - r_t^*\} + \varepsilon_{b_F} b_{Ft+1} + u_{ISt},$$

where $\varepsilon_{b_F} = (1 - g_y)[\sigma(1 - \omega_c) - \sigma^{open}]v_F$, and $u_{ISt} = g_y(g_t - \mathbb{E}_t g_{t+1}) + (1 - g_y)(c_t^* - \mathbb{E}_t c_{t+1}^*)$. This expression for the IS curve is the same as in the workhorse model (expression [25]) except that it involves the home country's net foreign asset position due to the presence of the intermediation cost. Since we set v_F to be very small, ε_{b_F} is very small and the IS curve is virtually unchanged vis-à-vis the workhorse model.

Under incomplete markets, however, the IS curve does not provide a complete description of aggregate demand. Intuitively, the IS curve determines how aggregate demand grows through time, but the current level is only pinned down by the intertemporal budget constraints of households, which at a national level constrains the evolution of net foreign assets. Accordingly, the aggregate demand block also includes a (log-linearized) law of motion specifying how net foreign assets b_{Ft+1} evolve given the home country's net savings ns_t:

$$(44) \qquad b_{Ft+1} = \frac{1}{\beta} b_{Ft} + \frac{1}{1 - g_y} ns_t,$$

where ns_t is the country's total income less household and government expenditures (i.e., $ns_t = [y_t - (1 - g_y)c_t - g_y g_{ct} - (1 - g_y)\omega_c \tau_t]$). Because consumption depends only on output and the terms of trade (given the resource constraint and equation for real net exports), net savings can also be expressed simply in terms of output and the terms of trade. Finally, the terms of trade are determined by a modified uncovered interest parity (UIP) condition, which is the same as in the workhorse model except that it reflects the presence of the intermediation cost:

$$(45) \qquad \tau_t = \mathbb{E}_t \tau_{t+1} + r_t^* - r_t - v_F b_{Ft+1} = (r_{Lt}^* - r_{Lt}) - v_F \mathbb{E}_t \sum_{j=0}^{\infty} b_{Ft+j+1},$$

where r_{Lt} corresponds to the domestic long-term real interest rate (see equation [24]).

Turning to aggregate supply, the MPL schedule remains unchanged under incomplete markets, as discussed in section 2.3. However, the MRS schedule is influenced by the country's ability to borrow and lend, so that changes in the home country's net foreign asset position influence aggregate supply.

In particular, the marginal rate of substitution (in product terms) can be written as:

$$(46) \qquad mrs_t = \chi l_t + \frac{1}{\sigma}\frac{1}{1-g_y}((1-\alpha)(l_t+z_t)-g_y g_t) - \frac{1}{\sigma}\frac{1}{1-g_y}ns_t - \left(\frac{1}{\sigma}-1\right)\tau_t.$$

This expression for the marginal rate of substitution is similar to the one for the closed economy (i.e., equation [29]), except for the inclusion of the last two terms involving net savings and the terms of trade. Clearly, for the special case of $\sigma = 1$, the terms of trade drops from equation (46) so that the only difference between the closed and open economy expression for the marginal rate of substitution involves the term in net savings. This net saving term can be regarded as adjusting the wealth effect on labor supply in an open relative to a closed economy. An increase in net savings is associated with a smaller wealth effect on labor supply, lowering the household's marginal rate of substitution, and depressing the potential real wage. By contrast, this effect is absent in a closed economy, since $ns_t = 0$.

The previous discussion suggests that the effects of domestic shocks may diverge considerably between a closed and open economy if the IS curve slope is sensitive to the degree of trade openness (for the same reasons discussed in section 2.3), or if the shocks exert large effects on net savings. To investigate the quantitative effects of openness under our benchmark calibration, the right column of figure 2.12 shows the responses of output, domestic inflation, and consumption to a persistent rise in technology (the AR[1] coefficient equals 0.97) for different degrees of trade openness under incomplete markets; for point of reference, corresponding results under complete markets are shown in the left column. Clearly, under either financial structure, technology shocks have somewhat larger effects on output and smaller effects on inflation, as the openness of the economy increases. This reflects that openness damps the expansion in consumption under either financial market structure: under complete markets, because of insurance arrangements, and while under incomplete markets it reflects an increase in desired saving because current income exceeds permanent income. As observed in section 2.3, the smaller implied wealth effect on labor supply translates into a larger output response, and mitigates the decline in inflation. Nevertheless, the differences in the responses of output and inflation appear fairly small given the large changes in openness examined. The modest size of the disparities reflects that home and foreign goods are not substitutable enough in our benchmark calibration to have large effects on the MRS schedule (i.e., net savings does not change enough to exert much of an effect on the MRS schedule given by equation [46]).

To demonstrate that there can potentially be large differences between an

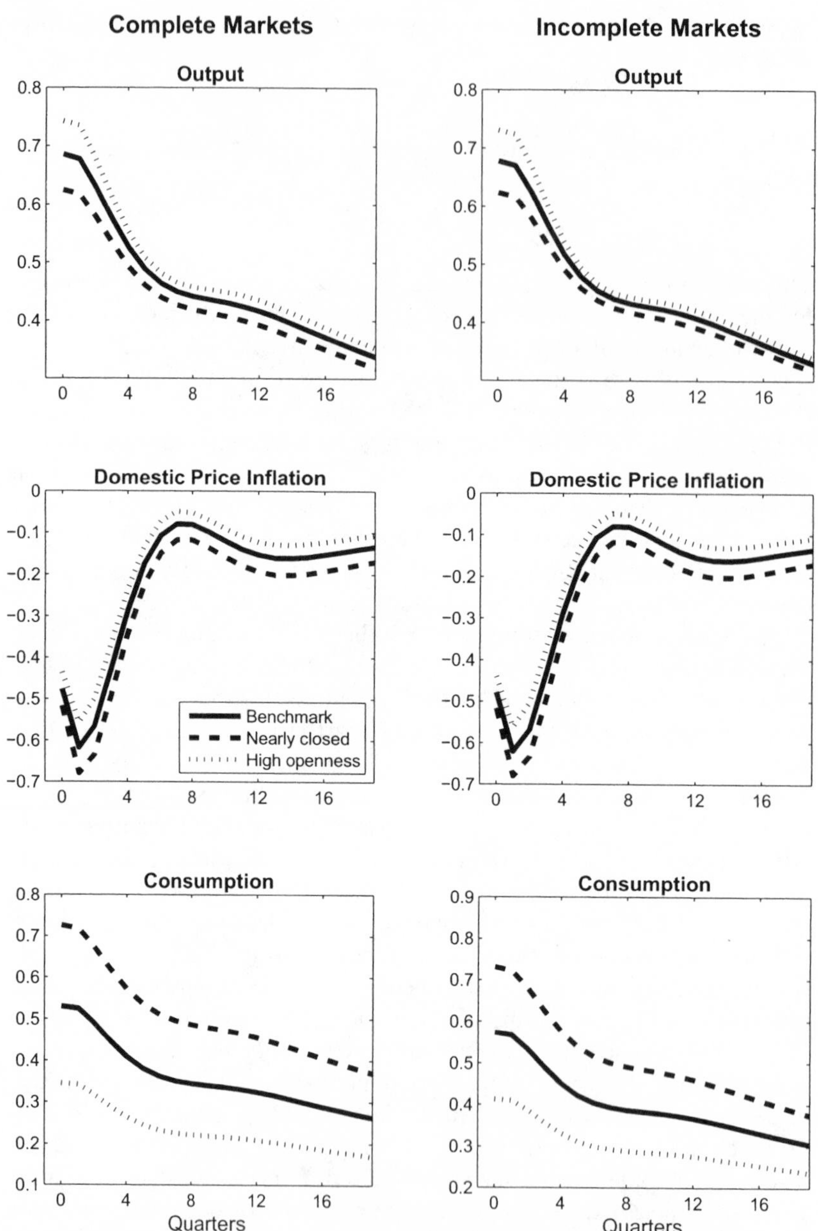

Fig. 2.12 Persistent increase in technology: Complete vs. incomplete markets

open and closed economy under incomplete markets, figure 2.13 shows the effects of a more transitory technology shock (the AR[1] coefficient equals 0.8) on output under three alternative calibrations of the trade price elasticity and the Frisch labor supply elasticity. We consider a transitory shock because it can potentially drive a larger wedge between current and permanent income, thus amplifying the differences in the wealth effect between a closed and open economy.

The top panel shows the effect on output under a trade price elasticity of 6 (keeping the Frisch elasticity at its benchmark value of 0.2, so $\chi = 5$). The combination of the more transient shock and greater substitutability between home and foreign goods generates a larger increase in net savings in the domestic economy; hence, larger output differences than under the benchmark calibration. As shown in the middle and lower panels, these differences in the output responses become even larger as the labor supply curve becomes more elastic (i.e., a lower value of χ) and as the trade price elasticity increases. However, it bears reiterating that rather extreme calibrations of the trade price elasticity (and a high Frisch elasticity) seem required for the responses to show large divergence based on openness.

2.4.2 Endogenous Investment

We next investigate the robustness of our results to include endogenous investment into the workhorse model of section 2.3. In the modified framework, households augment their stock of capital according to:

$$K_{t+1}(h) = (1 - \delta)K_t(h) + I_t(h), \tag{47}$$

where $I_t(h)$ and $K_t(h)$ denote household investment and the beginning of period t stock of capital, respectively. The household budget constraint is also modified to reflect investment purchases:

$$\begin{aligned} P_{Ct}C_t(h) + P_{Ct}I_t(h) + \int_s \xi_{t,t+1}B_{t+1}(h) = \\ W_t(h)N_t(h) + R_{Kt}K_t(h) + \Gamma_t(h) - T_t(h) + B_t(h) - P_{Dt}\phi_{It}(h). \end{aligned} \tag{48}$$

In equation (48), ϕ_{It} denotes an adjustment cost given by:

$$\phi_{It}(h) = \frac{\phi_I}{2}\frac{(I_t(h) - I_{t-1}(h))^2}{I_{t-1}(h)}. \tag{49}$$

Following Christiano, Eichenbaum, and Evans (2005), it is costly to change the level of investment from the previous period. Investment goods are produced using the same technology as final consumption goods (see equation [13]); hence, they require both the domestically produced composite good as well as imports. The import share of investment goods and elasticity of substitution between domestic goods and imports in the production function for investment is assumed to be the same as for consumption.

The inclusion of endogenous investment tends to markedly boost the

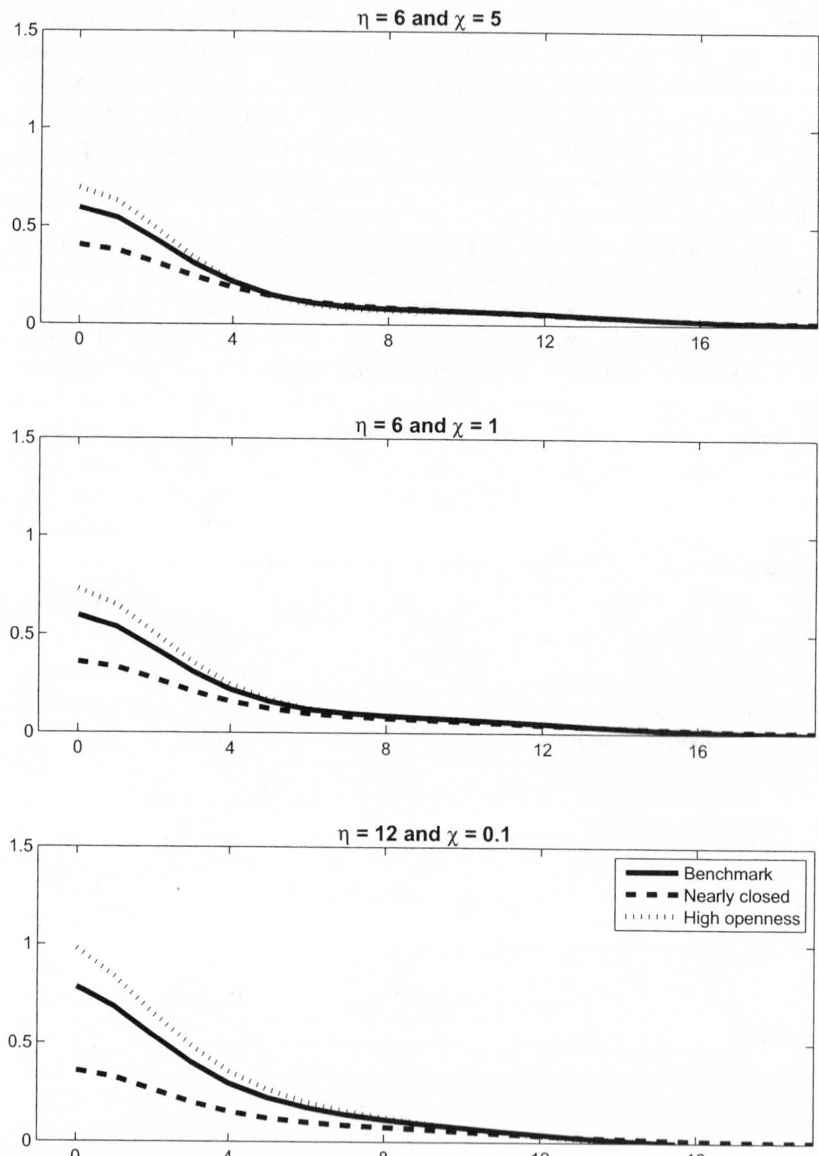

Fig. 2.13 The effect on output of a more transitory increase in technology (alternative calibrations of incomplete markets model)

interest sensitivity of domestic demand under plausible calibrations. Accordingly, as suggested by the SIGMA simulations in section 2.2, the interest sensitivity should be expected to rise less steeply with openness compared with the workhorse model; in fact, the aggregate interest sensitivity of the economy can even decline with greater openness if investment is sufficiently interest sensitive.

To illustrate these points, the upper panel of figure 2.14 reexamines the reduction in the inflation target shock in the augmented model with investment. The calibration in the top panel sets the adjustment cost on investment parameter $\phi_I = 0.2$, which effectively serves to equalize the interest elasticity of domestic demand and of real net exports (notwithstanding that the interest elasticity of consumption is unchanged from our benchmark calibration). In contrast to the model with fixed capital (see figure 2.6), which implied a modestly larger output contraction in the highly open economy relative to the closed economy, the response of both output and inflation is nearly invariant to trade openness. The virtually identical output responses reflect that the effective interest sensitivity of domestic demand is very close to that of real net exports, so that putting a higher weight on the latter as trade openness rises has little effect on the overall interest sensitivity of the economy. The similar output responses across the calibrations translate into commensurate effects on marginal cost and inflation.

The two lower panels consider alternative calibrations, which show that the general conditions highlighted in section 2.3 as potentially giving rise to large differences between closed and open economies continue to remain operative under endogenous capital accumulation. Thus, the middle panel considers the case in which the trade price elasticity is set to 6, rather than 1.5 as in our benchmark. In this case, the interest sensitivity of real net exports is much higher than that of domestic demand, so that the aggregate interest sensitivity of the economy rises with openness, and output shows a larger contraction as openness increases. The final panel keeps the trade price elasticity at its benchmark value of 1.5, but increases the effective interest sensitivity of domestic demand relative to the first panel by reducing the adjustment cost parameter ϕ_I to 0.01. In this case, output contracts by somewhat more in the closed than in the open economy.

2.4.3 Imported Materials

Our workhorse model treats imports as finished goods. However, many imported goods are used as intermediate inputs in production, and their use in production may alter the transmission of domestic shocks.

To investigate this possibility, we follow McCallum and Nelson (1999) and modify the production process of intermediate goods producers discussed in section 3.3 so that gross output of intermediate good i, $Y_t(i)$, is produced according to the CES gross production function:

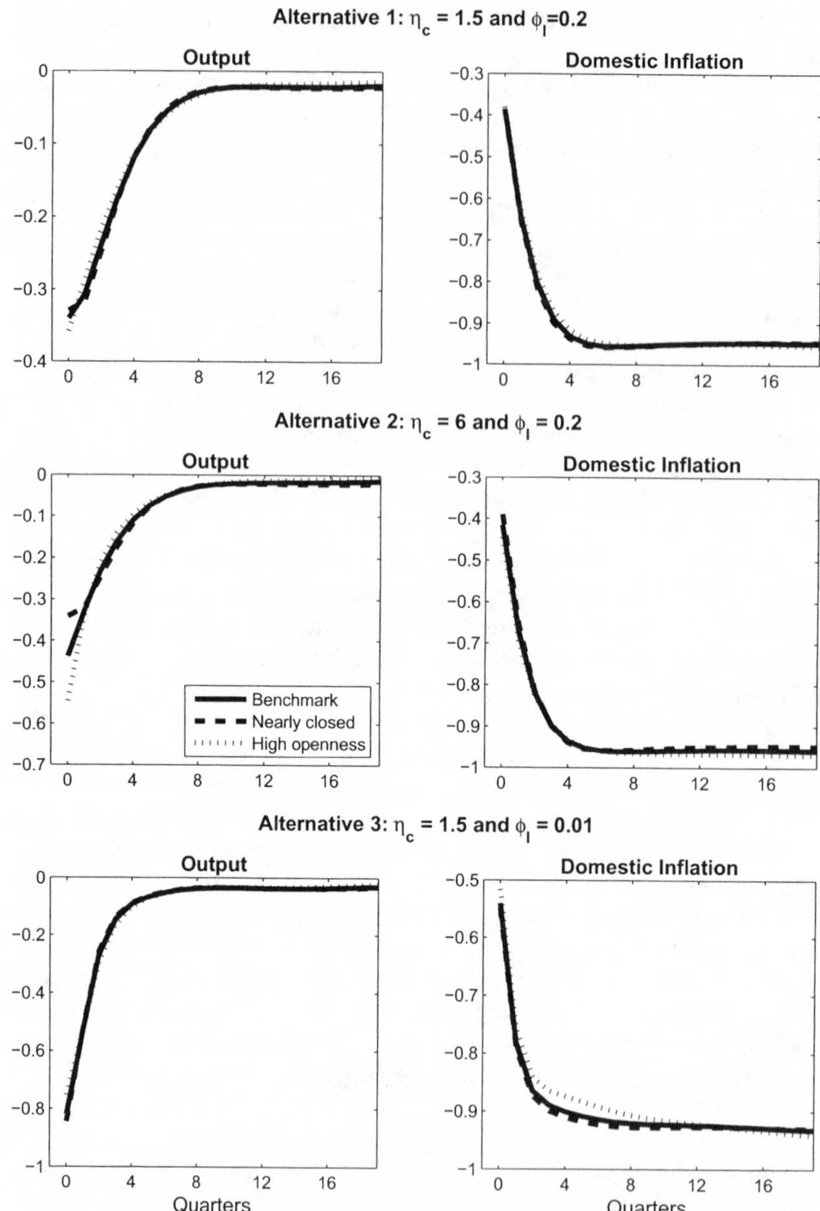

Fig. 2.14 Reduction in inflation target in endogenous investment model

(50) $$Y_t(i) = ((1-\omega_L)^{\rho L/(1+\rho_L)}(K_t(i)\alpha(Z_tL_t(i))^{1-\alpha})^{1/(1+\rho_L)} + \omega_L{}^{\rho_L/(1+\rho_L)}M_{Yt}(i)^{1/(1+\rho_L)})^{1+\rho_L}.$$

Thus, value-added for good i is produced via a Cobb-Douglas production function and combined with firm i's purchases of the foreign aggregate good $M_{Yt}(i)$, which is used as an intermediate input, to produce the gross output of good i. The parameter ω_L determines the share of imported materials in gross production, and $\eta_L = (1+\rho_L)/\rho_L$ is the elasticity of substitution between value-added and imported materials. We assume that capital, labor, and imported materials are perfectly mobile across firms within a country so that all firms have identical marginal costs per unit of gross output (MC_t):

(51) $$MC_t = ((1-\omega_L)MC_{Vt}^{-1/\rho_L} + \omega_L P_{Mt}^{-1/\rho_L})^{-\rho_L},$$

where MC_{Vt} is marginal cost per unit of value-added defined earlier in equation (10).

The inclusion of intermediate inputs in the model changes the home economy's resource constraint so that:

(52) $$Y_t = C_{Dt} + G_t + \frac{\zeta^*}{\zeta}(M^*_{Ct} + M^*_{Yt}),$$

where M^*_{Yt} denote exports of the domestic good used as intermediate inputs. Market clearing in the factor market for intermediate inputs implies:

(53) $$M_{Yt}\int_0^1 M_{Yt}(i)di.$$

The inclusion of material inputs alters the sensitivity of aggregate demand to interest rates. For the special case in which wages are flexible and value-added is linear in labor ($\alpha = 0$), it is possible to summarize how openness affects the interest sensitivity of aggregate demand through its effect on a single composite parameter. As shown in the appendix, under these conditions the open economy IS curve can be written:

(54) $$y_t = \mathbb{E}_t y_{t+1} - (1-g_y)\sigma_M^{open}\{r_t - r_t^*\} + u_{ISt},$$

where u_{ISt} is a term reflecting the government spending shock and foreign shocks. This expression parallels equation (25) in the workhorse model, with the composite parameter σ_M^{open} playing a role akin to σ^{open}; hence, it is interpretable as the effective interest sensitivity of aggregate demand. The elasticity σ_M^{open} can be related to σ^{open} according to $\sigma_M^{open} = \sigma^{open}(1-\omega_L) + \omega_L \eta_L/(1-g_y)$.[30] Thus, interest sensitivity of aggregate demand can be regarded as a weighted average of the interest sensitivity of consumption, real net exports of final goods, and intermediate imported inputs.

30. Following the logic of section 2.3, the price elasticity of demand for intermediate goods in effect can be translated directly into an interest sensitivity using the UIP relation.

The price elasticity of demand for intermediate goods, η_L, appears to be quite low relative to the price elasticity of demand for final traded goods, and is perhaps even lower than the intertemporal elasticity of substitution in consumption. Thus, using the same calibration as McCallum and Nelson (1999) which sets $\eta_L = 1/3$, the interest elasticity of aggregate demand σ_M^{open} declines under our benchmark calibration as the share of intermediate inputs in gross output (ω_L) rises. However, the quantitative implications are quite small, given that imported intermediate inputs appear to constitute only a small fraction of gross output for most countries. For example, given that the share of U.S. imports accounted for by materials (including oil and petroleum products) has averaged just under 25 percent during the past two decades (based on national income and product account [NIPA] data), this would suggest a value of ω_L in the range of 0.03. Using our benchmark calibration with $\sigma^{open} = 1.1$, and setting $\eta_L = 1/3$ and $\omega_L = .03$, the implied interest elasticity of aggregate demand in the model with imported intermediate goods σ_M^{open} only declines to 1.08.

The presence of imported materials also affects the pricing decisions of intermediate producers by altering their marginal costs. In particular, producers set gross output prices in a staggered fashion rather than value-added prices, and the first-order condition for the price of good i is:

$$(55)\qquad \mathbb{E}_t \sum_{j=0}^{\infty} \psi_{t,t+j}\xi_p^j \left(\frac{(1+\tau_p)V_{Dt+j}P_{Dt}(i)}{(1+\theta_p)} - MC_{Gt+j} \right) Y_{t+j}(i) = 0,$$

where $P_{Dt}(i)$ now has an interpretation as a gross output price and $V_{Dt+j} = \Pi_{h=1}^{j}\pi_{t+h-1}$. Equation (55) can be log-linearized and rewritten as:

$$(56)\qquad \pi_t - \pi_{t-1} = \beta(\pi_{t+1|t} - \pi_t) + \kappa_p[(1-\omega_L)(\zeta_t - mpl_t) + \omega_L\tau_t].$$

where $mpl_t = (1-\alpha)z_t - \alpha L_t$ corresponds to the marginal product of labor—in terms of value-added—described in section 2.3. The marginal cost term clearly depends on fluctuations in the terms of trade, although this influence depends on the share parameter ω_L, and hence, almost surely has small effects on marginal cost for most countries.

Figure 2.15 compares the effects of a technology shock in the workhorse model to that in the model with imported imports for different degrees of openness. In each case, we set $\eta_L = 1/3$, and calibrated ω_c and ω_L so that material imports account for roughly 25 percent of total imports in each economy.[31] As in the workhorse model, the highly open economy experiences a larger increase in output and smaller decline in inflation. The inclusion of intermediate inputs tends to dampen the fall in inflation in response

31. In the model with material imports, we vary both ω_c and ω_L to alter the ratio of imports to GDP in each scenario. As a result, the more open economy is characterized by larger values of both ω_c and ω_L; however, the fraction of material imports to overall imports is held fixed at 25 percent in all cases. Finally, the simulations shown in figure 2.15 restrict $\alpha = 0$, but otherwise adopt the values used in our benchmark calibration.

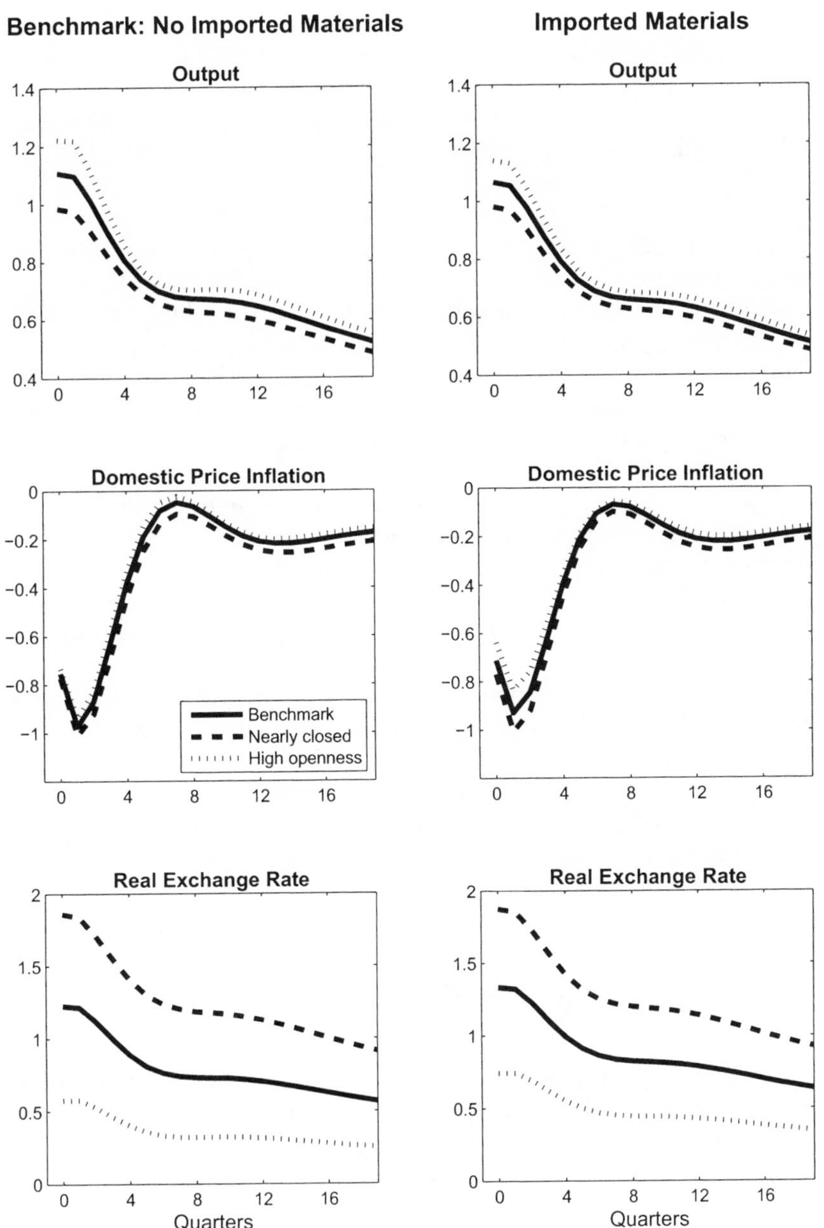

Fig. 2.15 Increase in technology: Workhorse model vs. imported materials model

to the technology shock, reflecting that the fall in unit labor costs is offset to a greater degree by higher import prices. However, the differences between the highly open economy and the closed economy do not appear large, so that the inclusion of intermediate goods only modestly amplifies the differences evident in the workhorse model.

2.4.4 Pricing to Market

Our workhorse model assumed that the law of one price holds for each intermediate good. However, there is considerable empirical evidence suggesting that the law of one price does not hold. A related literature emphasizes that U.S. import prices at the point of entry respond less than one for one with a change in the exchange rate (i.e., exchange rate pass-through to U.S. import prices is incomplete).[32] We now consider an alternative version of our model that can account for these findings.

In this alternative version, intermediate goods firms set different prices at home and abroad or "price to market." This pricing-to-market behavior arises for two reasons. First, we assume, as in Betts and Devereux (1996), that intermediate goods' prices are sticky in local currency terms. We also posit aggregators for intermediate goods that have nonconstant elasticities of demand as in Kimball (1995), implying that a firm may face different demand elasticities at home and abroad.[33]

To incorporate these features, we modify the problem of the consumption goods distributor in the workhorse model by replacing the CES production function in equation (13) with an alternative demand aggregator discussed in Gust, Leduc, and Vigfusson (2006). The implied demand functions of the consumption goods distributor for the imported and domestic good i are given by:

$$(57)\quad M_{Ct}(i) = \omega_c\left[\frac{1}{1-\nu}\left(\frac{P_{Mt}(i)}{P_{Mt}}\right)^{1/(1-\gamma)}\left(\frac{P_{Mt}}{P_{Ft}}\right)^{\rho/(\gamma-\rho)} - \frac{\nu}{1-\nu}\right](C_t + G_t),$$

$$(58)\quad C_{Dt}(i) = (1-\omega_c)\left[\frac{1}{1-\nu}\left(\frac{P_{Dt}(i)}{P_{Dt}}\right)^{1/(1-\gamma)}\left(\frac{P_{Dt}}{P_{Ft}}\right)^{\rho/(\gamma-\rho)} \frac{\nu}{1-\nu}\right](C_t + G_t).$$

As in Dotsey and King (2005), when $\nu \neq 0$ these demand curves have a linear term, which implies that the elasticity of demand of producer i depends on its price $P_{Dt}(i)$ relative to an index of the prices of its competitors (see the following). When $\nu = 0$, the demand elasticity is constant and $1/(1-\gamma)$ has the interpretation as the elasticity of substitution between home brands

32. For a survey of this literature, see Goldberg and Knetter (1997), and for more recent empirical evidence for the United States, see Marazzi, Sheets, and Vigfusson (2005).

33. See Bergin and Feenstra (2001) for a discussion of how the interaction of demand curves with nonconstant elasticities with sticky prices can be helpful in accounting for exchange rate dynamics.

(i.e., $(1-\gamma)/\gamma$ is equivalent to θ_P in the workhorse model). Price indexes of domestic and imported goods are P_{Mt} and P_{Dt}, given by:

$$(59) \quad P_{Dt} = \left(\int_0^1 P_{Dt}(i)^{\gamma/(\gamma-1)}di\right)^{(\gamma-1)/\gamma} \quad \text{and} \quad P_{Mt} = \left(\int_0^1 P_{Mt}(i)^{\gamma/(\gamma-1)}di\right)^{(\gamma-1)/\gamma},$$

while P_{Ft} is a price index consisting of all the prices of a firm's competitors:

$$(60) \quad P_{Ft} = [(1-\omega_c)P_{Dt}^{\gamma/(\gamma-\rho)} + \omega_c P_{Mt}^{\gamma/(\gamma-\rho)}]^{(\gamma-\rho)/\gamma}.$$

Intermediate goods producers sell their products to the consumption goods distributors and can charge different prices at home and abroad. These prices are determined according to Calvo-style contracts subject to indexation. The first-order condition associated with the optimal setting of the domestic price of intermediate good i (i.e., $P_{Dt}(i)$) is given by:

$$(61) \quad \mathbb{E}_t \sum_{j=0}^{\infty} \psi_{t,t+j}\xi_p^j \left[1 - \left(1 - \frac{MC_{t+j}}{(1+\tau_P)V_{Dt+j}P_{Dt}(i)}\right)\varepsilon_{Dt+j}(i)\right] V_{Dt+j}C_{Dt+j} = 0,$$

where the elasticity of demand for good i in the domestic market is:

$$(62) \quad \varepsilon_{Dt}(i) = \frac{1}{1-\gamma}\left[1 - \nu\left(\frac{P_{Dt}(i)}{P_{Dt}}\right)^{1/(1-\gamma)}\left(\frac{P_{Dt}}{P_{Ft}}\right)^{\rho/(\rho-\gamma)}\right]^{-1}.$$

With $\nu > 0$, as in Kimball (1995), $\varepsilon_{Dt}(i)$ may be an increasing function of a firm's price relative to its competitors, and a firm will not want its desired price (i.e., its optimal price in the absence of price rigidities) to deviate too far from its competitors.

Equation (61) can be log-linearized and expressed as:

$$(63) \quad \pi_t - \pi_{t-1} = \beta(\pi_{t+1|t} - \pi_t) + \kappa_p\Theta[\zeta_t - mpl_t + \nu\mu\omega_C\eta_c(p_{Mt} - p_{Dt})],$$

where $\mu = 1/(\varepsilon_D - 1)$ denotes the steady-state (net) markup over marginal cost, $\varepsilon_D = 1/[(1-\gamma)(1-\nu)]$ is the steady-state value of $\varepsilon_{Dt}(i)$, and $\eta_c = \rho/[(\rho-\gamma)(1-\nu)] > 0$ denotes (the absolute value of the) aggregate elasticity between home and foreign goods in steady state. The parameter $\Theta = 1/(1+\nu(1+\mu)) < 1$ reflects the degree of "strategic" complementarity in price setting (e.g., Woodford 2003). That is, with $\nu = 0$, a firm's demand elasticity is constant, and this expression is the same as in the workhorse model. With $\nu > 0$, there are variations in desired markups associated with changes in a firm's price relative to its competitors. In this case, inflation is less sensitive to marginal cost, and depends directly on import prices given that the composite coefficient $\nu\mu\omega_C\eta_C$ in equation (63) is positive. Clearly, the importance of import prices in affecting domestic inflation depends directly on the degree of openness, ω_C.

According to equation (63), foreign competition can influence domestic inflation through changes in desired markups. This expression is reminiscent of Dornbusch and Fischer (1984), who described how foreign competition could influence the desired markups of domestic firms and effectively change the slope of the Phillips curve. In particular, they argued that monetary shocks were likely to cause domestic prices in an open economy to respond more quickly, which they interpreted as a steepening of the slope of the Phillips curve. From a qualitative perspective, monetary policy shocks can also steepen the Phillips curve in our model with variable markups. In particular, a monetary contraction occurring in response to a decrease in the central bank's inflation target lowers marginal cost and generates a real appreciation of the domestic currency. This appreciation lowers import prices relative to domestic prices, and domestic producers respond by reducing their desired markups. As a result, domestic price inflation can appear more sensitive to the fall in demand associated with the monetary contraction.

However, we emphasize that the source of the shock in our framework has crucial bearing for the question of whether inflation becomes more or less sensitive to aggregate demand. For example, in response to a government spending shock, inflation can appear less sensitive to demand. Higher government spending puts upward pressure on marginal cost, but the real exchange rate appreciates. This appreciation reduces relative import prices, forcing domestic producers to lower their desired markups. This reduction in desired markups has the effect of making domestic price inflation less sensitive to the increase in aggregate demand.

A domestic firm also sets a sticky price in the local currency of the foreign economy. These prices are also determined according to Calvo-style contracts indexed to lagged foreign import price inflation, with the log-linearized first-order condition associated with domestic producer i's choice of a price to set in the foreign market given by:

$$(64) \qquad \pi^*_{Mt} - \pi^*_{Mt-1} = \beta(\pi^*_{Mt+1|t} - \pi^*_{Mt}) + \kappa_p\Theta[(\zeta_t - mpl_t - q_{Dt}) - \nu\mu(1 - \omega^*_C)\eta_c(P^*_{Mt} - P^*_{Dt})],$$

where $q_{Dt} = p^*_{Dt} + e_t - p_{Dt}$ is the real exchange rate in terms of domestic prices. This equation implies that foreign import prices (i.e., domestic export prices in units of the foreign currency) do not respond fully to changes in domestic marginal cost, or to changes in real exchange rates. In turn, the response of real trade flows is also muted. In contrast, in the workhorse model, changes in exchange rates have a relatively large effect on import prices and thus on real trade flows.

Figure 2.16 shows the effects of a technology shock for different degrees of openness in both the workhorse model with a constant elasticity of demand and the model with variable desired markups and pricing to market. For the model with variable desired markups, we set $\nu = 3$, ρ such that the aggregate trade price elasticity η_c equals its benchmark value of 1.5, and γ so that the steady-state markup is 20 percent. Under our benchmark calibration, the variation in desired markups mutes the responsiveness of import and export

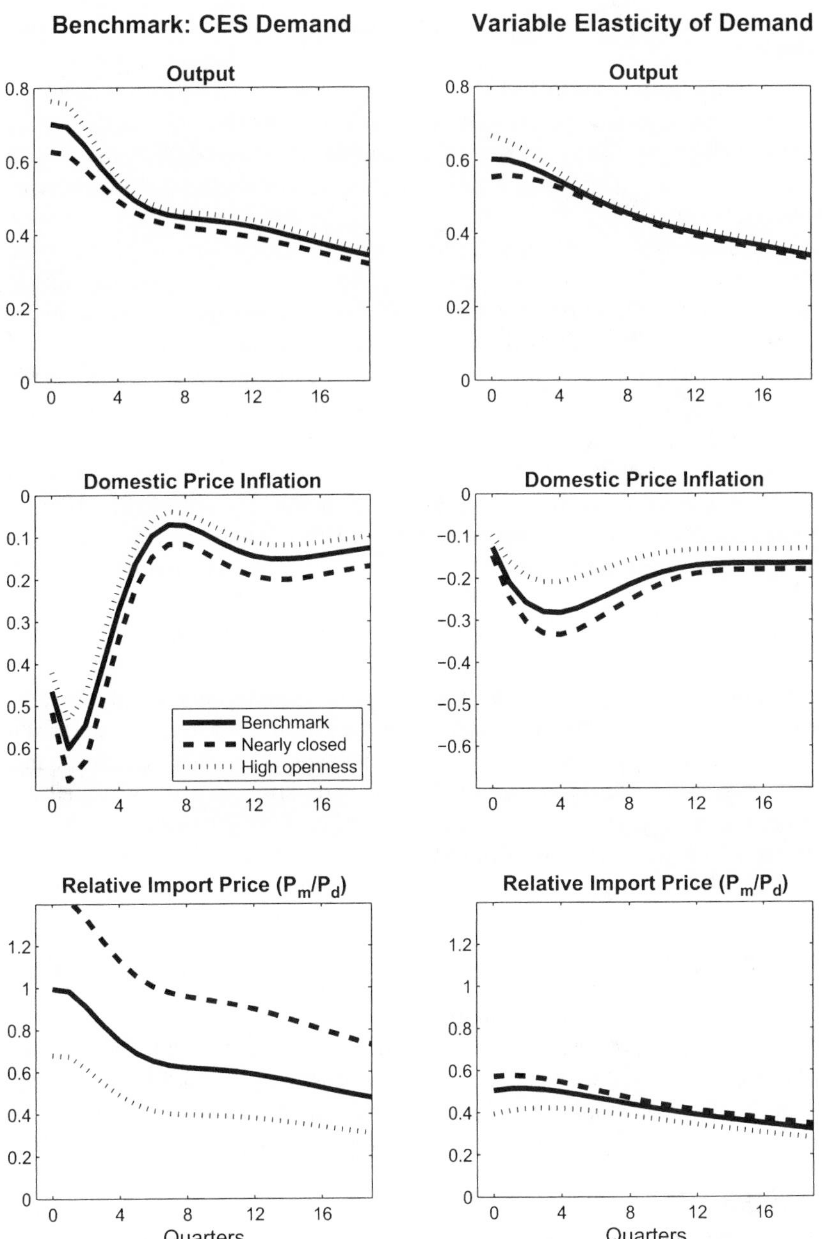

Fig. 2.16 Increase in technology: Workhorse model vs. variable desired markups model

prices to exchange rate changes and reduces the interest sensitivity of real trade flows.

Output responds more to the technology shock under calibrations with a high degree of trade openness in both the workhorse model and the model with variable markups. In particular, higher openness damps the wealth effect on labor supply, which causes potential output to respond more as openness rises.

The responses of inflation are uniformly smaller in the variable desired markups model than in the workhorse model for any level of openness, which mainly reflects that the former allows for strategic complementarity in price setting; this feature damps the response of inflation to real marginal cost. However, notwithstanding the smaller size of inflation responses in the variable desired markups model, there is noticeably greater variation with level of openness that is attributable to different incentives facing domestic price setters as openness changes in the variable markups framework. In particular, given that import prices rise as the home real exchange rate depreciates, domestic firms have an incentive to raise their markups in response to weaker competition from imports, thus mitigating the fall in domestic price inflation. This effect is clearly more important in a highly open economy than in a relatively closed economy, which accounts for the significant dampening in the inflation response as openness rises.

These considerations suggest that openness may have greater consequences for price setting than implied by the simple workhorse model. Even so, some of the spread between the inflation responses would be reduced in a richer dynamic model that allowed for trade adjustment costs, as this feature tends to retard variation in the desired markup. This helps account for why the inflation responses from the SIGMA model shown in figure 2.4 show noticeably less variation with openness than the responses in figure 2.16.

2.5 Conclusion

In this chapter, we have used an open economy DSGE modeling framework to explore how trade openness influences the transmission of domestic shocks. Our analysis focused on how openness can potentially affect transmission through changing the interest sensitivity of aggregate demand, and through influencing the supply block by affecting marginal costs and desired markups.

Perhaps surprisingly—and in contrast to some claims advanced in the ongoing debate about the effects of globalization—our results do not suggest much sensitivity of either aggregate demand or supply to trade openness. Based on our analysis, it still seems plausible that there may be noticeable differences between the response of a highly open economy, such as Canada, and a relatively closed economy, such as the United States, to certain domestic shocks. For example, as suggested in the previous section, inflation may fall less in response to a favorable supply shock in Canada than in the United States if the shock also makes imports less competitive due to exchange rate depreciation. However, it seems less plausible that the gradual rise in trade openness that has occurred in most industrial countries during the past few decades has had much influence on how domestic shocks, including monetary or fiscal policy changes, affect the economy.

As a corollary, it seems doubtful that globalization, interpreted narrowly as enhanced trade linkages, played much of a role in contributing to the "Great Moderation" by affecting the transmission channel of domestic shocks. Of course, this leaves open the possibility that some of the improved inflation and output performance experienced by a wide array of countries in the past two decades may be attributable to the combination of increased trade openness—which surely increases sensitivity to external shocks—and a generally favorable array of international shocks for much of that period.

In interpreting our results, it is important to caution that we have conditioned on a monetary rule that only responds to domestic price inflation (and the output gap) in order to focus on how openness affects transmission through the aggregate demand and supply blocks of the economy. Openness can potentially exert somewhat larger effects on the transmission of domestic shocks in the realistic case in which the monetary rule responds to consumer price inflation rather than domestic inflation. However, it is important to stress that to the extent that many models—including the workhorse model—impose complete pass-through of exchange rate changes to import prices, they probably exaggerate how openness affects transmission through the monetary policy rule. The difference between consumer price inflation and domestic price inflation does not vary as markedly with openness in models with variable desired markups such as SIGMA.

In this analysis, we have defined openness fairly narrowly as trade openness, and abstracted from the potential implications of the rapid increase in the size of cross border financial claims that have generally accompanied enhanced trade ties. It is quite plausible that changes in financial linkages could play a significantly larger role in influencing the transmission of domestic shocks than suggested by our analysis. This would seem an interesting extension for future research.

Appendix

This appendix describes how the presence of imported materials affect the overall elasticity of demand with respect to the real interest rate.

Proceeding as in section 2.3, simple algebraic manipulations allow us to obtain a relationship among domestic output, the terms of trade, and domestic and foreign shocks. A log-linear approximation to the aggregate resource constraint can be written as follows:

$$y_{Dt} = (1 - \omega_L)(1 - g_y)\{(1 - \omega_c)c_{Dt} + \omega_c m^*_{Ct}\} + \omega_L m^*_{Yt} + (1 - \omega_L)g_y g_t.$$

Following the steps used in section 2.3, the term in brackets $\{(1 - \omega_c)c_{Dt} + \omega_c m^*_{Ct}\}$ can be written in terms of foreign consumption and terms of trade (i.e., $(\sigma^{open}\tau_t - c^*_{Dt})(1 - g_y)(1 - \omega_L)$). The task, then, is to find an expression that relates m^*_{Yt} to foreign variables and the terms of trade. Import demand of materials in the foreign economy is given by*.

$$m^*_{Yt} = y^*_{Dt} + (1 - \omega^*_L)(1 - \omega^*_c)\eta_L[\xi^*_t - z^*_t + \tau_t].$$

Assuming that wages are flexible, we can use the MRS in the foreign economy to express the foreign product real wage in terms of foreign variables and the terms of trade. Thus, domestic demand can be written in a more compact way as follows:

$$y_{Dt} = (\sigma^{open}\tau_t - c^*_{Dt})(1 - g_y)(1 - \omega_L) + \omega L(1 - \omega^*_L)(1 - \omega^*_c)\eta_L\tau_t$$
$$+ (1 - \omega_L)g_y g_t + \omega_L f^*_t,$$

where f^*_t represents a combination of foreign variables. Relative to the benchmark model, the previous expression makes clear that fluctuations in imported materials introduce an additional effect of the terms of trade on domestic output, whose intensity depends upon the share of imported materials on gross production (ω_L), the share of imports of the foreign economy (ω^*_c), and the elasticity of substitution of materials (η_L) and value-added in gross production. The previous expression can be rearranged as follows:

$$y_{Dt} = (\sigma^{open}_M \tau_t - (1 - \omega_L)c^*_{Dt})(1 - g_y) + (1 - \omega_L)g_y g_t + \omega_L f^*_t,$$

where σ^{open}_M is given by:

$$\sigma^{open}_M = \sigma^{open}(1 - \omega_L) + \omega_L \frac{(1 - \omega^*_L)(1 - \omega^*_c)\eta_L}{(1 - g_y)}.$$

Assuming that the home economy is sufficiently small, we can rewrite this expression as:

$$\sigma^{open}_M = \sigma^{open}(1 - \omega_L) + \omega_L \frac{\eta_L}{(1 - g_y)}.$$

If $\omega_L = 0$, this expression is the same as the one for the workhorse model.

*For convenience, we assume that the value-added function is linear in labor ($\alpha = 0$).

References

Altonji, J. G. 1986. Intertemporal substitution in labor supply: Evidence from micro data. *Journal of Political Economy* 94 (3): 176–215.

Attanasio, O., and G. Weber. 1995. Is consumption growth consistent with intertemporal optimization? Evidence from the consumer expenditure survey. *Journal of Political Economy* 103 (6): 1121–57.

Attanasio, O., J. Banks, C. Meghir, and G. Weber. 1999. Humps and bumps in lifetime consumption. *Journal of Business and Economics Statistics* 17 (1): 22–35.

Ball, L. 1994. What determines the sacrifice ratio? In *Monetary policy,* ed. N. G. Mankiw, 155–82. Chicago: University of Chicago Press.

Barsky, R., F. Juster, M. Kimball, and M. Shapiro. 1997. Preferences parameters and behavioral heterogeneity: An experimental approach in the health and retirement study. *Quarterly Journal of Economics* 112: 537–79.

Benigno, G., and P. Benigno. 2003. Price stability in open economies. *Review of Economic Studies* 70 (4): 743–64.

Bergin, P. R., and R. C. Feenstra. 2001. Pricing-to-market, staggered contracts, and real exchange rate persistence. *Journal of International Economics* 54 (2): 333–59.

Betts, C., and M. B. Devereux. 1996. The exchange rate in a model of pricing-to-market. *European Economic Review* 40 (3–5): 1007–21.

Card, D. 1994. Intertemporal labor supply: An assessment. In *Advances in Econometrics, Sixth World Congress,* ed. Christopher Sims, 49–80. New York: Cambridge University Press.

Christiano, L. J., M. Eichenbaum, and C. L. Evans. 2005. Nominal rigidities and the dynamic effects of a shock to monetary policy. *Journal of Political Economy* 113 (1): 1–45.

Clarida, R., J. Galí, and M. Gertler. 1999. The science of monetary policy. *Journal of Economic Literature* 37 (2): 1661–1707.

———. 2001. Optimal monetary policy in open vs. closed economies. *American Economic Review* 91 (May): 253–57.

———. 2002. A simple framework for international monetary policy analysis. *Journal of Monetary Economics* 49 (5): 879–904.

Corsetti, G., and P. Pesenti. 2005. International dimensions of optimal monetary policy. *Journal of Monetary Economics* 52 (2): 281–305.

Devereux, M. B., and C. Engel. 2002. Exchange rate pass-through, exchange rate volatility, and exchange rate disconnect. *Journal of Monetary Economics* 49 (5): 913–40.

———. 2003. Monetary policy in the open economy revisited: Price setting and exchange rate flexibility. *Review of Economic Studies* 70 (4): 765–83.

Dornbusch, R. 1983. Flexible exchange rates and interdependence. *International Monetary Fund Staff Papers* 30 (1): 3–38.

Dornbusch, R., and S. Fischer. 1984. The open economy: Implications for monetary and fiscal policy. In *The American business cycle: Continuity and change,* ed. R. J. Gordon, 459–516. Chicago: University of Chicago Press.

Dotsey, M., and R. G. King. 2005. Implications of state-dependent pricing for dynamic macroeconomic models. *Journal of Monetary Economics* 52 (1): 213–42.

Erceg, C., L. Guerrieri, and C. Gust. 2006. SIGMA: A new open economy model for policy analysis. *Journal of International Central Banking* 2 (1): 1–50.

Erceg, C. J., D. W. Henderson, and A. T. Levin. 2000. Optimal monetary policy with staggered wage and price contracts. *Journal of Monetary Economics* 46 (2): 281–313.

Fleming, M. J. 1962. Domestic financial policies under fixed and floating exchange rates. *IMF Staff Papers* 9 (3): 369–79. Washington, DC: International Monetary Fund.
Galí, J., and T. Monacelli. 2005. Monetary policy and exchange rate volatility in a small open economy. *Review of Economic Studies* 72 (3): 707–34.
Goldberg, P. K., and M. M. Knetter. 1997. Goods prices and exchange rates: What have we learned? *Journal of Economic Literature* 35 (3): 1243–72.
Gust, C., S. Leduc, and R. J. Vigfusson. 2006. Trade integration, competition, and the decline in exchange-rate pass-through. International Finance Discussion Paper no. 864. Board of Governors of the Federal Reserve System.
Gust, C., and N. Sheets. 2006. The adjustment of global external imbalances: Does partial exchange rate pass-through to trade prices matter? Federal Reserve Board, International Finance Discussion Paper no. 850.
Hooper, P., K. Johnson, and J. Marquez. 2000. *Trade elasticities for the G-7 countries, Princeton Studies in International Economics.* Princeton, NJ: Princeton University Press.
Kimball, M. S. 1995. The quantitative analytics of the basic neomonetarist model. *Journal of Money, Credit, and Banking* 27: 1241–77.
Lane, P. R. 2001. The new open economy macroeconomics: A survey. *Journal of International Economics* 54 (2): 235–66.
MacCurdy, T. 1981. An empirical model of labor supply in a life-cycle setting. *Journal of Political Economy* 89 (6): 1059–85.
Marazzi, M., N. Sheets, and R. Vigfusson. 2005. Exchange rate pass-through to U.S. import prices: Some new evidence. Federal Reserve Board, International Finance Discussion Paper no. 833.
McCallum, B. T., and E. Nelson. 1999. Nominal income targeting in an open-economy optimizing model. *Journal of Monetary Economics* 43 (3): 553–79.
Mulligan, C. B. 1999. Substitution over time: Another look at life-cycle labor supply. In *NBER macroeconomics annual 1998,* vol. 13, ed. B. Bernanke and J. Rotemberg, 75–133. Cambridge, MA: MIT Press.
Mundell, R. A. 1962. The appropriate use of monetary and fiscal policy for internal and external stability. *IMF Staff Papers* 9 (1): 70–79. Washington, DC: International Monetary Fund.
Obstfeld, M., and K. Rogoff. 1995. Exchange rate dynamics redux. *Journal of Political Economy* 103 (3): 624–60.
Pencavel, J. 1998. The market work behavior and wages of women, 1975–94. *Journal of Human Resources* 33 (September): 771–804.
Pencavel, J. 2002. A cohort analysis of the association between work and wages among men. *The Journal of Human Resources* 37 (2): 251–74.
Ruhl, K. 2005. The elasticity puzzle in international economics. University of Texas at Austin, mimeo.
Smets, F., and R. Wouters. 2003. An estimated dynamic stochastic general equilibrium model of the euro area. *Journal of the European Economic Association* 1 (5): 1124–75.
Taylor, J. B. 1979. Estimation and control of a macroeconomic model with rational expectations. *Econometrica* 47 (5): 1267–86.
———. 1993. Discretion versus policy rules in practice. *Carnegie-Rochester Series on Public Policy* 39 (1): 195–214.
Turnovsky, S. J. 1985. Domestic and foreign disturbances in an optimizing model of exchange-rate determination. *Journal of International Money and Finance* 4 (1): 151–71.
Woodford, M. 2003. *Interest and prices.* Princeton, NJ: Princeton University Press.
———. 2007. Globalization and monetary control. NBER Working Paper no. 13329. Cambridge, MA: National Bureau of Economic Research, August.

Comment Malin Adolfson

Introduction

Opening up an economy to trade does not only subject it to international linkages in the form of spillovers of foreign disturbances, but also the propagation of purely domestically originated shocks may change because of, for example, expenditure switching effects. Christopher Erceg, Christopher Gust, and David Lopéz-Salido provide an excellent examination of the extent to which trade openness affects the diffusion of three domestic shocks (i.e., inflation target, government spending, and total factor productivity shocks), using a modern two-country dynamic stochastic general equilibrium model (DSGE) SIGMA. The authors also present a very clear understanding of the mechanisms at work by building intuition from a much more stylized model (à la Galí and Monacelli 2005). The chapter thus provides an important contribution to policymakers who need to know how macroeconomic fluctuations are affected and shaped by the increase in world trade.

Erceg, Gust, and Lopéz-Salido find that, under their preferred parameterization and model choice, a larger trade share has relatively small quantitative effects on the transmission of domestic shocks. Impulse responses of aggregate output and domestic prices are mainly unaffected by the degree of openness. In this comment, I will focus my discussion on two aspects that influence the chapter's findings. First, the authors' choice of parameterization, and in particular, the elasticity of substitution between domestic and imported goods, which critically governs the extent to which real quantities respond to disturbances and thereby also how these responses are affected by changes in trade openness. Second, I will discuss the role of monetary policy and how the monetary policy transmission mechanism changes with trade openness, which also influences how shocks are propagated into the economy.

Parameterization and Empirical Validation

The elasticity of substitution between domestic and imported goods is a crucial parameter for any open economy DSGE model since it affects how demand responds to relative prices between foreign and domestically produced goods. A low or a high elasticity has very different implications for the model economy, influencing, for example, the volatilities in international prices and quantities (see also the discussion in Corsetti, Dedola, and Leduc 2008).

Erceg, Gust, and Lopéz-Salido find in their stylized model that the elasticity of substitution between domestic and imported goods (together with

Malin Adolfson is a researcher at Sveriges Riksbank.

The views expressed in this chapter are solely the responsibility of the author and should not be interpreted as reflecting the views of the Executive Board of Sveriges Riksbank.

the Frisch elasticity of labor supply and the intertemporal elasticity of substitution in consumption) critically determines whether openness has large or small effects on output and inflation. This is because the elasticity of substitution between goods influences the slope of the labor supply curve in the same way as openness does; that is, flattening the curve the closer substitutes the goods are or the larger the trade share is. Consequently, with a low elasticity of substitution, consumers prefer not to change their domestic and imported quantities very much in order to smooth aggregate consumption. Because the consumption pattern is more or less fixed, this implies that the consumers do not take advantage of the enhanced possibilities to share risk internationally when the trade share increases. This, in turn, leads to very small effects on domestic responses. In addition, one should bear in mind that the SIGMA model also contains adjustment costs on changing the trade flows, which further limit the consumers' incentives to switch between internationally and domestically produced goods. In this sense it is not surprising that SIGMA responds more like a closed economy to the shocks, irrespective of the degree of trade openness, since there is no strong mechanism for the relative price differentials to propagate into the real economy.

However, as is well known, the elasticity of substitution between domestic and imported goods is notoriously difficult to estimate and the uncertainty in the literature is very large. Micro and macroeconomists reach very different conclusions, where estimates obtained from disaggregate time series and trade data usually are a lot larger than those resulting from macroeconomic data. For example, Harrigan (1993) finds values in the range of 5 to 12 using 3-digit Standard International Trade Classification (SITC) data for thirteen Organization for Economic Cooperation and Development (OECD) countries, Bernard et al. (2003) estimate the elasticity to about 4 using U.S. trade data, whereas Hooper, Johnson, and Marquez (2000) report price elasticities in the range of 0.3 to 1.5 for aggregate U.S. imports and exports.

The recent empirical DSGE literature has also produced very diverse estimates of the elasticity of substitution. Adolfson et al. (2007) show, using euro area data, that including imports among the observed variables in the estimation leads to a relatively high estimate of the elasticity of substitution (5, compared to about 0.5 when imports are excluded). Because imports are a lot more volatile than aggregate consumption, the model needs a high estimate of the elasticity of substitution to account for the fluctuations in both imports and consumption. Lubik and Schorfheide (2005), on the other hand, do not match their DSGE model against any traded quantities and report an estimate of around 0.4, whereas De Walque, Smets, and Wouters (2005) do include the real trade balance in their estimation and find estimates between 1.2 and 1.7 for the U.S. economy.

To get an idea about the robustness of Erceg, Gust, and Lopéz-Salido's results, figure 2C.1 shows the impulse response functions of some key macroeconomic variables to a one standard deviation (transitory) technology shock, using two different elasticities of substitution between domestic and imported goods (i.e., 5 and 1.5) in the model by Adolfson et al. (2008b). In contrast to SIGMA, this model does not contain trade adjustment costs so the difference between the open and closed economy responses are somewhat larger, also with a low elasticity of substitution.[1]

Which estimate should one then rely on when using a macromodel? Is an open economy with "fixed" consumption bundles more reliable than a closed economy specification, and do we believe that the consumers have an ability to substitute between goods? This is still very much an open question.

To determine whether the domestic effects of increased trade openness are quantitatively large or small is, in my view, ultimately an empirical question. Not only do we need to know how the transmission of domestic shocks changes with increased trade shares (which is studied here), but also which types of shocks matter most in the different setups. Even if increased trade openness changes the propagation of certain domestic disturbances, these disturbances may not contribute much to explaining the macroeconomic fluctuations in the open economy (see Adolfson et al. 2008a). An empirical variance decomposition could answer whether different shocks are important for the economic development in the open and closed economies. This could also simplify the parameterization. We know that matching the observed data can require different parameters than expected a priori. This means that conclusions based on a particular parameterization of the model may be overruled when taking the model to the data. As an illustration to this, figure 2C.2 shows the impulse response functions to a transitory technology shock under the prior and posterior modes using the model in Adolfson et al. (2008b). The figure shows that the a priori belief about the parameters has been updated by the data in the estimation, so that the responses obtained under the posterior are quite different from the ones generated by the prior.

The Role of Monetary Policy

Erceg, Gust, and Lopéz-Salido furthermore show that the interest rate sensitivity of aggregate demand increases with trade openness, because net exports are directly affected by the interest rate via the uncovered interest rate parity (UIP) condition and its implied expenditure switching effects. This suggests that the behavior of monetary policy is vital for the impulse responses obtained under different trade shares. By comparing variance trade-offs in the (domestic) inflation-output space and studying implied real interest rate volatilities, the authors conclude that the relatively small differences in responses between the closed and open economy specifications

1. The steady-state import share in the open economy is about 20 percent in the model by Adolfson et al., although it should be remembered that the value of the elasticity of substitution between the goods affects this share.

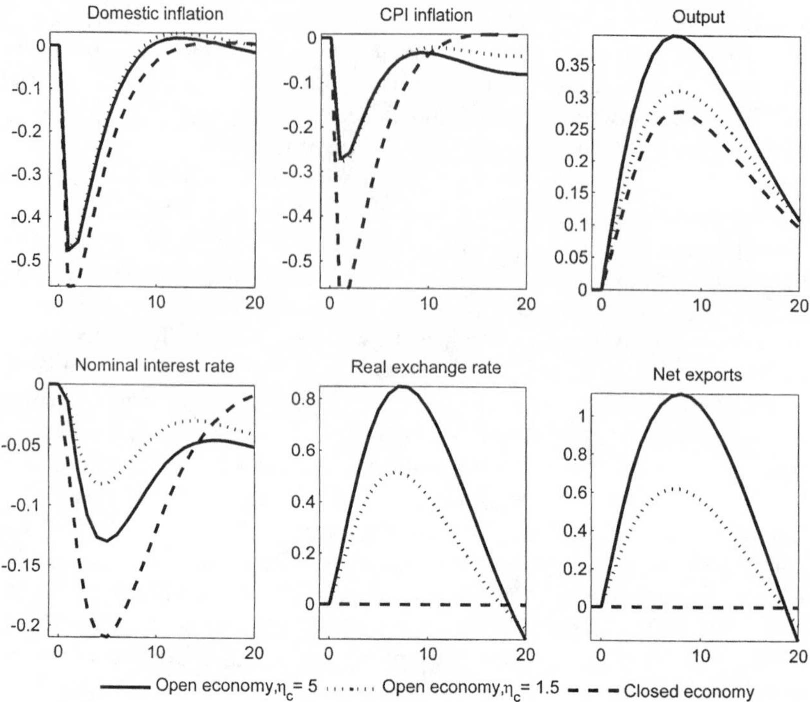

Fig. 2C.1 Impulse response functions to a transitory technology shock
Note: Percentage deviations from steady state

are mainly due to the aggregate demand block, since the inflation-output variance frontiers do not differ much whereas the implied interest rate volatility is a lot lower in the open economy.

I want to raise two comments in relation to this. First, conditioning the analysis upon an ad hoc quadratic loss function in only domestic inflation and the output gap implies that very large swings in the interest rate are permitted. In practice, however, interest rate smoothing appears to be an integral part of everyday central banking. Including an interest rate argument in the loss function would penalize the closed economy central bank more than that in the open economy, just because the exchange rate channel of monetary policy has less impact the lower the trade share is. This has consequences also for the variance trade-offs between inflation and output, since the closed economy policy becomes less efficient in stabilizing inflation and output in such a case, and the discrepancies between the closed and open economies would increase. To see how the exchange rate channel of transmitting monetary policy changes with openness, figure 2C.3 displays the impulse response functions to a monetary policy shock in the closed and

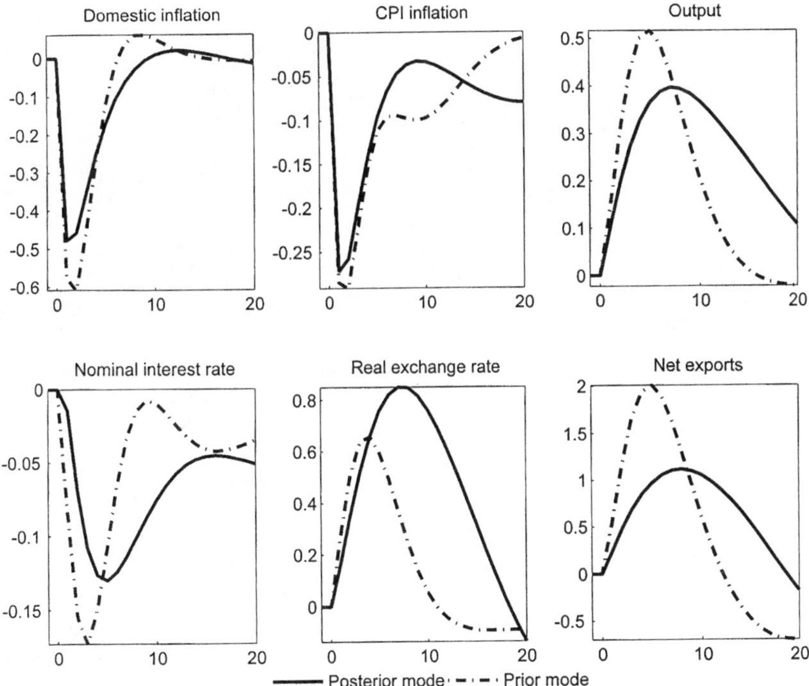

Fig. 2C.2 Impulse response functions to a transitory technology shock, prior and posterior mode

Note: Percentage deviations from steady state

open setup of the model in Adolfson et al. (2008b). The figure shows that the inflation rates respond much more to an interest rate increase of twenty-five basis points in the open economy than in the closed economy, which can be exploited by the central bank without an interest rate smoothing term in the loss function.

Second, the authors use *GDP deflator inflation* as the relevant inflation objective in their loss function, irrespective of the degree of openness. It should be remembered that the variance trade-off between *CPI inflation* and output is very different in the closed and open economies. In a similar framework to the stylized model here, Clarida, Galí, and Gertler (2001) show that the open economy monetary policy problem under the stated loss function is isomorphic to the closed economy policy problem, assuming that the law of one price holds. However, when there is incomplete exchange rate pass-through, as is the case in the SIGMA model, it can be welfare enhancing for the central bank to stabilize consumer price index (CPI) inflation rather than domestic inflation (Corsetti and Pesenti 2005). Because the households' consumption basket is specified in terms of both domestically produced goods and imported goods and there are distortions in the form of price stickiness

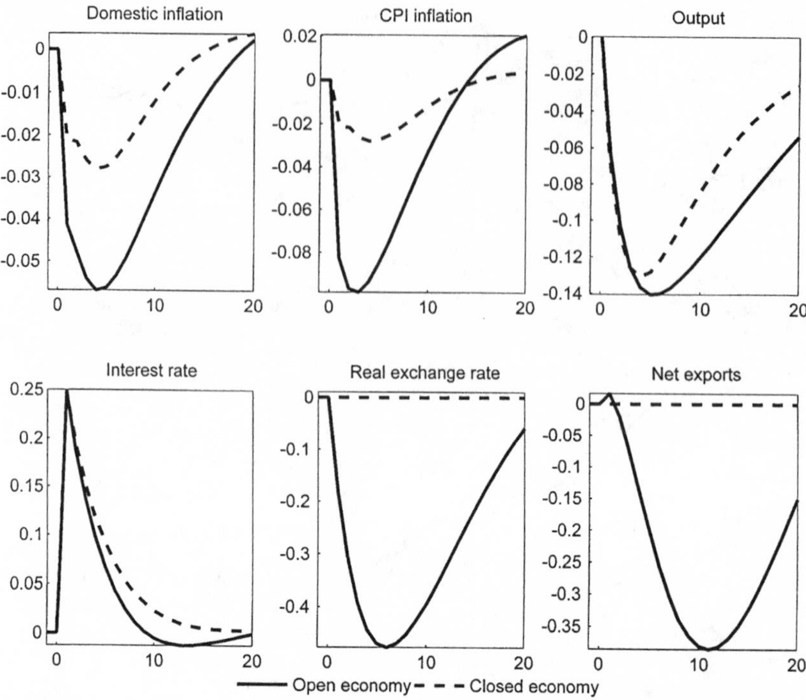

Fig. 2C.3 Impulse response functions to a monetary policy shock, closed and open economy

Note: Percentage deviations from steady state

in both sectors, the central bank should stabilize CPI inflation in this case. If this is accounted for here, there will be larger differences between the variance trade-offs in the closed and open economies and the intuition from the stylized model may not carry over to the more complex SIGMA model.

Final Remarks

To conclude, Erceg, Gust, and Lopéz-Salido have nicely argued that trade openness can have relatively modest effects on how domestic shocks affect the economy. Still, there is uncertainty about some of the key aspects that influence how international linkages operate, which is why I think more empirical work on these issues is desirable.

References

Adolfson, M., S. Laséen, J. Lindé, and M. Villani. 2007. Bayesian estimation of an open economy DSGE model with incomplete pass-through. *Journal of International Economics* 72 (2): 481–511.

———. 2008a. Empirical properties of closed and open economy DSGE models of the euro area. *Macroeconomic Dynamics* 12 (S1): 2–19.

———. 2008b. Evaluating an estimated new Keynesian small open economy model. *Journal of Economic Dynamics and Control* 32 (8): 2690–2721.

Bernard, A., J. Eaton, B. Jensen, and S. Kortum. 2003. Plants and productivity in international trade. *American Economic Review* 93 (4): 1268–90.

Clarida, R., J. Galí, and M. Gertler. 2001. Optimal monetary policy in open versus closed economies: An integrated approach. *American Economic Review* 91 (2): 248–52.

Corsetti, G., L. Dedola, and S. Leduc. 2008. International risk sharing and the transmission of productivity shocks. *Review of Economic Studies* 75 (2): 443–73.

Corsetti, G., and P. Pesenti. 2005. International dimensions of monetary policy. *Journal of Monetary Economics* 52: 281–305.

De Walque, G., F. Smets, and R. Wouters. 2005. An estimated two-country DSGE model for the euro area and the U.S. economy. National Bank of Belgium. Unpublished Manuscript.

Galí, J., and T. Monacelli. 2005. Monetary policy and exchange rate volatility in a small open economy. *Review of Economic Studies* 72 (3): 707–34.

Harrigan, J. 1993. OECD imports and trade barriers in 1983. *Journal of International Economics* 35 (1–2): 91–111.

Hooper, P., K. Johnson, and J. Marquez. 2000. *Trade elasticities for the G-7 countries, Princeton Studies in International Economics.* Princeton, NJ: Princeton University Press.

Lubik, T., and F. Schorfheide. 2005. A Bayesian look at new open economy macroeconomics. In *NBER Macroeconomics Annual,* ed. M. Gertler, and K. Rogoff, 313–66. Cambridge, MA: MIT Press.

3

International Transmission and Monetary Policy Cooperation

Günter Coenen, Giovanni Lombardo, Frank Smets, and Roland Straub

3.1 Introduction

The analysis of the implications of international economic interdependencies for the gains from cross-country cooperation between monetary authorities has a long history. More than three decades ago, Hamada (1976) recognized that "[m]ost traditional approaches do not seem to pay due attention to the interdependent nature of monetary policies." Hamada's seminal paper has spurred a large literature addressing this issue using a variety of models, methodologies, and game-theoretic concepts. The literature of the 1980s (e.g., Canzoneri and Gray 1985; Canzoneri and Henderson 1992) has shown that the potential gains from cooperation are proportional to the size of the international policy spillovers and these, in turn, depend on the parameter values of the model. Since then, open economy models have changed considerably, calling for a reconsideration of the earlier wisdom. In particular, efforts to give stronger microfoundations to the parameters of the model have resulted in the so-called New Open Economy Macroeconomics (NOEM) literature (Lane 2001). Using a stylized representative NOEM model, Obstfeld and Rogoff (2002) came to the conclusion that the gains

Günter Coenen is Head of Division of the Econometric Modelling division of the European Central Bank. Giovanni Lombardo is Senior Economist in the Monetary Policy Research division of the European Central Bank. Frank Smets is Director General of the Directorate General Research of the European Central Bank. Roland Straub is Senior Economist in the International Policy Analysis division of the European Central Bank.

This chapter was prepared for the NBER conference "International Dimensions of Monetary Policy," S'Agaró, Spain, 11–13 June 2007. We thank the organizers of the conference, Mark Gertler and Jordi Galí, the participants to the conference, and in particular our discussant Chris Sims, for their useful comments and suggestions. All remaining errors are our sole responsibility. The views expressed in this chapter do not necessarily reflect those of the European Central Bank.

from cooperation are at best very small. However, Canzoneri, Cumby, and Diba (2002) pointed out that the NOEM literature, per se, does not imply that self-oriented policy-making should be recommended. The results, once more, strongly depend on the value of some crucial parameters (see also Benigno [2002] and Sutherland [2004] on this point). Moreover, Benigno and Benigno (2006) argued that the gains from cooperation are also crucially dependent on the sources of the shocks affecting the economy, again a finding that was also true in the earlier literature. There is, therefore, a need to move away from the stylized NOEM models and consider richer models with a variety of shocks and frictions that have been calibrated or estimated to match international business cycle properties. In the end, whether the potential gains from cooperation are large or small is an empirical question. In this chapter, we attempt to move in that direction and therefore to close the circle with papers like Oudiz and Sachs (1984)—written two decades ago—that addressed similar issues using traditional large-scale models.[1] Two main differences with this older literature are that our analysis does not impose certainty equivalence and that the welfare measure is based on the preferences of the agents.

In order to quantify the gains from cooperation, we use a version of the New Area-Wide Model (NAWM) developed at the European Central Bank (ECB). The NAWM is a two-region dynamic stochastic general equilibrium (DSGE) model that is calibrated to represent the euro area (EA) and U.S. economies. The version used in this chapter is a simplified version of the model presented in Coenen, McAdam, and Straub (2007), which has been recalibrated in order to capture a number of empirical stylized facts. It contains nominal and real frictions such as nominal stickiness and indexation in intermediate goods prices, wages and import prices, monopolistic competition in goods and labor markets, habit formation, investment adjustment costs, home bias in consumption, and incomplete international financial markets. In addition, it features a number of different sources of shocks including technology, labor supply, investment, preference, markup, and exchange rate shocks.

We then use the model to derive the welfare-based optimal monetary policy under cooperation and under a particular definition of an open-loop Nash equilibrium. In this context, our chapter relates to the literature that addresses optimal monetary and/or fiscal policy in DSGE models with steady-state distortions, such as in Benigno and Woodford (2004a, 2004b) and Schmitt-Grohé and Uribe (2004a, 2004b, 2007a). We carry out a similar welfare-based optimal monetary policy analysis in a medium scale two-country open economy model, thereby complementing the analytical results in a very stylized version of a similar model in Clarida, Galí, and Gertler

1. De Fiore and Lombardo (2007) perform a similar analysis in a three-country DSGE model with trade in oil. They also find that the gains from cooperation are small.

(2002) and Benigno and Benigno (2003). In the benchmark Cournot-Nash game, we assume that each central bank takes the money growth path of the foreign central bank as given. However, we also discuss alternative choices of instruments and present results based on simple interest rate feedback rules.

Three conclusions of our benchmark analysis are worth highlighting. First, we show that the gains from cooperation are very sensitive to the degree of international economic integration. Given the current degree of openness of the U.S. and euro area economies, and in line with the recent literature, we find that the gains from cooperation are small. They amount to about 0.03 percent of steady-state consumption. This is an order of magnitude higher than the gains suggested by Obstfeld and Rogoff (2002), but nevertheless very small. Allowing for stronger economic integration between the two regions can bring about sizable gains from cooperation. For example, when the share of import in gross domestic product (GDP) is increased from 10 to 15 percent to about 32 percent in both regions, the gains from cooperation rise to about 1 percent of steady-state consumption. Second, by decomposing the sources of the gains from cooperation with respect to the various shocks, we confirm the findings of Benigno and Benigno (2006) that the markup shocks can bring about larger gains from cooperation. Overall, the gains from cooperation are an order of magnitude larger for the markup shocks than for each of the other shocks we consider. This may reflect the fact that those shocks are the most important source of inflation variability in the economy and that they are the most problematic for the monetary authorities in terms of creating policy trade-offs. Third, we perform a sensitivity analysis with respect to various key parameters of the model and find that the gains from cooperation become considerably larger when prices in the domestic intermediate goods sector become less sticky. With respect to most other parameters that we investigate, the gains from cooperation remain very small. For example, in line with the results of Obstfeld and Rogoff (2002), we find that complete international financial markets further reduce the gains from cooperation. It is also worth mentioning that in the benchmark model the gains from cooperation are quite symmetric. However, this result appears to be quite sensitive to the precise calibration of the model.

Not surprisingly, the discussion of the results of alternative assumptions regarding the strategy space (i.e., the open-loop Nash game and the simple closed-loop interest rate feedback Nash games) highlights that the size of the gains from cooperation depends very much on the definition of the noncooperative game. However, we argue that for the most reasonable definitions, the conclusions highlighted previously hold.

The rest of the chapter is structured as follows. Section 3.2 lays out the main structure of the two-region DSGE model. Section 3.3 discusses its calibration. Section 3.4 presents the two monetary policy games we study. Section 3.5 discusses the main results. Section 3.6 discusses the gains from cooperation when central banks follow simple feedback rules. Section 3.7 contains the conclusions.

3.2 A Two-Region DSGE Model

As discussed in the introduction, the model we use to investigate the gains from international monetary policy cooperation is a simplified version of the NAWM discussed in Coenen, McAdam, and Straub (2007). In particular, relative to Coenen, McAdam, and Straub (2007), three main differences are worth mentioning. First, it has only one type of representative household for each country. Second, the fiscal sector is simplified by assuming the budget is balanced at all times. And, third, there are no import adjustment costs. These simplifications were mainly done for computational reasons.

Nevertheless, in order to investigate the interaction between market imperfections and the gains of cooperation, the model consists of several real and nominal frictions. In particular, the domestic goods and import sector as well as the labor market are subject to monopolistic competition and staggered price and wage setting, respectively. Notice that we only allow for a stochastic markup in the domestic goods market. Furthermore, we also assume incomplete international asset markets in order to investigate the impact of imperfect risk-sharing on the gains of cooperation.

The model consists of two symmetric regions of normalized population size s and $1 - s$, respectively: the euro area (EA), denoted as home country, and the United States.[2] In each country, there are four types of economic agents: households, firms, a fiscal authority, and a monetary authority.

In the following, we outline the behavior of the different types of agents and state the market-clearing conditions and resource constraints that need to be satisfied in equilibrium. We focus on the exposition of the home country, with the understanding that the foreign country is similarly characterized. To the extent needed, foreign variables and parameters are indexed with an asterisk.

3.2.1 Households

The preferences of household i are described by the following intertemporal constant relative risk aversion (CRRA) utility function

$$(1)\quad E_t\left[\sum_{k=0}^{\infty}\beta^k\varepsilon_t^C\left(\frac{1}{1-\sigma}(C_{i,t+k}-\kappa C_{i,t+k-1})^{1-\sigma}\right.\right.$$
$$\left.\left.-\frac{\varepsilon_t^N}{1+\zeta}(N_{i,t+k})^{1+\zeta}+\frac{\varepsilon^M}{1-\psi}\left(\frac{M_{i,t}}{P_t}\right)^{1-\psi}\right)\right],$$

2. The model builds on recent advances in developing microfounded DSGE models suitable for quantitative policy analysis, as exemplified by the closed economy model of the euro area by Smets and Wouters (2003), the International Monetary Fund's Global Economy Model (GEM) (Bayoumi, Laxton, and Pesenti 2001) or the Federal Reserve Board's new open economy model named SIGMA (Erceg, Guerrieri, and Gust 2006).

where $C_{i,t}$ is a consumption index, $N_{i,t}$ denotes labor services (differentiated across households) and $M_{i,t}$ are nominal money balances; β is the discount factor, σ denotes the inverse of the intertemporal elasticity of substitution, and ζ is the inverse of the elasticity of work effort with respect to the real wage. The parameter κ measures the degree of habit formation in consumption, and ε_t^C and ε_t^N are AR(1) preference and labor supply shocks, respectively. Thus, the utility of the household depends positively on the quasi-difference between current and lagged individual consumption, and negatively on individual labor supply. Money is introduced in the utility function in order to obtain a money demand equation (used for monetary policy as described in the following). The inverse of the interest rate elasticity of money is denoted by ψ and the weight of money balances in the utility function is denoted by ε^M. The consumption price index (CPI) is P_t, defined later. Following most of the open economy related literature (e.g., Obstfeld and Rogoff 2002) we assume that the weight of real balances in the household preferences is negligible (i.e., $\varepsilon^M \to 0$).

Households face the following period-by-period budget constraint:

$$(1 + \tau_t^C)P_tC_{i,t} + P_tI_{i,t} + R_t^{-1}B_{i,t+1} + M_{i,t+1} + ((1 - \Gamma_{B^F}))R_{F,t})^{-1}S_tB_{i,t+1}^F$$
$$= (1 - \tau_t^N)W_{i,t}N_{i,t} + R_{K,t}K_{i,t} + D_{i,t} + T_{i,t} + B_{i,t} + S_tB_{i,t}^F + M_{i,t},$$

where R_t and R_t^F denote the riskless returns on domestic bonds and internationally traded bonds, respectively. Internationally traded bonds are denominated in foreign currency and thus, their domestic value depends on the nominal exchange rate S_t (expressed in terms of units of home currency per unit of foreign currency). The labor services provided to firms at wage rate $W_{i,t}$ is denoted by $N_{i,t}$, and $R_{K,t}$ indicates the rental rate for the capital services rented to firms $K_{i,t}$ and $D_{i,t}$ are the dividends paid by household-owned firms from the domestic production and import sector. Furthermore, we have introduced distortionary consumption and wage income taxes into the model, denoted by τ_t^c and τ_t^N, respectively.

Similarly, $\Gamma_{B^F}(B_t^F)$ represents a financial intermediation premium that households must pay when taking a position in the international bond market. The premium is a function of the aggregate net foreign asset position of the country and not of the single household's position. Finally, it is implicitly assumed that households hold state-contingent securities. These securities are traded among households and provide insurance against individual wage income risk. This guarantees that the marginal utility of consumption out of wage income is identical across individual households. As a result, all households will choose identical allocations in equilibrium (for simplicity these securities are not shown).

The capital stock owned by households evolves according to the following capital accumulation equation,

$$K_{i,t+1} = (1 - \delta)K_{i,t} + \left(1 - \Gamma_I\left(\frac{\varepsilon_t^I I_{i,t}}{I_{i,t-1}}\right)\right), I_{i,t},$$

where δ is the depreciation rate and $\Gamma_I(\varepsilon_t^I I_{i,t}/I_{i,t-1})$ is the adjustment cost function formulated in terms of changes in investment subject to a time varying AR(1) shock process ε_t^I.

Choice of Allocations

Defining as Λ_t/P_t and $\Lambda_t Q_t$, the Lagrange multipliers associated with the budget constraint and the capital accumulation equation, respectively, the first-order conditions for maximizing the household member's lifetime utility function with respect to $C_{i,t}$, $I_{i,t}$, $K_{i,t+1}$, $B_{i,t+1}$, $B_{i,t+1}^F$, $M_{i,t}$ are given by:

$$\frac{\Lambda_{i,t}}{P_t} = \varepsilon_t^C \frac{(C_{i,t} - \kappa C_{i,t-1})^{-\sigma}}{(1+\tau_t^C)}, \tag{2}$$

$$1 = Q_t\left(1 - \Gamma_I \frac{\varepsilon_t^I I_{i,t}}{I_{i,t-1}} - \Gamma'_I \frac{\varepsilon_t^I I_{i,t}}{I_{i,t-1}} \frac{\varepsilon_t^I I_{i,t}}{I_{i,t-1}}\right) + \beta \mathrm{E}_t\left(\frac{\Lambda_{i,t+1}}{\Lambda_{i,t}} Q_{t+1} \Gamma'_I \frac{\varepsilon_{t+1}^I I_{i,t+1}}{I_{i,t}} \frac{\varepsilon_{t+1}^I I_{i,t+1}^2}{I_{i,t}^2}\right),$$

$$Q_t = \beta \mathrm{E}_t \frac{\Lambda_{i,t+1} P_t}{\Lambda_{i,t} P_{t+1}}\left((1-\delta)Q_{t+1} \frac{R_{K,t+1}}{P_{t+1}}\right),$$

$$\beta R_t \mathrm{E}_t\left(\frac{\Lambda_{i,t+1}}{\Lambda_{i,t}} \frac{P_t}{P_{t+1}}\right) = 1,$$

$$\beta(1 - \Gamma_{B^F}(B_t^F))R_{F,t}\mathrm{E}_t\left[\frac{\Lambda_{i,t+1}}{\Lambda_{i,t}} \frac{P_t}{P_{t+1}} \frac{S_{t+1}}{S_t}\right] + \varepsilon_t^{UIP} = 1,$$

$$\Lambda_{i,t} = \varepsilon_t^C \varepsilon^M \left(\frac{M_{i,t}}{P_t}\right)^{-\psi} + \beta \mathrm{E}_t\left[\Lambda_{i,t+1} \frac{P_t}{P_{t+1}}\right],$$

where Λ_t is the marginal utility of consumption, Q_t measures the shadow price of a unit of the investment good (Tobin's Q), and ε_t^{UIP} stands for a white noise UIP shock.

Wage Setting

Households act as wage setters for their differentiated labor services $N_{i,t}$ in monopolistically competitive markets. We assume that the wages for the differentiated labor services, $\tilde{W}_t$, are determined by staggered nominal wage contracts à la Calvo (1983). Thus, households receive permission to optimally reset their nominal wage contract in a given period t with probability $1 - \xi_W$. All household members that receive permission to reset their wage contract choose the same wage rate $\tilde{W}_t$. Those households that do not receive permission are allowed to adjust the wage contract at least partially according to the following scheme:

$$W_{i,t} = \left(\frac{P_{t-1}}{P_{t-2}}\right)^{\chi W} \pi^{1-\chi W} W_{i,t-1},$$

where parameter χ_W measures the degree of indexation to past changes in the price level P_t, π is the steady-state inflation, and i is the index of an individual household.

Households that receive permission to optimally reset their wage contracts in period t are assumed to maximize lifetime utility, as represented by equation (1), taking into account the wage-indexation scheme and the demand for their labor services (the formal derivation of which we postpone until we consider the firms' problem).

Each household faces the following demand for its labor services:

$$N_{i,t} = \left(\frac{\tilde{W}_{i,t}}{W_t}\right)^{-\eta} N_t,$$

where η is the wage-elasticity of labor demand, W_t is the aggregate nominal wage index, and $N_t = \int_0^1 N_{i,t} di$.

Hence, we obtain the following first-order condition for the optimal wage setting decision in period t:

$$E_t\left[\sum_{k=0}^{\infty} \xi_W^k \beta^k \Lambda_{i,t+k}\left((1-\tau_t^N)\frac{\tilde{W}_{i,t}}{P_{t+k}}\left(\frac{P_{t+k-1}}{P_{t-1}}\right)^{\chi_W} \pi^{(1-\chi_W)k} - \frac{\eta}{\eta-1}\varepsilon_t^N (N_{i,t+k})^{\zeta}\right) N_{i,t+k}\right] = 0.$$

This expression states that in those labor markets in which wage contracts are reoptimized, the latter are set so as to equate the household's discounted sum of expected after-tax marginal revenues to the discounted sum of expected marginal disutility of labor.

3.2.2 Firms

There are three types of firms: a continuum of monopolistically competitive domestic firms, each of which produces a single tradable differentiated intermediate good, $Y_{f,t}$; a monopolistically competitive import sector receiving foreign goods "at the dock;" and a set of representative firms, which combine purchases of domestically produced intermediate goods with purchases of imported intermediate goods into a distinct nontradable intermediate good $Q_{f,t}$. All firms are indexed by $f \in [0, 1]$.

Intermediate Goods Firms

Each intermediate good firm f produces its differentiated output using a Cobb-Douglas technology,

$$(3) \qquad Y_{f,t} = z_t K_{f,t}^{\alpha} N_{f,t}^{(1-\alpha)},$$

utilizing as inputs homogeneous private capital services, $K_{f,t}$, that are rented from households in fully competitive markets, and labor services, N_t. The productivity processes, z_t and z_t^*, are assumed to follow a symmetric bivariate first-order autoregressive process defining global productivity with cross-correlated innovations, as in Backus and Crucini (2000).

Capital and Labor Inputs Taking the rental cost of capital $R_{K,t}$ and wage W_t as given, the firm's optimal demand for capital and labor services must solve the problem of minimizing total input cost $R_{K,t}K_{f,t} + W_tN_{f,t}$ subject to the technology constraint (3).

Defining as $MC_{f,t}$ the Lagrange multiplier associated with the technology constraint (3), the first-order conditions of the firm's cost minimization problem with respect to capital and labor inputs are given by

$$\alpha\frac{Y_{f,t}}{K_{f,t}}(1 - \tau_t^f)MC_{f,t} = R_{K,t}, \tag{4}$$

$$(1 - \alpha)\frac{Y_{f,t}}{N_{f,t}}(1 - \tau_t^f)MC_{f,t} = W_t, \tag{5}$$

where τ_t^f is a stochastic (i.i.d.) subsidy to firms. We introduce this subsidy à la Benigno and Benigno (2006) in order to generate cost-push shocks.[3] In what follows we refer to this shock as a markup shock.

The Lagrange multiplier $MC_{f,t}$ measures the nominal marginal cost. We note that, since all firms f face the same input prices and since they all have access to the same production technology, nominal marginal costs $MC_{f,t}$ are identical across firms; that is, $MC_{f,t} = MC_t$.

Price Setting Each firm f sells its differentiated output $H_{f,t}$ in the domestic markets or to foreign importers (the demand of which is denoted by $X_{f,t+k}$) under monopolistic competition and there is sluggish price adjustment due to staggered price contracts à la Calvo (1983). Accordingly, firm f receives permission to optimally reset its price in a given period t with probability $1 - \xi_H$.

Defining as $P_{H,f,t}$ the price of good f, all firms that receive permission to reset their price contracts in a given period t choose the same price. Those firms that do not receive permission are allowed to adjust their prices according to the following schemes:

$$P_{H,f,t} = \left(\frac{P_{t-1}}{P_{t-2}}\right)^{\chi_H}\pi^{1-\chi_H}P_{H,f,t-1};$$

that is, the price contracts are indexed to a convex combination of past changes in the aggregate price index, $P_{H,t}$, and the steady-state inflation rate, π, where χ_H is a constant indexation weight.

3. Often cost-push shocks are modeled as stochastic elasticity of substitution between goods (e.g., Smets and Wouters 2003). Such an assumption generates firm-specific pricing equations when solved to higher orders of approximation, making the model intractable.

Each firm f receiving permission to optimally reset its price in period t maximizes the discounted sum of its expected after-tax real profits,

$$E_t\left[\sum_{k=0}^{\infty} \Lambda_{t,t+k}(\xi_H^k D_{H,f,t+k})\right],$$

subject to the price indexation scheme and taking as given the aggregate domestic (H_t) and foreign (X_t) demand for home produced goods and subject to an elastic demand for its product defined as

$$Y_{f,t} = \left(\frac{P_{H,f,t}}{P_{H,t}}\right)^{-\theta}(H_t + X_t).$$

Here, $\Lambda_{t,t+k}$ is the firm's discount rate, defined as the households' real discount factor, while $D_{H,f,t} = (P_{H,f,t} - MC_t)Y_{f,t}$ are period-t nominal profits.

Hence, we obtain the following first-order condition characterizing the firm's optimal pricing decision for its output sold in the domestic and foreign market assuming producer currency pricing:

$$E_t\left[\sum_{k=0}^{\infty} \xi_H^k \Lambda_{t,t+k}\left(\tilde{P}_{H,t}\left(\frac{P_{t+k-1}}{P_{t-1}}\right)^{\chi_H}\pi^{(1-\chi_H)k} - \frac{(1-\tau_t^f)\theta}{\theta-1}MC_{t+k}\right)Y_{f,t}\right] = 0.$$

This expression states that in those intermediate good markets in which price contracts are reoptimized, the latter are set so as to equate the firms' discounted sum of expected revenues to the discounted sum of expected marginal cost.

Import Sector

In this section, we discuss briefly the optimization problem of the local importers who import foreign goods for which the law of one price holds; that is, $P_{IM,f,t}^D = S_t P_{F,f,t}$, as discussed in Monacelli (2005). Note $P_{IM,f,t}^D$ is the "price at the dock" of the imported good f, where perfect pass-through still holds. Imperfect exchange rate pass-through, however, is ensured via nominal rigidities in the import sector. This feature implies a deviation from both extreme assumptions on import pricing; namely, local versus producer currency pricing that characterize a wide array of the papers in the New Open Economy Macroeconomics literature. The empirical evidence appears to be in favor of the chosen specification, implying that the degree of pass-through is partial in the short-run but complete in the long-run, as demonstrated, for example, by Campa and Goldberg (2002).

In contrast to Monacelli (2005), however, in our setup imported, differentiated intermediate goods are combined at the dock to a composite of imported goods at the dock using a constant elasticity of substitution (CES) technology. The demand faced by each single importer is defined as

$$IM_{f,t} = \left(\frac{P_{IM,f,t}}{P_{IM,t}}\right)^{-\theta_{IM}} IM_t.$$

Price adjustment in the import sector is also sluggish due to staggered price contracts à la Calvo (1983). As a result, the following first-order condition characterizes the importer's optimal pricing decision:

$$E_t\left[\sum_{k=0}^{\infty}\xi_{IM}^k\Lambda_{t,t+k}\left(\tilde{P}_{IM,t}\left(\frac{P_{t+k-1}}{P_{t-1}}\right)^{\chi_{IM}}\pi^{(1-\chi_{IM})k}-\frac{\theta_{IM}}{\theta_{IM}-1}P_{IM,t}^D\right)IM_{f,t+k}\right]=0,$$

where $P_{IM,t}^D$ is the price of the composite of the infinite number of imported intermediate goods "at the dock," θ_{IM} is the elasticity of substitution between different types of imported goods, and $\tilde{P}_{IM,t}$ is the price chosen by importers that receive permission to reset their price contracts in a given period t. Note also that the Calvo-parameter ξ_{IM} can be interpreted as the degree of exchange rate pass-through in the model.

Final Good Firms

The representative final good firm (we neglect the indexation in what follows) produces the nontradable intermediate good, Q_t, combines purchases of a bundle of domestically produced intermediate goods, H_t, with purchases of a bundle of goods from the import sector, IM_t, using a constant returns to scale CES technology,

$$Q_t = (\nu^{1/\mu}H_t^{1-1/\mu} + (1-\nu)^{1/\mu}IM_t^{1-1/\mu})^{\mu/(\mu-1)}, \tag{6}$$

where the parameter μ denotes the intratemporal elasticity of substitution between the distinct bundles of domestic and imported goods, while $\nu \in (0, 1)$ is a measure of home bias in the production of the intermediate good. The demand function for domestic intermediate and imported goods are defined as:

$$H_t = \left(\frac{P_{H,t}}{P_t}\right)^{-\mu}Q_t,$$

$$IM_t = \left(\frac{P_{IM,t}}{P_t}\right)^{-\mu}Q_t,$$

where the corresponding price index (CPI) P_t is defined as

$$P_t = (\nu(P_{H,t})^{1-\mu} + (1-\nu)P_{IM_t,t}^{1-\mu})^{1/(1-\mu)}.$$

Note that we assume implicitly that the share of foreign goods in investment, consumption, and government spending are the same, and that there are no differences in the corresponding price indexes of the variables.

3.2.3 Fiscal and Monetary Authorities

The fiscal authority purchases the final good, G_t, and levies lump sum taxes T_t and distortionary taxes (subsidies) on households (firms). The fiscal authority's period-by-period budget constraint then has the following form:

$$P_tG_t = T_t + \tau_t^C P_t C_t + \tau_t^N W_t N_t + \tau_t^f D_t.$$

In the benchmark New Area-Wide Model the monetary authority is assumed to follow a Taylor-type interest rate rule (Taylor 1993) specified in terms of consumer price inflation and output,

$$R_t = \phi_R R_{t-1} + (1 - \phi_R)\left[R + \phi_\Pi\left(\frac{P_t}{P_{t-1}} - \Pi\right)\right] + \phi_{g_Y} Y_t + \varepsilon_{R,t},$$

where $R = \beta^{-1}\Pi$ is the equilibrium nominal interest rate, Π denotes the monetary authority's inflation target, and the term $\varepsilon_{R,t}$ represents a serially uncorrelated monetary policy shock.

3.2.4 Aggregation and Aggregate Resource Constraint

The model is closed by imposing market clearing conditions and formulating the aggregate resource constraint.

Aggregation

Aggregate Wage Dynamics With households setting their wage contracts W_t according to the described scheme, the aggregate wage index evolves according to

$$W_t = \left((1 - \xi_W)(\tilde{W}_t)^{1-\eta} + \xi_W\left(\left(\frac{P_{t-1}}{P_{t-2}}\right)^{\chi_W} \pi^{(1-\chi_W)} W_{t-1}\right)^{1-\eta}\right)^{1/(1-\eta)}.$$

Aggregate Price Dynamics With intermediate good firms f setting their price contracts for the differentiated products sold domestically, $P_{H,f,t}$, according to the described scheme, the aggregate nominal price index evolves according to

$$P_{H,t} = \left((1 - \xi_H)(\tilde{P}_{H,t})^{1-\theta} + \xi_H\left(\left(\frac{P_{t-1}}{P_{t-2}}\right)^{\chi_H} \pi^{(1-\chi_H)} P_{H,t-1}\right)^{1-\theta}\right)^{1/(1-\theta)}.$$

Similarly, the import prices $P_{IM,t}$ evolve according to:

$$P_{IM,t} = \left((1 - \xi_{IM})(\tilde{P}_{IM,t})^{1-\theta_{IM}} + \xi_{IM}\left(\left(\frac{P_{t-1}}{P_{t-2}}\right)^{\chi_{IM}} \pi^{(1-\chi_{IM})} P_{IM,t-1}\right)^{1-\theta_{IM}}\right)^{1/(1-\theta_{IM})}.$$

Aggregate Resource Constraint

The imposed market clearing conditions imply the following aggregate resource constraint:

$$\int_0^1 P_{f,t} Y_{f,t} = P_t C_t + P_t I_t + P_t G_t + TB_t,$$

where $TB_t = P_{H,t}X_t - P^D_{IM,t} IM_t$ is the home country's trade balance.

Given the aggregate resource constraint, the domestic holdings of internationally traded bonds (that is, the home country's [net] foreign assets) denominated in foreign currency, evolve over time according to

$$((1 - \Gamma_{B^F}(B_t^F))R_{F,t})^{-1}B_{t+1}^F = B_t^F + \frac{TB_t}{S_t}. \tag{7}$$

Overall, the model contains six domestic sources of stochastic shocks in each country: a productivity, an investment, a preference, a labor supply, a markup, and a monetary policy shock. In addition, there is a white-noise exchange rate shock (UIP) that results from variations in the costs of international financial intermediation. As mentioned earlier, the home and foreign productivity shocks are assumed to be partially cross-correlated.

3.3 Calibration

In order to be able to derive realistic empirical estimates of the gains from cooperation, ideally we would want to have an estimated version of the two-region model discussed previously. In the absence of such an estimated version, we have applied three different criteria for parametrizing the model.[4] First, our intention was to keep the impulse response functions of the model close to the extended NAWM as described in Coenen, McAdam, and Straub (2007). Therefore, we have left some of the parameters that are key in determining the dynamics of the model close to their values chosen in the NAWM. Second, we set the properties of the shocks and the parameter values of the model, such as: (a) to replicate the volatility and correlations of some relevant variables such as output, consumption, and investment; and (b) to generate realistic contributions of structural shocks to the variances of key endogenous variables. One benchmark in this respect is de Walque, Smets, and Wouters (2005).

We set the size of the home country to 0.43 corresponding to the size of the euro area's GDP relative to the U.S. GDP. The home bias in the euro area is set to 0.85 and in the United States to 0.9, reflecting the fact that the euro area is relatively more open than the United States. We have set the habit persistence parameter in both countries to 0.6, which is in line with a weighted average of estimates reported by Schorfheide and Lubik (2005) and de Walque, Smets, and Wouters (2005). The elasticity of labor supply is set to 2.5 in both countries. The inverse of the intertemporal elasticity of substitution σ is set to 2.5 in the euro area and to 2 in the United States, reflecting the observed relatively higher interest rate sensitivity in the United States.

The technology parameter α is set in both countries to 0.36, while the parameters determining the adjustment costs in investment are calibrated

4. In developing the NAWM, a two-track strategy is followed. A relatively large calibrated two-country version is used for policy analysis (as in Coenen, McAdam, and Straub [2007]). A simplified estimated version is used for projections (see Christoffel, Coenen, and Warne [2008]). The estimated version is still in development and treats the foreign block as exogenous and generated by a Vector Autoregression (VAR).

to 1.3 in the euro area and 1.1 in the United States, reflecting the lower investment volatility in the euro area data. At the same time, the parameter shaping the premium on foreign bond holdings equals 0.001. In both countries, we set the elasticity of substitution between different types of intermediate and imported goods to 6, while the elasticity of substitution between different labor types equals 3. Furthermore, in order to match the negative correlation between output and the trade balance in the data, we have calibrated the elasticity of substitution between home and imported goods to 0.7. Price and wage indexation are equal in both countries and are set to 0.6, while the Calvo probabilities in the domestic intermediate goods and import sector as well as in the labor market are set to 0.7, in line with the estimates of Schorfheide and Lubik (2005) and de Walque, Smets, and Wouters (2005). Finally, the simple monetary policy rule is calibrated as follows. We set the degree of interest rate smoothing at 0.7, the interest rate response to inflation at 1.7, and the interest rate response to output at 0.1, in both countries.

With regards to the tax rates, we have chosen the values reported, in Coenen, McAdam, and Straub (2007) that are based on Organization for Economic Cooperation and Development (OECD) data. Namely, we set the consumption tax rate at 0.183 in the euro area and at 0.077 in the United States, while labor income tax equals 0.24 in the euro area and 0.22 in the United States. Furthermore, the share of government spending in GDP is assumed to equal 20 percent in both regions. The subsidy to firms (τ^f) is set to zero in the steady state.

The calibrated standard deviations of the shocks are shown in table 3.1, while table 3.2 compares some of the moments generated by the model with the data for the euro area and the United States. The calibrated model gets the relative standard deviations of real GDP and its components more or less right. However, the standard deviation of inflation generated by the

Table 3.1 **Standard deviation of the shocks**

Preference shock home	0.018
Preference shock foreign	0.018
Investment home	0.044
Investment foreign	0.009
Monetary policy home	0.002
Monetary policy foreign	0.0026
Productivity home	0.0055
Productivity foreign	0.0055
Markup home	0.06
Markup foreign	0.06
Labor supply foreign	0.07
Labor supply home	0.06
UIP	0.01

Table 3.2 **Stylized facts of the model**

	Euro area				U.S.	
	Model	Data	Model	Data	Model	Data
Standard deviation						
GDP	0.89	0.93			1.01	1.02
Consumption	0.59	0.80			0.76	0.90
Investment	2.56	2.60			3.71	4.9
Inflation	0.53	1.05			0.57	1.20
Real exchange rate			1.98	7.00		
Net trade			0.26	0.46		
Cross-correlation over countries						
GDP			0.43	0.29		
Consumption			0.14	0.14		
Investment			0.25	0.17		
Cross-correlation within countries						
GDP—net trade	–0.28	–0.69			–0.47	–0.39
Consumption—net trade	–0.19	–0.75			–0.17	–0.45
Investment—net trade	–0.23	–0.79			–0.39	–0.51

model is too low (a bit more than half of that in the data). Also the volatility of the real exchange rate is too low in spite of the addition of uncovered interest rate parity shocks. Importantly for our purposes, the correlation of real GDP, consumption, and investment across the two regions is captured quite well. This is partly due to our assumption that productivity shocks have spillover effects across countries (the coefficient of correlation of the two shocks is about 0.74). As highlighted by Justiniano and Preston (2008), open economy DSGE models have difficulties explaining the comovement of business cycles in the absence of a common component in the underlying shocks. The model captures the negative correlation between GDP and net trade, although it is less than in the data.

Finally, as the source of the shocks is a potentially important determinant of the gains from cooperation, we also make sure that the contributions of the various shocks to the variance of the core macrovariables is reasonable. Tables 3.3 and 3.4 report the variance decomposition for the euro area and the United States, respectively. In line with estimated closed economy models, we observe that technology and labor supply shocks are the most important drivers of output in the long run.[5] Investment and preference shocks are important sources of variation of investment and consumption, respectively, but have only a significant short- to medium-run contribution to the variance of output. In both regions, the markup shocks in the domestic intermediate goods sector are the most important drivers of inflation,

5. See, for example, Smets and Wouters (2003, 2007).

Table 3.3 **Variance decomposition**

	Euro area				
	Output	Consumption	Investment	Inflation	REX
Euro area shocks					
Technology	55.4	26.3	41.1	27.4	11.6
Labor supply	19.5	6.79	15.7	8.03	9.43
Investment	0.93	0.75	6.06	0.14	0.36
Preferences	2.78	51.7	19.5	4.14	8.38
Markup	5.68	1.39	1.86	52.8	7.55
Monetary policy	1.00	0.41	0.57	1.63	4.48
U.S. shocks					
Technology	14.4	10.9	11.1	4.69	6.79
Labor supply	0.12	0.35	0.28	0.10	10.5
Investment	0.09	0.84	2.93	0.55	6.65
Preferences	0.06	0.28	0.44	0.19	4.06
Markup	0.03	0.12	0.03	0.17	9.02
Monetary policy	0.02	0.09	0.02	0.06	6.69
UIP	0.00	0.09	0.04	0.03	14.5

Table 3.4 **Variance decomposition**

	United States			
	Output	Consumption	Investment	Inflation
Euro area shocks				
Technology	11.2	10.0	6.38	4.02
Labor supply	0.04	0.15	0.07	0.03
Investment	0.00	0.02	0.06	0.01
Preferences	0.04	0.33	0.17	0.11
Markup	0.01	0.01	0.00	0.07
Monetary policy	0.00	0.04	0.00	0.01
U.S. shocks				
Technology	46.8	27.4	26.9	25.0
Labor supply	22.6	9.78	13.9	9.65
Investment	9.81	11.5	42.7	2.62
Preferences	2.36	38.4	7.05	2.77
Markup	5.34	1.51	1.73	53.1
Monetary policy	1.71	0.80	0.83	2.57
UIP	0.00	0.05	0.01	0.03

followed by technology shocks. The only shocks that have a nonnegligible impact on the variance decomposition of foreign output are the technology shocks. This is a result of the assumption that domestic technology shocks have spillover effects on foreign productivity, as in Backus, Kehoe, and Kydland (1994).

3.4 Definition of the Monetary Policy Game

The open economy dimension of our model gives rise to an international dimension of monetary policy. While we have used an empirical monetary policy reaction function to calibrate the two-region model, for the analysis of the gains from cooperation in the next section, we consider two concepts of equilibrium in the game played by the two central banks.[6] In the cooperative equilibrium, both central banks commit to implementing monetary policies that maximize the joint welfare of the euro area and the United States. The joint welfare is a population-weighted sum of the utility of the representative households in both economies. If we denote the aggregate welfare function of each country by $\mathbb{W}_t^i : i = \{EA, US\}$, the global cooperative objective function would be $\mathbb{W}_t^{coop} = s\mathbb{W}_t^{EA} + (1 - s)\,\mathbb{W}_t^{US}$.

In contrast, in the noncooperative equilibrium, each central bank maximizes the aggregate welfare function of its own country, taking as given the entire path of the foreign central bank's instrument. This corresponds to an open-loop Nash equilibrium (Blake and Westaway 1995).[7] The noncooperative equilibrium that emerges from the strategic game played by the central banks depends crucially on the instrument chosen by the two players, as discussed in Canzoneri and Henderson (1989), Henderson and Zhu (1990), Turnovsky and d'Orey (1989), and more recently in Lombardo and Sutherland (2006), among others.[8] It is well known that changing the strategy space (i.e., selecting different instrument variables) can give rise to different Nash equilibria. The current literature on this subject displays a variety of approaches.[9] For example, Obstfeld and Rogoff (2002) consider

6. Given the dimension of our model, we were forced to neglect optimal fiscal policy issues. Obviously, a complete normative analysis of optimal policies should take into account all available policy instruments. See Lombardo and Sutherland (2004) for a discussion of the global dimension of fiscal and monetary policy in a microfounded stylized two-period two-country model. Beetsma and Jensen (2005) discuss the monetary-fiscal interaction in a monetary union in a dynamic two-country model.

7. The open-loop Nash equilibrium implies that each central bank chooses the optimal allocation, taking as given the current and future choices of instrument by the foreign central bank (Blake and Westaway 1995). The alternative Nash equilibrium would be a closed-loop equilibrium "for which the sequence of foreign instruments is known to be dependent on (some of the) other system variables" (Levine, Pearlman, and Pierce 2008, 3341). Benigno and Benigno (2006), Levine, Pearlman, and Pierce (2008), and Clarida, Galí, and Gertler (2002) discuss open-loop equilibria. Feedback-loop (i.e., closed-loop) Nash equilibria have been studied in small models by Obstfeld and Rogoff (2002) and Lombardo and Sutherland (2004). In these models, as in most of the older literature, the distinction between open-loop and closed-loop is irrelevant as the models are essentially static (with preset prices). See Canzoneri and Henderson (1992) for examples of strategic setups in older models.

8. The different equilibrium allocation brought about by a Bertrand equilibrium as compared to, say, a Cournot equilibrium, exemplifies the effect that the choice of alternative instruments might have on the outcome.

9. The older literature on this subject focused more closely on the classical monetary policy instruments; that is, money supply or interest rates (Canzoneri and Henderson 1989). Rogoff (1985) discusses a special case in which taking the price of domestic goods as the strategic instrument is equivalent to using money supply. In general, though, this is not the case.

feedback money supply rules, while Benigno and Benigno (2006) define the strategies in terms of the inflation rate of the domestic GDP deflators. In this chapter, we assume that the central bank is able to control the money supply and we define the strategy space of the noncooperative equilibrium in terms of the growth rate of nominal money balances. The alternative option of choosing the nominal interest rate as the policy instrument does not deliver saddle-path stable equilibria in the open-loop Nash game (Blake and Westaway 1995), and therefore would produce a much inferior welfare outcome (at least locally).[10]

For the sake of comparison with the literature, in section 3.5.5 we also briefly consider open-loop Nash equilibria in which CPI and producer price index (PPI) inflation is chosen as the strategic policy variable. However, given that the central bank has a well-defined objective function that includes other variables than inflation, we think that these alternative assumptions regarding the strategy space are unwarranted in our model setup. We prefer to use the central bank's instrument (money supply) as our benchmark case. Nevertheless, it is worth emphasizing again that the size of the gains from cooperation depend, in general, on the particular definition of Nash equilibrium considered.

A brief description of the solution method is given in the appendix.

3.5 The Gains from Cooperation: Results

In the next section we report the welfare loss due to noncooperation (i.e., the difference between welfare under cooperation and welfare under noncooperation) in terms of the amount of consumption that the typical household would need to give up in order to incur the same loss in a deterministic world.[11]

3.5.1 Welfare Decomposition: Baseline Results

Table 3.5 presents our baseline results. The first two lines report the decomposition of the gains from monetary policy cooperation in the euro area and the United States (i.e., the difference in welfare between the cooperative and noncooperative equilibrium) into the different contributions of the shocks. Furthermore, the table also shows the difference between the conditional mean and variance of consumption, labor, real GDP, inflation, and the terms of trade in the cooperative and noncooperative equilibrium, as well

10. The equilibrium produced under such a game is locally explosive. One should note that when a central bank chooses the optimal allocation taking as given the foreign interest rate, a locally indeterminate equilibrium would emerge. We conjecture that the central bank would choose a best response to the exogenously given foreign rate such that a saddle-path equilibrium is reestablished. When two such strategies are combined together, they would produce too many unstable roots.

11. Denote Δ^W as the welfare gap produced by following two different monetary policies in a stochastic world. We then solve for λ such that $\Delta^W = (1-\beta)^{-1}\{U((1-\lambda)C_{ss}) - U(C_{ss})\}$.

Table 3.5 **Welfare decomposition: Benchmark calibration**

Variable	All shocks	*UIP*	mkp^{EA}	$prod^{EA}$	lab^{EA}	inv^{EA}	$pref^{EA}$	mkp^{US}	$prod^{US}$	lab^{US}	inv^{US}	$pref^{US}$
$E_{t0}[Welf^{EA}]$	0.0272	0.0015	0.0141	0.0016	0.0006	*0*	0.0001	0.0065	*–0.0001*	0.0021	0.0008	0
$E_{t0}[Welf^{US}]$	0.0294	0.003	0.0072	0.0002	0.0017	0	0.0002	0.014	0.0018	0.0012	*–0.0001*	0.0002
$E_{t0}[Cons^{EA}]$	0.0392	0.0012	0.0203	0.0024	0.0017	*0*	0.0003	0.0082	0.0007	0.0037	0.0006	0.0002
$Var_{t0}[Cons^{EA}]$	–0.0006	0	–0.0001	*0.0003*	–0.0002	0	*0*	–0.0004	*0.0001*	–0.0002	*0*	*0*
$E_{t0}[Cons^{US}]$	0.0415	0.002	0.0085	0.0009	0.0028	0	0.0004	0.0231	0.0026	0.0006	0.0003	0.0003
$Var_{t0}[Cons^{US}]$	–0.0003	–0.0001	–0.0002	*0.0003*	*0*	*0*	*0*	*0*	*0.0003*	–0.0007	0	*0*
$E_{t0}[Lab^{EA}]$	0.0491	0.0005	0.0221	0.0026	*–0.0026*	0	0.0005	0.0203	0.0006	0.0052	*–0.0004*	0.0003
$Var_{t0}[Lab^{EA}]$	–0.009	–0.0003	*0.0002*	–0.0018	–0.0034	*0*	*0.0001*	–0.004	–0.0001	*0.0001*	0	*0.0001*
$E_{t0}[Lab^{US}]$	0.0212	0.0009	0.0086	*–0.0004*	0.001	*0*	0.0002	0.0187	0.0016	*–0.0103*	0.0011	0
$Var_{t0}[Lab^{US}]$	–0.0093	–0.0005	–0.0015	–0.0001	*0.0006*	0	*0.0001*	*0.001*	–0.0009	–0.0079	0	0
$E_{t0}[Infl^{EA}]$	–0.0712	–0.0006	–0.0117	–0.0017	–0.0178	–0.0001	–0.0036	–0.0123	–0.0044	–0.016	–0.0003	–0.0026
$Var_{t0}[Infl^{EA}]$	–0.0003	0	–0.0001	0	–0.0001	*0*	0	–0.0001	0	0	*0*	0
$E_{t0}[Infl^{US}]$	–0.0528	–0.0003	–0.0038	–0.0029	–0.0125	0	–0.003	–0.0097	–0.0021	–0.0153	–0.0009	–0.0023
$Var_{t0}[Infl^{US}]$	–0.0002	0	0	0	0	*0*	0	0	*0*	–0.0002	*0*	0
$E_{t0}[GDP^{EA}]$	0.1099	0.0009	0.055	0.0052	0.0035	0.0001	0.0008	0.0299	0.002	0.0117	0.0002	0.0007
$Var_{t0}[GDP^{EA}]$	–0.0019	–0.0001	*0.0001*	*0.0006*	–0.0015	*0*	*0.0001*	–0.0016	*0.0005*	*0.0001*	0	*0*
$E_{t0}[GDP^{US}]$	0.0701	0.0013	0.0153	0.0005	0.0035	*0*	0.0005	0.0502	0.0034	*–0.0056*	0.0008	0.0002
$Var_{t0}[GDP^{US}]$	–0.003	–0.0002	–0.0006	*0.0006*	*0.0002*	0	*0*	*0.0004*	*0.0003*	–0.0037	0	0
$E_{t0}[tot]$	–0.0589	–0.0065	–0.0624	*0.0067*	–0.0096	*0.0003*	–0.0003	*0.0059*	–0.0007	*0.0118*	–0.0046	*0.0003*
$\mathrm{Var}_{t0}[tot]$	–0.1478	–0.0014	–0.0386	–0.0026	–0.0225	0	–0.0015	–0.0487	–0.0071	–0.0239	–0.0001	–0.0014

as the contribution of each of the shocks to these differences. The first two variables, consumption and labor, are of interest as they are the primitive arguments of the welfare function. Real GDP and inflation are of interest as they are often used in describing the objective function of central banks. In particular, in first generation models of monetary policy cooperation, inflation and output volatility were often used as the sole arguments of the central bank's objective function.[12] Moreover, inflation and output volatility may capture the cost from inefficient goods production due to staggered nominal prices. Finally, the terms of trade is a crucial variable in the strategic interaction between the two central banks. The welfare gains of cooperation ($E_{t0}[Welf^{EA}]$ and $E_{t0}[Welf^{US}]$) are expressed in permanent steady-state consumption units (percentages). The other variables are expressed as a percentage of their steady-state value. The first column of table 3.5 reports the values for the baseline calibration. The other columns display the values for each type of shock separately. Except for the conditional mean of welfare, the first column is the sum of all the subsequent columns. For welfare the sum is not identically equal to the first column due to the transformation in consumption units. For each single shock, the values that have a different sign from that obtained under all shocks have been underlined.

Based on table 3.5 a number of observations are worth highlighting. First of all, the first column of table 3.5 shows that the overall gains from cooperation are quite modest, thereby confirming much of the recent literature. For both countries they amount to about 0.03 percent of steady-state consumption. This value is about one order of magnitude larger than the values suggested by Obstfeld and Rogoff (2002) and within the range of values discussed by Benigno (2001).[13] For the sake of concreteness, making average pro-capita consumption equal to $28,000 per year, the gains from cooperation would amount to a mere $8.4 per year per head.

In spite of a number of cross-country asymmetries imposed in the calibration, the gains from cooperation are quite similar in both areas. Besides the differences in some of the values of the parameters and standard deviations, an important source of asymmetry is the fact that only dollar denominated bonds issued by the United States are assumed to be traded internationally. This assumption implies that the euro area and the United States are not treated symmetrically in terms of currency-risk hedging options

12. For example, Rogoff (1985), Canzoneri and Gray (1985), and Sachs (1983) on the second point and Woodford (2003) on the first point.

13. Oudiz and Sachs (1984), using large-scale multicountry econometric models, came to the conclusion that a coordinated expansion in the face of a global shock, like an oil-price shock of the magnitude seen in the 1970s, would increase U.S. GNP by about 0.5 percent ". . . [for] the next few years." Their results, as those of all the first generation literature on this topic, are based on rather different mechanisms than those highlighted by the current generation literature. In the new literature, certainty equivalence is not imposed so that ". . . the monetary policy rule does affect the expected trajectory of the economy via agents' responses to risk" (Obstfeld and Rogoff 2002).

(e.g., Devereux and Sutherland 2007) abstracting from the foreign asset return premium, for the U.S. internationally traded bonds provide the same return as domestically traded bonds. It should be noted that the asymmetry discussed here captures only one aspect of the issues related with the currency denomination of foreign assets. Another aspect would emerge had we assumed a nonzero initial (steady-state) net foreign asset position. In this case there would be a first-order effect of inflation on real income, as discussed by Benigno (2001). As we will show in the following, the results of broadly symmetric gains across the euro area and the United States do not appear to be very robust as we change some of the parameters.

Turning to some of the key variables in the welfare calculations such as consumption and labor, it is clear from the first column in table 3.5 that the gains in welfare come mostly from an increase in the average level of consumption by between 0.04 and 0.05 percent. This gain is partly offset by the fact that both euro area and U.S. households work more in the cooperative equilibrium. As a result, average GDP increases by 0.1 percent in the euro area and 0.07 percent in the United States. Overall, the volatility of the main variables is lower under cooperation, but generally not by much. Turning to inflation, inflation is on average lower in the cooperative equilibrium (by 0.07 and 0.05 percent, respectively, in the euro area and the United States). In other words, lack of cooperation leads to a small inflationary bias. On the other hand, cooperation leads to a small improvement of the terms of trade of the euro area by 0.05 percent.

A second important observation from table 3.5 is that the most important source of gains from cooperation are the markup shocks. In our model, all shocks produce policy trade-offs due to the large number of inefficiencies (incomplete markets, monopolistic competition, distortionary taxes, sticky wages, sticky prices, and imperfect exchange rate pass-through). As a result, cooperation is always better than noncooperation in response to all of the shocks. However, as argued by Benigno and Benigno (2006), some shocks produce larger incentives for the central banks to move the relative price to their own advantage. This is particularly true for markup shocks. This is confirmed by the analysis in table 3.5. The markup shocks explain more than three-fourths of the gains from cooperation. From the variance decomposition in tables 3.3 and 3.4, we know that markup shocks are also the single largest source of inflation volatility, while they account only for a modest share of the volatility of the real variables. In contrast, although productivity shocks play the major role in explaining the volatility in real activity of the euro area and U.S. economies, they do not generate wide discrepancies between the cooperative and the noncooperative allocations in terms of welfare. Similarly, the contribution of all the other shocks to the gains from cooperation is an order of magnitude smaller than those of the markup shocks.

As argued by Canzoneri, Cumby, and Diba (2002), the gains from coop-

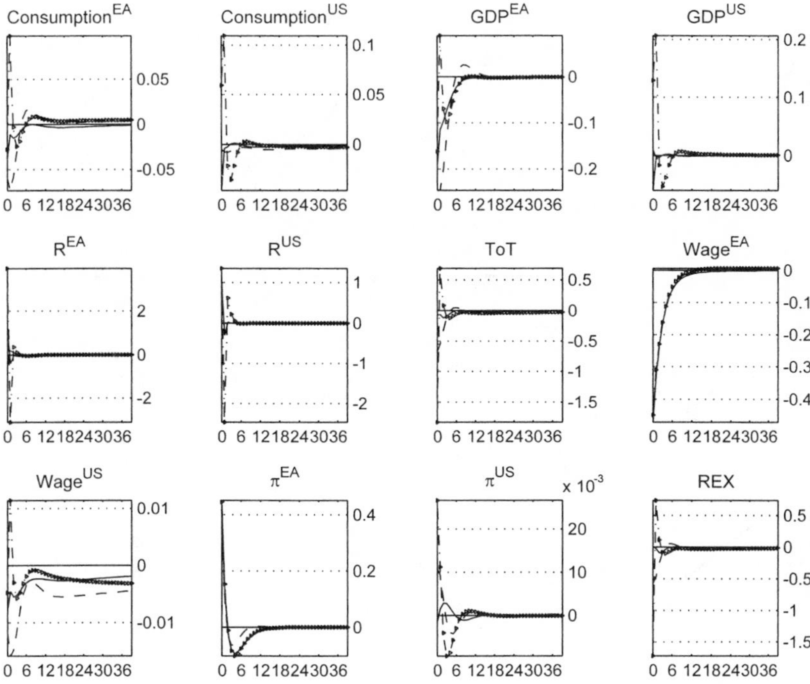

Fig. 3.1 Euro area markup shock: Coop. (solid), Nash (arrowed-dashed), Rule (dashed)

eration are increasing in the size of the policy trade-offs generated by the shocks. Shocks that can be easily offset by a self-oriented central bank do not produce international conflicts of interests. In that case, cooperation would not be welfare improving, as also argued by Obstfeld and Rogoff (2002). In contrast, shocks that produce large trade-offs generate strong incentives for the self-oriented central banks to export some of the costs to the other country. When both central banks pursue "beggar-thy-neighbor" policies, the net result will be a deterioration of global welfare. Cooperation, in this case, will be welfare improving.

Figures 3.1 and 3.2 compare the response of the euro area and U.S. economy to a markup shock and a productivity shock, respectively, under the cooperative and noncooperative equilibrium and the calibrated monetary policy reaction function. Under the cooperative equilibrium, a positive euro area markup shock has the usual negative impact on output and consumption in the euro area. Moreover, in order to stabilize inflation, the nominal interest rate increases and the terms of trade appreciate (although only marginally). More interestingly, the euro area markup shock generates positive comovement between euro area and U.S. GDP. In both countries inflation rises and the real wage falls.

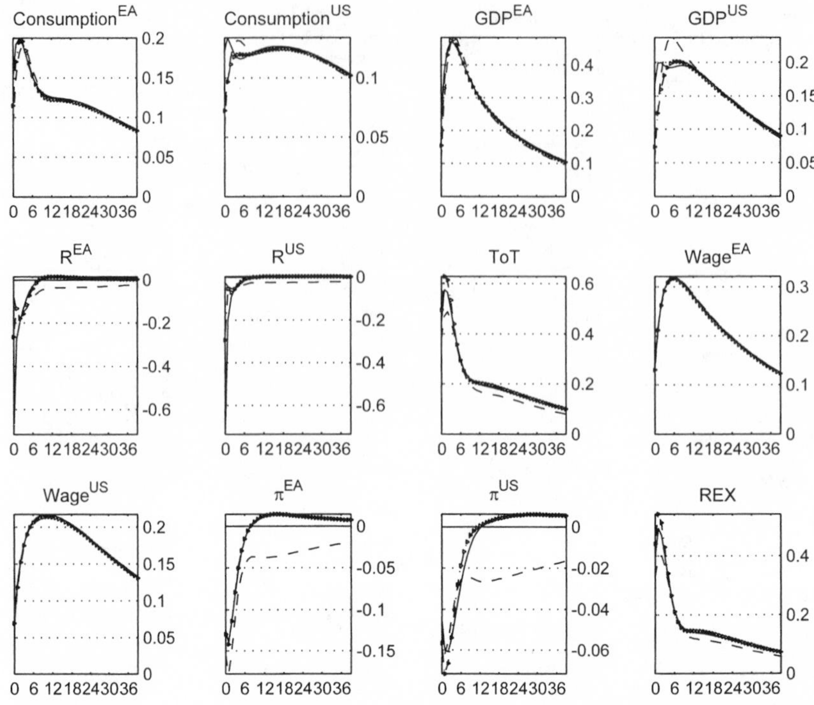

Fig. 3.2 Euro area productivity shock: Coop. (solid), Nash (arrowed-dashed), Rule (dashed)

The latter is in contrast with the impulse responses under the optimal cooperative policy derived by Benigno and Benigno (2006). In their much simpler open economy model, which only incorporates monopolistic competition and sticky prices, a domestic markup shock generates negative comovement between economic activity in both countries. As discussed by Benigno and Benigno (2006), in their simple model the crucial determinant of the sign of the international spillovers is the relative size of the intratemporal and intertemporal elasticity of substitution. If the intratemporal elasticity dominates, home and foreign goods are substitutes in the utility function (Corsetti and Pesenti 2001). In this case a foreign deterioration of the terms of trade will bring about a foreign expansion of production. In contrast, if the intertemporal elasticity of substitution dominates, the two goods are complements and both home and foreign production will contract.

These two parameters, though, are insufficient to describe the relative response of home and foreign output if capital accumulation is introduced in the model. In our model, as it would happen in the model developed by

Benigno and Benigno (2006) if extended with capital accumulation, the spillovers are positive under the optimal cooperative policy, at least on impact.

Qualitatively, the responses under the optimal cooperative policy are very similar to those under the calibrated monetary policy reaction functions. The discrepancy with the noncooperative policies is, however, quite large. The short-term interest rates and the terms of trade respond in a much more volatile fashion and this is reflected in a more volatile response of consumption and GDP. It is also clear that the initial response of GDP is negative in the euro area, but positive in the United States, as the euro area monetary authorities attempt to export some of the volatility in the labor costs to the foreign country.

A quite different picture is obtained in figure 3.2 regarding the effects of a productivity shock. In this case, the impulse responses under the cooperative and noncooperative equilibrium are quite similar, confirming the limited contribution of those shocks to the gains from cooperation. These impulse responses are also quite similar to those under the calibrated policy rule. As is to be expected, following a temporary positive productivity shock in both countries, consumption, output, and wages rise persistently, while nominal interest rates and inflation fall. The domestic terms of trade deteriorate as the productivity shock increases relative supply of the domestic goods.

As mentioned earlier, the single most important shock in accounting for the gains from cooperation (i.e., summing up the EA and U.S. welfare gains) is the markup shock. We should expect that the randomness in the home markup will partially spillover to the volatility of the home firms' optimal price. The home domestic price index is a concave function of individual prices. This implies that the expected home domestic price index is lower than its nonstochastic value. This is true also when we measure the expected home domestic price index relative to the CPI. The lower expected price implies a higher expected demand and, ceteris paribus, lower expected average profits, as firms expect, on average, to be off their supply curve. The expected foreign domestic price index, relative to the CPI, will be higher, as the CPI is partially affected by the drop in the home domestic price index. Therefore, demand is expected to switch partially from the foreign goods to the home goods. Whether this effect is welfare increasing or not will likely depend on the net increase in consumption and labor effort.[14] Each central bank, taken in isolation, will try to increase consumption while reducing labor effort.[15] The policymakers would attempt to do this by affecting the

14. That welfare could be higher in the stochastic equilibrium as compared to the nonstochastic equilibrium is a well-known fact in economics. Cho and Cooley (2003) offer a recent discussion of this result.

15. Using a simple two-country model à la Benigno and Benigno (2006), we can see that the optimizing (cooperative) central bank will try to increase consumption and labor more under an inefficient steady state than under an efficient steady state.

Table 3.6 Welfare decomposition: Nominal rigidities and indexation

Variable	All shocks	mkp^{EA}	mkp^{US}	Σ_{EA} other shocks	Σ_{US} other shocks
Lower price rigidity in intermediate-goods sector (Calvo pr. = 0.35)					
$E_{t0}[Welf^{EA}]$	10.9639	6.1409	5.397	0.1241	0.1271
$E_{t0}[Welf^{US}]$	18.0099	8.2732	11.0678	0.2592	0.2412
Higher exchange rate pass-through (Calvo pr. = 0.35)					
$E_{t0}[Welf^{EA}]$	0.0353	*–0.011*	0.0456	0.0003	0.0004
$E_{t0}[Welf^{US}]$	–0.0001	*0.0251*	–0.0266	*0.0011*	*0.0003*
Lower wage rigidity (Calvo pr. = 0.35)					
$E_{t0}[Welf^{EA}]$	0.0181	0.0078	0.0022	0.004	0.0041
$E_{t0}[Welf^{US}]$	0.0207	0.0046	0.0093	0.004	0.0028
No indexation of prices in intermediate goods sector					
$E_{t0}[Welf^{EA}]$	0.0376	0.051	*–0.0236*	0.0058	0.0045
$E_{t0}[Welf^{US}]$	0.0549	*–0.0217*	0.0629	0.008	0.0058
No indexation of import prices					
$E_{t0}[Welf^{EA}]$	0.0438	*–0.0115*	0.0486	0.0034	0.0033
$E_{t0}[Welf^{US}]$	0.0433	0.0487	*–0.0136*	0.0053	0.003
No indexation of wages					
$E_{t0}[Welf^{EA}]$	0.0271	0.0152	0.0052	0.004	0.0028
$E_{t0}[Welf^{US}]$	0.0294	0.0058	0.0149	0.0053	0.0034

(expected) terms of trade. When both banks act in this way, the net result will be a deterioration of welfare compared to the cooperative equilibrium.

3.5.2 Sensitivity Analysis with Respect to Nominal Rigidities

While table 3.5 shows the results for the calibrated (benchmark) model, tables 3.6 and 3.7 report the results from a sensitivity analysis. We report in each case the overall gain in welfare and its various components, as well as the contribution of the euro area and U.S. markup shock and the sum of the other shocks in each region. Also in these cases, the mark-up shocks are by far the most important contributors to the welfare gains. In interpreting many of these exercises, it is important to realize that the size of the welfare losses in general ceases to have a solid empirical basis. For example, imposing flexible prices, while maintaining all other parameters unchanged, gives the markup shocks a disproportionate effect on output.[16] These results, therefore, should only be taken as indicative of the sensitivity of the wel-

16. For example, the terms of trade would have a standard deviation about seven times larger than in the data. Euro area and U.S. GDP volatility would be twice as large as in the data, while they would be negatively cross-correlated. A number of other moments would be strongly altered. Finally, markup shocks would explain between 54 percent (EA) and 45 percent (U.S.) of the volatility of GDP (at twelve quarters).

Table 3.7 **Welfare decomposition: Further sensitivity analysis**

Variable	All shocks	mkp^{EA}	mkp^{US}	Σ_{EA} other shocks	Σ_{US} other shocks
Unitary intratemporal elasticity of substitution					
$E_{t0}[Welf^{EA}]$	0.0086	0.0061	*–0.0009*	0.0017	0.0018
$E_{t0}[Welf^{US}]$	0.0065	*–0.001*	0.0052	0.0015	0.0007
Higher intratemporal elasticity of substitution (1.7)					
$E_{t0}[Welf^{EA}]$	0.0031	0.0013	0.0005	0.0005	0.0008
$E_{t0}[Welf^{US}]$	0.0037	0.0007	0.0016	0.0009	0.0005
Equal intra- and intertemporal elasticities (0.7)					
$E_{t0}[Welf^{EA}]$	0.0016	*–0.0007*	*–0.0029*	0.0031	0.0021
$E_{t0}[Welf^{US}]$	0.0422	0.0148	0.0178	0.0074	0.0022
Equal country size and no home bias					
$E_{t0}[Welf^{EA}]$	21.5074	11.2688	10.0618	3.106	1.4399
$E_{t0}[Welf^{US}]$	24.8622	11.2348	13.0827	3.556	1.7581
Equal size and lower home bias (0.65)					
$E_{t0}[Welf^{EA}]$	0.7382	0.3876	0.1818	0.1384	0.0348
$E_{t0}[Welf^{US}]$	0.961	0.2237	0.5004	0.175	0.068
Complete markets (benchmark calibration)					
$E_{t0}[Welf^{EA}]$	0.0044	0.0026	*–0.0008*	0.0017	0.0009
$E_{t0}[Welf^{US}]$	0.0024	0.0005	0.0022	*–0.0002*	*–0.0001*
Complete markets, equal size, and lower home bias (0.65)					
$E_{t0}[Welf^{EA}]$	0.0269	0.0096	0.0158	0.0013	0.0002
$E_{t0}[Welf^{US}]$	0.0381	0.0219	0.0136	0.0016	0.001

fare losses to some of the parameters of the model. Deriving empirically sound confidence bands for the welfare losses would require a more complex approach that is beyond the scope of the present work and that we leave for future research.[17]

We first investigate the role of indexation in the intermediate goods sector (table 3.6). The table shows that without indexation, the gains from cooperation rise only marginally from about 0.05 to 0.09 percent of steady-state consumption. However, the cross-country "spillover effects" change sign: that is, while EA welfare gains increase in their own markup shock and decrease in the U.S. markup shock, the reverse happens in the foreign country. In other words, according to these results the euro area would be

17. In this regard the ranges suggested by Benigno (2001) should also be taken with a grain of salt, as they derive from varying some parameters without discussion of the implications for the empirical fit of the model.

better off not to adopt the cooperative policy if there were only U.S. markup shocks. Turning to the degree of price stickiness in the intermediate goods sector itself, table 3.6 shows the effect of reducing price stickiness by half in the intermediate goods sector. Higher flexibility in the intermediate goods sector increases the gains from cooperation quite drastically. In particular, halving the Calvo probability leads to welfare gains of 10 and 17 percent. As mentioned earlier, this result should be interpreted with particular caution, as reducing the degree of price rigidity increases the weight of markup volatility in the volatility of the whole economy beyond what we observe in the data.

It is also of particular interest to study the role of the incomplete pass-through of the exchange rate in generating gains from cooperation. In table 3.6, the degree of pass-through is increased by assuming that retail prices of imported goods are twice as flexible as in the benchmark model. A higher pass-through marginally reduces the overall gains from cooperation. However, under this assumption domestic markup shocks reduce the domestic welfare gains while they improve the foreign welfare gains.[18] Notice, furthermore, that the welfare gains associated with markup shocks cease to be symmetric. Table 3.6 shows what happens if import prices are not indexed to domestic CPI inflation. The sign of the contribution of markup shocks to the gain from cooperation is the same as in the previous case. In this case, though, symmetry is preserved.

Finally, we also had a look at the impact of changes in nominal wage rigidity and wage indexation. Somewhat surprisingly, those nominal rigidities do not seem to have a large impact on the gains from cooperation.

3.5.3 Degree of Openness

It is natural to expect that the gains from cooperation would be higher the higher the economic integration of the countries involved. Quoting Oudiz and Sachs (1984, 5–6), ". . . the direct effects of commodity trade on macroeconomic interdependence remain surprisingly small; at the core, it is these relatively small trade links that condition our conclusions regarding the returns to coordination." These authors were talking about export and import shares to GNP between the European Community and the United States (1982) of between 1.4 and 2.2 percent. While these numbers have increased somewhat since then, they remain relatively small. Our calibration implies that, in the nonstochastic steady state, U.S. exports to the EA

18. For the sake of comparison, we ran a similar experiment on the simple two-country model à la Benigno and Benigno (2006). This simple model would predict that domestic markup shocks are detrimental for domestic welfare gains from cooperation and beneficial for the foreign gains. This result is strongly sensitive to whether wages are flexible or not and to whether international financial markets are complete or not. The model dependence of these results makes a generalization of them nearly impossible.

are about 8 percent of U.S. GDP while U.S. imports from the EA are about 11 percent of U.S. GDP. The EA exports to the United States are about 14 percent of EA GDP, while EA imports from the United States are about 11 percent of EA GDP. Table 3.7 shows the polar case of equal sized countries and no home bias. Although this assumption might look extreme if compared with our benchmark parametrization, the variance decomposition of shocks and the moments (standard deviations and cross-correlations) of the model are not dramatically different from those obtained in our benchmark calibration. Nevertheless, the gains from coordination, absent home bias, are huge. They reach 21.5 percent for the euro area and 25.3 percent for the United States. Almost all of these gains are due to markup volatility.

Table 3.7 also offers an intermediate case, where the trade shares have been increased to about 32 percent of GDP in both countries (equal size and home-bias parameter set to 0.65). In this case the welfare gains are almost two orders of magnitude larger than in the benchmark calibration, reaching about 0.74 percent of steady-state consumption in the euro area and about 1.0 percent of steady-state consumption for the United States.

3.5.4 Some Other Critical Parameters

In this section, we discuss the implications of differences in some of the other parameters of our model that have received particular attention in the international monetary policy cooperation literature.

Inter- and Intratemporal Elasticity of Substitution

Corsetti and Pesenti (2001) show that the cross-country spillover effect of monetary policy crucially depends on the size of the intertemporal elasticity of substitution relative to the intratemporal elasticity (i.e., the elasticity of substitution between imported goods and domestically produced goods). With CES goods aggregators and CRRA utility function, the sign of the cross derivative of the utility function with respect to the domestically produced bundle of goods and the imported bundle of goods depends on the size of the intratemporal elasticity of substitution relative to the size of the intertemporal elasticity of substitution. If the former is larger than the latter, the two bundles are substitutes; if smaller, they are complements. If they have the same size, the consumption spillovers are nil. Nevertheless, even in the latter case, policy spillovers could still be present if monetary policy can affect the international distribution of labor effort. So, for example, an improvement of the terms of trade would tend to export labor effort abroad. While the extent of this effect increases in the intratemporal elasticity of substitution, the income gains decrease in this elasticity. In the spirit of the "optimum tariff" argument, the lower is the intratemporal elasticity of substitution, and the larger the monopolistic rent that the country can extract internationally.

Table 3.7 shows the welfare decomposition results for different values of the inter- and intratemporal elasticity of substitution. The main result of our chapter remains unchanged: the gains from cooperation are very modest.

A more detailed look at the results shows that the gains from cooperation seem to decrease in the intratemporal elasticity of substitution (table 3.7).[19]

Market Completeness

In Obstfeld and Rogoff (2002) the cooperative central banks face a trade-off between stabilization and increased tradable consumption risk-sharing.[20] This holds true also in our benchmark calibration, although the trade-off is more complex, involving a larger number of margins.

Increasing the degree of consumption risk-sharing is welfare improving. Nevertheless, without cooperation risk-sharing cannot be achieved. This fact, per se, will generate a gap between the cooperative and noncooperative allocations.

Table 3.7 reports the results of our decomposition of the welfare gains from cooperation when international financial markets are complete. Now the gains from cooperation are about one order of magnitude smaller than in the benchmark calibration. In the same table we show that a sizable reduction of the gains from cooperation is obtained by introducing market completeness in a model with larger trade shares.

3.5.5 Alternative Assumptions Regarding the Noncooperative Strategy Space

Benigno and Benigno (2006) define the strategy space of the Nash game in terms of the growth rate of the GDP deflator. In our model, we do not see any reason to assume that each central bank should take (any measure of) foreign inflation as given when solving its noncooperative policy problem. On the contrary, in the context of an open-loop noncooperative game, it sounds more reasonable to us to think that each central bank must take as given the choices of the other central bank regarding either the quantity or the price that clears the market in which the other central bank is active. Nevertheless, for the sake of comparison we computed the noncooperative equilibrium under two alternative specifications of the strategy space: in terms of the PPI inflation rates and in terms of the CPI inflation rates.

The Nash equilibrium brought about by the PPI inflation rates in the benchmark calibration is indeterminate, so that we should conclude that the gains from cooperation (in this case) are potentially huge.

In contrast, the Nash equilibrium brought about by the CPI inflation

19. Benigno (2001) shows that the gains are not monotonic in the intratemporal elasticity. We have considered also values of 2, 4, and 6 for the intratemporal elasticity, confirming that in this range the welfare gains seem to be lower the larger this elasticity.

20. In their model the risk-sharing motive is absent when the intertemporal elasticity of substitution is unitary.

rates is saddle-path stable, in the benchmark calibration. The gains from cooperation in this case are larger than those obtained when solving the game in terms of the money supplies. In particular, the gains from cooperation would be 0.32 percent for the euro area and 0.28 percent for the United States. Compared with the results reported in table 3.5, the gains are now one order of magnitude larger.

3.6 Performance of Simple Rules

Monetary policy is often described in terms of interest rate feedback rules of the type used in our calibration. Studying the gains from cooperation when central banks optimally choose the parameters of such feedback rules is not the main focus of our chapter. Nevertheless, in order to gain a sense of how our results would change if the policy problem is described in terms of particular interest rate rules, we have carried out two experiments. In the first, each central bank maximizes its objective function by choosing the coefficients of an inertial interest rate rule that responds to CPI inflation and real GDP, where the degree of inertia is the same as in the calibrated rule. This rule amounts to an inertial Taylor rule (Taylor 1993). This experiment shows that in both the cooperative and noncooperative equilibrium the central banks do not want to respond to output. This result is similar to the findings of Schmitt-Grohé and Uribe (2007a, 2007b), in a closed economy setting. The reason, we conjecture, is that the measure of output used in the model is the actual deviation of output from the steady state. The result would likely differ had we used the deviation of output from its efficient flexible price and wage level.

The second experiment assumes that the (inertial) interest rate rule responds to CPI inflation and wage inflation.[21] This rule is dictated by the results shown in Levin et al. (2006) that the optimal interest rate rule in a closed economy with wage and price stickiness attributes a large weight to wage inflation. This experiment shows that both the cooperative and the noncooperative central banks prefer to respond only to wage inflation.[22] In what follows, we therefore consider a closed-loop Nash game in the simple inertial wage inflation interest rate rules.

Figure 3.3 summarizes the results. The graph shows the contour plot of the EA and U.S. welfare functions (in utility units) in deviation from the steady-state value when the share of import (and export) in GDP is

21. Output is omitted on the basis of the result of the first experiment, thus easing the computational burden.

22. The search of the optimal response coefficients was done by imposing a grid for each parameter. The step size and the range of these grids has been adjusted in order to refine the results to a convincing degree. Given this procedure we cannot exclude that the optimal rule requires to respond to CPI inflation and GDP with very small coefficients. Given the purpose of our experiments we treat these small numbers as zero.

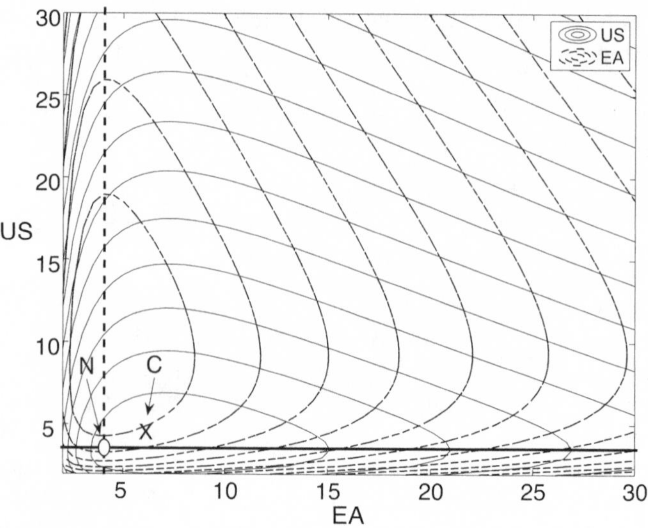

Fig. 3.3 Nash and cooperative equilibria under inertial interest rate rules reacting to wage inflation only

increased to about 32 percent.[23] The figure is reminiscent of the graphical analysis used by Hamada (1976) to derive the noncooperative equilibria in his monetary policy game. On the horizontal axis we have the EA response coefficient to wage inflation, while on the vertical axis we have the U.S. response coefficient. The straight lines crossing the contours represent the reaction functions of each central bank to the other bank's choice of reaction coefficient. As explained by Hamada (1976), the reaction function of the euro area passes through the point of tangency of each EA contour with horizontal lines. The reaction function of the United States passes through the point of tangency of each U.S. contour with vertical lines. The first interesting result is that the reaction functions are perpendicular: the Nash equilibrium involves strictly dominant strategies. This result suggests that, for the strategy space considered here, there is no monetary policy interdependence, although there are international monetary policy spillovers. The second interesting result is that the Nash equilibrium (denoted by "N" in the graph) differs from the cooperative equilibrium (denoted by "C" in the graph): the Nash equilibrium implies a weaker response to wage inflation than the cooperative equilibrium.

For the game described in figure 3.3 the gains from cooperation amount to 0.0013 percent for the euro area and 0.0021 percent for the United States (in consumption units). While these numbers are smaller than those presented in table 3.7 for the same degree of openness but under the open-

23. We consider this case because it makes the graphical analysis more visible.

Table 3.8 **Welfare decomposition: Cooperative policy vs. calibrated simple rules**

Variable	All shocks	mkp^{EA}	mkp^{US}	Σ_{EA} other shocks	Σ_{US} other shocks
$E_{t0}[Welf^{EA}]$	0.1366	0.0145	0.0248	0.055	0.0424
$E_{t0}[Welf^{US}]$	0.1067	*–0.0088*	*–0.0161*	0.0224	0.1092

loop Nash equilibrium, one should notice that the level of welfare obtained under cooperation with this simple rule is lower than that obtained under the Ramsey cooperative allocation. The difference between the former and the latter amounts to –0.4289 percent for the euro area and 0.2287 percent for the United States, making the simple rule suboptimal from the global point of view.

These experiments also confirm that under the benchmark model; that is, with a smaller degree of openness, the gains from cooperation are smaller, amounting to 0.00008 percent for the euro area and –0.00003 percent for the United States.

Finally, table 3.8 shows that the loss incurred in adopting the calibrated rule as opposed to the (Ramsey) optimal cooperative policy are not very large. Levin et al. (2006) in a closed economy model estimated with U.S. data, find that the loss incurred by adopting the estimated simple interest rate rule as opposed to the optimal policy implies a welfare cost of about 0.56 percent of steady-state consumption. We find a welfare cost that is about five times smaller.

3.7 Conclusion

In this chapter, we have analyzed the gains from monetary policy cooperation in a quantitative two-region DSGE model for the euro area and the United States. A number of recent papers have revived the debate about the gains from international monetary policy cooperation. None of these, nevertheless, has used large-scale DSGE models to quantify the gains from cooperation. Our chapter is a first attempt to fill this gap. Our analysis shows that the gains from cooperation are very sensitive to the degree of openness of the economies. Given the current degree of openness of the U.S. and euro area economies, and in line with the recent literature, we find that the gains from cooperation are small. They amount to about 0.03 percent of steady-state consumption. This is an order of magnitude higher than the gains suggested by Obstfeld and Rogoff (2002), but nevertheless very small. As we increase the degree of openness from 10 to 15 percent to about 32 percent, the gains from cooperation rise to a sizable level; that is, about 1 percent of steady-state consumption. Our analysis, therefore, suggests that the recent trends in international economic integration will be accompanied by larger gains from policy cooperation.

Our analysis also shows that markup shocks are the most important source of gains from international monetary policy cooperation. A deeper understanding of the sources of these type of disturbances will therefore be crucial for gauging the need for closer cooperation in the future.

There are various potentially fruitful avenues for further research. First, in the absence of a fully estimated two-region version of the NAWM, we have used a calibrated version of the model. Performing the same analysis on an estimated model would be useful in providing a benchmark for performing robustness and sensitivity analysis. In particular, one could use the posterior distribution of the model to calculate the empirically relevant range of the gains from cooperation given the structure of the economy. Second, we have focused on price markup shocks as the only inefficient sources of variation in the dynamics of the economy (with the exception of the exchange rate shocks). A full empirical analysis should also investigate the impact of markup shocks in the labor market and the imported goods sector. Third, we have focused our analysis of the noncooperative equilibrium to an open-loop Nash equilibrium where the monetary policy instruments are defined in terms of nominal money growth rates. An alternative and possibly more plausible game is one where each monetary authority takes the reaction function of the foreign central bank as given.

In section 3.6 we have taken a first step in that direction, analyzing closed-loop Nash equilibria in a few simple feedback rules. The results confirm our findings that in the benchmark case the gains from cooperation are small but increasing in the degree of trade integration. However, a more complete analysis using more complicated feedback rules is warranted. Fourth, the importance of markup shocks for the gains from cooperation raises questions about the microfoundations of those shocks. A deeper theory of why prices are sticky and what are the sources of the high-frequency variation in some prices would be important to gain more confidence in the welfare implications of such markup shocks.

Appendix

Description of the Solution Method

The cooperative and noncooperative (open-loop Nash) nonlinear first-order conditions of the policymakers' problem were derived using our Matlab code (compatible with DYNARE [Juillard 1996]). This code ("Lq-solution") is available from the authors on request. The derivation of the policymakers' first-order conditions is based on Benigno and Woodford (2006).

As money is neutral in the steady state of our model, the solution of the steady-state value of the endogenous variables is independent of the solution of the steady-state value of the Lagrange multipliers of the policy problem. The steady state of the structural equations was solved using a suite of nonlinear solvers (SolvOpt, by Kuntsevich and Kappel [1997], SA (simulated annealing) by Goffe [1996] and Matlab's fsolve with use of the analytical Jacobian of the model). The steady-state value of the Lagrange multipliers is then obtained by solving a least-squares problem.

The (first- and second-order accurate) state-space solution of the model (under the different specifications of monetary policy) was then obtained using Dynare (version 4).

The conditional moments were constructed by iterating the first- and second-order accurate state-space solutions returned by Dynare.

For the calibration exercise we used a combination of Dynare output and our own Matlab codes (including HP filtering).

References

Backus, D., P. Kehoe, and F. Kydland. 1994. Dynamics of the trade balance and terms of trade: The J-curve? *American Economic Review* 84 (1): 84–103.

Backus, D. K., and M. J. Crucini. 2000. Oil prices and the terms of trade. *Journal of International Economics* 50 (1): 185–213.

Bayoumi, T., D. Laxton, and P. Pesenti. 2001. Benefits and spillovers of greater competition in Europe: A macroeconomic assessment. European Central Bank (ECB) Working Paper no. 341.

Beetsma, R., and H. Jensen. 2005. Monetary and fiscal policy interactions in a micro-founded model of a monetary union. *Journal of International Economics* 67 (2): 320–52.

Benigno, G., and P. Benigno. 2003. Price stability in open economies. *Review of Economic Studies* 70 (4): 743–64.

———. 2006. Designing targeting rules for international monetary policy cooperation. *Journal of Monetary Economics* 53 (3): 473–506.

Benigno, P. 2001. Price stability with imperfect financial integration. Center for Economic Policy Research (CEPR) Discussion Paper no. DP2854.

———. 2002. A simple approach to international monetary policy coordination. *Journal of International Economics* 57 (1): 177–96.

Benigno, P., and M. Woodford. 2004a. Inflation stabilization and welfare: The case of a distorted steady state. Columbia University, Department of Economics Discussion Paper no. 0405-04.

———. 2004b. Optimal monetary and fiscal policy: A linear-quadratic approach. In *NBER Macroeconomics Annual,* ed. M. Gertler and K. Rogoff, 271–332. Cambridge, MA: MIT Press.

———. 2006. Linear-quadratic approximation of optimal policy problems. NBER Working Paper no. 12672. Cambridge, MA: National Bureau of Economic Research, November.

Blake, A. P., and P. F. Westaway. 1995. Time consistent policymaking: The infinite horizon linear-quadratic case. National Institute of Economic and Social Research (NIESR) Discussion Paper no. 86.

Calvo, G. A. 1983. Staggered prices in a utility-maximizing framework. *Journal of Monetary Economics* 12 (3): 383–98.
Campa, J., and L. S. Goldberg. 2002. Exchange rate pass-through into import prices: A macro or micro phenomenon? NBER Working Paper no. 8934. Cambridge, MA: National Bureau of Economic Research, May.
Canzoneri, M. B., R. E. Cumby, and B. T. Diba. 2002. The need for international policy coordination: What's old, what's new, what's yet to come. NBER Working Paper no. 8765. Cambridge, MA: National Bureau of Economic Research, February.
Canzoneri, M., and J. Gray. 1985. Monetary policy games and the consequences of non-cooperative behaviour. *International Economic Review* 26:547–64.
Canzoneri, M. B., and D. W. Henderson. 1989. Optimal choice of monetary policy instruments in a simple two country game. In *Dynamic policy games in economics,* ed. F. van der Ploeg and A. de Zeeuw, 547–64. Amsterdam: North-Holland.
———. 1992. *Monetary policy in interdependent economies: A game-theoretic approach.* Cambridge, MA: MIT Press.
Cho, J.-O., and T. F. Cooley. 2003. Business cycle uncertainty and economic welfare. Center for Economic Development (CED) Working Paper no. 0303.
Christoffel, K., G. Coenen, and A. Warne. 2008. The new area-wide model in the euro area: Specification, estimation and properties. ECB Working Paper no. 944.
Clarida, R., J. Galí, and M. Gertler. 2002. A simple framework for international monetary policy analysis. *Journal of Monetary Economics* 49 (5): 879–904.
Coenen, G., P. McAdam, and R. Straub. 2007. Tax reform and labour-market performance in the Euro area: A simulation-based analysis using the new area-wide model. ECB Working Paper no. 747.
Corsetti, G., and P. Pesenti. 2001. Welfare and macroeconomic interdependence. *Quarterly Journal of Economics* 116 (2): 421–45.
De Fiore, F., and G. Lombardo. 2007. The gains from monetary policy cooperation in a large DSGE model with oil. European Central Bank. Unpublished Manuscript.
de Walque, G., F. Smets, and R. Wouters. 2005. An estimated two-country DSGE model for the Euro area and the U.S. economy. National Bank of Belgium. Unpublished Manuscript.
Devereux, M. B., and A. Sutherland. 2007. Solving for country portfolios in open economy macro models. IMF Working Paper no. 07/284. Washington, DC: International Monetary Fund.
Erceg, C. J., L. Guerrieri, and C. Gust. 2006. SIGMA: A new open economy model for policy analysis. International Finance Discussion Paper no. 835. Board of Governors of the Federal Reserve System.
Goffe, W. L. 1996. SIMANN: A global optimization algorithm using simulated annealing. *Studies in Nonlinear Dynamics & Econometrics* 1 (3): 169–76.
Hamada, K. 1976. A strategic analysis of monetary interdependence. *Journal of Political Economy* 84 (4): 677–700.
Henderson, D. W., and N. Zhu. 1990. Uncertainty and the choice of instruments in a two-country monetary-policy game. *Open Economies Review* 1 (1): 39–65.
Juillard, M. 1996. Dynare: A program for the resolution and simulation of dynamic models with forward variables through the use of a relaxation algorithm. CEPREMAP Working Paper (Couverture Orange) no. 9602.
Justiniano, A., and B. Preston. 2008. Can structural small open economy models account for the influence of foreign disturbances? NBER Working Paper no. 14547. Cambridge, MA: National Bureau of Economic Research, December.
Kuntsevich, A., and F. Kappel. 1997. Solvopt: The solver for local nonlinear opti-

mization Problems. Institute for Mathematics, Karl-Franzens University of Graz. Unpublished Manuscript.
Lane, P. 2001. The new open economy macroeconomics: A survey. *Journal of International Economics* 54 (2): 235–66.
Levin, A. T., A. Onatski, J. C. Williams, and N. Williams. 2006. Monetary policy under uncertainty in micro-founded macroeconometric models. In *NBER Macroeconomics Annual 2005,* ed. M. Gertler and K. Rogoff, 229–312. Cambridge, MA: MIT Press.
Levine, P., J. Pearlman, and R. Pierce. 2008. Linear-quadratic approximation, external habit, and targeting rules. *Journal of Economic Dynamics and Control* 32 (10): 3315–49.
Lombardo, G., and A. Sutherland. 2004. Monetary and fiscal interactions in open economies. *Journal of Macroeconomics* 26 (2): 319–48.
———. 2006. Policy instrument choice and non-coordinated monetary policy in interdependent economies. *Journal of International Money and Finance* 25 (6): 855–73.
Monacelli, T. 2005. Monetary policy in a low pass-through environment. *Journal of Money, Credit, and Banking* 37:1047–66.
Obstfeld, M., and K. Rogoff. 2002. Global implications of self-oriented national monetary policy rules. *Quarterly Journal of Economics* 117:503–35.
Oudiz, G., and J. Sachs. 1984. Macroeconomic policy coordination among the industrial economies. *Brooking Papers on Economic Activity* 15 (1): 1–75. Washington, DC: Brookings Institution.
Rogoff, K. 1985. Can international monetary policy cooperation be counterproductive? *Journal of International Economics* 18 (3–4): 199–217.
Sachs, J. 1983. International policy coordination in a dynamic macroeconomic model. NBER Working paper no. 1166. Cambridge, MA: National Bureau of Economic Research, July.
Schmitt-Grohé, S., and M. Uribe. 2004a. Optimal operational monetary policy in the Christiano-Eichenbaum-Evans model of the U.S. business cycle. NBER Working Paper no. 10724. Cambridge, MA: National Bureau of Economic Research, September.
———. 2004b. Solving dynamic general equilibrium models using a second-order approximation to the policy function. *Journal of Economic Dynamics and Control* 28 (4): 645–858.
———. 2007a. Optimal inflation stabilization in a medium-scale macroeconomic model. In *Monetary policy under inflation targeting,* ed. K. Schmidt-Hebbel and F. S. Mishkin. 125–86. Santiago, Chile: Central Bank of Chile.
———. 2007b. Optimal simple, and implementable monetary and fiscal rules. *Journal of Monetary Economics* 54 (6): 1702–25.
Schorfheide, F., and T. A. Lubik. 2005. A Bayesian look at new open economy macroeconomics. In *NBER Macroeconomics Annual,* ed. M. Gertler and K. Rogoff, 313–66. Cambridge, MA: MIT Press.
Smets, F., and R. Wouters. 2003. An estimated stochastic dynamic general equilibrium model of the euro area. *Journal of the European Economic Association* 1:1123–75.
———. 2007. Shocks and frictions in U.S. business cycles: A Bayesia DSGE approach. *American Economic Review* 97 (3): 586–606.
Sutherland, A. 2004. International monetary policy coordination and financial market integration. CEPR Discussion Paper no. 4251.
Taylor, J. B. 1993. Discretion versus policy rules in practice. *Carnegie-Rochester Conference Series on Public Policy* 39:195–214.

Turnovsky, S., and V. d'Orey. 1989. The choice of monetary instrument in two interdependent economies under uncertainty. *Journal of Monetary Economics* 23 (1): 121–33.
Woodford, M. 2003. *Interest and prices: Foundations of a theory of monetary policy.* Princeton, NJ: Princeton University Press.

Comment Christopher A. Sims

The chapter sets up a state of the art two-country calibrated model in which monetary policy has welfare effects. It uses a second-order expansion to get accurate calculations of these effects, using the model's own agent utility functions, and thereby gives us a prototype of how this analysis should be done. But as the authors acknowledge in various caveats in the text, it is really only a prototype. There are many aspects of the model that are dubious and likely to be important to the conclusion. Most of my comments, therefore, point out questionable aspects of the chapter. At the end, I provide a constructive suggestion.

The Nature of the Game

The chapter models interaction of monetary authorities as a Nash equilibrium, but the nature of such an equilibrium depends crucially on what variables each player treats as given when choosing the player's own moves. The chapter's central case is that each monetary authority takes the entire past and future of the other's money stock as given in optimizing its own money stock choice. This is certainly unrealistic, and the chapter's own sensitivity analyses show that its conclusion that the welfare gains from cooperation are small is sensitive to this choice.

It is perhaps worthwhile to catalog the results of the chapter's sensitivity analysis: if the policy choice variables are the time paths of interest rates, the result is instability—in other words, extremely large welfare losses from noncooperation. The same is true if the policy choice variable is the producer price index (PPI). If the choice variable is consumer price index (CPI) path, the losses from noncooperation are finite, but ten times larger than in the case where the money time path is the choice variable. When the choice variables are the coefficients in a Taylor rule, the losses from noncooperation are minuscule, but "cooperation" in the choice of these coefficients leaves the equilibrium welfare far from the Ramsey optimal solution—by an amount

Christopher A. Sims is the Harold H. Helm '20 Professor of Economics and Banking at Princeton University and a research associate of the National Bureau of Economic Research.
This research was supported in part by National Science Foundation (NSF) grant SES-0719055.

of the same order of magnitude as the cost of noncooperation with the CPI choice variable.

This last observation suggests another reason to consider the chapter's results skeptically: except for the experiment with policy rule coefficients as choice variables, monetary authorities are assumed to set policy with complete information as to the nature of the shocks that have hit the economy, when in fact one of the key conundrums of monetary policy is the difficulty of being sure what the nature of recent shocks has been. This is why both the cooperative and noncooperative Taylor rule equilibria in the chapter give lower welfare than Ramsey: the Taylor rule policies depend only on a few clearly observable variables, while the Ramsey policies (and the other Nash policies in the chapter) do not impose such a constraint.

Notice that I have been talking about the "costs of noncooperation." It is traditional in this literature to study what are called "gains from cooperation." This suggests that we are studying the effects of doing something new in the way of cooperation. But in this chapter, and probably in reality, historically estimated policy rules give rise to behavior that is much closer to the fully cooperative equilibrium than to the noncooperative equilibrium. In fact, central banks are acutely aware of the likely reactions of other central banks to their own policy actions, and few now make policy, or assume that others make policy, based on M time paths. We are probably, therefore, in an equilibrium much more sophisticated than Nash equilibrium, with reputation playing an important role. Nonetheless, it is worth asking what could go wrong if central banks did attempt "beggar thy neighbor" policies, and the chapter should be considered in that light.

There is an interesting and consequential monetary policy game going on right now, involving international policy interactions that are not considered in this chapter. Will the United States take advantage of its ability to reduce domestic fiscal obligations by inflating away the value of its debt? Will non-U.S. monetary authorities be tempted to be the "first to unload" U.S. nominal debt? Doepke and Schneider (2006) argue that the benefits to the U.S. population as a whole of doing this are at an historic high. In the chapter's model, though, only U.S. nominal securities are traded. In fact, valuation effects depend on net positions in assets of both (all) denominations. These effects are large relative to those analyzed in this chapter.

Other Dubious Aspects of the Model and the Results

The model is calibrated to make about 70 percent of output explained by productivity and labor supply shocks in the long run. These long-run percentages are very poorly pinned down in the data; across different early Smets/Wouters papers the percentages jump around, in some cases with technology shocks given a minor role. At one- and two-year horizons, the percentages attributed to productivity shocks are usually much smaller. Is that true here? This chapter's percentages are at the upper end of the range in the literature fitting big, multishock models. The chapter cites papers by Smets and Wouters from 2003 and 2007 that display estimated dynamic stochastic general equilibrium (DSGE) models of the euro area and the United States, respectively, to support its specification that 70 percent of output variance is accounted for by technology and labor supply shocks. But in the first of those papers, for the euro area, the percentages of long-run variance in output accounted for by technology, labor supply, markup shocks, and monetary policy shocks are 8, 33, 3, and 28, respectively, whereas in the current chapter the corresponding percentages are 55, 20, 1, and 6. The percentages in the later paper, about the United States, are in line with the percentages in the current chapter, but in that paper the markup shocks account for almost no long-run variance, even for inflation.

Because technology shocks offer little room for monetary policy to offset them, it seems likely that the large role attributed to technology shocks might be a reason for the chapter's small estimates of the welfare effects of monetary policy coordination. In fact, the chapter's own discussion makes clear that "markup shocks" are the dominant source of gains from cooperation. It would have been useful, therefore, to see a sensitivity analysis in which the relative sizes of the shock variances were varied over the range observed in the empirical literature.

The model assumes full insurance of individual labor income fluctuations. Modeling the distribution of the heterogeneous effects of aggregate fluctuations on individuals may not be important for matching aggregate time series behavior, but for welfare evaluation it is critical. Despite habit in consumption, the model implies very limited welfare losses from volatile responses of interest rates, consumption, and gross domestic product (GDP) to markup shocks in the noncooperative solution. This conclusion would probably change if the limited insurability of the effects of most individual job losses were taken into account.

The chapter's model contains "markup shocks" and "uncovered interest parity" (UIP) shocks. The markup shocks play a central role in generating inflation, while in the calibrated model the UIP shocks, though large, are unimportant in explaining other variables. Because the interpretation of these shocks is unclear, the assumptions about their properties should be checked. The markup shocks are treated in the model as a varying subsidy to production, but there is obviously no such thing in reality. Of course other interpretations are possible, but since the shocks are somewhat ill-defined, the assumption that they are orthogonal to other shocks, and particularly policy shocks, should be checked. The same is true for the large UIP shocks. In both cases, it is assumed that the shocks are orthogonal to other shocks, but by calculating the implied values of the shocks in the actual data, it should be possible to check whether the estimated realized shocks are reasonably close to satisfying these assumptions.

The model does "microfounded" welfare calculations, using the model's own specification of agents' utility function. But in the model the household utility function and the technology include elements (habit persistence, investment adjustment costs, and shocks thereto) that help match macro time series facts but have little direct micro empirical support. The Calvo pricing leads to welfare costs arising from dispersion in output levels across firms. It is doubtful that this is the main source of costs of inflation, and there is again no empirical microfoundation for this aspect of the "microfounded" macro model. Idiosyncratic price volatility, combined with sluggish response of price aggregates to monetary policy, emerges naturally from information-theoretic models. But these would have very different welfare implications.

Because the welfare measure is therefore of uncertain value, it would be interesting to have more discussion of what the effects of noncooperation are on the behavior of the economy generally, as opposed to effects on the one-dimensional welfare measure. The responses of the economies to markup shocks are drastically different in the noncooperative Nash equilibrium. Interest rates, consumption, and GDP oscillate widely for several periods in response to these shocks, as the monetary authorities try, without success, to shift negative effects onto each other. If we thought the model reliable in predicting effects of policy changes on model variables, we might well characterize these differences between noncooperative and cooperative solutions as big, not small.

Reference

Doepke, M., and M. Schneider. 2006. Inflation and the redistribution of nominal wealth. *Journal of Political Economy* 114 (6): 1069–97.

II

Extending the Baseline Models to Address Policy Issues

4

Current Account Dynamics and Monetary Policy

Andrea Ferrero, Mark Gertler, and Lars E. O. Svensson

4.1 Introduction

A salient feature of the global economy is the emergence of significant global imbalances over the past decade, reflected principally by the large current account deficit of the United States, with the rest of the world portrayed in the top panel of figure 4.1. There has been considerable debate over the sources of these imbalances as well as over the implications they may have for future economic behavior. Perhaps most notably, Obstfeld and Rogoff (2005) (henceforth OR) argue that, regardless of origins of the recent U.S. current account deficit, a correction of this imbalance will require a real depreciation of the dollar on the order of 30 percent. While there is far from universal agreement with the OR hypothesis, the slide in the dollar over the past several years (bottom panel of figure 4.1) is certainly consistent with their scenario.

Despite the recent discussions about current account imbalances and exchange rates, much less attention has been paid to the implications for

Andrea Ferrero is an economist at the Federal Reserve Bank of New York. Mark Gertler is the Henry and Lucy Moses Professor of Economics at New York University and a research associate of the National Bureau of Economic Research. Lars E. O. Svensson is deputy governor of Sveriges Riksbank, a professor of economics at Princeton University, and a research associate of the National Bureau of Economic Research.

Prepared for the NBER conference on "International Dimensions of Monetary Policy" in Girona (Spain), June 2007. The authors are grateful to Gianluca Benigno, Paul Bergin, Luca Dedola, Maurice Obstfeld, and Paolo Pesenti for their discussions and also to participants at several conferences for helpful comments. Gertler thanks the National Science Foundation (NSF) and the Guggenheim Foundation for financial support. The views expressed in this chapter are those of the authors and do not necessarily reflect the position of the Federal Reserve Bank of New York, the Federal Reserve System, the Sveriges Riksbank, or the National Bureau of Economic Research.

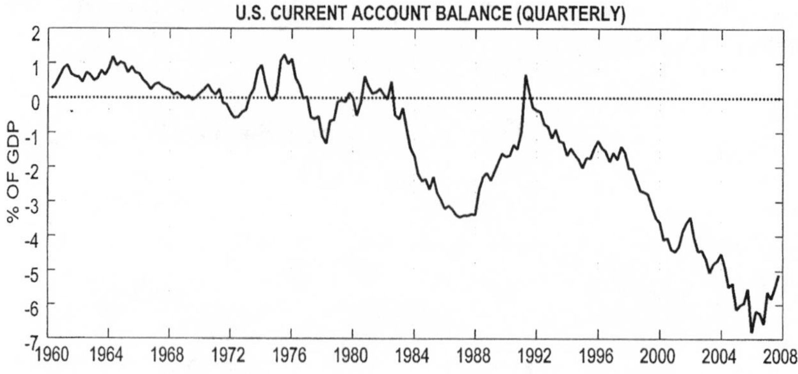

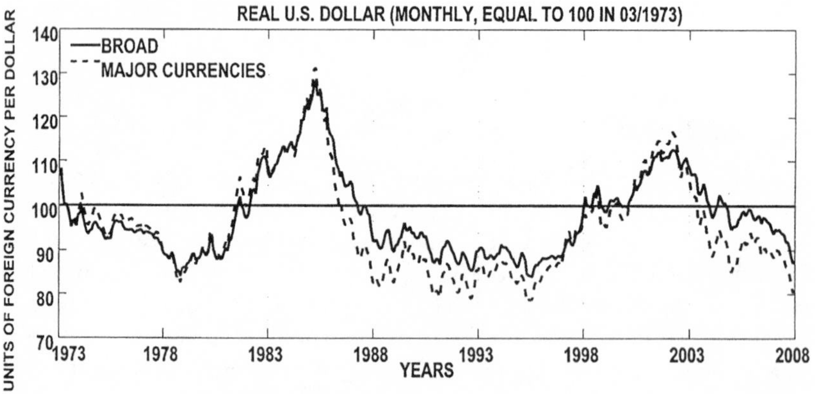

Fig. 4.1 U.S. Current Account and real exchange rate

Source: Bureau of Economic Analysis and Board of Governors of the Federal Reserve System.

monetary policy. At first blush, it may seem that any connection with monetary policy is at best indirect. Given that the U.S. current account deficit ultimately reflects saving/investment differences with the rest of the world, monetary policy management cannot be assigned any direct responsibility. Similarly, the adjustment of real exchange rates to correct these imbalances is beyond the direct province of monetary policy.

Nonetheless, while monetary policy is arguably not the cause of current account deficits and surpluses, there are potentially important implications of these imbalances for the management of monetary policy. For example, to the extent that OR are correct about the adjustment of exchanges rates, the depreciation of the dollar is potentially a source of inflationary pressure. To be sure, in the long run inflation is ultimately a monetary phenomenon and even in a global environment, the Federal Reserve retains full control over its monetary policy. Nonetheless, as Rogoff (2007) has suggested, movements in international relative prices may influence short-run inflation dynamics.

In the case of current account adjustment, any associated depreciation may force the central bank into choosing between maintaining price stability or output at potential. That is, even if the current account adjustment plays out smoothly, the depreciation of the dollar may induce extra pressure on consumer price index (CPI) inflation for a period of time that can only be offset by tightening of monetary policy, with potential repercussions for real activity.

Further, even if unlikely, it is not inconceivable that there might be a quick reversal of the U.S. current account, perhaps in response to some adverse news about the long-run growth prospects of the U.S. economy relative to the rest of the world. Under this "sudden stop" scenario, there would likely be a rapid depreciation of the dollar along with a sharp contraction in domestic spending required to bring the current account into line. These rapid and large adjustments could potentially create a complex balancing act for the Federal Reserve. Even if such a circumstance is remote, it is certainly worth exploring policy options under this kind of worst-case scenario.

In this chapter, accordingly, we explore the implications of current account imbalances for monetary policy. To do so, we develop a simple two-country monetary dynamic stochastic general equilibrium (DSGE) model. The framework nests the static endowment world economy that OR used to study the link between the current account and exchange rates. To this framework, we add explicit dynamics and consider production decisions under nominal rigidities. The end product is a framework where the current account, exchange rates, and both output and inflation within each country are determined endogenously. The behavior of each economy, further, depends on the monetary policy decisions of each country. We then use the model to study how different monetary policies affect aggregate economic behavior in light of current account developments.

We model the current account imbalance as the product of cross-country differences in expected productivity growth as well as differences in saving propensities, the two main factors typically cited as underlying the recent situation.[1] We initialize the model to approximately match the recent U.S. current account deficit, which is roughly 5 percent of gross domestic product (GDP). The expected depreciation the model predicts is then very close to the 30 percent estimate of OR. This is not entirely surprising since the way we calibrate our model is very consistent with OR's approach. In this regard, we stress that our goal is not to establish whether or not OR's forecast is correct. Rather, it is to consider various monetary policy strategies in an environment where current imbalances do exert pressures on the domestic

1. To be clear, we model differences in consumption/saving propensities as preferences shocks that are meant to be a catch-all for factors that could cause differences in national savings rates such as fiscal policies, demographics, and capital market frictions. For recent analyses of current account behavior, see, for example, Engel and Rogers (2006); Backus et al. (2006); Caballero, Fahri, and Gourinchas (2007); Ferrero (2007), Faruquee et al. (2005); and Mendoza, Quadrini, and Rios-Rull (2007).

economy of the type OR envision. Put differently, what we are engaged in should be regarded as "war-gaming" different scenarios that could prove challenging for monetary policy.

We consider two main scenarios. The first we refer to as the "slow burn." In this case the current account adjustment plays out slowly and smoothly. There are no major shocks along the way. Nonetheless, the steady depreciation of the dollar places persistent pressures on CPI inflation. In the second scenario, "the fast burn," there is a reversal of the current account deficit that plays out over the course of a year. We model the reversal as a revision in beliefs about future productivity growth in the home country relative to the foreign country. Under each scenario, we consider the implications of different monetary policies for the home and foreign countries.

There has been other work that examines monetary policies under different scenarios for current account adjustment. Several authors, for example, have employed the large scale Global Economy Model (GEM) developed by the International Monetary Fund (IMF) exactly for this purpose (e.g., Faruquee et al. 2005).[2] We differ by restricting attention to a small scale model, with the aim of developing a set of qualitative results. Thus, we abstract from many of the frictions present in the GEM framework that help tightly fit the data. Instead, we incorporate a relatively minimal set of frictions with the aim of a balance between facilitating qualitative analysis and at the same time permitting the model to generate quantitative predictions that are "in the ball park."

In section 4.2 we develop the basic model. It is a variation of the monetary two-country DSGE model with nominal rigidities developed by Obstfeld and Rogoff (2002), Clarida, Galí, and Gertler (2002), Corsetti and Pesenti (2005), Benigno and Benigno (2006), and others. The key differences involve (a) introducing incomplete international capital markets in order to study international lending and borrowing and (b) allowing for both tradable and nontradable goods in order to nest the OR model of the current account and real exchanges rates. We finish this section by analyzing the relation between our model and OR's specification. Section 4.3 presents the log-linear model and characterizes the monetary transmission mechanism in this kind of environment. Section 4.4 then discusses our numerical simulations under different scenarios for current account adjustment and explores the implications of different monetary rules. Our baseline case presumes perfect pass-through of exchange rates to import prices. Section 4.5 considers the implications of imperfect pass-through. Concluding remarks are in section 4.6.

4.2 The Model

We begin this section with a brief overview of the model, then present the details of the production sectors, and close with a description of the equilibrium.

2. For related work, see the references in the *IMF World Economic Outlook,* April 2007.

4.2.1 Overview

The framework is a variation of OR's model of current account adjustment and the exchange rate. Whereas OR studied a simple two-country endowment economy, we add production, nominal price rigidities, and monetary policy. In addition, while OR performed the static experiment of examining the response of the exchange rate to closure of the current account deficit, we examine the dynamic adjustment path. Our interest is to explore the implications of different adjustment scenarios for the appropriate course of monetary policy.

There are two countries: home (H) and foreign (F). Each country has one representative household that is assumed to behave competitively.[3] Within each country, the household consumes tradable and nontradable consumption goods. Tradable goods, further, consist of both home- and foreign-produced goods. For simplicity, there are no capital goods.

Each household consists of a continuum of workers of measure unity. Each member of the household consumes the same amount. Hence, there is perfect risk-sharing within each country. Each worker works in a particular firm in the country that produces intermediate tradable or nontradable goods. Therefore, there is a continuum of intermediate goods firms of measure unity. Because we want to allow for some real rigidity in price setting, we introduce local labor markets for each intermediate-goods firm (see, for instance, Woodford [2003]). A fraction of the workers work in the nontradable goods sector, while the rest work in the tradable goods sector.

Hence, there are two production sectors within each country: one for nontradable goods and one for a domestic tradable good. Within each sector, there are final and intermediate goods firms. Within each sector, competitive final goods firms produce a single homogenous good with a constant elasticity of substitution (CES) technology that combines differentiated intermediate goods. Intermediate goods firms are monopolistic competitors and set prices on a staggered basis.

Because we wish to study current account dynamics, we allow for incomplete financial markets at the international level. There is a single bond that is traded internationally and is denominated in units of home currency.[4] Foreign country citizens may also hold a bond denominated in units of foreign currency, but this bond is not traded internationally.[5]

3. We could alternatively consider a continuum of measure unity of identical households in each country.

4. The denomination of the international asset in U.S. currency is the only source of valuation effects in our model. If the dollar depreciates, the real value of U.S. foreign liabilities reduces, hence generating a capital gain. Cavallo and Tille (2006) discuss in detail how this mechanism can affect the rebalancing of the U.S. current account deficit in the context of the OR model. Bems and Dedola (2006) investigate the role of cross-country equity holdings and find that this channel can smooth the current account adjustment by increasing risk-sharing.

5. Since there is complete risk-sharing within a country, this bond is redundant. We simply add it to derive an uncovered interest parity condition.

While we allow for nominal price rigidities in both the nontradable and tradable sectors, for simplicity, we assume in our baseline case that across borders there is perfect exchange rate pass-through. Hence, the law of one price holds for tradable goods. There is of course considerable evidence of imperfect pass-through from exchange rates to import prices (see, for instance, Campa and Goldberg [2006]). Nonetheless, we think there are several reasons why in our baseline case it may be reasonable to abstract from this consideration. First, evidence that firms adjust prices sluggishly to "normal" exchange movements may not be relevant to situations where there are sudden large exchange rate movements, as could happen in a current account reversal. Second, under the baseline calibration, our model is broadly consistent with the evidence on low pass-through of exchange rates to final consumer prices. We obtain low pass-through to consumer prices because the calibrated import share is low, as is consistent with the evidence.[6] Nonetheless, it can be argued that the model with perfect pass-through misses out on some of the very high frequency dynamics between exchange rates, import prices, and final consumer prices. We accordingly extend the baseline model to allow for imperfect pass-through in section 4.6.

We next present the details of the model. We characterize the equations for the home country. Unless stated otherwise, there is a symmetric condition for the foreign country.

4.2.2 The Household

Let C_t be the following composite of tradable and nontradable consumption goods, C_{Tt} and C_{Nt}, respectively:

$$C_t \equiv \frac{C_{Tt}^{\gamma} C_{Nt}^{1-\gamma}}{\gamma(1-\gamma)}. \tag{1}$$

We employ the Cobb-Douglas specification to maintain analytical tractability. The implied elasticity of substitution of unity between tradables and nontradables, however, is not unreasonable from a quantitative standpoint and corresponds to the baseline case of OR.[7]

Tradable consumption goods, in turn, are the following composite of home tradables C_{Ht} and foreign tradables, C_{Ft}:

$$C_{Tt} \equiv [\alpha^{1/\eta}(C_{Ht})^{(\eta-1)/\eta} + (1-\alpha)^{1/\eta}(C_{Ft})^{(\eta-1)/\eta}]^{\eta/(\eta-1)}. \tag{2}$$

Following OR, we allow for home bias in tradables, that is, $\alpha > 0.5$. We use a CES specification as opposed to Cobb-Douglas, given that the elasticity of

6. Campa and Goldberg (2006) estimate an exchange rate pass-through elasticity to consumer prices of 0.08, which is close to the analogous value in our model. In our framework, the low value obtains because imports in the consumption bundle have small weight relative to nontraded goods and home tradables.

7. Model simulations suggest that varying this elasticity from 0.5 to 2.0 (the range considered by OR) does not have a major effect on the quantitative results.

substitution among tradables is likely to be higher than across tradables and nontradables. Further, as we will demonstrate, the departure from Cobb-Douglas permits the terms of trade to have a direct effect on the trade balance.

Given that the household minimizes expenditure costs given (1) and (2), the index for the nominal price of the consumption composite, P_t, is given by the following function of the price of tradables P_{Tt} and the price non-tradables P_{Nt}:

(3) $$P_t = P_{Tt}^{\gamma} P_{Nt}^{1-\gamma}.$$

Similarly, from cost minimization, we may express P_{Tt} as the following function of the price of home tradables P_{Ht}, and the (domestic currency) price of foreign tradables, P_{Ft}:

(4) $$P_{Tt} = [\alpha P_{Ht}^{1-\eta} + (1-\alpha) P_{Ft}^{1-\eta}]^{1/(1-\eta)}.$$

We assume that the law of one price holds for tradables. Let ε_t be the nominal exchange rate and let the superscript * denote the corresponding variable for the foreign country. Then, we have:

$$P_{jt} = \varepsilon_t P_{jt}^{*}$$

for $j = H, F$.

The household in each country consists of a continuum of workers who consume and supply labor. Within the household, a fraction γ of workers work in the tradable goods sector, while a fraction $1 - \gamma$ work in the nontradable goods sector. As we noted earlier, within each sector, labor markets are local, and we assume that each worker works in a particular firm within the sector.[8] Let $f \in (0, 1)$ index the intermediate goods firms, and let $f \in [0, \gamma)$ denote firms in the tradable goods sector and let $f \in (\gamma, 1)$ denote firms in the nontradable goods sector. Then we also let $f \in (0, 1)$ index workers in the household. Let $L_{kt}(f)$ denote hours worked by worker f in sector $k = H$, N (where $f \in [0, \gamma)$ for $k = H$ and $f \in (\gamma, 1)$ for $k = N$). Finally, let θ_t be the household's subjective discount factor. The preferences for the household in period t are then given by

(5) $$U_t \equiv E_t \sum_{s=0}^{\infty} \theta_{t+s-1} u_{t+s},$$

where the period utility u_t is given by

$$u_t \equiv \log C_t - \left[\int_0^{\gamma} \frac{L_{Ht}(f)^{1+\varphi}}{1+\varphi} df + \int_{\gamma}^{1} \frac{L_{Nt}(f)^{1+\varphi}}{1+\varphi} df \right].$$

The discount factor θ_t is endogenous and is defined by the recursion

8. To be clear, the household decides labor supply for each individual worker.

(6) $$\theta_t = \beta_t \theta_{t-1}$$

with

$$\beta_t \equiv \frac{e^{\varsigma t}}{1 + \psi(\log \overline{C}_t - \vartheta)},$$

where $\overline{C}_t$ is detrended consumption, treated as exogenous by the household, and hence, corresponding to an average across households in case we replace the representative household by an explicit continuum of identical households. Following Uzawa (1968), we make the discount factor endogenous to ensure a determinate steady state in the presence of incomplete markets and international lending and borrowing.[9] In particular, we choose the constant ψ to pin down the steady-state discount factor to the desired value and we choose the constant ϑ to ensure $\psi > 0$, which guarantees that the discount factor is decreasing in the level of average consumption.[10] Intuitively, under this formulation, there is a positive spillover from average consumption to individual consumption. Higher consumption within the community induces individuals to want to consume more today relative to the future; that is, β_t decreases. As in Uzawa (1968), indebtedness reduces borrowers' consumption, which raises their discount factor, thus inducing them to save, and vice versa. We stress, however, that this formulation is simply a technical fix. We parametrize the model so that the endogenous discount factor has only a negligible effect on the medium term dynamics by picking ψ to be sufficiently small.

Finally, the variable ς_t is a preference shock that follows a first-order autoregressive process with i.i.d. normal innovations

(7) $$\varsigma_t = \rho_\varsigma \varsigma_{t-1} + u_{\varsigma t}, \quad u_{\varsigma t} \sim \text{i.i.d. } N(0, \sigma_\varsigma^2).$$

The preferences for the foreign household are defined similarly.

Let B_t represent the nominal holdings at the beginning of period $t + 1$ of an internationally traded one-period riskless bond nominated in home currency. Let $W_{kt}(f)$ be the nominal wage in sector $k = H, N$ that worker $f \in [0, 1]$ faces. Finally, let Υ_t be dividends net of lump sum taxes. Then the household's budget constraint is given by

(8) $$P_t C_t + B_t = I_{t-1} B_{t-1} + \int_0^\gamma W_{Ht}(f) L_{Ht}(f) df + \int_\gamma^1 W_{Nt}(f) L_{Nt}(f) df + \Upsilon_t,$$

where I_{t-1} denotes the gross nominal domestic currency interest rate between period $t - 1$ and t.

9. For a recent survey of different approaches to introducing a determinate steady state with incomplete international financial markets, see Bodenstein (2006).

10. Nothing would change significantly if the discount factor depended on utility (perceived as exogenous) instead of consumption. We opt for consumption since it leads to a simpler dynamic relation for the discount factor. The effect on the quantitative performance of the model is negligible.

The household maximizes the utility function given by equation (5) subject to the budget constraint given by equation (8), as well as the definitions of the various composites, given by equations (1) and (2). The first-order necessary conditions of the household's problem are all reasonably conventional.

The allocation between tradables and nontradables is

$$C_{Tt} = \gamma\left(\frac{P_{Tt}}{P_t}\right)^{-1} C_t, \quad C_{Nt} = (1 - \gamma)\left(\frac{P_{Nt}}{P_t}\right)^{-1} C_t. \tag{9}$$

The allocation between home and foreign tradables is

$$C_{Ht} = \alpha\left(\frac{P_{Ht}}{P_{Tt}}\right)^{-\eta} C_{Tt}, \quad C_{Ft} = (1 - \alpha)\left(\frac{P_{Ft}}{P_{Tt}}\right)^{-\eta} C_{Tt}. \tag{10}$$

The consumption saving decisions depend upon a standard Euler equation,

$$\mathrm{E}_t\left[\beta_t I_t \frac{P_t}{P_{t+1}}\left(\frac{C_{t+1}}{C_t}\right)^{-1}\right] = 1. \tag{11}$$

Finally, the sectoral labor supply equations are

$$\frac{W_{kt}(f)}{P_t}\frac{1}{C_t} = L_{kt}(f)^{\varphi}. \tag{12}$$

We assume that the structure of the foreign country is similar, but with two differences. First, the realizations of the country specific shocks may differ across countries. Second, we assume that the foreign country bond is not traded internationally. Thus, while citizens of H trade only in domestic bonds, citizens of F may hold either domestic or foreign country bonds.

Accordingly, given that foreign country citizens must be indifferent between holding domestic and foreign bonds, we obtain the following uncovered interest parity condition:

$$E_t\left\{I_t \frac{\varepsilon_t P_t^*}{\varepsilon_{t+1} P_{t+1}^*}\left(\frac{C_{t+1}^*}{C_t^*}\right)^{-1}\right\} = E_t\left\{I_t^* \frac{P_t^*}{P_{t+1}^*}\left(\frac{C_{t+1}^*}{C_t^*}\right)^{-1}\right\}. \tag{13}$$

Note that, since there is only one representative household in country F, the foreign bond will be in zero net supply in equilibrium.

4.2.3 Firms

Final Goods Firms

As mentioned, $f \in [0, \gamma)$ and $f \in (\gamma, 1)$ denote intermediate goods firms in the tradable goods and nontradable goods sector, respectively. Within sector $k = \{H, N\}$, competitive final goods firms package together intermediate products to produce output, according to the following CES technology:

$$(14) \quad Y_{Ht} \equiv [\gamma^{-1/\sigma} \int_0^{\gamma} Y_{Ht}(f)^{(\sigma-1)/\sigma} df]^{\sigma/(\sigma-1)},$$
$$Y_{Nt} \equiv [(1-\gamma)^{-1/\sigma} \int_{\gamma}^{1} Y_{Nt}(f)^{(\sigma-1)/\sigma} df]^{\sigma/(\sigma-1)}.$$

The parameter σ is the elasticity of substitution among intermediate goods. We assume $\sigma > 1$.

From cost minimization:

$$(15) \quad Y_{Ht}(f) = \gamma^{-1}\left[\frac{P_{Ht}(f)}{P_{Ht}}\right]^{-\sigma} Y_{Ht}, \quad Y_{Nt}(f) = (1-\gamma)^{-1}\left[\frac{P_{Nt}(f)}{P_{Nt}}\right]^{-\sigma} Y_{Nt}.$$

Accordingly, the price index is:

$$(16) \quad P_{Ht} = [\gamma^{-1} \int_0^{\gamma} P_{Ht}(f)^{1-\sigma} df]^{1/(1-\sigma)}, \quad P_{Nt} = [(1-\gamma)^{-1} \int_{\gamma}^{1} P_{Nt}(f)^{1-\sigma} df]^{1/(1-\sigma)}.$$

Intermediate Goods Firms

Each intermediate goods firm produces output using only labor input. Let $Y_{kt}(f)$ be the output of intermediate goods firm f in sector k. Let $L_{kt}(f)$ be total input from the firm's local labor market (supplied by worker f) and let A_t be a productivity factor that is common within the country.[11] We assume that production is linear in labor inputs as follows:

$$(17) \quad Y_{kt}(f) = A_t L_{kt}(f).$$

Let Z_t be trend productivity and e^{a_t} be the cyclical component. Then A_t obeys

$$(18) \quad A_t = Z_t e^{a_t}$$

with

$$\frac{Z_t}{Z_{t-1}} = 1 + g,$$

where g is the trend productivity growth rate. We defer a full description of the cyclical component e^{a_t} to section 4.4.1, other than saying that this component is stationary.

Assuming that the firm acts competitively in the local labor market, cost minimization yields the following expression for the nominal marginal cost of firm f in sector k:

$$(19) \quad MC_{kt}(f) = \frac{W_{kt}(f)}{A_t}.$$

Firms set prices on a staggered basis. Each period a fraction ξ of firms do not adjust their price. These firms produce output to meet demand, assuming the price does not fall below marginal cost. For the fraction $1 - \xi$ that are able to change price, the objective is given by:

11. It is straightforward to allow for sector-specific productivity shocks as well.

$$(20)\qquad E_t \sum_{s=0}^{\infty} \xi^s \Lambda_{t,t+s}[P_{kt}(f) - MC_{k,t+s}(f)]Y_{k,t+s}(f),$$

where $\Lambda_{t,t+s} = \beta_{t+s}(C_{t+s}/C_t)^{-1}(P_t/P_{t+s})$ is the stochastic discount factor between t and $t + s$.

The firm maximizes the objective (20), given the demand for its product (15) and its production function (17). The first-order condition for the optimal reset price P^o_{kt} is given by (21)

$$(21)\qquad E_t\left\{\sum_{s=0}^{\infty} \xi^s \Lambda_{t,t+s}[P^o_{kt} - (1+\mu)MC_{k,t+s}(f)]Y_{k,t+s}(f)\right\} = 0,$$

where $\mu \equiv (\sigma - 1)^{-1}$.

Finally, from the law of large numbers, the price index in each sector evolves according to

$$(22)\qquad P_{kt} = [\xi P^{1-\sigma}_{k,t-1} + (1-\xi)(P^o_{kt})^{1-\sigma}]^{1/(1-\sigma)}.$$

4.2.4 Current Account Dynamics and the Real Exchange Rate

Total nominal domestic bond holdings, B_t, evolve according to

$$(23)\qquad \frac{B_t}{P_t} = \frac{I_{t-1}B_{t-1}}{P_t} + \mathrm{NX}_t,$$

where NX_t is the real value of net exports, given by:

$$(24)\qquad \mathrm{NX}_t \equiv \frac{P_{Ht}Y_{Ht} - P_{Tt}C_{Tt}}{P_t}.$$

The current account reflects the net change in real bond holdings:

$$(25)\qquad \mathrm{CA}_t \equiv \frac{B_t - B_{t-1}}{P_t}.$$

Finally, we define the real exchange rate as

$$(26)\qquad Q_t \equiv \frac{\varepsilon_t P^*_t}{P_t}.$$

4.2.5 Monetary Policy

In our benchmark framework we suppose that monetary policy obeys the following simple interest rate rule with partial adjustment:

$$(27)\qquad I_t = I^{\rho}_{t-1}\tilde{I}^{1-\rho}_t$$

where $\tilde{I}_t$ is the "full adjustment" nominal rate, which depends on the steady-state natural rate of interest in the frictionless zero inflation equilibrium, I, and on the gross inflation rate P_t/P_{t-1}

$$(28)\qquad \tilde{I}_t = I\left(\frac{P_t}{P_{t-1}}\right)^{\phi_\pi}.$$

We begin with this kind of rule as a benchmark because it provides the simplest empirical characterization of monetary policy by the major central banks over the past twenty years (see, for instance, Clarida, Galí, and Gertler [1998]). We will experiment with other rules, however, including targeting rules.

4.2.6 Equilibrium

For both home and foreign tradables, production must equal demand:

$$Y_{Nt} = C_{Nt}, \quad Y^*_{Nt} = C^*_{Nt}. \tag{29}$$

The production of home tradables must equal the sum of the demand from domestic and foreign residents:

$$Y_{Ht} = C_{Ht} + C^*_{Ht}, \tag{30}$$

where C^*_{Ht} denotes the demand for home tradable by the foreign household.

International financial markets must clear:

$$B_t + B^*_t = 0, \tag{31}$$

where B^*_t represents the nominal holdings of the domestic bond by the foreign household. Conditions (31) and (23) imply that the foreign trade balance in units of home consumption, $Q_t \text{NX}^*_t$, must equal the negative of the home trade balance, $-\text{NX}_t$.

Finally, if all these conditions are satisfied, by Walras' Law, the production of foreign tradables equals demand.

This completes the description of the model. There are two special cases to note. First, in the polar case where the probability that a price remains fixed is zero (i.e., $\xi = 0$), the economy converges to a flexible-price equilibrium. Second, with $\xi = 0$ and the Frisch elasticity of labor supply equal to zero (i.e., $\varphi = \infty$), the model converges to the dynamic version of the endowment economy in OR.

Because it will eventually prove convenient in characterizing the full log-linear model, before proceeding further we define aggregate domestic real output, $P_{Yt}Y_t/P_t$ as the sum of the value of the sectoral outputs:

$$\frac{P_{Yt}Y_t}{P_t} = \frac{P_{Ht}Y_{Ht} + P_{Nt}Y_{Nt}}{P_t}, \tag{32}$$

where P_{Yt} is the nominal domestic producer price index. In general, P_{Yt} may differ from P_t since domestic consumption may differ from domestic output. In steady state, however, the trade balance is zero, implying $P_{Yt} = P_t$ is the long-run equilibrium. Outside steady state, no arbitrage requires that P_{Yt} equals the output share weighted sum of the sectoral nominal prices.

4.2.7 International Relative Prices and Current Account: A Comparison with OR

In this section we present some intuition about the workings of our model. To do so, we first describe how our model nests OR's model of current accounts and exchange rates. We then outline how our modifications will influence the general equilibrium.

It is first convenient to define the following set of relative prices. Let $X_t \equiv P_{Nt}/P_{Tt}$ and $X_t^* \equiv P_{Nt}^*/P_{Tt}^*$ be the relative prices of nontradables to tradables in the home and foreign countries, respectively, and let $\mathcal{T}_t \equiv P_{Ft}/P_{Ht}$ be the terms of trade. After making use of the relevant price indexes and the definition of the real exchange rate, the real exchange rate may then be expressed as a function of these three relative prices:

$$Q_t = \left[\frac{\alpha \mathcal{T}_t^{1-\eta} + (1-\alpha)}{\alpha + (1-\alpha)\mathcal{T}_t^{1-\eta}}\right]^{1/(1-\eta)} \left(\frac{X_t^*}{X_t}\right)^{1-\gamma}. \tag{33}$$

Given home bias ($\alpha > 0.5$), the real exchange rate is increasing in $\mathcal{T}_t$. It is also increasing in X_t^* and decreasing in X_t.

We now turn the link between international relative prices and the current account. Substituting the demand functions for home tradables into the respective market-clearing condition yields:

$$\begin{aligned} Y_{Ht} = {} & \alpha[\alpha + (1-\alpha)\mathcal{T}_t^{1-\eta}]^{\eta/(1-\eta)} C_{Tt} \\ & + (1-\alpha)[\alpha \mathcal{T}_t^{1-\eta} + (1-\alpha)]^{\eta/(1-\eta)} C_{Tt}^*. \end{aligned} \tag{34}$$

Equating demand and supply in the home and foreign markets for nontradables yields:

$$Y_{Nt} = \frac{1-\gamma}{\gamma}(X_t)^{-1} C_{Tt}, \quad Y_{Nt}^* = \frac{1-\gamma}{\gamma}(X_t^*)^{-1} C_{Tt}^*. \tag{35}$$

Given that the international bond market clears, the trade balance in each country may be expressed as:

$$\mathrm{NX}_t = (X_t)^{\gamma-1}\{[\alpha + (1-\alpha)\mathcal{T}_t^{1-\eta}]^{1/(\eta-1)} Y_{Ht} - C_{Tt}\}, \tag{36}$$

$$-\frac{\mathrm{NX}_t}{Q_t} = (X_t^*)^{\gamma-1}\{[\alpha + (1-\alpha)\mathcal{T}_t^{\eta-1}]^{1/(\eta-1)} Y_{Ft}^* - C_{Tt}^*\}. \tag{37}$$

Finally, the current account may be expressed as:

$$\mathrm{CA}_t = (I_{t-1} - 1)\frac{B_{t-1}}{P_t} + \mathrm{NX}_t. \tag{38}$$

Obstfeld and Rogoff pursue the following strategy. They take as given the current account, CA_t, net interest payments, $(I_{t-1} - 1)B_{t-1}/P_t$, and the sectoral outputs in the home and foreign country, Y_{Ht}, Y_{Nt}, Y_{Ft}, and Y_{Nt}. Then, the six equations (33) through (38) determine net exports, NX_t, tradable consumption in the home and foreign countries, C_{Tt} and C^*_{Tt}, along with the four relative prices, $\mathcal{T}_t$, X_t, X_t^*, and Q_t.

Next, OR consider a set of comparative static exercises where the current account adjusts from a deficit to zero. Holding constant international relative prices and all the sectoral outputs, an improvement in the current account requires a decrease in domestic tradable consumption and a roughly offsetting increase in foreign tradable consumption. With home bias, the relative decrease in home tradable consumption causes a deterioration in the terms of trade; that is, an increase in $\mathcal{T}$. In addition, the drop in home tradable consumption required to bring the current account into balance reduces the demand for nontradables, causing a fall in the relative price of nontradables to tradables X. Conversely, the rise of tradable consumption in the foreign country pushes up the relative price of nontradables, X^*. The adjustment in each of the relative prices works to generate a depreciation of the home country's real exchange rate. Under their baseline calibration, for example, OR find that closing the current account from its current level would require a depreciation of the real exchange rate of about 30 percent. Of course, their results depend on the elasticities of substitution between nontradables and tradables and between home and foreign tradables, and require that sectoral outputs are fixed.

Our framework builds on OR and endogenizes the movement of the current account and sectoral outputs in the two countries. The current account is connected to aggregate activity in part through the impact of aggregate consumption on tradable consumption demand within each country:

$$C_T = \gamma(X_t)^{1-\gamma} C_t, \quad C_T^* = \gamma(X_t^*)^{1-\gamma} C_t^*. \tag{39}$$

Everything else equal, accordingly, a rise in aggregate consumption within a country raises the demand for tradable consumption, thus causing a deterioration in the trade balance.

The production of tradables and nontradables will of course also depend on aggregate economic activity. Within the flexible-price version of the model, labor demand and supply along the production technology within each sector determine sectoral outputs. Aggregate consumption and real interest rates within each country depend upon the respective economy-wide resource constraints and the respective consumption Euler equations. The relative pattern of real interest rates across countries and the real exchange rate, in turn, depend on the uncovered interest parity condition.

Within the sticky-price version of the model, for firms not adjusting price in a given period, output adjusts to meet demand so long as the markup is nonnegative. Given staggered price setting, the price index within each sector adjusts sluggishly to deviations of the markup from desired levels. As a consequence, there is stickiness in the movement of the overall index of domestic prices and also in the relative price of nontradables to tradables. The nominal stickiness, of course, implies that monetary policy influences the joint dynamics of output and inflation. There are potentially several extra complications from this open economy setup. Monetary policy can influence not only short-term real interest rates but also the real exchange rate. In addition, both domestic output and inflation depend on foreign economic behavior. Finally, stickiness in the movement of the relative price of nontradables to tradables may distort the efficient adjustments of the two sectors to international disturbances. In the numerical exercises that follow we illustrate these various phenomena.

We now turn to the log-linear model.

4.3 The Log-Linear Model

We consider a log-linear approximation of the model around a deterministic steady state. We first characterize the steady state and then turn to the complete log-linear model. Fortunately, the model is small enough so that the key mechanisms of current account and exchange rate determination as well as monetary policy transmission become quite transparent.

4.3.1 Steady State

The steady state is very simple. In the symmetric long-run equilibrium, each country grows at the steady-state productivity growth rate g. Both the trade balance and the stock of foreign debt are zero:

$$\mathrm{NX} = B = 0.$$

It is then straightforward to show these restrictions imply that in the symmetric deterministic steady state, all the relevant relative prices are unity:

$$\mathcal{T} = X = Q = 1.$$

In addition, for each country there are a simple set of relations that characterize the behavior of the real quantities. Given that the trade balance is zero, national output simply equals national consumption:

$$Y_t = C_t.$$

Next, since relative prices are unity, expenditures shares depend simply on preference parameters:

$$C_{Ht} = \alpha\gamma C_t, \quad C_{Ft} = (1-\alpha)\gamma C_t, \quad C_{Nt} = (1-\gamma)C_t.$$

Market clearing for output in each sector requires:

$$Y_{Ht} = C_{Ht} + C^*_{Ht}, \quad Y_{Nt} = C_{Nt}.$$

Similarly, market clearing for labor in each sector along with the respective production technologies pins down steady-state output with each sector

$$\frac{Y_{Ht}}{Z_t} = \gamma(1+\varphi)^{1/(1+\varphi)}, \quad \frac{Y_{Nt}}{Z_t} = (1-\gamma)(1+\varphi)^{1/(1+\varphi)},$$

where Z_t is trend productivity. Finally, the steady real interest rate, I^o, is given by:

$$I^o = \frac{1+g}{\beta},$$

where $1 + g$ is the gross growth rate of technology.

4.3.2 Log-Linear Model

We now characterize the log-linear system for the home country. A symmetric set of equations that we do not list here applies for the foreign country. Lowercase variables denote log deviations from a deterministic steady state, except as noted otherwise.[12]

We begin by expressing domestic real output as a linear combination of home tradable and nontradable output:

$$y_t = \gamma y_{Ht} + (1-\gamma) y_{Nt}. \tag{40}$$

The demand for home tradables depends positively on the terms of trade and on both relative prices of nontradables as well as on aggregate consumption in both countries:

$$y_{Ht} = 2\alpha(1-\alpha)\eta\tau_t + (1-\gamma)[\alpha x_t + (1-\alpha)x_t^*] + \alpha c_t + (1-\alpha)c_t^*. \tag{41}$$

In turn, the demand for nontradables may be expressed as:

$$y_{Nt} = -\gamma x_t + c_t, \tag{42}$$

where $x_t \equiv p_{Nt} - p_{Tt}$. The demand for home nontradables depends negatively on the relative price of nontradables and positively on aggregate consumption.

From the log-linear intertemporal Euler equation, consumption depends positively on expected future consumption, and inversely on the real interest rate and the time varying discount factor:

$$c_t = \mathrm{E}_t c_{t+1} - (i_t - \mathrm{E}_t \pi_{t+1}) - \hat{\beta} t, \tag{43}$$

where $\hat{\beta}_t$ denotes the percent deviation of β_t from steady state. The endogenous discount factor depends negatively on consumption according to

$$\hat{\beta}_t = \varsigma_t - \psi\beta c_t, \tag{44}$$

12. The approximation is performed about the steady state in which quantities are constant; that is, expressed relative to trend productivity Z_t.

where ς_t, the exogenous shock to the discount factor, obeys the autoregressive process given by equation (7). The presence of c_t reflects the consumption externality on the discount rate that ensure determinate model dynamics. As noted earlier, we pick ψ to be tiny to ensure that this feature has only a negligible effect on medium term dynamics.

One can view equations (40), (41), (42), (43), and (44) as determining aggregate demand for output, conditional on the real interest rate and international relative prices. Given nominal rigidities, of course, the real interest rate will depend on monetary policy. By adjusting the short-term interest rate, the central bank can also influence the terms of trade, as we show explicitly in the following.

Given that there is nominal inertia on both the tradable and nontradable sectors, τ_t and x_t evolve as follows:

$$\tau_t = \tau_{t-1} + (\Delta q_t + \pi^*_{Ft} - \pi^*_t) - (\pi_{Ht} - \pi_t), \tag{45}$$

$$x_t = x_{t-1} + \pi_{Nt} - \pi_{Ht} - \gamma(1 - \alpha)\Delta\tau_t. \tag{46}$$

Note, however, that because there is perfect pass-through in the tradable sector, there is an immediate effect of exchange rate adjustments on the terms of trade.

Let the superscript ^{o} denote the flexible-price equilibrium value of a variable. Then inflation in the tradable goods and nontradable goods sectors may be expressed as:

$$\pi_{Ht} = \kappa\left[(y_{Ht} - y^o_{Ht}) - \frac{1}{1+\varphi}(nx_t - nx^o_t)\right] + \beta E_t\pi_{H,t+1}, \tag{47}$$

$$\pi_{Nt} = \kappa(y_{Nt} - y^o_{Nt}) + \beta E_t\pi_{N,t+1}, \tag{48}$$

with $y^o_{Ht} = a_t + (1+\varphi)^{-1}nx^o_t$, $y^o_{Nt} = a_t$, and $\kappa = (1-\xi)(1-\beta\xi)(1+\varphi)/[\xi(1+\sigma\varphi)]$. Inflation in the nontradable sector depends on the current output gap within the sector and on anticipated future nontradable inflation, in analogy to the standard new-Keynesian Phillips curve (see, for instance, Woodford 2003). For the tradable goods sector, the "trade balance gap" matters as well. Roughly speaking, a higher trade deficit relative to the flexible-price equilibrium value is associated with higher marginal cost in the tradable goods sector resulting from this imbalance.

Overall CPI inflation depends not only on domestic inflation but also on the evolution of the price of imported goods:

$$\pi_t = \gamma\pi_{Ht} + (1-\gamma)\pi_{Nt} + \gamma(1-\alpha)\Delta\tau_t. \tag{49}$$

We next turn to interest rates and exchange rates. In the baseline case, the nominal interest rate follows a simple feedback rule with interest rate smoothing:

$$i_t = \rho i_{t-1} + (1-\rho)\phi_\pi\pi_t. \tag{50}$$

Uncovered interest rate parity implies the following link between real interest rates and real exchange rates:

$$(51)\qquad (i_t - E_t\pi_{t+1}) - (i_t^* - E_t\pi_{t+1}^*) = E_t q_{t+1} - q_t.$$

Finally, we turn to the trade balance and the evolution of net foreign indebtedness. Net exports depend inversely on the terms of trade and positively on the current and expected path of the discount factor shock:

$$(52)\qquad nx_t = \delta(\eta - 1)\tau_t + \sum_{s=0}^{\infty}(1-\alpha)E_t\hat{\beta}_{Rt+s},$$

with $\delta = 2\alpha(1-\alpha) > 0$, and where $\tau_t \equiv p_{Ft} - p_{Ht}$ and $\hat{\beta}_{Rt}$ is the difference between the home and foreign time varying discount factors. Since the steady-state value of net exports is zero, nx_t is net exports as a fraction of steady-state output. Equation (52) is obtained by combining the resource constraint, the market-clearing condition for home tradables, and the uncovered interest parity condition, along with the consumption Euler equations for the two countries.[13] Note that in the log case ($\eta = 1$), the trade balance is driven purely by the exogenous preference shock. In this instance, as emphasized by Cole and Obstfeld (1991) and others, the terms of trade adjusts to offset any impact on the trade balance of disturbances (other than shifts in consumption/saving preferences). This result also depends on having a unit elasticity of substitution between tradables and nontradables, as we have here.

Finally, the net foreign indebtedness evolves as follows:

$$(53)\qquad b_t = \frac{1}{\beta}b_{t-1} + nx_t,$$

where b_t is debt normalized by trend output.

The system thus far consists of fourteen equations that determine fourteen variables, $\{i_t, c_t, \hat{\beta}_t, y_t, y_{Ht}, y_{Nt}, x_t, \pi_t, \pi_{Ht}, \pi_{Nt}, q_t, nx_t, \tau_t, b_t\}$, conditional on the foreign economy and conditional on the exogenous shocks ς_t and a_t and the values of the predetermined variables b_{t-1}, τ_{t-1}, and x_{t-1}. The complete model consists of these equations plus nine more that help determine the foreign variables $\{i_t^*, c_t^*, \hat{\beta}_t^*0, y_t^*, y_{Ft}^*, y_{Nt}^*, x_t^*, \pi_t^*, \pi_{Ft}^*, \pi_{Nt}^*\}$, along with two foreign predetermined variables, τ_{t-1}^*, and x_{t-1}^*. These nine equations are the foreign counterparts of equations (41), (43), (44), (42), (46), (47), (48), (49), and (50). In addition, given the evolution of debt determined by the model, we may express the current account as:

$$(54)\qquad \mathrm{ca}_t = b_t - \frac{1}{1+g}b_{t-1},$$

13. From combining equations one obtains

$$nx_t = (1-\alpha)\hat{\beta}_{R,t} - \delta(\eta - 1)E_t\Delta\tau_{t+1} + E_t nx_{t+1}.$$

Given that $\hat{\beta}_{R,t}$ is stationary about a zero mean, one can iterate this relation forward to obtain equation (52).

where ca_t is the current account normalized by steady-state output.

The model is not small, but it is parsimonious (we think), given its objectives. In particular, it captures the link between international relative prices and the current account stressed by OR. Given our goal of studying the role of monetary policy, it goes beyond OR by endogenizing the determination of these variables within a two-country monetary general equilibrium framework.

The way monetary policy influences international relative prices and the current account further is fairly clear. Given that prices are sticky, an increase in the nominal interest rate causes an appreciation of the real exchange rate (holding constant expectations of the future) as the uncovered interest parity condition (51) makes clear. The appreciation of the exchange rate improves the terms of trade (i.e., τ_t falls), as equation (45) suggests. This in turn leads to a deterioration of the trade balance and hence, of the current account. The evolution of the current account and international relative prices will have implications for the behavior of output and inflation within each country and thus, implications for the appropriate course of monetary policy. It should also be clear that the monetary policy of one country has implications for the other.

We next employ the model to explore the implications of current account behavior for monetary policy.

4.4 Current Account Dynamics and Monetary Policy

We first describe how we calibrate the model. We then explore the behavior of the model economy in our benchmark case, where each country's central bank sets the short-term interest rate according to a Taylor rule with partial adjustment, as described by equation (50). We choose this formulation of monetary policy for our benchmark case because the evidence suggests it provides a reasonable way to describe the behavior of the major central banks during the past twenty-five years. We then proceed to consider alternative policy environments. For each policy environment, we consider two scenarios for current account adjustment. In the "slow burn" scenario, the adjustment is smooth and drawn out over time. In the "fast burn" scenario, instead, the current account is subject to a sharp reversal.

4.4.1 Calibration

We have in mind the United States as the home country and the rest of the world as the foreign country. This is somewhat problematic since the countries in the model are symmetric in size while the U.S. output is only about a quarter of world GDP. It is not hard to extend the model to allow for differences in country size, though at the cost of notational complexity. Thus, for this chapter, we stick with the simpler setup at the cost of some quantitative realism.

The model is quarterly. The three parameters that govern the open economy dimension of the model are the preference share parameter for tradables (γ), the preference share parameter for home tradables (α), and the elasticity of substitution between home and foreign tradables (η). Based on the evidence and arguments in OR, we set $\gamma = 0.25$, $\alpha = 0.7$, and $\eta = 2.0$. Note that our consumption composite imposes a unit elasticity of substitution between tradables and nontradables. This number is within the range of plausible values suggested by OR and is actually the benchmark case in their study.

There are five additional preference parameters, three of which are standard: the steady-state discount factor (β), the inverse of the Frisch elasticity of labor supply (φ), and the elasticity of substitution between intermediate inputs (σ). We set $\beta = 0.99$ and $\varphi = 2.0$. The latter implies a Frisch elasticity of labor supply of 0.5, which is squarely in the range of estimates from microdata. We set $\sigma = 11$ to deliver a 10 percent steady-state price markup in both the tradable- and nontradable-goods sectors. The other two preference parameters, ψ and ϑ, govern the spillover effect of aggregate consumption on the discount factor. We fix ψ consistently with our choice of β and we adjust ϑ so that ψ is small but positive. In particular, we arbitrarily set $\vartheta = -1{,}000$ and obtain $\psi = 7.2361 \cdot 10^{-6}$. Implicitly, we are simply ensuring that the endogeneity of the discount factor does not significantly influence medium term dynamics.

Next, we set the probability that a price does not adjust (ξ) at 0.66. This implies a mean duration that a price is fixed of 3 quarters, which is consistent with the micro evidence.

The two parameters of the policy rule are the feedback coefficient ϕ_π and the smoothing parameter ρ. Based on the evidence in Clarida, Galí, and Gertler (1998) and elsewhere, we set $\phi_\pi = 2.0$ and $\rho = 0.75$.

Finally, we turn to the parameters that govern the preference shock ς_t and the cyclical productivity shock a_t. As we discussed earlier, ς_τ is meant to be a simple way to capture structural factors that influence differences in consumption/saving propensities across countries, such as fiscal policy, demographics, and capital market development. In this regard, it is an object that is likely to persist over time. We thus set the serial correlation parameter that governs this process (ρ_ς) at 0.97.

We assume that trend productivity grows at a 2 percent annual rate (corresponding to $g = 0.5$ percent). Because we would like cyclical differences in productivity growth to contribute to current account dynamics, we model the cyclical component of technology, allowing for persistent forecastable periods of productivity movement away from trend that may vary over time. In particular, a_t is a combination of two processes, u_t and v_t, as follows:

$$a_t = u_t - v_t \tag{55}$$

with

$$u_t = \rho_u u_{t-1} + \varepsilon_t + \varepsilon_{ut}$$

$$v_t = \rho_v v_{t-1} + \varepsilon_t,$$

where $\rho_u = 0.999 > \rho_v$, and where ε_t and ε_{ut} are zero mean i.i.d. shocks.

The assumption that u_t is "near" unit root allows us to partition the shocks, roughly speaking, into one (ε_{ut}) that primarily affects the current level of productivity and another (ε_t) that affects its expected growth rate. Suppose we start at a steady state with $u_{t-1} = v_{t-1} = 0$. A positive innovation in ε_t has no direct effect on a_t in the first period. However, since $\rho_u > \rho_v$, a_t will grow steadily for a period of time. Because ρ_u is close to unity and greater than ρ_v, this period can be quite long. Thus, innovations in ε_t can induce growth cycles. By contrast, a shock to ε_{ut} has a direct affect on a_t but only generates a one-period blip in the growth rate since ρ_u is near unity. We can allow for ε_t and ε_{ut} to be correlated in any arbitrary fashion.

Similar to OR, we initialize the model to match roughly the current international situation; that is, a current account deficit for the home country (i.e., the United States) of approximately 5 percent of GDP (or equivalently 20 percent of tradable output) along with a stock of foreign debt approximately equal to 20 percent of GDP annualized (equivalent to 80 percent of tradable output).[14] We start with the flexible-price model and set the predetermined value of foreign indebtedness at its value in the data. We then adjust ε_t for the home country and ρ_v so that domestic productivity growth is expected to be roughly half percent above trend for the next decade. We adjust ε_t^* exactly in the opposite direction and set $\rho_v = \rho_v^*$. We fix the differential in expected productivity growth between the two countries at 1 percent based on the evidence from the G7 ex the United States over the past decade. It turns out that this accounts for roughly one-third of the U.S. current account deficit. We then add in a preference shock for both the home and foreign countries to explain the difference. Again, this preference shock is meant to account for factors that lead to different consumption/saving propensities across countries.

We then turn to the sticky-price model. We initialize the predetermined variables in the sticky-price model, τ_{t-1} and x_{t-1}, to match the values that arose in the first period of the flexible-price model. We then feed in the same size shocks as before to see whether we matched the current account evidence. If not, we adjust proportionately the sizes of all the shocks. We found that in all cases, only very tiny adjustments were necessary.

4.4.2 Baseline Case

We now analyze our baseline case where monetary policy in each country is given by a Taylor rule with partial adjustment, as described by equation

14. The recent current account deficit is more on the order of 6 percent of GDP, but we stick with the 5 percent number to maintain comparability with OR.

(50). We characterize the response of the home country economy in both the slow and fast burn scenarios. For the most part, we do not show the foreign country variables because to a first approximation their movement is of equal magnitude and is the opposite sign to those of the home country variables. This mirrored response arises because: (a) the countries are of equal size; (b) the shocks we feed in are of similar magnitude and opposite signs; and (c) for our baseline case, the two countries follow the same policy rule. It is true that one country is a debtor and the other a creditor. While this introduces a small difference in the low-frequency behavior of aggregate consumption across countries, it does not introduce any major differences in the comparative dynamics.

The Slow Burn Scenario

We start with the slow burn scenario. The top panel of figure 4.2 plots the response of a variety of "international" variables for this case, while the bottom panel of figure 4.2 plots mostly "domestic" variables. In each plot, the solid line presents the response of the model with nominal price rigidities. To provide a benchmark, the dotted line presents the response of the flexible-price model. The horizontal axis measures time in quarters from the initial period while, for the quantity variables and relative prices, the vertical axis measures the percent deviation from steady state. Inflation and interest rates are measured in annualized basis points.

To organize the discussion, it is useful to first describe the flexible-price case. As we noted earlier, we initialize the model with a current account deficit of 20 percent of tradable output. As the top panel of figure 4.2 shows, in the slow burn scenario the half life for adjustment of the current account is about seven years.[15] In the absence of any further shocks, after ten years the current account has closed by about 60 percent. The protracted current account deficit produces a sustained increase in net foreign indebtedness that does not level off until far in the future. Associated with the large current account deficit is a consumption boom in the home country (along with a consumption bust in the foreign country). Consumption is more than 3.5 percent above steady state in the home country, with the reverse being true in the foreign country. The sustained upward movement in consumption in the home country is due to the fact that for a sustained period productivity growth in the home country is above trend. Note in figure 4.2 that the upward movement in domestic output in percentage terms is nearly three times that of home country consumption. This differential helps account for why the current account is closing steadily over this period, despite the growth in consumption.

As figure 4.2 also shows, the current account imbalance implies an

15. Interestingly, this prediction is very close to that of the GEM model. See Faruqee et al. (2005).

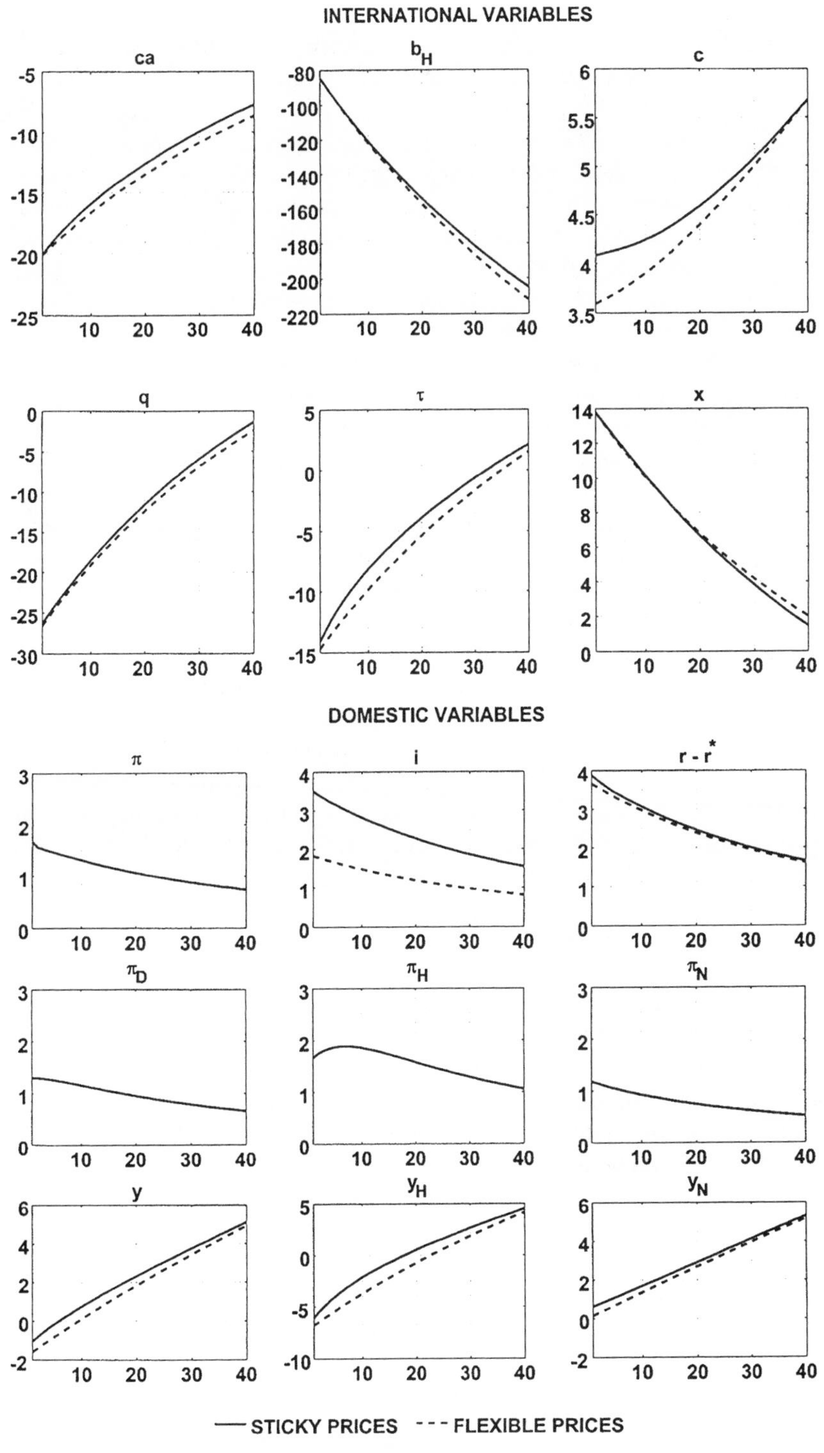

INTERNATIONAL VARIABLES

ca b_H c

q τ x

DOMESTIC VARIABLES

π i $r - r^*$

π_D π_H π_N

y y_H y_N

— STICKY PRICES - - - FLEXIBLE PRICES

Fig. 4.2 Baseline Taylor rule: Slow burn scenario

expected depreciation of almost 30 percent, in line with the estimates of OR. Under the slow burn scenario, the half life of this adjustment is roughly five years. The total expected exchange rate depreciation is accounted for by a 15 percent depreciation of the terms of trade and an expected decline in the relative price of nontradables to tradables of 14 percent, along with a symmetric increase in the foreign relative price of nontradables to tradables.[16] This decomposition is also in line with OR. Again, this correspondence is not that surprising since we are using a similar calibration of the international sector. Where we differ from OR is by providing a model of the dynamic adjustment path.

One other result worth noting for this case involves the real interest rate differential between the home and foreign country. As the bottom panel in figure 4.2 shows, in the initial period, the real interest rate for the flexible-price model is roughly two hundred basis points above steady state. It then steadily converges back to steady state. The foreign country interest rate is the mirror image, implying an initial real interest rate differential of roughly four hundred basic that erodes steadily over time. The source of these interest rate dynamics is the expected movement in the real exchange rate. Given that uncovered interest parity holds (at least in the model!), the home real interest must be sufficiently greater than the foreign real rate to compensate for the expected real depreciation of the home country currency. Of course, there is considerable evidence against uncovered interest parity. At the same time, the associated expected decline in the home country's short-term real interest rate suggests an inverted yield curve for the home country, everything else equal. Conversely, the expected rise in the foreign country suggests an upward sloping yield curve for this region. While certainly a host of other factors are at work, it is possible that these considerations may help account for the recent yield curve inversion in the United States, a phenomenon that has been largely specific to this country. In any event, as we discuss, the fact that current account adjustment influences the path of the natural rate of interest has potentially important implications for monetary policy.

We now turn to the sticky-price case. The first point we emphasize is that the behavior of the international variables does not differ dramatically from the flexible-price model. Put differently, in this baseline case, current account and real exchange rate behavior appear to depend mainly on real as opposed to monetary factors. Though there are some small differences, current account and real exchange rate dynamics are very similar across the sticky- and flexible-price models.

16. Given the calibrated elasticities of substitution, the relative price of nontradables explains about two-thirds of the overall movement of the real exchange rate. This is partly inconsistent with the last dollar depreciation episode (late 1980s) when the adjustment occurred mostly through the terms of trade. Relative to twenty years ago, however, the nontradable sector today represents a much larger share of the economy (Buera and Kaboski 2007). Therefore, it is not unlikely that the importance of the relative price of nontradables may increase significantly.

Under our baseline Taylor rule however, demand in the home country is high relative to the flexible-price equilibrium. In particular, both consumption and the current account are above their respective flexible-price equilibrium values (where the latter is driven primarily by the trade balance). Contributing to the positive current account gap is a systematic positive difference between the terms of trade and its flexible-price equilibrium value. In this respect, the terms-of-trade gap is another indicator that monetary policy is not sufficiently tight to curb excess demand in the baseline case. As figure 4.2 illustrates, the result is persistent inflation that averages almost a percent and a half (above target) over the first five years. There is also persistent inflation in both sectors, though it is nearly double in the tradable goods sector, due to the relative effect on demand in this sector stemming from the terms of trade gap. Finally, note the consumer price inflation is roughly thirty to forty basis points above domestic inflation, due to the added effect of the depreciation on import prices.

Note that persistent inflation emerges even though the central bank is aggressively adjusting interest rates in response to inflation (the Taylor rule coefficient is 2.0). A key reason that a conventional Taylor rule does not perform well in this environment is that it does not directly respond to the movement in the short-term natural rate of interest induced by the current account imbalance. At zero inflation, the rule fixes the nominal rate at its steady-state value. However, the current imbalance pushes up the short-term real rate, implying a monetary policy that is too expansionary in this instance. It is straightforward to show that allowing the target interest rate to also depend on an intercept equal to the natural rate of interest greatly improves the central bank's ability to contain inflation. The problem, of course, is that the natural rate is not directly observable. Later we present a rule based on observables that accomplishes much the same as a natural rate of interest augmented rule. In the meantime, we simply emphasize the general point that the current account imbalance may have implications for the natural rate of interest that must be factored into central bank policy, one way or another.

The Fast Burn Scenario

We now turn to the fast burn scenario. As we noted in the introduction, the probability does not seem high that the United States would suffer the kind of sudden current account reversal that many emerging market economies have experienced over the last twenty years. Given its well-developed financial markets, it does not seem likely that the United States would face rapid capital outflows and sharp increases in country risk spreads, as has been endured by a number of East Asian or South American countries. In this regard, if we are to imagine such a crisis arising, we think the most likely scenario is one where there is a sudden reversal of fortune in the growth prospects of the United States relative to the rest of the world.

In particular, we suppose that expected productivity growth in the home country over the next decade declines by an average of 0.75 percent and that the opposite happens in the foreign country. Thus, the initial 1.0 percent advantage in medium term productivity growth drops to a 0.5 disadvantage. Think of the productivity boom coming to a sudden end in the United States and at the same time picking up steam quickly abroad.[17] Because this is unlikely to happen instantly, we let the process play out over the course of the year. The shocks that reduce productivity growth in the home country and raise it in the foreign one are spaced out evenly over the course of four quarters.

Figure 4.3 portrays this scenario, both for the sticky- and flexible-price models. The hard landing begins in quarter 8 and plays out through quarter 12. For both models, the revision in expectations of relative productivity growth results in a current account reversal of roughly 70 percent in the year of the "crisis." The trade balance nearly closes, implying that most of the remaining current account deficit is due to interest payments. The real exchange rate drops nearly 20 percent in the flexible-price model. It drops by only three quarters of this amount, or 15 percent, in the sticky-price model. The somewhat smaller drop in the sticky-price model is due to the inertia in the movement of the relative price of nontradables to tradables in each country that is induced by the staggered nominal price setting within each sector. At the same time, there is a larger depreciation in the terms of trade in the sticky-price model relative to the flex price case, owing to a depreciation of the nominal exchange rate that outpaces the depreciation of the real exchange rate. This relative behavior of the terms of trade accounts for why at the end of the sharp reversal in expectations, the current account deficit is smaller by a modest margin in the sticky-price case.

How does the fast burn impact the domestic variables? In the flexible-price model domestic output actually continues to increase for a period. This somewhat perverse behavior arises because expectations of lower productivity growth reduce current domestic consumption, which in turn induces a positive wealth effect on labor supply. Thus, as emphasized in the recent literature on "news driven" business cycles, within a flexible-price model with standard preferences and technologies, shifts in expected productivity growth tend to move current output in the opposite direction.[18] Within our open economy framework, though, there is also a significant compositional effect, owing to the sharp depreciation of the real exchange rate. As a consequence, the modest rise in total output is accounted for by a sharp increase

17. For simplicity, we assume that the shift in relative productivity growth is the product of shifts within each country that are of equal absolute value but opposite sign. We would obtain virtually the same results if most or all of the shift in productivity growth occurs in one country.

18. See Beaudry and Portier (2004) and Jaimovich and Rebelo (2006) for recent analyses of news-driven business cycles within a flexible price neoclassical framework.

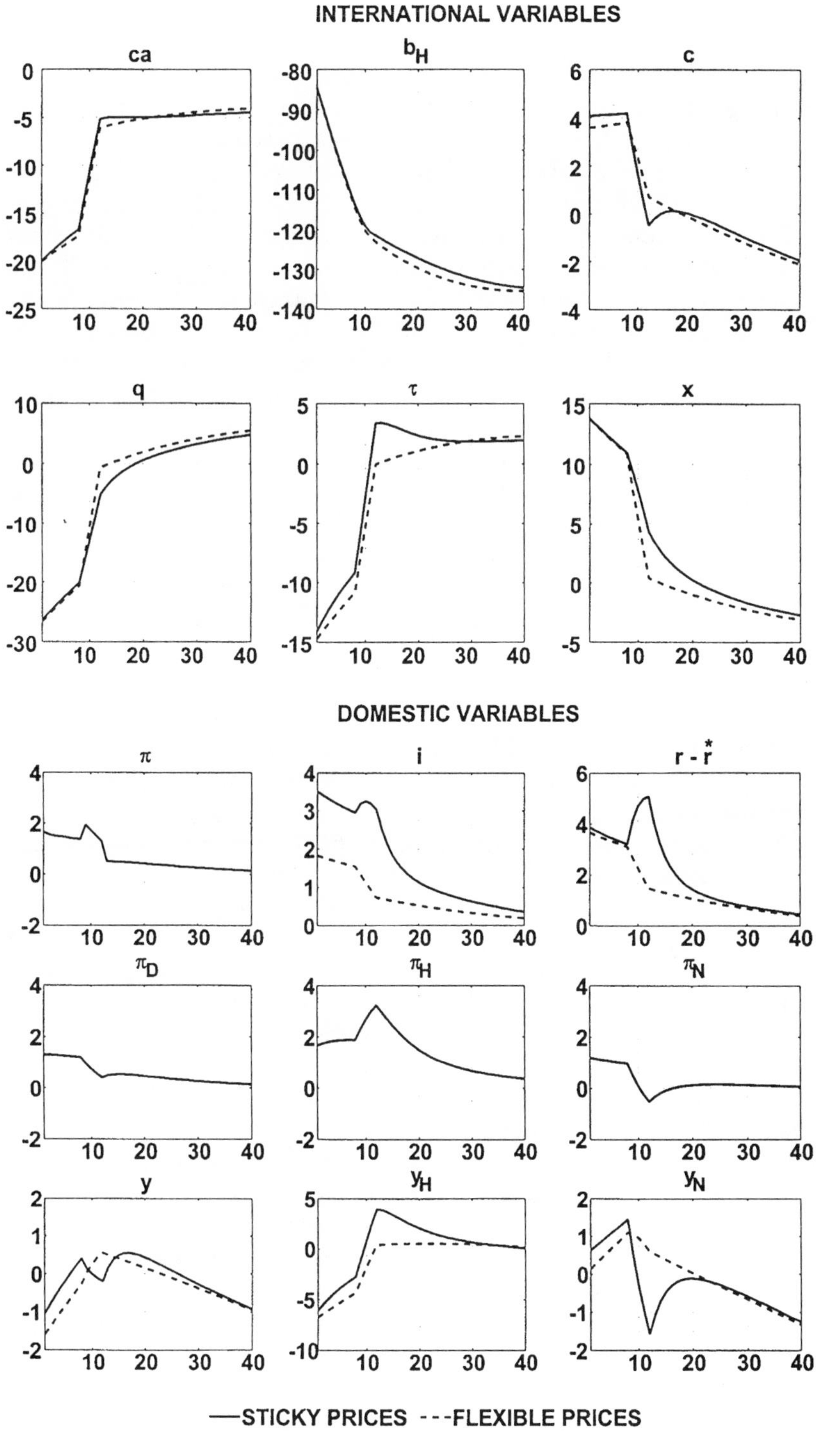

INTERNATIONAL VARIABLES

ca — b_H — c

q — τ — x

DOMESTIC VARIABLES

π — i — $r - r^*$

π_D — π_H — π_N

y — y_H — y_N

—STICKY PRICES - - -FLEXIBLE PRICES

Fig. 4.3 Baseline Taylor rule: Fast burn scenario

in tradable goods output. In contrast, nontradable output begins a steady decline at the onset of the revision in growth expectations.

In the sticky-price model, the fast burn produces a drop in output, albeit a modest one, roughly 0.5 percent over the year. Accompanying the output decline is a rise in inflation of roughly 50 basis points that stems from the exchange rate depreciation.

The small drop in aggregate output, however, masks a significant compositional effect. There is a major contraction in nontradable output, which drops more than 2.5 percent over the year. This sharp contraction opens up a gap with the potential level of nontradable output of more than 2.0 percent at the trough. What accounts for the modest decline in aggregate output is a sharp increase in tradable goods output, which jumps roughly 7.5 percent, nearly 3.0 percentage points larger than the rise in its potential value. The overreaction in the sectoral adjustment, of course, is a product of the stickiness in the relative price of nontradables and tradables. Thus, the modest decline in overall output relative to its potential level hides the efficiency losses stemming from the extra large sectoral adjustments.

There are, of course, a number of reasons why our baseline model likely understates the impact of the fast burn on aggregate output. Chief among these is that the model permits adjustment of the exchange rate to have an instantaneous effect on the demand and production of tradables. Adding factors that either slow down this adjustment or introduce a stronger complementarity with nontradable output will mute the ability of the tradable goods sector to soften the effect of the current account reversal on output. Indeed, in section 4.6 we illustrate how, under certain monetary policy rules, imperfect exchange rate pass-through can inhibit any stabilizing adjustment of the tradable goods sector.

Another consideration is that we abstract from any movement in risk premia. As we noted, owing to a more advanced financial structure, we would not expect a country risk premium for the United States to emerge that could come anywhere near to the levels reached in emerging market crises. Nonetheless, it is possible that some kind of premium could emerge that could have the effect of enhancing the crises. Modeling the movement of this premium in a satisfactory way, however, is beyond the scope of the chapter. Though we do not report the results here, we experimented, allowing the U.S. country risk premium to rise exogenously at the onset of a sudden stop. For increases in spread up to 200 basis points, the results we obtain are qualitatively very similar to our baseline case. The rise in the risk premium, of course, amplifies a bit the responses of all variables.

Finally, we note that the monetary policy rule is a key factor. The evidence suggests that countries that have experienced significant output drops typically have tied monetary policy to an exchange rate peg.[19] As a consequence, during the initial phase of the current account reversal, the central banks

19. See, for example, Gertler, Gilchrist, and Natalucci (2007) and Curdia (2007).

of these countries have usually raised short-term rates sharply in order to defend the peg. Large contractions in output have followed these large increases in short-term rates. By contrast, the baseline Taylor rule in our model economy induces only a tiny rise in current short-term rates, followed by a reasonably sharp decline in future short-term rates. This anticipated decline in short rates helps moderate the drop in aggregate output at the expense of a relatively modest increase in inflation. To illustrate the significance of the monetary policy rule on the overall output drop, following we provide two examples of monetary policy regimes that indeed produced a major contraction in aggregate economic activity.

4.4.3 Alternatives to the Baseline Case

We now explore the implications of some alternative monetary policy regimes. We first consider domestic producer inflation targeting as an example of a policy that works reasonably well in our framework. We next consider two policies that do not work well, at least in a fast burn scenario: consumer price inflation targeting and exchange rate targeting. As we show, under either of these policies, the fast burn produces a significant drop in aggregate output. Finally, we consider a case where monetary policy is asymmetric across the two countries: the home central bank follows a Taylor rule while the foreign central bank (for instance, the Bank of China) follows a strict peg.

Domestic Producer Inflation Targeting

We first consider a scenario where the central bank targets domestic producer inflation.[20] We do so for two reasons. First, as we noted in the previous section, the simple Taylor rule may not adequately account for shifts in the potential rate of interest generated by the current account imbalance. In contrast, the targeting rule requires that the central bank adjust its instrument to compensate for any impact that shifts in the natural interest rate may have on inflation. Second, as received wisdom suggests, it is desirable to stabilize prices in the sectors where prices are stickiest (see, for instance, Aoki [2001] and Benigno [2004]). Efficiency losses from relative price dispersion induced by inflation are greatest in these sectors.[21] In addition, by letting prices float

20. See Svensson (1999) for a discussion of inflation targeting as a monetary policy rule and Svensson and Woodford (2005) for a more detailed discussion of targeting rules and instrument rules.

21. It is possible to derive an explicit utility-based loss function to measure the welfare implications of different monetary policy rules by using the methods in Woodford (2003). In our case, the result is quite complicated due to the existence of two sectors in each country. We thus do not report it here. However, such an approach reveals that in this kind of framework it is producer inflation that is costly as opposed to consumer inflation, due to the costs of the associated relative price dispersion on production efficiency. Strictly speaking though, welfare losses depend on distortions at the sectoral level. Efficiency costs depend on squared deviations of output from its natural level in each sector as well as on squared deviations of inflation in each sector from zero. There is also a term that reflects the loss from incomplete international financial markets.

in flexible-price sectors, the central bank avoids costly output adjustments in the sticky-price sectors that may be required to stabilize an overall price index. For each country within our framework, domestic home tradable and nontradables constitute the sticky-price sectors. By contrast, due to perfect exchange rate pass-through, import prices are perfectly flexible. What this suggests is that within our framework, a domestic inflation target may be preferable to a consumer price inflation target. In this section and the next, we verify this conjecture.

We thus replace the simple Taylor rule for each country with the targeting rule for domestic producer inflation, π_{Dt}, given by

$$\pi_{Dt} = \gamma\pi_{Ht} + (1 - \gamma)\pi_{Nt} = 0. \tag{56}$$

The top panel of figure 4.4 reports the response of the model economy to a slow burn adjustment under this monetary rule. As we would expect, the rule is more effective than the simple Taylor rule in offsetting the inflationary impact of the current account deficit. In contrast to the previous case, there is only a very modest increase in consumer price inflation. The targeting rule fixes domestic producer inflation (which we do not report) at zero. This essentially coincides with fixing the larger component of consumer price inflation, given that the steady-state import share of consumer expenditures is only 7.5 percent under our baseline calibration. Thus, the only effective source of overall consumer price inflation is the terms of trade depreciation that boosts import prices. However, since the import share is small, the impact on overall consumer inflation is small, though tangible. The current account imbalance adds an average of 20 basis points to inflation over the first five years. Again, the aggregate statistics hide sectoral imbalances. The excess demand for tradable goods pushes up inflation in this sector by an average of 50 basis points. This effect is offset by a modest deflation in the nontradables goods sector.

In the fast burn scenario, the targeting rule eliminates the drop in aggregate output, as the bottom left panel of figure 4.4 shows. Under this rule, the nominal interest drops immediately through the course of the current account reversal, which works to offset any decline in aggregate demand. At the same time, though, the sharp depreciation induces a rise in consumer price inflation of roughly 1 percentage point over the course of the year.

While the rule moderates the aggregate impact of the fast burn, there remains a significant distortion of the sectoral reallocation. Though it is slightly more moderate than in the baseline case, nontradable goods output contracts roughly 2 percentage points over the course of the current account reversal. There is similarly a significant movement in tradable output above its potential level, which, if anything, is somewhat larger than in the baseline case.

Of course, some qualifications are in order. As in the baseline case, tradable goods output responds immediately and the crisis has no effect on the

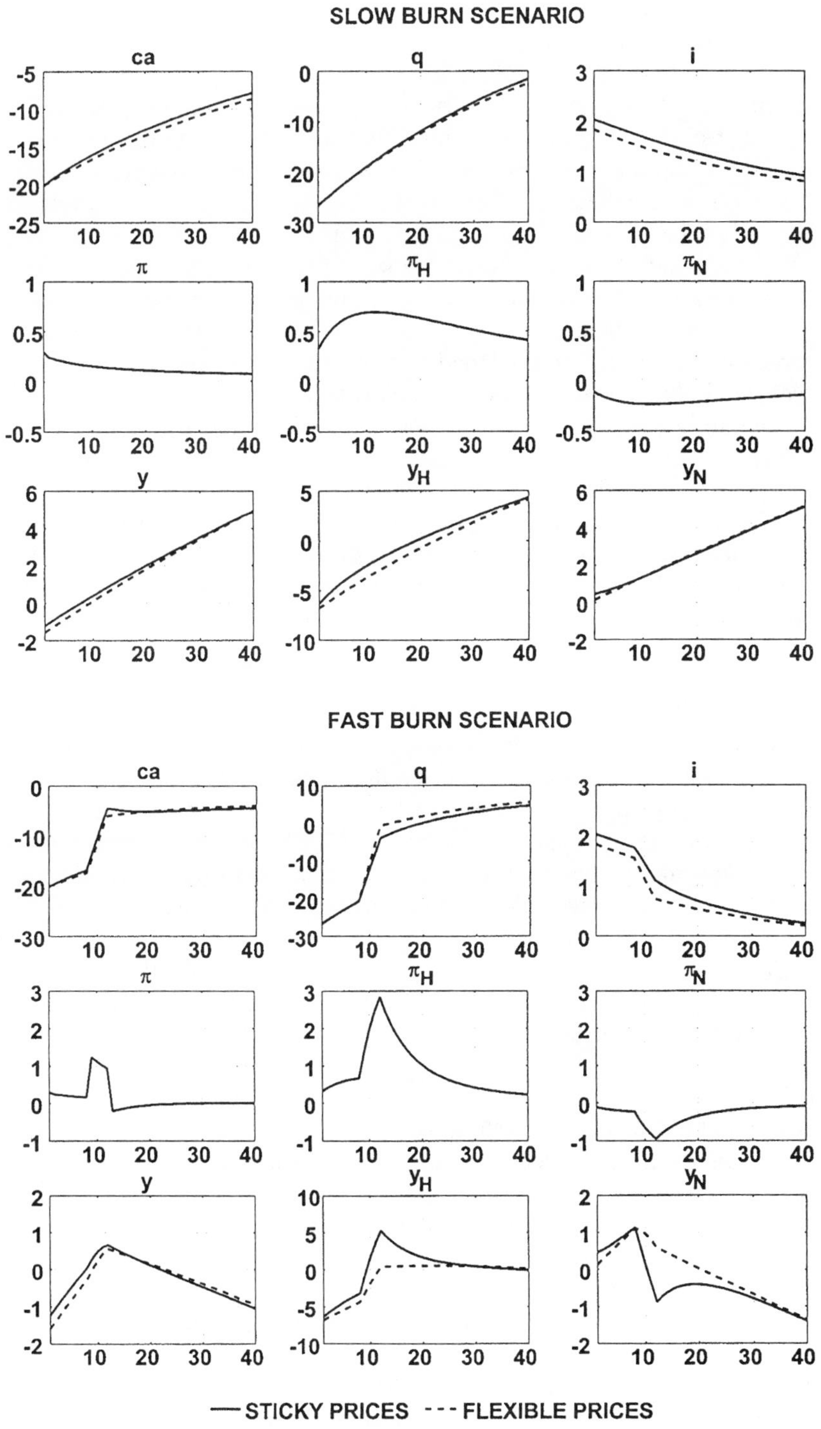

SLOW BURN SCENARIO

ca q i

π π_H π_N

y y_H y_N

FAST BURN SCENARIO

ca q i

π π_H π_N

y y_H y_N

— STICKY PRICES - - - FLEXIBLE PRICES

Fig. 4.4 Domestic inflation targeting

home country risk premium. As before, both these factors likely moderate the impact of the fast burn. It is also relevant that frictions introducing persistence in inflation such as wage rigidity or backward-looking price indexing are absent. Adding these frictions would likely make a rule that permitted inflation to deviate from target in response to movements in capacity utilization preferable to the strict inflation targeting rule that we have explored. At the same time, it is still likely to be the case that focusing on some measure of domestic inflation is preferable to incorporating overall consumer price inflation in the targeting rule. We elaborate on this point in the next section.

In the context of our model, we note that domestic producer inflation targeting corresponds to GDP deflator targeting. In making the leap to the real world, the issue may be more complex, since capital goods prices, which are absent in our model, enter the measure of the latter. To the extent that capital goods prices are roughly as sticky as those of consumer goods and services, it may suffice to use the GDP deflator as the appropriate index of producer prices to target. An alternative might be to develop a consumer price index that measures the prices of domestic goods exclusively. While in principle it is possible to construct such an index, doing so might involve considerable measurement error, especially given the need to account for complex input/output relationships.

Two Rules to Avoid in a Fast Burn: CPI and Exchange Rate Targeting

As we noted earlier, the effects on aggregate output of a fast burn depend critically on the monetary policy rule that is in act. We now give two examples of monetary policy regimes where the fast burn indeed generates a significant output contraction. In the first regime, the central bank targets overall consumer inflation as opposed to a measure of domestic inflation. In the second, it follows a Taylor rule that responds to exchange rate movements as well as inflation.

We begin with CPI targeting. We now suppose that a rule that fixes consumer price inflation at zero replaces our baseline Taylor rule. In particular, the "strict" CPI targeting rule is given by

$$\pi_t = \gamma\pi_{Ht} + (1 - \gamma)\pi_{Nt} + \gamma(1 - \alpha)\Delta\tau_t = 0. \tag{57}$$

It should be clear that stabilizing consumer price inflation in the presence of a terms-of-trade depreciation requires generating a deflation of domestic producer prices. Given that these prices are sticky, this deflation can occur only via an output contraction in at least one of the sectors. Indeed, this is exactly what happens in the fast burn scenario under this monetary policy regime.

As the top panel of figure 4.5 shows, under CPI targeting, the hard landing induces an output contraction on the order of 3 percent at the trough. In contrast to the case of domestic producer inflation targeting, the central bank immediately raises the short-term interest rate over 300 basis points, which

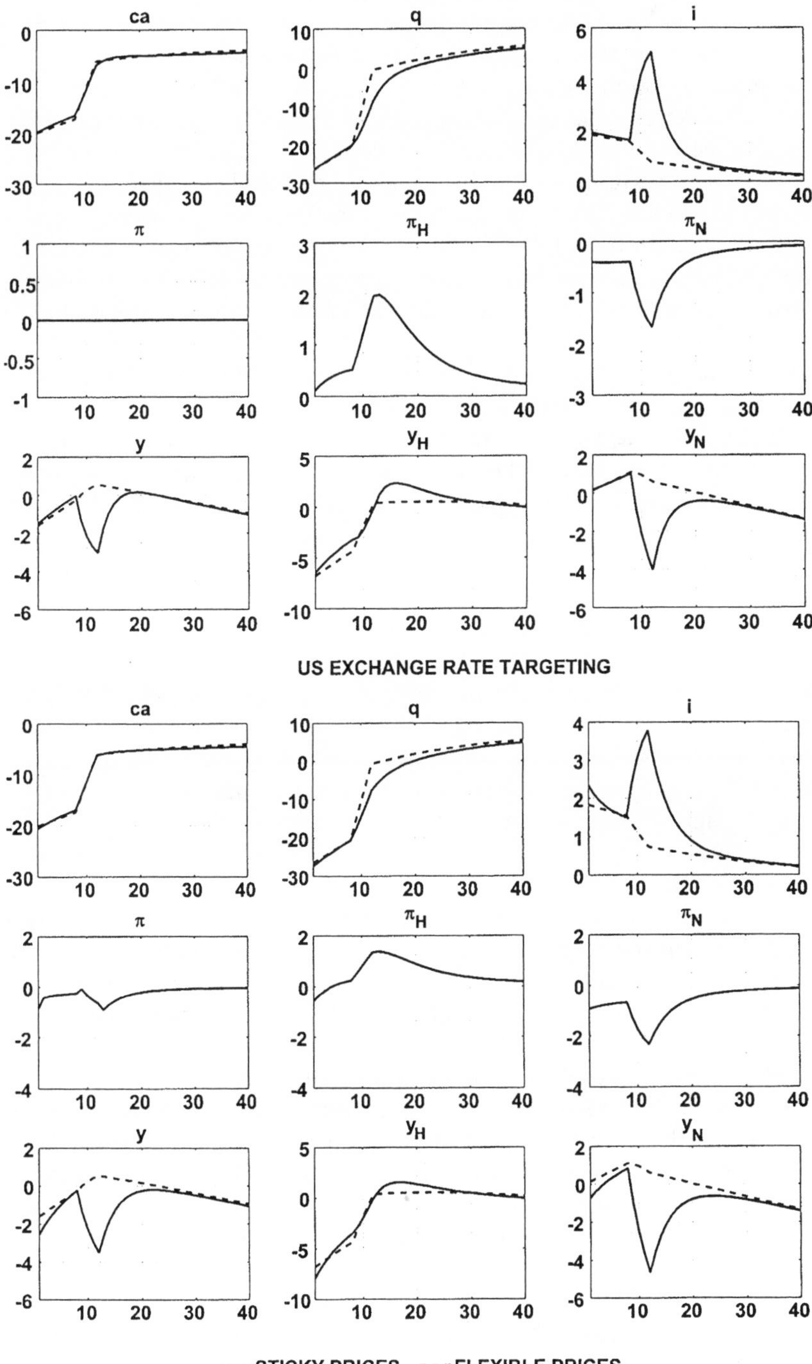

Fig. 4.5 Fast burn scenario under two different policy rules

enhances the contraction. In addition, the sectoral distortions intensify, many due to a nearly 4.5 percent contraction in nontradable goods output.

It thus appears that targeting a measure of domestic inflation is superior to targeting overall CPI inflation; though, as we noted earlier, coming up with a measure of the former that is appropriately distinct from the latter may not be a trivial undertaking.

We next turn to exchange rate targeting. As we noted, the emerging market economies that suffered large output contractions during current reversals typically had central banks that were following an exchange rate peg. For the Federal Reserve, of course, exchange rate considerations have played virtually no role in interest rate setting, at least in recent times. It is hard to say, however, whether or not during the kind of current account reversal we have been considering, pressures might mount for the central bank to respond even modestly to the depreciation.

In this spirit, we consider a variation of our baseline rule that permits the central bank to also respond to the exchange rate depreciation. Suppose the modified interest rate rule is given by

$$i_t = \bar{\imath}_t + \chi \Delta e_t \tag{58}$$

with

$$\bar{\imath}_t = \rho \bar{\imath}_{t-1} + (1 - \rho)\phi_\pi \pi_t.$$

Here, $\bar{\imath}_t$ is the rate the central bank would choose if it were to follow the baseline Taylor rule. The actual rate it sets is augmented by a factor that reflects the policy adjustment to the depreciation. We set $\chi = 0.1$, which suggests that a 10 percent exchange rate depreciation over the quarter would have the central bank increase the nominal interest rate by 100 basis points. Relative to a strict peg, the response of the policy rate to exchange rate movements is relatively modest.

The bottom panel of figure 4.5 portrays the hard landing scenario for this case. The drop in aggregate output is nearly 3.0 percent, as in the case of pure CPI targeting. Again, the reason for the contraction is that the policy rule forces a rise in short-term interest rates throughout the course of the current account reversal. Similarly, the nontradable goods sector is hit particularly hard. Output in this sector contracts nearly 5.0 percent.

Overall, policy regimes that produce large interest rate increases in response to the reversal can generate large output contractions. Even in the absences of large aggregate effects, though, there can be significant sectoral misallocations, with large positive output gaps opening up in the nontradable goods sectors and large negative ones in the tradable goods sectors.

A Foreign Exchange Rate Peg

We now return to our baseline case but assume that the foreign central bank abandons the Taylor rule and instead pegs its currency to that of the home country. We do this for two reasons. The first is to explore the implications of foreign monetary policy on current account adjustment. In our baseline case, the Taylor rule had the foreign central bank adjust interest rates in the opposite direction of the home central bank. During the fast burn experiment, the foreign interest rate behaved as the mirror image of the home country rate: it declined initially by a modest amount and then began a steady upward trajectory, enhancing the overall terms-of-trade depreciation for the home country. To what degree was this "cooperative" foreign monetary policy helpful in mitigating the impact of the fast burn on home country output? One way to get at the issue is to consider the case where the foreign central bank does not cooperate at all with exchange rate adjustment and simply follows a peg to the home country currency. A second consideration involves the impact of a foreign peg on current account dynamics. It has been widely speculated that by pegging its exchange rate to the dollar, China has been contributing to the U.S. current account deficits. While the other country in our model is meant to capture the rest of the world and not simply China, we can nonetheless shed some light on the issue by adopting the extreme assumption that the foreign country central bank adopts a peg.[22]

We accordingly return to the baseline case and, for foreign monetary policy, substitute a nominal exchange rate peg for the Taylor rule. From the uncovered interest parity condition, a pure nominal exchange rate peg simply requires that the foreign central bank sets its nominal rate equal to the home country rate:

$$i_t^* = i_t. \tag{59}$$

The top panel of figure 4.6 illustrates the response of a small set of domestic, foreign, and international variables for the case of the slow burn. Again, the dotted line reflects the flexible-price equilibrium. As a comparison of figures 4.2 and 4.6 suggests, the foreign country peg has virtually no impact on current account or real exchange rate dynamics. How can this be if the foreign country is fixing the nominal exchange rate? What causes the real exchange rate to adjust is a rapid increase in the foreign price level relative to the domestic level. By not letting its nominal exchange rate appreciate, the foreign country encourages excess demand in its tradable sector, which spills over to its nontradable sector. The end product is rapid domestic inflation, which provides the source of the exchange rate depreciation and the current account adjustment. In addition to the current account and the real exchange rate, the home country economy is also not affected much by the foreign country peg. Indeed, it is the foreign country economy that largely bears the brunt.

In a broad sense, the Chinese economy has behaved consistently with the model predictions. As figure 4.7 shows, output growth has climbed steadily since 2002, rising from 7 percent to almost 12 percent in 2007. Moreover,

22. Besides China, a number of oil producing countries, which, in recent years, have also substantially contributed to finance the U.S. current account deficit, peg their currency to the dollar, too.

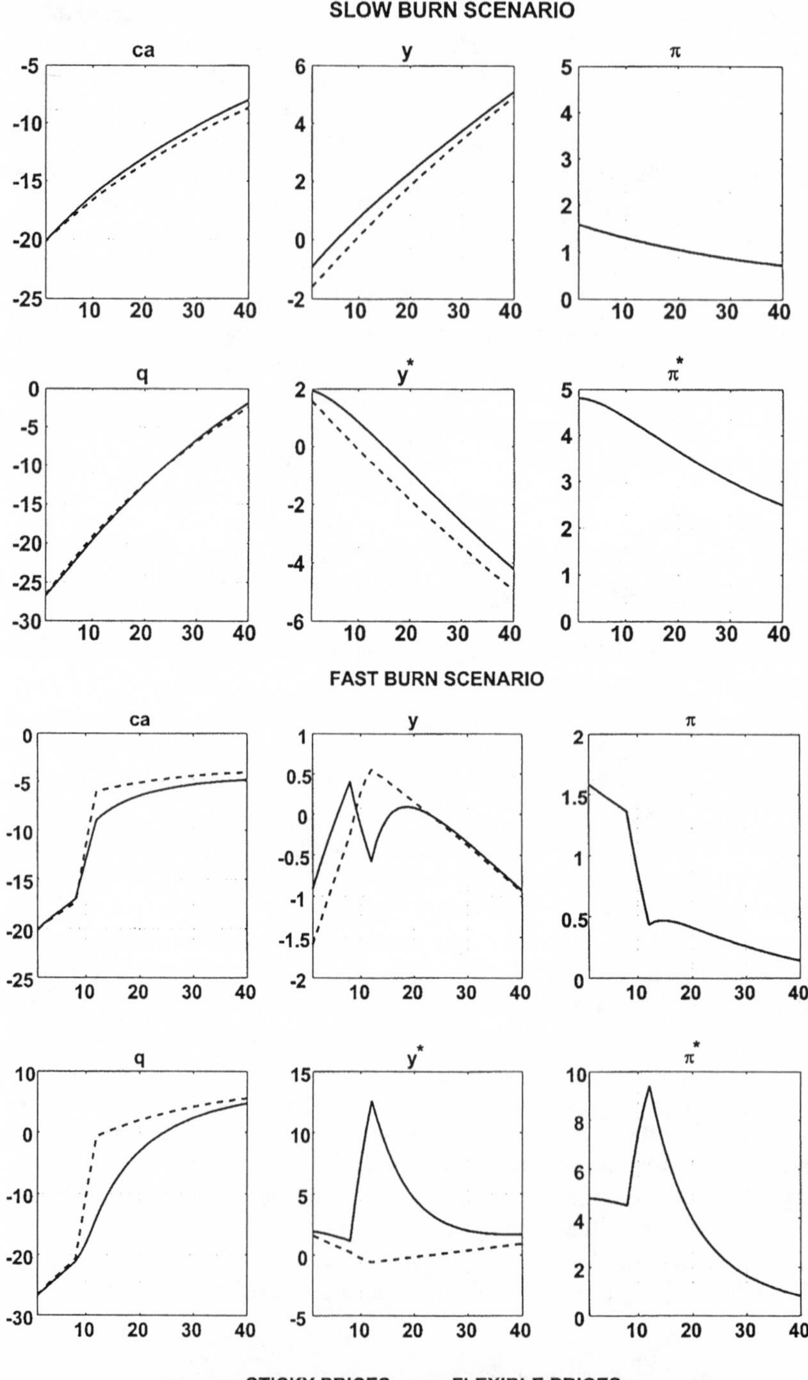

Fig. 4.6 Foreign exchange rate peg

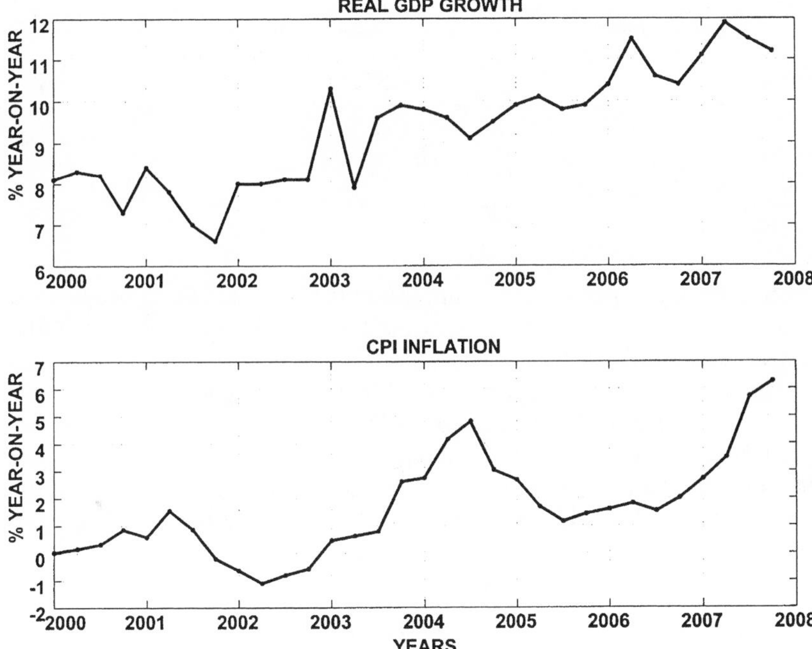

Fig. 4.7 China: Recent trends in GDP growth and inflation
Source: DLX/Haver Analytics.

there also has been a recent increase in CPI inflation from 1 to 6 percent in the last two years. Of course, there are a variety of factors such as price and capital controls that one would need to take into account before applying the model literally to China. In addition, since China only accounts for roughly one quarter of the U.S. current account deficit, we would need to appropriately adjust the calibration, which would likely work to dampen the predicted boom. Thus, the point to take away is that at least in our baseline slow burn scenario, the effect of a foreign peg is felt mainly by the foreign economy. There is little impact on the current account, the real exchange rate, or the home country economy.

Finally, the bottom panel of figure 4.6 portrays the fast burn scenario. Here there is a more significant impact of the foreign country peg. Intuitively, the sluggishness in nominal price adjustment becomes more significant when disturbances are sudden and large. During the crisis (quarters 8 to 12), the real exchange rate depreciates only by one-fourth as much as it did in the baseline case. Most of the adjustment occurs over the subsequent two years. The delayed response of the real exchange (and the terms of trade) leads to the current account closing only about 70 percent of the amount it did in the baseline case. The inertia in the real exchange rate leads to a larger

Table 4.1 Imperfect pass-through on import prices: 1992 ERM crises

	3 Quarters (%)	4 Quarters (%)	6 Quarters (%)	8 Quarters (%)
Italy	49	81	66	69
Sweden	66	53	68	72
United Kingdom	55	78	84	72

drop in aggregate domestic output than in the baseline case: a drop of 1.0 percent instead of 0.5 percent. At the same time, the main effect is felt by the foreign country through an enormous boom in output.

Again, it is important to keep in mind that our example is extreme in that we are assuming that the rest of the world is following a peg. We also abstract from some of the key frictions that may be relevant to an emerging market economy like China. Nonetheless, at least in our canonical framework, the main effects of the foreign peg are felt by the foreign economy, whether in the slow or fast burn scenarios.

4.5 Imperfect Exchange Rate Pass-Through

Our baseline model assumes perfect pass-through of exchange rate movements to import prices, but is calibrated to match the evidence on pass-through to the CPI. Much of this evidence, however, is based on an annual frequency, while our model is quarterly. In this respect, the baseline model may miss the quarterly link between exchange rate movements, import prices, and the CPI. For the slow burn scenario, this may not be problem, since the exchange rate depreciation plays out smoothly over a long period of time. However, it could be relevant to a situation where there is an abrupt large movement in the exchange rate, as for example would be likely to arise under a sudden stop.

To get a feel for how import prices respond to sharp exchange rate depreciations, we examine data from three countries—Italy, Sweden, and the United Kingdom—in the wake of the European Monetary System (EMS) crisis of 1992. Table 4.1 reports the degree of pass-through on import prices from three to eight quarters after the initial depreciation for the three countries in our sample. We conclude from the table that pass-through in response to a large depreciation is high, but delayed.[23]

In the model, we add imperfect pass-through following Monacelli (2005).

23. To the extent that importers face any distribution and/or transportation costs, we should expect any long-run exchange rate pass-through to be less than 100 percent. We abstract from distribution costs directly. However, we indirectly take account of how distribution costs may affect the link between exchange rates and final goods prices by adjusting the size of the nontraded goods sector.

We introduce monopolistically competitive retailers who import foreign tradables and sell them to domestic residents. The law of one price holds at the dock but not at the consumer level because local retailers set the price of imported goods in domestic currency on a staggered basis. Each period a fraction ξ of retailers hold their price constant while the remaining fraction $1-\xi$ solve an optimal dynamic pricing problem. In particular, those importers who change their price in period t choose P_{Ft} to maximize

(60) $$E_t \sum_{s=0}^{\infty} \xi^s \Lambda_{t,t+s}(P_{Ft} - \varepsilon_{t+s} P^*_{F,t+s}) C_{F,t+s},$$

subject to the demand equation (10). The first-order condition for this problem is

(61) $$E_t \left\{ \sum_{s=0}^{\infty} \xi^s \Lambda_{t,t+s}[P_{Ft} - (1+\tilde{\mu})\varepsilon_{t+s} P^*_{F,t+s})] C_{F,t+s} \right\} = 0,$$

where $\tilde{\mu} \equiv (\eta - 1)^{-1}$. The law of large numbers implies that the price index for imported goods becomes

(62) $$P_{Ft} = \xi P_{F,t-1} + (1-\xi) P^o_{Ft}.$$

Given the departure from the law of one price at the consumer level, it is useful to define the price gap as the ratio between the foreign price in domestic currency and the domestic price (also in domestic currency)

(63) $$\Psi_{Ft} \equiv \frac{\varepsilon_t P^*_{Ft}}{P_{Ft}}.$$

With perfect pass-through, Ψ_{Ft} equals unity.

Next we note that with imperfect pass-through, the terms of trade differs across countries. We keep the definition of the terms of trade from the perspective of the home country consistent with our baseline specification: $T_{Ht} = P_{Ft}/P_{Ht}$. Conversely, we define the foreign country terms of trade as $T_{Ft} \equiv P^*_{Ht}/P^*_{Ft}$.

In the loglinear model, the market demand for home tradables now accounts for the difference in the two countries' terms of trade

(64) $$y_{Ht} = \alpha(1-\alpha)\eta(\tau_{Ht} - \tau_{Ft}) + (1-\gamma)[\alpha x_t + (1-\alpha)x^*_t] + \alpha c_t + (1-\alpha)c^*_t.$$

The real exchange rate similarly accounts for the differences in country-specific terms of trade:

(65) $$q_t = \psi_{F,t} + \alpha\tau_{H,t} + (1-\alpha)\tau_{F,t} + (1-\gamma)(x^*_t - x_t).$$

Next, with imperfect pass-through, imported goods inflation is characterized by the following Phillips curve relation:

(66) $$\pi_{Ft} = \tilde{\kappa}\psi_{Ft} + \beta E_t \pi_{F,t+1},$$

where ψ_{Ft} is the log-linear deviation of the law of one price gap in (63) from its steady-state value (equal to one) and $\tilde{\kappa} \equiv (1 - \tilde{\xi})(1 - \beta\tilde{\xi})/\tilde{\xi}$.[24] The evolution of the law of one price gap depends on the depreciation of the nominal exchange rate as well as on the inflation rate differentials in the two countries

$$\Delta\psi_{Ft} = \Delta e_t + \pi^*_{F,t} - \pi_{F,t}. \tag{67}$$

As before, the percent change in the terms of trade depends on import inflation minus the inflation of domestic tradables. The difference in this case is that the relation for import inflation, equation (66), is based on imperfect exchange rate pass-through. There are an analogous set of relations that determine the evolution of the terms of trade for the foreign country. Keeping in mind the new country-specific definitions of the terms of trade, the remaining equations of the model are unchanged.

There is only one new parameter that we need to calibrate—the degree of price stickiness for importers, $1 - \tilde{\xi}$. We set this parameter at 0.66, the same value we used for domestic producers.

Figure 4.8 presents a comparison of imperfect versus perfect pass-through for the baseline case where each central bank obeys a simple Taylor rule. In each instance, the solid line reflects imperfect pass-through, while the dotted line reflects perfect pass-through. The top set of panels reflects the slow burn scenario. As we conjectured, the behavior of both the domestic and international variables is very similar across the two cases. As one might expect, inflation is a bit lower under imperfect pass-through since the impact of the exchange rate on the domestic price of imports is muted in this case. Though we do not report the results here, for the slow burn scenario imperfect pass-through does not have much effect on the behavior of any of the economic variables under the full set of policy experiments we considered for the benchmark model.

Imperfect pass-through is more relevant under the fast burn scenario. The bottom set of panels in figure 4.8 presents this case. Note first that current account is much slower to adjust under imperfect pass-through. In this instance the depreciation of the home currency has a much smaller effect on domestic exports. As a further consequence, there is a much sharper contraction in output relative to the case of perfect pass-through. In this latter case, the depreciation produces an export boom that softens the overall contraction in output. With imperfect pass-through, however, the export response is muted, which enhances the overall contraction in output.

As a check on our formulation of imperfect pass-through, we examine how the model captures the dynamics of exchange rates and import prices as compared to the experience of the Exchange Rate Mechanism (ERM)

24. For the same amount of nominal rigidities, the absence of labor inputs (and hence, of real rigidities) in the distribution sector implies that the slope of the imported goods Phillips curve is higher than for domestically produced goods.

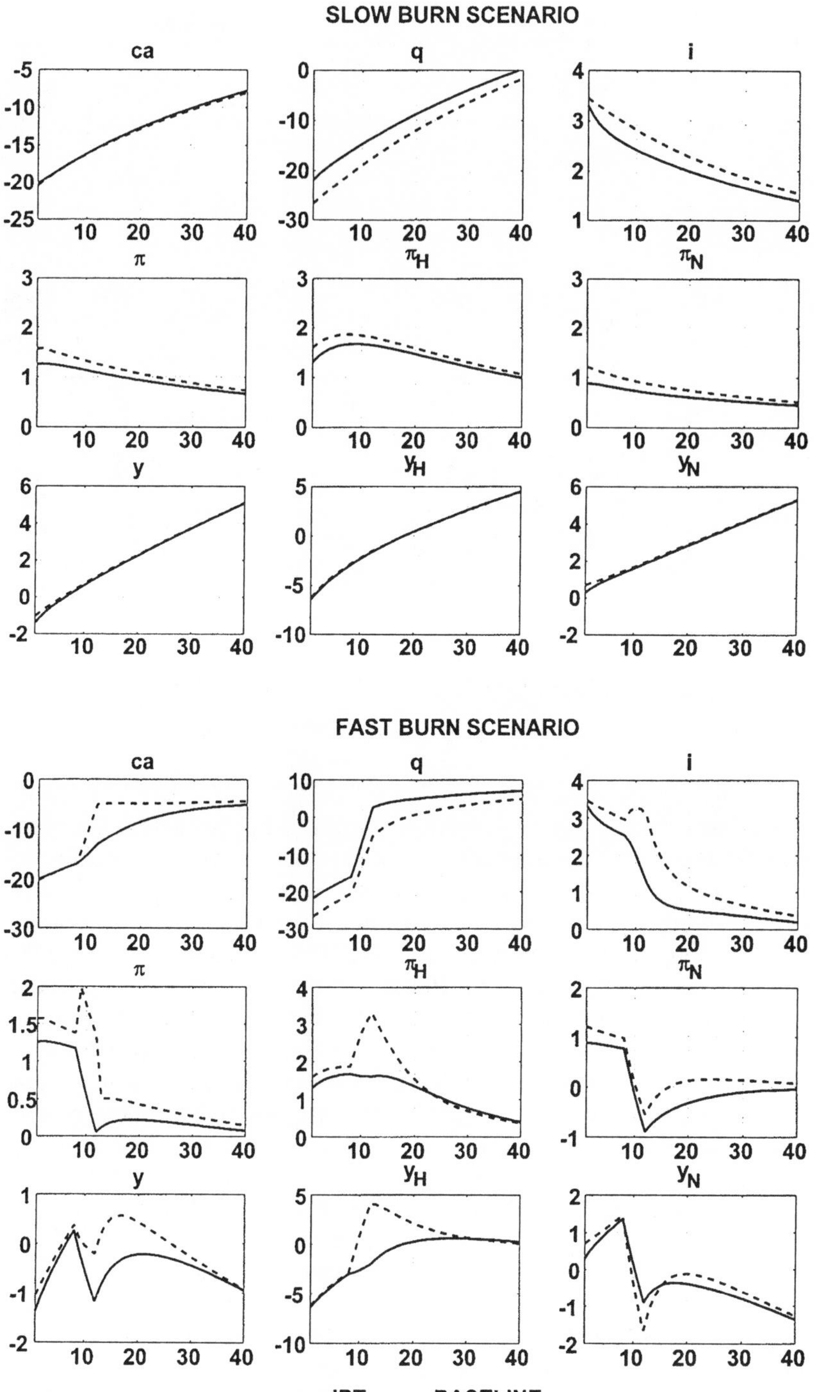

Fig. 4.8 Imperfect pass-through (Baseline Taylor rule)

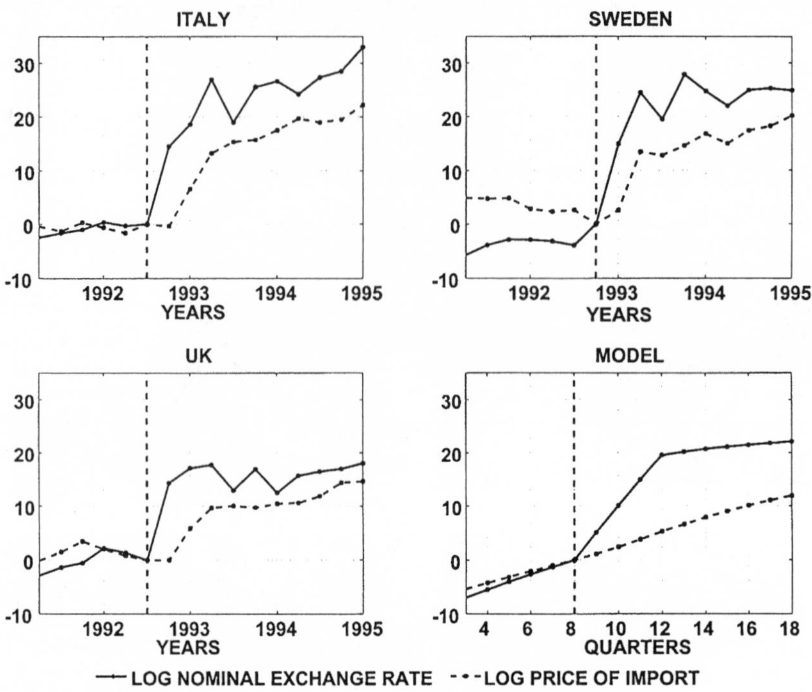

Fig. 4.9 Imperfect pass-through (1992 ERM crisis and model)
Source: IMF International Financial Statistics

crisis. The first three panels in figure 4.9 report the movement of the nominal exchange rate (the solid line) and import prices (the dotted line) for this period in the data. The vertical line shows the beginning of the crisis for each country. Both variables are normalized at zero at the start of the crisis. By construction, the exchange rate depreciations all begin in the first quarter following the start of the crisis. In each case, there is a delay of another quarter before import prices begin to move significantly. Though it varies a bit in each case, on average after a year or so, import prices increase by more than two-thirds of the exchange rate movement. The fourth panel displays the behavior of the correspondent variables in the model, given the appropriate normalization. Overall, the model is roughly consistent with the data.

Finally, as under perfect pass-through, domestic inflation targeting is reasonably effective in insulating the economy from the harmful effects of a sudden stop. As the solid line in the bottom left panel of figure 4.10 shows, under domestic inflation targeting there is no output drop under the sudden stop and only a mild increase in inflation. One difference from the case of perfect pass-through, however, is that CPI targeting is not as harmful. As the dotted line in the panel shows, there is a larger output drop under CPI target-

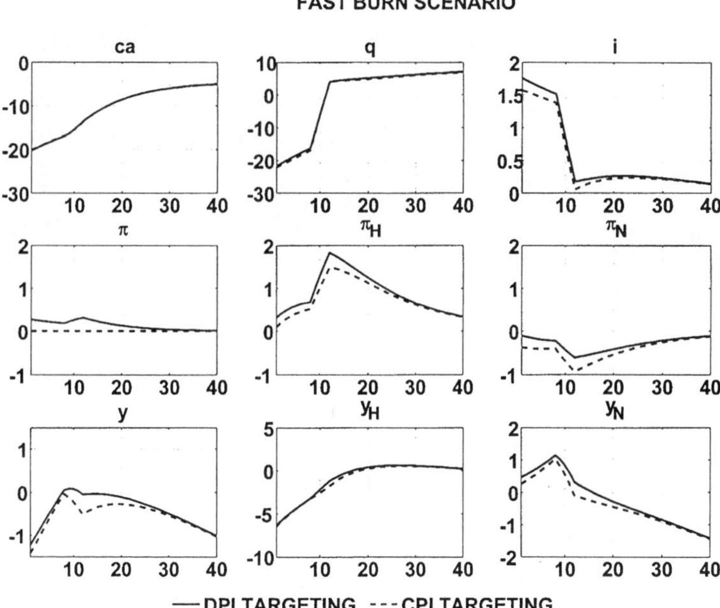

Fig. 4.10 Imperfect pass-through: DPI vs. CPI inflation targeting

ing relative to domestic inflation targeting, but the difference is not nearly as dramatic as under perfect pass-through. With imperfect pass-through the depreciation has less impact on CPI inflation, permitting a less aggressive increase in interest rates to maintain the inflation target.

4.6 Concluding Remarks

We have developed a simple two-country monetary DSGE model that is useful for analyzing the interplay between monetary policy and current account adjustment. We proceeded to use the framework to study the effects of different monetary policy regimes under two different adjustment scenarios: a "slow burn," where adjustment is smooth and plays out over a long period of time, and a "fast burn," where a sudden revision of the relative growth prospects of the home versus foreign country leads to a sharp current account reversal.

Our main finding is that the monetary policy regime has important consequences for the behavior of domestic variables (for instance, output and inflation), but much less so for international variables (for instance, the current account and real exchange rates). Among the policy rules we have examined, the policy rule that seems to work best overall has the central bank focus on targeting domestic (producer) inflation. This policy has the central bank accept the impact of the currency depreciation on import price inflation and instead focus on adjusting interest rates to keep producer prices stable. As a consequence, during the slow burn, inflation is very modest overall (since the import share of consumption is small) and aggregate output roughly equals its potential value. During the fast burn, the rule has each central bank adjust its policy rate rapidly to offset the sudden reallocation of demand across countries. This serves to dampen significantly the effect on aggregate output and inflation. One important caveat, though, is that the moderate aggregate behavior masks an inefficiently large sectoral reallocation. Due to the nominal rigidities, nontradable output falls significantly below its potential level, while the reverse happens in the tradable goods sector.

By contrast, two kinds of monetary regimes work very poorly during a current account reversal: targeting consumer price inflation and targeting the exchange rate. Each of the policies induces the home central bank to raise interest rates sharply to fend off a currency depreciation. This sharp increase in interest rates, in turn, leads to a major contraction in aggregate economic activity within the home country. The contraction is particularly severe in the nontradable goods sector, enhancing the inefficient sectoral reallocation.

While the response of domestic variables tends to be quite sensitive to the monetary policy regime, the same is not true of international variables. In most instances, the behavior of the current account and the real exchange rates does not vary significantly from what a flexible-price model would predict. Indeed, this is largely true even in an extreme case where the foreign country implements an exchange rate peg. In this case, the effect of the peg is largely absorbed by the foreign economy.

Our benchmark model allows for perfect pass-through of exchange rates to import prices but is calibrated to match pass-through to final consumer prices at the annual frequency. We show, however, that the main results are robust to allow for imperfect pass-through to capture the quarterly dynamics of exchange rates and import prices. Under the slow burn scenario, the degree of pass-through has little impact on economic behavior. Under the sudden stop, however, current account adjustment is much slower with imperfect pass-through and the output contraction is much steeper in the baseline case where each central bank obeys a simple Taylor rule. As in the case of perfect pass-through, however, domestic inflation targeting appears to have desirable stabilizing properties in the event of a current account crisis. Consumer price inflation targeting, though, is not as harmful as under perfect pass-through.

Finally, our model is designed to be sufficiently simple to afford qualitative insights, but at the same time to be sufficiently rich to give "ballpark" quantitative predictions. Next on the agenda is adding features that will improve the quantitative dimension.

References

Aoki, K. 2001. Optimal monetary policy response to relative price changes. *Journal of Monetary Economics* 48 (1): 55–80.

Backus, D., E. Henriksen, F. Lambert, and C. Telmer. 2006. Current account fact and fiction. Society for Economic Dynamics 2005 Meeting Paper no. 115.

Bems, R., and L. Dedola. 2006. Current account reversals and capital markets integration: The adjustment of the U.S. external position revisited. International Monetary Fund (IMF). Unpublished Manuscript.

Benigno, G., and P. Benigno. 2006. Designing targeting rules for international monetary policy coordination. *Journal of Monetary Economics* 53: 473–506.

Beaudry, P., and F. Portier. 2004. An exploration into Pigou's theory of cycles. *Journal of Monetary Economics* 51 (6): 1183–1216.

Benigno, P. 2004. Optimal monetary policy in a currency area. *Journal of International Economics* 63 (2): 293–320.

Bodenstein, M. 2006. Closing open economy models. International Finance Discussion Papers no. 867, Board of Governors of the Federal Reserve System.

Buera, F., and J. Kaboski. 2007. The rise of the service economy. Society for Economic Dynamics 2006 Meeting Paper no. 496.

Caballero, R., E. Farhi, and P.-O. Gourinchas. 2008. An equilibrium model of "Global Imbalances" and low interest rates. *American Economic Review* 98 (1): 358–93.

Campa, J., and L. Goldberg. 2006. Distribution margins, imported inputs, and the sensitivity of the CPI to exchange rates. NBER Working Paper no. 12121. Cambridge, MA: National Bureau of Economic Research, March.

Cavallo, M., and C. Tille. 2006. Current account adjustment with high financial integration: A scenario analysis. *Federal Reserve Bank of San Francisco Economic Review:* 31–46.

Clarida, R., J. Galí, and M. Gertler. 1998. Monetary policy rules in practice: Some international evidence. *European Economic Review* 42 (6): 1033–67.

———. 2002. A simple framework for international monetary policy analysis. *Journal of Monetary Economics* 49 (5): 879–904.

Cole, H., and M. Obstfeld. 1991. Commodity trade and international risk sharing: How much do financial markets matter? *Journal of Monetary Economics* 28 (1): 3–24.

Corsetti, G., and P. Pesenti. 2005. International dimensions of optimal monetary policy. *Journal of Monetary Economics* 52 (2): 281–305.

Curdia, V. 2007. Optimal monetary policy under sudden stop. Federal Reserve Bank of New York. Unpublished Manuscript.

Engel, C., and J. H. Rogers. 2006. The U.S. current account deficit and the expected share of world output. *Journal of Monetary Economics* 53: 1063–93.

Faruquee, H., D. Laxton, D. Muir, and P. Pesenti. 2005. Smooth landing or crash? Model-based scenarios of global current account rebalancing. In *G7 current account imbalances: Sustainability and adjustment,* ed. R. Clarida, 377–456. Chicago: University of Chicago Press.

Ferrero, A. 2007. The long-run determinants of the U.S. external imbalances. Federal Reserve Bank of New York Staff Reports no. 295.

Gertler, M., S. Gilchrist, and F. Natalucci. 2007. External constraints on monetary policy and the financial accelerator. *Journal of Money, Credit, and Banking* 39 (2–3): 295–330.

Jaimovich, N., and S. Rebelo. 2006. Can news about the future drive the business cycle. Stanford University. Unpublished Manuscript.

Mendoza, E., V. Quadrini, and V. Rios-Rull. 2007. Financial integration, financial deepness and global imbalances. University of Maryland. Unpublished Manuscript.
Monacelli, T. 2005. Monetary policy in a low pass-through environment. *Journal of Money Credit and Banking* 37 (December): 1047–66.
Obstfeld, M., and K. Rogoff. 2002. Global implications of self-oriented national monetary rules. *Quarterly Journal of Economics* 117 (2): 503–36.
———. 2005. The unsustainable U.S. current account position revisited. In *G7 current account imbalances: Sustainability and adjustment,* ed. Richard Clarida, 339–376. Chicago: University of Chicago Press.
Rogoff, K. 2007. Impact of globalization on monetary policy. In *The new economic geography: Effects and policy implications,* ed. Federal Reserve Bank of Kansas City, Kansas City: Federal Reserve Bank of Kansas City.
Svensson, L. E. O. 1999. Inflation targeting as a monetary policy rule. *Journal of Monetary Economics* 43 (3): 607–54.
Svensson, L. E. O., and M. Woodford. 2005. Implementing optimal policy through inflation-forecast targeting. In *The inflation-targeting debate,* ed. B. S. Bernanke and M. Woodford, 19–83. Chicago: University of Chicago Press.
Uzawa, H. 1968. Time preference, the consumption function and optimum asset holdings. In *Value, capital and growth: Papers in honor of Sir John Hicks,* ed. James Wolfe, Edinburgh, Scotland: University of Edinburgh Press.
Woodford, M. 2003. *Interest and prices.* Princeton, NJ: Princeton University Press.

Comment Paolo Pesenti

Arguably, the interaction between interest rate stance and current account imbalances is nowadays—and has been for quite a while—the key international dimension of monetary policy from the vantage point of the United States and its main trading partners. The point is not whether monetary policy can contribute significantly to closing the imbalances. The relevant question is rather what is the most suitable monetary response to sizable movements in global net saving. In the recent past, when U.S. interest rates were raised at the moderate and predictable pace of 25 basis points every Federal Open Market Committee (FOMC) cycle, a hotly debated issue among policy analysts was whether the path for the policy rate—other things equal—could have been steeper or looser because of considerations related to trade imbalances. Today, in light of highly differentiated patterns of net saving in the global economy, it remains highly relevant to investigate whether monetary policy in the United States and abroad is appropriately designed to deal with the macroeconomic implications of trade imbalances.

The answers to these broad questions, and to their more nuanced variants, are not obvious. In fact, it is possible to articulate a number of antithetical

Paolo Pesenti is vice president and head of the International Research Function at the Federal Reserve Bank of New York and a research associate at the NBER.

yet reasonable positions on these issues. A "dovish" take, for instance, would stress that, to the extent that net exports' contribution to gross domestic product (GDP) growth remains in negative territory and the current account deficit represents a persistent drag, a more stimulative policy action may be deemed as appropriate. Among other things, it would contribute to depreciate the exchange rate and support foreign demand for domestic goods and services. The alternative "hawkish" position would point out that, as the current account deficit reflects excess domestic demand, a tightening bias may be appropriate to preempt a build-up of inflationary pressures. This would help skewing incentives toward higher net saving by raising real rates. Then again, an "agnostic" view would argue that trade considerations are already accounted for in the central bank forecast, and there is no need to modify the policy path to account *specifically* for current account imbalances.

Against the backdrop of this debate, the chapter by Ferrero, Gertler, and Svensson (hereinafter FGS) draws a logically impeccable conclusion: "the current account imbalance may have implications for the natural rate of interest that have to factor into central bank policy, one way or another." Specifically, "a conventional Taylor rule does not perform well in this environment [because] it does not directly respond to the movement in the short term natural rate of interest rate induced by the current account imbalance. At zero inflation, the rule fixes the nominal rate at its steady-state value. However, the current imbalance pushes up the short term real rate, implying a monetary policy that is too expansionary in this instance."

Given the theme of this conference volume, and in the broader context of the current policy debate, these are important and compelling conclusions. It is important to understand carefully how we get there.

The chapter focuses on what I would define as a transfer problem on steroids. By this I mean that once we dig under the surface and the complexities of the dynamic stochastic general equilibrium (DSGE)-model apparatus, what we find is something Keynes and Ohlin would feel very familiar with. The current account adjustment process is substantially seen as a large-scale repayment from the debtor country (the United States) to the rest of the world. To support the transfer of real wealth and purchasing power, what is needed is that resources in the United States move from the nontradables sector to the tradable sector, and from the import-competing firms to the exporters. This requires changes in relative prices and the terms of trade.

The actual exercise can be summarized as follows. We know where we start from: a two-country world economy in which the home country runs a current account deficit in the order of 5 percent of GDP against the rest of the world. We know where we are going to end up: a steady state with zero net asset positions worldwide. To go from here to there, the authors suitably calibrate the dynamics of productivity and preferences and let the propagation mechanism of the model deliver the intertemporal details of the adjustment. It is worth emphasizing that, for the purpose of the exercise, global rebalancing is bound to take place even if its macroeconomic characteristics can differ across scenarios. In other words, adjustment can be smooth and easy (the slow burn scenario) or it can be fast and bumpy (the fast burn scenario), but it is in the cards and will happen no matter what. Foreigners want to be repaid. The U.S. residents will do whatever it takes to repay them. I will return to this point in a short time. Before, let me briefly comment on some of the more technical aspects of the exercise.

First, in terms of scale and detail, the FGS model occupies a somewhat intermediate position between the static framework of Obstfeld and Rogoff (2005, 2007)—in which sectoral outputs are fixed—and simulation exercises with large DSGE models, such as General Equilibrium Model (GEM).[1] With no capital, no investment, and no budget deficits for reasons of theoretical parsimony, a current account improvement in FGS can be achieved exclusively through a contraction of consumption relative to output. In reality, of course, current account dynamics are heavily affected by fluctuations in relative investment and ideally one would like to see the model extended to encompass this dimension. Nevertheless, I find interesting that the main results of FGS substantially confirm the findings of analogous exercises regardless of model size and characteristics (similar half-life for current account adjustment, similar cumulative size of real exchange rate adjustment, etc.). Is this cross-model similarity a sign of reliability and robustness of the underlying approach? Or rather, have the building blocks of recent open economy macro models become so similar in substance that their details can hardly make any difference?

Second, there is a potential issue of country size. The United States in the model represents 50 percent of the world economy. As a matter of fact the correct figure is somewhere between 25 and 30 percent. In the context of a general-equilibrium two-country model this asymmetry in country size may have important quantitative implications. Then again, one could argue that the relevant "rest of the world" for the purpose of this analysis is, in practice, heavily skewed toward emerging Asia and oil exporters (with third countries such as Europe approximately balanced vis-à-vis the United States). In this case, the United States may actually represent more than 50 percent of such "world" economy. It would be straightforward to carry out sensitivity analysis with respect to country size, and it is worth checking whether this element matters or not in practice.

Third, the world economy of the model approaches over time a steady state with a zero net asset position worldwide (as in Obstfeld and Rogoff [2005, 2007] and similar stylized "transfer problem" exercises such as Corsetti, Martin, and Pesenti [2008]). However, the model allows for steady-state growth, so that it would be possible for the home country to run a sustainable current account deficit even in the steady-state equilibrium. This of course

1. See, for example, IMF (2006, box 1.3).

would have implications for the overall size of the real depreciation associated with adjustment: the dollar correction required to close a trend deficit of 5 percent is potentially larger than the depreciation required to reduce the deficit from 5 to, say, only 2 percent of GDP.

Fourth, the FGS model (and, unfortunately, most models in the literature) assumes no loss of policy credibility no matter what course of action the policymakers take. Inflation converges to target at a relatively fast pace, and bygones are bygones. This may be especially relevant for the fast-burn scenario. The appropriate model-based monetary stance implies some short-term tolerance for higher consumer price index (CPI) inflation, which in "real-life" situations could be misperceived by markets as a sign that policymakers are dangerously falling behind the curve. As a result, inflation expectations may persistently deviate from the policy target if agents become concerned with the inability of the monetary authority to achieve price stability. By ignoring credibility issues *tout-court,* the model's potential for realistic policy evaluation ends up being severely curtailed.

Finally, the model abstracts from valuation effects (capital gains and losses related to exchange rate movements when gross assets and liabilities are denominated in different currencies), thus ignoring a potentially crucial aspect of the adjustment process.

Moving to the message of the chapter, there are two important lessons that require some discussion. First, domestic price (producer price index [PPI]) targeting turns out to be a better policy strategy than CPI targeting. Second, as far as the behavior of foreign authorities is concerned, a regime of limited exchange rate flexibility abroad turns out to be an inferior monetary strategy: in a nutshell, better dead than peg. Let's analyze these two results in some detail.

As the authors write, "within our framework, a domestic inflation target may be preferable to consumer price inflation target." Why? One could use a core inflation targeting argument here (a good starting point for any analysis of optimal monetary policy in closed and/or open economies). To make a long story short, optimal policies are expected to stabilize a weighted average of markups in labor and product markets, where the weights assigned to the different markups reflect to some extent the degree of nominal inertia associated with the underlying prices. In other words, the appropriate monetary stance pays more attention to sectors with more persistent nominal distortions, while it does not react to changes in sectors where adjustment is driven by flexible prices.

Now, if import prices are sufficiently flexible while domestic prices are sticky, it makes sense to target a basket of domestic prices only. In the context of the model (until section 4.5) PPI targeting is more appropriate than CPI targeting. This is because the law of one price holds and exchange rate pass-through is high, making import prices relatively close to the flexible benchmark.

The problem of course is that exchange rate pass-through is high in the model *by assumption,* not because it matches a stylized fact. In reality, pass-through to U.S. import prices is relatively low, even at the border level. Because of extensive invoicing of world exports in dollars, import prices in the United States have low sensitivity to exchange rate fluctuations. In a (realistic) "dollar pricing" world, terms of trade and import prices move much less than conventional wisdom would suggest in response to exchange rate fluctuations.

Some sensitivity analysis on this point is presented in section 4.5, and these new results provide a more reliable guideline for policy evaluation. In short, PPI targeting remains reasonably effective but CPI targeting yields substantially similar outcomes. In the future, it would be interesting to bring this analysis to the next step and provide a full account of optimal monetary policy according to the model, instead of restricting the analysis to the comparison between "simple" targeting rules.

Let us consider now the appropriate monetary behavior of the rest of the world. As the authors write, "by not letting its nominal exchange rate appreciate, the foreign country encourages excess demand in its tradable sector which spills over to its nontradable sector. The end product is rapid domestic inflation, which provides the source of the exchange rate depreciation and the current-account adjustment. In addition to the current account and the real exchange rate, the home country economy is also not much affected by the foreign-country peg. Indeed, it is the foreign country economy that largely bears the brunt."

Recall: the rest of the world pegs its *nominal* exchange rate to the home currency, but adjustment through the *real* exchange rate occurs no matter what. Because the rest of the world is unable or unwilling to prevent adjustment, the choice of the peg simply means that all the action goes through inflation differentials.[2]

As a feature of the process of global adjustment, these results are insightful and absolutely right. But they may overlook a few important elements that have contributed to the unfolding of global imbalances in the first place.

To make my point as simply as possible, think of a government in the rest of the world that is willing to accumulate official reserves for unexplained or extra-economic reasons (for instance, in order to maintain comfortable exchange rate levels for its exporters, protect market shares in the home market, and absorb excess labor force in the tradable sector as considered by the advocates of the so-called "Bretton Woods II" view[3]). Also assume that such a government is very successful at sterilizing its foreign exchange intervention. It is irrelevant to observe that this behavior may be suboptimal. Everything we need to know is simply that some agents somewhere in

2. Similar considerations hold in the case of GEM simulations. See Faruqee et al. (2007).
3. See, for example, Dooley, Folkerts-Landau, and Garber (2007).

the world economy are willing to support persistent capital inflows to the United States.

Under this scenario, the logic of the transfer problem is no longer valid. The rest of the world does not want to be repaid (at least for now). Its fixed exchange rate regime is not just a bad policy choice *given* the dynamics of adjustment. It is a policy that *changes* the dynamics of adjustment itself, and substantially prevents the rebalancing from taking place.

An analysis of the implications of this behavior requires a drastically different kind of simulation exercise, one in which the rest of the world is assumed to take the other side of the transaction and persistently provide the home country with the funds needed to finance its trade deficit. From the vantage point of the United States the policy implications can be severely different relative to the aforementioned ones, in fact different enough to reopen the question of whether the natural rate in the United States must actually increase if the rest of the world pegs its currency to the dollar.

Moving beyond academic speculation, concerns of this kind have been expressed in recent years by several policymakers. It seems appropriate to close with the following representative quote (my italics):

"*Insufficiently flexible exchange rate regimes* have the potential to *alter the pattern of capital flows* and the price of financial assets [. . .] The fact that official purchases of financial assets are determined by different factors than those influencing private investors suggests that we would probably see a somewhat different combination of capital flows, exchange rates and interest rates in the absence of official intervention. To the extent that *the factors affecting capital flows act to raise asset prices, lower interest rates and reduce risk premiums,* it is harder for the markets to assess how much of the currently very favorable conditions are likely to reflect fundamentals and prove more durable. *If the prevailing patterns of capital flows were to exert downward pressure on interest rates* and upward pressure on other asset prices, *they would contribute to more expansionary financial conditions* than would otherwise be the case. Among other things, *this outcome complicates our ability to assess the present stance of monetary policy.* It can change how monetary policy affects overall financial conditions and the economy as a whole" (Geithner 2006).

References

Corsetti, G., P. Martin, and P. Pesenti. 2008. Varieties and the transfer problem: The extensive margin of current account adjustment. NBER Working Paper no. 13795. Cambridge, MA: National Bureau of Economic Research, February.

Dooley, M. P., D. Folkerts-Landau, and P. Garber. 2007. Direct investment, rising real wages, and the absorption of excess labor in the periphery. In *G7 current account imbalances: Sustainability and adjustment,* ed. R. Clarida, 103–30. Chicago: University of Chicago Press.

Faruqee, H., D. Laxton, D. Muir, and P. Pesenti. 2007. Smooth landing or crash?

Model-based scenarios of global current account rebalancing. In *G7 current account imbalances: Sustainability and adjustment,* ed. R. Clarida, 377–456. Chicago: University of Chicago Press.

Geithner, T. 2006. Global economic and financial integration: Some implications for central banking. Remarks at the Columbia Business School Center on Japanese Economy and Business' 20th Anniversary Conference, Columbia University. 26 October, New York City.

International Monetary Fund. 2006. *World economic outlook. Financial systems and economic cycles.* Washington, DC: IMF, September.

Obstfeld, M., and K. Rogoff. 2005. Global current account imbalances and exchange rate adjustments. *Brookings Papers on Economic Activity* 1: 67–123. Washington, DC: Brookings Institution.

———. 2007. The unsustainable U.S. current account position revisited. In *G7 current account imbalances: Sustainability and adjustment,* ed. R. Clarida, 339–76. Chicago: University of Chicago Press.

5

Monetary Rules in Emerging Economies with Financial Market Imperfections

Nicoletta Batini, Paul Levine, and Joseph Pearlman

5.1 Introduction

Over the past twenty years there has been a marked shift toward more flexible exchange rate regimes and more open capital accounts by both industrial and emerging market countries. Exchange rate targets accounted for over half of monetary policy regimes in 1985, but declined to just 5 percent in 2005, while in emerging market and other developing countries the share fell from 75 percent to 55 percent.

The move to more flexible exchange rate regimes has been accompanied by a variety of frameworks to conduct monetary policy, including inflation targeting, monetary targeting, and more eclectic approaches involving multiple objectives. In industrial countries, exchange rate pegs and monetary targets have been replaced by eclectic regimes in G-3 countries, and by direct inflation targets almost everywhere else. In emerging market countries exchange rate pegs were replaced mainly by money targets through the mid-1990s. Since then, however, money targets as well as exchange rate pegs have been replaced by direct inflation targets.

Over the next few years, the trend toward adoption of flexible exchange

Nicoletta Batini is a Senior Economist at the IMF and a professor of economics at the University of Surrey. Paul Levine is a professor of economics at the University of Surrey. Joseph Pearlman is a professor of economics at London Metropolitan University.

Paper presented to the NBER conference on International Dimensions of Monetary Policy, S'Agaro, Catalonia, Spain, June 11–13, 2007. The chapter has benefited from comments of participants, particularly those of our discussant, Frederic Mishkin, and the conference organizers, Jordi Galí and Mark Gertler. We acknowledge financial support for this research from the ESRC, project no. RES-000-23-1126. We also acknowledge the Research Visitors Programme of the Central Reserve Bank of Peru for Paul Levine. Thanks are owed to the Central Bank of Peru for their hospitality and to Paul Castillo, Carlos Montoro, and Vicente Tuesta, in particular, for stimulating discussions.

rate regimes, and inflation targeting in particular, is expected to continue. A recent International Monetary Fund (IMF) survey of eighty-eight nonindustrial countries found that more than half expressed a desire to move to explicit or implicit quantitative inflation targets. Moreover, nearly three-quarters of these countries envisage a shift to full-fledged inflation targeting by 2010 (Batini, Breuer, and Kochhar 2006).

While there are undoubtedly countries where inflation targeting may not be a suitable framework, it is a flexible framework that can be adapted to particular needs of nonindustrial countries. Nonindustrial country inflation targeters face a number of challenges that differ in character or in degree from those faced in industrial economies. Calvo and Mishkin (2003) highlight five particularly important challenges for emerging market countries. These include: (a) weak public sector financial management; (b) weak financial sector institutions and markets; (c) low monetary policy credibility; (d) extensive dollarization of financial liabilities; and (e) vulnerability to sharp changes in capital flows and international investor sentiment. In addition, many of these countries face considerably greater uncertainty about the structure of their economies, the monetary policy transmission mechanism, and the cyclical position of the economy than is typical of industrial country inflation targeters.

Our goal in this chapter is to understand whether, for nonindustrial countries facing such challenges, inflation targets are better or worse than (fix or soft) exchange rate targets. In particular we try to answer two central questions:

1. How do financial frictions in emerging markets affect the transmission mechanism of monetary policy and the volatility of the economy?
2. Can and should central banks in emerging markets facing financial frictions and vulnerable to combination of internal and external shocks try to balance inflation and exchange rate stabilization objectives?

We address these questions by developing a two-bloc emerging market, a rest of the world dynamic stochastic general equilibrium (DSGE) model where, in the emerging market bloc there is a strong link between changes in the exchange rate and financial distress of household and firms. More precisely, we assume that: (a) there are financial frictions in the form of a "financial accelerator," since firms are obliged to finance at least part of their capital requirements in foreign currency (see Gertler, Gilchrist, and Natalucci [2003] and Gilchrist [2003]); (b) domestic households hold both local and foreign currency money balances for transaction purposes; and (c) the relative demand of foreign currency is endogenous to the extent of exchange rate stabilization by the central bank. The simultaneous assumption of (a) through (c) is novel in the literature.

We shock the model to understand how such financial frailties affect monetary transmission and inflation output trade-offs in the emerging market bloc. Using welfare analysis, we then compare the performance of monetary policy rules with different degrees of exchange rate flexibility and identify the rule for the emerging market central bank that responds to a combination of internal and external shocks at the smallest welfare cost.

The rest of the chapter is organized as follows. Section 5.2 presents the model. Section 5.3 sets out the form of monetary rules under investigation. In section 5.4 we study an analytically tractable form of the model without capital. The focus here is on the effects of transactions dollarization. In section 5.5 we explore the workings of the model and the monetary transmission mechanism in particular; we examine, under optimal policy, the volatility of key economic variables in the domestic economy and impulse response functions to a technology shock and to the country's borrowing premium shock. In section 5.6 we derive and compare alternative monetary policy rules that encompass various degrees of exchange rate flexibility, with, at one extreme, inflation targeting under a pure float, and at the other extreme, fixed exchange rates. Both domestic and consumer price inflation targets are examined. Section 5.7 addresses the requirement that monetary rules should be operational in the sense that, in the face of shocks, the zero lower bound constraint on the nominal interest rate is very rarely hit. Section 5.8 provides concluding remarks.

5.2 The Model

We start from a standard two-bloc microfounded model along the lines of Obstfeld and Rogoff (1995) to then incorporate many of the nominal and real frictions that have been shown to be empirically important in the study of closed economies (e.g., Smets and Wouters 2003). The blocs are asymmetric and unequally sized, each one with different household preferences and technologies. The single small open economy then emerges as the limit when the relative size of the larger bloc tends to infinity. Households work, save, and consume tradable goods produced both at home and abroad. At home there are three types of firms: wholesale, retail, and capital producers. As in Gertler et al. (2003), wholesale firms borrow from households to buy capital used in production and capital producers build new capital in response to the demand of wholesalers. Wholesalers' demand for capital in turn depends on their financial position which varies inversely with wholesalers' net worth.

There are four departures from the standard open economy model that lead to interesting results. First, money enters utility in a nonseparable way and results in a direct impact of the interest rate on the supply side.[1] Second, in the emerging market bloc, households derive utility from holding both domestic and foreign money (dollars) balances as in Felices and Tuesta

1. See Woodford (2003, chapter 4). A "cost channel," as in Ravenna and Walsh (2006), has a similar supply-side effect on the Phillips curve.

(2006). Third, along the lines of Gilchrist (2003) (see also Cespedes, Chang, and Velasco [2004]), firms face an external finance premium that increases with leverage and part of the debt of wholesale firms is financed in foreign currency (dollars), because it is impossible for firms to borrow 100 percent in domestic currency owing to "original sin"-type constraints. Finally, there are frictions in the world financial markets facing households as in Benigno (2001). Departures two and three add an additional dimension to openness itself, namely one whereby domestic agents not only hold foreign bonds and derive utility from consuming foreign produced goods, as in standard open economy models, but also borrow in foreign currency from domestic agents and derive utility from holding foreign money balances. Details of the model are as follows.

5.2.1 Households

Normalizing the total population to be unity, there are ν households in the "home," emerging economy bloc and $(1-\nu)$ households in the "foreign" bloc. A representative household h in the home bloc maximizes

$$(1) \quad E_t \sum_{t=0}^{\infty} \beta^t U\left(C_t(h), \frac{M_{H,t}(h)}{P_t}, \frac{M_{F,t}(h)S_t}{P_t}, L_t(h), \varepsilon_{C,t}, \varepsilon_{M_{\mathrm{H}},t}, \varepsilon_{M_{\mathrm{F}},t}, \varepsilon_{L,t}\right),$$

where E_t is the expectations operator indicating expectations formed at time t, β is the household's discount factor, $C_t(h)$ is a Dixit-Stiglitz index of consumption defined following in equation (5), $M_{H,t}(h)$ and $M_{F,t}(h)$ are end-of-period nominal domestic and foreign currency balances, respectively, P_t is a Dixit-Stiglitz price index defined in equation (11), S_t is the nominal exchange rate, and $L_t(h)$ are hours worked. A preference shock to the marginal utility of consumption is $\varepsilon_{C,t}$, and $\varepsilon_{M_{\mathrm{H}},t}$, $\varepsilon_{M_{\mathrm{F}},t}$, and $\varepsilon_{L,t}$ are shocks to demand for domestic currency, demand for foreign currency, and labor supply, respectively. An analogous symmetric intertemporal utility is defined for the foreign representative household and the corresponding variables (such as consumption) are denoted by $C_t^*(h)$, and so forth.

We incorporate financial frictions facing households as in Benigno (2001). There are two risk free one-period bonds denominated in the currencies of each bloc with payments in period t, $B_{H,t}$, and $B_{F,t}$, respectively, in (per capita) aggregate. The prices of these bonds are given by

$$P_{B,t} = \frac{1}{1+R_{n,t}}; \; P_{B,t}^* = \frac{1}{(1+R_{n,t}^*)\phi(S_tB_{F,t}/P_t)},$$

where $\phi(\cdot)$ captures the cost in the form of a risk premium for home households to hold foreign bonds. We assume $\phi(0) = 0$ and $\phi' < 0$. The nominal interest rate over the interval $[t, t+1]$ are denoted by $R_{n,t}$ and $R_{n,t}^*$. For analytical convenience, the home households can hold foreign bonds, but foreign households cannot hold home bonds. Then the net and gross foreign assets in the home bloc are equal. The representative household h must obey a budget constraint:

$$(2)\quad P_tC_t(h) + P_{B,t}B_{H,t}(h) + P^*_{B,t}S_tB_{F,t}(h) + M_{H,t}(h) + S_tM_{F,t}(h)TF_t = W_t(h)L_t(h) + B_{H,t-1}(h) + S_tB_{F,t-1}(h) + M_{H,t-1}(h) + S_tM_{F,t-1}(h) + \Gamma_t(h),$$

where $W_t(h)$ is the wage rate and $\Gamma_t(h)$ are dividends from ownership of firms. In addition, if we assume that households' labor supply is differentiated with elasticity of supply η, then (as we shall see following) the demand for each consumer's labor supplied by ν identical households is given by

$$(3)\qquad L_t(h) = \left(\frac{W_t(h)}{W_t}\right)^{-\eta} L_t,$$

where $W_t = [1/\nu \sum_{r=1}^{\nu} W_t(h)^{1-\eta}]^{1/(1-\eta)}$ and $L_t = [(1/\nu)\sum_{r=1}^{\nu} L_t(h)^{(\eta-1)/\eta}]^{\eta/(\eta-1)}$ are the average wage index and average employment, respectively.

Let the number of differentiated goods produced in the home and foreign blocs be n and $(1 - n)$, respectively, again normalizing the total number of goods in the world at unity. We also assume that the ratio of households to firms are the same in each bloc. It follows that n and $(1 - n)$ (or ν and $[1 - \nu]$) are measures of size. The per capita consumption index in the home bloc is given by

$$(4)\qquad C_t(h) = [\mathrm{w}^{1/\mu}C_{H,t}(h)^{(\mu-1)/\mu} + (1 - \mathrm{w})^{1/\mu}C_{F,t}(h)^{(\mu-1)/\mu}]^{\mu/(\mu-1)}$$

where μ is the elasticity of substitution between home and foreign goods,

$$C_{H,t}(h) = \left[\left(\frac{1}{n}\right)^{1/\zeta} \sum_{f=1}^{n} C_{H,t}(f, h)^{(\zeta-1)/\zeta}\right]^{\zeta/(\zeta-1)}$$

$$C_{F,t}(h) = \left[\left(\frac{1}{1-n}\right)^{1/\zeta} \left(\sum_{f=1}^{1-n} C_{F,t}(f, h)^{(\zeta-1)/\zeta}\right)\right]^{\zeta/(\zeta-1)},$$

where $C_{H,t}(f, h)$ and $C_{F,t}(f, h)$ denote the home consumption of household h of variety f produced in blocs H and F, respectively, and $\zeta > 1$ is the elasticity of substitution between varieties in each bloc. Analogous expressions hold for the foreign bloc, which are indicated with a superscript "*," and we impose $\zeta = \zeta^*$ for reasons that become apparent in the section on retail firms.[2] Weights in the consumption baskets in the two blocs are defined by

$$\mathrm{w} = 1 - (1 - n)(1 - \omega);\ \mathrm{w}^* = 1 - n(1 - \omega^*).$$

2. Consistently we adopt a notation where subscript H or F refers to goods H or F produced in the home and foreign bloc, respectively. The presence (for the foreign bloc) or the absence (for the home bloc) of a superscript "*" indicates where the good is consumed or used as an input. Thus, $C^*_{H,t}$ refers to the consumption of the home good by households in the foreign bloc. Parameter ω and ω^* refer to the home and foreign bloc, respectively, and so forth.

In equation (6), $\omega, \omega^* \in [0, 1]$ are parameters that capture the degree of bias in the two blocs. If $\omega = \omega^* = 1$, we have autarky, while $\omega = \omega^* = 0$ gives us the case of perfect integration. In the limit, as the home country becomes small, $n \to 0$ and $\nu \to 0$. Hence, $\mathrm{w} \to \omega$ and $\mathrm{w}^* \to 1$. Thus the foreign bloc becomes closed, but as long as there is a degree of home bias and $\omega > 0$, the home bloc continues to consume foreign produced consumption goods.

Denote by $P_{H,t}(f)$, $P_{F,t}(f)$ the prices in domestic currency of the good produced by firm f in the relevant bloc. Then the optimal intratemporal decisions are given by standard results:

$$(5)\quad C_{H,t}(r,f) = \left(\frac{P_{H,t}(f)}{P_{H,t}}\right)^{-\zeta} C_{H,t}(h);\quad C_{F,t}(r,f) = \left(\frac{P_{F,t}(f)}{P_{F,t}}\right)^{-\zeta} C_{F,t}(h)$$

$$(6)\quad C_{H,t}(h) = \mathrm{w}\left(\frac{P_{H,t}}{P_t}\right)^{-\mu} C_t(h);\quad C_{F,t}(h) = (1-\mathrm{w})\left(\frac{P_{F,t}}{P_t}\right)^{-\mu} C_t(h),$$

where aggregate price indexes for domestic and foreign consumption bundles are given by

$$(7)\quad P_{H,t} = \left[\frac{1}{n}\sum_{f=1}^{n} P_{H,t}(f)^{1-\zeta}\right]^{1/(1-\zeta)}$$

$$(8)\quad P_{F,t} = \left[\frac{1}{1-n}\sum_{f=1}^{1-n} P_{F,t}(f)^{1-\zeta}\right]^{1/(1-\zeta)},$$

and the domestic consumer price index P_t given by

$$(9)\quad P_t = [\mathrm{w}(P_{H,t})^{1-\mu} + (1-\mathrm{w})(P_{F,t})^{1-\mu}]^{1/(1-\mu)},$$

with a similar definition for the foreign bloc.

Let S_t be the nominal exchange rate. The law of one price applies to differentiated goods so that $S_t P^*_{F,t}/P_{F,t} = S_t P^*_{H,t}/P_{H,t} = 1$. Then it follows that the real exchange rate $RER_t = S_t P^*_t/P_t$ and the terms of trade, defined as the domestic currency relative price of imports to exports $\mathcal{T}_t = P_{F,t}/P_{H,t}$, are related by the relationship

$$(10)\quad RER_t \equiv \frac{S_t P^*_t}{P_t} = \frac{[\mathrm{w}^* + (1-\mathrm{w}^*)\mathcal{T}_t^{\mu^*-1}]^{1/(1-\mu^*)}}{[1-\mathrm{w}+\mathrm{w}\mathcal{T}_t^{\mu-1}]^{1/(1-\mu)}}.$$

Thus if $\mu = \mu^*$, then $RER_t = 1$ and the law of one price applies to the aggregate price indexes if $\mathrm{w}^* = 1 - \mathrm{w}$. The latter condition holds if there is no home bias. If there is home bias, the real exchange rate appreciates (RER_t falls) as the terms of trade deteriorates.

We assume flexible wages. Then maximizing equation (1) subject to equations (3) and (4), treating habit as exogenous, and imposing symmetry on households (so that $C_t(h) = C_t$, etc.) yields standard results:

(11) $$P_{B,t} = \beta E_t\left[\frac{U_{C,t+1}}{U_{C,t}}\frac{P_t}{P_{t+1}}\right]$$

(12) $$U_{M_H,t} = U_{C,t}\left[\frac{R_{n,t}}{1 + R_{n,t}}\right]$$

(13) $$U_{M_F,t} = U_{C,t}\left[\frac{R^*_{n,t}}{1 + R^*_{n,t}}\right]$$

(14) $$\frac{W_t}{P_t} = -\frac{\eta}{(\eta - 1)}\frac{U_{L,t}}{U_{C,t}},$$

where $U_{C,t}$, $U_{M_H,t}$, $U_{M_F,t}$, and $-U_{L,t}$ are the marginal utility of consumption, money holdings in the two currencies, and the marginal disutility of work, respectively. Taking expectations of (13), the familiar Keynes-Ramsey rule, and its foreign counterpart, we arrive at the *modified UIP condition*

(15) $$\frac{P_{B,t}}{P^*_{B,t}} = \frac{E_t[U_{C,t+1}(P_t/P_{t+1})]}{E_t[U_{C,t+1}(S_{t+1}P_t/S_tP_{t+1})]}.$$

In (14), the demand for money balances depends positively on the marginal utility of consumption and negatively on the nominal interest rate. If, as is common in the literature, one adopts a utility function that is separable in money holdings, then given the central bank's setting of the latter and ignoring seignorage in the government budget constraint money demand is completely recursive to the rest of the system describing our macromodel. However, separable utility functions are implausible (see Woodford [2003], chapter 3, section 3.4) and following Felices and Tuesta (2006) we will not go down this route. Finally, in (16) the real disposable wage is proportional to the marginal rate of substitution between consumption and leisure, $-U_{L,t}/U_{C,t}$, and the constant of proportionality reflects the market power of households that arises from their monopolistic supply of a differentiated factor input with elasticity η.

5.2.2 Firms

There are three types of firms: wholesale, retail, and capital producers. Wholesale firms are run by risk-neutral entrepreneurs who purchase capital and employ household labor to produce a wholesale good that is sold to the retail sector. The wholesale sector is competitive, but the retail sector is monopolistically competitive. Retail firms differentiate the wholesale goods at no resource cost and sell the differentiated (repackaged) goods to households. The capital goods sector is competitive and converts the final goods into capital. The details are as follows.

Wholesale Firms

Wholesale goods are homogeneous and produced by entrepreneurs who combine differentiated labor and capital with a technology

$$Y_t^W = A_t K_t^{\alpha} L_t^{1-\alpha}, \tag{16}$$

where K_t is beginning-of-period t capital stock,

$$L_t = \left[\left(\frac{1}{\nu}\right)^{1/\eta} \sum_{r=1}^{\nu} L_t(h)^{(\eta-1)/\eta}\right]^{\eta/(\eta-1)}, \tag{17}$$

where we recall that $L_t(h)$ is the labor input of type h, and A_t is an exogenous shock capturing shifts to trend total factor productivity in this sector.[3] Minimizing wage costs $\Sigma_{h=1}^{\nu} W_t(h)L_t(h)$ gives the demand for each household's labor as

$$L_t(h) = \left(\frac{W_t(h)}{W_t}\right)^{-\eta} L_t. \tag{18}$$

Wholesale goods sell at a price $P_{H,t}^W$ in the home bloc. Equating the marginal product and cost of aggregate labor gives

$$W_t = P_{H,t}^W (1 - \alpha)\frac{Y_t}{L_t}. \tag{19}$$

Let Q_t be the real market price of capital in units of total household consumption. Then noting that profits per period are $P_{H,t}^W Y_t - W_t L_t = \alpha P_{H,t}^W Y_t$, using equation (21), the expected return on capital, acquired at the beginning of period t over the period is given by

$$E_t(1 + R_t^k) = \frac{(P_{H,t}^W/P_t)\alpha(Y_t/K_t) + (1 - \delta)E_t[Q_{t+1}]}{Q_t}, \tag{20}$$

where δ is the depreciation rate of capital. This expected return must be equated with the expected cost of funds over $[t, t + 1]$, taking into account credit market frictions. Wholesale firms borrow in both home and foreign currency, with proportion of the former given by $\varphi \in [0, 1]$, so that this expected cost is

$$(1 + \Theta_t)\varphi E_t\left[(1 + R_{n,t})\frac{P_t}{P_{t+1}}\right] + (1 + \Theta_t)(1 - \varphi)E_t\left[(1 + R_{n,t}^*)\frac{P_t^*}{P_{t+1}^*}\frac{RER_{t+1}}{RER_t}\right] \tag{21}$$

$$= (1 + \Theta_t)\left\{\varphi E_t[(1 + R_t)] + (1 - \varphi)E_t\left[(1 + R_t^*)\frac{RER_{t+1}}{RER_t}\right]\right\}.$$

3. Following Gilchrist, Hairault, and Kempf (2002) and Gilchrist (2003), we ignore the managerial input into the production process and later, consistent with this, we ignore the contribution of the managerial wage in her net worth.

If $\varphi = 1$ or if UIP holds, this becomes $(1 + \Theta_t)E_t[1 + R_t]$. In (23), $RER_t \equiv P_t^* S_t / P_t$ is the real exchange rate, $R_{t-1} \equiv [(1 + R_{n,t-1})(P_{t-1}/P_t)] - 1$ is the ex post real interest rate over $[t - 1, t]$ and $\Theta_t \geq 0$ is the external finance premium given by

$$\Theta_t = \Theta\left(\frac{B_t}{N_t}\right);\ \Theta'(\cdot) > 0,\ \Theta(0) = 0,\ \Theta(\infty) = \infty, \tag{22}$$

where $B_t = Q_t K_t - N_t$ is bond-financed acquisition of capital in period t and N_t is the beginning-of-period t entrepreneurial net worth, the equity of the firm. Note that the ex post return at the beginning of period t, R_{t-1}^k, is given by

$$1 + R_{t-1}^k = \frac{(P_{H,t-1}^W / P_{t-1})\alpha(Y_{t-1}/K_{t-1}) + (1 - \delta)Q_t}{Q_{t-1}}, \tag{23}$$

and this can deviate from the ex-ante return on capital.

Assuming that entrepreneurs exit with a given probability $1 - \xi_e$, net worth accumulates according to

$$N_t = \xi_e V_t, \tag{24}$$

where V_t the net value carried over from the previous period is given by

$$V_t = \Bigg[(1 + R_{t-1}^k)Q_{t-1}K_{t-1} - (1 + \Theta_{t-1}) \cdot \left(\varphi(1 + R_{t-1}) + (1 - \varphi)(1 + R_{t-1}^*)\frac{RER_t}{RER_{t-1}}\right)(Q_{t-1}K_{t-1} - N_{t-1})\Bigg]. \tag{25}$$

Note that in (27), $(1 + R_{t-1}^k)$ is the ex post return on capital acquired at the beginning of period $t - 1$, $(1 + R_{t-1})$ is the ex post real cost of borrowing in home currency, and $(1 + R_{t-1}^*)RER_t/RER_{t-1}$ is the ex post real cost of borrowing in foreign currency. Also note that net worth N_t at the beginning of period t is a nonpredetermined variable since the ex post return depends on the current market value Q_t, itself a nonpredetermined variable.

Exiting entrepreneurs consume C_t^e, the remaining resources, given by

$$C_t^e = (1 - \xi_e)V_t, \tag{26}$$

of which consumption of the domestic good, as in equation (8), is given by

$$C_{H,t}^e = \mathrm{w}\left(\frac{P_{H,t}}{P_t}\right)^{-\mu} C_t^e. \tag{27}$$

Retail Firms

Retail firms are monopolistically competitive, buying wholesale goods and differentiating the product at a fixed resource cost F. In a free-entry equilibrium profits are driven to zero. Retail output for firm f is then $Y_t(f) = Y_t^W(f) - F$ where Y_t^W is produced according to production technology (18).

Retail firms set prices of differentiated goods according to the following. Assume that there is a probability of $1 - \xi_H$ at each period that the price of each good f is set optimally to $\hat{P}_{H,t}(f)$. If the price is not reoptimized, then it is held constant.[4] For each producer f the objective at time t is to choose $\hat{P}_{H,t}(f)$ to maximize discounted profits

$$E_t \sum_{k=0}^{\infty} \xi_H^k D_{t,t+k} Y_{t+k}(f)[\hat{P}_{H,t}(f) - P_{H,t+k} MC_{t+k}],$$

where $D_{t,t+k}$ is the discount factor over the interval $[t, t + k]$, subject to a common[5] downward sloping demand from domestic consumers and foreign importers of elasticity ζ as in (7), and $MC_t = P^W_{H,t}/P_{H,t}$ are marginal costs. The solution to this is

$$(28) \qquad E_t \sum_{k=0}^{\infty} \xi_H^k D_{t,t+k} Y_{t+k}(f)[\hat{P}_{Ht}(f) - \frac{\zeta}{(\zeta - 1)} P_{H,t+k} MC_{t+k}] = 0,$$

and by the law of large numbers the evolution of the price index is given by

$$(29) \qquad P^{1-\zeta}_{H,t+1} = \xi_H (P_{H,t})^{1-\zeta} + (1 - \xi_H)(\hat{P}_{H,t+1}(f))^{1-\zeta}.$$

Capital Producers

As in Smets and Wouters (2003), we introduce the delayed response of investment observed in the data. Capital producers combine existing capital, K_t, leased from the entrepreneurs to transform an input I_t, gross investment, into new capital according to

$$(30) \quad K_{t+1} = (1 - \delta)K_t + (1 - S(X_t))I_t;\ S', S'' \geq 0;\ S(1) = S'(1) = 0,$$

where $X_t \equiv I_t/(I_{t-1})$. This captures the ideas that adjustment costs are associated with *changes* rather than *levels* of investment.[6] Gross investment consists of domestic and foreign final goods

$$(31) \qquad I_t = [\mathrm{w}_I^{1/\rho_I} I_{H,t}^{(\rho_I - 1)/\rho_I} + (1 - \mathrm{w}_I)^{1/\rho_I} I_{F,t}^{(\rho_I - 1)/\rho_I}]^{\rho_I/(1-\rho_I)},$$

where weights in investment are defined as in the consumption baskets; namely

$$\mathrm{w}_I = 1 - (1 - n)(1 - \omega_I); \quad \mathrm{w}_I^* = 1 - n(1 - \omega_I^*),$$

with investment price given by

$$(32) \qquad P_{I,t} = [\mathrm{w}_I (P_{H,t})^{1-\rho_I} + (1 - \mathrm{w}_I)(P_{F,t})^{1-\rho_I}]^{1/(1-\rho_I)}.$$

4. Thus, we can interpret $1/(1 - \xi_H)$ as the average duration for which prices are left unchanged.

5. Recall that we have imposed a symmetry condition $\zeta = \zeta^*$ at this point; that is, the elasticity of substitution between differentiated goods produced in any one bloc is the same for consumers in both blocs.

6. In a balanced growth steady-state adjustment, costs are associated with change relative to trend so that the conditions on $S(\cdot)$ along the balanced growth path become $S(1 + g) = S'(1 + g) = 0$.

Capital producers choose the optimal combination of domestic and foreign inputs according to the same form of intratemporal first-order conditions as for consumption:

$$(33)\qquad I_{H,t} = \mathrm{w}_I\left(\frac{P_{H,t}}{P_{I,t}}\right)^{-\rho_I} I_t;\quad I_{F,t} = (1-\mathrm{w}_I)\left(\frac{P_{F,t}}{P_{I,t}}\right)^{-\rho_I} I_t.$$

The capital producing firm at time 0 then maximizes expected discounted profits[7]

$$E_t \sum_{t=0}^{\infty} D_{0,t}\left[Q_t(1 - S(X_t))I_t - \frac{P_{I,t}I_t}{P_t}\right],$$

which, with $X_t \equiv I_t/(I_{t-1})$, results in the first-order condition

$$(34)\quad Q_t(1 - S(X_t) - X_t S'(X_t)) + E_t\left[\frac{1}{(1+R_{t+1})} Q_{t+1} S'(X_t)\frac{I_{t+1}^2}{I_t^2}\right] = \frac{P_{I,t}}{P_t}.$$

5.2.3 The Equilibrium, Fiscal Policy, and Foreign Asset Accumulation

In equilibrium, goods markets, money markets, and the bond market are all clear. Equating the supply and demand of the home consumer good and assuming that government expenditure, taken as exogenous, goes exclusively on home goods, we obtain[8]

$$Y_t = C_{H,t} + C_{H,t}^e + I_{H,t} + \frac{1-\nu}{\nu}[C_{H,t}^* + C_{H,t}^{e*} + I_{H,t}^*] + G_t.$$

Fiscal policy is rudimentary: a balanced government budget constraint is given by

$$(35)\qquad P_{H,t}G_t = T_t + M_{H,t} - M_{H,t-1}.$$

Adjustments to the taxes, T_t, in response to shocks to government spending away from the steady state are assumed to be nondistortionary.

Let $\Sigma_{h=1}^{\nu} B_{F,t}(h) = \nu B_{F,t}$ be the net holdings by the household sector of foreign bonds. Summing over the household budget constraints (including entrepreneurs and capital producers), noting that net holdings of domestic bonds are zero (since home bonds are not held by foreign households), and subtracting (39), we arrive at the accumulation of net foreign assets:

$$\begin{aligned}(36)\quad P_{B,t}^* S_t B_{F,t} + S_t M_{F,t} &= S_t B_{F,t-1} + S_t M_{F,t-1} + W_t L_t + \Gamma_t + (1-\xi_e)P_t V_t \\ &\quad + P_t Q_t(1 - S(X_t))I_t - P_t C_t - P_t C_t^e - P_{I,t}I_t - P_{H,t}G_t \\ &\equiv S_t B_{F,t-1} + S_t M_{F,t-1} + TB_t,\end{aligned}$$

where the trade balance, TB_t, is given by the national accounting identity

7. This ignores leasing costs, which Gertler, Gilchrist, and Natalucci (2003) show to be of second-order importance.

8. Note that all aggregates, Y_t, $C_{H,t}$, and so forth are expressed in per capita (household) terms.

$$P_{H,t}Y_t = P_tC_t + P_tC_t^e + P_{I,t}I_t + P_{H,t}G_t + TB_t. \tag{37}$$

This completes the model. Given nominal interest rates $R_{n,t}$, $R^*_{n,t}$, the money supply is fixed by the central banks to accommodate money demand. By Walras' Law we can dispense with the bond market equilibrium condition. Then the equilibrium is defined at $t = 0$ as stochastic sequences C_t, C_t^e, $C_{H,t}$, $C_{F,t}$, $P_{H,t}$, $P_{F,t}$, P_t, $M_{H,t}$, $M_{F,t}$, $B_{H,t}$, $B_{F,t}$, W_t, Y_t, L_t, $P^0_{H,t}$, P^I_t, K_t, I_t, Q_t, V_t; foreign counterparts C^*_t, and so forth, RER_t, and S_t, given the monetary instruments $R_{n,t}$, $R^*_{n,t}$, and exogenous processes.

5.2.4 Specialization of the Household's Utility Function

The choice of utility function must achieve two objectives. The first, as in Felices and Tuesta (2006), is to provide a channel by which dollarization affects the marginal utility of consumption. This is achieved by a utility function that is nonseparable in consumption and money balances. The second objective is to have a model consistent with the balanced growth path (BGP) set out in previous sections. As pointed out in Barro and Sala-i-Martin (2004, chapter 9), this requires a careful choice of the form of the utility as a function of consumption and labor effort. Again, as in Gertler, Gilchrist, and Natalucci (2003), it is achieved by a utility function that is nonseparable, this time in the latter two arguments.

A utility function of the form

$$U \equiv \frac{(\varepsilon_t + 1)[\Phi(h)^{1-\varrho}(1 - L_t(h)(1 - \varepsilon_{L,t}))^{\varrho}]^{1-\sigma}}{1-\sigma} \tag{38}$$

where

$$\Phi_t(h) \equiv [b(C_t(h) - h_C C_{t-1})^{(\theta-1)/\theta} + (1 - b)Z_t(h)^{(\theta-1)/\theta}]^{\theta/(\theta-1)} \tag{39}$$

$$Z_t(h) \equiv \left[a\left(\frac{(\varepsilon_{M_H,t} + 1)M_{H,t}(h)}{P_t}\right)^{(\chi_M-1)/\chi_M} + (1-a)\left(\frac{(\varepsilon_{M_F,t} + 1)S_tM_{F,t}(h)}{P_t}\right)^{(\chi_M-1)/\chi_M}\right]^{\chi_M/(\chi_M-1)}, \tag{40}$$

and where labor supply, $L_t(h)$, measured as a proportion of a day, normalized at unity, satisfies these two requirements.[9] For this function, $U_{\Phi L} > 0$, so that consumption and money holdings together, and leisure (equal to $1 - L_t[h]$) are substitutes.

5.2.5 State Space Representation

We linearize around a deterministic zero inflation, balanced growth steady state. We can write the two-bloc model in state space form as

9. A balanced growth path (BGP) requires that the real wage, real money balances, and consumption grow at the same rate at the steady state with labor supply steady. It is straightforward to show that (42) has these properties.

$$(41)\qquad \begin{bmatrix} \mathbf{z}_{t+1} \\ E_t\mathbf{x}_{t+1} \end{bmatrix} = A\begin{bmatrix} \mathbf{z}_t \\ \mathbf{x}_t \end{bmatrix} + B\mathbf{o}_t + C\begin{bmatrix} r_{n,t} \\ r^*_{n,t} \end{bmatrix} + D\mathbf{v}_{t+1}$$

$$\mathbf{o}_t = H\begin{bmatrix} \mathbf{z}_t \\ \mathbf{x}_t \end{bmatrix} + J\begin{bmatrix} r_{n,t} \\ r^*_{n,t} \end{bmatrix},$$

where $\mathbf{z}_t$ is a vector of predetermined exogenous variables, $\mathbf{x}_t$ are nonpredetermined variables, and $\mathbf{o}_t$ is a vector of outputs.[10] Matrices A, B, and so forth are functions of model parameters. Rational expectations are formed assuming an information set $\{z_{1,s}, z_{2,s}, x_s\}, s \leq t$, the model and the monetary rule. Details of the linearization are provided in appendix B.

5.2.6 The Small Open Economy

Following Felices and Tuesta (2006), we can now model a small open economy by letting its relative size in the world economy $n \to 0$ while retaining its linkages with the rest of the world (ROW). In particular, the demand for exports is modeled in a consistent way that retains its dependence on shocks to the home and ROW economies. We now need a fully articulated model of the ROW. From (6) we have that $\mathrm{w} \to \omega$ and $\mathrm{w}^* \to 1$ as $n \to 0$. Similarly, for investment we have $\mathrm{w}_I \to \omega_I$ and $\mathrm{w}_I^* \to 1$ as $n \to 0$. It seems at first glance then that the ROW becomes closed and therefore exports from our small open economy must be zero. However, this is not the case. Consider the linearized form of the output demand equations in the two blocs:

$$(42)\quad y_t = \alpha_{C,H}c_t + \alpha^e_{C,H}c^e_t + \alpha^*_{C,H}c^*_t + \alpha_{I,H}i_t + \alpha^*_{I,H}i^*_t + \alpha_G g_t + [\mu(\alpha_{C,H} + \alpha^e_{C,H})(1 - \mathrm{w}) + \mu^*\alpha^*_{C,H}\mathrm{w}^* + \rho_I\alpha_{I,H}(1 - \mathrm{w}_I) + \rho^*_I\alpha^*_{I,H}\mathrm{w}^*_I]\tau_t$$

$$(43)\quad y^*_t = \alpha^*_{C,F}c^*_t + \alpha_{C,F}c_t + \alpha^e_{C,F}c^e_t + \alpha^*_{I,F}i^*_t + \alpha_{I,F}i_t + \alpha^*_G g^*_t - [\mu^*(\alpha^*_{C,F}(1 - \mathrm{w}^*) + \mu\alpha_{C,F}\mathrm{w} + \rho^*_I\alpha^*_{I,F}(1 - \mathrm{w}^*_I) + \rho_I\alpha_{I,F}\mathrm{w}_I]\tau_t,$$

where the elasticities and their limits as $n \to 0$ are given by

$$\alpha_{C,H} = \frac{\mathrm{w}(1 - s_e)C}{Y} \to \frac{\omega(1 - s_e)C}{Y}$$

$$\alpha^e_{C,H} = \frac{\mathrm{w}s_eC}{Y} \to \frac{\omega s_eC}{Y}$$

$$\alpha^*_{C,H} = \frac{(1 - \mathrm{w}^*)C^*}{Y^*}\,\frac{(1 - n)Y^*}{nY} \to \frac{(1 - \omega^*)C^*}{Y^*}\,\frac{Y^*}{Y}$$

$$\alpha_G = \frac{G}{Y}$$

10. We define all lowercase variables as proportional deviations from this baseline steady state except for rates of change, which are absolute deviations. That is, for a typical variable X_t, $x_t = X_t - X/X \simeq \log(X_t/X)$, where X is the baseline steady state. For variables expressing a rate of change over time such as the nominal interest rate $r_{n,t}$ and inflation rates, $x_t = X_t - X$.

$$\alpha_{I,H} = \frac{w_I I}{Y} \to \frac{\omega_I I}{Y}$$

$$\alpha^*_{I,H} = \frac{(1 - w^*_I)I^*}{Y^*}\frac{(1 - n)Y^*}{nY} \to \frac{(1 - \omega^*_I)I^*}{Y^*}\frac{Y^*}{Y}$$

$$\alpha^*_{C,F} = \frac{w^* C^*}{Y^*} \to \frac{C^*}{Y^*}$$

$$\alpha^{e*}_{C,F} = 0$$

$$\alpha_{C,F} = \frac{(1 - w)C}{Y}\frac{nY}{(1 - n)Y^*} \to 0$$

$$\alpha^e_{C,F} = \frac{(1 - w)(1 - \xi^e)n_k k_y}{\xi_e}\frac{nY}{(1 - n)Y^*} \to 0$$

$$\alpha^*_G = \frac{G^*}{Y^*}$$

$$\alpha^*_{I,F} = \frac{w^*_I I^*}{Y^*} \to \frac{I^*}{Y^*}$$

$$\alpha_{I,F} = \frac{(1 - w_I)I}{Y^*}\frac{nY}{(1 - n)Y^*} \to 0.$$

Thus, we see that from the viewpoint of the ROW our small open economy becomes invisible, but not vice versa. Exports to and imports from the ROW are now modeled explicitly in a way that captures all the interactions between shocks in the ROW and the transmission to the small open economy.

5.2.7 Calibration

Home Bias Parameters

The bias parameters we need to calibrate are: ω, ω^*, ω_I, and ω^*_I. Let in the steady state $C^e = s_e C$ be consumption by entrepreneurs, and $c_y = C/Y$. Let $cs_{imports}$ be the GDP share of imported consumption of the foreign (F) consumption good. Let $cs_{exports}$ be the GDP share of exports of the home (H) consumption good. Then we have that

$$\alpha_{C,H} = \frac{C_H}{Y} = \frac{\omega C}{Y} = (c_y - cs_{imports})(1 - s_e)$$

$$\alpha^e_{C,H} = \frac{C^e_H}{Y} = \frac{\omega C^e}{Y} = (c_y - cs_{imports})s_e$$

$$\alpha^*_{C,H} = \frac{C^*_H}{Y} = \frac{(1 - \omega^*)C^*}{Y^*}\frac{Y^*}{Y} = cs_{exports}.$$

Similarly, for investment define $is_{imports}$ to be the GDP share of imported investment of the F investment and $is_{exports}$ be the GDP share of exports of H investment good. Then with $i_y = I/Y$, we have

$$\alpha_{I,H} = \frac{I_H}{Y} = \frac{\omega_I I}{Y} = i_y - is_{imports}$$

$$\alpha^*_{I,H} = \frac{I^*_H}{Y} = \frac{(1-\omega^*_I)I^*}{Y^*}\frac{Y^*}{Y} = is_{exports}$$

in the steady state. We linearize around a zero trade balance $TB = 0$, so we require

$$cs_{imports} + is_{imports} = cs_{exports} + is_{exports} \tag{44}$$

in which case $\alpha_{C,H} + \alpha^e_{C,H} + \alpha^*_{C,H} + \alpha_{I,H} + \alpha^*_{I,H} = c_y + i_y$, as required. Thus, we can use trade data for consumption and investment goods, consumption shares, and relative per capita GDP to calibrate the bias parameters ω, ω^*, ω_I, and ω^*_I. We need the home country biases elsewhere in the model, but for the ROW we simply put $\omega^* = \omega^*_I = 1$ everywhere else, so these biases are not required as such.

Calibration of Household Preference Parameters

We now show how observed data on the household wage bill as a proportion of total consumption, real money balances as a proportion of consumption, and estimates of the elasticity of the marginal utility of consumption with respect to total money balances can be used to calibrate the preference parameters ϱ, b, and θ in (42).

Calibrating parameters to the BG steady state, we first note that from (16) we have

$$\frac{(\eta-1)}{\eta}\frac{W(1-L)}{PC} = \frac{\varrho\Phi}{C(1-h_C)\Phi_C(1-\varrho)}. \tag{45}$$

In (49), $W(1-L)/PC$ is the household wage bill as a proportion of total consumption, which is observable. From the definition of Φ in (43), we have that

$$\frac{\Phi}{C\Phi_C} = \frac{(1-b)cz^{(1-\theta)/\theta} + b}{b}, \tag{46}$$

where $cz \equiv (C(1-h_C))/Z$ is the effective-consumption–real money balance ratio (allowing for external habit). From (42), the elasticity the marginal utility of consumption with respect to total money balances, Ψ, say, is given by

$$\frac{ZU_{CZ}}{U_C} \equiv \Psi = \frac{(1-b)[(1-\varrho)(1-\sigma) - 1 + (1/\theta)]}{bcz(\theta-1)/\theta + 1 - b}. \tag{47}$$

From the first-order conditions in the steady state (A.26) and (A.27) with $R_n = R^*_n = R$ we have

$$\frac{b(1-h_C)}{1-b}cz^{-1/\theta} = \frac{1+R}{R}. \quad (48)$$

Thus, given σ, β, g, h_C, $(W(1-L))/PC$, cz, and Ψ, equations (49) through (52) can be solved for ϱ, b, and θ. Appendix C provides further details[11] of $\Psi \in [0, 0.01]$. Since $\Psi > 0$, we impose on our calibration the property that money and consumption are *complements*.

Remaining Parameters

As far as possible, parameters are chosen based on quarterly data for Peru. Elsewhere the parameters reflect broad characteristics of emerging economies. A variety of sources are used: for Peru we draw upon Castillo, Montoro, and Tuesta (2006) (henceforth, CMT). For emerging economies more generally and for parameters related to the financial accelerator we use Gertler, Gilchrist, and Natalucci (2003) (henceforth, GGN) and Bernanke, Gertler, and Gilchrist (1999) (henceforth, BGG). The rest of the world is represented by U.S. data. Here we draw upon Levin et al. (2006) (henceforth, LOWW). In places, we match Peru with European estimates using Smets and Wouters (2003) (henceforth, SW). Appendix C provides full details of the calibration.

5.3 Monetary Policy Interest Rate Rules

In line with the literature on open economy interest rate rules (see, for example, Benigno and Benigno [2004]), we assume that the central bank in the emerging market bloc has three options: (a) set the nominal interest to keep the exchange rate fixed (fixed exchange rates, "FIX"); (b) set the interest rate to minimize deviations of domestic or CPI inflation from a predetermined target (inflation targeting under fully flexible exchange rates, "FLEX(D)" or "FLEX(C)"); or finally, (c) follow a hybrid regime, in which the nominal interest rates respond to both inflation deviations from target and exchange rate deviations from a certain level (managed float, "HYB"). Many emerging market countries follow one or another of these options and most are likely to in the near future. Formally, the rules are as follows.

Fixed Exchange Rate Regime, "FIX" In a simplified model without an exchange rate premium as analyzed in section 5.4, we show this is implemented by

$$r_{n,t} = r^*_{n,t} + \theta_s s_t, \quad (49)$$

where any $\theta_s > 0$ is sufficient to the regime. In our full model with an exchange rate premium, we implement "FIX" as a "HYB" regime following, with feed-

11. See Woodford (2003, chapter 2) for a discussion of this parameter.

back coefficients chosen to minimize a loss function that includes a large penalty on exchange rate variability. (Note that values for the loss function reported shown in the following remove the latter contribution.)

Inflation Targets under a Fully Flexible Exchange Rate, "FLEX(D)" or "FLEX(C)" This takes the form of Taylor rule with domestic or CPI inflation and output growth targets:

$$r_{n,t} = \rho r_{n,t-1} + \theta_\pi E_t \pi_{H,t} + \theta_y \Delta y_t \tag{50}$$

$$r_{n,t} = \rho r_{n,t-1} + \theta_\pi E_t \pi_t + \theta_y \Delta y_t, \tag{51}$$

where $\rho \in [0, 1]$ is an interest rate smoothing parameter.

Managed Float, "HYB" In this rule the exchange rate response is direct rather than indirect as in the CPI inflation rule (55):[12]

$$r_{n,t} = \rho r_{n,t-1} + \theta_\pi E_t \pi_{H,t} + \theta_y \Delta y_t + \theta_s s_t. \tag{52}$$

In all cases we assume that the central bank in the emerging market bloc enjoys full credibility. Although this assumption may have been considered heroic a few years ago, today there are several emerging market countries that have succeeded in stabilizing inflation at low levels and have won the trust of economic agents at home and abroad including economies with a history of high or hyper-inflation (e.g., Brazil, Israel, Peru, and Mexico, among others. See Batini, Breuer, and Kochhar [2006]). Accounting for imperfect credibility of the central bank remains nonetheless important for many other emerging market countries, and can lead to higher stabilization costs than under full credibility (under inflation targeting and floating exchange rate, see Aoki and Kimura [2007]) or even sudden stops and financial crises (under fixed exchange rates, see IMF [2005]).

5.4 Transactions Dollarization in a Model without Capital

The stability and determinacy properties of various monetary rules provide a good indication of their stabilization performance. However, the full model with capital, the financial accelerator, and both transactions and liability dollarization has high-order dynamics and is not analytically tractable. In order to throw some light on the numerical results that follow, in

12. Rule (52) describes one of many possible specifications of a managed float, namely one where the central bank resists deviations of the exchange rate from a certain level—considered to be the equilibrium—as well as deviations of inflation from target and output from potential. An equally plausible specification involves a feedback on the rate of change of the exchange rate, in which case the central bank aim is to stabilize exchange rate volatility; that is, the pace at which the domestic currency appreciates or depreciates over time. For a discussion see Batini, Harrison, and Millard (2003). To limit the number of simulations and results to be compared, here we limit ourselves to one specification only.

this section we therefore study a special case of the model that suppresses capital, the associated financial accelerator, habit in consumption, and the exchange rate risk premium facing households (i.e., $h_C = \delta_r = 0$). The analysis provides results on the consequences of transactions dollarization for a simple current domestic inflation targeting rule in the form (54) with $\theta_y = 0$.

We are interested in establishing the conditions for this current domestic inflation rule to be saddle-path stable. Exogenous processes play no part in this property (so long as they themselves are stable or saddle-path stable, a property we assume). Ignoring these processes we can express the linearized system in terms of the marginal utilities of consumption, $u_{c,t}$ in deviation form,[13] and the marginal disutility of labor ($u_{l,t}$), which holds for any choice of utility function. After some effort this takes the form

$$E_t u_{c,t+1} = u_{c,t} - \omega(r_{n,t} - E_t \pi_{H,t+1}) \tag{53}$$

$$\beta E_t \pi_{H,t+1} = \pi_{H,t} - \lambda_H \left(u_{l,t} - \frac{1}{\omega} u_{c,t} \right) \tag{54}$$

$$y_t = l_t = \alpha_{C,H} c_t - \nu u_{c,t}, \tag{55}$$

where $\lambda_H = ((1 - \beta\xi_H)(1 - \xi_H))/\xi_H$ and $\nu = 1/\omega(\mu\alpha_{C,H}(1 - \omega) + \mu^*\alpha^*_{C,H})$. After further algebra, using the expressions for $u_{c,t}$, $u_{l,t}$, y_t, c_t in appendix B, we arrive at the following specification for $\pi_{H,t}$ expressed solely in terms of $u_{c,t}$ and $r_{n,t}$:

$$\beta E_t \pi_{H,t+1} = \pi_{H,t} + \gamma u_{c,t} - \kappa r_{n,t},$$

where

$$\gamma = \lambda_H \left(\frac{L}{1 - L} \frac{1 - \omega}{\omega} + \frac{L}{1 - L} \nu + \frac{(1 + (L/1 - L)\omega c_y)(1 + \nu)[\rho(\sigma - 1)L]/(1 - L)}{1 + (\sigma - 1)(1 - \rho) - \rho(\sigma - 1)\omega c_y (L/1 - L)} \right)$$

$$\kappa = \bar{a}\lambda_H \varpi_L + \frac{\bar{a}\lambda_H (1 + (L/1 - L)\omega c_y)\varpi}{1 + (\sigma - 1)(1 - \rho) - \rho(\sigma - 1)\omega c_y (L/1 - L)},$$

and ϖ, ϖ_L, b_1, $\bar{a}$ aand α are defined in appendix B.

We restrict ourselves to a range of parameter values for which $\sigma > 1$ and $(1 - \rho) - \rho\omega c_y L/(1 - L) > 0$. Because $\omega c_y\ L/(1 - L), \ll 1$ this is a very weak condition that our calibrated values easily satisfy. Then $\gamma > 0$. Furthermore, κ can be either positive or negative. By definition ϖ_L, the elasticity of the marginal utility of work effort with respect to the nominal interest rate is

13. Recall that all lower case variables are proportional deviations from the steady state, except for rates of change, which are absolute deviations. See note 12.

always positive. But the sign of ϖ, the corresponding elasticity of the marginal utility of consumption, depends on whether consumption and real balances are substitutes or complements. If they are substitutes then $\varpi > 0$ and then $\kappa > 0$. But here we assume that they are complements, in which case κ can take either sign. Our results following are sensitive to this.

In fact, for our chosen calibration, κ is comfortably positive. This means that the nominal interest rate impacts on the economy through two channels. First, given expectations of CPI inflation, an increase in the nominal interest rate reduces the expected real interest rate and reduces demand from consumption. This will cause the domestic inflation rate to fall in the usual way. But with a nonseparable utility function, there is a second channel of influence through the supply-side that sees marginal cost, and therefore the inflation rate, rise as the result of an increase in the interest rate. Thus, with $\kappa > 0$ *supply and demand effects work in opposite directions and the supply side effect will tend to undermine the stabilizing demand side effect.* However, κ depends on the degree of transactions dollarization, $\kappa = 0$, when there is complete dollarization ($a = \bar{a} = 0$) and therefore the supply effect closes down. This eliminates a destabilizing effect, so as we approach complete transactions dollarization we should witness a more effective form of monetary stabilization.

Equations (57) and (60) form the basis for the analysis of the next section. The important feature of the modified Phillips curve, (60), with a nonseparable utility function in money and consumption, is the manner in which the domestic interest rate impacts on domestic inflation.

5.4.1 Fixed Exchange Rate Regime (FIX)

For the model without capital and an exchange rate risk premium, the saddle-path stability of the FIX regime is unambiguous as the following proposition indicates:

PROPOSITION 1. *Under regime FIX:*
(a) The system is stable and determinate for all values of $\theta_s > 0$.
(b) The nominal exchange rate is fixed.

PROOF. See appendix D.

As Benigno and Benigno (2004) have stressed, the feedback from the exchange rate to the interest rate is not operative in the equilibrium because $s_t = 0$ at all times. Rather, it is the *belief* that the monetary authority responds in this way even for very small θ_s that maintains a fixed exchange rate. With such a regime, the domestic interest rate that enters the Phillips curve in (60) remains fixed too, so neither the nonseparable form of the utility function nor the existence of dollarization has an impact on the stability properties of the system.

5.4.2 Domestic Inflation Targeting Rule (FLEX (D))

Now consider the rule (54). In the rest of this section we focus on inflation-targeting interest rate rules that respond only to domestic inflation, but not to output growth. This makes the analysis tractable, but there are other reasons for examining such rules. First, pure inflation-targeting or inflation-targeting with a managed exchange rate corresponds to the objectives of many modern central banks. Second, it is of intrinsic interest to see to what extent an economy can be stabilized with the simplest possible form of rule that only tracks one nominal variable. With this form of rule we can then show the following.

PROPOSITION 2. *Under FLEX (D):*

(a) If $2\kappa > \omega\gamma > (1 - \rho)\kappa$, *then the system is stable and determinate for the range* $1 < \theta_\pi < ((1 + \rho)(2(1 + \beta) + \gamma\omega))/((1 - \rho)(2\kappa - \gamma\omega)) \triangleq \bar{\theta}_\pi$.

(b) If $\omega\gamma > 2\kappa$, *then any feedback* $\theta_\pi > 1$ *from current inflation leads to stability and determinacy.*

PROOF. See appendix D. An immediate corollary follows.

COROLLARY 1. *As* $\rho \to 1$ *and we approach an integral rule, then the range* $[1, \bar{\theta}_\pi]$ *in (a) becomes infinite.*

Thus, interest rate smoothing helps to induce determinacy—a result obtained in Batini, Levine, and Pearlman (2004) for both current and forward-looking inflation targeting rules. Furthermore, we show in appendix D that κ decreases with increasing dollarization in the range $0 < a < 1/2$, which leads to another corollary.

COROLLARY 2. *For high levels of dollarization* $a < 1/2$, *as dollarization increases further, then* κ *falls and the determinacy range for* θ_π *increases.*

Thus, for a current domestic inflation rule, a high degree of transactions dollarization poses no problems for stability and determinacy; in fact, it helps to avoid both problems. The intuition behind this result is that with $\kappa > 0$, a case easily supported by the calibration, supply and demand effects of nominal interest rate changes operate in opposite directions. But transactions dollarization closes down the supply-side effect and therefore helps the stabilization process.

Figure 5.1 illustrates our result using our central calibration. We see that condition (a) is just satisfied for all degrees of transactions dollarization, $a \in [0, 1]$, if $\rho > 0.25$, which is a very modest degree of interest rate smoothing. These results have been obtained for a simple model where many of the features in our full model have been suppressed. Nevertheless, they are suggestive of the effects of transactions dollarization on the stabilization properties of a simple current domestic inflation rule in the full model.

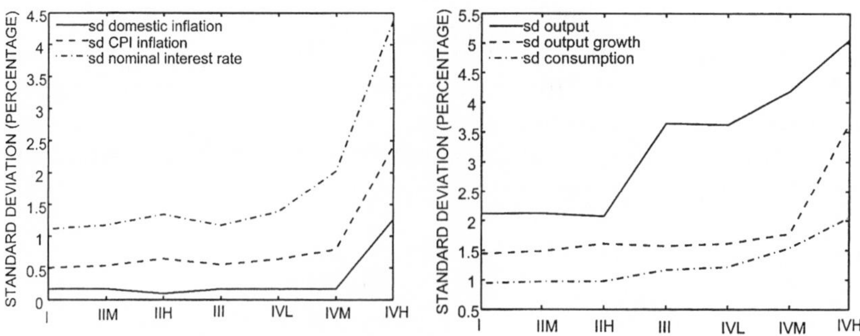

Fig. 5.1 Standard deviations of key variables

5.5 Optimal Monetary Policy, Volatility, and Impulse Responses

How do financial frictions and dollarization in emerging market economies affect the transmission mechanism of monetary policy and the volatilities of output, inflation, and other key variables? To answer this question we do two things. First, we parameterize four representations of the model with increasing frictions and dollarization, and solve them subject to the corresponding optimal monetary policy rule based on maximizing the household's utility. (Later, in section 5.6, this provides a benchmark against which to assess the welfare implications of the fixed exchange rate regime and various Taylor-type flexible exchange rate rules.) We then compare the volatilities delivered by each model for key macrovariables, including inflation and output. Second, we analyze how transmission of shocks is affected by frictions and dollarization by tracing impulse responses to two key shocks.

5.5.1 Optimal Monetary Policy and Volatilities

We adopt a linear-quadratic framework for the optimization problem facing the monetary authority. This is particularly convenient as we can then summarize outcomes in terms of unconditional (asymptotic) variances of macroeconomic variables and the local stability and determinacy of particular rules. The framework also proves useful for addressing the issue of the zero lower bound on the nominal interest rate.

Following Woodford (2003), we adopt a "small distortions" quadratic approximation to the household's single period utility that is accurate as long as the zero-inflation steady state is close to the social optimum. There are three distortions that result in the steady-state output being below the social optimum: namely, output and labor market distortions from monopolistic competition and distortionary taxes required to pay for government provided services. Given our calibration these features would make our distortions far from small. However, there is a further distortion, external habit in consumption, that in itself raises the equilibrium steady-state output above the social optimum. If the habit parameter h_C is large enough, the two sets of effects can cancel out and thus justify our small distortions approximation. In fact, this is the case in our calibration.[14]

From appendix E our quadratic approximation to the household's intertemporal expected loss function is given by

$$\Omega_0 = E_t\left[(1-\beta)\sum_{t=0}^{\infty}\beta^t L_t\right], \tag{56}$$

where

$$2L_t = w_c\left(\frac{c_t - h_C c_{t-1}}{1-h_C}\right)^2 + w_\tau \tau_t^2 + w_{cl}\left(\frac{c_t - h_C c_{t-1}}{1-h_C}\right)l_t + w_l l_t^2 \tag{57}$$

$$+ w_k(k_{t-1} - l_t)^2 - w_{ay} y_t a_t + w_{cir} ci_t \tau_t + w_{cls\tau} cls_t \tau_t + w_\pi \pi_{H,t}^2$$

$$ci_t \equiv \mu\omega(1-\omega)c_y c_t + \mu(1-\omega^*)c_y c_t^* + \rho_I\omega_I(1-\omega_I)i_y i_t + \rho_I^*(1-\omega_I^*)i_y i_t^*$$

$$cls_t \equiv [(1-\sigma)(1-\varrho)-1]\frac{c_t^* - hc_{t-1}^*}{1-h} - (1-\sigma)\varrho\frac{L^* l_t^*}{1-L^*},$$

and the weights w_c, w_τ, and so forth, are defined in appendix E. Thus, from (62) welfare is reduced as a result of volatility in consumption adjusted to external habit $c_t - h_C c_{t-1}$; the terms of trade τ_t, labor supply l_t, domestic inflation $\pi_{H,t}$, and foreign shocks. There are also some covariances that arise from the procedure for the quadratic approximation of the loss function. The policymaker's problem at time $t = 0$ is then to minimize (61) subject to the model in linear state-space form given by (45), initial conditions on predetermined variables z_0, and the Taylor rule followed by the ROW. Details of the optimization procedure are provided in Levine, McAdam, and Pearlman (2007).

We parameterize the model according to five alternatives, ordered by increasing degrees of frictions and dollarization:

- Model I: no transaction dollarization, no financial accelerator, and no liability dollarization. This is a fairly standard small open economy model similar to many in the new-Keynesian open economy literature with the only nonstandard features being a nonseparable utility function in money balances, consumption, and leisure consistent with a balanced growth path and a fully articulated ROW bloc.
- Model II: transaction dollarization (TD) only (where the degree of TD is captured by $1 - a$, where $a \in [0, 1]$).
- Model III: financial accelerator (FA) only.

14. See Levine, McAdam, and Pearlman (2007) and Levine, Pearlman, and Pierse (2006) for a discussion of these issues. The former paper provides details of all the optimization procedures in this chapter.

Table 5.1 **Expected welfare loss decomposition**

	I	II ($a = 0.5$)	III	IV ($\varphi = 0.5$)
a_t	0.8100	0.7779	0.6642	0.6980
g_t	0.0438	0.0416	0.0417	0.0475
g_t^*	0.0010	0.0001	0.0046	0.0046
$\epsilon_{UIP,t}$	0.0567	0.0520	0.0884	0.0863
$\epsilon_{R,t}^*$	0.0543	0.0240	0.0681	0.1406
$\epsilon_{P,t}$	0.0196	0.0197	0.1731	0.5970
All shocks	0.9855	0.9152	1.0400	1.5742

- Model IV: financial accelerator (FA) and liability dollarization (LD), assuming that firms borrow a fraction of their financing requirements $1 - \varphi \in [0, 1]$ in dollars.
- Model V: TD plus FA plus LD, where $a = \varphi = 0.5$; that is, medium level TD and LD.

We subject all these variants of the model to six exogenous and independent shocks. Three of these—total factor productivity (a_t), government spending (g_t), and the external risk premium facing firms, $\epsilon_{P,t}$—are domestic and three—a foreign demand counterpart to g_t^*, a country risk premium shock to the modified UIP condition, $\epsilon_{UIP,t}$, and shock to the foreign interest rate rule $\epsilon_{R,t}^*$—originate from the ROW. The foreign bloc is fully articulated, so the effect of these shocks impacts on the domestic economy through changes in the demand for exports. Since the domestic economy is small, however, there is no corresponding effect of domestic shocks on the ROW.[15]

The first question we pose is what is the relative importance of these six shocks for the welfare of domestic households under optimal monetary policy? Table 5.1 provides the answer by carrying out an expected welfare decomposition[16] with respect to the shocks for our four model variants. For both TD and LD we assume a degree of dollarization $1 - a = 1 - \varphi = 0.5$. Given our calibration, the most important shock is that to technology, irrespective of the existence of a FA or LD. But as these latter features are introduced in turn, the model economy becomes increasingly vulnerable to the three foreign shocks, with the contribution of technology falling from 82 percent in model I to 44 percent in model IV. Our earlier analysis of a model without capital suggested that TD improves stabilization. Table 5.1 confirms this for the full model—indeed, TD sees a reduction in the welfare loss emanating from all shocks.

15. Of course, the simulation results reported in the following depend on our calibration of both structural parameters and shocks, particularly on the parameters determining the exchange rate elasticity of trade and net worth. However, changing these with a plausible range does not affect the results qualitatively.

16. The expected welfare loss is the conditional loss in the vicinity of the steady state.

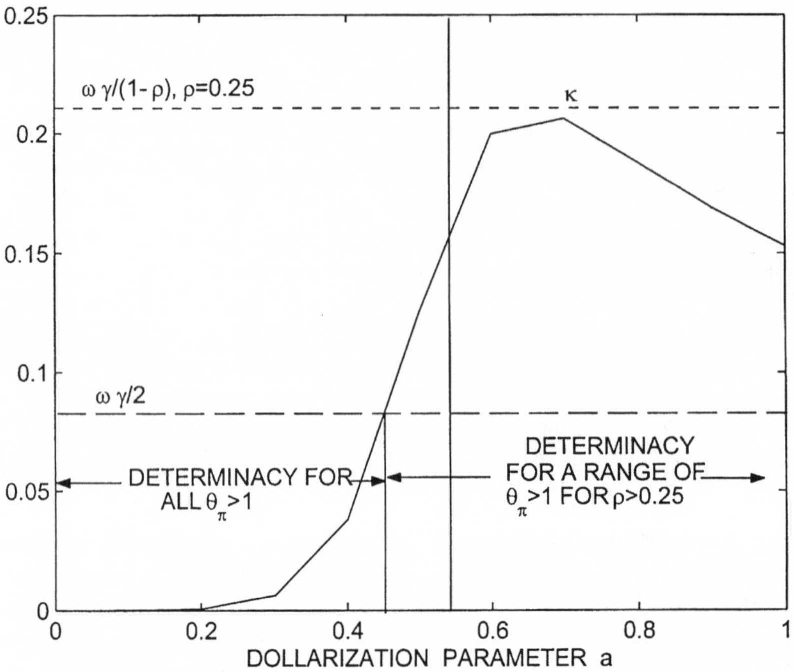

Fig. 5.2 Transactions dollarization and determinacy of current inflation rule

Figure 5.2 picks out some key variables and shows standard deviations associated with model I, model II with medium and high degrees of TD (IIM, IIH), and model III and model IV with low, medium, and high degrees of TD (IVL, IVM, IVH) under optimal policy.[17] Table 5.2 presents volatility results for all model variables. This broadly reaffirms the general result that more frictions and liability dollarization trigger greater economic volatility. Investment, net worth, interest rate, and real exchange variability are particularly high for even moderate degrees of liability dollarization and financial acceleration, compared to a world without such features.

A number of further features of these volatilities deserve highlighting. First consider TD proceeding from the baseline model with no TD to the opposite extreme of full TD. As mentioned previously, welfare does not deteriorate but indeed increases, and this is confirmed by the reduction in variances of consumption, the terms of trade (implied by the lower variance of the real exchange rate), and inflation, which feature in the loss function. However, this comes at a cost of an increase in the variance of the nominal interest rate since TD closes down one channel for monetary intervention.

17. We do not show model V because adding TD has no visible implications for volatilities in the chart.

Table 5.2 **Variances in percent² and expected welfare loss**

	I	II ($a = 0.5$)	II ($a = 0$)	III	IV ($\varphi = 0.75$)	IV ($\varphi = 0.5$)	IV ($\varphi = 0$)	V ($a = \varphi = 0.5$)
var(y_t)	4.50	4.53	4.31	13.3	13.1	17.5	25.6	17.8
var(c_t)	0.89	0.94	0.95	1.36	1.48	2.37	4.23	2.58
var(i_t)	9.67	9.78	9.72	139	117	138	44.2	135
var(q_t^k)	11.9	12.0	11.8	12.8	12.9	13.2	7.66	13.1
var(l_t)	0.72	0.58	0.39	1.19	1.22	1.83	30.3	1.61
var(rer_t)	3.66	3.61	3.54	3.82	4.33	5.89	16.9	5.68
var($\pi_{H,t}$)	0.03	0.03	0.01	0.03	0.03	0.03	1.59	0.03
var(π_t)	0.26	0.29	0.42	0.31	0.41	0.63	5.88	0.63
var($r_{n,t}$)	1.24	1.37	1.81	1.37	1.93	4.13	19.2	4.17
var(n_t)	0	0	0	227	207	274	118	270
var(θ_t)	1.33	1.33	1.33	2.02	2.03	2.19	1.67	2.18
var(Δy_t)	2.08	2.21	2.60	2.47	2.60	3.16	13.31	3.18
Ω_0	0.986	0.915	0.778	1.040	1.156	1.574	19.14	1.466

This higher interest rate has implications in terms of the zero lower bound (ZLB) constraint, an issue we return to in section 5.7.

Now consider the FA and LD. With the emergence of the FA we see an increase in the variances of all variables, which is marked in the case of output and investment. Variances increase further at first, as LD is introduced, but for complete LD, investment and net worth volatility are lower. We explore this phenomenon in our following discussion of impulse response functions. The combination of the FA and LD is a lethal cocktail for the welfare of households. Welfare loss increases sharply for high levels of LD with $\varphi > 0.5$. The variance of the nominal interest rate also increases substantially with further implications for welfare when we impose the ZLB.

To summarize these results:

- Inflation, consumption, and output volatility worsen markedly as financial frictions in the form of the FA, and eventually LD, are introduced. However, TD, even when complete, does not worsen volatility except for the nominal interest rate.
- Full liability dollarization combined with the financial accelerator leads to levels of real and nominal volatility that are several times larger than those present in an economy without such features, for the same shocks. As a result, the expected welfare loss increases sharply for high levels of LD with $\varphi < 0.5$.
- The central bank is more aggressive in its use of the nominal interest rate with both forms of dollarization. As a result, the variance of the nominal interest rate increases, and markedly so for LD. This has important further implications for welfare when we impose the interest rate zero lower bound.

How do these volatilities match up to data on financially dollarized economies? Probably the most definitive and wide-ranging work on empirical issues on dollarization is due to Levy Yeyati (2006), who analyzes a unique database. His cross-sectional time series data reveals a positive correlation between dollarization and the standard deviation of growth rates, which is a feature of the penultimate row of table 5.2. Without liability dollarization, devaluations lead to countercyclical behavior and eventually restore the economy to equilibrium. In the presence of LD, the balance sheet effect ultimately leads to lower borrowing and capital formation, and lower growth on average coupled with increased variability.[18]

5.5.2 Assessing the Impact of Key External and Internal Shocks

In this section we study impulse responses for two selected shocks, which our earlier results have shown have important welfare implications: a technology shock (a_t) and a shock to the country's external risk premium, $\epsilon_{UIP,t}$. These are shown in figures 5.3 through 5.6, which concentrate on the baseline model (no frictions/dollarization) and model variants where dollarization/frictions are most pernicious (models III and IVH). Although the analysis looks similar to Gilchrist (2003), it is in fact quite distinct in that here we are interested in comparing the transmission of shocks as frictions and dollarization increase, rather than in comparing the performance of flexible versus fixed exchange rates *given* frictions and liability dollarization.

To understand how the transmission of the shock changes for different levels of frictions and dollarization, we need first to take a step back and illustrate some of the mechanisms driving the real exchange rate, and the behavior of net worth of the wholesale firms sector.

Movements in the real exchange rate (and the related terms of trade) are critical for understanding our results. Linearization of the modified UIP condition (17) gives

$$rer_t = E_t rer_{t+1} + E_t(r_t^* - r_t) - \delta_r b_{F,t} + \epsilon_{UIP,t}, \tag{58}$$

Solving (63) forward, in time we see that the real exchange rate is a sum of future expected real interest rate differentials with the ROW plus a term proportional to the sum of future expected net liabilities plus a sum of expected future shocks $\epsilon_{UIP,t}$. The real exchange will depreciate (a rise in rer_t) if the sum of expected future interest rate differentials are positive and/or the sum of expected future net liabilities are positive and/or a positive shock to the risk premium, $\epsilon_{UIP,t}$ occurs.

Also crucial to the understanding of the effects of the FA and LD is the behavior of the net worth of the wholesale sector. In linearized form this is given by

18. However, Levy Yeyati (2006) is unable to pick up the balance sheet effects from the data.

$$(59)\quad n_t = \frac{\xi_e}{1+g}\left[\frac{1}{n_k} r^k_{t=1} + (1+\Theta)(1+R)n_{t-1} + \left(1 - \frac{1}{n_k}\right)\right.$$
$$\left. \cdot [(1+R)\theta_{t-1} + (1+\Theta)(\varphi r_{t-1} + (1-\varphi)(r^*_{t-1} + (1+R)(rer_t - rer_{t-1})]\right],$$

where the ex ante cost of capital is given by r^k_{t-1}. In (64) since leverage $1/n_k > 1$ we can see that net worth increases with the ex post return on capital at the beginning of period t, r^k_{t-1}, and decreases with the risk premium θ_{t-1} charged in period $t - 1$ and the ex post cost of capital in home currency and dollars, $\varphi r_{t-1} + (1 - \varphi)(r^*_{t-1} + (1 + R)(rer_t - rer_{t-1}))$, noting that $(rer_t - rer_{t-1})$ is the real depreciation of the home currency. Starting at the steady state at $t = 0$, from (64) at $t = 1$ we have

$$(60)\quad n_1 = \frac{\xi_e}{1+g}\left[(1-\delta)q_1 + \left(1 - \frac{1}{n_k}\right)(1+\Theta)(1-\varphi)(1+R)rer_1\right].$$

Thus, net worth falls if Tobin's Q falls and if some borrowing is in dollars ($\varphi < 1$). We see also that a *depreciation* of the real exchange rate ($rer_1 > 0$) brings about a further drop in net worth. However, an *appreciation* of the real exchange rate ($rer_1 < 0$) will offset the drop in net worth. Output falls through two channels: first, a drop in Tobin's Q and a subsequent fall in investment demand and, second, through a reduction in consumption by entrepreneurs.

Total Factor Productivity (TFP) Shock

Figures 5.3 and 5.4 illustrate the transmission channels in the model under optimal monetary policy in response to a negative 1 percent shock to total factor productivity. Because TD does not result in big differences in volatilities, we focus on only three variants: the baseline model with no TD nor FA, the model with a FA, and the model with both the FA and a high degree of LD. For all three models we have the following broad features: the shocks result in an immediate fall in consumption, output, and investment, a tightening of optimal monetary policy with a rise in the nominal and expected real interest rate, an appreciation of the real exchange rate (rer_t falls), a fall in the terms of trade ($p_{F,t} - p_{H,t} = \tau_t = rer_t/\omega$), a trade deficit, and a decline in net future assets. Investment falls because Tobin's Q (defined in the graphs as the real market price of capital relative to the price of capital goods, $q^k_t = q_t - p_{I,t} + p_t$) falls, which in turn responds to an anticipated future fall in profits relative to the cost of capital. With the FA switched on, the fall in Tobin's Q measured relative to the price of capital relative to the consumption good, q_t, causes net worth to fall, which in turn causes the external financing premium facing firms, θ_t, to rise. This exacerbates the increase in the cost of capital and Tobin's Q, and therefore investment, falls further. This is the familiar effect of a FA highlighted, for example, in Gertler, Gilchrist, and Natalucci (2003).

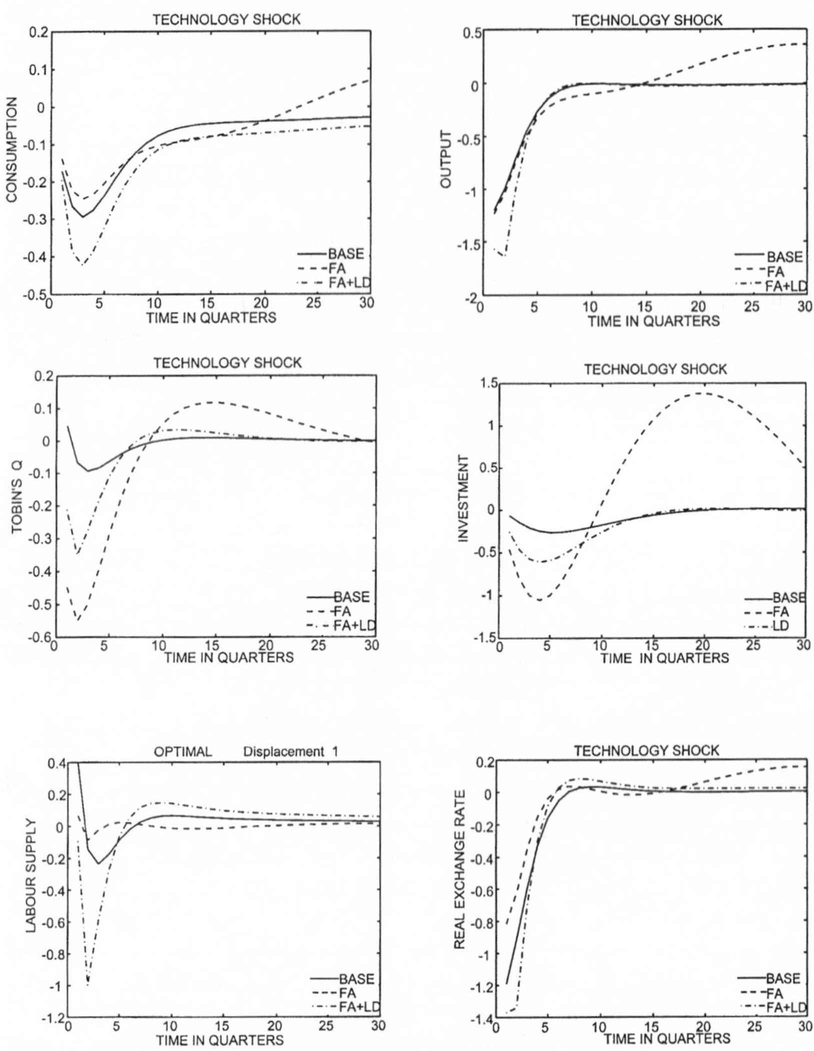

Fig. 5.3 Responses to a technology shock under optimal monetary policy

Now consider the FA plus LD where for the graphs we assume all borrowing by firms is in dollars ($\varphi = 0$). In this case, net worth and investment fall by far less, and net worth relative to the value of capital hardly changes, as can be seen from movements in the external risk premium. Why is this? The reason is the appreciation of the exchange rate which (from [65] with $\varphi < 1$) offsets the fall in net worth brought about by the fall in Tobin's Q. The policymaker responds to this by tightening more monetary condi-

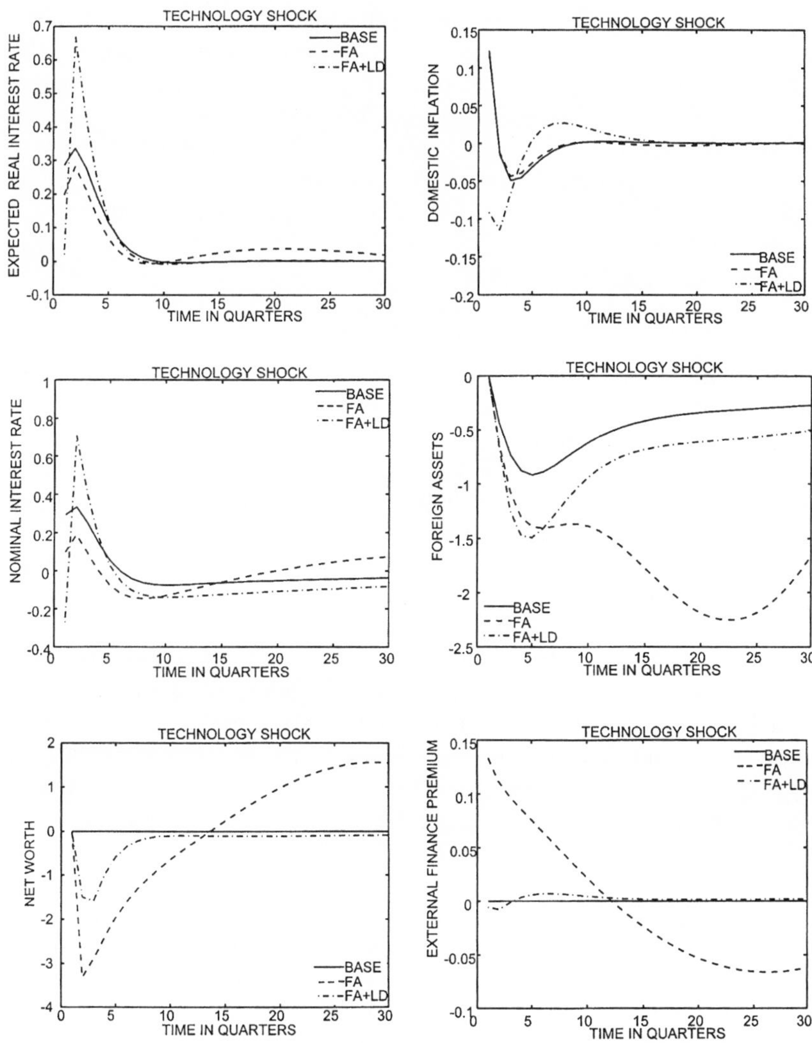

Fig. 5.4 Responses to a technology shock under optimal monetary policy

tions, so that the expected real interest rate rises relative to what happens in a model without LD. *Thus, the presence of LD induces a stronger monetary intervention* particularly in the short run. Another way to explain this is by saying that monetary policy is less effective under LD, other things equal, because the output gap channel of monetary transmission is weaker (since borrowing is partly in dollars, and so the cost of capital is less directly affected by changes in the interest rate), while the exchange rate channel is stronger (because under LD changes in the exchange rate generate balance sheet effects in addition to affecting net trade). As a result, the central bank uses the exchange rate more intensely as a stabilizing device, by creating domestic relative to abroad interest rate differentials. For big enough TFP shocks, however, use of the exchange rate channel to minimize "financial-accelerated" output fluctuations may clash with the objective of keeping inflation within a certain range. As indicated by the figure, it takes much longer for domestic inflation to return to target in a model with FA + LD than in a model without frictions or dollarization.

Country External Risk Premium Shock

Next, in figures 5.5 and 5.6, we turn to a 1 percent to the domestic country's external risk premium ϵ_{UIPt} in (63). Now the real exchange rate depreciates instead of appreciating, as was the case with the technology shock. The responses of all three variants of the model are again broadly similar, implying a drop in output, consumption, investment, a fall in Tobin's Q, a tightening of monetary policy, and a fall in net worth. The real depreciation of the exchange rate leads to a trade surplus and an accumulation of foreign assets. The effect of the FA on net worth, the external risk premium, and investment is pretty much the same as for the previous simulations. But when we combine the FA with LD an important difference emerges. Since the real exchange rate now depreciates instead of appreciating, the initial fall in net worth is exacerbated rather than attenuated by balance sheet effects, and the external risk premium rises by more. Monetary policy is tightened by more than in the TFP shock case, so the depreciation is short-lived because the interest rate differential relative to abroad is rapidly closed, and is eventually reversed, turning into an appreciation. With LD, the appreciation that follows the monetary tightening triggers a further balance sheet effect that has the effect of returning net worth back to its steady state faster than in the FA without LD. *Thus, LD has a long-stabilizing effect on movements in net worth.* Given that the external risk premium also returns faster to its equilibrium, forward-looking investment under LD behaves similarly to investment in the baseline, frictionless model. The immediate implication is that output returns faster to potential and generally contracts by less under FA + LD than in the baseline model with no frictions or in the FA-only model, a result that contrasts with the finding in Gertler, Gilchrist, and Natalucci (2003) using simple nonoptimized rules. The other key finding is that, once again, although FA and LD imply similar responses of investment, LD tends to make monetary policy more aggressive. Exactly as in the case of the TFP shock, this is optimal in that—under LD—the monetary authority can take advantage of the interest rate/exchange rate UIP channel to affect the exchange rate, and this way bring net worth and investment (and hence output and inflation) faster back to equilibrium.

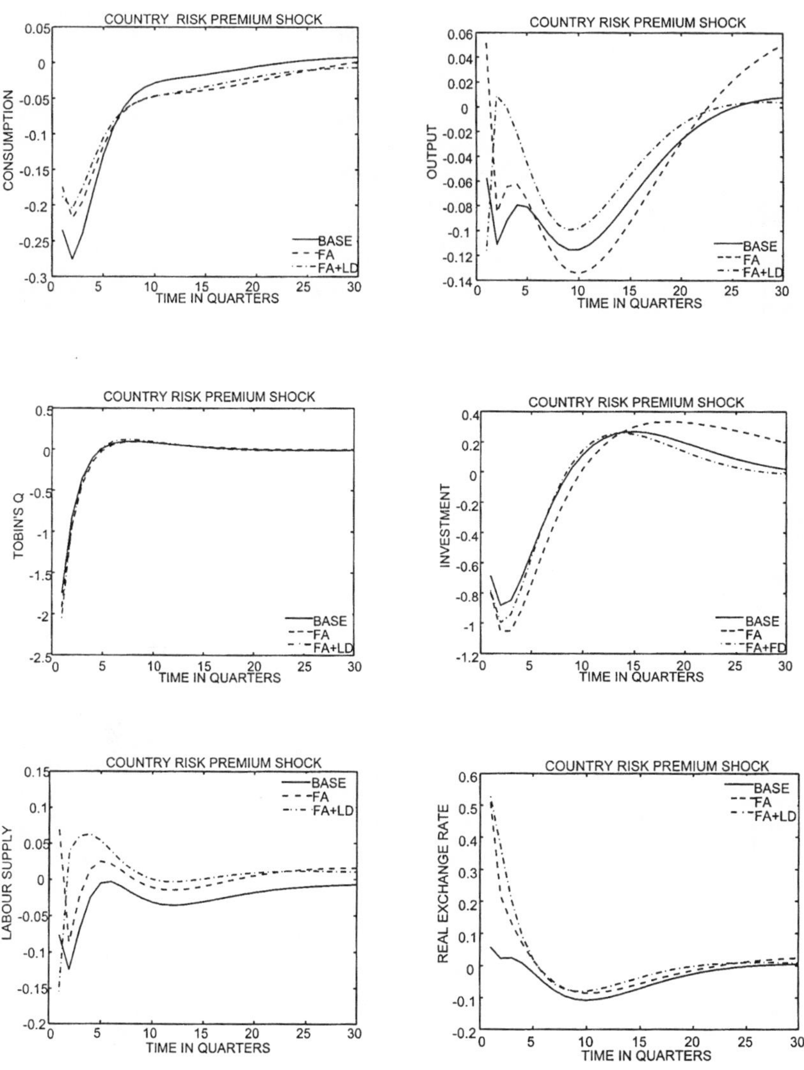

Fig. 5.5 Responses to a UIP shock under optimal monetary policy

5.6 The Fixed Exchange Rate Regime and Optimal Rules

What is left to understand now is what is hence the optimal degree of exchange rate stabilization (given inflation stabilization) in economies with frictions and dollarization. To this end we proceed to search simple optimized rules that maximize a welfare criterion based on households' utility under financial frictions and dollarization. We focus on the three regimes described previously, namely FIX, FLEX, and HYB. For the latter two

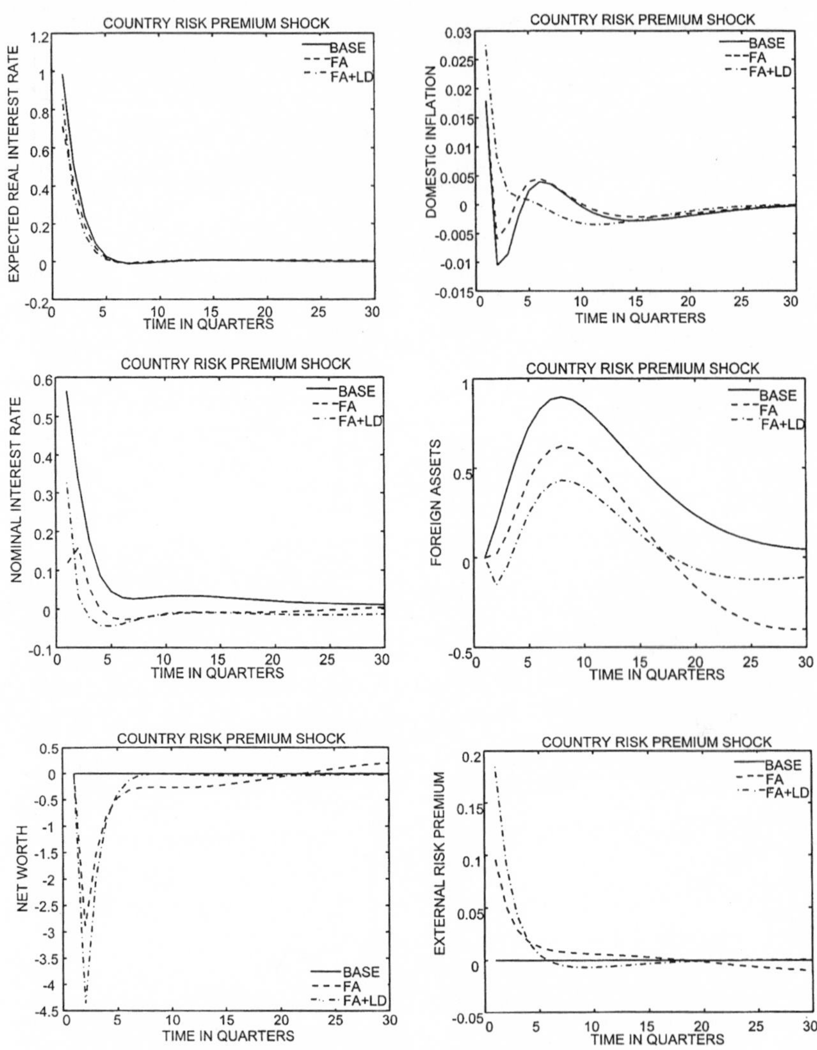

Fig. 5.6 Responses to a UIP shock under optimal monetary policy

regimes we compute optimized rules that minimize the expected welfare loss with respect to the feedback parameters $\rho \in [0, 1]$, π_θ, and π_s. We restrict our search to $\pi_\theta \in [1, 5]$: the lower bound ensures the rule satisfies the Taylor principle and the imposed upper bound avoids large initial jumps in the nominal interest rate.

We search simple rules that are optimal for four model variants (where in model II we set $a = 1/2$; i.e., moderate TD, in model IV we set $\varphi = 0.75$; i.e., a moderate LD).

Table 5.3 **Optimized rules**

Rule	ρ	θ_π	θ_y	θ_s
FLEX(D): Model I	1.0	5.0	0.32	0
FLEX(C): Model I	1.0	5.0	0.016	0
HYB: Model I	1.0	5.0	0.29	0.025
FLEX(D): Model II	1.0	5.0	0.25	0
FLEX(C): Model II	0.82	5.0	0.016	0
HYB: Model II	1.0	5.0	0.22	0.03
FLEX(D): Model III	0.95	5.0	0.44	0
FLEX(C): Model III	0.62	5.0	0.011	0
HYB: Model III	0.95	5.0	0.44	0
FLEX(D): Model IV	0.91	5.0	0.34	0
FLEX(C): Model IV	0.72	5.0	0.069	0
HYB: Model IV	0.91	5.0	0.34	0

Table 5.3 provides the parameter values that optimize the FLEX and HYB rules in these four cases.[19] Tables 5.4 through 5.7 report variances from simulating each model variant under all shocks for the corresponding simple optimized FIX, FLEX, and HYB rule.[20] A joint read of these tables points to some interesting results.

- Responding *directly* to the exchange rate, in addition to inflation and output growth, is not optimal under liability dollarization or in the presence of financial frictions (FA in particular): the optimal feedback from the exchange rate is zero, or close to zero across all models. Thus, central banks in countries with these features should not attempt to manage the exchange rate nor, more generally, attempt to balance inflation and exchange rate stability objectives. This finding restates the Gilchrist (2003) result obtained using simple nonoptimized rules. The reason is clear: financial dollarization weakens the output gap channel and strengthens the exchange rate channel of monetary policy transmission—which gets activated through the UIP via interest rate changes—because, in this case, the cost of capital on which output (and inflation) depend are a function of both the real interest rate and the real exchange rate. Because under financial dollarization exchange rate becomes the key adjustment variable, changes in it are necessary to stabilize inflation by attenuating the financial accelerator effects. Thus, fixing the exchange rate or reducing its volatility limits the ability of the central bank to enact stabilizing monetary interventions, and forces it to larger interest rate gyrations instead. These induce larger welfare losses both because the central bank now forgoes the possibility to use the exchange rate to

19. Note there is no "optimal" FIX regime since the parameter θ_s is simply set at a value sufficiently high to ensure a fixed exchange rate.

20. We omit to report results on model V for the reasons described previously.

Table 5.4 **Outcome of rules in model I (no TD, no FA)**

Rule	var(y_t)	var(c_t)	var(i_t)	var(q_t^k)	var(rer_t)	var($\pi_{H,t}$)	var(π_t)	var($r_{n,t}$)	var(θ_t)	Ω_0	c_e(%)
FIX	1.42	0.46	11.4	9.20	0.83	1.31	1.21	3.02	1.33	9.74	0.50
FLEX(D)	4.47	0.78	9.57	10.6	3.75	0.03	0.31	1.01	1.33	1.05	0.004
FLEX(C)	2.02	0.53	9.41	8.82	7.51	0.12	0.02	0.76	1.33	1.59	0.03
HYB	4.44	0.78	9.58	10.6	3.72	0.03	0.30	1.01	1.33	1.05	0.003
Optimal	4.50	0.89	9.67	11.9	3.66	0.03	0.26	1.24	1.33	0.986	0

Table 5.5 **Outcome of rules in model II (TD only)**

Rule	var(y_t)	var(c_t)	var(i_t)	var(q_t^k)	var(rer_t)	var($\pi_{H,t}$)	var(π_t)	var($r_{n,t}$)	var(θ_t)	Ω_0	c_e(%)
FIX	1.64	0.57	11.5	9.54	0.89	1.25	1.17	3.43	1.33	9.324	0.48
FLEX(D)	4.49	0.86	9.76	10.8	3.66	0.03	0.33	1.00	1.33	0.977	0.004
FLEX(C)	3.11	0.74	9.67	8.78	2.32	0.06	0.06	0.96	1.33	1.09	0.01
HYB	4.48	0.86	9.77	10.8	3.64	0.03	0.33	1.00	1.33	0.976	0.004
Optimal	4.53	0.94	9.78	12.0	3.61	0.03	0.29	1.37	1.33	0.915	0

Table 5.6 Outcome of rules in model III (FA, no TD)

Rule	var(y_t)	var(c_t)	var(i_t)	var(q_t^k)	var(rer_t)	var($\pi_{H,t}$)	var(π_t)	var($r_{n,t}$)	var(θ_t)	Ω_0	c_e(%)
FIX	57.7	54.3	977	61.3	10.9	2.19	1.59	9.83	5.96	19.8	1.07
FLEX(D)	17.5	1.76	217	15.9	4.62	0.03	0.23	1.60	2.56	1.24	0.01
FLEX(C)	22.1	2.27	347	29.1	5.63	0.17	0.03	3.07	3.36	2.94	0.101
HYB	17.5	1.76	217	15.9	4.62	0.03	0.23	1.60	2.56	1.24	0.01
Optimal	13.3	1.36	139	12.8	3.82	0.03	0.31	1.37	2.02	1.04	0

Table 5.7 Outcome of rules in model IV (FA, LD [$\varphi = 0.75$], no TD)

Rule	var(y_t)	var(c_t)	var(i_t)	var(q_t^k)	var(rer_t)	var($\pi_{H,t}$)	var(π_t)	var($r_{n,t}$)	var(θ_t)	Ω_0	c_e(%)
FIX	91.2	10.2	1,343	72.8	16.0	2.41	1.70	17.6	11.3	22.9	1.25
FLEX(D)	20.6	2.30	232	16.6	5.64	0.03	0.28	2.75	3.46	1.48	0.019
FLEX(C)	32.3	3.72	451	33.2	7.62	0.21	0.03	5.63	3.85	3.81	0.15
HYB	20.6	2.30	232	16.6	5.64	0.03	0.28	2.75	3.46	1.48	0.019
Optimal	13.1	1.48	117	12.9	4.33	0.03	0.41	1.93	2.03	1.16	0

undo financial accelerator effects and because aggressive changes in the interest rate generate adverse balance sheet effects at home by raising strongly the cost of capital, which in turn affects net worth and output.

- Responding *indirectly* to the exchange rate by choosing a consumer price rather than a domestic price inflation target, regime FLEX(C) is also severely suboptimal. The reasons for this are broadly the same as those for the failure of HYB to improve on FLEX(D).
- With flexible exchange rates, under FA + LD policy tends to be more aggressive, other things equal, with larger gyrations of the interest rate than under no frictions/dollarization. Adding an explicit feedback response to the exchange rate instills yet additional volatility to the interest rate with negative repercussions on all macrovariables (table 5.7) and a larger welfare loss. In the extreme case of exchange rate fixity (FIX) results are disastrous.
- The optimal parameters in our simple rules are similar across models, which means that a domestic inflation feedback rule with an added feedback for output is a robust rule with respect to any model uncertainty regarding financial frictions. Emerging market central banks do not have to significantly differentiate the way the monetary conditions are set from the way these are set in advanced, relatively frictionless economies.
- Finally, our results indicate that smoothing interest rate changes is desirable independently of the frictions/dollarization features of the economy—and indeed, integral rules always outperform proportional rules.[21]

Two questions remain. Given that there is little or no scope for targeting the nominal exchange rate, what is the welfare cost of maintaining a fixed rate? Second, the Taylor-type rules are only optimal given the constraints implied by the particular inflation and output growth targets, but is suboptimal compared with the fully optimal commitment rule. What, then, is the welfare cost of restricting rules in this way? Tables 5.4 through 5.8 provide answers to these questions. These tables provide outcomes in terms of unconditional variances of key variables where the maximized welfare losses Ω_0 are provided and compared with those for the optimal commitment policy. In the final column we provide the percentage consumption equivalent welfare loss compared with the optimal policy derived in appendix E and given by[22]

$$(61)\quad c_e = \frac{\Omega_0^i - \Omega_0^{OPT}}{(1-\rho)(1-h_C)c_y} \times 10^{-2}, i = \text{FIX, FLEX(D), FLEX(C)}.$$

A number of noteworthy points emerge from these results on welfare costs. First, the fixed exchange rate constraint imposes a cost in terms of a

21. As is shown in Batini, Levine, and Pearlman (2004) in an open economy context, interest rate smoothing is also desirable because it allows the rule to feedback strongly from the interest rate target without falling foul of determinacy.

22. Note that all welfare losses have been normalized by the terms $1 - \beta/FY$—see appendix E. In addition, all variances are in percent^2, so that c_e is in percent form.

permanent consumption equivalent of 0.48 through 0.50 percent for models I and II, rising to 1.25 percent in model IV. The introduction of the FA sees these consumption costs increase significantly and then rise again with the introduction of the LD at the moderate level of $\varphi = 0.75$ (meaning a quarter of the firms' borrowing is in dollars). Second, optimized domestic inflation Taylor-type rules mimic the fully optimal rule closely with a very small consumption equivalent loss. The latter rises with the introduction of the FA and again with LD, but remains small. So not only are optimized rules of this simple rule robust, they are only slightly suboptimal. Third, CPI inflation rules, however, impose far higher costs from 0.03 to 0.15 percent as one progresses from model I to model IV.

In one respect, the consumption equivalent costs reported up to now are misleading, especially for the FIX regime. The reason for this is to be seen for the unconditional variances reported in these, which are very large in the case of FIX and rise for all regimes when we introduce the FA and then LD. Such high variances imply that the interest rate under these optimized or optimal rules will hit the interest rate zero lower bound frequently.[23] The next section addresses this design fault in the rules.

5.7 Imposing the Nominal Interest Rate Zero Lower Bound

We now modify our interest rate rules to approximately impose an interest rate ZLB so that this event hardly ever occurs. Although so far only a few emerging market countries have experienced deflationary episodes (Peru and Israel in 2007 are examples of this), most inflation targeting emerging market countries have chosen low single digit inflation targets (see IMF [2005]), which makes the design of rules robust to ZLB problems germane. As in Woodford (2003, chapter 6), the ZLB constraint is implemented by modifying the single period welfare loss (62) to $L_t + w_r r_{n,t}^2$. Then following Levine, McAdam, and Pearlman (2007), the policymaker's optimization problem is to choose w_r and the unconditional distribution for $r_{n,t}$ (characterized by the steady-state variance) shifted to the right about a new nonzero steady state inflation rate and a higher nominal interest rate, such that the probability, p, of the interest rate hitting the lower bound is very low. This is implemented by calibrating the weight w_r *for each of our policy rules* so that $z_0(p)\sigma_r < R_n$, where $z_0(p)$ is the critical value of a standard normally distributed variable Z such that prob $(Z \leq z_0) = p$, $R_n = 1/(\beta(1 + g_{u_c}) - 1 + \pi^*$ is the steady-state nominal interest rate, $\sigma_r^2 = \text{var}(r_n)$ is the unconditional variance, and π^* is the new steady-state inflation rate. Given σ_r, the steady-state positive inflation rate that will ensure $r_{n,t} \geq 0$ with probability $1 - p$ is given by[24]

23. As Primiceri (2006) has pointed out, optimal rules with this feature are "not operational."

24. If the inefficiency of the steady-state output is negligible, then $\pi^* \geq 0$ is a credible new steady-state inflation rate. Note that in our LQ framework, the zero interest rate bound is very occasionally hit. Then, interest rate is allowed to become negative, possibly using a scheme proposed by Gesell (1934) and Keynes (1936). Our approach to the ZLB constraint (following

Table 5.8 **Optimal commitment with a nominal interest rate ZLB (Model IV with φ = 0.75)**

w_r	σ_r^2	$\tilde{\Omega}_0(w_r)$	$\tilde{\Omega}_0(0)$	π^*	$\overline{\Omega}_0(0)$	$\Omega_0(0)$
0	1.93	1.156	1.156	0.46	0.476	1.632
0.1	1.72	1.231	1.160	0.22	0.109	1.269
0.2	1.58	1.300	1.169	0.06	0.008	1.177
0.3	1.47	1.363	1.181	0	0	1.181
0.4	1.38	1.422	1.194	0	0	1.194

Notes: $\pi^* = \max[z_0(p)\sigma_r - (1/(\beta(1+g_{u_c}) - 1) \times 100, 0] = \max[3.00\sigma_r - 3.71, 0]$ with $p = 0.001$ probability of hitting the zero lower bound and $\beta = 0.99$, $g_{u_c} = -0.26$.
$\overline{\Omega}_0(0) = 1/2 w_\pi \pi^{*2} = 2.248\pi^{*2}$; $\Omega_0(0) = \tilde{\Omega}_0(0) + \overline{\Omega}_0(0)$.

$$(62) \qquad \pi^* = \max\left[z_0(p)\sigma_r - \left(\frac{1}{\beta(1+g_{uc})} - 1\right) \times 100, 0\right].$$

In our linear quadratic framework we can write the intertemporal expected welfare loss at time $t = 0$ as the sum of stochastic and deterministic components, $\Omega_0 = \tilde{\Omega}_0 + \overline{\Omega}_0$. Note that $\overline{\Omega}_0$ incorporates in principle the new steady-state values of all the variables; however, the NK Phillips curve being almost vertical, the main extra term comes from the π^2 term in equation (E.32). By increasing w_r we can lower σ_r, thereby decreasing π^* and reducing the deterministic component, but at the expense of increasing the stochastic component of the welfare loss. By exploiting this trade-off, we then arrive at the optimal policy that, in the vicinity of the steady state, imposes the ZLB constraint, $r_t \geq 0$, with probability $1 - p$.

Tables 5.8 and 5.9 show the results of this optimization procedure for the optimal commitment rules and the optimized simple rules, respectively, for the case of model IV. We choose $p = 0.001$. Given w_r, denote the expected intertemporal loss (stochastic plus deterministic components) at time $t = 0$ by $\Omega_0(w_r)$. This includes a term penalizing the variance of the interest rate that does not contribute to utility loss as such, but rather represents the interest rate lower bound constraint. Actual utility, found by subtracting the interest rate term, is given by $\Omega_0(0)$. The steady-state inflation rate, π^*, that will ensure the lower bound is reached only with probability $p = 0.001$, and is computed using (67). Given π^*, we can then evaluate the deterministic component of the welfare loss, $\overline{\Omega}_0$. Because in the new steady state the real interest rate is unchanged, the steady state involving real variables are also unchanged, so from (62) we can write $\overline{\Omega}_0(0) = w_\pi \pi^{*2}$. Both the ex ante optimal and the optimal time consistent deterministic welfare loss that guide

Woodford [2003]) in effect replaces it with a nominal interest rate variability constraint, which ensures the ZLB is hardly ever hit. By contrast, the work of a number of authors—including Adam and Billi (2007), Coenen and Wieland (2003), Eggertsson and Woodford (2003), and Eggertsson (2006)—study optimal monetary policy with commitment in the face of a nonlinear constraint $i_t \geq 0$, which allows for frequent episodes of liquidity traps in the form of $i_t = 0$.

Table 5.9 **Optimal FLEX (D) and FLEX (C) rule with a nominal interest rate ZLB**

			Model IV				
w_r	$[\rho, \theta_\pi, \theta_{\Delta y}]$	$\text{var}(r_{n,t})$	$\tilde{\Omega}_0(w_r)$	$\tilde{\Omega}_0(0)$	π^*	$\overline{\Omega}_0(0)$	$\Omega_0(0)$
			A FLEX (D)				
0	[0.91 5.0 0.39]	2.75	1.48	1.48	2.53	14.39	15.87
0.5	[1.0 5.0 0.54]	2.52	1.98	1.49	2.32	12.10	13.59
1	[1.0 5.0 0.64]	2.44	2.47	1.51	2.25	11.38	12.89
2	[1.0 5.0 0.78]	2.36	3.40	1.55	2.17	10.59	12.14
3	[1.0 5.0 0.87]	2.32	4.32	1.59	2.13	10.20	11.79
4	[1.0 5.0 0.94]	2.30	5.22	1.61	2.11	10.01	11.62
5	[1.0 5.0 0.99]	2.28	6.13	1.63	2.09	9.82	11.45
10	[1.0 5.0 1.13]	2.26	10.6	1.70	2.07	9.63	11.33
20	**[1.0 5.0 1.24]**	**2.24**	**19.48**	**1.75**	**2.05**	**9.45**	**11.20**
50	[1.0 5.0 1.34]	2.24	46.02	1.80	2.05	9.45	11.25
			B FLEX (C)				
0	[0.0 19.90 1.066]	5.21	3.67	3.67	3.14	22.16	25.83
5	[1.0 15.66 5.0]	4.04	11.73	3.99	2.32	12.10	16.09
10	[1.0 12.48 5.0]	3.99	19.38	4.15	2.28	11.68	15.83
15	**[1.0 11.27 5.0]**	**3.97**	**26.96**	**4.24**	**2.27**	**11.58**	**15.82**
20	[1.0 10.61 5.0]	3.97	34.43	4.30	2.27	11.58	15.88

the economy from a zero inflation steady state to $\pi = \pi^*$ differ from $\overline{\Omega}_0(0)$ (but not by much because the steady-state contributions by far outweigh the transitional one).

Table 5.10 summarizes the outcomes of optimized simple rules and the optimal rule with a ZLB approximately imposed in model IV. Comparing the last columns of tables 5.10 and 5.7 we can see that ZLB considerations create a substantial consumption equivalent loss for the fixed exchange rate, c_e, and smaller but significant one for the regimes FLEX(D) and FLEX(C), the latter being almost double the former. Under the FE there is no scope for trading off the variance of the nominal exchange rate with other macroeconomic variances that impact on welfare. Thus, the *only* way of reducing the probability of hitting the lower bound is to increase the steady-state inflation rate, which rises to 9 percent per quarter. This imposes a very large welfare loss, reflected in $c_e = 11.4$ percent.[25] For the Taylor rules there are some trade-offs between the variance of the nominal interest rate and the variances of inflation, consumption, and other variables impacting on welfare. Thus, for the optimized rule under a ZLB the variance of the nominal interest rate falls from 2.75 (percent)^2 to 2.24 (percent)^2 as w_r increases, at a steady-state inflation cost of 2.05 percent per quarter. The consumption equivalent loss

25. However, full dollarization, for example via a currency board, would result in $r_{n,t} = r^*_{n,t}$ and the ZLB then ceases to be a concern for the domestic country. This would still leave a significant welfare loss for the FIX regime (equal to that reported in table 5.7) of $c_e = 1.25$ percent. We are grateful to Marc Giannoni for pointing this out.

Table 5.10 **Summary of welfare outcome of rules with a nominal interest rate ZLB imposed**

	Model IV					
Rule	$\text{var}(r_{n,t})$	π^*	$\tilde{\Omega}_0(0)$	$\overline{\Omega}_0(0)$	$\Omega_0(0)$	$c_e(\%)$
FIX	17.6	8.88	22.9	177	200	11.4
FLEX(D)	2.24	2.05	1.75	9.45	11.2	0.57
FLEX(C)	3.97	2.27	4.24	11.58	11.82	0.83
Optimal	1.58	0.06	1.17	0.01	1.18	0

Note: c_e is the consumption equivalent welfare loss compared with the optimal policy given by $c_e = (\Omega^i(0) - \Omega^{OPT}(0))/((1-\varrho)(1-h_C)c_y) \times 10^{-2}$, i = FE, Taylor.

of the Taylor rules rises from 0.019 percent without ZLB concerns to 0.57 percent for FLEX(D) and 0.83 percent for FLEX(C), with such concerns.

5.8 Conclusions

Three clear results emerge from our analysis: first, given our calibration, the financial accelerator has a much larger impact on the performance of the optimized fixed exchange rate, Taylor, and hybrid interest rate rules than the presence of transactions dollarization. In particular, the costs of a fixed exchange rate regime rises significantly. Second, the introduction of liability dollarization alongside the financial accelerator increases these costs further. Finally, the zero lower bound constraint on the interest rate substantially increases the welfare cost of both the fixed exchange rate constraint, and restricts policy to an optimized Taylor, as opposed to a fully optimal monetary policy rule.

The message for monetary policymakers in emerging market economies struggling with frictions and dollarization is: do not try to achieve a double inflation exchange rate objectives, since this can backfire and lead to larger losses than commonly believed. You should fear to fix, not fear to float! Furthermore, central banks should not implicitly target the exchange rate by choosing a CPI rather than domestic price inflation target. Finally, the zero lower bound constraint on the interest rate substantially increases the welfare cost of the fixed exchange rate constraint, and restricts policy to an optimized flexible exchange rate Taylor-type rule, as opposed to a fully optimal monetary policy rule. As usual, central banks will have to carefully trade off in setting policy in a simple and monitorable way, with the costs of incurring in welfare losses from the higher risk of hitting the zero bound.

All our numerical results of course depend on both our choice of calibration and aspects of the modeling. On the former, while some experimentation suggests that the qualitative results should be robust with respect to a reasonable choice of alternatives, this will not be necessarily true of our quantitative findings on the welfare costs of various regimes. This suggests that future research could be usefully directed at a systems estimation of the model using Bayesian maximum likelihood methods now popular in the DSGE literature.[26] Nor can we assert that our results would withstand significant changes to the model, such as the introduction of a large commodity exporting sector (e.g., copper or oil) with prices fixed to the dollar and a consequent large imported share of consumables. Again, this suggests an item for future research.

Appendix A

The Steady State

The BGP zero inflation steady-state balanced growth path with consumption, wholesale output, the wage and capital stock growing at a rate g per period, must satisfy

$$\text{(A1)}\qquad \frac{\overline{K}_{t+1}}{\overline{K}_t} = \frac{\overline{Y}_{t+1}}{\overline{Y}_t} = \frac{\overline{C}_{t+1}}{\overline{C}_t} = \frac{\overline{W}_{t+1}}{\overline{W}_t} = 1 + g$$

$$\text{(A2)}\qquad \frac{\overline{A}_{t+1}}{\overline{A}_t} = 1 + g(1 - \alpha).$$

Since there are no investment adjustment costs at the steady state, it follows that

$$\text{(A3)}\qquad \overline{K}_{t+1} = (1 - \delta)\overline{K}_t + \overline{I}_t.$$

It follows from (A1) that

$$\text{(A4)}\qquad \overline{I}_t = (g + \delta)\overline{K}_t,$$

and hence, the previous assumptions regarding $\Phi(\cdot)$ become $\Phi(g + \delta) = g + \delta$ and $\Phi'(g + \delta) = 1$.

In what follows we denote the trended steady state of X_t by X. Then the rest of the steady state is given by

$$\text{(A5)}\qquad C_H = \mathrm{w}\left(\frac{P_H}{P}\right)^{-\mu} C$$

$$\text{(A6)}\qquad C_F = (1 - \mathrm{w})\left(\frac{P_F}{P}\right)^{-\mu} C$$

$$\text{(A7)}\qquad P = [\mathrm{w}P_H^{1-\mu} + (1 - \mathrm{w})P_F^{1-\mu}]^{1/(1-\mu)}$$

26. Castillo, Montoro, and Tuesta (2006) provides a promising first attempt at estimating a small open economy model, with many of the features of found in our chapter, using data for Peru.

(A8) $$\frac{W}{P} = -\frac{1}{1-(1/\eta)}\frac{U_L}{U_C}$$

(A9) $$1 = \beta(1+R_n)(1+g_{u_c}) = \beta(1+R)(1+g_{u_c}),$$

where g_{u_c} is the growth rate of the marginal utility of consumption in the steady state given by

(A10) $$g_{u_c} = (1+g)^{(1-\varrho)(1-\sigma)-1} - 1$$

and

(A11) $$1 + R^k = (1+\Theta)(1+R)$$

(A12) $$\Theta = \Theta\left(\frac{B}{N}\right) = \Theta\left(\frac{QK}{N} - 1\right)$$

(A13) $$Y = AK^{\alpha}L^{1-\alpha} - F$$

(A14) $$\frac{WL}{P_H^W Y} = 1 - \alpha$$

(A15) $$\frac{Q(R^k+\delta)K}{P_H^W Y} = \alpha$$

(A16) $$I = (g+\delta)K$$

(A17) $$I = [\mathrm{w}_I^{1/\rho_I} I_H^{(\rho_I-1)/\rho_I} + (1-\mathrm{w}_I)^{1/\rho_I} I_F^{(\rho_I-1)/\rho_I}]^{\rho_I/(1-\rho_I)}$$

(A18) $$\frac{I_H}{I_F} = \frac{\mathrm{w}_I}{1-\mathrm{w}_I}\left(\frac{P_H}{P_F}\right)^{-\rho_I}$$

(A19) $$P_I = [\mathrm{w}_I P_H^{1-\rho_I} + (1-\mathrm{w}_I)P_F^{1-\rho_I}]^{1/(1-\rho_I)}$$

(A20) $$Q\Phi'\left(\frac{I}{K}\right) = \frac{P_I}{P}$$

(A21) $$P_H = \hat{P}_H = \frac{P_H^W}{1-(1/\zeta)}$$

(A22) $$MC = \frac{P_H^W}{P_H} = 1 - \frac{1}{\zeta}$$

(A23) $$Y = C_H + \frac{1}{\nu}[C_H^e + C_H^{e*} + I_H + I_H^*] + \frac{1-\nu}{\nu}C_H^* + G$$

(A24) $$C_{H,t}^e = (1-\xi_e)V = (1-\xi_e)(1+R^k)N \equiv s_e C_{H,t}$$

(A25) $$T = G$$

(A26) $$U_{M_H} = U_C \frac{R_n}{1+R_n}$$

(A27) $$U_{M_F} = U_C \frac{R_n^*}{1 + R_n^*},$$

plus the foreign counterparts. Note that (A28) ignores seigniorage arising in a zero inflation from growth. The steady steady is completed with

(A28) $$\mathcal{T} = \frac{P_F}{P_H}$$

(A29) $$RER = \frac{SP^*}{P}$$

(A30) $$U_C = U_C^* \frac{z_0}{RER}.$$

Units of output are chosen so that $P_H = P_F = 1$. Hence, $\mathcal{T} = P = P_I = 1$. Hence, with our assumptions regarding $\Phi(\cdot)$, we have that $Q = 1$. We also normalize $S = 1$ in the steady state so that $P_F^* = P_H^* = P^* = P_I^* = 1$ as well. Then the steady state of the risk-sharing condition (A30) becomes $C = kC^*$, where k is a constant.

Appendix B

Linearization

Exogenous Processes

(B1) $$a_{t+1} = \rho_\alpha a_t + v_{a,t+1}$$

(B2) $$g_{t+1} = \rho_g g_t + v_{g,t+1}$$

(B3) $$g_{t+1}^* = \rho_g^* g_t^* + v_{g,t+1}^*$$

(B4) $$\varepsilon_{R,t+1}^* = \rho_R^* \varepsilon_{R,t}^* + v_{R,t+1}^*$$

(B5) $$\varepsilon_{P,t+1} = \rho_P \varepsilon_{P,t} + v_{P,t+1}$$

(B6) $$\varepsilon_{UIP,t+1} = \rho_{UIP} \varepsilon_{UIP,t} + v_{UIP,t+1}$$

Predetermined Variables

(B7) $$k_{t+1} = \frac{1 - \delta}{1 + g} k_t + \frac{\delta + g}{1 + g} i_t$$

(B8) $$k^*_{t+1} = \frac{1-\delta^*}{1+g}k^*_t + \frac{\delta^*+g}{1+g}i^*_t$$

(B9) $$n_t = \frac{\xi_e}{1+g}\left[\frac{1}{n_k}r^k_{t-1} + (1+\Theta)(1+R)n_{t-1} + \left(1-\frac{1}{n_k}\right)\cdot[(1+R)\theta_{t-1} + (1+\Theta)(\varphi r_{t-1}) + (1-\varphi)(r^*_{t-1}) + (1+R)(rer_t - rer_{t-1})]\right]$$

(B10) $$n^*_t = \frac{\xi^*_e}{1+g}\left[\frac{1}{n^*_k}r^{k*}_{t-1} + (1+\Theta^*)(1+R)n^*_{t-1} + \left(1-\frac{1}{n^*_k}\right)\cdot[(1+R)\theta^*_{t-1} + (1+\Theta^*)r^*_{t-1}]\right]$$

where $r_{t-1} = r_{n,t-1} - \pi_t$ and $r^*_{t-1} = r^*_{n,t-1} - \pi^*_t$ are the ex post real interest rates.

(B11) $$s_t = s_{t-1} + rer_t - rer_{t-1} + \pi_t - \pi^*_t$$

Nonpredetermined Variables

(B12) $$(1-\delta)E_t(q_{t+1}) = (1-R^k)q_t - (R^k+\delta)x_t + E_t(r^k_t)$$

(B13) $$(1-\delta^*)E_t(q^*_{t+1}) = (1+R^{k*})q^*_t - (R^{k*}+\delta^*)x^*_t + E_t(r^{k*}_t)$$

(B14) $$E_t u_{c,t+1} = u_{c,t} - \frac{r_{n,t}}{1+R} + E_t\pi_{t+1}$$

(B15) $$E_t u^*_{c,t+1} = u^*_{c,t} - \frac{r^*_{n,t}}{1+R} + E_t\pi^*_{t+1}$$

(B16) $$\beta E_t\pi_{H,t+1} = \pi_{H,t} - \lambda_H mc_t$$

(B17) $$\beta E_t\pi^*_{F,t+1} = \pi^*_{F,t} - \lambda^*_F mc^*_t$$

(B18) $$\left(1+\frac{1+g}{1+R}\right)i_t = \frac{1+g}{1+R}E_t i_{t+1} + i_{t-1} + \frac{1}{(1+g)^2 S''(1+g)}(q_t - p_{I,t} + p_t)$$

(B19) $$\left(1+\frac{1+g}{1+R}\right)i^*_t = \frac{1+g}{1+R}E_t i^*_{t+1} + i^*_{t-1} + \frac{1}{(1+g)^2 S''(1+g)}(q^*_t + p^*_{I,t} - p^*_t)$$

Instrument

(B20) $$r_{n,t} = \text{exogenous instrument}$$

Outputs

(B21) $$mc_t = u_{l,t} - u_{c,t} + l_t - \frac{1}{\phi_F}y_t + p_t - p_{H,t}$$

(B22) $$mc^*_t = u^*_{l,t} - u^*_{c,t} + l^*_t - \frac{1}{\phi^*_F}y^*_t + p^*_t - p^*_{F,t}$$

(B23) $$u_{c,t} = \frac{(1-\varrho)(1-\sigma)-1}{1-h_C}(c_t - h_C c_{t-1}) - \frac{L\varrho(1-\sigma)}{1-L} l_t + \varpi[\bar{a} r_{n,t} + (1-\bar{a}) r^*_{n,t}]$$

(B24) $$u^*_{c,t} = \frac{(1-\varrho^*)(1-\sigma^*)-1}{1-h^*_C}(c^*_t - h^*_C c^*_{t-1}) - \frac{L^*\varrho^*(1-\sigma^*)}{1-L^*} l^*_t + \varpi(1) r^*_{n,t}$$

(B25) $$u_{l,t} = \frac{1}{1-h_C}(c_t - h_C c_{t-1}) + \frac{L}{1-L} l_t + u_{c,t} + [\bar{a} r_{n,t} + (1-\bar{a}) r^*_{n,t}]$$

(B26) $$u^*_{l,t} = \frac{1}{1-h^*_C}(c^*_t - h^*_C c^*_{t-1}) + \frac{L^*}{1-L^*}(l^*_t - \varepsilon^*_{L,t}) + u^*_{c,t} + \varepsilon^*_{C,t} + \varpi^*_L r^*_{n,t}$$

(B27) $$y_t = \alpha_{C,H} c_t + \alpha^e_{C,H} c^e_t + \alpha^*_{C,H} c^*_t + \alpha_{I,H} i_t + \alpha^*_{I,H} i^*_t + \alpha_G g_t + [\mu(\alpha_{C,H} + \alpha^e_{C,H})(1-\mathrm{w}) + \mu^*\alpha^*_{C,H}\mathrm{w}^* + \rho_I \alpha_{I,H}(1-\mathrm{w}_I) + \rho^*_I \alpha^*_{I,H}\mathrm{w}^*_I]\tau_t$$

(B28) $$y^*_t = \alpha^*_{C,F} c^*_t + \alpha^{*e}_{C,F} c^{*e}_t + \alpha_{C,F} c_t + \alpha^e_{C,F} c^e_t + \alpha^*_{I,F} i^*_t + \alpha_{I,F} i_t + \alpha^*_G g^*_t - [\mu^*(\alpha^*_{C,F} + \alpha^{*e}_{C,F}) c^{*e}_t (1-\mathrm{w}^*) + \mu\alpha_{C,F}\mathrm{w} + \rho^*_I \alpha^*_{I,F}(1-\mathrm{w}^*_I) + \rho_I \alpha_{I,F}\mathrm{w}_I]\tau_t = c^*_y c^*_t + i^*_y i^*_t + g^*_y g^*_t.$$

(Note small open economy results: $\mathrm{w} = \omega$, $\mathrm{w}_I = \omega_I$, $\mathrm{w}^* = \mathrm{w}^*_I = 1$.)

(B29) $$c^e_t = n_t$$

(B30) $$c^{e*}_t = n^*_t$$

(B31) $$rer^r_t = u^*_{c,t} - u_{c,t}$$

(B32) $$\omega\tau_t = rer_t$$

(B33) $$\theta_t = \chi_\theta(n_t - k_t - q_t) + \epsilon_{P,t}$$

(B34) $$\theta^*_t = \chi^*_\theta(n^*_t - k^*_t - q^*_t) + \epsilon^*_{P,t}$$

(B35) $$E_t(r^k_t) = (1+R)\theta_t + (1+\Theta)(\varphi E_t(r_t) + (1-\varphi)E_t(r^*_t) + (1+R)(E_t(rer_{t+1}) - rer_t))$$

(B36) $$E_t(r^{k*}_t) = (1+R)\theta^*_t + (1+\Theta^*)E_t(r^*_t)$$

(B37) $$r^k_{t-1} = (1-\delta)q_t - (1+R^k)q_{t-1} + (R^k+\delta)x_{t-1}$$

(B38) $$r^{k*}_{t-1} = (1-\delta^*)q^*_t - (1+R^{k*})q^*_{t-1} + (R^{k*}+\delta^*)x^*_{t-1}$$

(B39) $$E_t(r_t) = r_{n,t} - E_t(\pi_{t+1})$$

(B40) $$E_t(r_t^*) = r_{n,t}^* - E_t(\pi_{t+1}^*)$$

(B41) $$p_t - p_{H,t} = (1 - w)\tau_t \to (1 - \omega)\tau_t \text{ as } n \to 0$$

(Note: $p_t^* - p_{F,t}^* = (1 - w^*)\tau^* \to 0$)

(B42) $$p_{I,t} - p_t = (w - w_I)\tau_t \to (\omega - \omega_I)\tau_t$$

(Note: $p_{I,t}^* - p_t^* = (1 - w_I^*)\tau_t \to 0$)

(B43) $$\pi_t = \pi_{H,t} + (1 - \omega)\Delta\tau_t$$

(B44) $$\pi_t^* = \pi_{F,t}^*$$

(B45) $$\pi_{F,t} = \pi_{H,t} + \Delta\tau_t$$

(B46) $$\pi_{H,t}^* = \pi_{F,t}^* - \Delta\tau_t$$

(B47) $$rf_t = \chi_R(r_{n,t} - r_{n,t}^*)$$

(B48) $$(1 - \alpha)l_t = \frac{1}{\phi_F}y_t - a_t - \alpha k_t$$

(B49) $$(1 - \alpha)l_t^* = \frac{1}{\phi_F^*}y_t^* - a_t^* - \alpha k_t^*$$

(B50) $$x_t = y_t + mc_t + p_{H,t} - p_t - k_t$$

(B51) $$x_t^* = y_t^* + mc_t^* - k_t^*$$

(B52) $$E_t\pi_{t+1} = wE_t\pi_{H,t+1} + (1 - w)E_t\pi_{F,t+1}$$

(B53) $$E_t\pi_{F,t+1} = E_t rer_{t+1} - rer_t + E_t\pi_{t+1} - E_t\pi_{t+1}^* + E_t\pi_{F,t+1}^*$$

(B54) $$E_t rer_{t+1} = E_t u_{c,t+1}^* - E_t u_{c,t+1} + E_t[rer_{t+1}^d]$$

(B55) $$r_{n,t}^* = \rho_i^* r_{n,t-1}^* + (1 - \rho_i^*)\theta_\pi^* \pi_{F,t}^* + \varepsilon_{R,t}^*$$

(B56) $$q_t^k = q_t - p_{I,t} + p_t$$

(Note: $q_t^{k*} = q_t^*$)

(Note: $X_t \equiv (P_{H,t}MC_tY_t)/(P_tK_t)$ in [B51].)

Foreign Asset Accumulation and Modified UIP

Linearizing around $B_F = TB = 0$ we define

(B57) $$b_{F,t} \equiv \frac{S_t(B_{F,t} + M_{F,t})}{P_{H,t}Y_t}$$

(B58) $$tb_t \equiv \frac{TB_t}{P_{H,t}Y_t}.$$

Then we have in linearized form

(B59) $$\beta b_{F,t} = \frac{1}{1+g} b_{F,t-1} + tb_t$$

$$tb_t = y_t - \alpha_{C,H} c_t - \alpha^e_{C,H} c^e_t - i_y i_t - g_y g_t - (c_y + i_y)(p_t - p_{H,t}) - i_y(p_{I,t} - p_t).$$

The real exchange rate is the risk-sharing value plus a risk premium deviation given by the system

(B60) $$rer_t = rer^r_t + rer^d_t$$

(B61) $$rer^r_t = u^*_{c,t} - u_{c,t}$$

(B62) $$E_t[rer^d_{t+1}] = rer^d_t + \delta_r b_{F,t} + \varepsilon_{UIP,t}.$$

Appendix C
Calibration and Estimation

We begin with estimates of the processes describing the exogenous shocks.

Shock Parameters

We require the AR1 persistence parameters ρ_a, ρ_g, ρ^*_g, ρ^*_r, ρ_P, ρ_{UIP}, and the corresponding standard deviations of white noise processes, sd_a, sd_g, and so forth. The following have been estimated by ordinary least squares (OLS).

Peru's TFP shock (A_t): AR coefficient: 0.59, SE = 1.1 percent
Peru's fiscal shock (G_t/Y_t): AR coefficient: 0.97, SE = 0.2 percent
U.S. fiscal shock (G_t/Y_t): AR coefficient: 0.78, SE = 0.8 percent
U.S. Taylor Rule:

(C1) $$r^*_{n,t} = 0.94 r^*_{n,t-1} + 0.069\pi^*_{F,t} + 0.22(y^*_t - y^*_{t-1}) + \epsilon^*_{R,t}.$$

SE(ϵ_R) = 0.36 percent. Note that the long run of this rule satisfies the Taylor principle that the real interest rate should respond positively to an increase in inflation.

UIP shock: AR coefficient = 0.96, SE = 0.32 percent

External finance premium shock: In the absence of any estimates in the literature this shock is calibrated to take central values for financial shocks: AR coefficient = 0.95, SE = 0.5 percent.

Preferences

Risk Aversion Parameters: Estimates in the literature suggest the range $\sigma \in [2, 5]$. However, for the United States, Bayesian estimates suggest a range $\sigma^* \in [2, 3]$. Our central estimates are $\sigma = 3$, $\sigma^* = 2$.

Discount Factors: A standard choice is $\beta = \beta^* = 0.99$

Working Day: A standard value is $L^* = 0.40$ for the United States. We choose a slightly higher value $L = 0.5$ for Peru.
Habit Parameters: $h_C = 0.7$ (CMT), $h_C^* = 0.5$ (LOWW)
Substitution Elasticity: A standard choice for small open economies is $\mu = \mu^* = 1.5$.
Elasticity of the marginal utility of consumption with respect to money balances Ψ, Ψ^*: We examine a range $\Psi, \Psi^* \in [0.01, 0.03]$ for which money balances and consumption are complements.
Home currency consumption transactions: $a \in [0, 1]$, $\chi_M = 4$. Estimated by CMT.

Technology

Depreciation Rates: A standard choice is $\delta = \delta^* = 0.025$.
Common World Growth Rate: We choose a realistic common world growth rates: $g = g^* = 3$ percent per annum.
Investment Adjustment Costs: We match Peru with European data using an estimate from SW, for United States we use LOWW obtaining $S''(1 + g) = 6.0$, $[S''(1 + g)]^* = 4.0$ from SW.
Capital Shares: $\alpha = 0.5$ (CMT), $\alpha^* = 0.33$(*LOWW*)
Investment Substitution Elasticities: $\rho_I = \rho_I^* = 0.25$

Financial Accelerator

Elasticity: $\chi_\theta = -0.065$, $\chi_\theta^* = -0.05$ (BGG)
Home currency borrowing for capital: $\varphi \in [0, 1]$
Survival rate: $\xi_e = \xi_e^* = 0.93$ (GGN)
Asset/Debt Ratio: $n_k = 0.4$, $n_k^* = 0.7$ (BGG)
FA Risk Premium: $\Theta = 0.035$, $\Theta^* = 0.05$ (BGG)
UIP Risk Premium: $\delta_r = 0.01$

Market Power

Labor Market Power: $\eta = 3$ (SW), corresponding to a 50 percent markup, $\eta^* = 6$, corresponding to a 20 percent markup.
Product Market Power: $\zeta = 7.67$ corresponding to a 15 percent (SW, LOWW).

Pricing

Calvo Contract: A standard value $\xi_H = \xi_F^* = 0.66$, corresponding to 3 quarter price contracts on average (see CMT).

Consumption, Investment, Money Balance, and Trade Shares

Standard values for the United States are $c_y^* = 0.6$, $i_y^* = 0.2$, $g_y = 0.2$, and $z_y = 0.25$ (the latter $z_y = Z/PY$ is money stock as a proportion of quarterly GDP). For Peru we choose $c_y = 0.7$, $i_y = 0.15$, $g_y = 0.1.5$, and $z_y = 0.25$ (as for the United States).

Trade Shares: Total exports and imports are around 25 percent for Peru so $0.25 = cs_{imports} + is_{imports} = cs_{exports} + is_{exports}$ for balanced trade. Data on consumption and capital goods exports show $is_{imports}/cs_{imports} = 1.6$ and $is_{exports}/cs_{exports} = 0.1$. Hence, we choose $cs_{imports} = 0.10$, $is_{imports} = 0.15$, $cs_{exports} = 0.23$, and $is_{exports} = 0.02$.

Derived Parameters

Given these estimates and data observations, we can now calibrate the following parameters. Preference Parameters (b, θ, ϱ) are found by solving the set of equations

$$\frac{W(1-L)}{PC} = \frac{(1-\alpha)(1-L)}{c_y L}$$

$$\Psi = \frac{(1-b)[(1-\varrho)(1-\sigma) - 1 + (1/\theta)}{bcz[(\theta-1)/\theta] + 1 - b}$$

$$\frac{\Phi}{C\Phi_C} = \frac{(1-b)cz^{(1-\theta)/\theta} + b}{b}$$

$$cz \equiv \frac{C(1-h_C)}{Z}$$

$$\varrho = \frac{[1-(1/\eta)]W(1-L)/PC}{\Phi/(C(1-h_C)\Phi_C) + [1-(1/\eta)]W(1-L)/PC}$$

$$\frac{b(1-h_C)}{1-b}cz^{-1/\theta} = \frac{1+R}{R}.$$

For central values of σ, assuming $\Psi = 0.01$, we obtain: $b = 0.95$, $\theta = 0.28$, $\varrho = 0.17$ for Peru data and $b^* = 0.99$, $\theta = 0.39$, and $\varrho = 0.66$ for U.S. data.

Demand elasticities calibrated from trade data:

$$\alpha_{C,H} = (c_y - cs_{imports})(1 - s_e)$$

$$\alpha^e_{C,H} = (c_y - cs_{imports})s_e$$

$$\alpha^*_{C,H} = cs_{exports}$$

$$\alpha_{I,H} = i_y - is_{imports}$$

$$\alpha^*_{I,H} = is_{exports}$$

$$\alpha^*_{C,F} = c^*_y$$

$$\alpha^{e*}_{C,F} = 0$$

$$\alpha_{C,F} = 0$$

$$\alpha^*_{I,F} = i^*_y$$

$$\alpha_{I,F} = 0$$

$$\alpha_G = g_y$$

$$\alpha^*_G = g^*_y.$$

Note the small open economy implication that $\alpha_{C,F} = \alpha_{I,F} = 0$. Then we have

$$\omega = \frac{\alpha_{C,H} + \alpha^{e}_{C,H}}{c_y} = \frac{c_y - cs_{imports}}{c_y}$$

$$\omega_I = \frac{\alpha_{I,H}}{i_y}.$$

Remaining calibrated parameters are:

$$g_{u_c} = (1+g)^{(1-\varrho)(1-\sigma)-1} - 1$$

$$R = \frac{1}{\beta(1+g_{u_c})} - 1$$

$$R^k = (1+\Theta)(1+R) - 1$$

$$\bar{a} = \bar{a}(a) = \frac{a^{\chi_M}}{a^{\chi_M} + (1-a)^{\chi_M}}$$

$$\alpha = (a + a^{1-\chi}(1-a)^{\chi})^{\theta/(\chi-1)}\left(\frac{(1-b)a}{b(1-\beta)}\right)^{\theta}$$

$$= \left(\frac{(1-b)}{b(1-\beta)}\right)^{\theta} \text{ for } a = 1 \text{ and } a \to 0$$

$$= \frac{1}{2^{\theta}}\left(\frac{(1-b)}{b(1-\beta)}\right)^{\theta} \text{ for } a = \frac{1}{2}$$

$$\alpha^* = \left(\frac{(1-b^*)}{b^*(1-\beta)}\right) \text{(Note: } a^* = 1)$$

$$b_1 = b_1(a) = \frac{b}{(b + (1-b)\alpha^{(\theta-1)/\theta})}$$

$$\varpi = \varpi(a) = \frac{\beta}{1-\beta}[(1-(1-\varrho)(1-\sigma))\theta - 1](1-b_1)$$

$$\lambda_H = \frac{(1-\beta\xi_H)(1-\xi_H)}{\xi_H}$$

$$\chi_R = \frac{\chi_M}{R_n(1+R_n)}$$

$$k_y = \frac{i_y}{g+\delta}$$

$$s_e = \frac{(1-\xi_e)n_k k_y}{\xi_e c_y}$$

$$\varpi_L = \varpi_L(a) = \frac{\beta}{1-\beta}(1-\theta)(1-b_1).$$

Appendix D
Proof of Propositions 1, 2 and Corollary 2

PROPOSITION 1. *To study the FIX regime, we need to augment the system with a definitional equation relating the change in the nominal exchange rate to the change in the terms of trade and inflation. First, we assume that foreign prices are fixed, so in log terms* $0 = \Delta p^*_{F,t} = \Delta(p_{F,t} - s_t) = \Delta(p_{H,t} + \tau_t - s_t)$, *where* τ_t *is the terms of trade in deviation form. Thus,*

$$s_t = s_{t-1} + \tau_t - \tau_{t-1} + \pi_{Ht}. \tag{D1}$$

In addition, from the first-order conditions for consumption, we have a relationship between the real exchange rate and marginal utility of consumption $rer_t = u^*_{c,t} - u_{c,t}$, and linearization of (10) yields $rer_t = \omega\tau_t$. Hence,

$$s_t = s_{t-1} - \frac{1}{\omega}[u_{ct} - u_{c,t-1} - (u^*_{c,t} - u^*_{c,t-1})] + \pi_{Ht}. \tag{D2}$$

Note that the implication of this equation is that feedback on the nominal exchange rate via (52) is a form of "integral control" (i.e., a sum of all past values) on inflation. It is known that integral control rules are very robust in terms of their stabilization properties.

Now put $r_{n,t} = r^*_{n,t} + \theta_s s_t$, as discussed previously; it is now easy to show that taken together with (62), this implies

$$E_t s_{t+1} = (1 + \theta_s)s_t, \tag{D3}$$

from which we deduce that the nominal exchange rate is given by $s_t = 0$ for all t. Note that this implies from (D2) that $u_{c,t}$ and $\pi_{H,t}$ are related under this feedback regime and therefore cannot "jump" independently of one another. Thus, we require that the part of the system that describes the joint behavior of these two variables must have one stable and one unstable eigenvalue. It is easy now to ascertain that their joint characteristic equation becomes

$$(z - 1)(\beta z - 1) - \gamma\omega z = 0, \tag{D4}$$

where z is the forward operator. It is also easy to show that one root of this equation is greater than 1, and the other lies between 0 and 1. Hence, proposition 1 follows.

PROPOSITION 2. *Ignoring all exogenous and stochastic variables, yields a characteristic equation for (60), (65), and (62) given by*

$$(z - \rho)[(z - 1)(\beta z - 1) - \gamma\omega z] + (1 - \rho)\theta_\pi z[\kappa(z - 1) + \omega\gamma] = 0. \tag{D5}$$

The effects of dollarization can be assessed through the variation in κ, which is a function of a, where $1 - a$ is the degree of dollarization.

As pointed out in the previous section, the case of no dollarization is easily seen to be equivalent to that of a separable utility function. Indeed, for the case $\omega = 1$, this is equivalent to the case of a closed economy. For the case of a partially dollarized economy, $\kappa > 0$ is possible when consumption and real balances are complements, and it turns out that the results depend on the degree of dollarization.

For determinacy, since there are two jump variables, we require exactly two unstable roots. First note that when $\theta_\pi = 0$, the eigenvalues of the system are given by ρ and the roots of $(z - 1)(\beta z - 1) - \gamma\omega z$; it is easy to show that one of the latter roots is greater and the other is less than 1, so the system is indeterminate. As $\theta_\pi \to \infty$, the roots tend to $-\infty$ and $1 - \omega\gamma/\kappa$, so that the system has two unstable roots if $1 - \omega\gamma/\kappa < -1$, as in (b), as required for determinacy, but only one unstable root for (b).

Equation (D.9) describes the root locus method that enables to track the path of the roots in the complex plane as θ_π changes. In this case, it is easy to show that the smaller of the two stable roots heads for $z = 0$ as θ_π increases to ∞. Also, as θ_π increases to a value slightly beyond 1, the other two roots move closer to one another. They merge into a double root at a value of $z > 1$; to show this, we note that $z = 1$ when $\theta_\pi = 1$, so we need to prove that increasing θ_π beyond 1 leads to a root larger than 1. It is trivial to show that this follows from the fact that

$$\text{(D6)} \qquad \left.\frac{\partial z}{\partial \theta_\pi}\right|_{\theta_\pi = z = 1} = \frac{\gamma\omega}{\gamma\omega + (1 - \rho)(1 - \beta - \kappa)}.$$

This is greater than 0 for both (a) and (b). From this double root there are then two branches out into the complex plane, which merge for a much larger value of θ_π on to the negative part of the real axis, and then the roots diverge, one to $-\infty$, and the other to $1 - \omega\gamma/\kappa$. Thus for case (b), there are two unstable roots for all θ_π, provided that the root locus does not pass through the unit circle. Likewise for (a), if it does not pass through the unit circle, then there are two unstable roots for $1 < \theta_\pi < \overline{\theta}_\pi$, where $\overline{\theta}_\pi$ is the value of θ_π such that there is a root at $z = -1$; there is an additional proviso, that the root locus passes through the point -1 from the left. But this follows from

$$\text{(D7)} \qquad \left.\frac{\partial z}{\partial \theta_\pi}\right|_{z=-1} = \frac{(1-\rho)(2\kappa - \gamma\omega)}{(1+\rho)(1-\beta) + (2(1+\beta) = \beta\omega)[\gamma\omega - (1-\rho)\kappa]/(2\kappa - \gamma\omega)}$$

which is also greater than 0 for case (b). Finally we need to show that when the root locus is off the real line, it does not cross the unit circle, which is characterized by $z = e^{i\psi} = \cos\psi + i\sin\psi$. To find a potential crossing, we substitute this into (D5) (with $\rho = 0, j = 0$), then multiply by $e^{i\psi}$ and equate real and imaginary parts to 0. These yield

$$\text{(D8)} \qquad 0 = \beta\cos 2\psi - (1 + \beta + \omega\gamma + \rho + \rho\beta)\cos\psi + 1 + \rho(1 + \beta + \omega\gamma) + \theta_\pi(1 - \rho)(\kappa\cos\psi + \omega\gamma - \kappa)$$

(D9) $0 = \beta \sin 2\psi - (1 + \beta + \omega\gamma - \rho + \rho\beta) \sin \psi + \theta_\pi(1 - \rho)\kappa \sin \psi.$

There are obviously roots at $\sin \psi = 0$, which corresponds to (i) $z = 1, \theta_\pi = 1$, which explains why we there is indeterminacy for $\theta_\pi < 1$ (ii) $z = -1$, which only corresponds to positive θ_π for case (a). The alternative, after removing the factor $\sin \psi$ from (D9), is that $0 = 2\beta \cos \psi - (1 + \beta + \omega\gamma - \rho + \rho\beta) + \theta_\pi(1 - \rho)\kappa$. Substituting for $\cos \psi$ from this expression into (D8) yields a unique value of θ_π. But for the locus to branch at a value of $z > 1$, and return to the real line at a value of $z < -1$, it needs to cross the unit circle twice, but this is ruled out by this unique value of θ_π.[27]

Corollary 2. *First note that of all the parameters in (D5), only* κ *is dependent on dollarization, via the term* $\bar{a}(1 - b_1)$. *The effect of increasing a on this term is given by*

$$\text{(D10)} \quad \frac{d(\bar{a}(1 - b_1))}{da} = \frac{\chi_M B(a^{\chi_M} + (1 - a)^{\chi_M})^{(\theta-1)/(\chi_M-1)}}{(a^{\chi_M} + (1 - a)^{\chi_M})^2(b + B(a^{\chi_M} + (1 - a)^{\chi_M})^{(\theta-1)/(\chi_M-1)})^2}$$
$$\left[a^{\chi_M-1}(1 - a)^{\chi_M-1}(b + B(a^{\chi_M} + (1 - a)^{\chi_M})^{(\theta-1)/(\chi_M-1)}) + \frac{\theta - 1}{\chi_M - 1} b a^{\chi_M}(a^{\chi_M-1} - (1 - a)^{\chi_M-1})\right],$$

where $B = (1 - b)^\theta b^{1-\theta}(1 - \beta)^{1-\theta}$.

Given that $\theta < 1$, and in our calibrations we use $\chi_M > 1$, it is easy to see that this is increasing for $a < 1/2$. But dollarization is associated with decreasing a, which leads to a decrease in κ as a decrease from 1/2 to 0. Thus, we have corollary 2 in the main text.

Appendix E
Quadratic Approximation of the Welfare Loss

The basic idea is to obtain the quadratic approximation to the social planner's problem, coupled with a term in inflation, which arises from price dispersion. We adopt a "small distortions" approximation, which is accurate as long as the zero inflation steady-state is close to the social optimum. As we have noted in the main text, the existence of external habit offsets the distortions in the product and labor markets. For our calibrated high value for the

27. For the case $(1 - \rho)\kappa > \gamma\omega$, the unit circle could be crossed once by the root locus, implying that there may be a limited range of determinacy.

habit parameter h_C, this leaves the steady state of the decentralized economy close to the social optimum, justifying the small distortions approximation.

Consider the social planner's problem to maximize

$$\text{(E1)} \qquad \sum_{t=0}^{\infty} \beta^t \frac{(C_t - h_C C_{t-1})^{(1-\varrho)(1-\sigma)}(1 - L_t)^{\varrho(1-\sigma)}}{1 - \sigma},$$

subject to the (resource) constraints:

$$\text{(E2)} \quad 1 - \omega + \omega T_t^{\mu-1} = E_t^{\mu-1} \quad 1 - \omega_I + \omega_I T_t^{\rho_I-1} = E_{It}^{\rho_I-1} \quad K_t = (1 - \delta)K_{t-1} + I_t$$

$$\text{(E3)} \quad Y_t + \Phi = A_t K_{t-1}^{\alpha} L_t^{1-\alpha} = \omega E_t^{-\mu} T_t^{\mu} C_t + (1 - \omega^*) T_t^{\mu} C_t^* + \omega_I E_{It}^{-\rho_I} T_t^{\rho_I} I_t + (1 - \omega_I^*) T_t^{\rho_I^*} I_t^* + G_t$$

where the terms of trade are given by $T = P_F/P_H$, and the real exchange rate as $E = SP^*/P$, so that $E^{1-\mu} = P_F^{1-\mu}/[\omega P_H^{1-\mu} + (1-\omega)P_F^{1-\mu}]$. There is a risk-sharing condition given by

$$\text{(E4)} \quad E_t = \frac{U_{C_t^*}^*}{U_{C_t}} \quad E_t C_t^{(1-\varrho)(1-\sigma)-1}(1 - L_t)^{\varrho(1-\sigma)} = C_t^{*(1-\varrho)(1-\sigma)-1}(1 - L_t^*)^{\varrho(1-\sigma)}$$

where we assume initial wealth per capita is the same in each country.

The Lagrangian for the problem may be written as

$$\text{(E5)} \quad \sum_{t=0}^{\infty} \beta^t \Bigg[\frac{(C_t - Z_t)^{(1-\varrho)(1-\sigma)}(1 - L_t)^{\varrho(1-\sigma)}}{1 - \sigma} + \lambda_{1t}(Z_t - h_C C_{t-1}) + \lambda_{2t}(\omega E_t^{-\mu} T_t^{\mu} C_t + (1 - \omega^*) T_t^{\mu} C_t^* + \omega_I E_{It}^{-\rho_I} T_t^{\rho_I} I_t + (1 - \omega_I^*) T_t^{\rho_I^*} I_t^* + G_t - A_t K_{t-1}^{\alpha} L_t^{1-\alpha}) + \lambda_{3t}(1 - \omega + \omega T_t^{\mu-1} - E_t^{\mu-1}) + \lambda_{4t}(1 - \omega_I + \omega_I T_t^{\rho_I-1} - E_{It}^{\rho_I-1}) + \lambda_{5t}(E_t C_t^{(1-\varrho)(1-\sigma)-1}(1 - L_t)^{\varrho(1-\sigma)} - U_{C^*}) + \lambda_{6t}(K_t - (1 - \delta)K_{t-1} - I_t) \Bigg].$$

First-order conditions with respect to C, Z, E, T, E_I, I, L, and K yield

$$\text{(E6)} \quad 0 = (1 - \varrho)(C - Z)^{(1-\varrho)(1-\sigma)-1}(1 - L)^{\varrho(1-\sigma)} - \beta\lambda_1 h_C + \lambda_2 \omega E^{-\mu} T^{\mu} + \lambda_5[(1 - \sigma)(1 - \varrho) - 1]E(C - Z)^{(1-\varrho)(1-\sigma)-1}(1 - L)^{\varrho(1-\sigma)}$$

$$\text{(E7)} \quad 0 = -(1 - \varrho)(C - Z)^{(1-\varrho)(1-\sigma)-1}(1 - L)^{\varrho(1-\sigma)} + \lambda_1 + \lambda_5[(1 - \sigma)(1 - \varrho) - 1]E(C - Z)^{(1-\varrho)(1-\sigma)-1}(1 - L)^{\varrho(1-\sigma)}$$

$$\text{(E8)} \quad 0 = -\lambda_2 \mu \omega E^{-\mu-1} T^{\mu} C - \lambda_3(\mu - 1)E^{\mu-2} + \lambda_5(C - Z)^{(1-\varrho)(1-\sigma)-1} \cdot (1 - L)^{\varrho(1-\sigma)}$$

$$\text{(E9)} \quad 0 = \lambda_2 T^{\mu-1}(\omega E^{-\mu} C + (1 - \omega)C^*) + \lambda_2 \rho_I T^{\rho_I-1}(\omega_I E_I^{-\rho_I} I + (1 - \omega_I)I^* + \lambda_3 \omega(\mu - 1)T^{\mu-2} + \lambda_4 \omega_I(\rho_I - 1)T^{\rho_I-2}$$

(E10) $0 = -\lambda_2\rho_I\omega_I E_I^{-\rho_I - 1}T^{\rho_I}I - \lambda_4(\rho_I - 1)E_I^{\rho_I}$

(E11) $0 = \lambda_2\omega_I E_I^{-\rho_I}T_{\rho_I} - \lambda_6$

(E12) $0 = -\varrho(C - Z)^{(1-\varrho)(1-\sigma)}(1 - L)^{\varrho(1-\sigma)-1} - \lambda_2 A(1 - \alpha)K^{\alpha}L^{-\alpha}$

$$- \lambda_5\varrho(1 - \sigma)E(C - Z)^{(1-\varrho)(1-\sigma)-1}(1 - L)^{\varrho(1-\sigma)-1}$$

(E13) $0 = \lambda_2\alpha AK^{\alpha-1}L^{1-\alpha} + \lambda_6\left(\frac{1}{\beta} - 1 + \delta\right).$

In steady state these satisfy

(E14) $\alpha A\left(\frac{L}{K}\right)^{1-\alpha} = \omega_I\left(\frac{1}{\beta} - 1 + \delta\right) = \omega_I R_K \quad \lambda_4(1 - \rho_I) = \lambda_2\rho_I\omega_I I$

(E15) $\lambda_3\omega(1 - \mu) = \lambda_2(\mu_C + \rho_I(1 - \omega_I^2)I) \quad (1 - \beta h_C)\lambda_1 = -\omega\lambda_2$

(E16) $\lambda_5 F = -\frac{\lambda_2}{\omega}[\mu(1 - \omega^2)C + \rho_I(1 - \omega_I^2)I]$

where

(E17) $F = (C(1 - h_C))^{(1-\varrho)(1-\sigma)-1}(1 - L)^{\varrho(1-\sigma)}.$

Also define

(E18) $F_1 = (C(1 - h_C))^{(1-\varrho)(1-\sigma)}(1 - L)^{\varrho(1-\sigma)} = C(1 - h_C)F.$

It can be shown that the second-order expansion is given by the sum of the following terms

(E19) $$\frac{F_1}{2}\left(\frac{(1 - \varrho)[(1 - \sigma)(1 - \varrho) - 1](c_t - h_C c_{t-1})^2}{(1 - h_C)^2} - 2\frac{(1 - \sigma)(1 - \varrho)\varrho L(c_t - h_C c_{t-1})lt}{(1 - h_C)(1 - L)} + \frac{\varrho[(1 - \sigma)\varrho - 1]L^2 l_t^2}{(1 - L)^2}\right)$$

(which is negative definite)

(E20) $$\left(\frac{\lambda_2 C\mu}{2}[2\omega^3 - 3\omega + 1 + \mu\omega(1 - \omega)^2] + \frac{\lambda_2 I\rho_I}{2}[(1 - \omega_I)^2(\mu\omega - 3\omega - \mu) + 1 - \omega_I^3 + \rho_I(1 - 3\omega_I^2 + 2\omega_I^3]\right)\tau_t^2$$

(E21) $\frac{\lambda_2 A\alpha(1 - \alpha)K^{\alpha}L^{1-\alpha}}{2}(k_{t-1} - l_t)^2 - \lambda_2 AK^{\alpha}L^{1-\alpha}[(1 - \alpha)l_t + \alpha k_{t-1}]a_t$

(E22) $$\lambda_2(\mu\omega(1 - \omega)Cc_t + \mu(1 - \omega^*)Cc_t^* + \rho_I\omega_I(1 - \omega_I)Ii_t + \rho_I^*(1 - \omega_I^*)Ii_t^*)\tau_t$$

(E23) $$\lambda_2(\mu(1-\omega^2)C+\rho_I(1-\omega^2)I)\cdot\left([(1-\sigma)(1-\varrho)-1]\frac{c_t^*-h_C c_{t-1}^*}{1-h_C}-(1-\sigma)\varrho\frac{L^* l_t^*}{1-L^*}\right)\tau_t.$$

Price dispersion arising from price setting behavior by firms yields a second-order term

(E24) $$-\frac{\varrho L F_1}{2(1-L)}\frac{\zeta\xi_H}{(1-\xi_H)(1-\beta\xi_H)}\pi_t^2.$$

Finally, we require an expression for λ_2, which is obtained from

(E25) $$\lambda_2\left(A(1-\alpha)\left(\frac{K}{L}\right)^\alpha+\frac{\varrho(1-\sigma)}{\omega(1-L)}[\mu(\omega^2-1)C+\rho_I(\omega_I^2-1)I]\right)=-\frac{\varrho C(1-h_C)F}{1-L}.$$

If $\sigma > 1$, it follows that $\lambda_2 < 0$. Note, too, that we may write

(E26) $$\lambda_2=-\frac{\varrho c_y(1-h_C)F}{[(1-\alpha)R_K\omega_I k_y/\alpha][(1-L)/L]+[\varrho(1-\sigma)/\omega][\mu(\omega^2-1)c_y+\rho_I(\omega_I^2-1)i_y]}.$$

Finally we can divide all terms by FY, and by writing $F_1 = FY(1-h_C)c_y$, we can obtain all weights in terms of ratios c_y, i_y, k_y, $(1-L)/L$, and parameters.

Note that there is an issue here of which values C, L we use in all of these expressions. There is an additional representation of λ_2 for the social planner's problem, which leads ultimately to a linear relationship between C and L, and then via the goods market equation to a complete expression for each of these. One can go through this procedure, or just use the steady-state values of observed ratios C/Y, I/Y, and G/Y. We choose to do the latter.

To obtain the quadratic form, define

(E27) $$cmcl_t=\frac{c_t-h_C c_{t-1}}{1-h_C}$$

(E28) $$kml_t=k_{t-1}-l_t$$

(E29) $$ccii_t=\mu\omega(1-\omega)c_y c_t+\mu(1-\omega^*)c_y c_t^*+\rho_I\omega_I(1-\omega_I)i_y i_t+\rho_I^*(1-\omega_I^*)i_y i_t^*$$

(E30) $$ccsls_t=[(1-\sigma)(1-\varrho)-1]\frac{c_t^*-h_C c_{t-1}^*}{1-h_C}-(1-\sigma)\varrho\frac{L^* l_t^*}{1-L^*}.$$

And define

(E31) $$\lambda=\frac{\varrho c_y(1-h_C)}{[(1-\alpha)R_K\omega_I k_y/\alpha][(1-L)/L]+[\varrho(1-\sigma)/\omega][\mu(\omega^2-1)c_y+\rho_I(\omega_I^2-1)i_y]}.$$

Converting the welfare approximation into welfare loss, and dividing by FY leads to

$$\text{(E32)}\quad 2W = -(1-h_C)c_y\Bigg((1-\varrho)[(1-\sigma)(1-\varrho)-1]cmcl_t^2 - 2(1-\sigma)\varrho(1-\varrho)cmcl_t\frac{Ll_t}{1-L} + \frac{\varrho[(1-\sigma)\varrho-1]L^2l_t^2}{(1-L)^2}\Bigg)$$
$$-\left(\lambda c_y\mu[2\omega^3-3\omega+1+\mu\omega(1-\omega)^2]+\frac{\lambda i_y\rho_I}{2}\right.$$
$$\left.\cdot[(1-\omega_I)^2(\mu\omega-3\omega-\mu)+1-\omega_I^3+\rho_I(1-3\omega_I^2+2\omega_I^3)]\right)\tau_t^2$$
$$-\lambda\frac{\Phi+Y}{Y}\alpha(1-\alpha)kml_t^2+2\lambda\frac{\Phi+Y}{Y}y_ta_t-2\lambda ccii_t\tau_t$$
$$-2\lambda ccsls_t\tau_t+\frac{\varrho L(1-h_C)}{(1-L)}\frac{\zeta\xi_H}{(1-\xi_H)(1-\beta\xi_H)}\pi_t^2,$$

which corresponds to (57) in the main text.

The change in welfare for a small change in consumption-equivalent over all periods is given by

$$\text{(E33)}\quad \Delta\Omega = (1-\rho)\sum_{t=0}^{\infty}\beta^tC(1-h_C)^{(1-\sigma)(1-\rho)-1}(1-L)^{\rho(1-\sigma)}(\Delta C-h_C\Delta C)$$
$$=\frac{(1-\rho)(1-h_C)c_y}{1-\beta}FYc_e.$$

Ignoring the term in $FY = C(1-h_C)^{(1-\sigma)(1-\rho)-1}(1-L)^{\rho(1-\sigma)}Y$, since all the welfare loss terms have been normalized by this, we can rewrite this as

$$\text{(E34)}\qquad c_e = \frac{(1-\beta)\Delta\Omega}{(1-\rho)(1-h_C)c_y}.$$

Furthermore, if all welfare loss terms have been further normalized by $(1-\beta)$, and that all variances are expressed in percent^2, it follows that we can write c_e in percent terms as

$$\text{(E35)}\qquad c_e = \frac{\Delta\Omega}{(1-\rho)(1-h_C)c_y}\times 10^{-2},$$

which corresponds to (61) in the main text.

References

Adam, K., and R. M. Billi. 2007. Discretionary monetary policy and the zero lower bound on nominal interest rates. *Journal of Monetary Economics* 54 (3): 728–52.

Aoki, K., and T. Kimura. 2007. Uncertainty about perceived inflation target and monetary policy. Paper presented at the Bundesbank-Federal Reserve Bank of

Cleveland Conference Monetary Policy: Old and New Challenges. 6–7 June, Frankfurt am Main.
Barro, R., and X. Sala-i-Martin. 2004. *Economic growth,* 2nd ed. New York: McGraw-Hill.
Batini, N., P. Breuer, and K. Kochhar. 2006. Inflation targeting and the IMF. International Monetary Fund Board Paper. Washington, DC: IMF.
Batini, N., R. Harrison, and S. Millard. 2003. Monetary policy rules for open economies. *Journal of Economic Dynamics and Control* 27 (11–12): 2059–94.
Batini, N., P. Levine, and J. Pearlman. 2004. Indeterminancy with inflation-forecast-based rules in a two-bloc model. European Central Bank (ECB) Discussion Paper no. 340 and Federal Reserve Board (FRB) Discussion Paper no. 797, presented at the International Research Forum on Monetary Policy. 14–15 November, Washington, DC.
Benigno, P. 2001. Price stability with imperfect financial integration. CEPR Discussion Paper no. 2854.
Benigno, G., and P. Benigno. 2004. Exchange rate determination under interest rate rules. Revised version of Center for Economic Policy Research (CEPR) Discussion Paper no. 2807, 2001.
Bernanke, B., M. Gertler, and S. Gilchrist. 1999. The financial accelerator in quantitative business cycles. In *Handbook of macroeconomics,* vol. 1C, ed. M. Woodford and J. B. Taylor, Amsterdam: Elsevier Science.
Calvo, G., and F. Mishkin. 2003. The mirage of exchange rate regimes for emerging market countries. *Journal of Economic Perspectives* 17 (4): 99–118.
Castillo, P., C. Montoro, and V. Tuesta. 2006. An estimated stochastic general equilibrium model with partial dollarization: A Bayesian approach. Central Bank of Chile Working Paper no. 381.
Cespedes, L. F., R. Chang, and A. Velasco. 2004. Balance sheets and exchange rate policy. *American Economic Review* 94 (4): 1183–93.
Coenen, G., and V. Wieland. 2003. The zero-interest rate bound and the role of the exchange rate for monetary policy in Japan. *Journal of Monetary Economics* 50 (5): 1071–1101.
Eggertsson, G. 2006. The deflation bias and committing to being irresponsible. *Journal of Money, Credit and Banking* 36 (2): 283–322.
Eggertsson, G., and M. Woodford. 2003. The zero interest-rate bound and optimal monetary policy. *Brooking Papers on Economic Activity* 1: 139–211. Washington, DC: Brookings Institution.
Felices, G., and V. Tuesta. 2006. Monetary policy in a partially dollarized economy. Mimeo.
Gertler, M., S. Gilchrist, and F. M. Natalucci. 2003. External constraints on monetary policy and the financial accelerator. NBER Working Paper no. 10128. Cambridge, MA: National Bureau of Economic Research, December.
Gesell, S. 1934. *The natural economic order.* Trans. Philip Pye. San Antonio, TX: Free-Economy Publishing.
Gilchrist, S. 2003. Financial markets and financial leverage in a two-country word-Economy. Central Bank of Chile Working Paper no. 228.
Gilchrist, S., J.-O. Hairault, and H. Kempf. 2002. Monetary policy and the financial accelerator in a monetary union. European Central Bank Working Paper no. 175.
International Monetary Fund. 2005. Does inflation targeting work in emerging markets? In *World economic outlook,* chapter 4. Washington, DC: IMF, fall.
Keynes, J. M. 1936. The general theory of employment, interest and money. New York: Macmillan.
Levin, A., A. Onatski, J. C. Williams, and N. Williams. 2006. Monetary policy under

uncertainty in micro-founded macroeconomic models. In *NBER Macroeconomics Annual, 2005,* ed. M. Gertler and K. Rogoff, 229–387. Cambridge, MA: MIT Press.

Levine, P., P. McAdam, and J. Pearlman. 2007. Quantifying and sustaining welfare gains from monetary commitment. ECB Working Paper no. 709. Presented at the 12th International Conference on Computing in Economics and Finance. June, Cyprus.

Levine, P., J. Pearlman, and R. Pierse. 2006. Linear-quadratic approximation, efficiency and target-implementability. Paper presented at the 12th International Conference on Computing in Economics and Finance. June, Cyprus.

Levy Yeyati, E. 2006. Financial dollarization: Evaluating the consequences. *Economic Policy* 21 (45): 61–118.

Obstfeld, M., and K. Rogoff. 1995. Exchange rate dynamics redux. *Journal of Political Economy* 103 (3): 624–60.

Primiceri, G. 2006. Comment on "Monetary policy under uncertainty in micro-founded macroeconomic models." In *NBER macroeconomics annual, 2005,* ed. M. Gertler and K. Rogoff, 289–296. Cambridge, MA: MIT Press.

Ravenna, F., and C. E. Walsh. 2006. Optimal monetary policy with the cost channel. *Journal of Monetary Economics* 53 (2): 199–216.

Smets, F., and R. Wouters. 2003. An estimated Stochastic Dynamic General Equilibrium Model of the euro area. *Journal of the European Economic Association* 1 (5): 1123–75.

Woodford, M. 2003. *Foundations of a theory of monetary policy.* Princeton, NJ: Princeton University Press.

Comment Frederic S. Mishkin

There are several key features of emerging market economies that make them very different from advanced economies: they have weak fiscal, monetary policy, and financial institutional frameworks that lead to high levels of transactions and liabilities denominated in foreign currencies (dollarization) and larger credit market imperfections.[1] The chapter by Batini, Levine, and Pearlman is very nice because, given the special features of emerging market economies, it asks exactly the right questions in examining macroeconomic policy issues in these economies: (a) How do financial frictions affect macroeconomic volatility and monetary policy? (b) Because of extensive dollarization, should the exchange rate have a special role in monetary policy?

In my discussion of the chapter, I will first discuss what it does, as well as

Frederic S. Mishkin is the Alfred Lerner Professor of Banking and Financial Institutions, Graduate School of Business, Columbia University, and a research associate of the National Bureau of Economic Research.

For presentation at the NBER conference on International Dimensions of Monetary Policy S'Agaró, Catalonia, Spain, June 12, 2007. The views expressed in this chapter are exclusively those of the author and do not necessarily reflect those of Columbia University, the National Bureau of Economic Research, the Board of Governors, or the Federal Reserve System.

1. For example, see Calvo and Mishkin (2003) and Mishkin (2006).

their model, describe their results, and then ask whether the results are right and what policy conclusions should we draw from them.

The Model

The chapter develops a small open economy dynamic stochastic general equilibrium (DSGE) model along the lines of Gertler, Gilchrist, and Natalucci (2007) to examine the effects of volatility and monetary policy from (a) transactions dollarization (TD), (b) credit market imperfections (financial accelerator [FA], and (c) liability dollarization (the denomination of debts in foreign currency, often dollars, which they refer to as financial dollarization [FD].[2] Their model has several unique features that distinguish it from the standard open economy model: (a) money enters the utility function in a nonseparable way so there is an effect of interest rate on aggregate supply; (b) households derive utility from both domestic and foreign (dollar) money holdings; (c) firms have some of their debt in foreign currency (liability dollarization); and (d) there is a financial accelerator because there are financial frictions.

While I applaud the basic framework of their model, I have concerns about their approach to modeling transactions dollarization using money in the utility function. I have always been skeptical of deriving the demand for money and thinking about the monetary transmission mechanism using money in the utility function. The results from this approach are very dependent on the exact form of the utility function, about which we know little. For example, in their model, utility is nonseparable in all its arguments and there are strong assumptions about cross derivatives and second derivatives that are not immediately obvious. In addition, putting money in the utility function does not always provide us with good intuition as to what is going on. An alternative way to go is transactions-based approaches, which might provide clearer intuition on the role of money, and therefore make it easier for us to evaluate results. However, embedding a transactions-based approach to the role of money may not be easy to do in their model, and transactions-based approaches can have their own problems if they make unattractive assumptions to make them tractable. Nonetheless, their use of money in the utility function casts some doubt on particular results, as I will discuss later.

The second set of issues with their modeling approach is that their results are likely to be highly dependent on the modeling assumptions, especially on their choices about the values of calibrated parameters. Let me give four examples. First, expenditure-switching effects from exchange rate changes are apparently small in their model, relative to balance sheet effects, because

2. Batini, Levine, and Pearlman use the nonstandard term "financial dollarization," which I think is confusing because it could encompass dollarization of transactions while the authors mean for it to refer to dollarization of liabilities only.

of their calibration choices. Expenditure-switching and balance sheet effects work in opposite directions, so this feature of their model has important implications. In contrast to their paper, Céspedes, Chang, and Velasco (2004) find that in emerging market economies with small or moderate debt to net worth, exchange rate depreciation is actually expansionary in an emerging market economy because the stimulus from expenditure-switching effects are greater than the contractionary balance sheet effects. Second, the inflation measure used in the Taylor rule is a domestic rather than an aggregate measure like the consumer price index (CPI). This is quite nonstandard because most Taylor rules use aggregate inflation measures. Third, the pass-through from exchange rate changes appears to be complete in their model. Fourth, the loss function for welfare comparisons is affected by calibration choices.

The bottom line is that to really be convinced by the results, we need to see them exposed to a robustness analysis for key parameters in the model involving habit persistence, trade elasticities, shares of imported goods in investment, debt to net worth, and so forth. The authors are aware of this and indicate that they do plan to do this in future research.

Results

There are five major results derived from the model in the chapter. First, transactions dollarization is not a big deal. Transactions dollarization has little impact on volatility. Indeed, the welfare loss even falls with greater transactions dollarization because the supply-side effect from interest rate changes declines, making monetary policy more effective. Second, the financial accelerator and liability dollarization are a "lethal cocktail for welfare." Third, the simple Taylor rule as a guide to monetary policy is only slightly suboptimal. Fourth, fixed exchange rate regimes are very bad. Fifth, in a flexible exchange rate regime, the monetary authorities should not respond to the exchange rate in their Taylor rule.

Are Their Conclusions Right?

Let's look at each of these results in turn. The result that transactions dollarization is not very important to how the economy in an emerging market country behaves sounds right to me. Even with a different model, it is hard to think that the form of the transactions medium is a big deal to welfare. On the other hand, my skepticism about using money in the utility function as a modeling strategy makes me suspicious of the result that more transactions dollarization makes the economy better off. A different transactions-based model or different assumptions about the utility function might lead to a different result.

I strongly believe that the result that credit market imperfections and liability dollarization in emerging market economies is a "lethal cocktail" is right on the money. Other theoretical models[3] and detailed studies of financial crises in emerging market countries that I have described in my recent book (Mishkin 2006) strongly supports this conclusion. The lethal cocktail leads to two important policy conclusions that I stress in my book. First, it is imperative that emerging market countries promote reforms to improve their institutional framework—legal system, disclosure of information, and prudential supervision of the financial system. Not only are these reforms crucial to economic growth, but they also reduce lower credit market imperfections and make the economy more financially robust; that is, less susceptible to financial crises.

Second, emerging market countries need to take steps to limit *currency mismatch* (debts denominated in foreign currency when the value of production is denominated in domestic currency). One way of doing this is through prudential regulation and supervision, which can be used to restrict financial institutions from lending in foreign currency to firms whose output is denominated in domestic currency. In their model, they do not allow for indexation of debt. Reducing currency mismatch can also be promoted by encouraging debt that is indexed to inflation, as was done in Chile, which then decreases the incentives for denominating debt in foreign currency (liability dollarization). Good monetary policy that results in both low and stable inflation also can help discourage liability dollarization.

I also strongly agree with the conclusion that fixed exchange rate regimes are usually a bad idea for emerging market economies. Financial crises are far more likely in emerging market countries that have fixed exchange rates for the reasons outlined in their model. Fixed exchange rate regimes are subject to speculative attacks and if these attacks are successful, the collapse of the domestic currency is usually much larger, more rapid, and more unanticipated than when a depreciation occurs under a floating exchange rate regime. Then, as the mechanisms in the model in this chapter illustrate, fixed exchange rate regimes make an emerging market economy especially vulnerable to the twin crises of Kaminsky and Reinhart (1999), in which the currency collapses, destroys firms' and households' balance sheets, and then provokes a financial crisis and a sharp economic contraction. Supporting this view is the fact that countries exiting from pegged exchange rate regimes are more prone to higher cost financial crises and large declines in output the longer the exchange rate peg has been in place.[4]

However, there are additional reasons why fixed exchange rate regimes are likely to lead to more financially fragile economies in emerging market countries that the chapter does not explore. In their model, the level of liability dollarization is exogenous and so they do not allow for another channel

3. For example, Calvo and Mendoza (2000); Aghion, Bacchetta, and Banerjee (2000, 2001); Céspedes, Chang, and Velasco (2004); Eichengreen and Hausmann (2004); Schneider and Tornell (2004); and Caballero and Krishnamurthy (2005).

4. Aizenman and Glick (2008); Eichengreen and Masson (1998); and Eichengreen (1999).

that causes fixed exchange rate regimes to lower welfare. Fixed exchange rate regimes are likely to encourage liability dollarization.[5] Then as Batini, Levine, and Pearlman indicate, greater liability dollarization leads to greater macroeconomic volatility and much lower welfare.

Furthermore, by providing a more stable value of the currency, an exchange rate peg can lower the perceived risk for foreign investors and thus encourage capital inflows. Although these capital inflows might be channeled into productive investments and stimulate growth, the presence of a government safety net and weak bank supervision can lead instead to excessive lending. An outcome of the capital inflow is then likely to be a lending boom, an explosion of nonperforming loans and an eventual financial crisis as is described in the case studies in my recent book (Mishkin 2006).

A fixed exchange rate regime also can also make it easier for countries to tap foreign markets for credit and so make it easier for the government to engage in irresponsible fiscal policy because it is easier for it to sell its debt. Argentina provides a graphic example of this problem (Mussa 2002). When its fiscal policy became unsustainable, it provoked a disastrous crisis that pushed it into a great depression.

Given the experience with fixed exchange rate regimes, Stanley Fischer—who was the first deputy managing director of the International Monetary Fund (IMF)—has stated that, "The adoption of flexible exchange rate systems by most emerging market countries is by far the most important emerging market crisis prevention measure." (Fischer 2003, 19). A flexible exchange rate regime has the advantage that movements in the exchange rate are much less nonlinear than in a pegged exchange rate regime. Indeed, the daily fluctuations in the exchange rate in a flexible exchange rate regime have the advantage of making clear to private firms, banks, and governments that there is substantial risk involved in issuing liabilities denominated in foreign currencies. Furthermore, a depreciation of the exchange rate may provide an early warning signal to policymakers that their policies may have to be adjusted to limit the potential for a financial crisis.[6]

The finding in the chapter that the Taylor rule for monetary policy should not respond to the exchange rate leads the authors to make the following remarkable claim: "Emerging market central banks should not differentiate the way they set monetary conditions from the way they are set in advanced, frictionless economies." Given the fact that exchange rate fluctuations have a major impact on firms' balance sheets in emerging market economies because there is liability dollarization, this claim is counterintuitive. Are they right?

One caveat for their claim is that the result that the Taylor rule should not have a term involving the exchange rate may not withstand robustness tests

5. See Levy-Yeyati (2003) and Broda and Levy-Yeyati (2006).
6. For example, Mishkin (1998).

using different calibrations of their model. There is, however, a stronger reason to doubt their conclusion: the economy may be very nonlinear.

In "tranquil" times, their conclusion may well be right because in this environment, the economy may be reasonably characterized as linear and so their linear quadratic (LQ) approach, which depends on linearity, will provide the right intuition. Not responding to the exchange rate in this environment also makes a lot of sense because, as is emphasized in Mishkin and Savastano (2001), a focus on the exchange rate may lead to a weakening of the inflation target as a nominal anchor.[7]

The conclusion that the exchange rate should not have a special role in the conduct of monetary policy in emerging market countries, however, is likely to be very wrong in a nonlinear world with sudden stops (Calvo 2006), which Batini, Levine, and Pearlman do not model at all. In a sudden stop episode when capital abruptly stops flowing into the country, the normal interest rate Taylor rule, which Calvo (2006) calls "interest rate tweaking" may not work. Interest rate manipulation may not have the usual effect on the exchange rate in these kinds of episodes, with the result that the value of the currency would collapse in a nonlinear way, leading to huge negative balance sheet effects that cause a financial crisis and an economic collapse. In situations like this, it might make sense to temporarily suspend the interest rate rule and conduct foreign exchange rate interventions to prop up the exchange rate.

The bottom line is that benign neglect of the exchange rate could be bad policy when a country faces a sudden stop, but in normal, more tranquil times, I am sympathetic to their view that the monetary authorities in emerging market countries should not focus too much on the exchange rate.

References

Aghion, P., P. Bacchetta, and A. Banerjee. 2000. A simple model of monetary policy and currency crises. *European Economic Review, Papers and Proceedings* 44 (6): 728–38.

———. 2001. Currency crisis and monetary policy in an economy with credit constraints. *European Economic Review* 45 (7): 1121–50.

Aizenman, J., and R. Glick. 2008. Pegged exchange rate regimes—A Trap? *Journal of Money, Credit, and Banking* 40 (4): 817–35.

Bernanke, B. S., T. Laubach, F. S. Mishkin, and A. S. Posen. 1999. *Inflation targeting: Lessons from the international experience.* Princeton, NJ: Princeton University Press.

Broda, C., and E. Levy-Yeyati. 2006. Endogenous deposit dollarization. *Journal of Money, Credit, and Banking* 38 (4): 963–88.

Caballero, R., and A. Krishnamurthy. 2005. Exchange rate volatility and the credit channel in emerging markets: A vertical perspective. *International Journal of Central Banking* 1 (1): 207–45.

7. See Bernanke et al. (1999); Mishkin and Savastano (2001), and Jonas and Mishkin (2005) for examples.

Calvo, G. 2006. Monetary policy challenges in emerging markets: Sudden stop, liability dollarization, and lender of last resort. NBER Working Paper no. 12788. Cambridge, MA: National Bureau of Economic Research, December.
Calvo, G., and E. Mendoza. 2000. Capital markets crises and economic collapse in emerging markets: An informational-frictions approach. *American Economic Review, Papers & Proceedings* 90 (2): 59–64.
Calvo, G., and F. S. Mishkin. 2003. The mirage of exchange rate regimes for emerging market countries. *Journal of Economic Perspectives* 17 (4): 99–118.
Céspedes, L., R. Chang, and A. Velasco. 2004. Balance sheets and exchange rate policy. *American Economic Review* 94 (4): 1183–93.
Eichengreen, B. 1999. Kicking the habit: Moving from pegged exchange rates to greater exchange rate flexibility. *Economic Journal* 109 (454): 1–14.
Eichengreen, B., and R. Hausmann. 2004. *Other people's money: Debt denomination and financial instability in emerging market economies.* Chicago: University of Chicago Press.
Eichengreen, B., and P. Masson. 1998. Exit strategies: Policy options for countries seeking greater exchange rate flexibility. IMF Occasional Paper no. 98/168. Washington, DC: International Monetary Fund.
Fischer, S. 2003. Globalization and its challenges. *American Economic Review* 93 (2): 1–30.
Gertler, M., S. Gilchrist, and F. Natalucci. 2007. External constraints on monetary policy and the financial accelerator. *Journal of Money Credit and Banking* 39 (2–3): 295–330.
Jonas, J., and F. S. Mishkin. 2005. Inflation targeting in transition countries: Experience and prospects. In *Inflation targeting,* ed. M. Woodford, 353–413. Chicago: University of Chicago Press.
Kaminsky, G., and C. Reinhart. 1999. The twin crises: The causes of banking and balance-of-payments problems. *American Economic Review* 89 (3): 473–500.
Levy-Yeyati, E. 2003. Financial dollarization: Where do we stand? Paper presented at the IADB/World Bank Conference, Financial Dedollarization: Policy Options. 1–2 December, Washington, DC.
Mishkin, F. S. 1998. The dangers of exchange-rate pegging in emerging market countries. *International Finance* 1 (1): 81–101.
———. 2006. *The next great globalization: How disadvantaged nations can harness their financial systems to get rich.* Princeton, NJ: Princeton University Press.
Mishkin, F. S., and M. Savastano. 2001. Monetary policy strategies for Latin America. *Journal of Development Economics* 66 (2): 415–44.
Mussa, M. 2002. *Argentina and the fund: From triumph to tragedy.* Washington, DC: Institute for International Economics.
Schneider, M., and A. Tornell. 2004. Balance sheet effects, bailout guarantees and financial crises. *Review of Economic Studies* 71 (7): 883–913.

6

Optimal Monetary Policy and the Sources of Local-Currency Price Stability

Giancarlo Corsetti, Luca Dedola, and Sylvain Leduc

6.1 Introduction

The high degree of stability of import prices in local currency, documented both at the border and at consumer level, vis-à-vis large movements in exchange rates, raises issues at the core of the design of national monetary policies in a globalizing world economy.[1] On the one hand, a low elasticity of import prices with respect to the exchange rate can result from the presence of costs incurred locally before the imported goods reach the consumers, such as distribution costs or assembling costs; that is, costs of combining imported intermediated inputs with domestic inputs. By the same token, it may result from optimal markup adjustment by monopolistic firms, which maximize profits through price discrimination across national markets ("pricing to market"). These are real sources of local currency price stability of imports, which influence pricing even in the absence of nominal rigidities.

Giancarlo Corsetti is Pierre Werner Chair, joint professor at the Robert Schuman Centre for Advanced Studies and the Department of Economics at the European University Institute, and a research Fellow of the Centre for Economic Policy Research (CEPR). Luca Dedola is a senior economist at the European Central Bank. Sylvain Leduc is a research advisor at the Federal Reserve Bank of San Francisco

Prepared for the NBER conference on International Dimensions of Monetary Policy, S'Agaró, Catalonia, Spain, June 11–13, 2007. We thank our discussant Philippe Bacchetta and participants in the European Central Bank (ECB) macro seminar, and the University of Amsterdam for comments. We thank Francesca Viani for superb research assistance. Giancarlo Corsetti's work on this chapter is part of the Pierre Werner Chair Programme on Monetary Union at the European University Institute. Hospitality by De Nederlandsche Bank while working on this project is gratefully acknowledged. The views expressed here are those of the authors and do not necessarily reflect the positions of the ECB, the Board of Governors of the Federal Reserve System, or any other institutions with which the authors are affiliated.

1. See, for example, Engel and Rogers (1996); Goldberg and Knetter (1997); Campa and Goldberg (2005); and Frankel, Parsley, and Wei (2005).

Although these factors may result in inefficiencies—like deviations from the law of one price due to pricing to market—they also shield price and wage dynamics from currency volatility, thus helping central banks maintain a low and stable headline inflation. On the other hand, stable import prices and low exchange rate pass-through can also stem from nominal frictions impeding desired markup adjustment, thus interfering with equilibrium movements in relative prices. When local currency price stability of imports is due to price stickiness, it creates policy trade-offs between competing objectives; for example, between stabilizing the prices of domestically produced goods as opposed to the (relative) price of imported goods, which raise the importance of international considerations in the conduct of monetary policy.

In this chapter we reconsider these policy trade-offs in economies where stable import prices in local currency result from both nominal rigidities and endogenous destination-specific markup adjustment. We specify a two-country model where each economy produces an array of country-specific, differentiated traded goods. In each country, we model local downstream firms as using one intermediate traded good, and possibly local inputs, to produce nontradable final goods. In other words, each intermediate good is produced by an upstream monopolist and sold to a continuum of monopolistic downstream firms, active in each country, from which local consumers can directly buy further differentiated final varieties. Thus, because both upstream and downstream firms have monopoly power, final prices reflect double marginalization. We posit that markets are segmentated across national borders, so that intermediate producers price-discriminate between domestic and foreign local downstream producers as a group, although not among individual local producers (charging different prices within the same country).

As in standard monetary models, we assume that firms set prices in local currency, adjusting them infrequently according to the Calvo mechanism.[2] Different from the previous literature, however, we explicitly model strategic interactions among upstream and downstream firms: upstream firms exercise their monopoly power by taking into account country-specific differences in the properties of the demand for their products. Relative to the literature already modeling vertical interactions between exporters and local firms (e.g., Bacchetta and Van Wincoop 2005; Corsetti and Dedola 2005; Devereux and Engel 2007; Monacelli 2005), an important novel contribution of this chapter consists of analyzing the effects of staggered price setting at the downstream level on the optimal price (and markup) chosen by upstream producers.

Specifically, our analysis establishes three key characteristics of the perceived demand elasticity by upstream producers when nominal rigidities constrain price decisions by downstream firms. *First,* this elasticity is a

2. See the literature review in section 6.2.

decreasing function of the rate of change of final prices in each industry: the higher this rate (thus the higher the price dispersion among final producers selling an industry product), the higher the intermediate producer's equilibrium markup. *Second,* the perceived demand elasticity is market-specific, depending on differences in industry-specific inflation rates across the domestic and the export market. Sticky prices at consumer level create an incentive for upstream firms to price discriminate across borders, which leads to equilibrium deviations from the law of one price, independently of the degree of nominal rigidities in the upstream firms' own prices. *Third,* if either local inputs in downstream production are a good substitute of intermediate imported goods, or their share in the downstream firms' costs is low, the demand elasticity is decreasing in the price charged by upstream producers. In other words, downstream nominal rigidities magnify the price response to shocks by upstream monopolists who optimally reset their price in any given period. This generates strategic substitutability among upstream producers: a rise in marginal costs will lead to an increase in their desired markups.

These results have at least two notable implications for policy modeling and design. *First,* by shedding light on the link between optimal price adjustment at the dock and domestic inflation rates, our results suggest a specific reason why, in line with the observations by Taylor (2000), lower consumer price index (CPI) inflation volatility and price dispersion may result in a lower degree of exchange rate pass-through: stable inflation reduces at the margin the producers' incentives to price discriminate across countries, decreasing the sensitivity of their "desired markup" to cost changes.

Second, by showing that downstream price rigidities result into strategic substitutability among upstream producers, our results emphasize that adding several layers of nominal rigidities do not necessarily result in more price inertia. Strategic interactions among vertically integrated firms with sticky prices may create incentive for large price adjustment, feeding back into inflation volatility.

In addition, our model specification implies an important dimension of heterogeneity across firms that has a bearing on optimal monetary policy. In contrast to standard models, the marginal costs of our downstream firms are generally not symmetric, not even when the economy is completely closed to foreign trade and there are no markup shocks. Thus, monetary authorities are not able to achieve complete stabilization of final prices.[3]

The mechanism underlying these results is different from that emphasized by the previous literature focusing on vertical interactions between upstream and downstream firms, but that stresses real determinants of the local cur-

3. In standard models with cost-push and markup shocks, monetary authorities can achieve complete price stability, but face trade-offs that motivate deviations from it—see, for instance, the discussion in Woodford (2003). In our model, instead, stability of all prices is unfeasible to start with.

rency price stability of imports. In previous work of ours, we assume that local firms produce consumer goods by combining intermediate tradable goods with local inputs (Corsetti and Dedola 2005; Corsetti, Dedola, and Leduc 2008b). In this framework, provided that the tradable goods and the local inputs are poor substitutes in production, the presence of local inputs tends to mute the response of upstream prices to shocks (corresponding to a case of strategic complementarity), and makes the exchange rate pass-through incomplete, even in the absence of nominal rigidities. Building an example of an economy encompassing both channels, we analyze conditions under which the properties of the demand elasticity faced by upstream producers are dominated by the effect of local inputs in production, as opposed to the effect of downstream nominal rigidities.

We characterize the optimal cooperative monetary policy under commitment. In order to reduce inefficiencies due to price stickiness, monetary policy does mitigate fluctuations in the major components of consumer price inflation. However, it falls short of stabilizing completely either the CPI, or the price of domestic intermediate goods.[4]

Optimal monetary policies address different trade-offs, specific to both the international and the domestic dimensions of the economy. First, as in Corsetti and Pesenti (2005), nominal rigidities in local currency at the upstream level lead benevolent monetary authorities to attach a positive weight to stabilizing the consumer price of imports, and thus deviate from perfect stabilization of the final prices of domestic goods. Second, downstream technology shocks prevent perfect stabilization of all consumer prices, because vertical interactions with upstream firms, which may or may not adjust their prices, induce heterogeneity of marginal costs at retail level. This effect is compounded in an open economy setting, because of the response of the intermediate price of imports to exchange rate fluctuations. Third, the elasticity of the producer's demand curve falls with the industry's dispersion of final goods prices, motivating policy emphasis on final price stabilization.

None of these trade-offs, however, entail specific prescriptions regarding the volatility of the real exchange rate. In the literature, optimal monetary policy in models with nominal rigidities in local currency is sometimes associated with a limited degree of real exchange rate volatility, relative to the terms of trade (see, e.g., Devereux and Engel 2007). In contrast, we find that implementing the optimal policy in our economy with nominal rigidities leads the real exchange rate to be more volatile, and the terms of trade to be less volatile, than in the same economy under flexible prices. This is because of the combined effects of nominal rigidities, and the presence of

4. In our model economy the isomorphism between optimal monetary policy in closed and open economies characterized by Clarida, Galí, and Gertler (2002) obviously does not hold, as policymakers face several trade-offs that make perfect stabilization of domestic inflation suboptimal.

nontradable components in final goods. We take these findings as a caution against strong policy prescriptions on the need to curb the volatility of the real exchange rate. The point is that, while there are good reasons to expect optimal policies to contain the volatility of the terms of trade, these reasons cannot be mechanically extended to the real exchange rate, whose volatility is bound to depend on a number of structural features of the economy.

This chapter is organized as follows. In the next section, we will briefly survey the literature on pricing to market and monetary policy, with the goal of clarifying our contributions to it. Section 6.3 specifies the model, while section 6.4 provides analytical results on the link between price stickiness and price discrimination arising from vertical interactions. Section 6.5 describes our calibration of the model. Section 6.6 presents the equilibrium dynamics of prices in response to shocks, while section 6.7 discusses the allocation under the optimal policy, relative to alternative policy rules and the case of flexible prices. Section 6.8 concludes. An appendix provides analytical details on the model and the derivation of the main results.

6.2 Local Currency Price Stability and Efficient Monetary Stabilization

In this section we briefly reconstruct the main development of recent debates on the local currency price stability of imports—and their implications for the international transmission and the optimal design of monetary policy—with the goal of clarifying our contribution to the literature. A core issue underlying these debates is whether monetary policy should react to international variables, such as the exchange rate or the terms of trade, beyond the influence that these variables have on the domestic output gap (for example, via external demand) and on the domestic good prices—so that it would have a specific "international dimension." As discussed in the following, models stressing the stability of import prices in local currency have provided one possible answer to this question stressing the implications of nominal rigidities for monetary transmission and stabilization policy.

6.2.1 Nominal Rigidities and the International Dimensions of Optimal Monetary Policy

At the heart of the international dimension of monetary policy lies the role of the exchange rate in the international transmission mechanism. Consistent with traditional open macroeconomic models, the seminal contribution to the New Open Economy Macroeconomics (henceforth NOEM) by Obstfeld and Rogoff (1995) embraces the view that exchange rate movements play the stabilizing role of adjusting international relative prices in response to shocks, when frictions prevent or slow down price adjustment in the local currency. The idea is that nominal depreciation transpires into real depreciation, making domestic goods cheaper in the world markets, hence redirecting world demand toward them: exchange rate movements therefore have "expenditure switching effects." Accordingly, NOEM contributions after Obstfeld and Rogoff (1995) draw on the Mundell–Fleming and Keynesian tradition, and posit that firms preset the price for their products in domestic currency, implying that export prices are sticky in the currency of the producers—this is why such hypothesis is commonly dubbed "producer currency pricing" (henceforth PCP). Under this hypothesis, nominal import prices in local currency move one-to-one with the exchange rate and pass-through is perfect. In the baseline model with preset prices, to the extent that the demand elasticities are identical across countries, there is no incentive for producers to charge different prices in different markets: in equilibrium there would be no deviations from the law of one price even if national markets were segmented.

In model economies with PCP, optimal monetary policy rules tend to be "inward-looking" (and isomorphic to the rules derived in closed economy models): welfare-maximizing central banks pursue the stabilization of domestic producers marginal costs and markups—hence, they aim at stabilizing the GDP deflator—while letting the consumer price index (CPI) fluctuate with efficient movements in the relative price of imports. There is no need for monetary policies to react to international variables—a result that in the baseline NOEM model after Corsetti and Pesenti (2001) goes through under different assumptions regarding nominal rigidities, including staggered price setting and partial adjustment (see, for example, Clarida, Galí, and Gertler (2002), or Benigno and Benigno (2003) for a generalization of the baseline model).

The high elasticity of import prices to the exchange rate underlying the contributions after Obstfeld and Rogoff (1995), however, is clearly at odds with a large body of empirical studies showing that the exchange rate pass-through on import prices is far from complete in the short run, and deviations from the law of one price are large and persistent (see, for example, Engel and Rogers [1996]; Goldberg and Knetter [1997]; Campa and Goldberg [2005]). Based on this evidence, several contributions have engaged in a thorough critique of the received wisdom on the expenditure switching effects of the exchange rate. Specifically, Betts and Devereux (2000) and Devereux and Engel (2003), among others, posit that firms preset export prices in the currency of the market where they sell their goods. This assumption, commonly dubbed "local currency pricing" (henceforth LCP), attributes local currency price stability of imports entirely to nominal frictions. The far-reaching implications of LCP for the role of the exchange rate in the international transmission mechanism have been widely discussed by the literature (see, e.g., Engel [2003]).

To the extent that import prices are sticky in the local currency, a Home depreciation does not affect the price of Home goods in the world markets; hence, it has no expenditure switching effects. Instead, it raises the ex-post markups on Home exports: at given marginal costs, revenues in domestic currency from selling goods abroad rise. In contrast with the received wisdom, nominal depreciation strengthens a country's terms of trade: if export prices are preset during the period, the Home terms of trade improves when the Home currency weakens.

As opposed to earlier literature, models assuming LCP unveil a clear-cut argument in favor of policies with an "international dimension." One way to present the argument is as follows. To the extent that exporters' revenues and markups are exposed to exchange rate uncertainty, firms' optimal pricing strategies internalize the monetary policy of the importing country. In the benchmark model by Corsetti and Pesenti (2005) for instance, foreign firms optimally preset the price of their goods in the Home market one period ahead, by charging the equilibrium markup over expected marginal costs evaluated in Home currency. The preset price of Home imports then depends on the joint distribution of Home monetary policy and Foreign productivity shocks: in the model, it is increasing in the variance of nominal marginal costs.

The reason why the isomorphism between closed economy and open economy monetary rules breaks down is apparent. Suppose that the Home monetary authorities ignore the influence of their decisions on the price of Home imports. Incomplete stabilization of Foreign firms' marginal costs and markup in local currency will translate into inefficiently high local prices of their product. On the other hand, if Home monetary authorities wanted to stabilize Foreign firms' marginal costs, they could only do so at the cost of raising costs and markup uncertainty for Home producers, resulting in inefficient Home good prices. It follows that, to maximize Home welfare, Home policymakers should optimally trade-off the stabilization of marginal costs of all producers (domestic and foreign) selling in the Home markets. The optimal response to Foreign shocks by domestic policymakers depends, among other factors, on the degree of openness of the economy, as indexed by the overall share of imports in the CPI (see Corsetti and Pesenti [2005], and Sutherland [2005], for a discussion of intermediate degrees of pass-through).

In section 6.7 of this chapter we will show that these basic principles of the international dimensions of optimal monetary policies go through in models assuming LCP and staggered price adjustment. Namely, in our model monetary authorities will optimally attempt to stabilize the CPI, although CPI stabilization will not be complete because of the asymmetry in shocks hitting different economies and different sectors of the same national economy, creating the need for relative price adjustment. At an optimum, welfare-maximizing policymakers will thus trade-off inefficient misalignment of import prices, with inefficient relative price dispersion among domestic and foreign goods (see also Smets and Wouters [2002] and Monacelli [2005]).

6.2.2 Interactions of Nominal and Real Determinants of Local Currency Price Stability of Imports

While most of the discussion in the NOEM literature has focused on incomplete pass-through as an implication of nominal rigidities, a low pass-through, in itself, is not necessarily incompatible with expenditure switching effects—a point stressed by Obstfeld (2002), among others. In this respect, Obstfeld and Rogoff (2000) point out that, in the data (and consistent with the received wisdom), nominal depreciation does tend to be associated with deteriorating terms of trade. This piece of evidence clearly sets an empirical hurdle for LCP models: specifications that assume a very high degree of price stickiness in local currency cannot pass this test (see Corsetti, Dedola, and Leduc [2008a], for a quantitative assessment). Interestingly, estimates of LCP models attributing incomplete pass-through exclusively to nominal rigidities in local currency tend to predict that the degree of price stickiness is implausibly higher for imports than for domestic goods—a result suggesting model misspecification (see, for example, Lubik and Schorfheide [2006]).

The key issue is the extent to which the evidence of local currency price stability of imports can be explained by nominal rigidities. In the literature, it is well understood that the low elasticity of import prices at the retail level, with respect to the exchange rate, is in large part due to the incidence of distribution (see Burstein, Eichenbaum, and Rebelo [2006] for a recent reconsideration of this point). Namely, suppose that import prices at the dock move one-to-one with the exchange rate, but the distribution margin accounts for 50 percent of the retail price, mostly covering local costs. A 1 percent depreciation of the currency will then affect the final price of the imported good only by 0.5 percent.

In addition, several macro and micro contributions have emphasized that import prices at the dock do not move one-to-one with the exchange rate because of optimal destination-specific markup adjustment by monopolistic firms. Instances of these studies include Dornbusch (1987), stressing market structure, as well as previous work by two of us (Corsetti and Dedola 2005), where upstream monopolists sell their tradable goods to downstream firms, which combine them with local inputs before reaching the consumer. The latter contribution establishes that, to the extent that the tradable goods and the local inputs are not good substitutes in the downstream firms' production, the demand elasticity faced by upstream monopolists will be (a) market-specific, causing optimal price discrimination across markets, and (b) increasing in the monopolists price, thus leading to incomplete exchange rate pass-through independent of nominal rigidities. Based on this principle, that paper then generalizes the model with distribution by Burstein, Neves, and Rebelo (2003) as to encompass local currency price stability due to endogenous movements of markups implied by the presence of distribution services intensive in local inputs. The same principle nonetheless can be applied to models where intermediate imported inputs are assembled using local inputs—a case analyzed by Bacchetta and Van Wincoop (2003). Whether one has in mind markets with high distribution margins (such as the market for cups of coffee at Starbucks in the United States), or markets for goods with a relatively high incidence of imported parts (such as the market for cars "made in the United States"), incomplete exchange rate pass-through can be traced back to some degree of complementarity between imported goods and local input/services.

Analyses of the relative importance of these different sources of import price stability (especially local costs) are provided by several market-specific studies—such as Goldberg and Verboven (2001), Goldberg and Hellerstein (2007), and Hellerstein (2005). The main result emerging from these partial equilibrium contributions is that real factors can explain a large extent of local currency price stability of imports. Most interestingly, similar conclusions can be reached using quantitative, general equilibrium models, as suggested by the numerical exercises in Corsetti and Dedola (2005).

Yet quantitative studies incorporating these factors also corroborate the idea that a realistic degree of nominal rigidities can improve substantially the performance of the model. In Corsetti, Dedola, and Leduc (2005), we show that a model assuming LCP, together with vertical interaction between producers and distributors, can pass the empirical hurdle set by Obstfeld and Rogoff (2000), provided that the average frequency of price adjustment is consistent with the evidence by Bils and Klenow (2004).

Research is therefore increasingly focused on the interaction between real and monetary determinants of low exchange rate pass-through and deviations from the law of one price. A first early instance of research focused on such interaction is provided by contributions that emphasize the need to treat the currency denomination of exports as an endogenous choice by profit-maximizing firms. Bacchetta and Van Wincoop (2005), Devereux, Engel, and Storgaard (2004), and Friberg (1998) have developed models where firms can choose whether to price export in domestic or in foreign currency, knowing that price updates will be subject to frictions. A number of factors—from the market share of exporters to the incidence of distribution, and the availability of hedging instruments—potentially play a crucial role in this choice (see Engel (2006) for a synthesis).

Although most of these models are developed assuming an arbitrary monetary policy, the role of optimal stabilization policy in the choice between LCP and PCP is addressed by Corsetti and Pesenti (2001). The main idea is that expansionary monetary shocks unrelated to fundamental shocks (e.g., productivity) raise nominal wages and marginal costs while depreciating the currency. Consider a firm located in a country with noisy monetary policy; that is, hit by frequent monetary shocks unrelated to fundamentals. For such a firm, pricing its exports in foreign currency (i.e., choosing LCP) is attractive in the following sense: it ensures that revenues from exports in domestic currency will move in parallel with nominal marginal costs, with stabilizing effects on the markup. This is because any expansionary monetary shock depreciating the Home currency would simultaneously raise wages and the domestic currency revenue from unit sales abroad (at an unchanged local price). This observation may help explain why exporters from countries with relatively unstable domestic monetary policies (e.g., some developing countries) prefer to price their exports to developed countries in the importers' currency. The same argument, however, suggests that LCP is not necessarily optimal for exporters producing in countries where monetary policy systematically stabilizes marginal costs (see Goldberg and Tille [2008] for empirical evidence). For firms located in these countries, real factors arguably become more relevant in the choice.

A second instance of the new directions taken by the literature consists of studies taking the LCP choice as given, and combining it with different determinants of pricing to market and incomplete pass-through. This is the approach we take in this chapter. In contrast from previous contributions, where price stickiness is not linked to price discrimination (e.g., Monacelli 2005), or where nominal rigidities and price discrimination coexist without feeding into each other (e.g., Corsetti, Dedola, and Leduc 2005), we specify a model building on the intuitive idea that the frequency of price changes by local downstream firms selling products to consumers is bound to affect the elasticity of demand perceived by upstream producers of intermediate goods (or tradable inputs). The novel result of our study is that, looking at the interactions between nominal and real determinants of price discrimination in an otherwise standard monetary model, nominal rigidities at the retail level do not necessarily lower the equilibrium reaction of final prices to exchange rate movements, thus increasing price inertia. As mentioned in the introduction, downstream price rigidities tend to generate strategic substitutability among upstream producers and an overall larger sensitivity of all prices to exchange rate changes.

6.3 The Model Economy

The world economy consists of two countries of equal size, H and F. Each country specializes in one type of tradable good, produced in a number of differentiated industries defined over a continuum of unit mass. Tradable goods are indexed by $h \in [0, 1]$ in the Home country and $f \in [0, 1]$ in the Foreign country. In each industry, the firm producing the tradable good h (or f) is a monopolistic supplier of one good, using labor as the only input to production. These firms set prices in local currency units and in a staggered fashion as in Calvo (1983).

A distinctive feature of our setting is that we model a downstream sector in each country. Specifically, we assume that each producer's good h is sold to consumers in many varieties by a continuum of local firms indexed by

$r_h \in [0, 1]$. These firms buy the h tradable goods and turn them into consumer goods—which are not traded across borders—with random productivity. We will distinguish between two cases: one in which local firms use domestic labor as an input; the other in which they do not. Similar to upstream producers, downstream also operate under monopolistic competition and set prices in a staggered fashion as in Calvo (1983).

By the logic of the Calvo adjustment, local downstream firms buying goods from upstream producers charge different prices to final users, with a constant fraction of them reoptimizing prices in each period. In principle, one could assume that upstream firms exercise their monopoly power by charging individual prices that are specific to each downstream firm. However, we find it more realistic and convincing to assume that upstream producers are not able to price discriminate across individual local firms, but only across groups of them—namely, across domestic and foreign local firms. So we assume that upstream producers exercise their monopoly power and set prices by taking into account the total demand for their product in each market, at Home and in the Foreign country.

In what follows, we describe our setup, focusing on the Home country, with the understanding that similar expressions also characterize the Foreign economy—variables referred to Foreign firms and households are marked with an asterisk.

6.3.1 The Household's Problem

Preferences

The representative Home agent maximizes the expected value of her lifetime utility, given by the following standard functional form:

$$(1) \qquad V_0 = E \sum_{t=0}^{\infty} \beta^t U \left[\frac{C_t^{1-\sigma}}{1-\sigma} + \chi \frac{(M_{t+1}/P_t)^{1-\sigma}}{1-\sigma} + \kappa \frac{(1-L_t)^{1-\upsilon}}{1-\upsilon} \right],$$

where instantaneous utility U is a function of a consumption index, C_t; leisure, $(1 - L_t)$; and real money balances M_{t+1}/P_t. Households consume both domestically produced and imported goods. We define $C_t(h, r_h)$ as the Home agent's consumption as of time t of the variety r_h of the Home good h, produced and distributed by the firm r_h; similarly, $C_t(f, r_f)$ is the Home agent's consumption of the variety r_f of the good f, produced and distributed by firm r_f. For each good h (or f), we assume that one final good variety r_h (r_f) is an imperfect substitute for all other final good varieties, with constant elasticity of substitution $\eta > 1$:

$$C_t(h) \equiv \left[\int_0^1 C_t(h, r_h)^{(\eta-1)/\eta} dr \right]^{\eta/(\eta-1)}, \quad C_t(f) \equiv \left[\int_0^1 C_t(f, r_f)^{(\eta-1)/\eta} dr \right]^{\eta/(\eta-1)},$$

where $C_t(h)$ is the consumption of (all varieties of) the Home good h, by the Home agent, at time t; similarly, $C_t(f)$ is the same agent's consumption of the Foreign good *f*. We then assume that the good produced by the *h* industry is an imperfect substitute for all other goods produced by the Home industries, with the same constant elasticity of substitution $\eta > 1$ as between final good varieties. Aggregate consumption of Home and Foreign goods by the Home agent is thus defined as:

$$C_{\mathrm{H},t} \equiv \left[\int_0^1 C_t(h)^{(\eta-1)/\eta} dh\right]^{\eta/(\eta-1)}, \quad C_{\mathrm{F},t} \equiv \left[\int_0^1 C_t(f)^{(\eta-1)/\eta} df\right]^{\eta/(\eta-1)},$$

The full consumption basket, C_t, in each country, aggregates Home and Foreign goods according to the following standard constant elasticity of substitution (CES) function:

$$(2) \qquad C_t \equiv [a_{\mathrm{H}}^{1-\phi} C_{\mathrm{H},t}^{\phi} + a_{\mathrm{F}}^{1-\phi} C_{\mathrm{F},t}^{\phi}]^{1/\phi}, \quad \phi < 1,$$

where a_{H} and a_{F} are the weights on the consumption of Home and Foreign traded goods, respectively, and $1/(1-\phi)$ is the constant elasticity of substitution between $C_{\mathrm{H},t}$ and $C_{\mathrm{F},t}$.

Budget Constraints and Asset Markets

For simplicity, we posit that domestic and international asset markets are complete and that only domestic residents hold the Home currency, M_{t+1}. Households derive income from working, $W_t L_t$, from domestic firms' profits, and from previously accumulated units of currency, as well as from the proceeds from holding state-contingent assets, B_t. They pay nondistortionary (lump-sum) net taxes $\mathbb{T}$, denominated in Home currency. Households use their disposable income to consume and invest in state-contingent assets. The individual flow budget constraint for the representative agent *j* in the Home country is therefore:

$$(3) \quad \mathbb{P}_{\mathrm{H},t} C_{\mathrm{H},t} + \mathbb{P}_{\mathrm{F},t} C_{\mathrm{F},t} + \int_s p_{bt,t+1} B_{t+1} + M_{t+1} \leq W_t L_t + M_t + B_t$$
$$+ \int_0^1 \Pi(h) dh + \int_0^1 \int_0^1 \Pi(h, r_h) dh dr_h + \int_0^1 \int_0^1 \Pi(f, r_f) df dr_f + \mathbb{T}_t,$$

where $\Pi(.)$ denotes the agent's share of profits from all firms *h* and *r* in the economy. The price indexes are as follows: $\mathbb{P}_{\mathrm{H},t}$ denotes the consumer price of the aggregate Home traded good; $\mathbb{P}_{\mathrm{F},t}$ denotes the consumer price of aggregate Home imports. We will also denote the overall consumer price index (CPI) by P_t. All these indexes are defined in the following.

The household's problem consists of maximizing lifetime utility, defined by (1), subject to the constraint (3).

6.3.2 Production Structure and Technology

International price discrimination is a key feature of the international economy captured by our model. In what follows we show that, even if Home and Foreign consumers have identical constant elasticity preferences for consumption, vertical interactions between upstream and downstream firms cause differences in the elasticity of demand for the h (f) product at wholesale level across national markets. Upstream firms will thus want to charge different prices at Home and in the Foreign country. We will focus our analysis on Home firms—optimal pricing by Foreign firms can be easily derived from it. To distinguish between upstream and downstream firms, we will denote variables referred to the former with an upper bar.

We begin by specifying the technology used by upstream firms producing Home tradables. These firms employ domestic labor to produce a differentiated product h according to the following linear production function:

$$\overline{Y}(h) = \overline{Z} \cdot \overline{L}(h),$$

where $\overline{L}(h)$ is the demand for labor by the producer of the good h and $\overline{Z}$ is a technology shock common to all upstream producers in the Home country, which follows a statistical process to be specified later. The letter h will be indifferently referred to an upstream producer selling to downstream firms r_h, or the corresponding "industry."

In each industry h, downstream firms r_h combine the traded input, bought from upstream producers, with some local nontraded input. For analytical convenience, in most of our analysis we do not model the local nontraded input explicitly, but posit that the production function of firms r_h is linear in the traded input only

$$Y(h, r_h) = ZX(h, r_h), \tag{4}$$

where $X(h, r_h)$ is the demand for tradable good h by firm r_h, Z is a random technology component that affects the amount of traded input required to produce the variety r_h and distribute it to consumers. This random shock is country-specific, and hits symmetrically all national downstream firms.

The use of the local input is consequential for our results, to the extent that it is a poor substitute with X. This case has been made in previous work of ours (see Corsetti and Dedola [2005]; Corsetti, Dedola, and Leduc [2005]) in which we have assumed that downstream firms in an industry h combine the tradable good h with a local input according to a fixed-proportion production function, such as

$$Y(h, r_h) = Min[X(h, r_h), ZL(h, r_h)]. \tag{5}$$

Here, $L(h, r_h)$ is the demand for labor by the downstream firm r_h, and the random technology component Z now affects the amount of labor required to produce the variety r_h and distribute it to consumers.

In our previous contributions, we have shown that this specification can generate endogenous movements in upstream firms' markups and cross-border price discrimination independent of nominal price rigidities. In this chapter, we make a different, but complementary, point. Namely, we show that vertical interactions among upstream and downstream firms can lead to price discrimination *exclusively* as a consequence of nominal rigidities. To focus sharply on the mechanism underlying this new result, throughout our analysis we specify the production function of downstream firms as in (4), abstracting from the local nontraded input. For the sake of comparison, however, in the next sections we will also show analytical results for the production function (5).

6.3.3 The Problem of Downstream Firms

Both upstream and downstream firms are subject to nominal rigidities à la Calvo. Hence, at any time t downstream firms will buy either from a producer h, which updates its price in the same period, or from a producer still charging an old price. Conversely, in each period, upstream producers updating their price will need to consider that only a fraction of downstream firms buying their products will also reoptimize in the period. In characterizing optimal pricing decisions, it is instructive to go over these cases one by one. Let θ be the probability that a downstream firm within the industry h keeps its price fixed—in each period a firm r_h sets a new price with probability $(1 - \theta)$. The corresponding probabilities for the upstream producers will be denoted by $\overline{\theta}$ and $(1 - \overline{\theta})$.

Consider first the optimization problem of the downstream firms, r_h, which can reset their product prices in the current period t. The representative firm r_h chooses $P_t(h, r_h)$ to maximize the expected discounted sum of profits:

$$\pi(h) = E_t\left\{\sum_{k=0}^{\infty} p_{bt,t+k}\theta^k(P_t(h, r_h)C_{t+k}(h, r_h) - MC_{t+k}(h)C_{t+k}(h, r_h))\right\},$$

where $p_{bt,t+k}$ is the firm's stochastic nominal discount factor between t and $t + k$. This firm faces the following final demand:

$$C_t(h, r_h) = \left(\frac{P_t(h, r_h)}{\mathbb{P}_t(h)}\right)^{-\eta}\left(\frac{\mathbb{P}_t(h)}{\mathbb{P}_{H,t}}\right)^{-\eta} C_{H,t},$$

where $\mathbb{P}_t(h)$ is the price index of the good (or industry) h, and $\mathbb{P}_{H,t}$ is the price index of all Home goods. The optimal price charged to consumers can then be written in the following standard form:

$$(6) \qquad P_t^o(h, r_h) = \frac{\eta}{\eta - 1}\frac{E_t\sum_{k=0}^{\infty} p_{bt,t+k}\theta^k MC_{t+k}(h)C_{t+k}(h, r_h)}{E_t\sum_{k=0}^{\infty} p_{bt,t+k}\theta^k C_{t+k}(h, r_h)}.$$

where, depending on whether we consider (4) or (5), the firm's marginal cost, $MC_t(h)$, will be given by either of the following expressions:

$$MC_t(h) = \frac{\overline{P}_t(h)}{Z_t}$$

$$MC_t(h) = \overline{P}_t(h) + \frac{W_t}{Z_t},$$

where $\overline{P}_t(h)$ is the price of good h charged by the producer in the industry.

Now, if the downstream firm operates in an industry in which the upstream producer does not reoptimize its product price during the period, the price $\overline{P}_t(h)$ in the previous expression will coincide with the price charged in the previous period; that is, $\overline{P}_t(h) = \overline{P}_{t-1}(h)$. Conversely, if the downstream firm r_h operates in an industry h in which the upstream firm has also reset the price of its product during the same period, the marginal cost will be depending on the new, optimized price, discussed in the following section. This has the noteworthy implication that downstream firms in different industries will be facing different marginal costs even in the face of common productivity shocks Z_t—a key feature of our model that will be important in determining the characteristics of the optimal monetary policy.

6.3.4 Price Indexes and Market Clearing

Price Indexes

Before getting to the analytical core of our contribution and delving into our numerical experiments, we conclude the presentation of the model by formally defining the price indexes repeatedly used in the analysis so far, and writing down the market-clearing conditions in the goods market. In an industry in which the producer updates its price, the price index of the good h at consumer level is given by.[5]

$$\mathbb{P}_t(h) = \left[\int_0^1 P_t(h, r_h)^{1-\eta} dr_h\right]^{1/(1-\eta)} = [(1-\theta)P_t^o(h)^{1-\eta} + \theta\mathbb{P}_{t-1}(h)^{1-\eta}]^{1/(1-\eta)}.$$

Denoting with a tilde the prices in an industry in which the producer does not update its price, the price index is:

$$\tilde{\mathbb{P}}_t(h) = \left[\int_0^1 P_t(h, r_h)^{1-\eta} dr_h\right]^{1/(1-\eta)} = [(1-\theta)\tilde{P}_t^o(h)^{1-\eta} + \theta\tilde{\mathbb{P}}_{t-1}(h)^{1-\eta}]^{1/(1-\eta)}.$$

The price index of Home tradables consumed at home thus becomes:

$$\mathbb{P}_{H,t} = \left[\int_0^1 \mathbb{P}_t(h)^{1-\eta} dh\right]^{1/(1-\eta)} =>$$

$$\begin{aligned}
\mathbb{P}_{H,t}^{1-\eta} &= [(1-\overline{\theta})\mathbb{P}_t(h)^{1-\eta} + \overline{\theta}\tilde{\mathbb{P}}_t(h)^{1-\eta}] \\
&= (1-\theta)[(1-\overline{\theta})P_t^o(h)^{1-\eta} + \overline{\theta}\tilde{P}_t^o(h)^{1-\eta}] \\
&\quad + \theta[(1-\overline{\theta})\mathbb{P}_{t-1}(h)^{1-\eta} + \overline{\theta}\tilde{\mathbb{P}}_{t-1}(h)^{1-\eta}] \\
&= (1-\theta)[(1-\overline{\theta})P_t^o(h)^{1-\eta} + \overline{\theta}\tilde{P}_t^o(h)^{1-\eta}] + \theta\mathbb{P}_{H,t-1}^{1-\eta}.
\end{aligned}$$

The price index associated with the consumption basket, C_t, is:

$$P_t = [a_H \mathbb{P}_{H,t}^{\phi/(\phi-1)} + a_F \mathbb{P}_{F,t}^{\phi/(\phi-1)}]^{(\phi-1)/\phi}.$$

5. We drop the index r_h in our notation of the optimal final prices, since in any given industry firms that can update their price will choose the same optimal one.

Let $\mathcal{E}_t$ denote the Home nominal exchange rate, expressed in units of Home currency per unit of Foreign currency. The real exchange rate is costumarily defined as the ratio of CPIs expressed in the same currency; that is, $\mathcal{E}_t P_t^*/P_t$. The terms of trade are instead defined as the relative price of domestic imports in terms of exports, namely $\mathbb{P}_{F,t}/\mathcal{E}_t\mathbb{P}_{H,t}^*$.

Equilibrium in the Goods Market

To characterize the equilibrium conditions in the goods market, we equate supply to demand at each firm level. Integrating over all downstream firms in a given industry we get:

$$\begin{aligned} \overline{Y}_t(h) &= a_H\left(\frac{\mathbb{P}_t(h)}{\mathbb{P}_{H,t}}\right)^{-\eta}\left(\frac{\mathbb{P}_{H,t}}{P_t}\right)^{1/(\phi-1)}\frac{C_t}{Z_t}S_t(h) \\ &= +(1-a_H)\left(\frac{\mathbb{P}_t^*(h)}{\mathbb{P}_{H,t}^*}\right)^{-\eta}\left(\frac{\mathbb{P}_{H,t}^*}{P_t^*}\right)^{1/(\phi-1)}\frac{C_t^*}{Z_t^*}S_t^*(f), \end{aligned}$$

where $S_t(h)$ denotes industry h's relative price dispersion at the consumer level:

$$S_t(h) = \int\left(\frac{P_t(h, r_h)}{\mathbb{P}_t(h)}\right)^{-\eta} dr_h.$$

Integrating over all industries, aggregate output is:

$$\overline{Y}_t = a_H\left(\frac{\mathbb{P}_{H,t}}{P_t}\right)^{1/(\phi-1)}\frac{C_t}{Z_t}\overline{S}_t + (1-a_H)\left(\frac{\mathbb{P}_{H,t}^*}{P_t^*}\right)^{1/(\phi-1)}\frac{C_t^*}{Z_t^*}\overline{S}_t^*,$$

where the price dispersion term, $\overline{S}_t$, is defined as:

$$\overline{S}_t = \int\left(\frac{\mathbb{P}_t(h)}{\mathbb{P}_{H,t}}\right)^{-\eta} S_t(h)dh.$$

Observe that $\overline{S}_t$ captures the relative price dispersion within and across industries. Because $\overline{S}_t$ and $S_t(h)$ are bounded below by 1, price dispersion implies a real resource cost.

6.4 Modeling the Sources of Local Currency Price Stability: Price Discrimination and Nominal Rigidities

In this section we fully characterize pricing to market by upstream firms as a function of final prices. A crucial feature of our model is that the demand price elasticity perceived by upstream producers is time varying as a function of downstream price inflation. Because results differ depending on the specification of the downstream firms' production function, we will characterize the optimal producer price $\overline{P}_t^o(h)$, and discuss its main properties, looking first at the case of downstream linear (Cobb-Douglas) production, then at the case of downstream Leontief production.

6.4.1 The Problem of the Upstream Firms

Consistent with the logic of the Calvo model, we posit that, when upstream producers update their prices, they do so simultaneously in the Home and in the Foreign market, in the respective currencies. The maximization problem is then as follows:

$$(7)\quad Max_{\overline{p}(h),\overline{p}^*(h)}E_t$$

$$\cdot\left\{\sum_{k=0}^{\infty} p_{bt,t+k}\theta^k([\overline{P}_t(h)D_{t+k}(h) + \mathcal{E}_t\overline{P}_t^*(h)D_{t+k}^*(h)] - \overline{MC}_{t+k}(h)[D_{t+k}(h) + D_{t+k}^*(h)])\right\}$$

where the marginal cost of the producer is given by:

$$\overline{MC}(h) = \frac{W_t}{\overline{Z}_t},$$

and, depending on the production function downstream, the Home and Foreign demands for the firm's variety are given by:

$$D_t(h) = \frac{1}{Z_t}\int\left(\frac{P_t(h, r_h)}{\mathbb{P}_t(h)}\right)^{-\eta}\left(\frac{\mathbb{P}_t(h)}{\mathbb{P}_{\mathrm{H},t}}\right)^{-\eta}C_{\mathrm{H},t}dr_h$$

$$D_t^*(h) = \frac{1}{Z_t^*}\int\left(\frac{P_t^*(h, r_h^*)}{\mathbb{P}_t^*(h)}\right)^{-\eta}\left(\frac{\mathbb{P}_t^*(h)}{\mathbb{P}_{\mathrm{H},t}^*}\right)^{-\eta}C_{\mathrm{H},t}^*dr_h^*$$

in our linear production specification, or

$$D_t(h) = \int\left(\frac{P_t(h, r_h)}{\mathbb{P}_t(h)}\right)^{-\eta}\left(\frac{\mathbb{P}_t(h)}{\mathbb{P}_{\mathrm{H},t}}\right)^{-\eta}C_{\mathrm{H},t}dr_h$$

$$D_t^*(h) = \int\left(\frac{P_t^*(h, r_h^*)}{\mathbb{P}_t^*(h)}\right)^{-\eta}\left(\frac{\mathbb{P}_t^*(h)}{\mathbb{P}_{\mathrm{H},t}^*}\right)^{-\eta}C_{\mathrm{H},t}^*dr_h^*$$

for the case of Leontief production function. In these expressions, $\mathbb{P}_t^*(h)$ and $\mathbb{P}_{\mathrm{H},t}^*$ denote the price index of industry h and of Home goods, respectively, in the Foreign country, expressed in Foreign currency. In comparing the two sets of the previous demands, recall that in the linear production case (4) the firm's productivity affects the quantity of tradable good h needed to satisfy a given final demand for each variety r_h: hence, the demand for the monopolist's product is scaled by productivity.

For each industry h, we can write the relative price dispersion at the consumer level as:

$$S_t(h) = (1 - \theta)\left(\frac{P_t(h)}{\mathbb{P}_t(h)}\right)^{-\eta} + \theta\pi_t^{\eta}(h)S_{t-1},$$

where $\pi_t^{\eta}(h) = \mathbb{P}_t(h)/\mathbb{P}_{t-1}(h)$.[6] Using this result, we can rewrite the demand faced by each upstream producer as a function of price dispersion. In other words,

6. See appendix for details.

the producer's demand curve depends on the price dispersion at the consumer level, induced by infrequent price adjustment by downstream firms.[7]

By the first-order condition of the producer's problem, the optimal price $\overline{P}_t^o(h)$ in domestic currency charged to domestic downstream firms is:

$$\overline{P}_t^o(h) = \frac{E_t \sum_{k=0}^{\infty} \overline{\theta}^k p_{bt,t+k} \varepsilon_{t+k}(h) D_{t+k}(h) \overline{MC}_{t+k}(h)}{E_t \sum_{k=0}^{\infty} \overline{\theta}^k p_{bt,t+k} (\varepsilon_{t+k}(h) - 1) D_{t+k}(h)}; \tag{8}$$

while the price (in foreign currency) charged to downstream firms in the foreign country is:

$$\overline{P_t^{*o}}(h) = \frac{E_t \sum_{k=0}^{\infty} \overline{\theta}^k p_{bt,t+k} \varepsilon_{t+k}^*(h) D_{t+k}^*(h) (\overline{MC}_{t+k}(h) / \mathcal{E}_{t+k})}{E_t \sum_{k=0}^{\infty} \overline{\theta}^k p_{bt,t+k} (\varepsilon_{t+k}^*(h) - 1) D_{t+k}^*(h)};$$

where the elasticities

$$\varepsilon_{t+k}(h) = -\frac{\partial D_{t+k}(h)}{\partial \overline{P}_t(h)} \frac{\overline{P}_t(h)}{D_{t+k}(h)}$$

$$\varepsilon_{t+k}^*(h) = -\frac{\partial D_{t+k}^*(h)}{\partial \overline{P}_t^*(h)} \frac{\overline{P}_t^*(h)}{D_{t+k}^*(h)}$$

summarize how the price set by the producer as of t, will affect the choice of downstream firms that will have a chance to change their prices in the current period and in the future.

Now, it is well understood that when $\overline{P}_t(h)$ and $\overline{P}_t^*(h)$ are sticky in local currency, exchange rate movements translate into systematic violation of the law of one price. However, comparing the expressions for the optimal prices, it is apparent that the law of one price is bound to be systematically violated even when the firm has a chance to reset its prices, reflecting differences in the two market elasticities $\varepsilon(h)$ and $\varepsilon^*(h)$. In this respect, it is worth emphasizing that in our economy, deviations from the law of one price across markets are not an exclusive implication of nominal rigidities in local currency. They also depend on the way vertical interactions among upstream and downstream monopolists affect optimal pricing by producers, as shown in the following.

6.4.2 Demand Price Elasticities, Price Variability, and Strategic Interactions

We now characterize the elasticities in equation (9) for our specification in which the downstream firms' production function is linear in the traded good, as in equation (4), and discuss its main properties and implications for pricing. The derivative of the producer's demand with respect to its own price is:

7. In the Leontief case, for instance, the demand curve can be written as:

$$D_{t+k}(h) = [(1-\theta)P_{t+k}^{-\eta}(h) + \theta \mathbb{P}_{t+k-1}^{-\eta}(h) S_{t+k-1}(h)] \mathbb{P}_{H,t+k}^{\eta} C_{H,t+k}.$$

$$\frac{\partial D_{t+k}(h)}{\partial \overline{P}_t(h)} = \sum_{s=0}^{k} \frac{\partial C_{t+k}(h, r_h)}{\partial P_{t+k-s}(h, r_h)} \frac{\partial P_{t+k-s}(h, r_h)}{\partial \overline{P}_t(h)}$$
$$= -\eta(1-\theta)\sum_{s=0}^{k} \theta^s \left(\frac{P^o_{t+k-s}(h)}{\mathbb{P}_{\mathrm{H},t+k}}\right)^{-\eta} \frac{C_{\mathrm{H},t+k}}{Z_{t+k}} \frac{1}{P^o_{t+k-s}(h)} \frac{\partial P^o_{t+k-s}(h)}{\partial \overline{P}_t(h)},$$

where the partial derivative $\partial P^o_{t+k}(h)/\partial \overline{P}_t(h)$ captures the extent to which current and future optimal pricing decision by firms r_h are affected by the current producer pricing decision—here, $P^o_{t+k}(h)$ denotes the optimal price set by the downstream firms, which will reoptimize in each period $t + k$, while facing the traded input price $\overline{P}_t(h)$.

In the appendix, we show that this derivative is simply equal to the ratio of the two prices themselves; for example, at time t we have $\partial P^o_t(h)/\partial \overline{P}_t(h) = P^o_t(h)/\overline{P}_t(h)$. Using this fact, the impact on current and future demand of a price change by the producer can be simplified as follows:[8]

$$\frac{\partial D_{t+k}(h)}{\partial \overline{P}_t(h)} = -\eta(1-\theta)\frac{C_{\mathrm{H},t+k}}{Z_{t+k}} \frac{\mathbb{P}^{\eta}_{\mathrm{H},t+k}}{\overline{P}_t(h)} \sum_{s=0}^{k} \theta^s (P^o_{t+k-s}(h))^{-\eta}$$
$$= -\eta(1-\theta)\frac{C_{\mathrm{H},t+k}}{Z_{t+k}} \frac{\mathbb{P}^{\eta}_{\mathrm{H},t+k}}{\mathbb{P}^{\eta}_{t+k}(h)} \frac{1}{\overline{P}_t(h)} \sum_{s=0}^{k} \theta^s \left(\frac{P^o_{t+k-s}(h)}{\mathbb{P}_{t+k}(h)}\right)^{-\eta}$$
$$= -\eta\frac{C_{\mathrm{H},t+k}}{Z_{t+k}} \frac{\mathbb{P}^{\eta}_{\mathrm{H},t+k}}{\mathbb{P}^{\eta}_{t+k}(h)} \frac{1}{\overline{P}_t(h)} \left(S_{t+k}(h) - \theta^{k+1}\frac{\mathbb{P}^{\eta}_{t+k}(h)}{\mathbb{P}^{\eta}_{t-1}(h)} S_{t-1}(h)\right).$$

The sum $\sum_{s=0}^{k} \theta^s (P^o_{t+k-s}(h)/\mathbb{P}_{t+k}(h))^{-\eta}$ in the second line of this expression reflects the fact that, when setting the optimal price as of t, upstream monopolists internalize its effects on final demand in each future period between t and $t + k$. Observe that in the last line in the previous expression, this sum has been substituted out using the definition of $S_{t+k}(h)$.[9]

8. We note here that this result is due to the fact that for prices P_{t+k} reset optimally as of

$$t + k, \frac{\partial MC_{t+k+s}(h)}{\partial \overline{P}_t(h)} = \frac{1}{Z_{t+k+s}} = \frac{MC_{t+k+s}(h)}{\overline{P}_t(h)}, \forall s > 0, \text{ and}$$

$$\frac{\partial C_{t+k+s}(h, r_h)}{\partial \overline{P}_t(h)} = -\eta \frac{C_{t+k+s}(h, r_h)}{P_{t+k}(h)} \frac{\partial P_{t+k}(h)}{\partial \overline{P}_t(h)}.$$

See appendix for details.

9. Namely:

$$S_{t+k}(h) \equiv \int \left(\frac{P_{t+k}(h, r_h)}{\mathbb{P}_{t+k}(h)}\right)^{-\eta} dr = (1-\theta)\mathbb{P}^{\eta}_{t+k}(h) \sum_{j=0}^{\infty} \theta^j P_{t+k-j}(h)^{-\eta}$$

$$(1-\theta)\mathbb{P}^{\eta}_{t+k}(h) \sum_{j=0}^{k} \theta^j P_{t+k-j}(h)^{-\eta} = S_{t+k}(h) - (1-\theta)\mathbb{P}^{\eta}_{t+k}(h) \sum_{j=k+1}^{\infty} \theta^j P_{t+k-j}(h)^{-\eta}$$
$$= S_{t+k}(h) - (1-\theta)\frac{\mathbb{P}^{\eta}_{t+k}(h)}{\mathbb{P}^{\eta}_{t-1}(h)} \mathbb{P}^{\eta}_{t-1}(h)\theta^{k+1} \sum_{j=0}^{\infty} \theta^j P_{t-1-j}(h)^{-\eta}$$
$$= S_{t+k}(h) - \theta^{k+1}\left(\frac{\mathbb{P}_{t+k}(h)}{\mathbb{P}_{t-1}(h)}\right)^{\eta} S_{t-1}(h).$$

Using again the definition of $S_{t+k}(h)$, the price elasticity of demand at each point in time as perceived by the producer $\varepsilon_{t+k}(h)$ becomes:

$$(9)\quad \varepsilon_{t+k}(h) = -\frac{\partial D_{t+k}(h)}{\partial \overline{P}_t(h)} \frac{\overline{P}_t(h)}{D_{t+k}(h)}$$

$$= \eta \frac{C_{H,t+k}}{Z_{t+k}} \frac{\mathbb{P}^{\eta}_{H,t+k}}{\mathbb{P}^{\eta}_{t+k}(h)} \left(S_{t+k}(h) - \theta^{k+1} \frac{\mathbb{P}^{\eta}_{t+k}(h)}{\mathbb{P}^{\eta}_{t-1}(h)} S_{t-1}(h) \right) \frac{1}{D_{t+k}(h)}$$

$$= \eta \left(1 - \frac{\theta^{k+1} (\mathbb{P}_{t+k}(h) / \mathbb{P}_{t-1}(h))^{\eta} S_{t-1}(h)}{S_{t+k}(h)} \right).$$

This demand elasticity is a function of the producer price $\overline{P}_t(h)$ only indirectly, through the impact of $P^o_{t+k}(h)$ on the final price level $\mathbb{P}_{t+k}(h)$: absent downstream nominal rigidities ($\theta = 0$), the price elasticity of the producer would be constant and proportional to that perceived by the downstream firm, η—the final price charged would simply be $[\eta/(\eta - 1)]\overline{P}_t(h)/Z_t$.

In equation (9), the implications for the demand elasticity of nominal rigidities at the downstream level are captured by the negative term inside the brackets. An important and novel result is that the demand price elasticity perceived by upstream firms under sticky prices is time varying and, up to first order[10] a decreasing function of the cumulated rate of inflation at the consumer level, $\mathbb{P}_{t+k}(h)/\mathbb{P}_{t-1}(h)$. Namely, with positive inflation such elasticity will be lower than with flexible prices (in which case it is constant and equal to η). Any change in the consumer prices within a specific h industry—either in response to productivity shocks hitting downstream firms, or in response to price changes by the upstream firms—modifies the elasticity of the demand faced by upstream producers in the same industry. A notable implication is that differences in national inflation rates will induce differences in demand price elasticities for a product, creating an incentive for producers to price-to-market across borders.

To provide an intuitive account of these results, observe that, from the vantage point of an upstream producer of tradables h, the marginal revenue from a price change reflects the fact that only some downstream firms update their prices in any given period. Specifically, the upstream monopolist does not know which individual firm r_h will be updating its price in the period, but knows that a fraction $1 - \theta$ of them will do so, while a fraction θ will keep their price unchanged. Because of the latter, the upstream producers will optimally respond to shocks to own marginal costs by charging a price that is higher than she or he would ideally charge if all downstream producers set new prices.

This leads to *strategic substitutability* among producers: namely, a rise in their marginal costs will lead to an increase in the desired markups by pro-

10. We show in the following that up to first-order price dispersion $S_t(h)$ is equal to 1 around a zero inflation steady state.

ducers. Strategic substitutability in our model is important because it implies that producer prices will be more reactive to shocks to their demand conditions and to marginal costs: when vertical interactions among firms with sticky prices are considered, it may not be necessarily the case that several layers of nominal rigidities bring about more inertia in prices.

It is worth stressing that, if monetary policy stabilized consumer prices completely, removing any within-industry price dispersion for each good h, such policy would make the producer's demand elasticity and thus its desired markup constant. To wit: in this case, the producer's demand elasticity would be given by $\eta(1 - \theta^{k+1})$. Through price stabilization, monetary authorities would therefore eliminate the incentive to price discriminate. However, observe that the elimination of consumer price variability (and consumer price dispersion) would not make the producer's markups independent of downstream price rigidities. The steady-state markup of upstream firms would still be a function of θ, and equal to $\eta/(\eta - (1 - \theta\beta\overline{\theta})/(1 - \theta))$, implying that the steady-state elasticity is lower than η, and equal to

$$\varepsilon_{ss} = \eta\frac{1 - \theta}{1 - \theta\beta\overline{\theta}} < \eta.$$

6.4.3 Inflation Variability, Optimal Markups, and Exchange Rate Pass-Through

To characterize further firms' equilibrium behavior, we log-linearize expression (8) around a zero inflation steady-state. Using standard procedures, the optimal price charged by updating upstream producers can be approximated as follows:

$$\widehat{\overline{P}_t^o}(h) = (1-\beta\overline{\theta})\left[\widehat{\overline{MC}}_t(h) - \frac{\hat{\varepsilon}_t(h)}{\varepsilon_{ss} - 1}\right] + \beta\overline{\theta}E_t\widehat{\overline{P}_{t+1}^o}(h),$$

where in turn the elasticity as of t is approximately given by

$$\hat{\varepsilon}_t(h) = -\theta\eta\hat{\pi}_t(h),$$

with $\hat{\pi}_t(h)$ denoting downstream inflation deviations from steady state in sector h. Because downstream inflation changes depend on the final price set by firms adjusting during the period

$$\hat{\pi}_t(h) = (1 - \theta)\widehat{P_t^o}(h),$$

it is clear that the elasticity $\hat{\varepsilon}_t(h)$ will ultimately be a decreasing function of the upstream price. Using the difference equation for optimally reset downstream prices,

$$\widehat{P_t^o}(h) = (1 - \beta\theta)\widehat{MC}_t(h) + \beta\theta E_t\widehat{P_{t+1}^o}(h),$$

together with the fact that $\widehat{MC}_t(h) = \widehat{\overline{P}_t^o}(h) - \hat{Z}_t$, we can characterize downstream inflation in each industry h as

$$\hat{\pi}_t(h) = (1-\theta)(1-\beta\theta)[\widehat{\bar{P}_t^o}(h) - \hat{Z}_t] + \theta\beta E_t \hat{\pi}_{t+1}(h),$$

and thus derive a dynamic expression for the optimal pricing by upstream firms:

$$\widehat{\bar{P}_t^o}(h) = (1-\beta\bar{\theta})\left(\widehat{\overline{MC}}_t(h) + \frac{\eta\theta}{\varepsilon_{ss}-1}[(1-\theta)(1-\beta\theta)(\widehat{\bar{P}_t^o}(h) - \hat{Z}_t) + \theta\beta E_t \hat{\pi}_{t+1}(h)]\right)$$
$$+ \beta\bar{\theta}E_t\widehat{\bar{P}_{t+1}^o}(h)$$
$$= \frac{(1-\beta\bar{\theta})(\widehat{\overline{MC}}_t(h) + \frac{\varepsilon_{ss}}{\varepsilon_{ss}-1}(1-\beta\bar{\theta})\theta[-(1-\theta)(1-\beta\theta)\hat{Z}_t + \theta\beta E_t\hat{\pi}_{t+1}(h)])}{1 - \frac{\varepsilon_{ss}}{\varepsilon_{ss}-1}\theta(1-\beta\theta)(1-\beta\bar{\theta})^2}$$
$$+ \frac{\beta\bar{\theta}E_t\widehat{\bar{P}_{t+1}^o}(h)}{1 - \frac{\varepsilon_{ss}}{\varepsilon_{ss}-1}\theta(1-\beta\theta)(1-\beta\bar{\theta})^2}.$$

The term $1-\varepsilon_{ss}/(\varepsilon_{ss}-1)\,\theta\,(1-\beta\theta)\,(1-\beta\bar{\theta})^2$ in the denominator of the previous expression is lower than 1.[11] This means that, as already discussed, the time varying elasticity due to downstream nominal rigidities will transpire into a larger response of the optimal price to changes in marginal costs, relative to the case in which the upstream price elasticity is constant.

Now the price charged to foreign downstream firms by domestic upstream producers will be:

$$\widehat{P^{*o}_t}(h) = \frac{(1-\beta\bar{\theta})(\widehat{\overline{MC}}_t(h) - \hat{\mathcal{E}}_t + \frac{\varepsilon_{ss}}{\varepsilon_{ss}-1}\theta(1-\beta\bar{\theta})[-(1-\beta\theta)(1-\theta)\widehat{Z^*}_t + \theta\beta E_t\widehat{\pi^*}_{t+1}(h)])}{1 - \frac{\varepsilon_{ss}}{\varepsilon_{ss}-1}\theta(1-\beta\theta)(1-\beta\bar{\theta})^2}$$
$$+ \frac{\beta\bar{\theta}E_t\widehat{P^{*o}_{t+1}}(h)}{1 - \frac{\varepsilon_{ss}}{\varepsilon_{ss}-1}\theta(1-\beta\theta)(1-\beta\bar{\theta})^2}.$$

The coefficient multiplying exchange rate deviations $\hat{\mathcal{E}}_t$ in this expression, which we write for convenience here

$$\frac{1-\beta\bar{\theta}}{1-\varepsilon_{ss}/(\varepsilon_{ss}-1)\theta(1-\beta\theta)(1-\beta\bar{\theta})^2},$$

11. It is also possible to show that this term will be positive as long as the upstream markup is not too large. A sufficient condition is that

$$\frac{\varepsilon_{ss}}{\varepsilon_{ss}-1} < 4\beta \Leftrightarrow \eta > \frac{4\beta}{4\beta-1}\,\frac{1-\theta\beta\bar{\theta}}{1-\theta}.$$

measures the structural exchange rate pass-through, as defined in Corsetti, Dedola, and Leduc (2005). This coefficient highlights the two mechanisms determining how exchange rate movements are passed through into local prices according to our analysis. On the one hand, upstream nominal rigidities ($\bar{\theta} > 0$) tend to lower short-run pass-through irrespective of vertical interactions. But, as we previously noted, downstream nominal rigidities ($\theta > 0$) lower the denominator in the prior expression below 1 because of strategic substitutability. Thus, the response of the optimal price to exchange rate changes will be stronger when the elasticity is time varying due to downstream nominal rigidities, relative to the case of a constant elasticity. For instance, if upstream prices were fully flexible—corresponding to $\bar{\theta} = 0$—the structural pass-through coefficient would be larger than 1 per effect of the vertical interactions with downstream sticky price firms. However, for any given value of θ, a sufficiently large $\bar{\theta}$ will generally reduce exchange rate pass-through (ERPT) below 100 percent in the short run—unless the upstream steady-state markup is unreasonably large.[12]

6.4.4 Price Rigidities Versus Local Costs (the Leontief Technology Case)

As already mentioned, in previous work (Corsetti, Dedola, and Leduc 2005) we have analyzed a different model specification, assuming that the production function of the downstream firm includes a local input, which is a poor substitute for the traded intermediate goods. We showed that the demand price elasticity faced by upstream producers is also market-specific in this case (independently of nominal rigidities). The properties of this model are, however, quite different from the ones discussed so far. In the rest of this subsection, we analyze these differences within a single analytical framework. Our main conclusion is that the presence of local inputs (which are weak substitutes for intermediate goods) in downstream production leads to an attenuation of the main effect of price stickiness on upstream producers' optimal markups, without necessarily overturning it.

When the technology of the downstream firms is as in equation (5), the derivative of the producer demand with respect to its price becomes:

12. Precisely, it can be shown that a sufficient condition for the ERPT coefficient to be less than one is that:

$$\bar{\theta} \geq \frac{1}{\beta} - \frac{\varepsilon_{ss} - 1}{\varepsilon_{ss}}\left(\sqrt{1 + \frac{2}{\beta}\frac{\varepsilon_{ss}}{\varepsilon_{ss} - 1}} - 1\right).$$

If it is also assumed that the markup is not too large (e.g., $\varepsilon_{ss}/(\varepsilon_{ss} - 1) \leq 2\beta$), which is reasonable for β close to 1, then a sufficient condition for incomplete ERPT in the short run is:

$$\bar{\theta} \geq \frac{2 - \sqrt{3}}{\beta} = \frac{0.268}{\beta}.$$

Finally, observe that the ERPT coefficient is also a nonmonotonic function of the degree of downstream price rigidity, θ.

$$\frac{\partial D_{t+k}(h)}{\partial \overline{P}_t(h)} = -\eta(1-\theta)\sum_{s=0}^{k}\theta^s\left(\frac{P^o_{t+k-s}(h)}{\mathbb{P}_{H,t+k}}\right)^{-\eta}\frac{C_{H,t+k}}{P^o_{t+k-s}(h)}\frac{\partial P^o_{t+k-s}(h)}{\partial \overline{P}_t(h)}.$$

This is similar to the expression derived for the linear case, except that the right-hand side is not scaled by downstream firms' productivity. After some simplifications (detailed in the appendix), the derivative of the final price to the producer price can be shown to be a constant depending on η. Evaluating this derivative at time t we can write:[13]

$$\frac{\partial P^o_t(h)}{\partial \overline{P}_t(h)} = \frac{\eta}{\eta-1}.$$

Intuitively, the effect of an increase in the upstream producer price (and thus of the marginal cost) on the price optimally charged by downstream firms in the same period will be proportional to the markup charged by the latter, $\eta/(\eta-1)$; a clear instance of double marginalization.

The derivative of current and future demands with respect to the wholesale price becomes:[14]

$$\begin{aligned}\frac{\partial D_{t+k}(h)}{\partial \overline{P}_t(h)} &= -\frac{\eta^2}{\eta-1}(1-\theta)\sum_{s=0}^{k}\theta^s\left(\frac{P^o_{t+k-s}(h)}{\mathbb{P}_{H,t+k}}\right)^{-\eta}\frac{C_{H,t+k}}{P^o_{t+k-s}(h)}\\ &= -\frac{\eta^2}{\eta-1}C_{H,t+k}\frac{\mathbb{P}^{\eta}_{H,t+k}}{\mathbb{P}^{\eta+1}_{t+k}(h)}(1-\theta)\sum_{s=0}^{k}\theta^s\left(\frac{P^o_{t+k-s}(h)}{\mathbb{P}_{t+k}(h)}\right)^{-\eta-1}\\ &= -\frac{\eta^2}{\eta-1}C_{H,t+k}\frac{\mathbb{P}^{\eta}_{H,t+k}}{\mathbb{P}^{\eta+1}_{t+k}(h)}\left[\tilde{S}_{t+k}(h)-\theta^{k+1}\left(\frac{\mathbb{P}_{t+k}(h)}{\mathbb{P}_{t-1}(h)}\right)^{\eta+1}\tilde{S}_{t-1}(h)\right].\end{aligned}$$

13. Using the same reasoning as in the appendix and the fact that $\partial MC_{t+k}(h)/\partial \overline{P}_t(h) = 1$, and

$$\begin{aligned}\frac{\partial C_{t+k}(h,r_h)}{\partial \overline{P}_t(h)} &= -\eta\left(\frac{P_t(h)}{\mathbb{P}_{H,t+k}}\right)^{-\eta}C_{H,t+k}\frac{1}{P_t(h)}\frac{\partial P_t(h)}{\partial \overline{P}_t(h)}\\ &= -\eta\frac{C_{t+k}(h,r_h)}{P_t(h)}\frac{\partial P_t(h)}{\partial \overline{P}_t(h)}.\end{aligned}$$

14. The following is due to the fact that for retail prices P_{t+k} reset as of $t+k$, it will still be true that $\partial MC_{t+k+s}(h)/\partial \overline{P}_t(h) = 1$ and

$$\frac{\partial C_{t+k+s}(h,r_h)}{\partial \overline{P}_t(h)} = -\eta\frac{C_{t+k+s}(h,r_h)}{P_{t+k}(h)}\frac{\partial P_{t+k}(h)}{\partial \overline{P}_t(h)}.$$

Moreover, define:

$$\tilde{S}_{t+k}(h) \equiv \int\left(\frac{P^o_{t+k}(h,r_h)}{\mathbb{P}_{t+k}(h)}\right)^{-\eta-1}dr = (1-\theta)\mathbb{P}^{\eta+1}_{t+k}(h)\sum_{j=0}^{\infty}\theta^j P^o_{t+k-j}(h)^{-\eta-1}$$

$$\begin{aligned}(1-\theta)\mathbb{P}^{\eta+1}_{t+k}(h)\sum_{j=0}^{k}\theta^j P^o_{t+k-j}(h)^{-\eta-1} &= \tilde{S}_{t+k}(h)-(1-\theta)\mathbb{P}^{\eta+1}_{t+k}(h)\sum_{j=k+1}^{\infty}\theta^j P_{t+k-j}(h)^{-\eta-1}\\ &= \tilde{S}_{t+k}(h)-(1-\theta)\frac{\mathbb{P}^{\eta+1}_{t+k}(h)}{\mathbb{P}^{\eta+1}_{t-1}(h)}\mathbb{P}^{\eta+1}_{t-k}(h)\theta^{k+1}\sum_{j=0}^{\infty}\theta^j P_{t-j}(h)^{-\eta-1}\\ &= \tilde{S}_{t+k}(h)-\theta^{k+1}\left(\frac{\mathbb{P}_{t+k}(h)}{\mathbb{P}_{t-1}(h)}\right)^{\eta+1}\tilde{S}_{t-1}(h).\end{aligned}$$

The price elasticity of demand at each point in time as perceived by the upstream producer is then given by:

$$(10)\qquad \varepsilon_{t+k}(h) = \frac{\eta^2}{\eta - 1}\frac{\bar{P}_t(h)}{\mathbb{P}_{t+k}(h)}\left[\tilde{S}_{t+k}(h) - \theta^{k+1}\left(\frac{\mathbb{P}_{t+k}(h)}{\mathbb{P}_{t-1}(h)}\right)^{\eta+1}\tilde{S}_{t-1}(h)\right],$$

where again it is true that

$$\tilde{S}_t(h) = (1 - \theta)\left(\frac{P_t(h)}{\mathbb{P}_t(h)}\right)^{-\eta-1} + \theta\pi_t^{\eta+1}(h)\,\tilde{S}_{t-1}(h).$$

In contrast to the linear production case, the demand elasticity is now a function of the wholesale price $\bar{P}_t(h)$ not only indirectly, through the final price index $\mathbb{P}_{t+k}(h)$, but also directly. Specifically, this elasticity reflects three effects.

The first arises from the double marginalization due to the presence of two vertically integrated monopolists and is captured by the term $\eta/(\eta - 1)$ in (10): absent nominal rigidities ($\theta = 0$) and the nontraded input among downstream firms, the price elasticity of the producer would be constant and equal to that perceived by these firms, η—the price charged to consumers by all firms would simply be $\eta/(\eta - 1)\bar{P}_t(h)$.

The second effect, arising from nominal rigidities, is captured by the term in brackets in (10) and has already been discussed extensively in the previous subsection—it links the demand elasticity to downstream price inflation and price dispersion among final producers. Its presence tends to make the demand elasticity an *increasing* function of $\bar{P}_t(h)$.

The third and last effect arises from the assumption that downstream firms combine the traded and labor inputs in fixed proportion and is captured by the term $\bar{P}_t(h)/\mathbb{P}_{t+k}(h)$: absent downstream nominal rigidities this ratio would be equal to $\bar{P}_t(h)/((\eta/(\eta - 1)(\bar{P}_t(h) + W_t/Z_t))$, as in Corsetti and Dedola (2005). However, in contrast to our previous results, this last effect tends to make the demand elasticity *decreasing* in $\bar{P}_t(h)$.

Summing up: our analysis suggests that price stickiness and local inputs, which are complement to intermediate tradables in final good production, affect producers' markups in different ways: the former makes the producers' demand elasticity decreasing, the latter increasing, in the producer price. Under what conditions would one effect prevail over the other?

Taking a log-linear approximation to the upstream price and the elasticity, we find as before that

$$\widehat{\bar{P}_t^o}(h) = (1 - \beta\bar{\theta})\left[\widehat{MC}_t(h) - \frac{\hat{\varepsilon}_t(h)}{\varepsilon_{ss} - 1}\right] + \beta\bar{\theta}E_t\widehat{\bar{P}_{t+1}^o}(h),$$

where the elasticity as of t is now given by:

$$\hat{\varepsilon}_t(h) = \widehat{\bar{P}_t^o}(h) - (1 + \theta\eta)\widehat{P_t^o}(h).$$

and

$$\varepsilon_{ss} = \eta\delta\frac{1-\theta}{1-\theta\beta\bar{\theta}}.$$

Relative to our previous analysis, this steady-state elasticity depends on δ, which is defined as the steady-state share of the upstream product in the downstream firms' costs, with $0 < 1 - \delta < 1$. Because downstream marginal cost can be approximated as

$$\widehat{MC}_t(h) = \delta\widehat{\bar{P}^o_t}(h) + (1-\delta)(\hat{W}_t - \hat{Z}_t),$$

the expression for the optimal upstream price becomes:

$$\widehat{\bar{P}^o_t}(h) = (1-\beta\bar{\theta})\left[\widehat{MC}_t(h) - \frac{\hat{\varepsilon}_t(h)}{\varepsilon_{ss}-1}\right] + \beta\bar{\theta}E_t\widehat{\bar{P}^o_{t+1}}(h)$$

$$= (1-\beta\bar{\theta})\left[\widehat{MC}_t(h) - \frac{\widehat{\bar{P}^o_t}(h) - (1+\theta\eta)((1-\beta\theta)(\delta\widehat{\bar{P}^o_t}(h) + (1-\delta)(\hat{W}_t - \hat{Z}_t)) + \beta\theta E_t\widehat{P^o_{t+1}}(h))}{\varepsilon_{ss}-1}\right]$$

$$+ \beta\bar{\theta}E_t\widehat{\bar{P}^o_{t+1}}(h),$$

or

$$\widehat{\bar{P}^o_t}(h) = \frac{(1-\beta\bar{\theta})\left[\widehat{MC}_t(h) - \dfrac{(1+\theta\eta)((1-\beta\theta)(1-\delta)(\hat{W}_t - \hat{Z}_t) + \beta\theta E_t\widehat{P^o_{t+1}}(h))}{\varepsilon_{ss}-1}\right]}{1 + \dfrac{1-\delta(1+\theta\eta)(1-\beta\bar{\theta})(1-\beta\theta)}{\varepsilon_{ss}-1}}$$

$$+ \frac{\beta\bar{\theta}E_t\widehat{\bar{P}^o_{t+1}}(h)}{1 + \dfrac{1-\delta(1+\theta\eta)(1-\beta\bar{\theta})(1-\beta\theta)}{\varepsilon_{ss}-1}}.$$

The denominator of the coefficient multiplying marginal costs can now have either sign; that is, the time varying elasticity can either magnify or mute the response of the optimal upstream price to marginal costs. This means that we can have either strategic substitutability (the denominator is negative, as was in the previous subsection) or strategic complementarity (positive). A sufficient condition for strategic complementarity is:

$$\delta < \frac{1}{1+\theta\eta}.$$

In other words, the share of local inputs in downstream firms should be sufficiently high. Observe that the previous inequality is more likely to hold when η is low (markups are high), or θ is low, so that downstream prices are not too sticky.

6.5 Calibration

This section describes the benchmark calibration for our numerical experiments, which we assume symmetric across countries. We used Dynare++ to solve for the optimal monetary policy and to simulate our different economies. In each exercise, we report statistics averaged over 500 simulations of 100 periods each.

6.5.1 Preferences and Production

We posit that the period-by-period utility function has the form already shown by equation (1), that we reproduce here for convenience:

$$U\left[C_t, \frac{M_{t+1}}{P_t}, L_t\right] = \frac{C_t^{1-\sigma}}{1-\sigma} + \chi\frac{(M_{t+1}/P_t)^{1-\sigma}}{1-\sigma} + \kappa\frac{(1-L_t)^{1-\upsilon}}{1-\upsilon}. \tag{11}$$

We set κ so that in steady state, one-third of the time endowment is spent working. In our benchmark calibration, we assume υ equal to σ (risk aversion), which we in turn set to 2. Because the utility function is separable in consumption and real money balances, money demand is determined residually and does not play any role in our results. We therefore set χ arbitrarily to 0.1.

We set the constant elasticity of substitution across brands, η, so that the markup of downstream firms in steady state is 15 percent. Following Backus, Kehoe, and Kydland (1992), we chose ϕ so that the trade elasticity is 1.5. As regards the weights of domestic and foreign tradables in the consumption basket, a_H and a_F (normalized $a_H + a_F = 1$) are set such that imports are 10 percent of aggregate output in steady state, roughly in line with the average ratio for the United States in the last thirty years. We pick the steady-state value of Z to ensure that the price of traded goods accounts for 50 percent of the final price in steady state. This value corresponds to the empirical estimates by Burstein, Neves, and Rebelo (2003) for the distribution margin only. In our specification, downstream firms can do more than distribute goods to final users, suggesting that the value we select is on the conservative side.

As benchmark, we set the probability that upstream and downstream firms update their prices to 0.5. This overall frequency of price adjustment is in line with the evidence in Bils and Klenow (2004) and Nakamura and Steinsson (2008), if sales are treated as price changes.

6.5.2 Productivity Shocks

Let the vector $\mathbf{Z} \equiv \{Z, \overline{Z}, Z^*, \overline{Z^*}\}$ represent the sectoral technology shocks in the domestic and foreign economies. We assume that sectoral disturbances to technology follow a trend-stationary AR(1) process

$$\mathbf{Z}' = \boldsymbol{\lambda}\mathbf{Z} + \mathbf{u}, \tag{12}$$

whereas **u** has variance-covariance matrix $V(\mathbf{u})$, and $\boldsymbol{\lambda}$ is a 4×4 matrix of coefficients describing the autocorrelation properties of the shocks, that are the same for both sectoral shocks. Since we assume a symmetric economic structure across countries, we also impose symmetry on the autocorrelation and variance-covariance matrices of the previous process. Because of lack of sectoral data on productivity, we posit that sectoral shocks follow a rather conventional process. First, in line with most of the international business cycle literature—for example, Backus, Kehoe, and Kydland (1992)—we assume that these shocks are very persistent, and set their autocorrelation to 0.95. Second, the standard deviation of the innovations is set to 0.007. For simplicity, we set the shock correlation and the spillovers across countries and sectors to zero.

6.5.3 Monetary Policy

To characterize the optimal monetary policy, we let the planner choose the growth rates of money in the Home and Foreign economies, to maximize the world welfare subject to the first-order conditions for households and firms and the economy-wide resource constraints. We assume that the planner places equal weights on Home and Foreign welfare, so that world welfare is given by the following expression:

$$Welfare = \frac{V_0 + V_0^*}{2},$$

where V_0 and V_0^* do not take into account utility accruing from real balances in (11). We follow an approach similar to that in Khan, King, and Wolman (2003) and consider an optimal policy that has been in place for a long enough time that initial conditions do not matter. When solving our economies, we assume the presence of fiscal subsidies, financed via lump-sum taxation, to ensure that all prices would equal marginal costs if prices were fully flexible.

In describing our results, we also compare the optimal policy to other well-known policy rules. We first consider a Taylor-type rule that sets the short-term nominal interest rate as a function of the deviations of CPI inflation and real GDP from steady-state values:

$$(13) \qquad R_t = \rho R_{t-1} + \chi(1-\rho)E(\pi_t - \pi^{ss}) + \gamma(1-\rho)(y_t - y^{ss}).$$

We conventionally parameterize the policy rule using the estimates in Lubik and Schorfheide (2004): $\rho = 0.84$, $\chi = 2.19$, $\gamma = 0.3$. We also consider inflation targeting rules in which the central bank stabilizes either the inflation rate at the final or intermediate level, which we label CPI and GDP inflation targeting, respectively.[15]

15. Our price index of Home intermediates is a CES function of the price of Home intermediates in the Home market and the price of Home intermediates sold abroad (expressed in Home currency). We set the weights over those prices to be the same as in the CPI.

6.6 The Response of Producers and Consumer Prices to Shocks

In this section, we use our quantitative framework to discuss key properties of our model regarding the behavior of prices and markups in response to productivity shocks. Figures 6.1 and 6.2 show the impulse responses of prices, markups, and inflation—all in percentage deviations from their

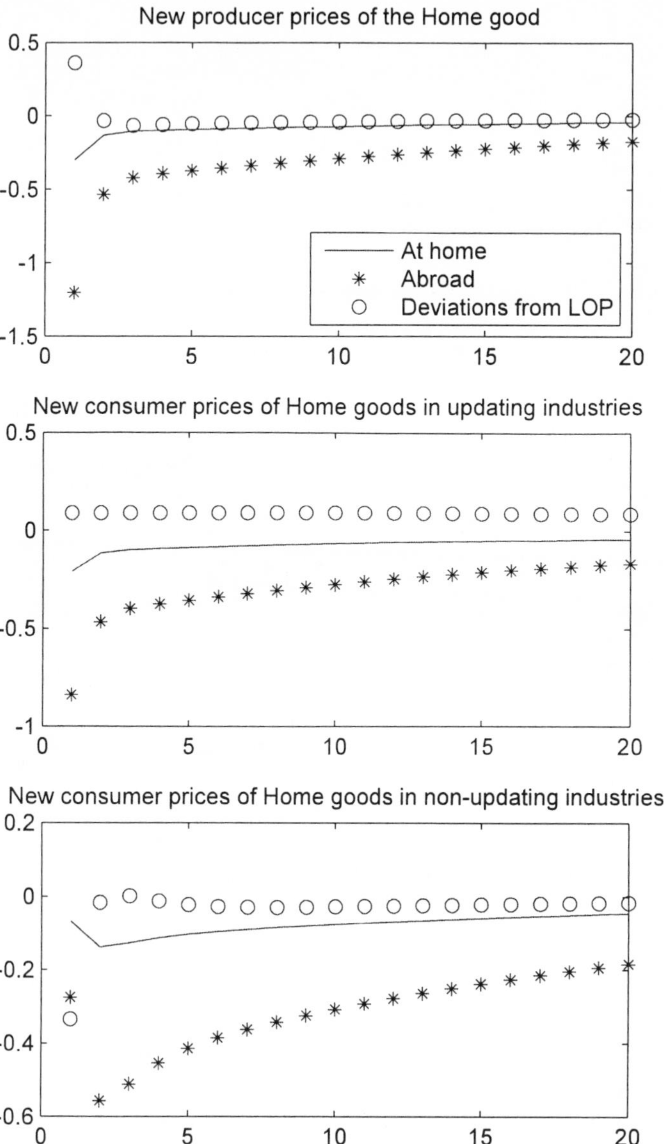

Fig. 6.1 Productivity shock to home upstream production

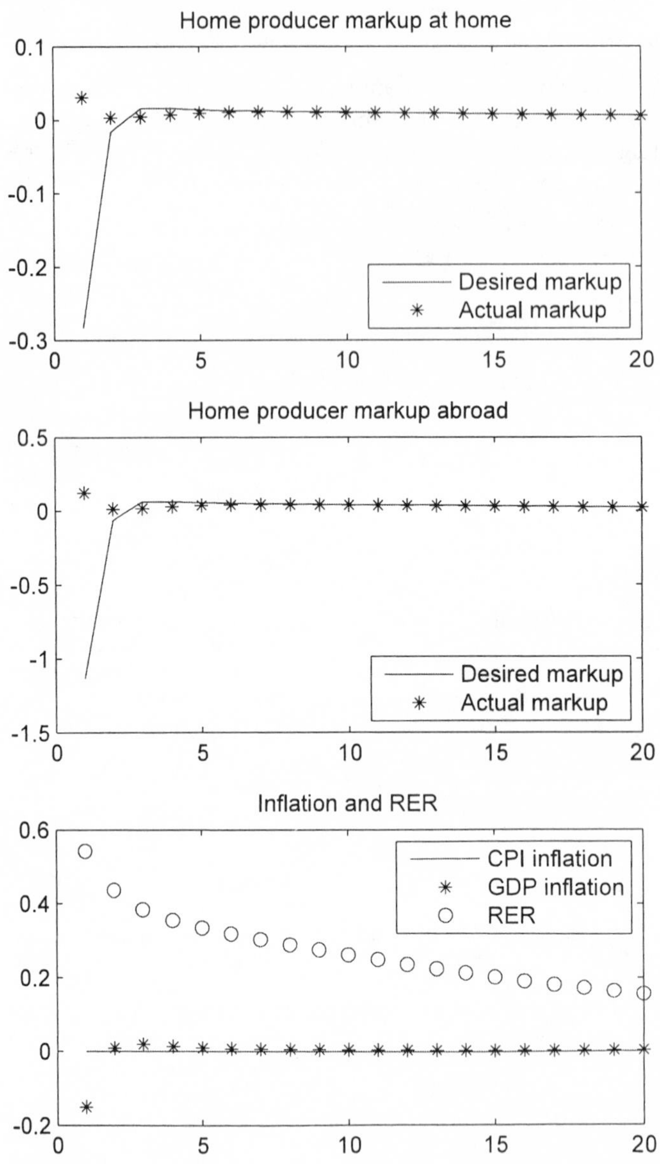

Fig. 6.1 (cont.)

steady-state values—to productivity shocks, distinguishing between the intermediate and final production sectors. Throughout these exercises we assume that central banks in the two countries set monetary policy to implement a strict CPI inflation targeting. Similar results can be obtained however, assuming that central banks implement the optimal policy, discussed in the next section.

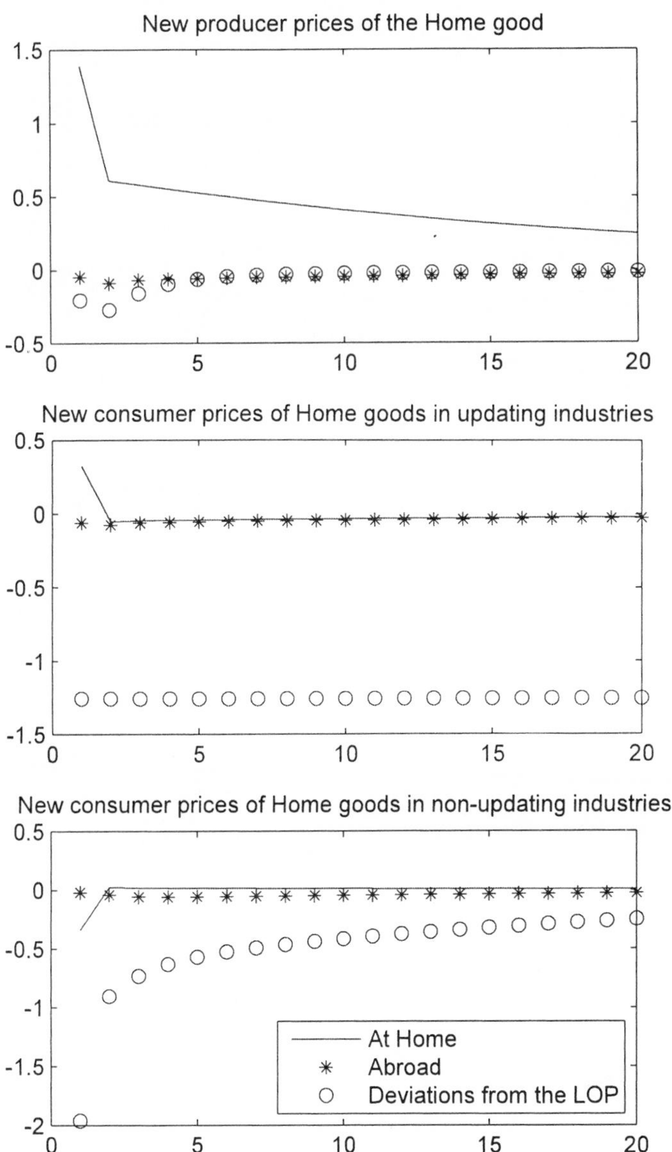

Fig. 6.2 Productivity shock to home downstream production

6.6.1 Technology Shocks to Upstream Firms

Figure 6.1 focuses on the effects of an unexpected and persistent productivity increase in the Home tradable goods sector. Consistent with strict inflation targeting, the monetary authorities react to the shock by expanding the country's monetary stance in line with productivity, causing a depreciation of the nominal exchange rate—given CPI inflation targeting, the

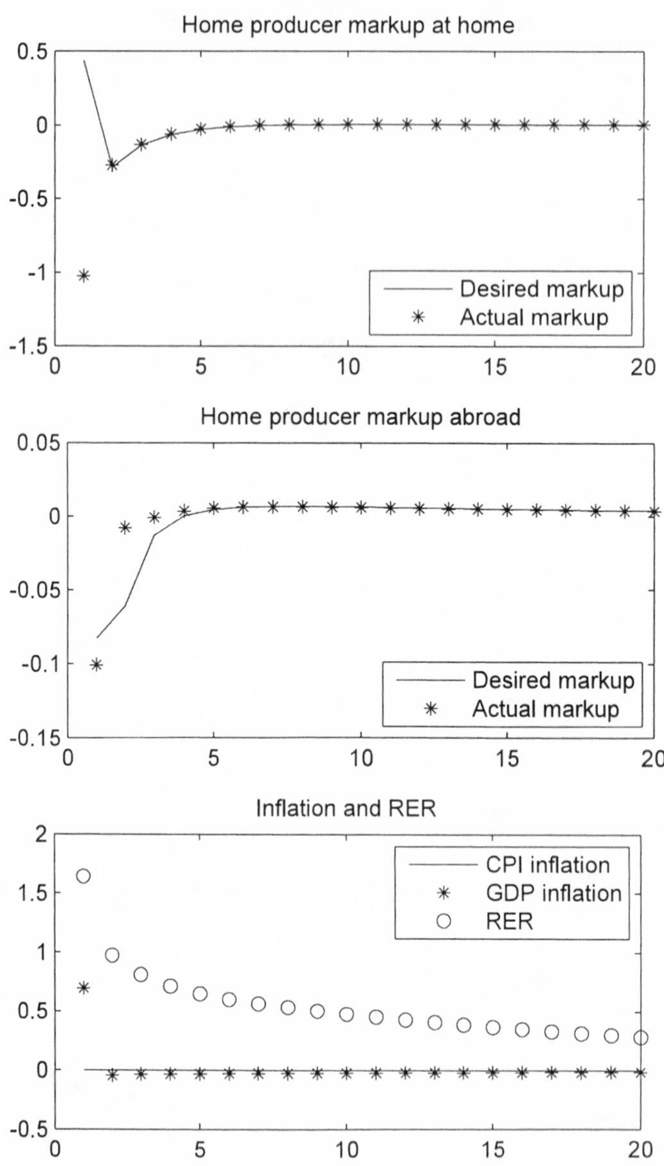

Fig. 6.2 (cont.)

nominal and real exchange rate move together (see the graph in the lower right corner of figure 6.1).

As shown by figure 6.1, upstream producers that update their prices lower them both in the domestic and the foreign market (see the first chart on the upper left corner of the figure). The fall in the home good price is, however, larger abroad than in the domestic market, in violation of the law of one price. In the graph, a positive deviation from the law of one price means that domestic prices are higher than foreign prices.

The behavior of prices is mirrored by the response of the desired and actual markups of the upstream Home producers, shown by the fourth and fifth graphs of figure 6.1. As discussed in section 6.4, downstream nominal rigidities lead to pricing substitutability at the level of upstream producers. As a result, the *desired markup* by these producers fall with their prices in either market, but relatively more in the Foreign one.[16] Nonetheless, since prices are sticky in local currency, the nominal depreciation of the Home exchange rate raises export revenues in the exporters' own currency: the *average markup* in the country actually rises.

The impact of the same shock on *consumer prices* clearly differs, depending on whether the upstream monopolist in a particular industry *h* updates its price, or leaves it unchanged. In the former case (shown in the second graph of figure 6.1), downstream firms face a drop in their marginal costs. Hence, those firms that can reset prices will lower them, both domestically and abroad. As we have seen previously, the intermediate good price falls more in the Foreign country. Thus, Foreign downstream firms decrease their price by more than the domestic ones, so that deviations from the law of one price have the same sign at both consumer prices' and producer prices' level.

Interestingly, our results show that consumer prices fall also in industries in which the upstream producers *do not* update their prices during the period—albeit by a smaller amount than in the other case (see the third graph of figure 6.1). This is so for two reasons. First, although marginal costs of downstream firms in these industries do not fall in the period, these firms nonetheless take into account that the productivity shock is persistent: they thus anticipate that their marginal costs are likely to decrease in the future. Second, a lower price helps these firms respond to increasing competition by firms operating in the other industries, where the price of intermediate product have already gone down.

In these industries, the deviations from the law of one price are larger, but of the opposite sign, relative to the industries in which the upstream price is updated. This is because, for a constant upstream price, consumer prices decrease on impact by more at Home than abroad. To wit: in the first period, the sign of the deviations from the law of one price is positive in the second graph, and negative in the third graph of figure 6.1.

6.6.2 Technology Shocks to Downstream Firms

Figure 6.2 displays the responses to an unexpected persistent increase in the productivity of Home downstream firms. As in the previous case, under

16. Recall that we also show that this result is attenuated when the production function includes local labor input, with a low degree of substitutability with the intermediate tradable goods.

the assumed strict CPI inflation targeting the Home monetary authorities react with an expansion, which leads to nominal and real depreciation of the Home currency (see last graph of figure 6.2).

Recall that downstream technology shocks are also country-specific: they lower the marginal costs of downstream firms at Home, but do not affect the costs of downstream firms in the industry located in the Foreign country. So, in all industries in which the upstream producers do not update their current price within the period, domestic downstream firms updating their prices will optimally lower them, while downstream firms abroad will keep their prices virtually unchanged. This is at the root of the deviations from the law of one price shown in the third graph of figure 6.2, which are further magnified by the fact that monetary authorities react to the shock by engineering Home currency depreciation.

More complex is the case of industries in which upstream producers change their prices (second graph in the figure), since the overall effects of the shock will depend on a number of general equilibrium effects. Key to understanding these effects is the fact that higher productivity by downstream firms causes an increase in their output, and thus in real domestic consumption. In our model specification, the increase in downstream output does not affect the labor market and thus the real wage directly—under the linear production function previously specified, a higher downstream output has no direct impact on the demand for labor, since these firms are assumed not to employ any labor input. However, it does so indirectly: higher domestic consumption is associated with a positive income effect, which reduces labor supply and ultimately translates into a downward shift in hours worked. Given that at the same time the demand for intermediate products is increasing, the labor market tightens, causing a rise in real wages. Facing higher labor costs, upstream firms that can reoptimize their prices raise them, thus increasing the marginal costs of downstream firms. Somewhat surprisingly, as shown in the second graph of figure 6.2, the feedback effect on consumer prices is positive.

This transmission mechanism was discussed early on by Friedman, in his celebrated critical analysis of cost-push inflation (see, e.g., Nelson [2007] and references within). In the industries where upstream producers adjust their prices, they raise them in response to higher costs in the form of higher nominal wages. Yet one key factor raising wages is the demand expansion engineered by monetary policymakers in response to productivity improvement at retail level. Changes in prices that appear to be motivated by costs consideration are actually the result of a demand stimulus working its way up through the vertical links between downstream and upstream producers, and ultimately raising the price of scarce production inputs supplied in competitive markets.

Observe that domestic upstream producers slightly lower their wholesale prices in foreign currency. Nonetheless, because of currency depreciation, these prices in Home currency are higher than the ones charged in the domestic market, again in violation of the law of one price. Consistently, the desired markup of Home producers increases in the Home market, while it falls abroad—in line with the change in prices. The average markup nonetheless falls everywhere in the economy, per effect of nominal rigidities.

6.7 International Dimensions of Optimal Stabilization Policy

This section is devoted to the analysis of stabilization policies under the assumption of cooperation between the Home and Foreign monetary authorities and full commitment. In order to shed light on how policy works in our model, we find it useful to discuss the problem of stabilizing economies hit by shocks to upstream or downstream shocks in isolation, and then proceed to present results for our complete baseline calibration. Thus, results are shown in three tables. For a set of macrovariables, table 6.1 and 6.2 report volatilities conditional on shocks to upstream and downstream productivity, respectively; table 6.3 reports results when both shocks are considered. In each table, the first column shows the result for the flexible price benchmark, in which monetary policy targets a zero rate of CPI inflation at all times; the other columns refer to economies with price rigidities under different policy regimes. Tables 6.1 and 6.2 only show results under the optimal cooperative policy, including a case in which there is no home bias in consumption expenditure (i.e., $a_H = a_F = 1/2$). Table 6.3, instead, includes the alternative monetary policies specified in section 6.5—CPI inflation targeting, GDP inflation targeting, and the Taylor-type rule. As we assume subsidies that exactly offset steady-state markups, under the optimal policy long-run inflation is zero. To facilitate comparison across experiments, we also posit that steady-state inflation is nil when solving the model under the alternative policies.

6.7.1 Upstream Shocks Only

Starting from the simplest case, consider first the problem of stabilizing technology shocks to upstream production only. As an important benchmark, we first establish that, if our Home country were a closed economy, monetary authorities would be able to stabilize completely upstream marginal costs, and therefore upstream prices, preventing any dispersion in the prices charged by adjusting and nonadjusting firms. Monetary authorities can do so by matching any change in upstream marginal costs driven by productivity with a change in the monetary stance in the opposite direction, which ultimately moves nominal wages in tandem with productivity. The specific reason why such a policy would stabilize all sticky prices (at both producer and consumer level) is that, in our specification, fluctuations in nominal wages are not consequential for downstream firms, by virtue of our assumption that these firms employ no labor resources in producing final goods. So, downstream marginal costs only change with the intermediate goods' prices, or with downstream productivity: without shocks to the latter, once upstream prices are constant in equilibrium, so are downstream prices. Similarly to the standard closed economy monetary model, the policy just described would replicate the allocation under flexible prices—this policy is optimal in our environment since we assume that steady-state monopolistic distortions in production are corrected with fiscal instruments.[17]

The optimality of complete price stabilization, however, does not carry over to an open economy setting, as shown in table 6.1. With an optimal monetary policy in place (second column of the table), the variability of the CPI is close to, but not zero—domestic and imported goods prices are actually much more variable than the CPI. Observe that prices and markups in both countries fluctuate much less for domestic goods than for imported goods. This corresponds to the fact that monetary policymakers concentrate their efforts to reduce the volatility of markups of domestic producers selling in the domestic markets. The reason has already been laid out in section 6.2.1, but is worth reconsidering here in the framework of our model with staggered price setting.

By mirroring the logic of Corsetti and Pesenti (2005), assume an equilibrium where there is no price dispersion in either domestic market for domestically produced goods: the monetary authority completely stabilizes the marginal costs of *upstream* firms, once again matching any increase in productivity with an appropriate expansion in the Home monetary stance. While domestic goods prices remain constant and identical to each other, at both intermediate and final level, any monetary decision affecting the nominal exchange rate would create import price dispersion at consumer level (since a fraction $\bar{\theta}$ of Foreign producers would react to, for example, Home depreciation, by raising the price they charge to Home downstream firms). At the margin, depending on the degree of openness of the economy, it would be optimal to move away from such equilibrium. Specifically, it is efficient to stabilize the marginal costs of domestic intermediate producers by less, as to reduce the incentive to move prices in the import sector. Monetary authorities can raise welfare by trading-off lower import price

17. It is worth stressing that, had we assumed that downstream firms use labor, complete stability of upstream prices would be incompatible with complete stability of downstream prices. Even if prices of intermediate goods were held constant, movements in nominal wages in response to endogenous monetary policy changes would additionally affect marginal costs of final good producers, creating an immediate incentive for these to reset prices when possible, thus generating price variability at the retail level. As a result, relative to our baseline model specification, introducing a labor input in final good production implies that welfare-maximizing monetary authorities would face a trade-off between stabilization of upstream marginal costs and downstream price dispersion. They would therefore tend to react by less to upstream productivity shocks, with the objective of containing price dispersion at consumer level. As should become clear in the rest of the text, abstracting from labor inputs in downstream production is helpful in focusing most sharply on the policy trade-offs arising specifically from vertical interactions between downstream and upstream firms.

Table 6.1 **Volatility under optimal policy: Upstream shocks only (in percent)**

	Economies		
	With home bias		Without home bias
Standard deviation	Flexible prices	Optimal policy	Optimal policy
Inflation rates			
CPI	0	0.01	0
Domestic final goods	0.19	0.11	0.25
Imported final goods	0.74	0.43	0.25
Domestic intermediate prices	0.19	0.19	0.50
Import intermediate prices	0.74	0.87	0.50
Export intermediate prices	0.74	0.87	0.50
International prices			
Real exchange rate (CPI based)	1.38	1.62	0
Terms of trade	2.30	2.10	2.06
Deviations from the LOP			
Home goods at producer level	0	0.57	0
Home goods at consumer level	0	0.39	0
Home markups			
Domestic intermediate goods	0	0.06	0.17
Exported intermediate goods	0	0.26	0.17
Domestic final goods	0	0.24	0.65
Imported final goods	0	1.12	0.65
Quantities			
Home consumption	0.87	0.90	0.81
Home hours	0.41	0.43	0.47
Real GDP	1.42	1.43	1.54

dispersion, against some price dispersion in the Home markets for domestic goods.

We observe here that optimal Foreign monetary policy would mimick Home monetary policy in response to Home shocks, for essentially the same reason. For a given Foreign monetary policy, a Home currency depreciation generates price variability in local currency of Foreign imports from Home, as Home exporters updating their price will lower them. An expansion allows the Foreign monetary authorities to contain import price variability, at the cost of some price dispersion in the domestic market for domestic goods. This is exactly what underlies our numerical results in table 6.1.

As is well understood in the literature, with LCP endogenous changes in monetary stance across countries tend to be positively correlated. In the limiting case in which there is no home bias in consumption (the case reported in the third column in table 6.1), domestic and foreign goods in the Home and the Foreign consumer price indexes have exactly the same weights. This implies that, in response to disturbances to upstream productivity, national monetary policy stances react to the same weighted average of shocks, becoming perfectly correlated in the optimum. As a result, the nominal exchange rate does not respond to shocks (in the third column of table 6.1, the volatility of the real exchange rate is 0), even if shocks are country-specific and uncorrelated—a finding discussed at length by the literature surveyed in section 6.2. What induces optimal exchange rate variability under cooperation is home bias in consumption, which obviously raises the importance of stabilizing the marginal costs of domestic producers relative to those of the importers (the case shown in the second column in table 6.1). In this respect, our results generalize the point discussed by Corsetti (2006) to an environment with staggered price adjustment.

By comparing the first and the second column of table 6.1, it is apparent that the positive comovements in optimal national monetary policies induced by LCP distortions curb the *volatility of the terms of trade,* relative to the case of flexible prices. With LCP, nominal exchange rate movements do not help correct international relative prices. The only way in which a nominal expansion cum exchange rate depreciation can reduce the price of domestic goods sold abroad is via price adjustment in foreign currency, but by the Calvo mechanism only a subset of firms can reduce their prices. For all the other firms, the terms of trade actually move in the direction of an appreciation. Hence, any "expenditure-switching effect" from a monetary expansion has nothing to do with exchange rate movements, and comes at the cost of import price dispersion (which is then the main concern of national monetary authorities). This is why, depending on the relative weight of domestic and imported goods in the CPI, optimal stabilization policy tends to contain international relative prices and thus terms of trade variability.

However, observe that in our results the volatility of the real exchange rate, like that of consumption and hours worked, is higher with nominal rigidities (under the optimal policy), than with flexible prices—the opposite of our results on the terms of trade. We will return on this important point in the following.

6.7.2 Downstream Shocks Only

Shocks hitting final good producers substantially modify the monetary policy problem in at least two respects. First, in our baseline specification without labor input in downstream production, monetary authorities would never be able to achieve complete stability of final prices, not even in a closed economy environment. In other words, these shocks create policy trade-offs among competing objectives, independent of openness. The problem is that complete price stability at consumer level requires monetary policy to respond to technology shocks downstream. Because the resulting fluctuations in wages (see section 6.6.2) induce (inefficient) price dispersion among upstream firms, it follows that final producers will face different costs of their intermediate input, depending on which industry they operate in. In this sense, vertical interactions in our model bring about an important dimension of heterogeneity across firms, which should be appropriately emphasized. Differently from standard sticky price models, the marginal costs of our downstream firms are generally not symmetric, not even when the economy is completely closed to foreign trade, and there are no markup shocks; due, for example, to stochastic preferences.

Second, since final producers differentiate locally the products they bring to consumers, downstream shocks add an important element of nontradability to consumer goods. Hence, even when consumer expenditure is not biased toward domestic goods, consumption baskets would still be effectively different across countries. When the expenditure weights a_H and a_F are identical—a case of no home bias in terms of upstream products—monetary authorities would efficiently provide the same degree of stabilization across all categories of domestic and imported goods. Yet in contrast to the case of upstream disturbances only, the optimal monetary stance will be sufficiently different across countries as to induce nominal and real exchange rate fluctuations in response to country-specific shocks at downstream level. This result is a generalization of Duarte and Obstfeld (2008), who also stress nontradability as a reason for nominal exchange rate flexibility. However, they include nontradables as a separate sector in the economy (as they abstract from vertical interactions), and focus on the case of one period preset prices (hence abstract from forward-looking price setting).

The previous discussion is clearly reflected in the results in table 6.2. When we focus on downstream shocks only, the variability of CPI inflation is not zero, and remains remarkably stable for different degrees of home bias in consumption. What instead varies considerably with the degree of home bias is the variability of markups across sectors, since home bias shifts the weight of monetary stabilization away from imported goods. Precisely, observe that in the third column—the case of no home bias—markups are equally stabilized at the retail level, for both domestic and foreign goods. In the second column, instead, the markup of final producers is much less volatile if they sell domestic goods than if they sell imported goods.

Relative to the case of upstream shocks, there are two notable differences regarding exchange rate volatility. First, because of nontradability, the real exchange rate is now much more volatile than the terms of trade, even in the flexible price allocation. Second, relative to the flexible price allocation, an economy with nominal rigidities and the optimal policy in place will be characterized by more volatility in both the real exchange rate and the terms of trade. The fact that these patterns are quite different from those discussed in the previous subsection makes it clear that optimal monetary policies do not translate into any general prescription about the relative volatility of these international prices.

Table 6.2 Volatility under optimal policy: Downstream shocks only (in percent)

	Economies		
	With home bias		Without home bias
Standard deviation	Flexible prices	Optimal policy	Optimal policy
Inflation rates			
CPI	0	0.12	0.13
Domestic final goods	0.02	0.13	0.12
Imported final goods	0.09	0.11	0.12
Domestic intermediate prices	0.69	0.38	0.39
Import intermediate prices	0.77	0.44	0.39
Export intermediate prices	0.77	0.44	0.39
International prices			
Real exchange rate (CPI based)	2.62	2.91	2.75
Terms of trade	0.27	0.72	0.78
Deviations from the LOP			
Home goods at producer level	0	0.27	0.29
Home goods at consumer level	2.46	2.68	2.66
Home markups			
Domestic intermediate goods	0	0.58	0.57
Exported intermediate goods	0	0.56	0.57
Domestic final goods	0	0.04	0.04
Imported final goods	0	0.11	0.04
Quantities			
Home consumption	0.99	1.08	1.05
Home hours	0.51	0.47	0.42
Real GDP	1.21	1.30	1.46

6.7.3 Baseline Economy

We now have all the basic elements to analyze our baseline economy with all shocks combined. Results are shown in table 6.3. Observe that the combination of downstream and upstream shocks raises the volatility in our artificial economy reasonably close to the data for the United States and other large industrial economies: for instance, the standard deviations of real GDP is (realistically) around 2 percent, regardless of nominal rigidities.

Consider first the flexible-price benchmark, shown in the first column of the table. With flexible prices, the demand elasticity facing producers, and thus the markups they charge, are constant; therefore the law of one price holds at the dock (the volatility of deviations from the law of one price at the dock is correspondingly zero). Nonetheless, the law of one price cannot (and does not) hold for final goods: country-specific productivity shocks hitting the downstream firms drive a wedge between final goods' prices across countries (expressed in a common currency). As a result, and in accord to stylized facts, the real exchange rate is more volatile than the terms of trade; the correlation between the real (and nominal) exchange rate is high and

Table 6.3 **Volatility under alternative policies: Baseline calibration (in percent)**

	Policies				
Standard deviation	Flexible prices	Optimal policy	CPI inflation targeting	GDP inflation targeting	Taylor rule
Inflation rates					
CPI	0	0.12	0	0.41	0.38
Domestic final goods	0.19	0.17	0.11	0.41	0.43
Imported final goods	0.75	0.45	0.44	0.64	0.48
Domestic intermediate prices	0.71	0.49	0.95	0	0.51
Import intermediate prices	1.09	0.99	1.13	1.04	0.76
Export intermediate prices	1.09	0.99	1.13	1.04	0.76
International prices					
Real exchange rate (CPI based)	2.97	3.35	3.78	3.14	3.62
Terms of trade	2.31	2.21	2.55	2.26	2.04
Deviations from the LOP					
Home goods at producer level	0	0.63	0.78	1.41	1.21
Home goods at consumer level	2.47	2.71	3.14	2.76	3.19
Home markups					
Domestic intermediate goods	0	0.60	1.06	0.87	0.82
Exported intermediate goods	0	0.63	0.96	0.90	0.89
Domestic final goods	0	0.25	0.61	0.59	0.72
Imported final goods	0	1.13	1.24	1.38	0.97
Quantities					
Home consumption	1.39	1.47	1.58	1.44	1.57
Home hours	0.61	0.60	0.61	0.62	0.54
Real GDP	1.93	2.00	1.98	1.90	1.98

positive—despite the fact that upstream and downstream technology shocks are assumed not to be correlated. Recall that, in our flexible-price economy, we posit that monetary policy keeps the CPI constant: consistent with this monetary regime, sectoral inflation rates are more volatile at producer level than at the final level, and for imported goods than for domestically produced goods, respectively. The latter result clearly reflects the low weight of foreign goods in the CPI.

The second column of table 6.3 displays results for our sticky-price economy with the optimal policy in place. In order to reduce inefficiencies due to price stickiness, monetary policy mitigates fluctuations in the major components of consumer price inflation. However, it falls short of completely stabilizing either the CPI or domestic intermediate prices inflation. Key to understanding this result are the different trade-offs discussed in our text. First, as in Corsetti and Pesenti (2005), LCP at upstream level leads benevolent monetary authorities to attach a positive weight to stabilizing the consumer price of imports, and thus to deviate from perfect stabilization of the final prices of domestic goods. Second, downstream technology shocks prevent perfect stabilization of all consumer prices, because of the heterogeneity of marginal costs implied by vertical interactions. This effect is of course worse in an open economy setting, because of the response of the intermediate price of imports to exchange rate fluctuations. Third, the elasticity of the producer's demand curve depends on the industry's dispersion of final goods prices, motivating policy emphasis on final price stabilization. The implications of these trade-offs for the volatilities of prices and markups, real exchange rates, and terms of trade are discussed following, together with a comparative analysis of the optimal policy relative to other policy rules.

Prices and Markups

Because of limited price adjustment, it is not surprising that real variables generally display more volatility in the sticky-price economy (with the optimal monetary policy in place), than in the flexible-price economy.[18] Notable exceptions are the terms of trade and hours worked. The reduced volatility of the terms of trade is a consequence of LCP at the intermediate level, as discussed in section 6.7.1. A reduced volatility of hours worked is already a feature of optimal monetary policy with downstream shocks only in table 6.2, and is essentially a consequence of our assumption that downstream firms do not employ labor.

What is most interesting, instead, is the very large discrepancy in volatilities of producers' and distributors' average markups, which are constant in the flexible-price allocation. The markup of domestically produced goods is two-and-a-half times as volatile at the upstream level as at the downstream level. This is remarkable in light of the fact that, in our experiments, we assume the same degree of nominal rigidities at either level. The volatility differential reflects the real components of markup movements in producers' prices, arising from vertical interactions. Conversely, the markup of imported goods is more volatile at the downstream level than at the upstream level—almost twice as much. Such differential reflects the fact that optimal policy attaches a large weight to stabilizing domestically produced goods at the retail level—the bulk of households' consumption.

We should stress here that fluctuations in markups translate into inefficient deviations in the law of one price, both at the border and at the consumer level. Observe that the volatility of deviations from the law of one price in final prices is quite similar to the one in the economy with flexible prices,

18. The volatility differential between our economies with and without nominal rigidities is by no means uniform across sectors. Namely, for domestically produced goods, the ratio in volatility of upstream and downstream prices is 4 in the flexible price allocation, but it falls down to 2.5 with nominal rigidities. A similar drop can be found in the ratio of volatility of imports prices to domestic goods prices. Conversely, the volatility of the producer price of imported goods, though lower than in the flexible price economy, is now twice that of domestically produced goods.

notwithstanding that, per effect of the exchange rate movements, the markups of Home downstream firms selling imported goods have the highest volatility.

Real Exchange Rates and Terms of Trade

A notable international dimension of the optimal policy in table 6.3 is that the real exchange rate is more volatile in the economy with nominal frictions than under flexible prices, while the terms of trade are less volatile, reflecting the effects of LCP and nontradability previously discussed. These findings clearly caution against suggestions to drastically curb the volatility of nominal and real exchange rates. For instance, they caution against the strong policy prescription derived by Devereux and Engel (2007), who argue that under pervasive LCP the optimal stabilization policy should reduce the variability of the real exchange rate significantly below that of the terms of trade. In these authors' view, the fact that we observe the opposite pattern in the data suggests that policymakers around the world fail to stabilize currency movements efficiently. As we argued previously, the problem with this and similar views is that, while there are good theoretical reasons to expect optimal policies under LCP to contain the volatility of the terms of trade, these reasons cannot be mechanically applied to the real exchange rate, whose volatility is bound to depend on a number of structural features of the economy.[19]

Simple Rules

The last three columns of table 6.3 report results for alternative policy rules; namely, CPI inflation targeting, GDP inflation targeting, and a standard Taylor rule. Compared to the optimal policy, these alternative simple rules bring about noticeably larger volatility in most real variables, particularly in the markups and the deviations from the law of one price for both consumer prices and prices at the dock.

Focus first on the strict CPI inflation targeting regime, presented in the third column of table 6.3: such monetary policy regime leads to more volatility in the upstream prices of all goods (imported and domestically produced). Relative to the optimal policy, the economy displays higher volatility of markups, terms of trade, and the real exchange rate. This is so because complete stabilization of headline consumer price inflation brings about suboptimally large movements in sectoral (i.e., domestic and imported goods) inflation rates at retail level, which ultimately affect the desired markups by upstream producers.

19. As discussed previously, in our model the optimal ranking of volatility between the real exchange rate and the terms of trade depends, among other things, on the relative degree of price stickiness among upstream and downstream producers. If producer prices are assumed to be completely flexible, the real exchange rate becomes less volatile than the terms of trade—in line with the case discussed by Devereux and Engel (2007).

Likewise, stabilizing the prices of domestically produced goods—the case dubbed GDP inflation targeting in the fourth column of table 6.3—also leads to too much volatility in sectoral inflation rates, especially in inflation of imported goods at the border as well as at the consumer level. Interestingly, consumption and real GDP are less volatile than under the optimal policy, but this is achieved by generating more volatility in all other real variables, especially in hours worked and in the terms of trade, because of the suboptimally low weight attached to stabilizing export and import goods prices.

Finally, a Taylor rule (following a quite standard parameterization) improves on the strict CPI inflation target by producing less volatility in consumption and hours. However, relative to the optimal policy, both the CPI and its individual components are too volatile, since too much importance is attached to output stabilization. As a result, the volatility of consumption is excessive, and that of hours is too low.

6.8 Concluding Remarks

The literature in international economics and open macro has so far pursued two distinct explanations of the observed stability of import prices in local currency. According to one modeling strategy, this is the result of optimal markup adjustment by monopolistic firms, which optimize profits through price discrimination across national markets. In this case, market segmentation is attributed to real factors. According to an alternative modeling strategy, local currency price stability reflects nominal rigidities, which imply suboptimal variations in firms' profits in response to shocks. By considering vertically integrated firms, our chapter emphasizes that a rigid distinction between these two approaches is unwarranted, since optimal markup adjustments and nominal frictions are likely to act as intertwined factors in causing stable import prices in local currency. Specifically, we build a model where, because of market-specific nominal rigidities at the downstream level, different dynamics in final prices provide an incentive for upstream producers to price discriminate across countries, exacerbating the distortions from monopoly power. At the same time, the use of local nontradable inputs by firms selling goods to final users mutes the response of final prices to exchange rate movements.

There are at least three potentially important implications of our findings for policymaking. First, by creating price discrimination at the border, consumer price movements feed back to deviations from the law of one price across markets. The transmission mechanism from consumer price inflation to price discrimination provides monetary authorities with an additional reason to stabilize final prices. In this respect, our analysis sheds light on one possible reason why the progressive stabilization of inflation in the last decade may have contributed to the observed fall in exchange rate pass-through. By reducing movements in consumer prices, policymakers indirectly affect the demand elasticity faced by upstream producers, reducing opportunities for exercising monopoly power through price discrimination.

Yet complete CPI stabilization will never be desirable in our economies, because of both international and domestic policy trade-offs. Specifically, in addition to the international dimensions of monetary policy already discussed in the literature, we show that, with vertical interactions among industries adjusting prices in a staggered fashion, domestic price stability is actually unfeasible. This is due to the fact that nominal rigidities inducing staggered pricing by upstream producers inherently lead to cost heterogeneity among downstream firms.

Finally, as shown by the literature, nominal rigidities in local currency induce positive comovements in the optimal monetary stance across countries, which tend to curb the volatility of the terms of trade. However, our results make it clear that, at an optimum, the real exchange rate can be more or less volatile than the terms of trade, depending on a number of structural features of the economy, like home bias in expenditure and local components of marginal costs in consumer goods. In this sense, the empirical regularity that real exchange rates are typically more volatile than the terms of trade does not automatically suggest that policymakers fall short of stabilizing exchange rates efficiently.

Appendix

In this appendix we provide details on the derivation of a few results used extensively in the text.

Price Dispersions

We can write the within-industry price dispersion of consumer prices as:

$$S_t(h) \equiv \int \left(\frac{P_t(h, r_h)}{\mathbb{P}_t(h)} \right)^{-\eta} dr_h.$$

$$= \mathbb{P}_t^{\eta}(h) \sum_{j=0}^{\infty} (1 - \theta)\theta^j P_{t-j}(h)^{-\eta}$$

$$= (1 - \theta)\left(\frac{P_t(h)}{\mathbb{P}_t(h)} \right)^{-\eta} + \theta\pi_t^{\eta}(h) S_{t-1}(h).$$

Similarly, we can express the across-industry dispersion in consumer prices as follows:

$$\overline{S}_t = \int \left(\frac{\mathbb{P}_t(h)}{P_{H,t}} \right)^{-\eta} S_t(h)dh$$
$$= \int \left(\frac{\mathbb{P}_t(h)}{P_{H,t}} \right)^{-\eta} (1-\theta) \left(\frac{P_t(h)}{\mathbb{P}_t(h)} \right)^{-\eta} dh + \int \left(\frac{\mathbb{P}_t(h)}{P_{\mathrm{H},t}} \right)^{-\eta} \theta \pi_{t-1}^{\eta}(h) S_{t-1}(h)dh$$
$$= (1-\theta) \int \left(\frac{P_t(h)}{P_{\mathrm{H},t}} \right)^{-\eta} dh + \int \left(\frac{\mathbb{P}_t(h)}{P_{\mathrm{H},t}} \right)^{-\eta} \theta \pi_t^{\eta}(h) S_{t-1} dh$$
$$= (1-\theta) \left[(1-\overline{\theta}) \left(\frac{P_t(h)}{P_{\mathrm{H},t}} \right)^{-\eta} + \overline{\theta} \left(\frac{\tilde{P}_t(h)}{P_{\mathrm{H},t}} \right)^{-\eta} \right] + \theta \pi_{\mathrm{H},t}^{\eta} \overline{S}_{t-1}.$$

The Derivative of the Optimal Downstream Price with Respect to Upstream Prices

We now show that $\partial P_t^o(h)/\partial \overline{P}_t(h) = P_t^o(h)/\overline{P}_t(h)$. First, take the derivative

$$\frac{\partial P_t(h)}{\partial \overline{P}_t(h)} = \frac{\eta}{\eta - 1} \left\{ \frac{E_t \sum_{k=0}^{\infty} p_{bt,t+k} \theta^k \left[\frac{\partial MC_{t+k}(h)}{\partial \overline{P}_t(h)} C_{t+k}(h,r_h) + \frac{\partial C_{t+k}(h,r_h)}{\partial \overline{P}_t(h)} MC_{t+k}(h) \right]}{E_t \sum_{k=0}^{\infty} p_{bt,t+k} \theta^k C_{t+k}(h,r_h)} + \right.$$
$$\left. - \frac{\left[E_t \sum_{k=0}^{\infty} p_{bt,t+k} \theta^k C_{t+k}(h,r_h) MC_{t+k}(h) \right] \left[E_t \sum_{k=0}^{\infty} p_{bt,t+k} \theta^k \frac{\partial C_{t+k}(h,r_h)}{\partial \overline{P}_t(h)} \right]}{\left[E_t \sum_{k=0}^{\infty} p_{bt,t+k} \theta^k C_{t+k}(h,r_h) \right]^2} \right\}.$$

Noting that $\partial MC_{t+k}(h)/\partial \overline{P}_t(h) = 1/Z_{t+k} = MC_{t+k}(h)/\overline{P}_t(h)$, and

$$\frac{\partial C_{t+k}(h, r_h)}{\partial \overline{P}_t(h)} = -\eta \left(\frac{P_t(h)}{\mathbb{P}_{\mathrm{H},t+k}} \right)^{-\eta} C_{\mathrm{H},t+k} \frac{1}{P_t(h)} \frac{\partial P_t(h)}{\partial \overline{P}_t(h)}$$
$$= -\eta \frac{C_{t+k}(h, r_h)}{P_t(h)} \frac{\partial P_t(h)}{\partial \overline{P}_t(h)},$$

we obtain

$$\frac{\partial P_t(h)}{\partial \overline{P}_t(h)} = \frac{\eta}{\eta - 1}$$
$$\cdot \left\{ \frac{\frac{1}{\overline{P}_t(h)} E_t \sum_{k=0}^{\infty} p_{bt,t+k} \theta^k C_{t+k}(h,r_h) MC_{t+k}(h) - \eta \frac{\partial P_t(h)}{\partial \overline{P}_t(h)} \frac{1}{P_t(h)} E_t \sum_{k=0}^{\infty} p_{bt,t+k} \theta^k C_{t+k}(h,r_h) MC_{t+k}(h)}{E_t \sum_{k=0}^{\infty} p_{bt,t+k} \theta^k C_{t+k}(h,r_h)} + \right.$$
$$\left. - \frac{\left[E_t \sum_{k=0}^{\infty} p_{bt,t+k} \theta^k C_{t+k}(h,r_h) MC_{t+k}(h) \right] \left[-\eta \frac{\partial P_t(h)}{\partial \overline{P}_t(h)} \frac{1}{P_t(h)} E_t \sum_{k=0}^{\infty} p_{bt,t+k} \theta^k C_{t+k}(h,r_h) \right]}{\left[E_t \sum_{k=0}^{\infty} p_{bt,t+k} \theta^k C_{t+k}(h,r_h) \right]^2} \right\};$$

which after further simplification becomes

$$\frac{\partial P_t(h)}{\partial \bar{P}_t(h)} = \left\{ \frac{P_t(h)}{\bar{P}_t(h)} - \eta \frac{\partial P_t(h)}{\partial \bar{P}_t(h)} + \frac{\partial P_t(h)}{\partial \bar{P}_t(h)} \right\}$$

$$= \frac{P_t(h)}{\bar{P}_t(h)}.$$

References

Bacchetta, P., and E. van Wincoop. 2005. A theory of the currency denomination of international trade. *Journal of International Economics* 67 (2): 295–319.

———. 2003. Why do consumer prices react less than import prices to exchange rates? *Journal of the European Economic Association, Papers and Proceedings* 1: 662–70.

Backus, D. K., P. J. Kehoe, and F. E. Kydland. 1992. International real business cycles. *Journal of Political Economy* 100: 745–75.

Benigno, G., and P. Benigno. 2003. Price stability in open economy. *Review of Economic Studies* 70: 743–64.

Betts, C., and M. Devereux. 2000. Exchange rate dynamics in a model of pricing to market. *Journal of International Economics* 50 (1): 215–44.

Bils, M., and P. J. Klenow. 2004. Some evidence on the importance of sticky prices. *Journal of Political Economy* 112 (5): 947–85.

Burstein, A. T., M. Eichenbaum, and S. Rebelo. 2006. Large devaluations and the real exchange rate. *Journal of Political Economy* 113 (4): 742–84.

Burstein, A. T., J. Neves, and S. Rebelo. 2003. Distribution costs and real exchange rate dynamics during exchange-rate-based stabilizations. *Journal of Monetary Economics* 50 (6): 1189–1214.

Calvo, G. A. 1983. Staggered prices in a utility-maximizing framework. *Journal of Monetary Economics* 12 (3): 383–98.

Campa, J., and L. Goldberg. 2005. Exchange rate pass through into import prices. *Review of Economics and Statistics* 87 (4): 679–90.

Clarida, R., J. Galí, M. Gertler. 2002. A simple framework for international policy analysis. *Journal of Monetary Economics* 49: 879–904.

Corsetti, G. 2006. Openness and the case for flexible exchange rates. *Research in Economics* 60 (1): 1–21.

Corsetti, G., and L. Dedola. 2005. A macroeconomic model of international price discrimination. *Journal of International Economics* 67 (1): 129–56.

Corsetti, G., L. Dedola, and S. Leduc. 2008a. High exchange-rate volatility and low pass-through. *Journal of Monetary Economics* 55 (6): 1113–28.

———. 2008b. International risk sharing and the transmission of productivity shocks. *Review of Economic Studies* 75 (2): 443–73.

Corsetti, G., and P. Pesenti. 2001. Welfare and macroeconomic interdependence. *Quarterly Journal of Economics* 116 (2): 421–46.

———. 2005. International dimension of optimal monetary policy. *Journal of Monetary Economics* 52 (2): 281–305.

Devereux, M. B., and C. Engel. 2003. Monetary policy in open economy revisited: Price setting and exchange rate flexibility. *Review of Economic Studies* 70: 765–83.

———. 2007. Expenditure switching vs. real exchange rate stabilization: Competing objectives for exchange rate policy. *Journal of Monetary Economics,* forthcoming.

Devereux, M. B., C. Engel, and P. E. Storgaard. 2004. Endogenous exchange rate pass-through when nominal prices are set in advance. *Journal of International Economics* 63: 263–91.

Dornbusch, R. 1987. Exchange rates and prices. *American Economic Review* 77 (1): 93–106.

Duarte, M. and M. Obstfeld. 2008. Monetary policy in the open economy revisited: The case for exchange-rate flexibility restored. *Journal of International Money and Finance* 27 (6): 949–57.

Engel, C. 2003. Expenditure switching and exchange rate policy. *NBER Macroeconomics Annual 2002,* vol. 17, ed. M. Gertler and K. Rogoff, 231–72. Cambridge, MA: MIT Press.

———. 2006. Equivalence results for optimal pass-through, optimal indexing to exchange rates, and optimal choice of currency for export pricing. *Journal of the European Economics Association* 4 (December): 1249–60.

Engel, C., and J. H. Rogers. 1996. How wide is the border? *American Economic Review* 86 (December): 1112–25.

Frankel, J., D. Parsley, and S.-J. Wei. 2005. Slow pass-through around the world: A new import for developing countries? NBER Working Paper no. 11199. Cambridge, MA: National Bureau of Economic Research, March.

Friberg, R. 1998. In which currency should exporters set their prices? *Journal of International Economics* 45 (1): 59–76.

Goldberg, L., and C. Tille. 2008. Macroeconomic interdependence and the international role of the dollar. Federal Reserve Bank of New York Staff Report no. 316.

Goldberg, P. K., and R. Hellerstein. 2007. A framework for identifying the sources of local-currency price stability with empirical application. Federal Reserve Bank of New York Staff Report no. 287.

Goldberg, P. K., and M. M. Knetter. 1997. Goods prices and exchange rates: What have we learned? *Journal of Economic Literature* 35 (3): 1243–72.

Goldberg, P. K., and F. Verboven. 2001. The evolution of price dispersion in the European car market. *Review of Economic Studies* 68 (4): 811–48.

Hellerstein, R. 2005. A decomposition of the sources of incomplete cross-border transmission: The case of beer. Federal Reserve Bank of New York. Working Paper.

Khan, A., R. G. King, and A. L. Wolman. 2003. Optimal monetary policy. *Review of Economic Studies* 70: 825–60.

Lubik, T., and F. Schorfheide. 2004. Testing for indeterminacy: An application to U.S. monetary policy. *American Economic Review* 94 (1): 190–217.

———. 2006. A Bayesian look at new open economy macroeconomics. *NBER Macroeconomics Annual 2005,* vol. 20, ed. M. Gertler and K. Rogoff, 313–66. Cambridge, MA: MIT Press.

Monacelli, T. 2005. Monetary policy in a low pass-through environment. *Journal of Money, Credit and Banking* 37: 1047–66.

Nakamura, E., and J. Steinsson. 2008. Five facts about prices: A reevaluation of menu cost models. *Quarterly Journal of Economics* 123 (4): 1415–64.

Nelson, E. 2007. Milton Friedman and U.S. monetary history: 1961–2006. *Federal Reserve Bank of St. Louis Review* 89 (3): 153–82.

Obstfeld, M. 2002. Inflation-targeting, exchange rate pass-through, and volatility. *American Economic Review* 92 (2): 102–7.

Obstfeld, M., and K. Rogoff. 1995. Exchange rate dynamics redux. *Journal of Political Economy* 103 (3): 624–60.

———. 2000. New directions for stochastic open economy models. *Journal of International Economics* 50 (1): 117–54.
Smets, F., and R. Wouters. 2002. Openness, imperfect exchange rate pass-through and monetary policy. *Journal of Monetary Economics* 49 (5): 947–81.
Sutherland, A. 2005. Incomplete pass-through and the welfare effects of exchange rate variability. *Journal of International Economics* 65 (2): 375–99.
Taylor, J. 2000. Low inflation, pass-through, and the pricing power of firms. *European Economic Review* 44 (7): 1389–1408.
Woodford, M. 2003. *Interest and prices.* Princeton, NJ: Princeton University Press.

Comment Philippe Bacchetta

General Comments

This chapter fits well the major theme of the conference, which is the impact of openness (or globalization) on monetary policy. An open issue is how the exchange rate and foreign prices should be considered in the conduct of monetary policy. The debate is present both at the policy and at the theoretical level. Should the central bank stabilize the exchange rate above and beyond its impact on inflation and output? At the theoretical level, a crucial element is how exchange rate changes are channeled through domestic prices. Because different transmission channels have potentially different implications for optimal monetary policy, it is important to investigate these various channels. The chapter by Corsetti, Dedola, and Leduc contributes to the literature by examining a new channel.

Since the version of the chapter appearing in the conference book already incorporates several of my comments made during the conference, my discussion will be brief. In particular, I will not discuss the link of the chapter to the literature: the second section of the chapter already gives a very nice overview of this literature.

One can label the model presented in the chapter as a "small shop" model: upstream producers sell their product to a large number of distributors, the downstream firms, who sell the product to consumers. This perspective can be contrasted with the "cup of coffee" model and the "auto parts" model mentioned in the literature review. A characteristic of the small shop model is double marginalization: since both the upstream producers and the distributors have market power, they both charge a markup. Moreover, since there is price stickiness at both levels, it is impossible to reach a first best with monetary policy.

Philippe Bacchetta is a professor of economics at the University of Lausanne.

Optimal Monetary Policy

The chapter examines the implications of global welfare-maximizing monetary policy and compares it with the implications of simple rules. In such a rich model, the results are derived by simulating a calibrated version of the model. While the results are interesting, it is difficult to see the main mechanisms at work. But we know that in the context of open economy neo-Keynesian models, the main objective of optimal policy should be to lower the price level (see Bacchetta and van Wincoop 2000; Devereux and Engel 2003; Corsetti and Pesenti 2005). To better understand the issue, consider first a context where firms set prices one period ahead (instead of Calvo pricing). In this context the price is generally given by:

$$price = \phi \frac{E\lambda Costs}{E\lambda Sales}, \tag{1}$$

where ϕ is a markup and λ is a stochastic discount factor used to compute the certainty equivalent of marginal costs and revenues. The price can therefore be written as a markup over the certainty equivalent of costs, divided by the certainty equivalent of sales. Thus, optimal monetary policy will lower the markup and the certainty equivalent of costs and increase the certainty equivalent of sales. In Corsetti, Dedola, and Leduc's chapter, the price set by an exporting producer would be given by:

$$\overline{P}_t = \phi_t \frac{E_t \lambda_t W_t D_t / \overline{Z}_t}{E_t \lambda_t \xi_t D_t}. \tag{2}$$

The optimal policy can increase the certainty equivalent of sales in particular by increasing the correlation between the nominal exchange rate ξ_t and demand. It can also attempt to decrease the correlation between the wage and demand to decrease the certainty equivalent of costs. As for the markup, however, monetary policy does not seem to have much of an impact.

This is where we need to abandon the assumption of one period ahead price setting and use the Calvo pricing assumption. This leads to equation (9) in the chapter. As is well explained in the chapter, this pricing assumption implies a dispersion in the prices of distribution firms and affects the demand elasticities faced by exporters. A higher price dispersion decreases the elasticity faced by exporters and, ceteris paribus, increases the price level. Since price dispersion increases with domestic inflation, this gives an additional incentive for central banks to stabilize inflation. Thus, we can expect that optimal inflation should be more stable than under a Taylor rule.

The previous reasoning shows that a crucial aspect in determining the welfare impact of monetary policy is the *level* of prices and of inflation as well as the correlation among major variables. Unfortunately, the authors do not give indications on these features in their numerical simulation. They only provide us with standard deviations. While this is valuable information, it would have been even better to provide the other types of information. We would have gained a clearer insight about optimal monetary policy.

Some Further Comments

For the analysis of the chapter to be useful for policy analysis in the open economy, more work is needed. First, how does one implement optimal policy? Should policymakers solve the full model and their optimization problem or is there a more practical way to implement this policy? If we come back to the role of the exchange rate, to what extent should it affect monetary policy? The numerical results show that real exchange rate volatility is lower under optimal monetary policy than under a Taylor rule, but the difference is small. This would still imply that it is optimal to stabilize the exchange rate to some extent. More generally, how should we interpret these results?

Second, what would be the outcome under noncooperative policies? The analysis focuses on optimal cooperative policies. While this is a useful theoretical benchmark, it would be more realistic to look at noncooperative policies. Third, what is the welfare impact of the various policies? The welfare levels are not given in the numerical analysis, but it would be very useful to compare the welfare levels between the optimal policy and the other rules. This would give us a sense of how much is lost by not considering the international dimension of monetary policy. Finally, how do the implications for optimal monetary policy differ across the various models of exchange rate pass-through? It is not clear at this stage whether the alternative model presented by the authors has significantly different implications for monetary policy.

To summarize, Corsetti, Dedola, and Leduc offer a useful contribution to the literature. They develop a new perspective of exchange rate pass-through and examine optimal monetary policy in this context. While many of the results are interesting, more work is required to determine the usefulness of their approach and its policy implications.

References

Bacchetta, P., and E. van Wincoop. 2000. Does exchange rate stability increase trade and welfare? *American Economic Review* 90 (5): 1093–1109.

Corsetti, G., and P. Pesenti. 2005. International dimensions of optimal monetary policy. *Journal of Monetary Economics* 52 (2): 281–305.

Devereux, M. B., and C. Engel. 2003. Monetary policy in the open economy revisited: Exchange rate flexibility and price setting behavior. *Review of Economic Studies* 70 (4): 765–83.

III

Empirical Issues in International Monetary Policy Analysis

7

The Macroeconomic Effects of Oil Price Shocks
Why Are the 2000s so Different from the 1970s?

Olivier J. Blanchard and Jordi Galí

7.1 Introduction

Since the 1970s, and at least until recently, macroeconomists have viewed changes in the price of oil as an important source of economic fluctuations, as well as a paradigm of a global shock, likely to affect many economies simultaneously. Such a perception is largely due to the two episodes of low growth, high unemployment, and high inflation that characterized most industrialized economies in the mid and late 1970s. Conventional accounts of those episodes of stagflation blame them on the large increases in the price of oil triggered by the Yom Kippur war in 1973, and the Iranian revolution of 1979, respectively.[1]

The events of the past decade, however, seem to call into question the relevance of oil price changes as a significant source of economic fluctuations. The reason: since the late 1990s, the global economy has experienced two oil shocks of sign and magnitude comparable to those of the 1970s but, in contrast with the latter episodes, both gross domestic product (GDP) growth

Olivier J. Blanchard is the Class of 1941 Professor at the Massachusetts Institute of Technology and a research associate of the National Bureau of Economic Research. Jordi Galí is the Director of the Center for Research in International Economics (CREI), a professor of economics at the Universitat Pompeu Fabra, and a research associate of the National Bureau of Economic Research. We are grateful for helpful comments and suggestions to Julio Rotemberg, John Parsons, Lutz Kilian, José de Gregorio, Gauti Eggertsson, Carlos Montoro, Tomaz Cajner, and participants at NBER ME Meeting, the NBER conference on International Dimensions of Monetary Policy, and seminars at CREI-UPF, LSE, GIIS (Geneva), Fundación Rafael del Pino, and Bank of Portugal. We thank Davide Debortoli for excellent research assistance, and the NSF and the Banque de France Foundation for financial assistance. This version updates an earlier version, using data up to 2007:3 and corrected oil shares.

1. Most undergraduate textbooks make an unambiguous connection between the two oil price hikes of 1973 and 1974 and 1979 and 1980 and the period of stagflation that ensued. (See, e.g., Mankiw [2007, 274].)

and inflation have remained relatively stable in much of the industrialized world.

Our goal in this chapter is to shed light on the nature of the apparent changes in the macroeconomic effects of oil shocks, as well as on some of their possible causes. Disentangling the factors behind those changes is obviously key to assessing the extent to which the episodes of stagflation of the 1970s can reoccur in response to future oil shocks and, if so, to understanding the role that monetary policy can play in order to mitigate their adverse effects.

One plausible hypothesis is that the effects of the increase in the price of oil proper have been similar across episodes, but have coincided in time with large shocks of a very different nature (e.g., large rises in other commodity prices in the 1970s, high productivity growth, and world demand in the 2000s). That coincidence could significantly distort any assessment of the impact of oil shocks based on a simple observation of the movements in aggregate variables around each episode.

In order to evaluate this hypothesis one must isolate the component of macroeconomic fluctuations associated with exogenous changes in the price of oil. To do so, we identify and estimate the effects of an oil price shock using structural Vector Autoregression (VAR) techniques. We report and compare estimates for different sample periods and discuss how they have changed over time. We follow two alternative approaches. The first one is based on a large VAR, and allows for a break in the sample in the mid-1980s. The second approach is based on rolling bivariate VARs, including the price of oil and one other variable at a time. The latter approach allows for a gradual change in the estimated effects of oil price shocks, without imposing a discrete break in a single period.

Two conclusions clearly emerge from this analysis: first, there were indeed other adverse shocks at work in the 1970s; the price of oil explains only part of the stagflation episodes of the 1970s. Second, and importantly, the effects of a given change in the price of oil have changed substantially over time. Our estimates point to much larger effects of oil price shocks on inflation and activity in the early part of the sample; that is, the one that includes the two oil shock episodes of the 1970s.

Our basic empirical findings are summarized graphically in figure 7.1 (we postpone a description of the underlying assumptions to section 7.3). The left-hand graph shows the responses of U.S. (log) GDP and the (log) consumer price index (CPI) to a 10 percent increase in the price of oil, estimated using pre-1984 data. The right-hand graph displays the corresponding responses, based on post-1984 data. As the figure makes clear, the response of both variables has become more muted in the more recent period. As we show following, that pattern can also be observed for other variables (prices and quantities) and many (though not all) other countries considered. In sum, the evidence suggests that economies face an improved

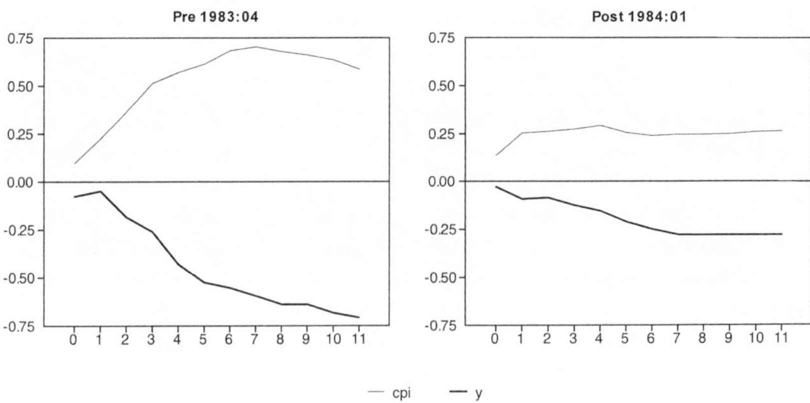

Fig. 7.1 U.S.—Impulse response to an oil price shock

trade-off in the more recent period, in the face of oil price shocks of a similar magnitude.

We then focus on the potential explanations for these changes over time. We consider three hypotheses, not mutually exclusive. First, real wage rigidities may have decreased over time. The presence of real wage rigidities generates a trade-off between stabilization of inflation and stabilization of the output gap. As a result, and in response to an adverse supply shock and for a given money rule, inflation will generally rise more and output will decline more, the slower real wages adjust. A trend toward more flexible labor markets, including more flexible wages, could thus explain the smaller impact of the more recent oil shocks.

Second, changes in the way monetary policy is conducted may be responsible for the differential response of the economy to the oil shocks. In particular, the stronger commitment by central banks to maintaining a low and stable rate of inflation, reflected in the widespread adoption of more or less explicit inflation targeting strategies, may have led to an improvement in the policy trade-off that would make it possible to have a smaller impact of a given oil price increase on both inflation and output simultaneously.

Third, the share of oil in the economy may have declined sufficiently since the 1970s to account for the decrease in the effects of its price changes. Under that hypothesis, changes in the price of oil have increasingly turned into a sideshow, with no significant macroeconomic effects (not unlike fluctuations in the price of caviar).

To assess the merits of the different hypotheses we proceed in two steps. First, we develop a simple version of the new-Keynesian model where (imported) oil is both consumed by households and used as a production input by firms. The model allows us to examine how the economy's response to an exogenous change in the price of oil is affected by the degree of real wage rigidities, the nature and credibility of monetary policy, and the share of oil in production and consumption. We then look for more direct evidence pointing to the relevance and quantitative importance of each of those hypotheses. We conclude that all three are likely to have played an important role in explaining the different effects of oil prices during the 1970s and during the last decade.

The chapter is organized as follows. Section 7.1 gives a short summary of how our chapter fits in the literature. Section 7.2 presents basic facts. Section 7.3 presents results from multivariate VARs. Section 7.4 presents results from rolling bivariate VARs. Section 7.5 presents the model. Section 7.6 uses the model to analyze the role of real rigidities, credibility in monetary policy, and the oil share. Section 7.7 concludes.

7.1 Relation to the Literature

Our chapter is related to many strands of research. The first strand is concerned with the effects of oil price shocks on the economy. The seminal work in that literature is Bruno and Sachs (1985), who were the first to analyze in depth the effects of oil prices of the 1970s on output and inflation in the major industrialized countries. They explored many of the themes of our chapter, the role of other shocks, the role of monetary policy, and the role of wage setting.

On the empirical side, Hamilton showed in a series of contributions (see, in particular, Hamilton [1983, 1996]) that most of U.S. recessions were preceded by increases in the price of oil, suggesting an essential role for oil price increases as one of the main causes of recessions. The stability of this relation has been challenged by a number of authors, in particular Hooker (1996). Our finding that the effects of the price of oil have changed over time is consistent with the mixed findings of this line of research.

On the theoretical side, a number of papers have assessed the ability of standard models to account for the size and nature of the observed effects of oil price shocks. Thus, Rotemberg and Woodford (1996) argued that it was difficult to explain the sheer size of these effects in the 1970s. They argued that something else was going on; namely, an endogenous increase in the markup of firms, leading to a larger decrease in output. Finn (2000) showed that effects of the relevant size could be generated in a perfectly competitive real business cycle (RBC) model, by allowing for variable capital utilization. Neither mechanism would seem to account for the depth of the effects of the 1970s and not in the 2000s. The latter observation motivates our focus on the role of real wage rigidities, and the decline in these rigidities over time, an explanation we find more convincing than changes in either the behavior of markups or capacity utilization over time. In following this line, we build on our earlier work on the implications of real wage rigidities and their interaction with nominal price stickiness (Blanchard and Galí 2007).

A second strand of research related to the present chapter deals with the possible changes over time in the effects of oil shocks. Of course, that strand is in turn related to the literature on the "Great Moderation," a term used to refer to the decrease in output fluctuations over the last thirty years (e.g., Blanchard and Simon 2001; Stock and Watson 2003). The latter literature has tried to assess to what extent the declines in volatility have been due to "good luck" (i.e., smaller shocks) or changes in the economy's structure (including policy changes). In that context, some authors have argued that the stagflations of the 1970s were largely due to factors other than oil. Most prominently, Barsky and Kilian (2002) argue that they may have been partly caused by exogenous changes in monetary policy, which coincided in time with the rise in oil prices. Bernanke, Gertler, and Watson (1997) argue that much of the decline in output and employment was due to the rise in interest rates, resulting from the Fed's endogenous response to the higher inflation induced by the oil shocks.

While our evidence suggests that oil price shocks can only account for a fraction of the fluctuations of the 1970s, our findings that the dynamic effects of oil shocks have decreased considerably over time, combined with the observation that the oil shocks themselves have been no smaller, is consistent with the hypothesis of structural change.

We know of four papers that specifically focus, as we do, on the changing impact of oil shocks. Hooker (2002) analyzes empirically the changing weight of oil prices as an explanatory variable in a traditional Phillips curve specification for the U.S. economy. He finds that pass-through from oil to prices has become negligible since the early 1980s, but cannot find evidence for a significant role of the decline in energy intensity, the deregulation of energy industries, or changes in monetary policy as a factor behind that lower pass-through. De Gregorio, Landerretche, and Neilson (2007) provide a variety of estimates of the degree of pass-through from oil prices to inflation, and its changes over time, for a large set of countries. In addition to estimates of Phillips curves along the lines of Hooker (2002), they also provide evidence based on rolling VARs, as we do in the present chapter, though they use a different specification and focus exclusively on the effects on inflation. Their paper also examines a number of potential explanations, including a change in the response of the exchange rate (in the case of non-U.S. countries), and the virtuous effects of being in a low inflation environment. In two recent papers, developed independently, Herrera and Pesavento (2007) and Edelstein and Kilian (2007) also document the decrease in the effects of oil shocks on a number of aggregate variables using a VAR approach. Herrera and Pesavento, following the approach of Bernanke, Gertler, and Watson (1997), explore the role of changes in the response of monetary policy to oil shocks in accounting for the more muted effects of those shocks in the recent period. Their answer is largely negative: their findings point to a more stabilizing role of monetary policy in the 1970s relative to the recent period. Edelstein and Kilian focus on changes in the composition of U.S. automobile production, and the declining importance of the U.S. automobile sector. Given that the decline in the effects of the price of oil appears to be present in a large number of Organization for Economic Cooperation and Development (OECD) countries, this explanation appears perhaps too U.S.-specific.

7.2 Basic Facts

Figure 7.2 displays the evolution of the price of oil since 1970. More specifically, it shows the quarterly average price of a barrel of West Texas Intermediate, measured in U.S. dollars.[2] The figure shows how a long spell of stability came to an end in 1973, triggering a new era characterized by large and persistent fluctuations in the price of oil, punctuated with occasional sharp run-ups and spikes, and ending with the prolonged rise of the past few years. The shaded areas in the figure correspond to the four large oil shock episodes discussed following.

Figure 7.3 displays the same variable, now normalized by the U.S. GDP deflator, and measured in natural logarithms. This transformation gives us a better sense of the magnitude of the changes in the real price of oil. As the figure makes clear, such changes have often been very large, and concentrated over relatively short periods of time.

It is useful to start with descriptive statistics associated with the large oil shocks visible in the previous figures. We define a large oil shock as an episode involving a cumulative change in the (log) price of oil above 50 percent, sustained for more than four quarters. This gives us four episodes, starting in 1973, 1979, 1999, and 2002, respectively. Exact dates for each run-up are given in table 7.1 (given our definition, the largest price changes need not coincide with the starting date, and, indeed, they do not). For convenience we refer to those episodes as O1, O2, O3, and O4, respectively. Note that this criterion leaves out the price rise of 1990 (triggered by the Gulf War), due to its quick reversal. We also note that O3 is somewhat different, since it is preceded by a significant price decline.

Table 7.1 lists, for each episode: (a) the run-up period; (b) the date at which the cumulative log change attained the 50 percent threshold (which we use as a benchmark date in the following); and (c) the percent change from trough to peak (measured by the cumulative log change), both in nominal

2. The description of the stylized facts discussed following is not altered significantly if one uses alternative oil price measures, such as the PPI index for crude oil (used, e.g., by Hamilton [1983] and Rotemberg and Woodford [1996]) or the price of imported crude oil (e.g., Kilian 2006).

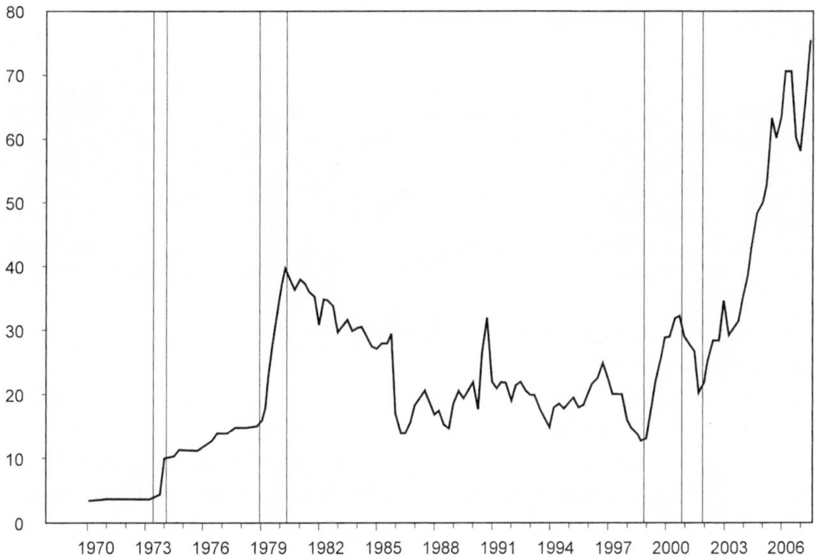

Fig. 7.2 Oil price ($ per barrel)

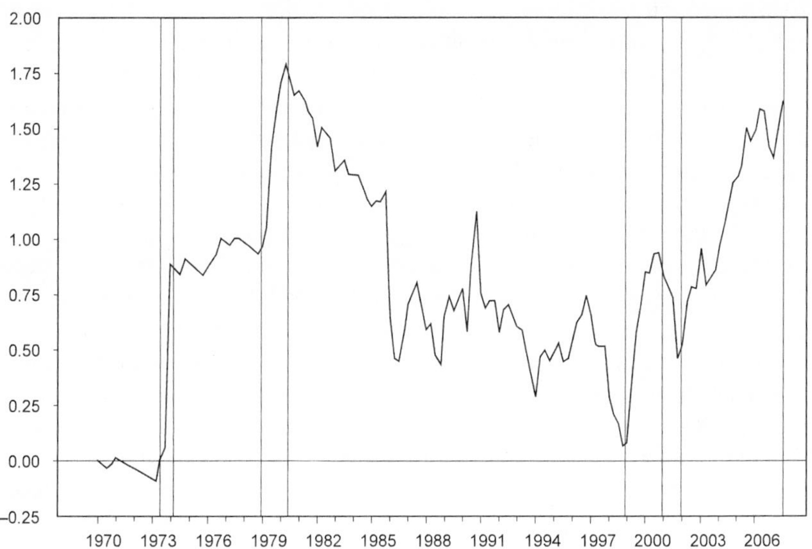

Fig. 7.3 Log real oil price

Table 7.1 Postwar oil shock episodes

	Run-up period	50% rise date	Max log change ($) (%)	Max log change (real) (%)
O1	1973:3–1974:1	1974:1	104	96
O2	1979:1–1980:2	1979:3	98	85
O3	1999:1–2000:4	1999:3	91	87
O4	2002:1–2007:3	2003:1	125	110

and real terms. The duration of the episodes ranges from three quarters (O1) to twenty quarters (O4).[3]

Interestingly, the size of the associated nominal price rise is roughly similar across episodes—around 100 percent. A similar characterization emerges when we use the cumulative change in the real price of oil (with the price normalized by the GDP deflator), except for O2, where the rise is somewhat smaller because of the high rate of inflation during that episode. In short, the four episodes involve oil shocks of a similar magnitude. In particular, the numbers do not seem to justify a characterization of the two recent shocks as being milder in size than the shocks of the 1970s.

In spite of their relatively similar magnitude, these four oil shock episodes have been associated with very different macroeconomic performances. Figures 7.4 and 7.5, which show, respectively, the evolution of (annual) CPI inflation and the unemployment rate in the United States over the period 1970:1 through 2007:3, provide a visual illustration.

Each figure shows, in addition to the variable displayed, the (log) real price of oil and the four shaded areas representing our four oil shock episodes. Note that the timing of O1 and O2 coincide with a sharp increase in inflation, and mark the beginning of a large rise in the unemployment rate. In each case, both inflation and unemployment reached a peak a few quarters after the peak in oil prices (up to a level of 11.3 percent and 13.4 percent, respectively, in the case of inflation; 8.8 percent and 10.6 percent for the unemployment rate). The pattern of both variables during the more recent oil shock episodes is very different. First, while CPI inflation shows a slight upward trend during both O3 and O4, the magnitude of the changes involved is much smaller than that observed for O1 and O2, with the associated rises in inflation hardly standing out relative to the moderate size of fluctuations shown by that variable since the mid-1980s. Second, the variation in the unemployment rate during and after O3 and O4 is much smaller in size than that observed in O1 and O2. The timing is also very different:

3. While our sample ends in 2007:3, it is clear that episode (04) has not ended yet. The price of oil has continued to increase, in both 2007:4 and 2008:1.

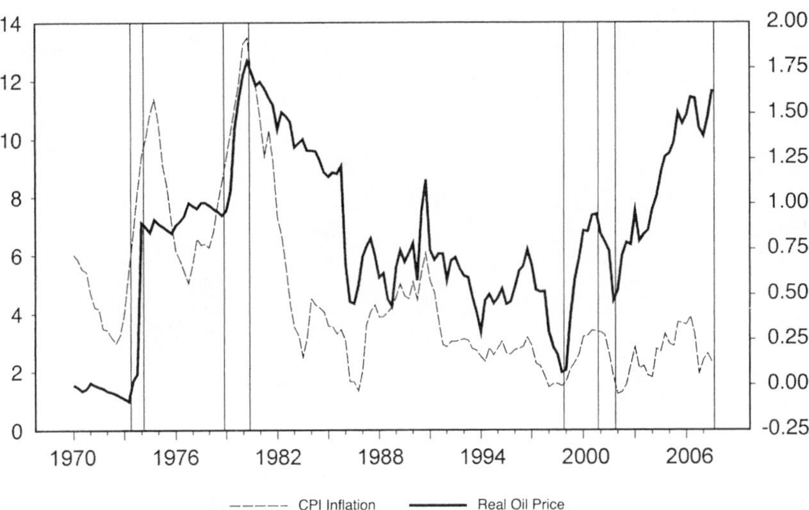

Fig. 7.4 Oil shocks and CPI inflation

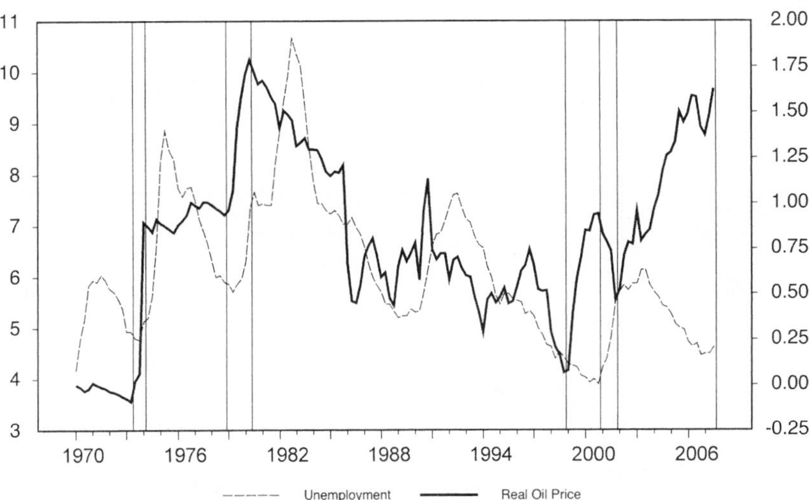

Fig. 7.5 Oil shocks and unemployment

while O1 and O2 lead to a sharp rise in unemployment, the latter variable keeps declining during the length of the O3 episode, with its rebound preceding O4. Furthermore, after a persistent (though relatively small) increase, unemployment starts declining in the midst of O4; that is, while the price of oil is still on the rise.

Tables 7.2 and 7.3 provide related evidence for each of the G7 countries as well as for three aggregates (the G7, the euro-12, and the OECD

Table 7.2 **Oil shock episodes: Change in inflation**

	O1	O2	O3	O4	AVG (1,2)	AVG (3,4)
Canada	4.7	1.8	2.2	0.5	3.3	1.4
Germany	0.1	2.6	1.1	–0.2	1.4	0.4
France	5.4	3.1	1.3	0.5	4.2	0.9
U.K.	10.2	4.3	0.0	0.5	7.3	0.3
Italy	7.7	5.6	1.0	–0.1	6.6	0.4
Japan	7.9	1.0	–1.7	0.9	4.4	–0.4
U.S.	4.9	4.0	1.7	–0.2	4.5	0.7
G7	4.8	1.9	0.3	0.0	3.3	0.2
Euro12	4.3	2.7	1.3	–0.5	3.5	0.4
OECD	4.9	1.8	0.1	–0.5	3.4	–0.2

Table 7.3 **Oil shock episodes: Cumulative GDP change**

	O1	O2	O3	O4	AVG (1,2)	AVG (3,4)
Canada	–8.3	–1.0	–1.5	3.2	–4.6	0.8
Germany	–9.6	–3.5	1.3	–2.5	–6.6	–0.6
France	–7.6	–4.4	0.6	1.2	–6.0	0.9
U.K.	–16.4	–9.2	0.4	2.5	–12.8	1.4
Italy	–8.6	0.4	3.0	–2.0	–4.1	0.5
Japan	–16.1	–4.4	7.6	3.3	–10.3	5.4
U.S.	–13.3	–11.8	–3.7	7.1	–12.5	1.7
G7	–12.6	–7.7	–0.2	3.9	–10.2	1.8
Euro12	–9.1	–2.9	1.0	–0.4	–6.0	0.3
OECD	–11.2	–6.5	0.1	4.1	–8.9	2.1

countries).[4] More specifically, table 7.2 displays, for each country and episode, the average rate of inflation over the eight quarters following each episode's benchmark date (at which the 50 percent threshold oil price rise is reached) *minus* the average rate of inflation over the eight quarters immediately preceding each run-up. Note that the increase in inflation associated with O1 is typically larger than the one for O2. The most striking evidence, however, relates to O3 and O4, which are typically associated with a change in inflation in their aftermath of a much smaller size than that following O1 and O2.[5] The last two columns, which average the inflation change for O1–O2 and O3–O4, makes the same point in a more dramatic way.

The evidence on output across episodes is shown in table 7.3, which reports for each country and episode (or averages of two episodes in the

4. We use quarterly data from OECD's Economic Outlook Database. For the purpose of this exercise, inflation is the annualized quarter-to-quarter rate of change in the CPI. These two tables have not been updated, and use data up to the end of 2005 only.

5. Even for Canada and Germany, the largest change in inflation occurs in either O1 or O2.

case of the last two columns) the cumulative GDP gain or loss over the eight quarters following each episode's benchmark date, relative to a trend given by the cumulative GDP growth rate over the eight quarters preceding each episode. The pattern closely resembles that shown for inflation: O1 and O2 are generally associated with GDP losses that are much larger than those corresponding to O3 and O4 (with the latter involving some small GDP gains in some cases). When averages are taken over pairs of episodes the pattern becomes uniform, pointing once again to much larger output losses during and after the oil shocks of the 1970s.

The evidence previously presented is consistent with the hypothesis that the macroeconomic effects of oil price shocks have become smaller over time, being currently almost negligible (at least in comparison with their effects in the 1970s). But it is also consistent with the hypothesis that other (non-oil) shocks have coincided in time with the major oil shocks, either reinforcing the adverse effects of the latter in the 1970s, or dampening them during the more recent episodes. In order to sort out those possibilities we turn next to a more structured analysis of the comovements between oil prices and other variables.

7.3 Estimating the Effects of Oil Price Shocks Using Structural VARs

In this section we provide more structural evidence on the macroeconomic effects of oil price shocks, and changes over time in the nature and size of those effects. We provide evidence for the United States, France, Germany, the United Kingdom, Italy, and Japan, using a six-variable VAR. In the next section we turn to a more detailed analysis of the U.S. evidence, using a battery of rolling bivariate VARs.

Our baseline VAR makes use of data on the nominal price of oil (in dollars), three inflation measures (CPI, GDP deflator, and wages) and two quantities (GDP and employment). By using a multivariate specification, we allow for a variety of shocks in addition to the oil shock that is our focus of interest. We identify oil shocks by assuming that unexpected variations in the nominal price of oil are exogenous relative to the contemporaneous values of the remaining macroeconomic variables included in the VAR. In other words, we take the oil shock to correspond to the reduced form innovation to the (log) nominal oil price, measured in U.S. dollars.

This identification assumption will clearly be incorrect if economic developments in the country under consideration affect the world price of oil contemporaneously. This may be either because the economy under consideration is large, or because developments in the country are correlated with world developments. For example, Rotemberg and Woodford (1996), who rely on the same identification assumption as we do when studying the effects of oil shocks on the U.S. economy, restrict their sample period to end in 1980 on the grounds that variations in the price of oil may have a significant endogenous component after that date. We have therefore explored an alternative assumption; namely, letting the price of oil react contemporaneously to current developments in the two quantity variables (output and employment), while assuming that quantity variables do not react contemporaneously to the price of oil. Because the contemporaneous correlations between quarterly quantity and oil price innovations are small, the results are nearly identical, and we do not report them in the text.

Another approach would be to use, either in addition or in substitution to the oil price, a more exogenous variable to proxy for oil shocks. This is the approach followed by Kilian (2008), who constructs and uses a proxy for unexpected movements in global oil production. What matters, however, to any given country is not the level of global oil production, but the price at which firms and households can purchase oil, which in turn depends also on world demand for oil. Thus, if the price of oil rises as a result of, say, higher Chinese demand, this is just like an exogenous oil supply shock for the remaining countries. This is indeed why we are fairly confident in our identification approach: the large residuals in our oil price series are clearly associated either with identifiable episodes of large supply disruptions or, in the more recent past, with increases in emerging countries' demand. These observations largely drive our estimates and our impulse response functions.

For each of the six countries, we estimate a VAR containing six variables: the dollar price of oil (expressed in log differences), CPI inflation, GDP deflator inflation, wage inflation, and the log changes in GDP and employment.[6] We use the dollar price of oil rather than the real price of oil to avoid dividing by an endogenous variable, the GDP deflator. For the same reason, we do not convert the price of oil into domestic currency for non-U.S. countries. For the United States, the data are taken from the USECON database, and cover the sample period 1960:1 to 2007:3. For the remaining countries, the data are drawn from OECD's Economic Outlook database, with the sample period being 1970:1 to 2007:3. Our three inflation measures are quarter-to-quarter, expressed in annualized terms. Each equation in our VAR includes four lags of the six aforementioned variables, a constant term, and a quadratic trend fitted measure of productivity growth.

Some of the oil price changes, and by implication, some of the residuals in the price of oil equation, are extremely large. The change in the price of oil for 1974:1, for example, is equal to eight times its standard deviation over the sample. Such large changes are likely to lead to small sample bias when estimating the oil price equation: the best ordinary least squares (OLS) fit is achieved by reducing the size of these particular residuals; thus, by spuri-

6. For the United States we use nonfarm business hours instead of employment, and the wage refers to nonfarm business compensation per hour. For simplicity we use the term employment to refer to both hours (in the case of the United States) and employment proper (for the remaining countries).

ously linking these very large realizations to movements in current or past values of the other variables in the regression. This in turn overstates the endogenous component of the price of oil, and understates the size of the true residuals. We deal with this issue by estimating the oil price equation using a sample that excludes all oil price changes larger than three standard deviations. (These large changes in oil prices are clearly essential in giving us precise estimates of the effects of oil prices on other variables. Thus, we use the complete sample when estimating the other equations.)

7.3.1 Impulse Responses

Figure 7.6, panels A through F, display the estimated impulse response functions (IRFs) for the different variables of interest to an oil price shock where, as discussed previously, the latter is identified as the innovation in the oil price equation. Estimates are reported for two different sample periods: 1970:1 to 1983:4 (1960:1 to 1983:4 for the United States) and 1984:1 to 2007:3 (1984:1 to 2005:4 for Germany and Italy). The break date chosen corresponds roughly to the beginning of the Great Moderation in the United States, as identified by several authors (e.g., McConnell and Pérez-Quirós (2000). Note that each subperiod contains two of the four large oil shock episodes identified in the previous section.

One standard deviation confidence intervals, obtained using a Monte Carlo procedure, are shown on both sides of the point estimates. The estimated responses of GDP and employment are accumulated and shown in levels. The size of the shock is normalized so that it raises the price of oil by 10 percent on impact. This roughly corresponds to the estimated standard deviations of oil price innovations for the two subsamples, which are very similar.[7] In all cases, the real price of oil shows a near-random walk response (not shown here); that is, it jumps on impact, and then stays around a new plateau.

The estimates for the United States, shown in panel A of figure 7.6, fit pretty well the conventional wisdom about the effects of a rise in oil prices. (figure 7.1, presented in the introduction, corresponds to panel A, with the results for the CPI shown in levels rather than rates of change.) For the pre-1984 period, CPI inflation shifts up immediately, and remains positive for a protracted period. The response of GDP inflation and wage inflation is similar, though more gradual. Output and employment decline persistently, albeit with a lag. Most relevant for our purposes, the responses of the same variables in the post-1984 period are considerably more muted, thus suggesting a weaker impact of oil price shocks on the economy. The only exception to this pattern is given by CPI inflation, whose response on impact is very similar across periods (though its persistence is smaller in the second period).

7. The estimated standard deviation of oil price innovations is 9.4 percent in the pre-1984 period, 12.4 percent in the post-1984 period.

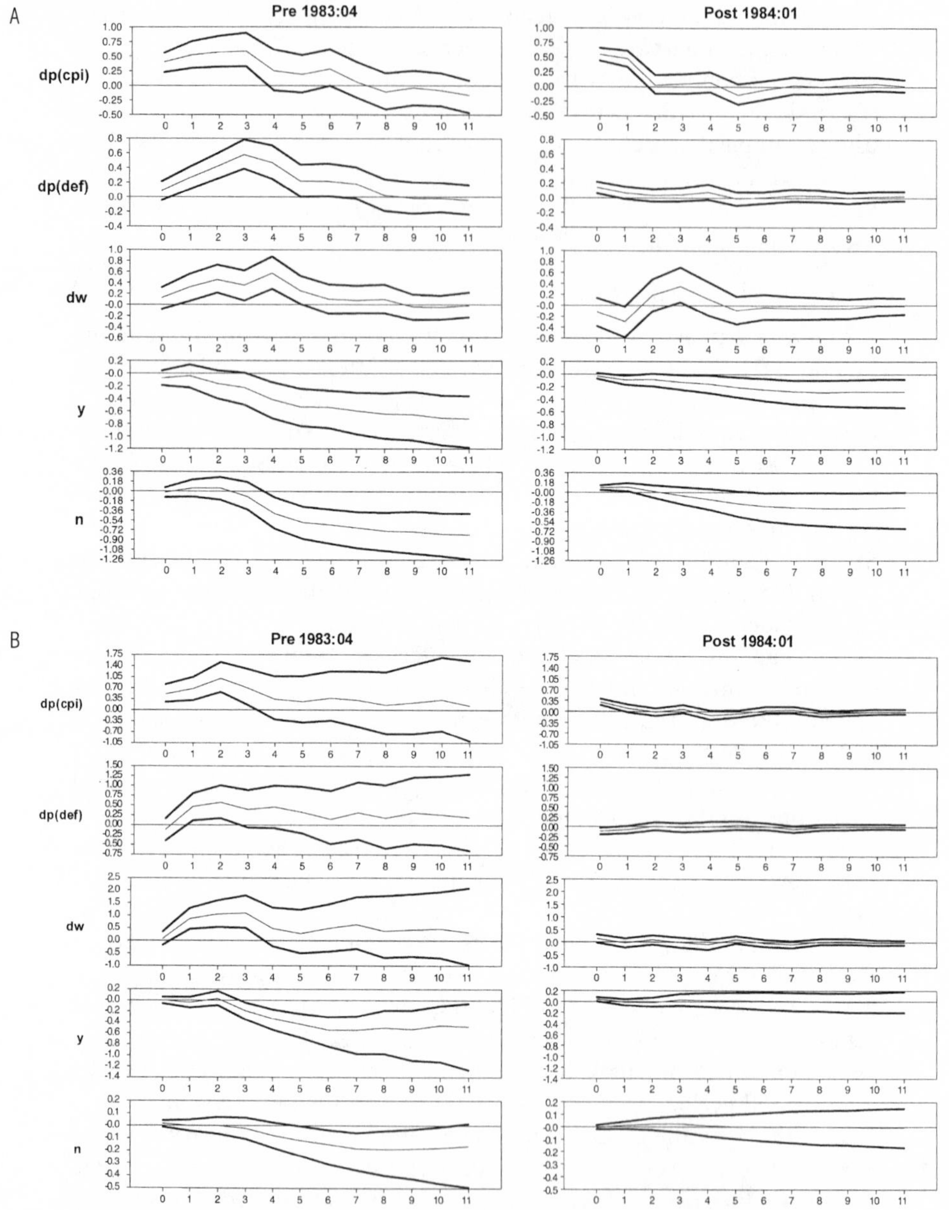

Fig. 7.6 Impulse response to an oil price shock *A*, United States; *B*, France; *C*, United Kingdom; *D*, Germany; *E*, Italy; *F*, Japan

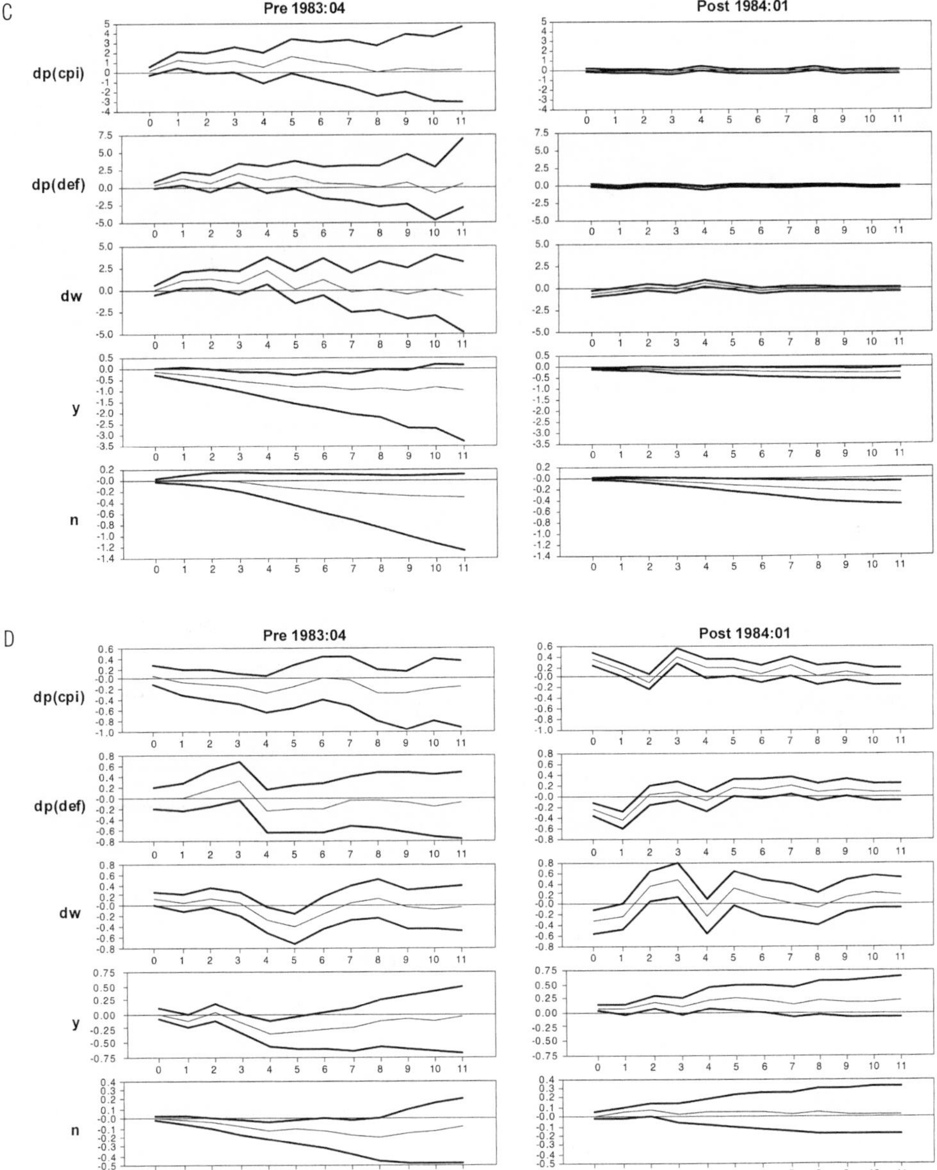
C
Pre 1983:04
Post 1984:01
dp(cpi)
dp(def)
dw
y
n
D
Pre 1983:04
Post 1984:01
dp(cpi)
dp(def)
dw
y
n

Fig. 7.6 (cont.)

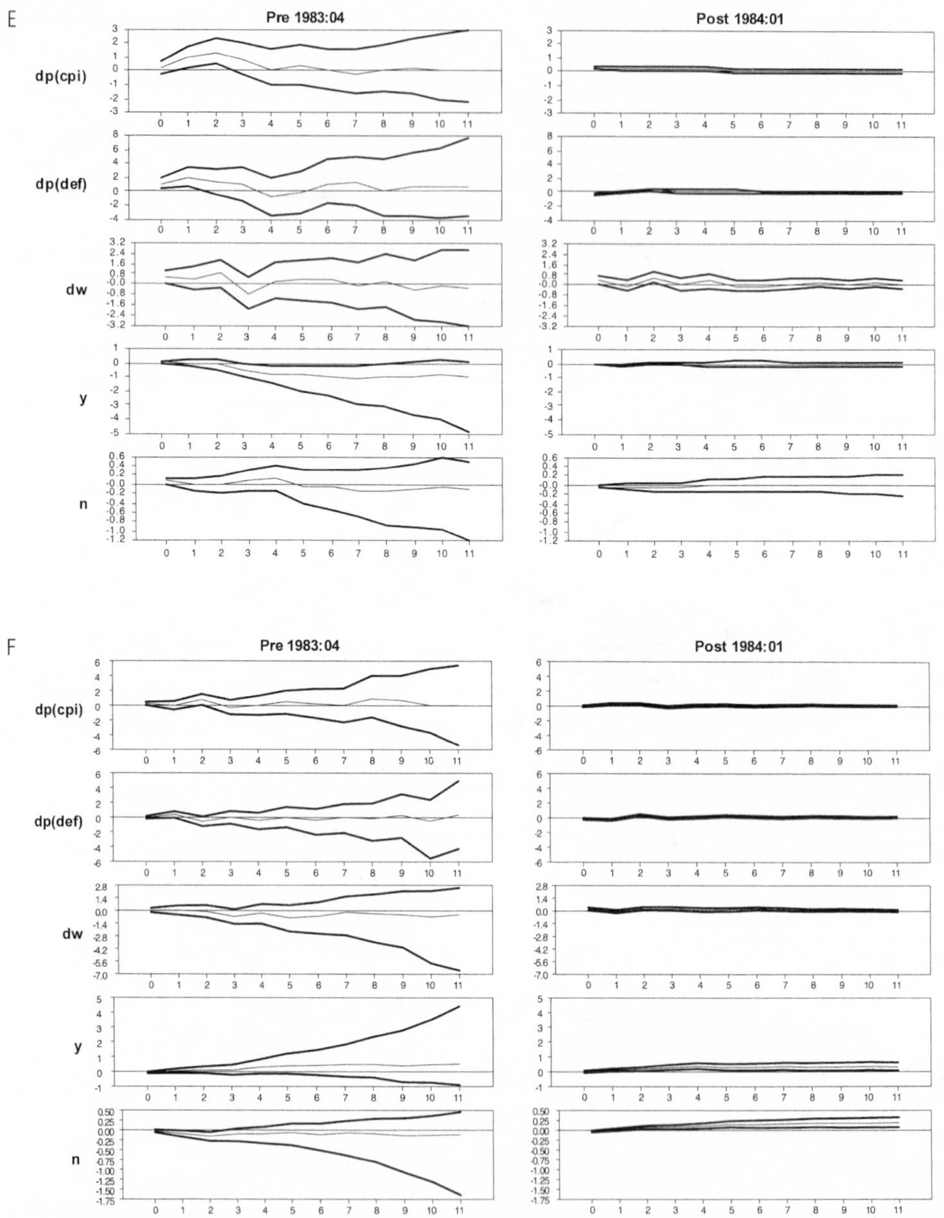

Fig. 7.6 (cont.) Impulse response to an oil price shock *A*, United States; *B*, France; *C*, United Kingdom; *D*, Germany; *E*, Italy; *F*, Japan

This may not be surprising since part of the increase in oil prices is reflected mechanically in the oil component of the CPI.

The estimates for France and the United Kingdom show a pattern very similar to that of the United States. In the case of France, the contrast between the early and the late periods is particularly strong, both in terms of the size and the persistence of the effects, and for both prices and quantities. In the case of the United Kingdom, the response of inflation variables is almost nonexistent in the latter period, though in contrast with France, there is some evidence of a decline in output and employment (albeit smaller than in the first sample period).

Some of the estimated responses for Germany and Italy fit conventional wisdom less well. The inflation measures in Germany hardly change in response to the rise in oil prices in either period, though the impact on output and employment is more adverse in the pre-1984 period. This is consistent with a stronger anti-inflationary stance of the Bundesbank, relative to other central banks. The slight increase in employment and output in the post-1984 period goes against conventional wisdom. In the case of Italy, there is barely any employment response in the pre-1984 period. Still, for both countries the sign of most of the responses accord with conventional wisdom, and the responses are smaller in the post-1984 period.

The story is different for Japan. The sign of many of the responses to the rise in oil prices is often at odds with standard priors. Also, the uncertainty of the estimates is much larger, as reflected in the wider bands. The effect on inflation is weak and does not have a clear sign in either period. There is a (slight) rise in output in both periods, and of employment in the post-1984 period.

In short, except for Japan (and to some extent, for Germany), most of the responses fit conventional wisdom rather well: an increase in the price of oil leads to more wage and price inflation, and to a decrease in employment and output for some time. In all cases, however, the effects on both inflation and activity are considerably weaker in the second subsample than in the first.

7.3.2 Variance and Historical Decompositions

How important are oil shocks in accounting for the observed fluctuations in inflation, output, and employment in the U.S. economy? Table 7.4 and figure 7.7 answer this question by using the decomposition associated with the estimated six-variable VAR, with data starting in 1960. For each variable and sample period, they compare the actual time series with the component of the series that results from putting all shocks, except the identified oil price shocks, equal to zero. Series for GDP and employment are accumulated, so the resulting series are in log-levels. All series are then Hodrick-Prescott (HP)-filtered so that the series can be interpreted as deviations from a slowly moving trend. Table 7.4 provides statistics for the role

Table 7.4 **The contribution of oil shocks to U.S. economic fluctuations, 1960:1–2007:3**

	Conditional standard deviation			Conditional SD / Unconditional SD	
	60:1–83:4	84:1–07:3	Ratio	60:1–83:4	84:1–07:3
Oil price (real)	12.9	15.4	1.19	0.82	0.88
CPI inflation	0.89	0.74	0.83	0.43	0.55
GDP inflation	0.71	0.15	0.24	0.50	0.25
Wage inflation	0.69	0.56	0.81	0.41	0.23
GDP	0.59	0.28	0.48	0.34	0.31
Hours	0.76	0.43	0.57	0.42	0.30

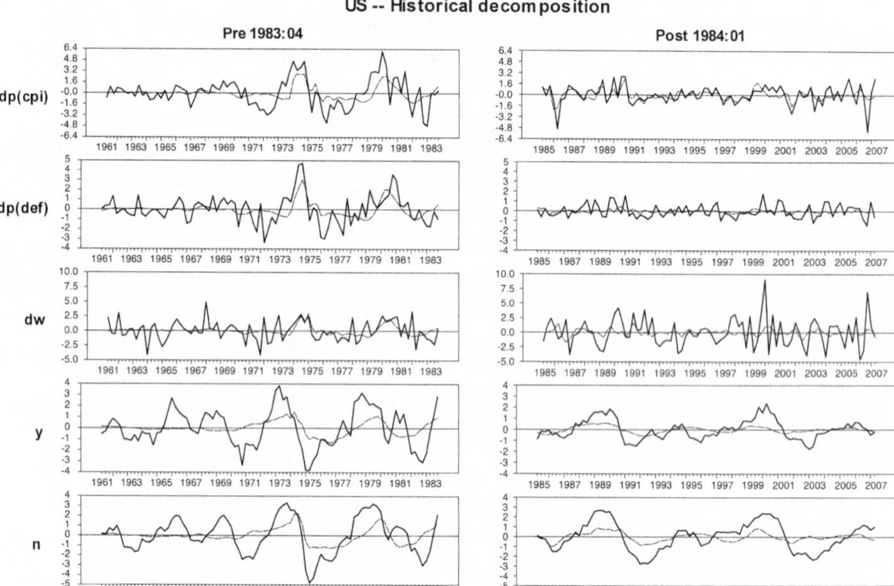

Fig. 7.7 The role of oil price shocks

of oil shocks as a source of fluctuations, including its percent contribution to the volatility of each variable (including the real price of oil, measured relative to the GDP deflator), both in absolute and relative terms. Figure 7.7 plots the series over time.

The estimated standard deviations of the oil-driven component of the different variables ("conditional standard deviations"), given in the first three columns of table 7.4, show that the volatility of fluctuations caused by oil shocks has diminished considerably for all variables, except for the real price of oil itself. In fact, the standard deviation of the exogenous component of the latter variable is about 20 percent larger in the second sample period. This can be explained to a large extent by the limited variation in the real price of oil before the 1973 crisis, and despite the two large spikes in that year and during 1979 and 1980.

This evidence reinforces our earlier Impulse response function (IRFs)-based findings of a more muted response of all variables to an oil shock of a given size. Thus, the change in the way the economy has responded to oil shocks has contributed to the dampening of economic fluctuations since the mid-1980s, the phenomenon known as the Great Moderation. Interestingly, our estimates suggest that this has been possible in spite of the slightly larger volatility of oil prices themselves.

The next two columns of table 7.4 give the relative contribution of oil shocks to movements in the various variables, measured as the ratio of the conditional to the unconditional standard deviation. The estimates suggest that the relative contribution of oil shocks to fluctuations in quantity variables (GDP and employment) has remained roughly unchanged over time, at around one-third. In the case of wage inflation and GDP deflator inflation, the contribution of oil shocks has declined to one-fourth in both cases, from a level close to one-half. In contrast, the contribution of oil shocks to CPI inflation has increased in the recent period. Note that this is consistent with a relatively stable core CPI, with oil price changes being passed through to the energy component of the CPI, and accounting for, according to our estimates, as much as 60 percent of the fluctuations in overall CPI inflation.

Figure 7.7 allows us to focus on the contribution of oil prices to the 1973 to 1974 and 1979 to 1981 episodes. It shows the substantial but nonexclusive role of exogenous oil shocks during each of the two episodes. In particular, while for our three inflation variables the oil price shocks seem to have accounted for the bulk of the increases in 1973 to 1974 and 1979 to 1981, no more than a half of the observed decline in employment and output during those episodes can be attributed to the oil shocks themselves. Thus, our findings suggest that other shocks played an important role in triggering those episodes.

Within our six-variable VAR, our partial identification approach does not allow us to determine what those additional underlying shocks may have been. Yet when we replace the price of oil by the broader producer price index (PPI) for crude materials in our six-variable VAR, the estimates of GDP and employment driven by exogenous shocks to that broader price index track more closely the movements of the actual time series themselves in the pre-1984 period, including the two large oil shock episodes contained in that period, as shown in figure 7.8. In particular, those shocks account for more than half of the fluctuations in all variables over the pre-1984 period. On the other hand, such broader supply shocks play a very limited role in accounting for the fluctuations in output and employment in the post-1984 period (though they play a more important one in accounting for variations in CPI inflation, in a way consistent with earlier evidence).

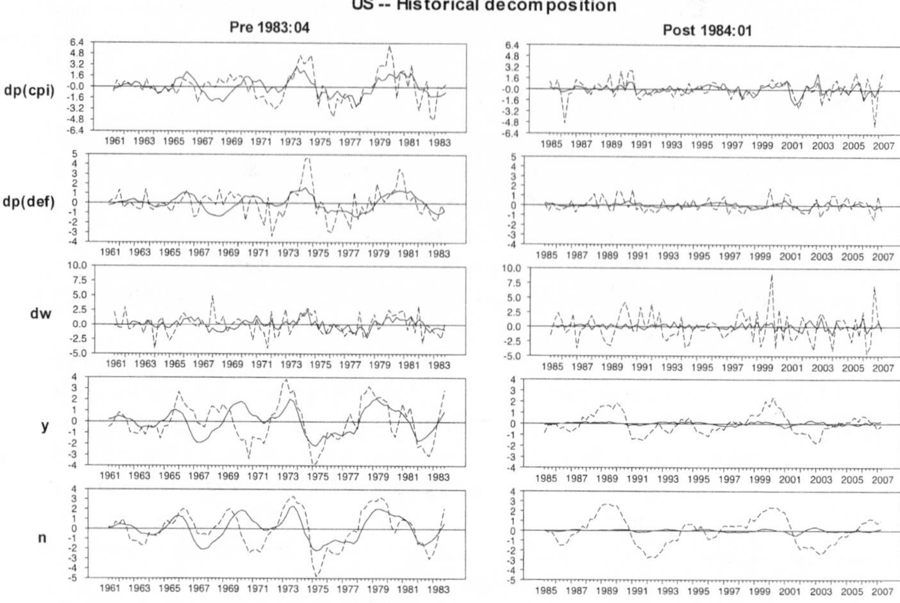

Fig. 7.8 The role of shocks to crude materials prices

7.4 U.S. Evidence Based on Rolling Bivariate Regressions

So far, we have analyzed the macroeconomic effects of oil price shocks and their change over time under the maintained assumption of a discrete break sometime around the mid-1980s. While the findings reported previously are largely robust to changes in the specific date of the break, some of the potential explanations (discussed following) for the change in the effects of oil price shocks are more likely to have been associated with a more gradual variation over time. This leads us to adopt a more flexible approach, and estimate rolling IRFs to oil price shocks, based on a simple dynamic equation linking a variable of interest to its own lags and the current and lagged values of the change in the (log) oil price. We do this using a moving window of 40 quarters, with the first moving window centered in 1970.

More specifically, letting y_t and p_t^o denote the variable of interest and the price of oil, respectively, we use OLS to estimate the regression:

$$y_t = \alpha + \sum_{j=1}^{4} \beta_j y_{t-j} + \sum_{j=0}^{4} \gamma_j \Delta p_{t-j}^o + u_t$$

and use the resulting estimates to obtain the implied dynamic response of y_t (or a transformation thereof) to a permanent 10 percent (log) change in the price of oil, thus implicitly assuming in the simulation that Δp_t^o is an i.i.d. process (which is roughly consistent with the random walk-like response of the price of oil obtained using our multivariate model).

Relative to the multivariate model analyzed in the previous section, correct identification of oil price shocks is obviously more doubtful in the present bivariate model, given the lower dimension specification of the economy's dynamics. This shortcoming must be traded-off with the possibility of estimating the VAR with much shorter samples and, hence, being able to obtain our rolling IRFs. In order to check the consistency with our earlier results, we first computed the average IRFs across moving windows within each of the subperiods considered earlier (pre-1984 and post-1984), and found the estimated IRFs (not shown) to be very similar to the ones obtained earlier. In particular, both the inflation variables, as well as output and employment, show a more muted response in the more recent period.

Figure 7.9, panels A through E, display the rolling IRFs for our three inflation measures, output, and employment. Several features stand out in the figure.

Consumer price index inflation appears quite sensitive to the oil shock over the entire sample period, but particularly in the late 1970s, when inflation is estimated to rise more than 1 percentage point two/three quarters after a 10 percent rise in the oil price. The response becomes steadily more muted over time and, perhaps as important, less persistent, especially in the more recent period (in a way consistent with our earlier evidence based on the six-variable VAR). The evolution over time in the response of GDP deflator inflation to an oil price shock is similar to that of CPI inflation, but shows a more dramatic contrast, with the response at the end of our sample being almost negligible. The response of wage inflation is rather muted all along, except for its large persistent increases in the late 1970s and early 1980s, and a similar spike in the 1990s.

The most dramatic changes are in the responses of output and employment (see figure 7.9, panels D and E). In the early part of the sample, output is estimated to decline as much as 1 percent two years after the 10 percent change in the price of oil. The estimated response, however, becomes weaker over time, with the point estimates of that response becoming slightly positive for the most recent period. A similar pattern can be observed for employment.

The previous evidence thus reinforces the picture that emerged from the earlier evidence, one which strongly suggests a vanishing effect of oil shocks on macroeconomic variables, both real and nominal. In the next section we try to uncover some of the reasons why.

7.5 Modeling the Macroeconomic Effects of Oil Price Shocks: A Simple Framework

We now develop a simple model of the macroeconomic effects of oil price shocks. Our focus is on explaining the different response of the economy to oil price shocks in the 1970s and the 2000s. With this in mind, we focus on three potential changes in the economy.

A

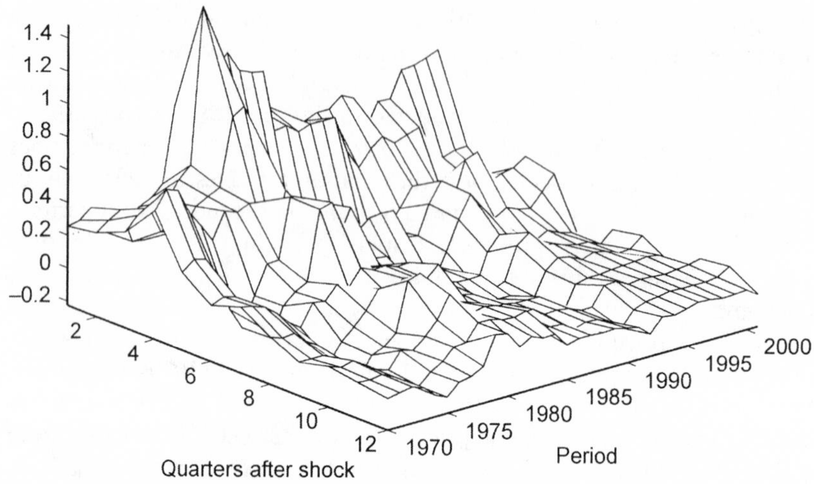

B

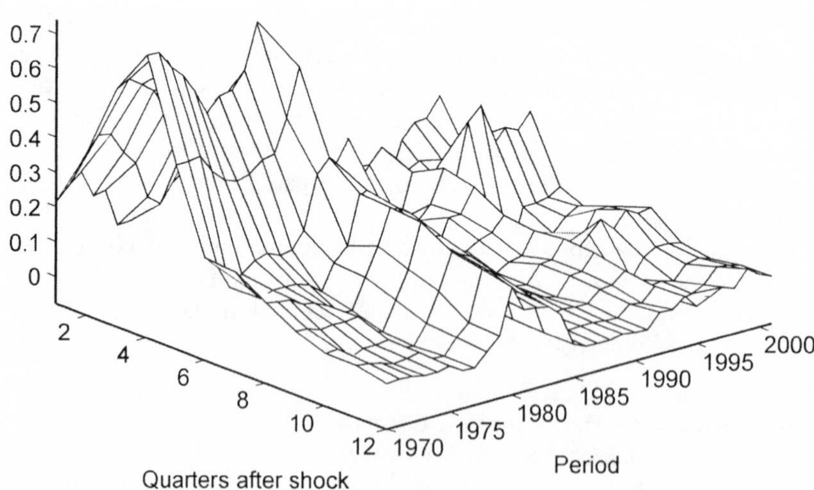

Fig. 7.9 Response of inflation, GDP, and employment

C

Response of Wage Inflation

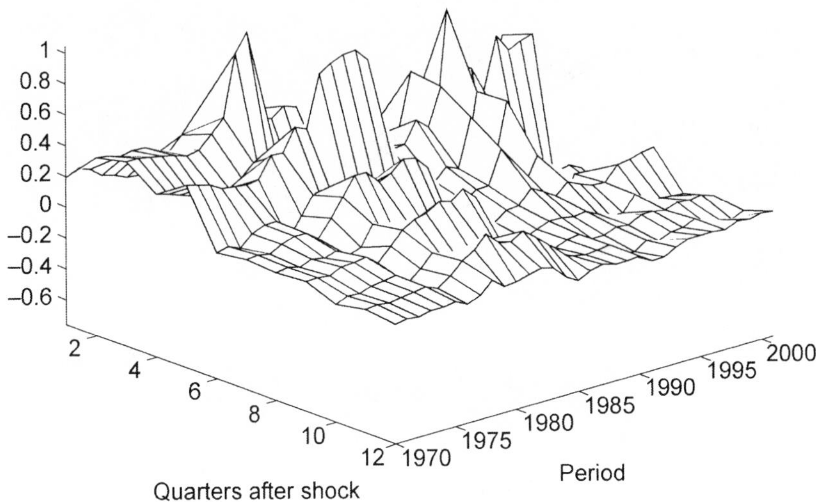

D

Response of GDP

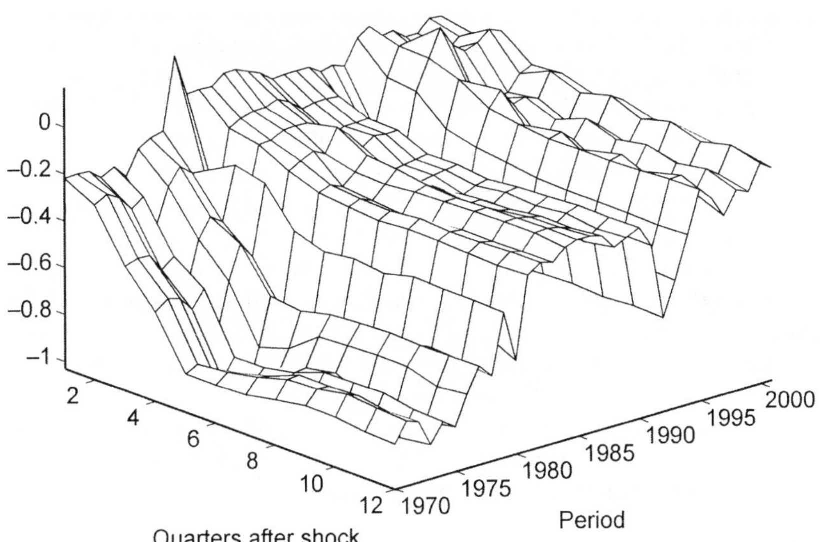

Fig. 7.9 (cont.)

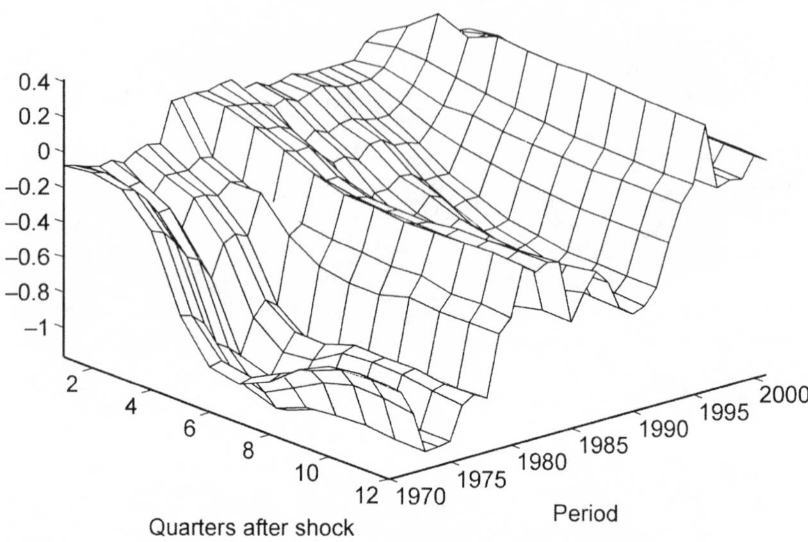

Fig. 7.9 (cont.)

First, the behavior of wages. To us, this looks a priori like the most plausible candidate. The 1970s were times of strong unions and high wage indexation. In the 2000s, unions are much weaker, and wage indexation has practically disappeared.

The second potential change is the role of monetary policy. Faced with a new type of shock, the central banks of the 1970s did not know at first how to react, policy mistakes were made, and central bank credibility was low. In the 2000s, supply shocks are no longer new, monetary policy is clearly set, and credibility is much higher.

Third, and trivially, is the quantitative importance of oil in the economy. Increases in the price of oil have led to substitution away from oil, and a decrease in the relevant shares of oil in consumption and in production. The question is whether this decrease can account for much of the difference in the effects of oil prices in the 1970s and the 2000s.[8]

We start from the standard new-Keynesian model and introduce two modifications. First, we introduce oil both as an input in consumption and as an input in production. We assume the country is an oil importer, and that

8. Some observers have suggested another factor—an increase in hedging against oil price shocks by oil users. What is known about hedging by airlines suggests, however, that while hedging is more prevalent than in the 1970s, its extent remains limited, with few hedges going beyond a year. See, for example, Carter, Rogers, and Simkins (2006a, 2006b).

the real price of oil (in terms of domestic goods) follows an exogenous process. Second, we allow for real wage rigidities, along the lines of our earlier work (Blanchard and Galí 2007). We present only log-linearized relations in the text, leaving the full derivation to appendix A. Lower case letters denote logarithms of the original variables, and for notational simplicity, we ignore all constants.

7.5.1 The Role of Oil

Oil is used both by firms in production and by consumers in consumption. Production is given by

$$q_t = a_t + \alpha_n n_t + \alpha_m m_t,$$

where q_t is (gross) domestic output; a_t is an exogenous technology parameter; n_t is labor; m_t is the quantity of imported oil used in production; and $\alpha_n + \alpha_m \leq 1$.[9]

Consumption is given by

$$c_t \equiv (1 - \chi)\, c_{q,t} + \chi\, c_{m,t},$$

where c_t is consumption; $c_{q,t}$ is the consumption of domestically produced goods (gross output); and $c_{m,t}$ is the consumption of imported oil.

In this environment, it is important to distinguish between two prices, the price of domestic output $p_{q,t}$, and the price of consumption $p_{c,t}$. Let $p_{m,t}$ be the price of oil, and $s_t \equiv p_{m,t} - p_{q,t}$ be the real price of oil. From the definition of consumption, the relation between the consumption price and the domestic output price is given by

$$p_{c,t} = p_{q,t} + \chi\, s_t. \tag{1}$$

Increases in the real price of oil lead to an increase in the consumption price relative to the domestic output price.

7.5.2 Households

The behavior of households is characterized by two equations. The first is an intertemporal condition for consumption:

$$c_t = E_t\{c_{t+1}\} - (i_t - E_t\{\pi_{c,t+1}\}), \tag{2}$$

where i_t is the nominal interest rate, and $\pi_{c,t} \equiv p_{c,t} - p_{c,t-1}$ is CPI inflation.

The second condition characterizes labor supply. If the labor market was perfectly competitive, labor supply would be implicitly given by

$$w_t - p_{c,t} = c_t + \phi\, n_t,$$

9. We use a Cobb-Douglas specification for convenience. It has the counterfactual implication that the share of oil in output remains constant. So, in our framework, when looking at changes in the share over time, we must attribute it to a change in the parameter α_m. For our purposes, this appears innocuous.

where w_t is the nominal wage, and n_t is employment. This is the condition that the consumption wage must equal the marginal rate of substitution between consumption and leisure; ϕ is the inverse of the Frisch elasticity of labor supply.

We formalize real wage rigidities by modifying the previous equation to read

$$w_t - p_{c,t} = (1 - \gamma)(c_t + \phi n_t), \tag{3}$$

where we interpret the parameter $\gamma \in [0, 1]$ as an index of the degree of real wage rigidities. While clearly ad-hoc, equation (3) is meant to capture in a parsimonious way the notion that real wages may not respond to labor market conditions as much as implied by the model with perfectly competitive markets. We have explored the implications of a dynamic version of equation (3), in which the wage adjusts over time to the marginal rate of substitution. This alternative is more attractive conceptually, and gives richer dynamics. However, it is also analytically more complex, and we have decided to present results using the simpler version presented earlier.

7.5.3 Firms

Given the production function, cost minimization implies that the firms' demand for oil is given by $m_t = -\mu_t^p - s_t + q_t$, where μ_t^p is the price markup. Using this expression to eliminate m_t in the production function gives a reduced-form production function

$$q_t = \frac{1}{1 - \alpha_m}(a_t + \alpha_n n_t - \alpha_m s_t - \alpha_m \mu_t^p). \tag{4}$$

Output is a decreasing function of the real price of oil, given employment and technology.

Combining the cost minimization conditions for oil and for labor with the aggregate production function yields the following factor price frontier:

$$(1 - \alpha_m)(w_t - p_{c,t}) + (\alpha_m + (1 - \alpha_m)\chi)\, s_t + (1 - \alpha_n - \alpha_m)\, n_t - a_t + \mu_t^p = 0. \tag{5}$$

Given productivity, an increase in the real price of oil must lead to one or more of the following adjustments: (a) a lower consumption wage, (b) lower employment, and (c) a lower markup. Under our assumed functional forms, it can be shown that with flexible prices and wages, the entire burden of the adjustment in response to an increase in s_t falls on the consumption wage, with employment and the markup remaining unchanged. But, as we discuss next, things are different when we allow the markup to vary (as a result of sticky prices), and wages to respond less than their competitive labor markets counterpart.

Firms are assumed to set prices à la Calvo (1983), an assumption that yields the following log-linearized equation for domestic output price inflation (domestic inflation for short)

$$\pi_{q,t} = \beta\, E_t\{\pi_{q,t+1}\} - \lambda_p\, \mu_t^p, \tag{6}$$

where $\lambda_p \equiv [(1-\theta)(1-\beta\theta)/\theta][(\alpha_m + \alpha_n)/(1 + (1-\alpha_m + \alpha_n)(\varepsilon - 1))]$, where θ denotes the fraction of firms that leave prices unchanged, β is the discount factor of households, and ε is the elasticity of substitution between domestic goods in consumption.

Note that this specification assumes a constant desired markup of firms. By doing so, we rule out a mechanism examined by Rotemberg and Woodford (1996) who argue that, to explain the size of the decline in output observed in response to oil shocks, one must assume countercyclical markups. We do so not because we believe the mechanism is irrelevant, but because we do not think that variations in the degree of countercyclicality of markups are likely to be one of the main factors behind the differences between the 1970s and the 2000s.

7.5.4 Equilibrium

The real wage consistent with household choices (cum real wage rigidities) is given by equation (3), and depends on consumption and employment.

The real wage consistent with the firms' factor price frontier is given by equation (5) and depends on the real price of oil, the markup, and employment.

Together, these two relations imply that the markup is a function of consumption, employment, and the real price of oil. Solving for consumption by using the condition that trade be balanced gives:

$$c_t = q_t - \chi\, s_t + \eta\, \mu_t^p, \tag{7}$$

where $\eta \equiv \alpha_m/(\mathcal{M}^p - \alpha_m)$, with $\mathcal{M}^p$ denoting the steady-state gross markup (now in levels). Combining this equation with the reduced-form production function gives consumption as a function of employment, productivity, the real price of oil, and the markup

$$c_t = \frac{1}{1-\alpha_m} a_t + \frac{\alpha_n}{1-\alpha_m} n_t - \left(\chi + \frac{\alpha_m}{1-\alpha_m}\right) s_t + \left(\eta - \frac{\alpha_m}{1-\alpha_m}\right) \mu_t^p.$$

If the steady-state markup is not too large, the last term is small and can safely be ignored. Replacing the expression for consumption in equation (3) for the consumption wage and then replacing the consumption wage in the factor price frontier gives an expression for the markup

(8) $$\mu_t^p = -\Gamma_n n_t - \Gamma_s s_t + \Gamma_a a_t,$$

where

$$\Gamma_n \equiv \frac{(1-\alpha_n-\alpha_m)\gamma + (1-\alpha_m)(1-\gamma)(1+\phi)}{1-(1-\gamma)(\alpha_m-(1-\alpha_m)\eta)} \geq 0$$

$$\Gamma_a \equiv \frac{\gamma}{1-(1-\gamma)(\alpha_m-(1-\alpha_m)\eta)} \geq 0$$

$$\Gamma_s \equiv \frac{\gamma\,(\alpha_m+(1-\alpha_m)\chi)}{1-(1-\gamma)(\alpha_m-(1-\alpha_m)\eta)} \geq 0.$$

Using this expression for the markup in equations (6) and (2) gives the following characterization of domestic inflation

(9) $$\pi_{q,t} = \beta\, E_t\{\pi_{q,t+1}\} + \lambda_p \Gamma_n n_t + \lambda_p \Gamma_s s_t - \lambda_p \Gamma_a a_t.$$

Under our assumptions, the first best level of employment can be shown to be invariant to the real price of oil—substitution and income effects cancel.[10] If $\gamma = 0$; that is, if there are no real wage rigidities, then Γ_a and Γ_s are both equal to zero, and domestic inflation only depends on employment. Together, these two propositions imply that stabilizing domestic inflation is equivalent to stabilizing the distance of employment from first best—a result we have called elsewhere the "divine coincidence."

Positive values of γ lead instead to positive values of Γ_a and Γ_s. The higher γ, or the higher $(\alpha_m + (1-\alpha_m)\chi)$—an expression that depends on the shares of oil in production and in consumption—the worse the trade-off between stabilization of employment and stabilization of domestic inflation in response to oil price shocks.

7.5.5 Implications for GDP and the GDP Deflator

Note that the characterization of the equilibrium did not require introducing either value added or the value-added deflator. But these are needed to compare the implications of the model to the data.

The value-added deflator, $p_{y,t}$, is implicitly defined by $p_{q,t} = (1-\alpha_m)\,p_{y,t} + \alpha_m\,p_{m,t}$. Rearranging terms gives

(10) $$p_{y,t} = p_{q,t} - \frac{\alpha_m}{1-\alpha_m} s_t,$$

thus implying a negative effect of the real price of oil on the value-added deflator, given domestic output prices.

10. To see this, we can just determine equilibrium employment under perfect competition in both goods and labor markets, corresponding to the assumptions $\mu_t = 0$ for all t and $\gamma = 0$, respectively.

The definition of value added, combined with the demand for oil, yields the following relation between value added and output:

(11) $$y_t = q_t + \frac{\alpha_m}{1 - \alpha_m} s_t + \eta \, \mu_t^p.$$

This in turn implies the following relation between value added and consumption:

(12) $$y_t = c_t + \left(\frac{\alpha_m}{1 - \alpha_m} + \chi \right) s_t.$$

An increase in the price of oil decreases consumption given value added both because (imported) oil is used as an input in production, and used as an input in consumption.

Under the same approximation as before; that is, $(\eta - \alpha_m/(1 - \alpha_m)) \, \mu_t^p \simeq 0$, equations (4) and (11) imply the following relation between value added and employment:

(13) $$y_t = \frac{1}{1 - \alpha_m} (a_t + \alpha_n n_t).$$

Note that, under this approximation, the relation between value added and employment does not depend on the real price of oil.

7.5.6 Quantifying the Effects of Oil Price Shocks

Equations (1), (2), (9), (12), and (13) describe the equilibrium dynamics of prices and quantities, given exogenous processes for technology and the real price of oil, and a description of how the interest rate is determined (i.e., an interest rate rule). We now use these conditions to characterize the economy's response to an oil price shock.

Assume that $a_t = 0$ for all t (i.e., abstract from technology shocks). It follows from (13) and the previous discussion that the efficient level of value added is constant (and normalized to zero) in this case. Assume further that the real price of oil follows an AR(1) process

(14) $$s_t = \rho_s \, s_{t-1} + \varepsilon_t.$$

We can then summarize the equilibrium dynamics of value added and domestic inflation through the system:

(15) $$\pi_{q,t} = \beta \, E_t\{\pi_{q,t+1}\} + \kappa \, y_t + \lambda_p \Gamma_s \, s_t$$

(16) $$y_t = E_t\{y_{t+1}\} - (i_t - E_t\{\pi_{q,t+1}\}) + \frac{\alpha_m (1 - \rho_s)}{1 - \alpha_m} s_t,$$

where $\kappa \equiv \lambda_p \, \Gamma_n \, (1 - \alpha_m)/\alpha_n$.

These two equations must be complemented with a description of monetary policy. Assume an interest rate rule of the form

$$i_t = \phi_\pi \pi_{q,t}, \tag{17}$$

where $\phi_\pi > 1$. Note that in our model, $\pi_{q,t}$ corresponds to core CPI inflation, a variable that many central banks appear to focus on as the basis for their interest rate decisions.

We can then solve for the equilibrium analytically, using the method of undetermined coefficients. This yields the following expressions for domestic inflation and output:

$$\pi_{q,t} = \Psi_\pi s_t$$

$$y_t = \Psi_y s_t$$

where

$$\Psi_\pi = \frac{(1-\rho_s)(\kappa\alpha_m/(1-\alpha_m) + \lambda_p\Gamma_s)}{(1-\rho_s)(1-\beta\rho_s) + (\phi_\pi - \rho_s)\kappa}$$

and

$$\Psi_y = \frac{\alpha_m/(1-\alpha_m)(1-\rho_s)(1-\beta\rho_s) - (\phi_\pi - \rho_s)\lambda_p\Gamma_s}{(1-\rho_s)(1-\beta\rho_s) + (\phi_\pi - \rho_s)\kappa}.$$

Domestic inflation and GDP follow AR(1) processes with the same first-order coefficient as the real price of oil. Their innovations are proportional to the innovation in the real price of oil, with the coefficient of proportionality depending on the parameters of the model.

Expressions for CPI inflation and employment can be obtained using (1) and (13), respectively:

$$\pi_{c,t} = \Psi_\pi s_t + \chi \Delta s_t$$

$$n_t = \Psi_y \frac{1-\alpha_m}{\alpha_n} s_t.$$

With these equations, we can turn to the discussion of the potential role of the three factors we identified earlier—real wage rigidities, monetary policy, and the quantitative importance of oil in the economy—in explaining the differences between the 1970s and the 2000s. In all cases we use the evidence we presented earlier for the United States as a benchmark.

7.6 Three Hypotheses on the Changing Effects of Oil Price Shocks

In order to assess quantitatively the potential for oil price shocks to generate significant macroeconomic fluctuations, we first need to calibrate our model. We assume the following parameter values:

The time unit is a quarter. We set the discount factor β equal to 0.99. We set the Calvo parameter, θ, to 0.75. We choose the elasticity of output with respect to labor, α_n, equal to 0.7. We assume $\phi = 1$, thus implying a unitary Frisch labor supply elasticity.

As discussed in previous sections, changes in the volatility of the real price of oil are unlikely to lie behind the changes in the size of the effects of oil shocks. Thus, for simplicity, we assume an unchanged process for the real price of oil. Based on the conditional standard deviation of the price of oil for the period 1984:1 to 2005:4, we assume $var(s_t) = (0.16)^2$. We set $\rho_s = 0.97$.[11] Also, and unless otherwise noted, we set the shares of oil in production and consumption (α_m and χ) to equal 0.017 and 0.012, respectively, which correspond to their values in 1997.[12]

Most of the aforementioned parameters are kept constant across all the simulations presented following. The exceptions, as well as our treatment of the remaining parameters, varies depending on the hypothesis being considered in each case.

7.6.1 Changes in Real Wage Rigidities

In the previously mentioned framework, the presence of some rigidity in the adjustment of real wages to economic conditions is a necessary ingredient in order to generate significant fluctuations in measures of inflation and economic activity. Figure 7.10 illustrates this point by showing the range of volatilities of CPI inflation (annualized, and expressed in percent) and GDP implied by our calibrated model under the assumption of perfectly competitive labor markets ($\gamma = 0$), and under two alternative calibrations. The first calibration assumes a relatively favorable environment, with the two shares of oil at their "low" values prevailing in 1997, and no credibility gap in monetary policy ($\delta = 0$; the discussion of credibility and the definition of δ will be given following). The second calibration assumes a less favorable environment, with the shares of oil at their "high" values prevailing in 1973 (see appendix B), and the presence of a credibility gap in monetary policy ($\delta = 0.5$). For each calibration, the figure plots the standard deviations of CPI inflation and value added, as the coefficient on inflation in the Taylor rule, ϕ_π, varies from 1 to 5, a range of values that covers the empirically plausible set (conditional on having a unique equilibrium). The exercise yields two conclusions.

First, the slope of the relation between the standard deviation of GDP and the standard deviation of CPI inflation is positive. This should not be surprising: in the absence of real wage rigidities, there is no trade-off between inflation and value-added stabilization. Hence, a policy that seeks

11. The price of oil would be better characterized as nonstationary. But we would then have to extend our formalization of real wage rigidities to allow the wage to eventually converge to the marginal rate of substitution. Thus, we assume the value of ρ to be high, but less than one.

12. See appendix B for details of construction. We thank Carlos Montoro for pointing out an error in the computation of the oil shares in earlier versions of the chapter.

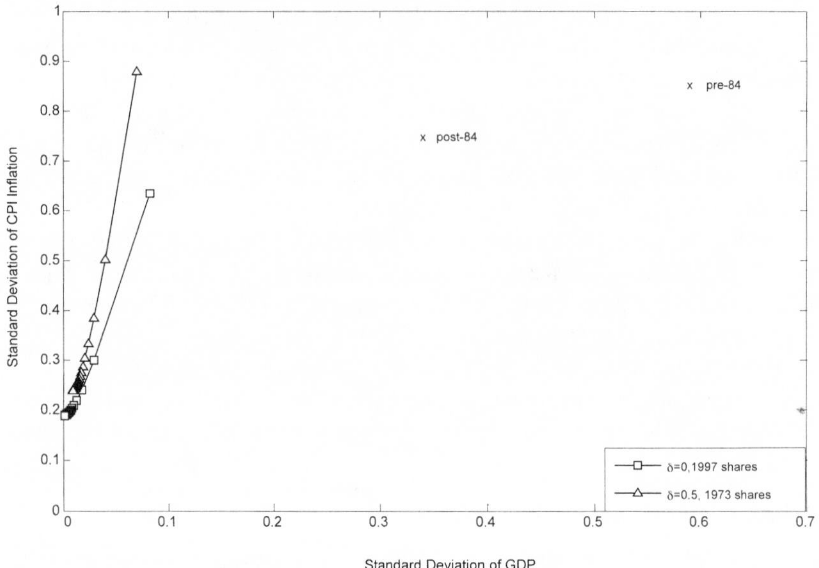

Fig. 7.10 Volatility ranges under flexible wages

to stabilize domestic inflation more aggressively also stabilizes value added. In fact, one can reduce the volatility of both variables by choosing ϕ_π to be arbitrarily large (this is what we called the "divine coincidence" in an earlier chapter). Under the assumed rule, on the other hand, CPI inflation faces a lower bound to its volatility, since it is affected directly by any change in the price of oil, in proportion to the share of oil in the consumption basket.

Second, the model has a clear counterfactual implication. While finite values of ϕ_π yield positive standard deviations for both GDP and CPI inflation, they also imply a positive response of both GDP and CPI inflation to an increase in the price of oil, an implication obviously at odds with the data.

Figure 7.11 shows that the introduction of real wage rigidities alters that picture substantially. It plots three loci, corresponding to three different values of the real wage rigidity parameter: $\gamma = 0.0$, $\gamma = 0.6$, and $\gamma = 0.9$. In the three cases, we assume an otherwise favorable environment, with the 1997 oil shares and full credibility of monetary policy. As before, each locus is obtained by varying ϕ_π from 1 to 5. Several results are worth pointing out.

First, the trade-off generated by the presence of real wage rigidities is apparent in the negative relationship between inflation volatility on the one hand and GDP volatility on the other when γ is positive.

Second, while the introduction of real wage rigidities raises the volatility of all variables (for any given ϕ_π), the model's predictions still fall short of

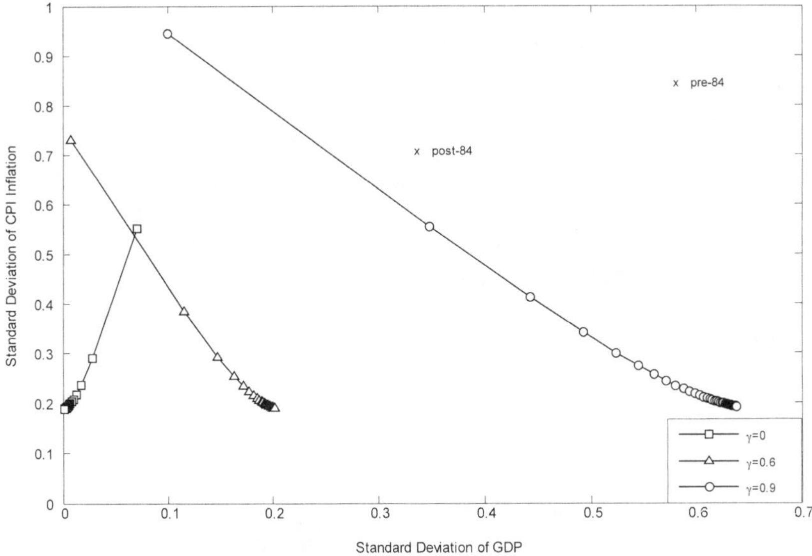

Fig. 7.11 Real wage rigidities and policy trade-offs

matching the (conditional) standard deviations of CPI inflation and GDP in our two samples, represented by the two crosses.

Finally, and that shortcoming notwithstanding, the figure also makes clear that a moderate reduction in the degree of real wage rigidities (e.g., a shift of γ from 0.9 to 0.6) can account for a substantial improvement in the policy trade-off and hence on a simultaneous reduction in the volatility of inflation and GDP resulting from oil price shocks (or supply shock, more generally).

To what extent a reduction in the degree of real wage rigidities may have been a factor behind the more muted effects of oil shocks in recent years? We rely again on the bivariate rolling VAR approach used earlier to try to answer this question, by seeking evidence of faster wage adjustment in recent years. In particular, we use this approach to estimate the responses of the real consumption wage, the unemployment rate, and the wage markup, defined as the gap between the (log) consumption wage, $w_t - p_{c,t}$, and the (log) marginal rate of substitution, $c_t + \phi n_t$, with $\phi = 1$, as in our baseline calibration. In response to a rise in the real price of oil, we would expect this markup to increase in the presence of real wage rigidities, which in turn should be associated with a rise in unemployment.

Figure 7.12, panels A through C, display the relevant IRFs representing, as before, the estimated response of each variable to a permanent 10 percent increase in the dollar price of oil. Panel A shows that the consumption wage tends to decline in response to the oil shock. While the response shows some variability over time, it does not show a tendency

A

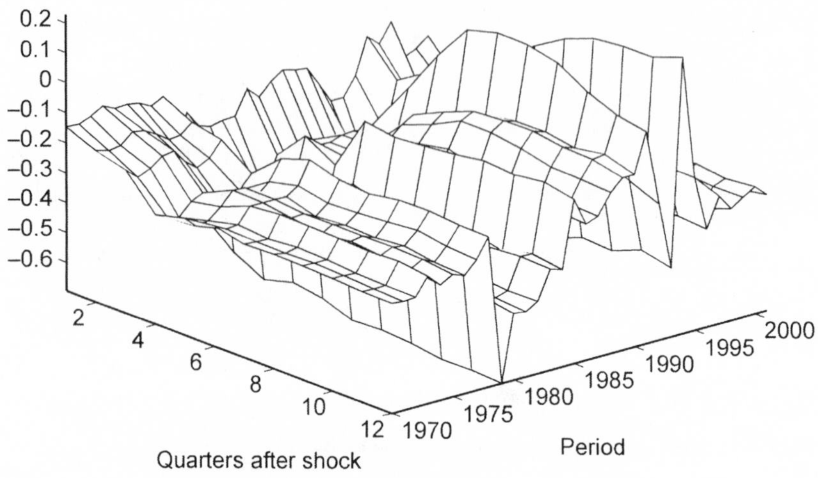

B

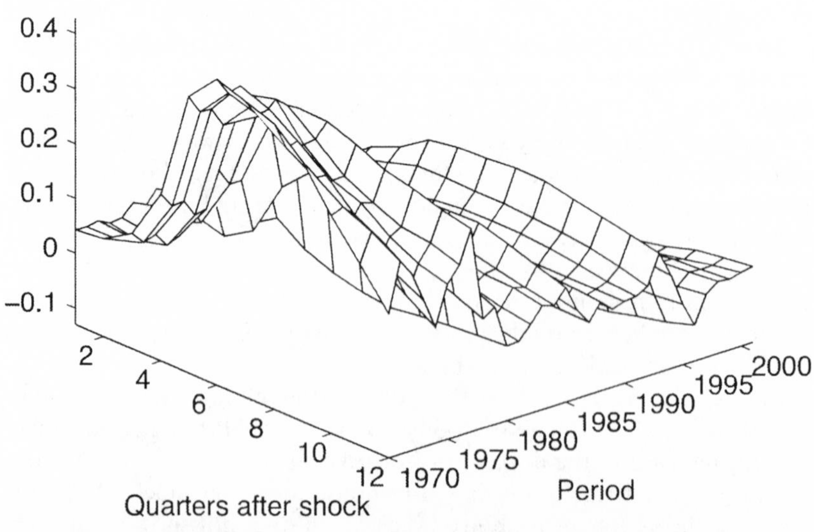

Fig. 7.12 Response of real wage, unemployment rate, and wage markup

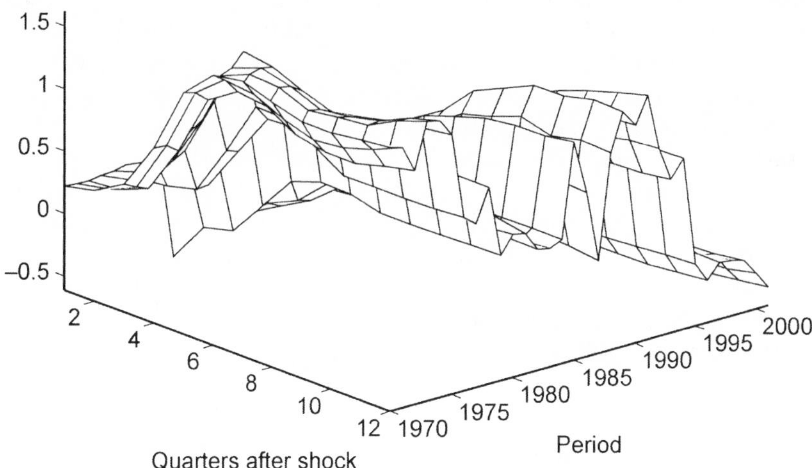

Fig. 7.12 Response of real wage, unemployment rate, and wage markup

toward a larger response of the consumption wage over time. Panel B shows that unemployment tends to increase in response to the oil shock. It also shows that this response has declined dramatically over time. An interpretation of these two evolutions is that the decrease in real wages, which required a large increase in unemployment in the 1970s, is now achieved with barely any increase in unemployment today. This suggests, in turn, a decrease in real wage rigidities. Another way of making the same point, within the logic of the model, is to look at the evolution of the wage markup. This is done in panel C. An increase in the oil price leads to an increase in the wage markup; that is, the decrease in the consumption wage is smaller than the decrease in the marginal rate of substitution. The effect has become, however, steadily smaller over time, very rapidly so in the more recent period. This suggests that the real consumption wage moves today much more in line with the marginal rate of substitution than it did in the 1970s.[13]

7.6.2 Changes in Monetary Policy

A number of studies (e.g., Clarida, Galí, and Gertler 2000) have provided evidence of a stronger interest rate response to variations in inflation over the

13. At least from a qualitative point of view, the previous evidence is robust to variations in the calibration of parameter ϕ within a plausible range (which we take to be given by the interval [0.5, 5]).

past two decades, relative to the 1960s and 1970s. It should be clear, however, from the simulations of our previously presented model that, other things equal, a stronger anti-inflationary stance should have reduced the volatility of inflation, but increased that of GDP. In other words, that evidence cannot explain—at least by itself—the lower volatility of both inflation and economic activity in response to oil price shocks.

In addition to this change in behavior, captured by the literature on empirical interest rate rules, there is also widespread agreement that central banks' commitment to keeping inflation low and stable has also become more credible over the past two decades, thanks to improved communications, greater transparency, the adoption of more or less explicit quantitative inflation targets, and ultimately, by the force of deeds. In this section we use the framework developed earlier to study the role that such an improvement in credibility may have had in accounting for the reduced impact of oil shocks.

We model credibility as follows: as in our baseline model, we assume that the central bank follows an interest rate rule

$$i_t = \phi_\pi \pi_{q,t}.$$

The public, however, is assumed to perceive that interest rate decisions are made according to

$$i_t = \phi_\pi(1 - \delta)\, \pi_{q,t} + v_t,$$

where $\{v_t\}$ is taken by the public to be an exogenous i.i.d monetary policy shock, and $\delta \in [0, 1]$ can be interpreted as a measure of the credibility gap. In the following, we restrict ourselves to calibrations that guarantee a unique equilibrium, which requires that the condition $\phi_\pi (1 - \delta) > 1$ be met.[14]

In addition to the prior actual and perceived policy rules, the model is exactly as the one developed previously, with the dynamics of value added, domestic inflation, and the real price of oil summarized by equations (14) through (16). Solving the model for domestic inflation and value added gives:

$$\pi_{q,t} = a\, s_t + b v_t,$$

$$y_t = c\, s_t + d v_t,$$

where a, b, c, and d are given by:

$$a = \frac{(1 - \rho_s)(\kappa\alpha_m(1 - \alpha_m)^{-1} + \lambda_p \Gamma_s)}{(1 - \rho_s)(1 - \beta\rho_s) + (\phi_\pi(1 - \delta) - \rho_s)\kappa} > 0$$

14. The hypothesis of an indeterminate equilibrium (and, hence, the possibility of sunspot fluctuations) in the first part of the sample could also potentially explain the greater volatility in both inflation and GDP, as emphasized by Clarida, Galí, and Gertler (2000). We choose to pursue an alternative line of explanation here, which does not rely on multiplicity of equilibria.

$$b = -\frac{\kappa}{1 + \phi_\pi(1-\delta)\kappa} < 0$$

$$c = \frac{\alpha_m(1-\alpha_m)^{-1}(1-\rho_s)(1-\beta\rho_s) - (\phi_\pi(1-\delta) - \rho_s)\lambda_p\Gamma_s}{(1-\rho_s)(1-\beta\rho_s) + (\phi_\pi(1-\delta) - \rho_s)\kappa}$$

$$d = -\frac{1}{1 + \phi_\pi(1-\delta)\kappa}.$$

Imposing $v_t = \delta\phi_\pi\pi_{H,t}$ into the solution (so that the central bank actually adheres to its chosen rule) we get

$$\pi_{q,t} = \frac{a}{1 - b\delta\phi_\pi} s_t,$$

thus implying that CPI inflation is

$$\pi_{c,t} = \frac{a}{1 - b\delta\phi_\pi} s_t + \chi\,\Delta s_t.$$

Value added is then given by:

$$\begin{aligned} y_t &= c\,s_t + d\phi_\pi\delta\,\pi_{q,t} \\ &= \left(c + \frac{da\phi_\pi\delta}{1 - b\delta\phi_\pi}\right)s_t. \end{aligned}$$

Figure 7.13 displays the loci of standard deviations of CPI inflation and GDP associated with $\delta = 0$ and $\delta = 0.5$; that is, corresponding to a full

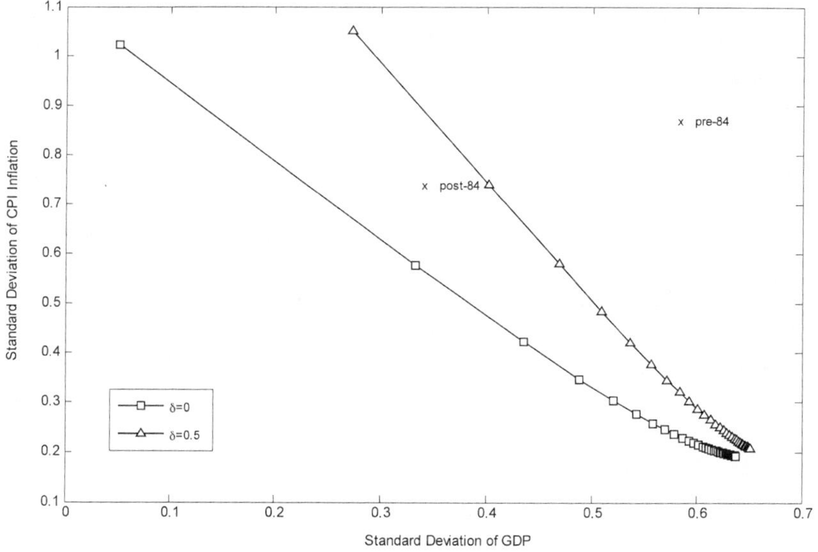

Fig. 7.13 Credibility and policy trade-offs

credibility and a low credibility environment, respectively. In both cases we restrict ϕ_π to values above two in order to guarantee a unique equilibrium. We set γ equal to 0.9, and calibrate the oil shares to their 1997 values. Two points are worth noting.

First, allowing for both real wage rigidities and poor credibility, the model's predictions come closer but still fall somewhat short of matching the (conditional) standard deviations of CPI inflation and GDP in the pre-1984 sample. Given the primitive nature of the model, this may not be overly worrisome.

Second, credibility gains can improve the trade-off facing policymakers significantly. The quantitative gains, however, do not seem sufficient to account, by themselves, for the observed decline in macro volatility in the face of oil shocks, documented earlier in the chapter. But they show that improved credibility may certainly have contributed to that decline.

Figure 7.14, panels A through C, provides some evidence of the changes in the Fed's response to oil price shocks, as well as an indicator of potential changes in its credibility. The rolling IRFs displayed are based on estimated bivariate VARs with the price of oil and, one at a time, a measure of inflation expectations over the next twelve months from the Michigan Survey, the three-month Treasury Bill rate, and the real interest rate (measured as the difference between the previous two variables).

First, and most noticeable, the response of expected inflation to an oil price shock of the same size (normalized here to 10 percent rise) has shrunk dramatically over time, from a rise of about 50 basis points in the 1970s, to about 20 basis points since the mid-1980s, and has remained remarkably stable after that.

Second, and perhaps surprisingly, the strength of the response of the nominal interest rate has not changed much across sample periods. The shrinking response of expected inflation implies, however, that the response of the real rate to an oil price shock has become stronger over time. In fact, the real rate appears to decline significantly in response to an oil price shock in the 1970s, an observation consistent with the (unconditional) evidence in Clarida, Galí, and Gertler (2000). This decline may have contributed to the large and persistent increase in inflation. It also suggests that had the Fed pursued a stronger anti-inflationary policy (keeping credibility unchanged) the adverse effects on output and inflation would have been even larger.[15]

To summarize the lessons from the previous analysis: while the weak

15. Note that, for the most recent period, the real interest rate shows very little change in response to an oil price shock. There are several explanations for this finding. First, as shown before, several measures of inflation (including expected inflation and GDP deflator inflation) hardly change in response to the oil price rise. If the Fed responds to those measures, the required adjustment in the nominal and real rates will be relatively small. Secondly, the Fed may also adjust rates in response to measures of economic activity. The decline in GDP and employment may thus have induced an interest rate movement in the opposite direction, with the net effect being close to zero.

A

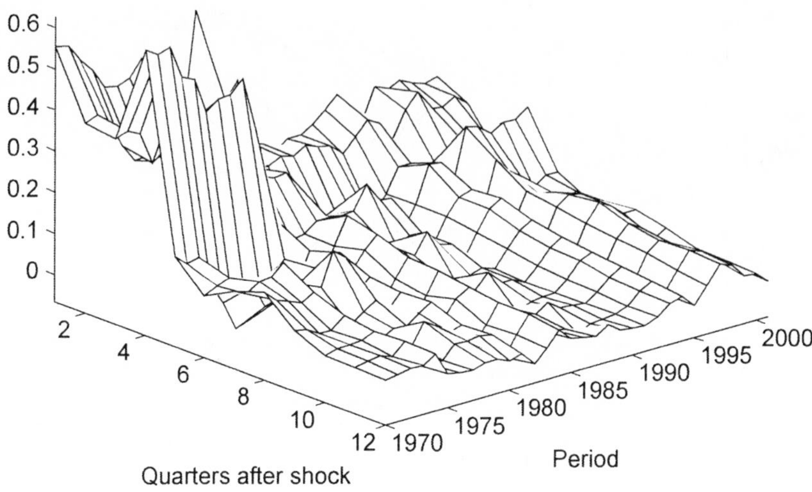

B

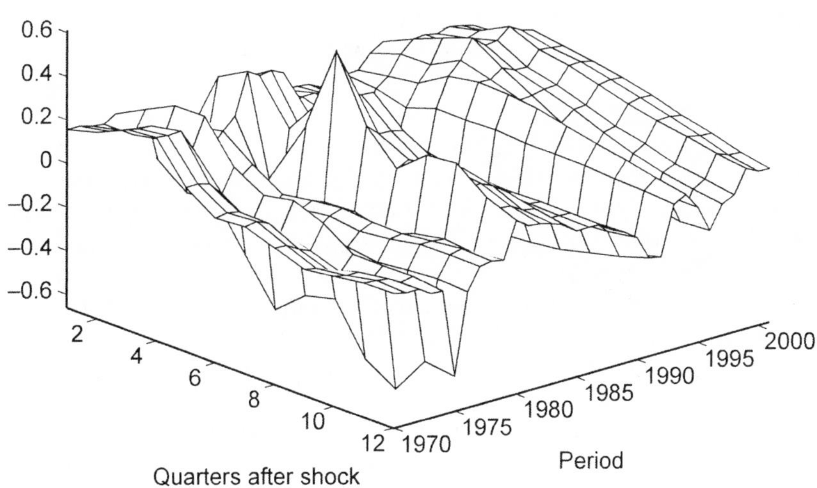

Fig. 7.14 Response of expected inflation, nominal rate, and real rate

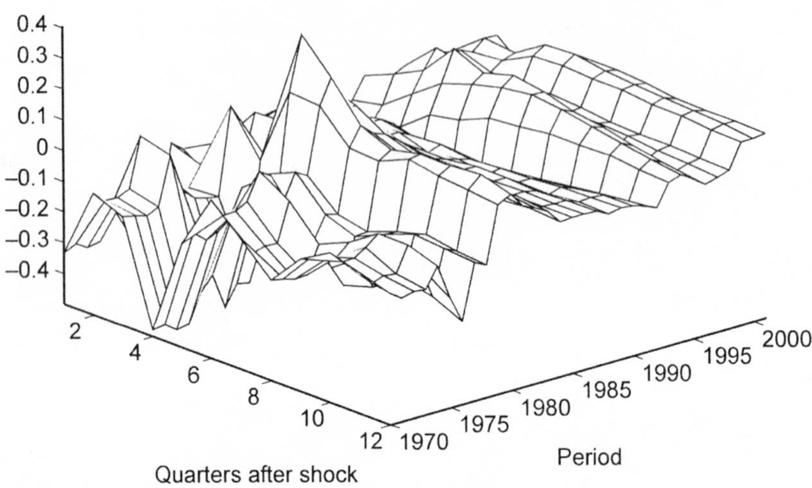

Fig. 7.14 (cont.)

response of inflation to oil price shocks in recent years is often interpreted as a consequence of a stronger anti-inflation stance by the Fed (a higher ϕ_π, in the context of our model), the evidence of a smaller decline in employment and GDP suggests that an enhanced anti-inflation credibility may also have played a role. The sharp decline in the response of inflation expectations to an oil price shock is certainly consistent with this view.

7.6.3 Declining Oil Shares

A third hypothesis for the improved policy trade-off is that the share of oil in consumption and in production is smaller today than it was in the 1970s. To examine the possible impact of these changes we simulate two alternative versions of our model, with α_m and χ calibrated using 1973 and 1997 data on the share of oil in production costs and consumption expenditures (see appendix B for details of construction). In light of this evidence we choose $\alpha_m = 2.3$ percent and $\chi = 1.5$ percent (1973 data) for the 1970s, and $\alpha_m = 1.7$ percent and $\chi = 1.2$ percent (based on data for 1997) for our two calibrations.

Figure 7.15 displays CPI inflation and GDP volatility for the two calibrations, keeping the index of real wage rigidities unchanged at $\gamma = 0.9$ (and $\delta = 0$). The conclusion is similar to those reached for the other two candidate

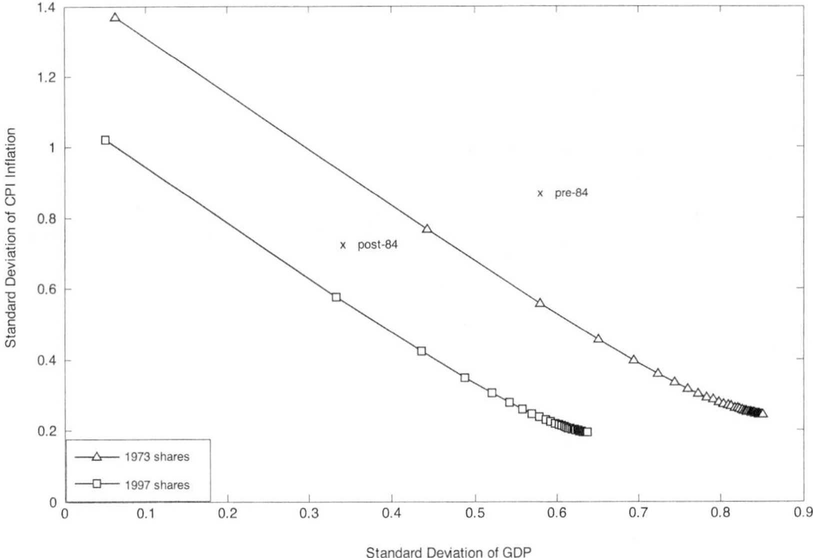

Fig. 7.15 Changing oil shares and policy trade-offs

explanations. The reduction in the oil shares in consumption and production cannot account for the full decline in volatility, but it clearly accounts for part of it. (The values of α_m and χ in 1977, thus after the first but before the second oil shock, were 3.6 percent and 1.8 percent, respectively. This suggests that, other things equal, the second oil shock should have had larger effects than the first. As we saw earlier, the opposite appears to be true.)

The previous analysis has examined the effects on CPI inflation and GDP volatility of changes in one parameter at a time. Figure 7.16 shows the combined effect of a simultaneous change in the three parameters. The first calibration, which is meant to roughly capture the 1970s environment, assumes strong wage rigidities ($\gamma = 0.9$), limited central bank credibility ($\delta = 0.5$), and the 1973 oil shares. The second calibration assumes milder wage rigidities ($\gamma = 0.6$), full credibility ($\delta = 0$), and the 1997 oil shares. The figure shows that the combination of the three changes in the environment we have focused on can in principle more than account for the improvement in the trade-off observed in the data.

7.7 Concluding Comments

We have reached five main conclusions. First is that the effects of oil price shocks must have coincided in time with large shocks of a different nature. Given our partial identification strategy, we have not identified these other

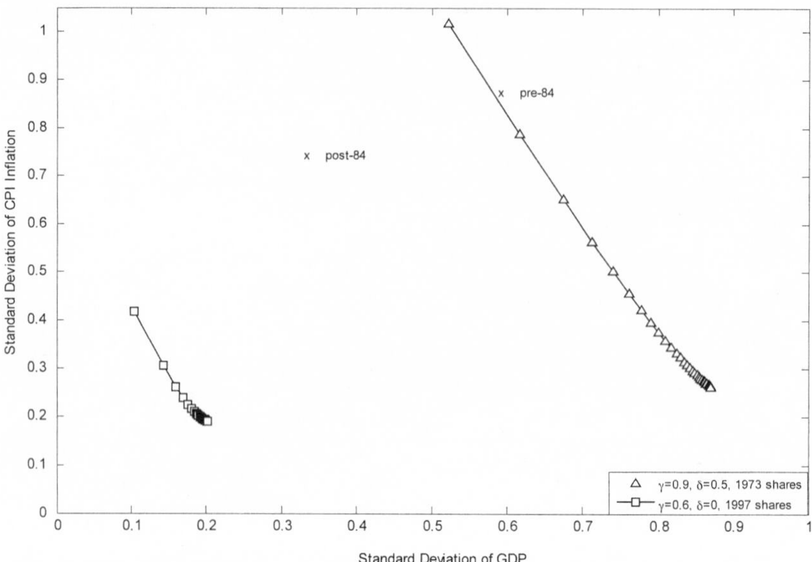

Fig. 7.16 Combined effects

shocks. We have given some evidence that increases in other commodity prices were important in the 1970s. We have not identified the other shocks for the 2000s.

Second, the effects of oil price shocks have changed over time, with steadily smaller effects on prices and wages, as well as on output and employment.

The third conclusion is that a first plausible cause for these changes is a decrease in real wage rigidities. Such rigidities are needed to generate the type of large stagflation in response to adverse supply shocks such as those that took place in the 1970s. We have shown that the response of the consumption wage to the marginal rate of substitution, and thus to employment, appears to have increased over time.

Fourth is that a second plausible cause for these changes is the increased credibility of monetary policy. We have offered a simple formalization of lack of credibility and its effect on the volatility frontier. We have shown that the response of expected inflation to oil shocks has substantially decreased over time.

And finally, the fifth conclusion is that a third plausible cause for these changes is simply the decrease in the share of oil in consumption and in production. The decline is large enough to have quantitatively significant implications.

Despite the length of the chapter, we are conscious, however, of the limitations of our arguments. Some of the evidence—for example, the IRF evidence for Japan—does not fit our story. The model we have developed is too primitive in many dimensions, and its quantitative implications must be taken with caution. The development of a richer model, at least with respect to the specification of production, and of real wage rigidities and its estimation, seem the natural next steps to check the conclusions reached previously. The different implications of the various candidate hypotheses for the shape of impulse response functions in response to changes in the price of oil makes us hopeful that structural estimation can succeed in identifying their respective importance.

Appendix A

A New-Keynesian Model for an Oil-Importing Economy

The present appendix describes in more detail the model used in section 7.5 and derives the equilibrium conditions underlying the simulations in the main text.

Households

We assume a continuum of identical infinitely-lived households. Each household seeks to maximize

$$E_0 \sum_{t=0}^{\infty} \beta^t \, U(C_t, N_t),$$

where

$$C_t \equiv \Theta_\chi \, C_{m,t}^{\chi} \, C_{q,t}^{1-\chi},$$

and where $C_{m,t}$ denotes consumption of (imported) oil, $C_{q,t} \equiv (\int_0^1 C_{q,t}(i)^{1-1/\varepsilon} di)^{\varepsilon/(\varepsilon-1)}$ is a CES index of domestic goods, N_t denotes employment or hours worked, and $\Theta_\chi \equiv \chi^{-\chi}(1-\chi)^{-(1-\chi)}$.

We assume that period utility is given by

$$U(C_t, N_t) \equiv \log C_t - \frac{N_t^{1+\phi}}{1+\phi}.$$

The period budget constraint, conditional on optimal allocation of expenditures among different domestic goods (not derived here) is given by:

$$P_{q,t}C_{q,t} + P_{m,t}C_{m,t} + Q_t^B B_t = W_t N_t + B_{t-1} + \Pi_t,$$

where $P_{q,t} \equiv (\int_0^1 P_{q,t}(i)^{1-\varepsilon} di)^{1/(1-\varepsilon)}$ is a price index for domestic goods, $P_{m,t}$ is the price of oil (in domestic currency), and W_t is the nominal wage. The price of a one-period nominally riskless domestic bond Q_t^B, paying one unit of domestic currency; B_t denotes the quantity of that bond purchased in period t. For simplicity, we assume no access to international financial markets.

The optimal allocation of expenditures between imported and domestically produced good implies

$$P_{q,t}C_{q,t} = (1 - \chi)\, P_{c,t}C_t$$

$$P_{m,t}C_{m,t} = \chi\, P_{c,t}C_t,$$

where $P_{c,t} \equiv P_{m,t}^{\chi}\, P_{q,t}^{1-\chi}$ is the CPI index. Note that χ corresponds, in equilibrium, to the share of oil in consumption. Note also that $P_{c,t} \equiv P_{q,t}\, S_t^{\chi}$, where $S_t \equiv P_{m,t}/P_{q,t}$ denotes the real price of oil, expressed in terms of domestically produced goods. Taking logs,

$$p_{c,t} = p_{q,t} + \chi\, s_t,$$

where $s_t \equiv p_{m,t} - p_{q,t}$ is the log of the real price of oil (measured in terms of domestic goods).

Furthermore, and conditional on an optimal allocation between the two types of goods, we have $P_{q,t}C_{q,t} + P_{m,t}C_{m,t} = P_{c,t}C_t$, which can be substituted into the budget constraint. The resulting constraint can then be used to derive the household's remaining optimality conditions. The intertemporal optimality condition is given by:

$$Q_t^B = \beta\, E_t\left\{\frac{C_t}{C_{t+1}}\,\frac{P_{c,t}}{P_{c,t+1}}\right\}.$$

Under the assumption of perfect competition in labor markets (to be relaxed following), the household's intratemporal optimality condition is given by

$$\frac{W_t}{P_{c,t}} = C_t\, N_t^{\phi} \equiv MRS_t,$$

which is the perfectly competitive labor supply schedule. The log-linearized version of the previous two equations, found in the text, are given by:

$$c_t = E_t\{c_{t+1}\} - (i_t - E_t\{\pi_{c,t+1}\} - \rho) \tag{18}$$

$$w_t - p_{c,t} = c_t + \phi\, n_t \tag{19}$$

where we use lowercase letters to denote the logarithms of the original variables, and where $\pi_{c,t} \equiv p_{c,t} - p_{c,t-1}$ represents CPI inflation.

Firms

Each firm produces a differentiated good indexed by $i \in [0, 1]$ with a production function

$$Q_t(i) = A_t\, M_t(i)^{\alpha_m}\, N_t(i)^{\alpha_n},$$

where $\alpha_m + \alpha_n \leq 1$.

Independently of how prices are set, and assuming that firms take the price of both inputs as given, cost minimization implies that firm i's nominal marginal cost $\Psi_t(i)$ is given by:

$$\Psi_t(i) = \frac{W_t}{\alpha_n(Q_t(i)/N_t(i))} = \frac{P_{m,t}}{\alpha_m(Q_t(i)/M_t(i))}. \tag{20}$$

Letting $\mathcal{M}_t^p(i) \equiv P_{q,t}(i)/\Psi_t(i)$ denote firm i's gross markup, we have

$$\mathcal{M}_t^p(i)\, S_t M_t(i) = \alpha_m\, Q_t(i)\, \frac{P_{q,t}(i)}{P_{q,t}}.$$

Let $Q_t \equiv (\int_0^1 Q_t(i)^{1-1/\varepsilon}\, di)^{\varepsilon/(\varepsilon-1)}$ denote aggregate gross output. It follows that

$$M_t = \frac{\alpha_m\, Q_t}{\mathcal{M}_t^p\, S_t} \tag{21}$$

where we have used the fact that $Q_t(i) = (P_{q,t}(i)/P_{q,t})^{-\varepsilon}\, Q_t$ (the demand schedule facing firm i), and defined $\mathcal{M}_t^p$ as the average gross markup, weighted by firms' input shares.

Taking logs and ignoring constants

$$m_t = -\mu_t^p - s_t + q_t,$$

where $\mu_t^p \equiv \log \mathcal{M}_t^p$. The latter expression can be plugged back into the (log-linearized) aggregate production function to yield the reduced form gross output equation

$$q_t = \frac{1}{1-\alpha_m}(a_t + \alpha_n n_t - \alpha_m s_t - \alpha_m \mu_t^p). \tag{22}$$

Consumption and Gross Output

Note that in an equilibrium with balanced trade (and hence $B_t = 0$) the following relation must hold:

$$\begin{aligned} P_{c,t} C_t &= P_{q,t} Q_t - P_{m,t} M_t \\ &= \left(1 - \frac{\alpha_m}{\mathcal{M}_t^p}\right) P_{q,t} Q_t, \end{aligned}$$

where we have used (21) to derive the second equality. Taking logs and using the relations between the different price indexes, we obtain

$$c_t = q_t - \chi\, s_t + \eta\, \mu_t^p, \tag{23}$$

where $\eta \equiv \alpha_m/(\mathcal{M}^p - \alpha_m)$ and $\mathcal{M}^p$ denotes the steady-state markup.

Combining (22) and (23), and invoking the fact that $(\alpha_m/(\mathcal{M}^p - \alpha_m) - \alpha_m/(1-\alpha_m))\, \mu_t^p \simeq 0$ for plausibly low values of α_m and the net markup measures $\mathcal{M}^p - 1$ and μ_t^p, we can write

(24) $$c_t = \frac{1}{1-\alpha_m} a_t + \frac{\alpha_n}{1-\alpha_m} n_t - \left(\frac{\alpha_m}{1-\alpha_m} + \chi\right) s_t.$$

Gross Output, Value Added, and the GDP Deflator

The GDP deflator $P_{y,t}$ is implicitly defined by

$$P_{q,t} \equiv (P_{y,t})^{1-\alpha_m}(P_{m,t})^{\alpha_m}.$$

Taking logs and using the definition of the terms of trade s_t

$$p_{y,t} = p_{q,t} - \frac{\alpha_m}{1-\alpha_m} s_t.$$

Value added (or GDP), Y_t, is then defined by

$$P_{y,t} Y_t \equiv P_{q,t} Q_t - P_{m,t} M_t$$

$$P_{y,t} Y_t = \left(1 - \frac{\alpha_m}{\mathcal{M}_t^p}\right) P_{q,t} Q_t,$$

which can be log-linearized to yield

$$y_t = q_t + \frac{\alpha_m}{1-\alpha_m} s_t + \eta\, \mu_t^p$$

$$= \frac{1}{1-\alpha_m}(a_t + \alpha_n n_t),$$

where the last equality uses the previous invoked approximation.

Note that combining these expressions for consumption and value added we can obtain the following relation between the two

$$c_t = y_t - \left(\frac{\alpha_m}{1-\alpha_m} + \chi\right) s_t.$$

Price Setting

Here we assume that firms set prices in a staggered fashion, as in Calvo (1983). Each period only a fraction $1 - \theta$ of firms, selected randomly, reset prices. The remaining firms, with measure θ, keep their prices unchanged. The optimal price setting rule for a firm resetting prices in period t is given by

(25) $$E_t\left\{\sum_{k=0}^{\infty} \theta^k \Lambda_{t,t+k} Q_{t+k|t} (P_t^* - \mathcal{M}^p \Psi_{t+k|t})\right\} = 0,$$

where P_t^* denotes the price newly set at time t, $Q_{t+k|t}$ and $\psi_{t+k|t}$ are, respectively, the level of output and marginal cost in period $t + k$ for a firm that last set its price in period t, and $\mathcal{M}^p \equiv \varepsilon/(\varepsilon - 1)$ is the desired gross markup.

Note that the latter also corresponds to the gross markup in the zero inflation perfect foresight steady state.

The domestic price level evolves according to the difference equation

$$P_{q,t} = [\theta\,(P_{q,t-1})^{1-\varepsilon} + (1-\theta)\,(P_t^*)^{1-\varepsilon}]^{1/(1-\varepsilon)}. \tag{26}$$

Combining the log-linearized version of (25) and (26) around a zero inflation steady state yields the following equation for domestic inflation, $\pi_{q,t} \equiv p_{q,t} - p_{q,t-1}$:

$$\pi_{q,t} = \beta\, E_t\{\pi_{q,t+1}\} - \lambda_p\, \hat{\mu}_t^p, \tag{27}$$

where $\hat{\mu}_t^p \equiv \mu_t^p - \mu^p$ denotes the (log) deviation of the average markup from its desired level, and $\lambda_p \equiv ((1-\theta)(1-\beta\theta))/\theta\,(1-\alpha_k)/(1-\alpha_k+\alpha_k\varepsilon)$.

Appendix B

Computation of the Oil Share

We think of the U.S. economy as having two sectors, an oil-producing sector and a nonoil producing sector. We define the oil producing sector as the sum of the "oil and gas extraction" sector (North American Industry Classification NAIC code 211) and the "petroleum and coal" sector (NAIC code 324). ("Petroleum refineries," a subsector of "petroleum and coal" is available only for benchmark years, the last available one being 1997. It represents 85 percent of the gross output of the "petroleum and coal" sector.) We define the nonoil producing sector as the rest of the economy.

To compute relevant numbers for 2005, we use data from the Input-Output (I-O) tables from the Bureau of Economic Analysis (BEA) site.

In 2005, "oil and gas extraction" output was \$227b, imports were \$223b, for a total of \$450b. Of this total, \$5b was for domestic final uses, \$440b was for intermediates, of which \$259 went to "petroleum and coal," and \$181b went to the non-oil sector. Petroleum and coal output was \$402b, imports were \$65b, for a total of \$467b. Of this total, \$167 was for domestic final uses, \$279b for intermediates to the non-oil producing sector.

In 2005, total U.S. value added was \$12,455b. Value added by "oil and gas" was \$12b, value added by "petroleum and coal" was \$12b, so value added in the non-oil producing sector was \$12,431b.

These numbers imply a value for α_m of (181 + 279)/(12,431 + 181 + 279) = 3.6 percent, and an estimate for χ of (5 + 167)/(12,431 + 181 + 279) = 1.3 percent.

The shares obviously depend very much on the price of oil. The same computation for the benchmark year of 1997 (which allows us to use "petroleum refining" rather than "petroleum and coal" together) gives 1.7 percent and 1.2 percent, respectively.

For the years 1973 and 1977. sectors are classified according to industry number codes. We construct the oil-producing sector as the of "crude petroleum and natural gas" (1977 industry number 8) and "petroleum refining" (1977 industry number 31). The same steps as before yield $\alpha_m = 2.3$ percent and $\chi = 1.5$ percent in 1973, and $\alpha_m = 3.6$ percent and $\chi = 1.8$ percent in 1977.

References

Barsky, R., and L. Killian. 2002. Do we really know that oil caused the great stagflation? A monetary alternative. *NBER macroeconomics annual 2001,* ed. B. S. Bernanke and K. S. Rogoff, 137–83. Cambridge, MA: MIT Press.

Bernanke, B., M. Gertler, and M. Watson. 1997. Systematic monetary policy and the effects of oil shocks. *Brookings Papers on Economic Activity* 1: 91–157. Washington, DC: Brookings Institution.

Blanchard, O., and J. Galí. 2007. Real wage rigidities and the new-Keynesian model. *Journal of Money, Credit, and Banking* 39 (supplement, 1): 35–66.

Blanchard, O., and J. Simon. 2001. The long and large decline in U.S. output volatility. *Brookings Papers on Economic Activity* 1: 135–74. Washington, DC: Brookings Institution.

Bruno, M., and J. Sachs. 1985. *Economics of worldwide stagflation.* Cambridge, MA: Harvard University Press.

Calvo, G. 1983. Staggered contracts in a utility-maximizing framework. *Journal of Monetary Economics* 12 (September): 383–98.

Carter, D., D. Rogers, and B. Simkins. 2006a. Does fuel hedging make economic sense? The case of the U.S. airline industry. *Financial Management* 35–1 (Spring): 53–86.

———. 2006b. Hedging and value in the U.S. airline industry. *Journal of Applied Corporate Finance* 18 (4): 21–33.

Castelnuovo, E., S. Nicoletti-Altimari, and D. Rodriguez-Palenzuela. 2003. Definition of price stability, range and point inflation targets: The anchoring of long term inflation expectations *Background studies for the ECB's evaluation of its monetary policy strategy.* European Central Bank Report. Frankfurt, Germany: ECB.

Clarida, R., J. Galí, and M. Gertler. 2000. Monetary policy rules and macroeconomic stability: Evidence and some theory. *Quarterly Journal of Economics* 115-1 (February): 147–80.

De Gregorio, J., O. Landerretche, and C. Neilson. 2007. Another passthrough bites the dust? Oil prices and inflation. Central Bank of Chile and University of Chile. Unpublished Manuscript.

Edelstein, P., and L. Kilian. 2007. Retail energy prices and consumer expenditures. University of Michigan. Center for Economic Policy Research (CEPR) Discussion Paper no. 6255.

Finn, M. G. 2000. Perfect competition and the effects of energy price increases on economic activity. *Journal of Money Credit and Banking* 32 (3): 400–16.

Hamilton, J. 1983. Oil and the macroeconomy since World War II. *Journal of Political Economy* (April): 228–48.

———. 1996. This is what happened to the oil price macroeconomy relationship. *Journal of Monetary Economics* 38 (2): 215–20.

Herrera, A. M., and E. Pesavento. 2007. Oil price shocks, systematic monetary policy, and the great moderation. Michigan State University. Unpublished Manuscript.
Hooker, M. A. 1996. What happened to the oil price macroeconomy relationship? *Journal of Monetary Economics* 38 (2): 195–213.
———. 2002. Are oil shocks inflationary? Asymmetric and nonlinear specifications versus changes in regime. *Journal of Money, Credit and Banking* 34 (2): 540–61.
Kilian, L. 2006. Not all oil price shocks are alike: Disentangling demand and supply shocks in the crude oil market. CEPR Discussion Paper no. 5994.
———. 2008. A comparison of the effects of exogenous oil supply shocks on output and inflation in the G7 countries. *Journal of the European Economic Association* 6 (1): 78–121.
Mankiw, N. G. 2007. *Macroeconomics,* 6th ed. New York: Worth Publishers.
McConnell, M., and G. Perez-Quiros. 2000. Output fluctuations in the United States; What has changed since the early 1980s? *American Economic Review* 90-5 (December): 1464–76.
Rotemberg, J., and M. Woodford. 1996. Imperfect competition and the effects of energy price increases on economic activity. *Journal of Money, Credit, and Banking* 28 (4): 549–77.
Stock, J., and M. Watson. 2003. Has the business cycle changed and why? In *NBER Macroeconomics Annual 2002, vol. 17,* ed. M. Gertler and K. S. Rogoff, 159–230. Cambridge, MA: MIT Press.

Comment Julio J. Rotemberg

Using a battery of compelling statistical methods, this chapter shows that the statistical effect of oil price shocks on output and inflation is more muted after 1984 than it was in the post-war period up to that point. As it happens, a small response of the economy to oil price increases is more consistent with standard macroeconomic models. There is thus a sense in which developments in the economy may lead this issue to lose its allure. In my opinion, however, it is precisely because we observed puzzling responses to what were arguably exogenous disturbances, that this topic is a great laboratory for understanding central features of the economy as a whole. Thus, I very much welcome this chapter's effort to disentangle the causes of this change in response.

The chapter offers three basic stories for the decline in the response to the price of oil. These are: (a) that "real wage rigidity" was more important in the past than it is today; (b) that "monetary policy credibility" was weaker in the past than it is today, and (c) that the share of energy in the economy was larger in the past than it is today. The message of this chapter is thus optimistic in that it suggests a transformation in U.S. institutions has inoculated the economy against the responses that we saw in the past.

Julio J. Rotemberg is the William Ziegler Professor of Business Administration at Harvard Business School and a research associate of the National Bureau of Economic Research.

In this discussion, I articulate some concerns about all three mechanisms introduced by Blanchard and Galí. First, I see the "real wage rigidity" emphasized in this chapter as being of relatively limited use in explaining the large responses observed in the past. Moreover, I see very little evidence that such rigidities have become less prevalent more recently, as required for this story to explain the reduction in the importance of oil shocks. Second, the model of low credibility of central banks that the authors introduce has counterfactual implications for the response of real interest rates to oil price shocks, so it does not seem compelling as an explanation of past responses. Third, while I agree with Blanchard and Galí that the value of energy has fallen relative to gross domestic product (GDP), the importance of this phenomenon is not easy to quantify. After devoting three sections to spelling out my reactions to the three mechanisms emphasized by Blanchard and Galí, my comment closes with some alternative interpretations for the reduction in the measured effect of oil price increases on the economy.

The Importance of Reductions in Real Wage Rigidity

Blanchard and Galí suppose that, if there were no real wage rigidities, households would be indifferent between consuming one additional hour of leisure and working this extra hour in exchange for consuming the proceeds. With log utility for consumption and a Frisch labor supply of 1, this would imply that the log of real wages is equal to the sum of the log of employment plus the log of consumption. As a result, the wage should rise by considerably more than 1 percent every time that GDP rises by 1 percent. In practice, real wages are only slightly procyclical.[1]

It thus seems difficult to disagree with the notion that this model is inaccurate as a description of labor market equilibrium. Moreover, the equation that Blanchard and Galí propose to use instead is a paragon of simplicity. They suppose that

$$w_t - p_{c,t} = (1 - \gamma)(c_t + \phi n_t),$$

where w_t, $p_{c,t}$, c_t, and n_t represent, respectively, the nominal wage, the consumer price index, consumption, and employment at t. While this is a convenient simplification of labor markets, it fits far from perfectly, and this makes it difficult to estimate γ or its change. Nonetheless, Blanchard and Galí argue that the parameter γ that represents real wage rigidity has fallen in the United States. Blanchard and Galí defend this claim by noting that real wage declines after energy price increases were similar in the pre- and post-1984 period while the reductions in $(c_t + \phi n_t)$ were much larger in the earlier period. They interpret this as suggesting that wages are now more (procyclically) sensitive to employment and consumption so that γ is smaller.

1. My interpretation of the relevant empirical findings can be found in Rotemberg (2006).

Unfortunately, we do not know that real wages respond only to $(c_t + \phi n_t)$ as opposed to responding also to other variables. And, since letting $\gamma \neq 0$ is an ad hoc emendation of a model that fits badly, there is no a priori reason to suppose that wages do indeed respond only to this variable. An alternative hypothesis, therefore, is that firms were, and remain, able to reduce consumption wages when oil prices rise for reasons having nothing to do with this model of wage determination while the response of wages to employment and consumption has remained unchanged. To see which of these alternatives is more valid one could look at other shocks that move consumption and employment and study whether these now have larger procyclical effects on wages.

A crude way of doing this is to run a regression of $(w_t - p_{c,t} - c_t - n_t)$ on $(c_t + n_t)$. According to the Blanchard-Galí interpretation, this coefficient should be more negative in the earlier period when wages were unresponsive to $(c_t + n_t)$, while it should be closer to zero in the more recent one. Using that data that Blanchard and Galí have graciously provided, the earlier period yields a coefficient of –.917 while the latter yields –1.057. Thus, by this metric, real wages have become slightly less procyclical and γ has risen over time. This is precisely contrary to the Blanchard-Galí conclusion that "the response of the consumption wage to the marginal rate of substitution [. . .] appears to have increased over time."

In any event, real wage rigidity (and its changes) cannot be the whole story even though the idea that the failure of wages to adjust played an important role in the recessions induced by oil price increases has a distinguished history. As Bruno and Sachs (1985) pointed out, oil price increases necessitate a reduction in real wages because they lead workers to produce a lower value of "net output." Thus, an unwillingness of workers to reduce their wages would lead firms to curtail their employment. As Rotemberg and Woodford (1996) have stressed, however, the amount by which wages must fall for firms to keep their employment unchanged is extremely small.

To see this, follow Rotemberg and Woodford and consider a general constant returns to scale production function that relates output Y_t to value added $V(H_t)$ and energy inputs E_t, where H_t is the volume of employment

$$Y_t = Q(V(H_t), E_t).$$

Constant returns then implies that

$$Y = Q_{Vt}V_t + Q_{Et}E_t.$$

The first-order conditions for profit maximization are

$$Q_{Et} = \mu_t p_{Et} \qquad \text{and} \qquad Q_{Vt}V_H(H_t) = \mu_t W_t,$$

where μ_t is the markup of price over marginal cost, p_{Et} is the price of energy relative to the price of final output, and W_t is the real wage in terms of final output. The left-hand side of the second of these equations falls with employment. Thus, this equation says that employment will fall if either the real wage or the markup rise.

These equations can be used to study the extent to which the real wage W_t needs to fall to keep employment constant. One way of demonstrating that this change is quite small is to focus on the wage deflated by the value-added deflator defined as

$$P_{Vt} \equiv \frac{Y_t - P_{Et}E_t}{V(H_t)}.$$

With perfect competition, $\mu_t = 1$ so the previous equations imply that $P_{Vt} = Q_{Vt}$. Thus, the second equation in (1) becomes

$$V_H(H_t) = \frac{W_t}{P_{Vt}}.$$

This says that employment would stay constant as long as the wage deflated by the value-added deflator stayed constant as well. The wage deflated by the price of total output does indeed have to decline. However, the required percentage drop in wages equals the percent increase in the price of energy times the share of the value of energy in the value of output. Since this share is about 3 percent, the amount by which the wage must decline is trivial.

What is more, both the impulse responses in Rotemberg and Woodford (1996) and those in the current chapter show that the wage deflated by the value-added deflator actually fell after the pre-1984 energy price increases. Thus, the resulting decline in employment and output is inexplicable unless markups rose. While Blanchard and Galí do not explicitly grant markup variations a large role, such variations stand behind the power of monetary policy in their model. As in all new-Keynesian models with sticky prices, increases in interest rates lower output because price rigidity prevents firms from cutting prices right away, and this raises markups.

A second reason to worry about the role of real wages in the pre-1984 recessions is that this does not seem to explain international differences in responses. French wages, for example, seem to have increased in the impulse response functions reported in this chapter. Yet the output decline in France does not appear to have been significantly larger than the output decline in the United States.

Blanchard and Galí's Model of Markup Increases: Noncredible Monetary Policy

As discussed previously, an explanation of why output fell more after the pre-1984 oil price increases is likely to be incomplete without a theory of why these earlier shocks led to larger increases in markups. This chapter's theory exacerbates the effect of sticky prices on markup variation through an ingenious model of monetary policy failure.

The idea is that monetary policy was set by having

$$i_t = \phi_\pi \pi_t,$$

where i_t and π_t represent the nominal interest rate and inflation at t, respectively, and where $\phi_\pi > 1$. Price setters, on the other hand, believed that the interest rate was set according to

$$i_t = \phi_\pi(1 - \delta)\pi_t + v_t,$$

where $\delta > 0$ and v_t was believed to be i.i.d. Since price setters correctly perceived both current interest rates and current inflation, they used their beliefs regarding $\phi_\pi(1 - \delta)$ to compute v_t, with the result that this always turned out to equal $\phi_\pi \delta \pi_t$.

For the parameters used in this chapter the effect of $\delta > 0$ is to make firms raise their prices too much in response to oil price increases. Firms do so because they attribute the contemporaneous rise in interest rates to a monetary policy disturbance that will soon be corrected so that they expect the monetary authority to conduct a fairly loose monetary policy in the future. Markups are high, resulting in a recession, because of false expectation that the currently high interest rates will quickly be rescinded.

While providing a very elegant theory of stagflation, this model seems counterfactual both regarding the behavior of the ex-ante real rate and of the "real rate" one obtains by subtracting the current inflation rate from the current interest rate. Because $\phi_\pi > 1$, the model predicts that this latter "real rate" should have been very high after an inflationary episode induced by an oil price increase. However, while pre-1984 oil shocks did raise inflation and lower output, they were associated with low rather than high values of $i_t - \pi_t$.

Blanchard and Galí point out that surveys of expectations show that these shocks were associated with increases in expected inflation. This is consistent with the idea that people expected monetary policy to be relatively loose. The difficulty for the model is that monetary policy was in fact loose as well. Moreover, people seem to have noticed this in the sense that ex-ante real rates constructed with their own inflation expectations were low. This seems impossible to square with the reductions in output that are observed (because aggregate demand should not have been low). Not being consistent with output declines, this behavior of ex-ante rates is not consistent with markup increases either. Rotemberg and Woodford's (1996) theory, by contrast, is designed to offer an alternative reason that markups should have increased and thereby reduced output.

My view remains, as in Rotemberg (1983), that implicating tight monetary policy for the output declines that followed oil price increases is difficult. The reason is that oil price increases led to rises in inflation, and these rises in inflation suggest that monetary policy was too loose rather than too tight. The idea that monetary policy was to blame for these recessions is not unique to Blanchard and Galí's work, however. Barsky and Kilian (2002) also proposed a model that seeks to explain post-oil shock recessions in this way, though their model of price setting involves more inertial elements than those found in the current chapter. Even so, the Barsky and Kilian (2002) model also has trouble explaining how output declines could have been so large in a period of negative real rates.

Changes in the Share of Energy

As a final factor, Blanchard and Galí note that energy's importance in the economy has waned. There is good prima facie evidence for this decline, with the U.S. Energy Information Administration reporting a drop in the "energy intensity" of GDP from an index value of 100 in 1980 to a value of about 62 in 2000.[2] I am thus inclined to believe that this structural transformation could be an important factor. It turns out, however, that measuring the importance of this factor is nontrivial.

To see this, recall that the Blanchard and Galí model supposes that utility depends on the log of consumption, which is in turn given by

$$c_t = (1 - \chi)c_{q,t} + \chi c_{m,t},$$

where c_t, $c_{q,t}$ and $c_{m,t}$ represent, respectively, the logarithms of total consumption, consumption of domestically produced goods, and consumption of energy at t. The share parameter χ is then literally the ratio of the value of energy consumption over the value of total consumption. With these preferences, this share is constant and independent of the price of energy.

Similarly, Blanchard and Galí suppose that the production function for domestic output takes the Cobb-Douglas form

$$q_t = a_t + \alpha_n n_t + \alpha_m m_t,$$

where q_t, n_t, and m_t represent, respectively, the logarithm of domestically produced output of employment and of the energy input at t. Here too, the technological parameter α_m ought to equal the ratio of the value of energy inputs to the value of domestic output and this ratio ought to be independent of the real price of energy.

As is well known and as the Blanchard-Galí calculations in appendix B make clear, increases in the price of energy raise the ratio of energy expenditures of households over total expenditures as well as raising the ratio of the value of energy inputs over the value of produced output. This suggests that the elasticity of demand for energy is less than one and that the constant share models are not ideal. If, as is done in Blanchard and Galí, one calibrates the "constant shares" χ and α_n on the basis of particular yearly observations (they choose 1973 for the pre-1984 period and 1997 for the post-1984 period), the year that is chosen for this calibration is important.

2. See http://www.eia.doe.gov/oiaf/1605/gg05rpt/stopics.html.

It seems possible that one might be able to obtain more robust estimates by considering explicitly a model with less substitutability between energy and other goods.

Alternatives

Blanchard and Galí's question of why the output response to oil price increases dampened after 1984 is important, and is only made more urgent if one does not find all the explanations offered in this chapter entirely convincing. One possible alternative explanation, stressed in Rotemberg and Woodford (1996), is that the earlier movements in the price of oil were exogenous to the behavior of the U.S. economy (and induced either by the Texas Railroad Commission or by developments in the Middle East), while the more recent ones were endogenous.

Blanchard and Galí argue that they are considering exogenous changes in the price of oil because they are letting oil be influenced contemporaneously by other variables in their VAR and treating the residuals as the oil price shock. Unfortunately, this technique is not compelling in the case of the price of a durable commodity such as oil. In a free market, the price of such commodities is strongly affected not only by variables that affect current GDP but also by expectations of future demand. Thus, the expectation that China will demand a great deal of oil in the future would drive up the price of oil today. Blanchard and Galí assert that, from the point of view of the United States, an oil price increase fueled by Chinese demand is equivalent to one fueled by a supply disruption. This is questionable, however. Increases in Chinese demand can also lead to increases in the demand for U.S. output in a way that oil supply disruptions need not. This expansionary effect of Chinese demand may then counteract the negative effect of oil price increases. This point is perhaps best understood at the world level, where an increase in the price of oil that is due to factors that raise world output is much less likely to lead to output reductions than an exogenous increase in the price of oil.

While separation of exogenous from endogenous oil price changes seems essential for progress on this issue, the task appears to be a difficult one. Kilian (2008) proposes a method for detecting the exogenous changes in the quantity of oil sold by Organization of the Petroleum Exporting Countries (OPEC) members by comparing the output of countries subject to shocks to the output of other countries that he deems immune to these shocks. These exogenous changes turn out to be associated with only small subsequent movements in output and inflation both in the early period and in the Kuwait-Iraq War of 1990. While very attractive methodologically, this approach creates puzzles of its own. Consider, for example, the well known 1973 to 1974 "OPEC shock." From September 1973 to January 1974, the official price of Saudi crude went from $2.59 per barrel to $11.65 per barrel and then remained high for a long time. In Kilian's (2008) narrative, quantity supplied did decline in the last quarter of 1973, but rose so much thereafter that OPEC output was back to normal by March 1974 (so that a favorable supply shock in the first quarter of 1974 fully offset the unfavorable one of the last quarter of 1973).

In addition to being much more likely to be endogenous, recent changes in the price of oil seem more likely to have been seen as transitory. It is apparent from figure 7.1 in their chapter that the price of oil experienced several transitory up-and-down movements between 1995 and 2001, and that these movements are of a different character than those that came before. Of course, it is still an open question whether a coherent model can be developed where transitory endogenous movements in the price of oil are less correlated with subsequent movements in output and inflation than are more permanent exogenous movements in the price of oil. Given the importance of making sense of the pre-1984 correlations between oil prices and the economy, such an effort would seem very worthwhile.

Lastly, Blanchard and Galí may well be right when they think that the markup variations due to repeated oligopolistic interactions that are discussed in Rotemberg and Woodford (1996) do not help explain why oil shocks now seem to matter less. It is worth noting, however, that the period since 1982 has been one where many firms have faced renewed international competition. This may have destabilized, perhaps only temporarily, the oligopolistic arrangements studied in that paper.

References

Barsky, R. B., and L. Kilian. 2002. Do we really know that oil caused the great stagflation? A monetary alternative. In *NBER macroeconomics annual 2001,* ed. B. S. Bernanke and K. S. Rogoff, 137–83. Cambridge, MA: MIT Press.

Bruno, M., and J. Sachs. 1985. *Economics of worldwide stagflation.* Cambridge, MA: Harvard University Press.

Kilian, L. 2008. Exogenous oil supply shocks: How big are they and how much do they matter for the U.S. economy. *Review of Economics and Statistics* 90 (2): 216–40.

Rotemberg, J. J. 1983. Supply shocks, sticky prices and monetary policy. *Journal of Money, Credit and Banking* 15 (4): 489–98.

———. 2006. Cyclical wages in a search and bargaining model with large firms. *NBER international seminar on macroeconomics 2006,* ed. L. Reichlin and K. D. West, 65–107. Chicago: University of Chicago Press.

Rotemberg, J. J., and M. Woodford. 1996. Imperfect competition and the effects of energy price increases on economic activity. *Journal of Money, Credit, and Banking* 28 (4): 549–77.

8

Global Forces and Monetary Policy Effectiveness

Jean Boivin and Marc P. Giannoni

8.1 Introduction

In many respects, the economic integration of the U.S. economy with the rest of the world has deepened in the last two decades. International trade has continued to expand more rapidly than economic activity in industrialized countries. For the United States, the amount of goods and services imported and exported that represented 18 percent of gross domestic product (GDP) in the mid-1980s represents more than 27 percent in 2005. But the globalization of finance has shown a much more dramatic development. During the same period, the ratio of foreign assets and liabilities to GDP has increased from approximately 80 percent to more than 300 percent in the twenty-three most industrialized economies, according to Lane and Milesi-Ferretti (2006). As global economic integration spreads, it is often argued that macroeconomic variables in one country—whether they pertain to measures of economic activity, inflation, or interest rates—should increasingly reflect events occurring in the rest of the world.[1]

Jean Boivin is Chair in Monetary Policy and Financial Markets at the Institute of Applied Economics, HEC-Montréal, and a faculty research fellow of the National Bureau of Economic Research. Marc P. Giannoni is the Roderick H. Cushman Associate Professor of Business at the Columbia Business School and a faculty research fellow of the National Bureau of Economic Research.

Prepared for the NBER conference on International Dimensions of Monetary Policy in Girona (Spain), June 2007. We thank conference participants, in particular Olivier Blanchard, Jordi Galí, Mark Gertler, Larry Meyer, Benoît Mojon, Lucrezia Reichlin, Chris Sims, and Michael Woodford for very valuable discussions and comments, and Guilherme Martins for excellent research assistance. We are also grateful to the National Science Foundation for financial support (SES-0518770).

1. For example, the President of the Federal Reserve Bank of Dallas, Richard Fisher, and Michael Cox (2007) have argued that domestic inflation may be increasingly determined in the rest of the world. Advocating a "new inflation equation," they conclude that "globalization

Such developments naturally raise two sets of questions, which we attempt to address in this chapter. First, to what extent have international factors affected the determination of key macroeconomic variables in the U.S. economy? Is it the case that with the recent globalization, this economy has become more strongly affected by international factors? Second, has the very rapid globalization of finance weakened the ability of U.S. monetary policy to influence domestic financial market conditions, and through it, the rest of the economy? In other words, does a change in the Federal Funds rate have a smaller impact on the U.S. economy now than it used to?

Central bankers and economists in the financial press have pointed out the fact that while the U.S. central bank raised the Federal funds rate target by 425 basis points between June 2004 and July 2006, long-term rates remained at historically low levels, with the ten-year Treasury bond yield increasing by less than 40 basis points and the twenty-year yield actually falling by 20 basis points during that time. This phenomenon, which former Federal Reserve Chairman Alan Greenspan labeled "conundrum," highlights the fact that U.S. long-term interest rates may have become more dependent on international factors than had been observed historically. As then-governor Bernanke (2005) explained, a more extensive global financial integration and the increased amount of savings outside the U.S.—in particular in developing economies—may have resulted in a "global saving glut," which may have put downward pressures on long-term interest rates. A casual look at such recent historical episodes raises the possibility that the long-term yields may respond less to changes in Federal funds rates than in the past. Given that monetary policy does at least in part affect the economy through its effect on long-term rates, it is natural to wonder about the implications of the globalization of finance for the effectiveness of monetary policy. Certainly, the answers to such questions have key implications for a proper understanding of the determinants of economic fluctuations, and for policy.

To address these questions, we provide in this chapter an empirical assessment of the synchronization between international factors and key U.S. economic variables. We then investigate whether the importance of these global forces has changed for the U.S. economy over the last two decades, and how such a possible change has affected the transmission of monetary policy.

The general empirical framework that we consider is a factor-augmented vector autoregression model (FAVAR), as described in Bernanke, Boivin, and Eliasz (2005), but extended to explicitly include international or "global" factors. One of its key features is to provide estimates of macroeconomic factors that affect the data of interest by systematically exploiting all infor-

has been changing how we consume as well as the way we do business. It's high time economic doctrine caught up." *The Economist* (2005), citing Stephen Roach, chief economist of Morgan Stanley, and the 2005 annual report of the Bank for International Settlements, suggests that global forces have become more important relative to domestic factors in determining inflation in individual countries.

mation from a large set of economic indicators. In our application, we estimate the empirical model based on the information from a large number of macroeconomic indicators and disaggregated data for the United States, as well as a large set of macroeconomic indicators for the fifteen major U.S. trade partners. By identifying U.S. monetary policy shocks, this framework allows us to uncover the transmission of such shocks to a large set of macroeconomic indicators. Our interest in studying the responses to monetary policy shocks does not reside in the fact that these shocks are important. In fact, it is well-known that they contribute only a little to U.S. output fluctuations. Rather, we find the responses to such shocks interesting as they allow us to trace out the effects of monetary policy on the economy.

Many studies have provided evidence that key macroeconomic variables display substantial comovements across countries. For instance, Kose, Otrok, and Whiteman (2003), analyzing output, consumption, and investment data from sixty countries over the 1960 to 1990 period, document that a large fraction of business cycles fluctuations of developed economies is accounted by a common world factor. The latter factor—a component of economic activity that is common to all countries considered—explains more than one-third of output fluctuations in the United States and in Europe.[2] Ciccarelli and Mojon (2005) argue that inflation in industrialized economies is also largely a global phenomenon: they find that on average, about 70 percent of inflation variance is attributable to a common global factor given by the component of inflation that is common across countries. Moreover, Ehrmann, Fratzscher, and Rigobon (2005) show that shocks to money, bond, and equity markets result in substantial spillovers between the United States and Europe.

Other researchers have recently examined whether the importance of such comovements across regions has changed over time. The evidence regarding the output synchronization is mixed. Kose, Prasad, and Terrones (2003)

2. Similar comovements in economic activity have been documented for more restricted sets of countries. Gerlach (1988) found that industrial production is positively correlated across several Organization for Economic Cooperation and Development (OECD) countries. Backus, Kehoe, and Kydland (1995) and Baxter (1995) found that business cycles share similarities in major industrial economies. Gregory, Head, and Raynauld (1997) in an early estimation of a factor model on economic activity data for the G7 countries, detected a significant common factor across countries. Bergman, Bordo, and Jonung (1998), analyzing more than one-hundred years of data, found that the synchronization in activity across thirteen industrialized countries remains strong regardless of the monetary regime. Forni et al. (2000), proposing a generalized dynamic factor model and applying it to data of ten European economies, find that a common European activity factor explains between 35 percent and 96 percent of the volatility in countries' GDP. Clark and Shin (2000) similarly find that a common factor accounts substantial variations in industrial production of European economies, and Lumsdaine and Prasad (2003), examining correlations between industrial output in seventeen OECD countries and a common component, find evidence of a world business cycle and of a European business cycle. Canova, Ciccarelli, and Ortega (2004), estimating a Bayesian panel VAR model on G7 data, find also a significant world business cycle, but find no evidence of a cycle specific to the euro area, in contrast to some of the other studies.

report evidence of stronger comovements of output in industrialized countries with a world factor (since the early 1980s) than in the preceding two decades. However, Doyle and Faust (2005), testing for changes in comovements among real activity measures for the G7 countries, find very few statistically significant changes over the 1960 to 2000 period. When looking at their point estimates, they even find some evidence of a fall in the correlation across countries since the early 1980s. Such a reduced synchronization is in fact consistent with findings of Helbling and Bayoumi (2003); Monfort, Renne, Ruffer, and Vitale (2003); Heathcote and Perri (2004); Stock and Watson (2005); and Kose, Otrok, and Whiteman (2005). According to Stock and Watson (2005), and Kose, Otrok, and Whiteman (2005), the fact that the output correlations across countries were particularly high in the 1970s may reflect unusually strong common shocks—such as large movements in oil prices—during that period. These authors thus argue that the reduction in the volatility of common international shocks since in the early 1980s, compared to the 1960s and 1970s, provides an important explanation for the reduced synchronization among G7 countries since the early 1980s, and that the correlation in output across countries would have been larger, had the international common shocks been as important in the 1980s and the 1990s, as they were in the 1960s and 1970s.

In addition, some authors have argued that the development of trade in goods and services, especially with low cost producing economies such as China and India, may have altered the relationship between some measure of the output gap and domestic inflation (see, e.g., Rogoff 2004, Borio and Filardo 2006, Ihrig et al. 2007).

While we also seek to characterize changes in U.S. macroeconomic dynamics due to global forces, our chapter distinguishes itself from the papers just mentioned in several respects.

First, in general, global comovements among macrovariables could arise from the presence of exogenous global—or worldwide—shocks, or from the international transmission of domestic shocks. Our central focus in this chapter is the implications for monetary policy of the changes in the role of global forces. It is thus important to stress that, while we allow for the presence of global shocks like in many of the papers just cited, our interest will be mainly on the characterization of the international transmission of regional shocks. In particular, we determine to what extent the transmission of U.S. monetary policy shocks—as measured by exogenous changes in the Federal funds rate—to key U.S. economic variables such as long-term interest rates, output, inflation, and so on, has been altered by global forces.

Second, in order to identify the monetary transmission mechanism, we jointly model multiple dimensions of the U.S. economy. Thus, rather than restricting ourselves to the comparison of a single type of measures across regions of the world—for example, only economic activity measures or only inflation measures—we adopt a more general and encompassing approach that allows us to compare a set of factors summarizing the U.S. macroeconomic dynamics with those summarizing the rest of the world's macroeconomic dynamics. Another contribution is to consider a much broader set of macroeconomic indicators than has been used before in order to document the changes in the importance of global forces for the determination of U.S. measures of real activity, inflation, interest rates, and various other series.

Finally, we focus on the evolution since 1984. Our sample includes the period during which the globalization of financial flows accelerated significantly and allows us to sidestep an important issue: the considerable changes that occurred in the preceding decade. The period of large common shocks, in the 1970s and the early 1980s, during which the business cycles of many countries were strongly correlated, was followed in the United States by a rapid adjustment—called "great moderation"—to a regime characterized by lower output volatility.[3] Some studies have explained the reduction in volatility with a reduced volatility of shocks (e.g., Stock and Watson 2002a, Sims and Zha 2006, Smets and Wouters 2007, Justiniano and Primiceri 2008). In addition, as documented in Clarida, Galí, and Gertler (2000), Boivin (2006), Cogley and Sargent (2002, 2005), and Boivin and Giannoni (2002, 2006b), the systematic response of U.S. monetary policy to fluctuations in inflation and output changed significantly around 1980, revealing a greater tendency to stabilize inflation fluctuations. As Boivin and Giannoni (2006b) emphasize, such a change in policy can explain in large part why the responses of output and inflation to an unexpected change in the Federal funds rate of a given size have been much smaller since the early 1980s than they were in the 1960s and 1970s. By considering the period after 1984; that is, a period during which both the variance of the shocks may reasonably be assumed to have remained constant and the systematic monetary policy rule has not been found to have dramatically changed, we hope to better isolate the effect of international factors.

It is important to stress, however, that our sample is relatively short: it contains a bit more than twenty years of quarterly data. We expect a priori that this will make statistical relationships harder to detect and will constitute an important constraint on the richness of the models that we can contemplate in the empirical exercise following. This is an important sense in which we see our analysis as an exploration of how important global forces might have become for the U.S. economy. But as the results seem to suggest, there is still sufficient statistical information in the sample that allows us to learn something useful about changes in the economy in the recent past.

Our findings can be summarized as follows. First, we find that common

3. Many researchers have documented a sharp drop in the volatility of the U.S. real GDP in the early 1980s (see, e.g., McConnell and Perez-Quiros 2000; Blanchard and Simon 2001; Boivin and Giannoni 2002; Stock and Watson 2002a). Stock and Watson (2005) show that other G7 countries, with the exception of France, have similarly experienced lower output volatility since the mid-1980s, compared to the previous decades.

factors capture, on average, a sizable fraction of the fluctuations in U.S. macroeconomic indicators. This provides support for the use of our empirical model. Second, there is evidence that the role of international factors in explaining U.S. variables has been changing over the 1984 to 2005 period, but this evolution is not systematic across series, and it is difficult to see a pattern suggesting that they have become generally more important. Some variables such as the long-term interest rates, as well as import and export prices, however, do display a systematic increase of their correlation with global factors throughout our sample.

We do not find strong statistical evidence of a significant change in the transmission mechanism of monetary policy due to global forces. Taking our point estimates literally, global forces do not seem to have played an important role in the U.S. monetary transmission mechanism between 1984 and 1999. Also, since 2000, the initial response of the U.S. economy following a monetary policy shock—the first six to eight quarters—is essentially the same as the one that has been observed in the 1984 to 1999 period. However, point estimates suggest that the growing importance of global forces might have contributed to reducing some of the persistence in the responses, two or more years after the shocks.

Overall, we conclude that if global forces have had an effect on the monetary transmission mechanism, this is a recent phenomenon. This means, however, that we will need more data before we can get strong statistical conclusions on this question.

The rest of the chapter is organized as follows. In section 8.2, we describe the econometric framework adopted and the estimation approach. In section 8.3, we present empirical results on the comovements between international factors and U.S. data, and document changes in these relationships over the last two decades. In section 8.4, we document to what extent the role of global factors has changed the transmission mechanism of monetary policy. Section 8.5 concludes.

8.2 Econometric Framework: FAVAR

One key objective of this study is to evaluate the importance of the rest of the world in the transmission of U.S. monetary policy. That is, we seek to estimate to what extent the response of the rest of the world's economy enhances or mitigates the effect of U.S. monetary policy on the U.S. economy, and, importantly, whether this has changed over time. The FAVAR model described in Bernanke, Boivin, and Eliasz (2005) (henceforth, BBE) provides a natural framework to address these questions. In this section, we describe the empirical model and our estimation approach.

8.2.1 Description of FAVAR

The econometric framework that we consider is based on the FAVAR, extended to include international factors. We consider two regions: the U.S.

economy and the rest of the world, which we denote with *. We assume that in each region, the state of the economy, which is possibly unobserved, can be summarized by a $K \times 1$ vector C_t in the United States, and a $K^* \times 1$ vector C_t^* for the rest of the world. We measure the state of the economy in each region with large vectors of macroeconomic indicators, denoted by X_t for the United States, and X_t^* for the rest of the world. These vectors are of dimension $N \times 1$ and $N^* \times 1$, respectively. The indicators are assumed to relate to the state of the economy in each region according to the observation equations

$$X_t = \Lambda C_t + e_t \tag{1}$$

$$X_t^* = \Lambda^* C_t^* + e_t^*, \tag{2}$$

where Λ and Λ^* are matrices of factor loadings of appropriate dimensions, and the $N \times 1$ (respectively, $N^* \times 1$) vectors e_t and e_t^* contain (mean zero) series-specific components that are uncorrelated with the common components C_t (respectively, C_t^*), but are allowed to be serially correlated and weakly correlated across indicators. The number of common factors is assumed to be small relative to the number of indicators; that is, $N > K$ and $N^* > K^*$.

Under this structure, C_t and C_t^* constitute two sets of components that are common to all data series in the respective region and in general correlated across regions. Equations (1) and (2) reflect the fact that the common factors represent pervasive forces that drive the common dynamics of the data, and summarize at each date the state of the economy in each region. The variables in X_t are thus noisy measures of the underlying unobserved factors C_t. Note that it is in principle not restrictive to assume that X_t depends only on the current values of the factors, as C_t can always capture arbitrary lags of some fundamental factors.[4] The unobserved factors should reflect general region-specific economic conditions such as "economic activity," the "general level of prices," the level of "productivity," and key dimensions of the interest rate term structure, which may not easily be captured by a few time series, but rather by a wide range of economic variables.

The dynamics of the common factors are modeled as a structural Vector Autoregression (VAR)

$$\Phi_0 \begin{bmatrix} C_t^* \\ C_t \end{bmatrix} = \Phi(L) \begin{bmatrix} C_{t-1}^* \\ C_{t-1} \end{bmatrix} + \begin{bmatrix} v_t^* \\ v_t \end{bmatrix}, \tag{3}$$

where Φ_0 is a matrix of appropriate size on which we will later impose some restrictions, $\Phi(L)$ is a conformable lag polynomial of finite order, and the "structural" shocks v_t and v_t^* are assumed to be i.i.d. with mean zero and diagonal covariance matrix Q and Q^*, respectively. While these shocks are

4. This is why Stock and Watson (1999) refer to (1) as a dynamic factor model.

uncorrelated, anyone of these shocks may affect common factors of the other region immediately or over time, through the off-diagonal elements of Φ_0 and $\Phi(L)$. This structural VAR has a reduced-form representation obtained by premultiplying on both sides of (3) by Φ_0^{-1}:

$$\begin{bmatrix} C_t^* \\ C_t \end{bmatrix} = \begin{bmatrix} \Psi_{11}(L) & \Psi_{12}(L) \\ \Psi_{21}(L) & \Psi_{22}(L) \end{bmatrix} \begin{bmatrix} C_{t-1}^* \\ C_{t-1} \end{bmatrix} + \begin{bmatrix} u_t^* \\ u_t \end{bmatrix}, \tag{4}$$

where the reduced-form innovations u_t and u_t^* are cross-correlated.

Because we will ultimately be interested in characterizing the effects of monetary policy on the economy, we include in the vector of U.S. common components an observable measure of the monetary policy stance. As in most related VAR applications, we assume that the Federal funds rate, R_t, is the policy instrument. The latter will be allowed to have pervasive effect throughout the economy and will thus be considered as a common component of all U.S. data series. We thus write

$$C_t = \begin{bmatrix} F_t \\ R_t \end{bmatrix},$$

where F_t is a vector of latent macroeconomic factors summarizing the behavior of the U.S. economy.

8.2.2 Interpreting the FAVAR Structure in an International Context

The empirical model we just laid out is a dynamic factor model that links a large set of observable indicators to a small set of common components through the observation equations (1) and (2). The evolution of these common components is specified by the transition equation (3) or its reduced-form representation (4). It is useful to spell out more clearly the economic interpretation of this empirical model and, in particular, the relationship with possible underlying structural models.

As in Bernanke, Boivin, and Eliasz (2005) and in Boivin and Giannoni (2006a), we interpret the unobserved factors, C_t and C_t^*, as corresponding to theoretical concepts or variables that would enter a structural macroeconomic model. For instance, open economy dynamic general equilibrium models such as those of Benigno and Benigno (2001), Clarida, Galí, and Gertler (2002), Lubik and Schorfheide (2006), and those of many papers collected in this volume fully characterize the equilibrium evolution of inflation, output, interest rates, net exports, and other variables in two regions. In terms of the notation in our empirical framework, all of these variables would be in C_t and C_t^*. The dynamic evolution of these variables implied by such open economy models can be approximated by an unrestricted VAR of the form (4).[5] If all of these macroeconomic concepts were perfectly

5. For a formal description of the link between the solution of a dynamic stochastic general equilibrium (DSGE) model in state-space form and a VAR (see, e.g., Fernández-Villaverde et al. [2007] and references therein).

observed, the system (4) would boil down to a standard multicountry VAR and could be estimated directly, as in, for example, Eichenbaum and Evans (1995), Grilli and Roubini (1995, 1996), Cushman and Zha (1997), Kim and Roubini (2000), and Scholl and Uhlig (2006). In such a case, there would be no need to use the large set of indicators X_t.

However, there are reasons to believe that not all relevant concepts are perfectly observed. First, some macroeconomic concepts are simply measured with error.[6] Second, some of the macroeconomic variables that are key for the model's dynamics may be fundamentally latent. For instance, the concept of "potential output," often critical in monetary models, cannot be measured directly. By using a large data set, one is able to extract empirically the components that are most important in explaining fluctuations in the entire data set. While each common component does not need to represent any single economic concept, the common components C_t and C_t^* should constitute a linear combination of all of the relevant latent variables driving the set of noisy indicators X_t and X_t^*, to the extent that we extract the correct number of common components from the data set.

An advantage of this empirical framework is that it provides, both for the U.S. and the international data sets, summary measures of the state of these economies at each date, in the form of factors that may summarize many features of the economy. We thus do not restrict ourselves simply to measures of inflation or output. Another advantage of our approach, as BBE argue, is that this framework should lead to a better identification of the monetary policy shock than standard VARs, because it explicitly recognizes the large information set that the Federal Reserve and financial market participants exploit in practice, and also because, as just argued, it does not require to take a stand on the appropriate measures of prices and real activity that can simply be treated as latent common components. Moreover, for a set of identifying assumptions, a natural by-product of the estimation is to provide impulse response functions for any variable included in the data set. This is particularly useful in our case, since we want to understand the effect of globalization on the transmission of monetary policy to a wide range of economic variables.

The empirical model (1) and (2) and (4) provides a convenient decomposition of all data series into components driven by the U.S. factors C_t (i.e., the Federal funds rate and other U.S. latent factors F_t), non-U.S. latent factors C_t^*, and by series-specific components unrelated to the general state of the economies, e_t or e_t^*. For instance, (1) specifies that indicators of measures of U.S. economic activity or inflation are driven by the Federal funds rate R_t, U.S. latent factors F_t, and a component that is specific to each individual series (representing, e.g., measurement error or other idiosyncrasies of each series). The dynamics of the U.S. common components are in turn specified by (4).

6. Boivin and Giannoni (2006a) argue, for example, that inflation is imperfectly measured by any single indicator, and that it is important to use multiple indicators of it for proper inference.

Note that the factors C_t and C_t^* summarizing macroeconomic conditions in the U.S. respectively, in the rest of the world, may be affected both by their own region-specific shocks and by worldwide or "global" shocks. In fact, since reduced-form innovations u_t and u_t^* may be cross-correlated, they could be expressed as the sum of a component that is common both the U.S. and the rest of the world, possibly due to "global" shocks and a component that is exclusively region-specific. The reduced-form VAR may thus be rewritten as

$$C_t^* = \Psi_{11}(L)C_{t-1}^* + \Psi_{12}(L)C_{t-1} + \Gamma_1 g_t + \varepsilon_t^* \tag{5}$$

$$C_t = \Psi_{21}(L)C_{t-1}^* + \Psi_{22}(L)C_{t-1} + \Gamma_2 g_t + \varepsilon_t, \tag{6}$$

where g_t is a vector of "global" exogenous shocks, and ε_t^*, ε_t are disturbances that are specific to each region and uncorrelated across regions.[7]

8.2.3 Estimation

As in Stock and Watson (2002b) and BBE, we estimate our empirical model using a variant of a two-step principal component approach that we briefly outline here. We refer to these papers for a more detailed description.

The first step consists of extracting principal components from X_t and X_t^* to obtain consistent estimates of the common factors under the structure laid out. In the second step, the Federal funds rate is added to the estimated factors and the VAR in equation (4) is estimated. Note that in the first step, BBE do not impose the constraint that the Federal funds rate is one of the common components. So if this interest rate is really a common component, it should be captured by the principal components. To remove the Federal funds rate from the space covered by the principal components, in the second step BBE perform a transformation of the principal components exploiting the different behavior of what they call "slow moving" and "fast moving" variables. Our implementation is slightly different, however. We adopt a more direct approach, which consists of imposing the constraint that Federal funds rate is one of the factors in the first-step estimation. This guarantees that the estimated latent factors recover dimensions of the common dynamics not captured by the Federal funds rate.[8] To do so, we adopt the following procedure in the first step of the estimation. Starting from an initial estimate of F_t, denoted by $F_t^{(0)}$ and obtained as the first $K-1$ principal components of X_t, we iterate through the following steps:

1. Regress X_t on $F_t^{(0)}$ and R_t, to obtain $\hat{\lambda}_R^{(0)}$.

7. In this respect, C_t and C_t^* have a different interpretation than the world factors estimated by, for example, Gregory, Head, and Reynauld (1997), Forni et al. (2000), Kose, Otrok, and Whiteman (2003), and Ciccarelli and Mojon (2005). While these authors estimate a world factor and orthogonal region-(or country)-specific factors, our estimated C_t and C_t^* contain both fluctuations in regional and world factors.

8. We thank Olivier Blanchard for pointing us in that direction.

2. Compute $\tilde{X}_t^{(0)} = X_t - \hat{\lambda}_R^{(0)} R_t$.
3. Estimate $F_t^{(1)}$ as the first $K - 1$ principal components of $\tilde{X}_t^{(0)}$.
4. Back to 1.

Having estimated the factors C_t and C_t^* and the factor loadings Λ, Λ^*, we can estimate the VAR (4). As we will argue in section 8.4, the matrix polynomial $\Psi_{21}(L)$ will be of particular interest to us, as it captures the effects of international factors on domestic variables. For now, note that the VAR coefficients $\Psi_{ij}(L)$ are identified provided that the variance-covariance matrix of the innovations $[u_t^{*\prime}, u_t^{\prime}]^{\prime}$ is nonsingular. A sufficient condition for this is that the variance-covariance matrices of ε_t^* and ε_t are both full-ranked in the VAR representations (5) and (6).[9] In that case, C_t^* Granger causes C_t, and the domestic factors C_t do not constitute sufficient statistics to uncover the dynamics of the domestic economy. In other words, the domestic economy is not a statistical "island." Alternatively, if the rest of the world had no region-specific shocks, so that $E(\varepsilon_t^* \varepsilon_t^{*\prime}) = 0$, then $\Psi_{21}(L)$ would not be identified, as international factors would bring no additional information. The estimate of the VAR coefficients $\Psi_{21}(L)$ will thus rely on the presence of independent variations originating in the rest of the world, and the Granger-causality tests that we report following will guarantee that there is indeed sufficient such variation.

8.2.4 Data

The data we use for the estimation of the FAVAR are a balanced panel of 720 quarterly series for the period running from 1984:1 to 2005:2. The data series are listed in the appendix. They comprise 671 U.S. series. Among these, there are 129 macroeconomic indicators that measure economic activity, employment, prices, interest rates, exchange rates, and other key financial variables. In addition, we include the 542 series of disaggregate consumption, and consumer and producer price series used in Boivin, Giannoni, and Mihov (2009). As discussed in that paper, disaggregate price data provide useful information for the appropriate estimation of the monetary policy shocks, and are found to mitigate the price puzzle obtained in conventional VARs or factor models that omit that information. For the rest of the world, we consider a panel of forty-nine quarterly data series for the fifteen main U.S. trade partners. This data set includes—for each country—measures of economic activity, prices, and short- and long-term interest rates (if available). All data series have been transformed to induce stationarity, and the transformations applied are indicated in the appendix.

8.2.5 Preferred Specification of the FAVAR

For the model selection, there are two important observations to keep in

9. In terms of instrumental variables (IV) intuition, to estimate $\Psi_{12}(L)$, we need some independent variation in C_t^* in order to be able to use it as an instrument for itself in equation (6). For a formal treatment of this argument, see Hausman and Taylor (1983).

mind. First, the sample size severely constrains the class of specifications we can consider, especially the number of lags in (4), as the number of factors gets large. Second, in trying to identify the monetary policy transmission mechanism, we are more worried about bias than efficiency. Available information criteria for selecting the number of factors are thus not clearly adequate in that respect. Our general approach for selecting our preferred specification has thus been to try with up to twenty domestic factors and up to ten foreign factors.

It turns out that irrespective of the number of factors that we include, the Bayesian information criterion selects 1 lag in (4) over the post-1984 sample. We found that including more than ten domestic factors and four global factors did not change substantially the dynamic response of the economy to monetary policy, although, obviously, the uncertainty around the estimates increases with more factors. In fact, very similar results are obtained with as few as six domestic factors and three foreign factors, although point estimates suggest some price puzzle for some of the price series.

Our preferred specification thus includes ten domestic latent factors and four global factors, and the transition equation (4) has 1 lag.

8.3 International Factors and U.S. Economic Dynamics

Several studies have recently attempted to determine the degree of comovement of a few macroeconomic series across countries. For instance, Kose, Otrok, and Whiteman (2003, 2005) and Stock and Watson (2005) study the comovement of economic activity measures, and Ciccarelli and Mojon (2005) focus on inflation. In this chapter, rather than restricting ourself to the comparison of a single type of measure across regions of the world, we use our FAVAR framework to compare how the factors summarizing the U.S. macroeconomic dynamics relate to the rest of the world's factors.[10] If global forces are important to describe the dynamics of the U.S. economy, they should be captured by the latent factor space of the FAVAR. We use the common factors extracted from our large data set and determine the fraction of fluctuations in U.S. indicators of real activity, inflation, and interest rates that can be explained by U.S. and global factors, respectively. After showing to what extent key U.S. economic variables comove with U.S. and international factors, we determine whether these relationships have changed since the mid-1980s. We then attempt to measure whether foreign factors do "cause" (in a Granger sense) fluctuations in U.S. factors. In the next section, we report how monetary policy shocks affect a large number of variables, how the transmission mechanism has changed over time, and to what extent the change is due to international factors.

10. Justiniano (2004) similarly studies the comovement of multiple macroeconomic series between Canada, Australia, and the rest of the world.

8.3.1 Comovements between U.S. and International Factors

We first start by determining to what extent U.S. variables are correlated with U.S. and foreign factors. Table 8.1 reports the fraction of the volatility in the series listed in the first column that is explained by the eleven U.S. factors C_t (i.e., ten latent factors and the Federal funds rate), the four foreign factors C_t^*, and all factors taken together. This corresponds to the R^2 statistics obtained by the regressions of these variables on the appropriate set of factors for the entire 1984:1 to 2005:2 sample. Note that since the U.S. and international factors are allowed to be correlated, the fraction of the variance in any given variable explained by the U.S. factors (first column) plus that explained by the international factors (second column) do not correspond to the fraction of the variance explained jointly by both sets of factors (third column). However, by comparing the numbers in the third column to the sum of the other two columns, we may have a rough sense of how the determinants of the variable of interest may be correlated across countries.

Looking at table 8.1, several observations are worth mentioning. First,

Table 8.1 **R2 for regressions of selected U.S. series on various sets of factors (sample 1984:1–2005:2)**

	U.S. factors	Intl. factors	All factors
All U.S. data X_t (average over all U.S. data)	0.39	0.13	0.45
Selected U.S. indicators			
Interest rate (Federal funds)	1.00	0.65	1.00
GDP	0.30	0.18	0.37
Consumption	0.28	0.14	0.33
Investment	0.50	0.08	0.51
Exports	0.38	0.31	0.57
Imports	0.45	0.18	0.55
GDP deflator	0.54	0.33	0.69
Consumption deflator (PCE)	0.66	0.37	0.70
Investment deflator	0.53	0.11	0.58
Export deflator	0.58	0.08	0.65
Import deflator	0.42	0.06	0.49
Consumer price index (CPI)	0.50	0.23	0.56
Producer price index (PPI)	0.78	0.03	0.81
Industrial production	0.79	0.12	0.84
Employment (total nonfarm)	0.84	0.34	0.85
Real personal expenditures: durable goods	0.29	0.01	0.29
Real personal expenditures: nondurable goods	0.77	0.09	0.80
Price of personal expenditures: durable goods	0.58	0.43	0.68
Price of personal expenditures: nondurable goods	0.85	0.03	0.87
Price of personal expenditures: services	0.67	0.46	0.74
Long-term interest rate (10 years)	0.91	0.86	0.93
U.S. dollar (trade-weighted nominal exchange rate)	0.74	0.27	0.78

the entire U.S. data set X_t is on average quite strongly correlated with the common factors. On average, all factors explain 45 percent of the variance of U.S. series. Most of the common fluctuations in U.S. series is, however, provided by U.S. factors, as the R^2 for these factors amounts to 0.39. However, foreign factors do also appear to be correlated with U.S. data series, with an R^2 of 0.13. Note that, at this point, we do not attempt to determine the origin of the fluctuations in the factors and the direction of causality between U.S. and international factors. We realize that, in general, U.S. variables may be affected by global economic shocks that impact simultaneously U.S. and international factors. Instead, we attempt to assess to what extent international factors can explain fluctuations in various U.S. macroeconomic variables with information that is not contained in U.S. factors.

Looking at selected U.S. indicators, we find that quarterly growth rates of measures of real economic activity, such as quarterly averages of industrial production and employment, display very high correlations with the U.S. factors (R^2 statistics of 0.79 and 0.84, respectively). It may be surprising that other activity measures such as real GDP or consumption from the national income accounts do not appear as strongly correlated with the U.S. factors, especially when compared with existing evidence based on similar factor models. However, this is purely an artifact of our use of quarterly growth for GDP components mixed with quarterly averages of monthly data. In fact, the quarterly growth rates of the GDP components display more high-frequency variability than those of (the quarterly averages of) employment and industrial production. Because that variability is not well captured by U.S. factors, a large fraction of these series volatility is explained by the idiosyncratic terms. Were we to consider year-over-year growth rates of the variables, GDP and consumption would display much larger contributions of U.S. factors. The important point, however, is that most of the fluctuations in industrial production, consumption, investment, or employment indicators are determined by domestic factors. While these indicators display some correlation with the international factors, the additional explanatory power of the latter factors is relatively low. In fact, the R^2 obtained for these variables by them regressing on all factors are not much higher than those found by regressing only on the U.S. factors.

Quite naturally, the picture is different for U.S. real exports and imports, as they appear to be much more strongly related to international factors. Adding the international factors to the U.S. factors increases the fraction of the variance of exports explained from 0.38 to 0.57, and raises the R^2 of imports from 0.45 to 0.55. These global factors thus contain substantial information not already contained in U.S. factors, and that is correlated with real exports and imports. Real GDP then reflects the descriptions of its underlying components: while domestic factors are certainly key, adding the international factors increases the R^2 by 7 percentage points.

For U.S. quarterly inflation rates, the importance of international factors varies sensibly depending on the price index used. Inflation of the producer price index (PPI), for instance, is well described by U.S. factors and displays very little correlation with international factors. However, growth rates of the U.S. GDP deflator and of consumer prices, whether based on the consumer price index (CPI) or the personal personal consumption expenditure (PCE) deflator, are more correlated with international factors. The latter factors explain 37 percent of fluctuations in inflation of the PCE deflator. Nonetheless, the international factors do not seem to explain much more of consumer price inflation than what is explained by U.S. domestic factors. This suggests that the U.S. and international factors that explain well inflation are strongly correlated. This is consistent with Ciccarelli and Mojon (2005), who find that an important component of consumer price inflation is shared globally. For the GDP deflator, however, global factors contain information not included in U.S. factors. In fact, regressing this indicator on all factors raises the R^2 to 0.69, compared to 0.54, when we consider only U.S. factors. One possible explanation is that export prices depend sensibly on international factors in a way that is not captured by U.S. factors. The inflation rate of the exports' deflator does not however, appear to be strongly correlated with international factors over our entire sample. As we will see following, this low correlation with international factors is deceptive, as it appears to be due to considerable instability over the sample.

The nominal exchange rate is strongly correlated with domestic factors, and the R^2 with international factors is 0.27, but these global factors seem to contain surprisingly little information not already contained in the domestic factors, and the R^2 with all factors is only a little higher than the one with only U.S. factors.

Finally, for nominal interest rates, the Federal funds rate is by assumption a U.S. factor, but it is also strongly correlated with international factors. Similarly, the long-term U.S. interest rate is very strongly correlated with U.S. and international factors. This suggests that all of the countries considered in our data set are affected by a common factor resembling U.S. interest rates.

8.3.2 Have U.S. and International Forces Become More Strongly Correlated?

Overall, the evidence reported in table 8.1 indicates that most selected key U.S. variables are strongly correlated with U.S. factors and, to a lesser extent, with international factors. Such results have been obtained for the sample that runs from 1984:1 to 2005:2. As mentioned in the introduction, though, the U.S. economy's trade in goods and services with the rest of the world has expanded considerably, and the financial globalization, as measured by the sum of external assets and liabilities, has developed at an unprecedented pace during this period.

Such dramatic developments are likely to have affected the relationship between U.S. variables and international factors. To date, however, the evidence about change in the synchronization of the U.S. economy with the rest of the world is mixed. While Kose, Prasad, and Terrones (2003) find stronger comovements of output in industrialized countries with a world factor (since the early 1980s) than in the preceding two decades, Doyle and Faust (2005) find little evidence of statistically significant changes, and Helbling and Bayoumi (2003), Monfort et al. (2003), Heathcote and Perri (2004), Stock and Watson (2005), and Kose, Otrok, and Whiteman (2005) find reductions in the synchronization of output fluctuations across countries. In addition, these studies typically consider the period subsequent to the mid-1980s as a whole, and do not allow for changes during that period.

Several observers have nonetheless suggested that key macroeconomic variables might have become more dependent on the state of the economy in the rest of the world in the last few years. Chairman Bernanke (2007) pointed out that long-term interest rates in the United States have become sensibly more correlated with those of Germany and other industrialized economies. Some have argued that U.S. inflation may have become more strongly affected by international developments, such as the rise of China as a source of goods and services sold in the United States (see, e.g., Rogoff 2003; Kamin, Marazzi, and Schindler 2006; Borio and Filardo 2006; Ihrig et al. 2007). While some U.S. variables may well have become more strongly correlated with international factors, our framework allows us to assess whether a large number of macroeconomic variables in the United States have become systematically more synchronized with the factors of its major trade partners.

It is important to keep in mind that a formal empirical analysis of the recent changes due to the greater globalization is difficult, and faces limits, as the data samples are still very short. Nevertheless, our framework provides a rich account of these changes since 1984, which can show to what extent the global components have revealed changes in the correlations with U.S. variables. Figure 8.1, panels A and B, document the comovement of U.S. variables with global forces over time. They show the fraction of the variability in U.S. variables explained by the global factors, where the estimation is done using a ten-year rolling window. The dates correspond to the midpoint of that window.

These figures reveal several interesting results. First, they show that international factors have *not* become more strongly correlated with a *broad* set of U.S. variables since 1984. The regressions of the U.S. common components on all international components result in R^2 statistics that have not increased on average. Second, despite a fairly constant correlation between international and U.S. factors, when taken as a whole, the importance of global forces on some individual U.S. variables has varied considerably over the sample. Part of that variation certainly reflects the short samples, and may exaggerate the nature of the true changes. Nonetheless, the R^2 of the

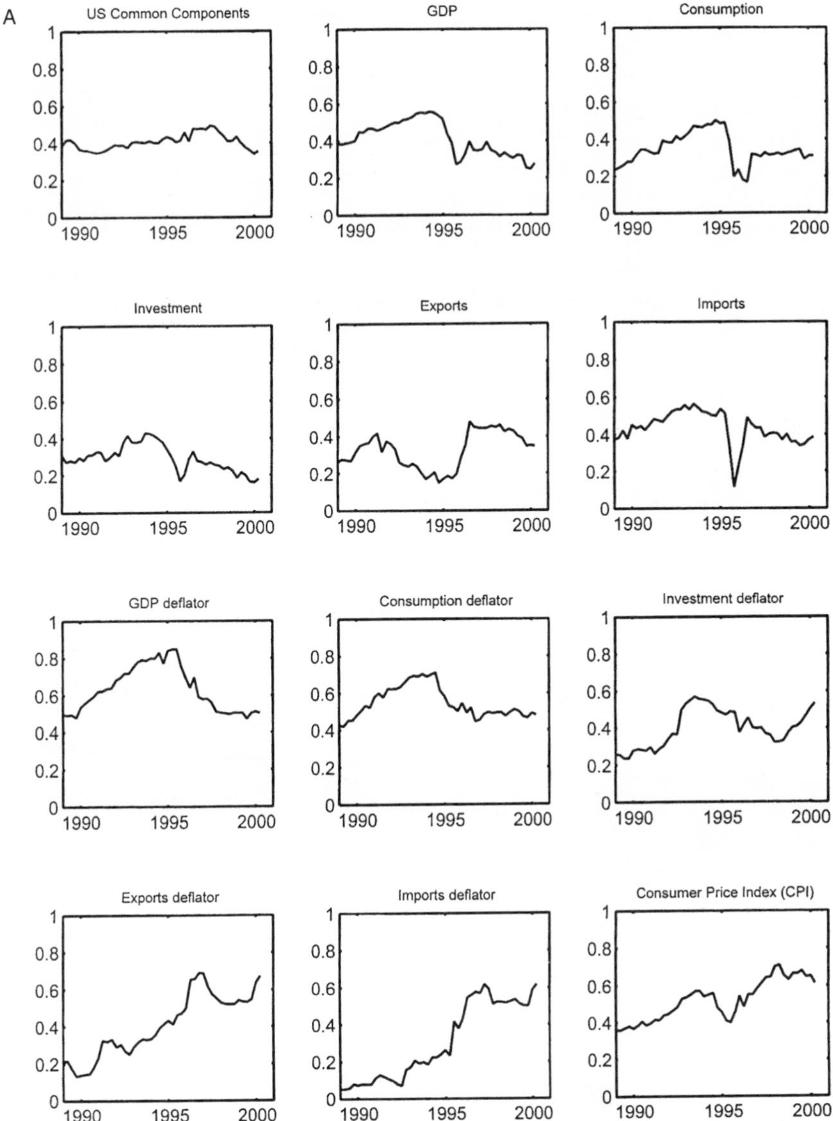

Fig. 8.1 Fraction of the variance of individual series explained by global factors, in regressions with 10-year rolling windows

regression of real GDP growth on international factors fell from 1995 (corresponding to the period that spans 1990 to 2000) to 2000 (i.e., the period that spans 1995 to 2005). A similar evolution can be found for consumption, investment, and imports, though the R^2 found at the end of the sample are not very different from those obtained at the beginning of the sample. The

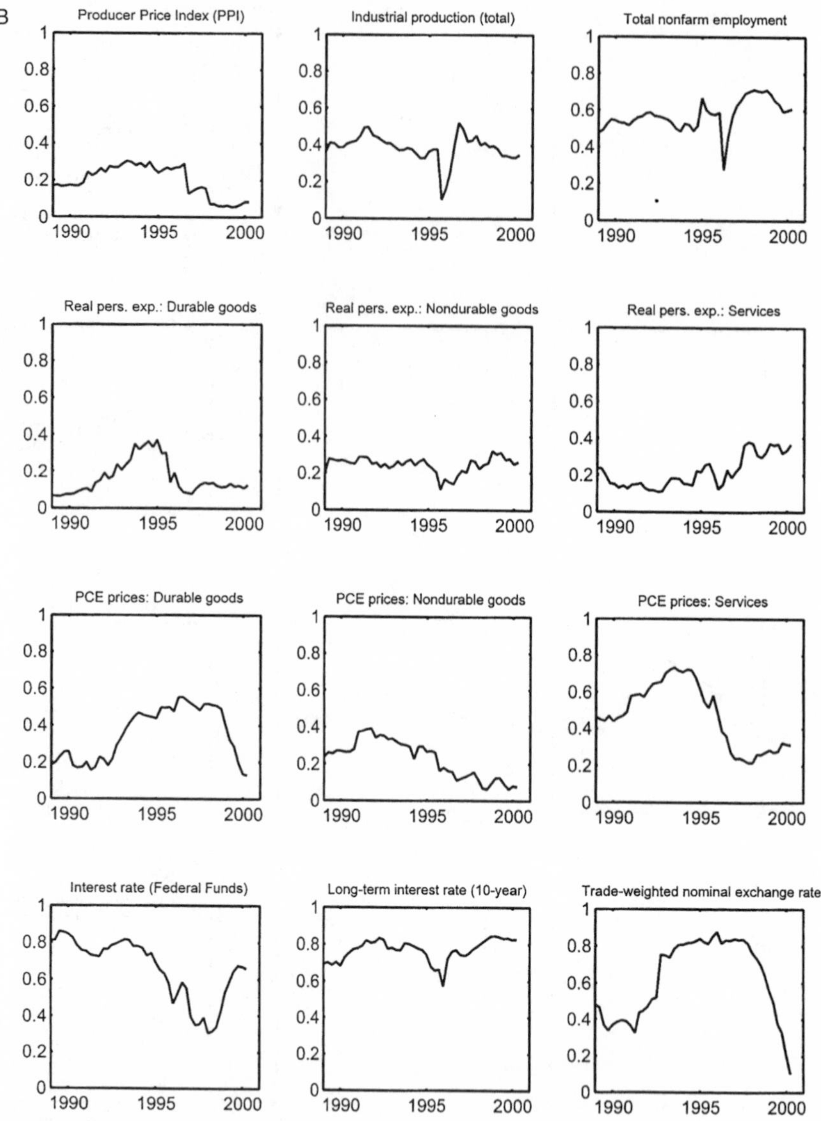

Fig. 8.1 (cont.)

U.S. exports, however, do seem to be more strongly correlated with international factors after the mid-1990s, with R^2 doubling from approximately 0.20 to 0.40.

In terms of prices, inflation in export prices is increasingly more correlated with the international factors throughout the sample. While international factors explain only about 20 percent of the variance of the export prices' inflation rate around 1990, they explain close to 70 percent of this variance a decade later. Import prices similarly see their correlation with international factors steadily increase over time. This is consistent with the idea that import prices have been rising more slowly than other consumer prices, due in part to an increase in imports from low-cost emerging economies. In fact, Kamin, Marazzi, and Schindler (2006) find that trade with China has reduced inflation in import prices by about 1 percentage point. This ends up being reflected in a greater correlation of the international factors with U.S. inflation as measured by the CPI, but surprisingly, there is no such effect on the inflation rate of PCE prices. In addition, there is no evidence that the GDP deflator has become more strongly correlated with international factors since the mid-1990s. If anything, the R^2 statistic has decreased since 1995 for the inflation based on the GDP deflator and on the PCE deflator. These findings contrast sharply with the claims often made that U.S. inflation may have become increasingly determined in the rest of the world (e.g., Borio and Filardo 2006), but are consistent with the results of Ihrig et al. (2007).

Regarding interest rates, the Federal funds rate appears very strongly correlated with international factors until mid-1995, and again by the year 2000. But in the second half of the 1990s, the Federal funds rate appears to disconnect from the international factors for several years. For ten-year rates, the correlation with international factors seems to increase by the late 1990s, a fact consistent with the finding by Bernanke (2007) that long-term yields in industrialized countries have become more strongly correlated in the last few years. While we do not attempt to determine why that correlation has increased, we note that it does not necessarily imply that U.S. rates are determined to a greater extent on foreign capital market. In fact, such a finding is also consistent with the idea that U.S. monetary policy may now have larger effects on international bond markets at the same time as it affects U.S. financial markets (see Ehrmann, Fratzscher, and Rigobon 2005; Faust et al. 2007).

Finally, while the value of the U.S. dollar seems to have been strongly correlated with international factors for a large part of the 1990s, the recent decline in the value of the dollar appears to have had little relation with global factors. Instead, it has been much more determined by U.S. domestic factors.

While table 8.1 and figure 8.1 have provided an interesting account of the relationship between various U.S. macroeconomic variables and international factors, the numbers reported are, however, merely correlations, and do not imply that fluctuations in U.S. variables such as the Federal funds rate are caused by changes in international conditions. It may well be that changes in U.S. conditions may be sufficiently important to cause changes in foreign factors.

Table 8.2 **Granger-causality tests for international factors affecting U.S. factors**

	Full sample	84:1–94:4	95:1–05:2
Factors			
1	0.00	0.00	0.00
2	0.00	0.00	0.00
3	0.00	0.00	0.18
4	0.04	0.06	0.01
5	0.07	0.24	0.35
6	0.00	0.00	0.00
7	0.01	0.10	0.00
8	0.03	0.29	0.04
9	0.05	0.38	0.00
10	0.00	0.00	0.03
Fed. funds rate	0.00	0.00	0.00

Note: Table reports p-values.

8.3.3 Testing the Relevance of Global Forces for U.S. Fluctuations

Granger Causality Tests

To check formally whether global forces do matter for U.S. fluctuations, we now turn to Granger causality tests. Results are presented in table 8.2. We test whether the lags of all international factors, C^*_{t-1}, jointly have predictive power for the current values of U.S. factors C_t listed in the first column, over and beyond lags of domestic factors, C_{t-1}. Under the null hypothesis, foreign factors have no predictive power. The table suggests that all but one U.S. common factors, including the Fed funds rate, are Granger-caused by international factors at the 5 percent level over the entire sample considered. The evidence is somewhat weaker when we perform the test over the 1984:1 to 1994:4 period. At this stage, this might only be reflecting lower power of the test over the smaller subsamples. Interestingly, however, combined with the evidence that we report in section 8.4, it seems that global factors were not very important to explain U.S. economic dynamics before the late 1990s. This evidence implies that the feedback from the rest of the world to the U.S. economy as measured by $\Psi_{21}(L)$, and to which we return in section 8.4, are identified.

Has the Influence of International Factors on U.S. Factors Increased over the Last Two Decades?

As the comparison of the Granger causality tests between the two subsamples crudely suggests, the relationship of the global factors with the U.S. economy might have changed over time. In fact, if there is any content to the claims that the greater economic integration between the U.S. and the rest of the world has affected the dynamics of U.S. economic variables, the Granger causality relationship must have changed over time.

Table 8.3 **Stability tests for Granger-causality coefficients of international factors affecting future U.S. factors**

	Joint-Global
Factors	
1	41.59**
2	85.17**
3	47.53**
4	38.14**
5	102.15**
6	34.92**
7	30.90**
8	20.78**
9	17.44*
10	62.20**
Fed. funds rate	15.94

Note: Table reports QLR statistics and confidence level.
**Significant at the 5 percent level.
*Significant at the 10 percent level.

One way to get formal evidence on this question is to test for the stability of the Granger causality relationships. We do so using the Quandt likelihood ratio test (QLR), the asymptotic distribution of which has been derived by Andrews (1993).[11] We apply the test jointly to all global factors.

The results are reported in table 8.3. As is clear from the table, we reject stability at the 5 percent level in most cases. Based on this, one important observation is that even though we have a fairly short sample, the latter contains sufficient information to allow us to detect statistically significant changes. It remains to be investigated whether these changes have been sufficiently important, economically speaking, to affect the transmission mechanism of monetary policy. Interestingly, the Federal funds rate is the only variable for which the stability is not rejected. The data thus suggests that while the setting of the Federal funds rate has been affected by global factors, the role of the latter factors does not seem to have changed significantly in our sample.

8.4 Implications for the Monetary Transmission Mechanism

In the last section, we determined that some of U.S. factors have become more synchronized with international factors over the last two decades. A

11. In doing so, we ignore the uncertainty in the factor estimates. When the cross section of macro indicators is large, the uncertainty in the factor estimates should be negligible asymptotically (see Bai and Ng 2006).

natural question that arises, then, is to what extent has U.S. monetary policy become more constrained by the expansion of international trade, and to a larger extent by the much greater globalization of finance. Do global forces mitigate the effects of U.S. monetary policy more than they used to?

There is little doubt that, despite this globalization, the Federal Reserve has retained its capacity to align the Federal funds rate with its target rate by managing the supply of funds in the interbank market. It is thus still reasonable to think of the Federal funds rate as being the instrument of monetary policy. As other short-term rates, such as yields on three-month or six-month U.S. Treasury securities, remain very strongly correlated with actual Federal funds rate (the correlation between the Federal funds rate and three-month securities is above 0.99 for the period 1984 to 2007 and has remained as high since 2000) they can still be viewed as primarily affected by monetary policy.

Clearly, longer-term interest rates reflect, at least in part, expectations of future short-term rates, and depend on announcements provided by central bankers. Longer-term rates have, however, become more strongly correlated with international factors in recent years, as mentioned before. Part of this change may reflect a greater influence of international capital markets on U.S. long-term rates.[12] Alternatively, U.S. factors may have more impact on international capital markets (see Ehrmann, Fratzscher, and Rigobon 2005; Faust et al. 2007). At the same time, since monetary policy's effect on other variables such as economic activity and inflation is believed to depend partly on long-term rates, it is possible that these other variables might have become less affected by Federal funds rate movements. In addition, the increase in international trade in goods and services may explain why U.S. import and export prices have become more correlated with international factors. A natural question, then, is what are the implications of these changes for the transmission of U.S. monetary policy?

8.4.1 Empirical Strategy

In the context of our FAVAR framework, we can characterize the transmission mechanism of monetary policy by computing the response of selected macroeconomic series to an identified monetary policy shock. In the spirit of VAR analyses, we impose only the minimum number of restrictions needed to identify the policy shock. This allows us to document some facts about the evolution of the monetary transmission mechanism that should not be otherwise contaminated by auxiliary assumptions.

Recall that the structural representation of our VAR transition equation takes the form (3), where again $C_t = [F_t', R_t]'$. To identify monetary policy shocks (i.e., the surprise changes in the Federal funds rate) we assume that

12. See, for example, Bernanke (2005) for an argument that increased saving in emerging economies and in oil-producing countries has contributed to maintaining low long-term U.S. interest rates.

the latent factors F_t and C_t^* cannot respond to innovations in R_t in the period of the shock. The Fed funds rate, however, is allowed to respond to contemporaneous fluctuations in such factors. We thus impose the restriction that the matrix Φ_0 in (3) has ones on the main diagonal, and zeroes in the last column, except for the lower right element, which is one. This has the implication that the monetary policy shock enters only in the last element of the innovations vector $\boldsymbol{u}_t$ in the reduced-form VAR (4), which we repeat here for convenience:

$$\begin{bmatrix} C_t^* \\ C_t \end{bmatrix} = \begin{bmatrix} \Psi_{11}(L) & \Psi_{12}(L) \\ \Psi_{21}(L) & \Psi_{22}(L) \end{bmatrix} \begin{bmatrix} C_{t-1}^* \\ C_{t-1} \end{bmatrix} + \begin{bmatrix} u_t^* \\ u_t \end{bmatrix}.$$

As mentioned previously, the matrix polynomials $\Psi_{12}(L)$ and $\Psi_{21}(L)$ determine the magnitude of the spillovers between the U.S. and the rest of the world's economic variables. When $\Psi_{21}(L) = 0$, the rest of the world has no spillovers on the U.S. economy, meaning that fluctuations in foreign economic variables do not cause (in the sense of Granger) any fluctuations in U.S. variables. Following a U.S. monetary policy shock, $\Psi_{21}(L)$ measures the extent to which the rest of the world contributes to the transmission of the U.S. monetary policy domestically.

Our strategy involves computing impulse response functions to a monetary policy shock in the aforementioned system, and comparing them to those obtained with different values of $\Psi_{21}(L)$. The difference between these impulse responses provides a measure of the importance of the endogenous response of the rest of the world in the U.S. transmission of monetary policy. (Note that in both cases, C_t^* is allowed to move only in response to the monetary shock.) In addition, to the extent that the greater integration of the world economies has changed the role played by the rest of the world in the transmission of U.S. monetary policy, this should imply a change in $\Psi_{21}(L)$. Consequently, by documenting the changes over time in $\Psi_{21}(L)$ and its implications on the impulse response functions, it is possible to evaluate whether globalization has reduced the ability of U.S. monetary policy to affect domestic variables.

To illustrate more directly the exercise we perform, let us consider a simplified version of this model in which the macroeconomic factors are actually observed. To fix ideas more concretely, think of the set of relevant domestic factors C_t as being given by the domestic (or world) interest rate R_t, and domestic real activity Y_t, and the foreign factors C_t^* as corresponding foreign real activity Y_t^*. Let us assume that the structural model relating these variables is as follows:

$$Y_t^* = \psi_{11} Y_{t-1}^* + \psi_{12} Y_{t-1} + \psi_{13} R_{t-1} + g_t + \varepsilon_t^*$$

$$Y_t = \psi_{21} Y_{t-1}^* + \psi_{22} Y_{t-1} + \psi_{23} R_{t-1} + g_t + \varepsilon_t$$

$$R_t = \phi Y_{t-1} + \eta_t,$$

where ε_t^* and ε_t are region-specific output shocks and g_t is a worldwide shock. The first two equations are reduced-form equations determining output in both regions, while the third equation can be interpreted as an interest rate rule, so that η_t can be viewed as a monetary policy shock.

In this context, our approach consists of comparing the impulse response functions of Y_t and R_t implied by this unrestricted system, with those obtained for different values of ψ_{21}. For instance, setting $\psi_{21} = 0$ is equivalent to assuming that domestic variables are not affected by international developments. Comparing the two sets of impulse response functions thus provides a way to assess the importance of the "feedback" or "spillover" from the rest of the world in explaining the transmission mechanism of monetary policy.

Whether or not our strategy identifies the effect of international factors (i.e., the effect of Y_t^*) in the transmission mechanism of monetary policy depends solely on whether the parameter ψ_{21} is identified. As mentioned in section 8.2, ψ_{21} is identified provided that the variances of ε_t and ε_t^* are nonzero. If $var(\varepsilon_t^*)$ were equal to zero, the system would be reduced-ranked and it would not be possible to identify separately all the parameters ψ_{ij}, as Y_t^* and Y_t would be perfectly collinear. Notice that the condition that $var(\varepsilon_t) > 0$ and $var(\varepsilon_t^*) > 0$ is equivalent to saying that Y_t^* Granger causes Y_t (conditional on past values of Y_t).

It is important to note that our analysis does not identify directly "worldwide shocks," which would affect simultaneously domestic and international factors (such as the shock g_t) in the previous example, in the absence of further restrictions. It is, however, not necessary to identify such global shocks in order to quantify the effects of international factors of the transmission of U.S. monetary policy shocks.

For illustration purposes, in this simple example, we assumed that the factors C_t and C_t^* were perfectly observed. In our application, however, these factors are unobserved and relate to a large set of informative variables according to (1) and (2). This does not change any of the arguments just made in the context of the simple example. Once we have estimates of C_t and C_t^*, we are back in the world described in the previous example. The matrix polynomial $\psi_{21}(L)$ is similarly identified when the matrix $var(\varepsilon_t^*)$ is full rank or, alternatively, provided that C_t^* Granger causes C_t.

8.4.2 Implementation

In estimating the FAVAR over the sample 1984:1 to 2005:2, we allow for the possibility that the international factors may affect U.S. variables differently after the year 2000. More specifically, we expand the VAR system of our FAVAR with a dummy variable interacted with all the lags of the foreign factors. More precisely, we estimate the following system

$$\begin{bmatrix} C_t^* \\ C_t \end{bmatrix} = \begin{bmatrix} \Psi_{11}(L) & \Psi_{12}(L) \\ \Psi_{21}(L) & \Psi_{22}(L) \end{bmatrix} \begin{bmatrix} C_{t-1}^* \\ C_{t-1} \end{bmatrix} + \begin{bmatrix} \Psi_{11}^d(L) \\ \Psi_{21}^d(L) \end{bmatrix} d_t C_{t-1}^* + \begin{bmatrix} u_t^* \\ u_t \end{bmatrix},$$

where d_t takes the value 0 for the period 1984:1 to 1999:4 and 1 after. This means that the coefficients on the lag international factors in the equations for C_t are equal to $\psi_{21}(L)$ for 1984:1 to 1999:4, and to $\psi_{21}(L) + \psi_{21}^{d}(L)$ thereafter. Given that our preferred specification has only one lag, notice that allowing for this form of instability requires estimating four additional parameters per equation, so it is not too costly in terms of degrees of freedom.

8.4.3 The Effects of Monetary Policy Shocks

Figure 8.2, panels A and B, show the estimated impulse responses of a set of macroeconomic indicators to a tightening of monetary policy; that is, an innovation in the Federal funds rate corresponding to an unexpected increase of 25 basis points. The solid lines represent the responses computed using the relationship between the U.S. factors and the international factors as estimated during the 1984:1 to 1999:4 period, along with the 70 percent confidence intervals.[13] The dashed lines, instead, display the responses using the same FAVAR, but assuming that the U.S. and international factors relate as estimated after 2000. A comparison of these two sets of impulse responses allows us to gauge the effects on the monetary transmission mechanism of the changes in the relationship between international factors and U.S. variables. In fact, between the two sets of responses, the only relationships that are allowed to change are those that describe how foreign factors end up affecting U.S. data. Note that by doing so, we maximize the length of our sample in the estimation, yet we allow for a change in the role of international factors.

As the impulse responses based on the effects of international factors estimated for the 1984:1 to 1999:4 sample reveal in figure 8.2, an unexpected tightening in monetary policy results in a gradual decline in real GDP, which tends to revert back to the original level after about three years. Other measures of activity, such as industrial production and employment, both respond in a similar way. Consumption also shows a similar although smaller response, while investment falls much more. Together with the fall in domestic demand, imports fall in response to the interest rate increase. The reduction in imports appears to be reinforced by a significant appreciation in the value of the U.S. dollar, lasting about two years following the shock. Exports to the rest of the world also fall significantly following the monetary tightening. This is consistent with the fact that the U.S. dollar appreciates, and that output in foreign trade partners falls (not reported).

All price indexes (reported in levels) show little response on impact, but also tend to fall progressively, and in a persistent way, following the monetary tightening. However, while the import and export price deflators seem to respond rapidly to the shock, it takes about three quarters for the GDP deflator and the CPI to show any movement. While the import price response may reflect a slowing domestic economy, the response of export prices may

13. The confidence intervals were obtained using Kilian's (1998) bootstrap procedure.

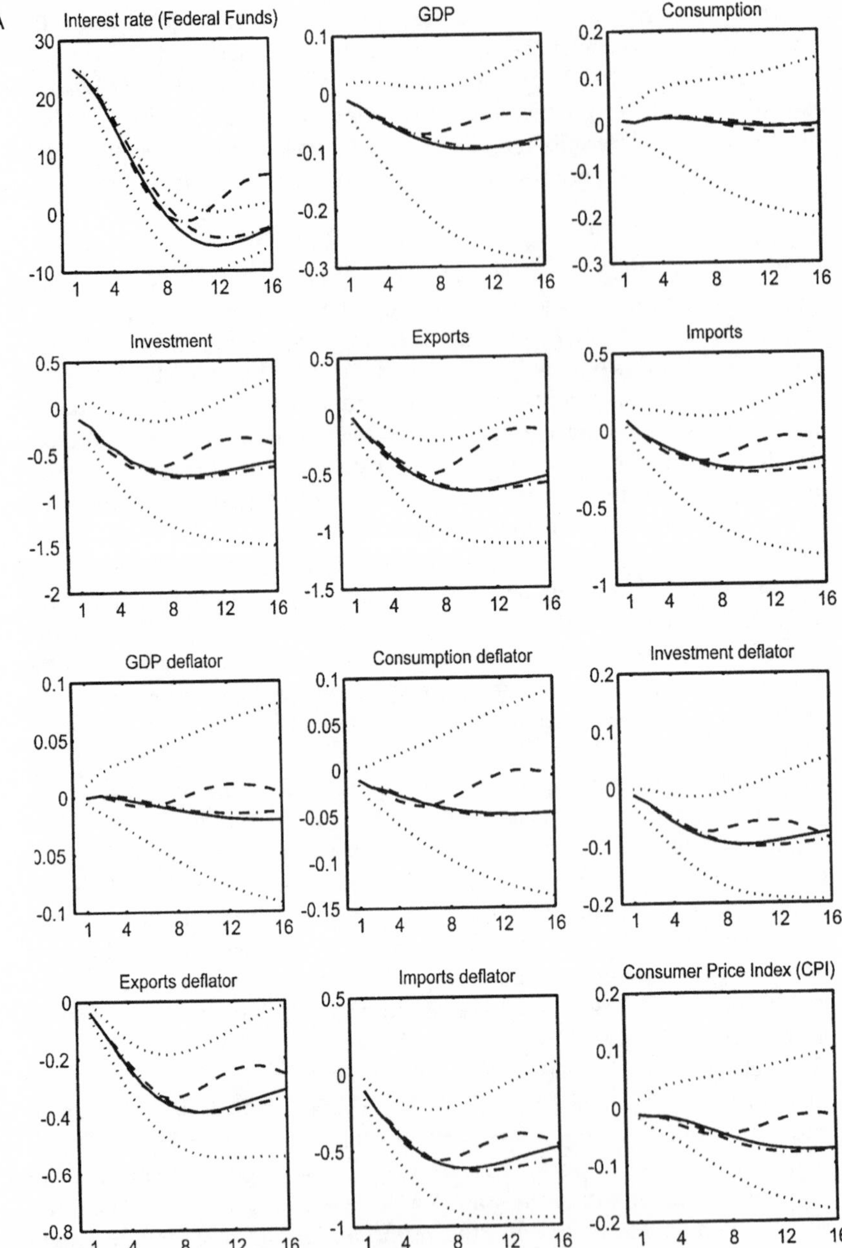

Fig. 8.2 Impulse responses to an identified monetary policy shock

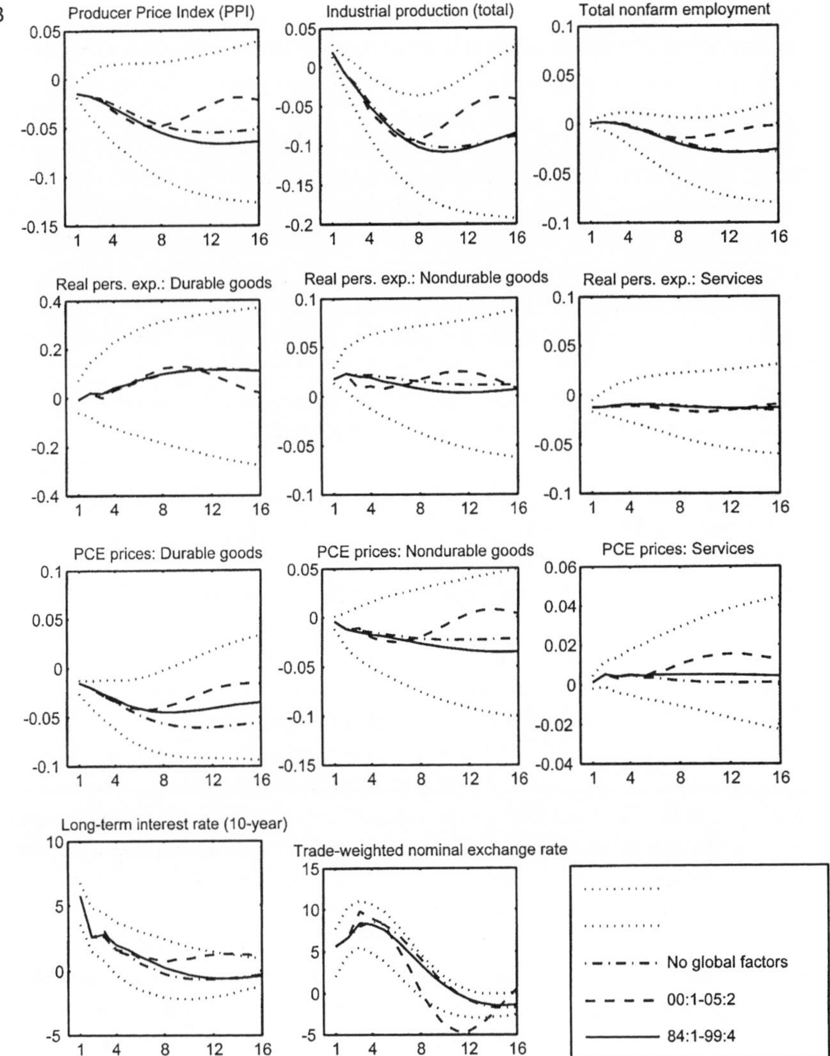

Fig. 8.2 (cont.)

be explained by a drop in foreign demand for U.S. goods, due both to an appreciating U.S. dollar and to a slowing foreign economy.

8.4.4 Has the Role of Global Forces on the U.S. Monetary Transmission Changed?

We find little overall evidence that global forces have had an important effect on the U.S. monetary transmission mechanism, and find little evidence of change over the last several years. To determine to what extent the response of macroeconomic variables to a monetary tightening has changed recently, we compare the impulse responses based on the FAVAR involving the link between domestic and international factors as estimated since 2000 (dashed lines) to those based on international factors in the 1984 to 1999 period (solid lines). One interesting conclusion that emerges from this exercise is that the variables display in both cases almost identical responses in the first six to seven quarters following the shock. After that, the responses based on the most recent international factors reveal a slightly more rapid return to the initial level. The output and various measures of prices, for instance, show less persistent responses to the monetary tightening. But most changes are not statistically significant. Only for the Federal funds rate, the long-term interest rate, and the exchange rate do we have sharper evidence that the impulse responses have changed after three or four years, when using the more recent factors. And the expectation of a higher Federal funds rate three or more years following the shock is reflected in a slightly higher value of the ten-year yield.

The changes in the impulse responses just documented were obtained by allowing a different relationship between the U.S. and international factors starting in year 2000. For robustness, we checked with alternative break dates, and found that in all cases, the changes were similar or smaller than those reported in the figures. This suggests that if there has been a change in the response to monetary policy shock, this phenomenon is very recent.

In brief, we found no evidence that the responses of a large number of key U.S. variables to monetary policy shocks have changed in the first six to seven quarters following the shock. However, we found some evidence that the relationship between U.S. and international factors has changed in such a way as to imply a lower persistence in the response to monetary policy shocks eight or more quarters after the shock.

How important are global forces for the monetary transmission? When the Federal Reserve changes the course of monetary policy, it affects both U.S. and international factors. The response of the latter may in turn constrain the response of the U.S. economy. A crude way of assessing the role of global forces in the transmission of U.S. monetary policy is to report the responses of U.S. macroeconomic variables to a monetary policy shock, but assume that the U.S. factors do not respond to global factors. Specifically, we compute the responses of the monetary shock by setting to zero the submatrices ψ_{21} and ψ_{21}^{d}, referring to the international factors C_t^*. These impulse responses that abstract from international factors are shown with dashed-dotted lines in figure 8.2, panels A and B.

A striking conclusion is that these responses almost perfectly replicate those estimated with the international factors in the 1984 to 1999 period (solid lines). It follows that the global factors in that period do not seem to have more than a marginal impact on the response of the U.S. economy to monetary shocks. Of course, we are *not* saying that global factors do not have an impact on the economy, and that the Federal Reserve does not need to give any consideration to the international economic situation. In fact, as we reported in the previous section, several key variables *are* strongly correlated with international factors. Our results suggest, however, that *conditional on changing the Federal funds rate* in a particular way, the response of the main U.S. macroeconomic variables have been little affected by the response of international factors.

It is important, however, to keep in mind that in the counterfactual experiment just described, as well as in our assessment of the change over time in the effect of foreign factors, we assume that the coefficients measuring the response of U.S. variables to U.S. factors as well as those characterizing the dynamics of the U.S. factors do not change. While we would in principle want to allow for possible changes over time in the latter coefficients, such exercises are unfortunately unlikely to provide reliable results in our empirical model, given the number of extra parameters that we would need to estimate, and given our relatively short sample. Such an assumption may well not be satisfied. For instance, several authors have argued that the slope of the Phillips curve relating U.S. inflation to domestic measures of marginal costs or of activity may have changed following the greater economic integration of the United States with the rest of the world. However, Sbordone (chapter 10, this volume) and Woodford (chapter 1, this volume) argue, in simple calibrated models, that such changes are unlikely to be large. Another possibility is that the processes determining expectations about future domestic variables be altered by the greater openness of the domestic economy. By not letting the relationships among domestic variables change in our empirical model with the increased globalization, we are technically subject to the Lucas critique. One would thus need a fully-specified forward-looking structural model to account for this issue.

8.5 Conclusion

It has been widely documented that international trade has continued to advance, and that the globalization of finance has seen an extraordinary expansion since the mid-1980s. In this context, several observers have argued that global factors may now have a greater influence than in the past on the determination of key U.S. macroeconomic variables, and that conditions in international capital markets may impose more constraints on the transmission of monetary policy.

In this chapter, we have attempted to quantify the changes in the relationship between international forces and the U.S. economy over the 1984 to 2005 period. To do so, we have used an empirical model that allows us to summarize the macroeconomic conditions of the U.S. economy and of the rest of the world with a small number of factors. This framework allows us to quantify the extent of comovement between many key U.S. macroeconomic variables and international factors. It allows us to characterize empirically the transmission of monetary policy shocks to a large set of macroeconomic indicators.

Our findings can be summarized as follows. First, we find that common factors capture, on average, a sizable fraction of the fluctuations in U.S. macroeconomic indicators. This provides support to the use of our empirical model. Second, there is evidence that the role of international factors in explaining U.S. variables has been changing over the 1984 to 2005 period, but this evolution is not systematic across series, and it is difficult to see a pattern suggesting that international factors have become generally more important. Some variables such as the long-term interest rates, as well as import and export prices, however, do display a systematic increase of their correlation with global factors throughout our sample.

We do not find strong statistical evidence of a significant change in the transmission mechanism of monetary policy due to global forces. Taking our point estimates literally, global forces do not seem to have played an important role in the U.S. monetary transmission mechanism between 1984 and 1999. This does not mean that global factors do not have an impact on the economy, as other shocks, such as international shocks, may have an important effect on U.S. economic variables. However, our results suggest that *conditional on a monetary policy shock* in the United States, the response of the main U.S. macroeconomic variables have been little affected by the response of international factors.

In addition, since the year 2000, the initial response of the U.S. economy following a monetary policy shock—the first six to eight quarters—is essentially the same as the one that has been observed in the 1984 to 1999 period. However, point estimates suggest that the growing importance of global forces might have contributed to reducing some of the persistence in the responses, two or more years after the shocks.

Overall, we conclude that if global forces have had an effect on the monetary transmission mechanism, this is a recent phenomenon. This means, however, that we will need more data before we can get strong statistical conclusions on this question.

Appendix

Data Sets

1—U.S. Macroeconomic Series

Format contains series number; series mnemonic; data span (in quarters); transformation code; and series description as appears in the database. The transformation codes are: 1—no transformation; 2—first difference; 4—logarithm; 5—first difference of logarithm. Second differencing of logarithms was not used. Our main data set contains seventeen quarterly series and 112 monthly series with no missing observations. Quarterly averages of monthly series were taken. The series were taken from DRI/McGraw Hill's Basic Economics database, and Data Insight's U.S. Central database.

National Income and Products Accounts (NIPA)

1	GDPR.Q	1983:4–2005:2	5	Real Gross Domestic Product Billions of Chained (2000) Dollars, SAAR
2	CR.Q	1983:4–2005:2	5	Real Personal Consumption Expenditures Billions of Chained (2000) Dollars, SAAR
3	IR.Q	1983:4–2005:2	5	Real Gross Private Domestic Investment Billions of Chained (2000) Dollars, SAAR
4	XR.Q	1983:4–2005:2	5	Real Exports Billions of Chained (2000) Dollars, SAAR
5	MR.Q	1983:4–2005:2	5	Real Imports Billions of Chained (2000) Dollars, SAAR
6	GR.Q	1983:4–2005:2	5	Real Government Consumption Exp. & Gross Invest., Bil. of Chained (2000) Dollars, SAAR
7	X.Q	1983:4–2005:2	5	Exports of Goods and Services Billions of Dollars, SAAR
8	XFY.Q	1983:4–2005:2	5	Income Receipts from the Rest of the World Billions of Dollars, SAAR
9	M.Q	1983:4–2005:2	5	Imports of Goods and Services Billions of Dollars, SAAR
10	MFY.Q	1983:4–2005:2	5	Income payments to the Rest of the World Billions of Dollars, SAAR
11	MTAXATRF.Q	1983:4–2005:2	5	Current Taxes And Transfer Payments to Rest of the World (net) Bil. of Dollars, SAAR
12	JPGDP.Q	1983:4–2005:2	5	Gross Domestic Product Price Index (2000 = 100), SA
13	JPC.Q	1983:4–2005:2	5	Personal Consumption Expenditures Price Index (2000 = 100), SA
14	JPI.Q	1983:4–2005:2	5	Gross Private Domestic Investment Price Index (2000 = 100), SAAR
15	JPX.Q	1983:4–2005:2	5	Exports Price Index (2000 = 100), SA
16	JPM.Q	1983:4–2005:2	5	Imports Price Index (2000 = 100), SA
17	JPG.Q	1983:4–2005:2	5	Government Consumption Expenditures & Gross Investment Price Index (2000 = 100), SA

OUT—Real Output and Income

18	IPS11	1983:4–2005:2	5	Industrial Production Index–Products, Total
19	IPS299	1983:4–2005:2	5	Industrial Production Index–Final Products
20	IPS12	1983:4–2005:2	5	Industrial Production Index–Consumer Goods

21	IPS13	1983:4–2005:2	5	Industrial Production Index–Durable Consumer Goods
22	IPS18	1983:4–2005:2	5	Industrial Production Index–Nondurable Consumer Goods
23	IPS25	1983:4–2005:2	5	Industrial Production Index–Business Equipment
24	IPS32	1983:4–2005:2	5	Industrial Production Index–Materials
25	IPS34	1983:4–2005:2	5	Industrial Production Index–Durable Goods Materials
26	IPS38	1983:4–2005:2	5	Industrial Production Index–Nondurable Goods Materials
27	IPS43	1983:4–2005:2	5	Industrial Production Index–Manufacturing (SIC)
28	IPS67e	1983:4–2005:2	5	Industrial Production Index–Mining NAICS = 21
29	IPS68e	1983:4–2005:2	5	Industrial Production Index–Electric and Gas Utilities
30	IPS10	1983:4–2005:2	5	Industrial Production Index–Total Index
31	PMI	1983:4–2005:2	5	Purchasing Managers' Index (SA)
32	PMP	1983:4–2005:2	5	NAPM Production Index (Percent)
33	PYQ	1983:4–2005:2	5	Personal Income (Chained) (Bil 2000$, SAAR)
34	MYXPQ	1983:4–2005:2	5	Personal Income Less Transfer Payments (Chained) (Bil 2000$, SAAR)
35	IPS307	1983:4–2005:2	5	Industrial Production Index–Residential Utilities
36	IPS316	1983:4–2005:2	5	Industrial Production Index–Basic Metals
EMP—Employment and Hours				
37	LHEL	1983:4–2005:2	5	Index of Help-Wanted Advertising in Newspapers (1967 = 100; SA)
38	LHELX	1983:4–2005:2	4	Employment: Ratio; Help-Wanted Ads: No. Unemployed Clf
39	LHEM	1983:4–2005:2	5	Civilian Labor Force: Employed, Total (Thous., SA)
40	LHNAG	1983:4–2005:2	5	Civilian Labor Force: Employed, Nonagric. Industries (Thous., SA)
41	LHUR	1983:4–2005:2	1	Unemployment Rate: All Workers, 16 Years & Over (%, SA)
42	LHU680	1983:4–2005:2	1	Unemploy. by Duration: Average (Mean) Duration in Weeks (SA)
43	LHU5	1983:4–2005:2	1	Unemploy. by Duration: Persons Unempl. Less Than 5 Wks (Thous., SA)
44	LHU14	1983:4–2005:2	1	Unemploy. by Duration: Persons Unempl. 5 To 14 Wks (Thous., SA)
45	LHU15	1983:4–2005:2	1	Unemploy. by Duration: Persons Unempl. 15 Wks + (Thous., SA)
46	LHU26	1983:4–2005:2	1	Unemploy. by Duration: Persons Unempl. 15 To 26 Wks (Thous., SA)
47	BLS_LPNAG	1983:4–2005:2	5	Total Nonfarm Employment (SA)–CES0000000001

48 BLS_LP	1983:4–2005:2	5	Total Private Employment (SA)–CES0500000001
49 BLS_LPGD	1983:4–2005:2	5	Goods-Producing Employment (SA)–CES0600000001
50 BLS_LPMI	1983:4–2005:2	5	Natural Resources and Mining Employment (SA)–CES1000000001
51 BLS_LPCC	1983:4–2005:2	5	Construction Employment (SA)–CES2000000001
52 BLS_LPEM	1983:4–2005:2	5	Manufacturing Employment (SA)–CES3000000001
53 BLS_LPED	1983:4–2005:2	5	Durable Goods Manufacturing Employment (SA)–CES3100000001
54 BLS_LPEN	1983:4–2005:2	5	Nondurable Goods Manufacturing Employment (SA)–CES3200000001
55 BLS_Ser.-EMP	1983:4–2005:2	5	Service-Providing Employment (SA)–CES0700000001
56 BLS_Tra.EMP	1983:4–2005:2	5	Trade, Transportation, and Utilities Employment (SA)–CES4000000001
57 BLS_Ret.-EMP	1983:4–2005:2	5	Retail Trade Employment (SA)–CES4200000001
58 BLS_Whol. EMP	1983:4–2005:2	5	Wholesale Trade Employment (SA)–CES4142000001
59 BLS_Fin.-EMP	1983:4–2005:2	5	Financial Activities Employment (SA)–CES5500000001
60 BLS_P-Ser.EMP	1983:4–2005:2	5	Private Service-Providing Employment (SA)–CES0800000001
61 BLS_LPGOV	1983:4–2005:2	5	Government Employment (SA)–CES9000000001
62 BLS_LPHRM	1983:4–2005:2	1	Manufacturing Average Weekly Hours of Production Workers (SA)–CES3000000005
63 BLS_LPMOSA	1983:4–2005:2	1	Manufacturing Average Weekly Overtime of Production Workers (SA)–CES3000000007
64 PMEMP	1983:4–2005:2		NAPM Employment Index (Percent)

HSS—Housing Starts and Sales

65 HSFR	1983:4–2005:2	4	Housing Starts: Nonfarm (1947–1958); Total Farm & Nonfarm (1959–); (Thous. U., SA)
66 HSNE	1983:4–2005:2	4	Housing Starts: Northeast (Thous. U., SA)
67 HSMW	1983:4–2005:2	4	Housing Starts: Midwest (Thous. U., SA)
68 HSSOU	1983:4–2005:2	4	Housing Starts: South (Thous. U., SA)
69 HSWST	1983:4–2005:2	4	Housing Starts: West (Thous. U., SA)
70 HSBR	1983:4–2005:2	4	Housing Authorized: Total New Private Housing Units (Thous., SAAR)
71 HMOB	1983:4–2005:2	4	Mobile Homes: Manufacturers' Shipments (Thous. U., SAAR)

INV—Real Inventories and Inventory-Sales Ratios

72 PMNV	1983:4–2005:2	1	NAPM Inventories Index (Percent)

ORD—Orders and Unfilled Orders

73 PMNO	1983:4–2005:2	1	NAPM New Orders Index (Percent)
74 PMDEL	1983:4–2005:2	1	NAPM Vendor Deliveries Index (Percent)
75 MOCMQ	1983:4–2005:2	5	New Orders (Net)–Consumer Goods & Materials, 1996 Dollars (BCI)
76 MSONDQ	1983:4–2005:2	5	New Orders, Nondefense Capital Goods, In 1996 Dollars (BCI)

SPR—Stock Prices

77 FSPCOM	1983:4–2005:2	5	S&P's Common Stock Price Index: Composite (1941–1943 = 10)
78 FSPIN	1983:4–2005:2	5	S&P's Common Stock Price Index: Industrials (1941–1943 = 10)
79 FSDXP	1983:4–2005:2	1	S&P's Composite Common Stock: Dividend Yield (% Per Annum)
80 FSPXE	1983:4–2005:2	1	S&P's Composite Common Stock: Price-Earnings Ratio (%, NSA)
81 FSDJ	1983:4–2005:2		Common Stock Prices: Dow Jones Industrial Average

EXR—Exchange Rates

82 JRXTWCNS@06.M	1983:4–2005:2	1	Trade-weighted value of the U.S. Dollar (Nominal, 1995 = 100)
83 EXRSW	1983:4–2005:2	5	Foreign Exchange Rate: Switzerland (Swiss Franc Per U.S.$)
84 EXRJAN	1983:4–2005:2	5	Foreign Exchange Rate: Japan (Yen Per U.S.$)
85 EXRUK	1983:4–2005:2	5	Foreign Exchange Rate: United Kingdom (Cents Per Pound)
86 EXRCAN	1983:4–2005:2	5	Foreign Exchange Rate: Canada (Canadian $ Per U.S.$)

INT—Interest Rates

87 FYFF	1983:4–2005:2	1	Interest Rate: Federal Funds (Effective) (% Per Annum, NSA)
88 FYGM3	1983:4–2005:2	1	Interest Rate: U.S. Treasury Bills, Sec Mkt, 3–Mo. (% Per Ann., NSA)
89 FYGM6	1983:4–2005:2	1	Interest Rate: U.S. Treasury Bills, Sec Mkt, 6–Mo. (% Per Ann., NSA)
90 FYGT1	1983:4–2005:2	1	Interest Rate: U.S. Treasury Const Maturities, 1–Yr. (% Per Ann., NSA)
91 FYGT5	1983:4–2005:2	1	Interest Rate: U.S. Treasury Const Maturities, 5–Yr. (% Per Ann., NSA)
92 FYGT10	1983:4–2005:2	1	Interest Rate: U.S. Treasury Const Maturities, 10–Yr. (% Per Ann., NSA)
93 FYAAAC	1983:4–2005:2	1	Bond Yield: Moody's AAA Corporate (% Per Annum)
94 FYBAAC	1983:4–2005:2	1	Bond Yield: Moody's BAA Corporate (% Per Annum)
95 SFYGM3	1983:4–2005:2	1	Spread FYGM3–FYFF

96 SFYGM6	1983:4–2005:2	1	Spread FYGM6–FYFF
97 SFYGT1	1983:4–2005:2	1	Spread FYGT1–FYFF
98 SFYGT5	1983:4–2005:2	1	Spread FYGT5–FYFF
99 SFYGT10	1983:4–2005:2	1	Spread FYGT10–FYFF
100 SFYAAAC	1983:4–2005:2	1	Spread FYAAAC–FYFF
101 SFYBAAC	1983:4–2005:2	1	Spread FYBAAC–FYFF

MON—Money and Credit Quantity Aggregates

102 FM1	1983:4–2005:2	5	Money Stock: M1(Curr, Trav.Cks, Dem Dep, Other Ck'able Dep) (Bil$, SA)
103 FM2	1983:4–2005:2	5	Money Stock: M2(M1 + O'nite Rps, Euro$, G/P&B/D Mmmfs&SAv&Sm Time Dep (Bil$, SA)
104 FM3	1983:4–2005:2	5	Money Stock: M3(M2 + Lg Time Dep, Term Rp's&Inst nnly Mmmfs) (Bil$, SA)
105 FM2DQ	1983:4–2005:2	5	Money Supply–M2 in 1996 Dollars (BCI)
106 FMFBA	1983:4–2005:2	5	Monetary Base, Adj for Reserve Requirement Changes (Mil$, SA)
107 FMRRA	1983:4–2005:2	5	Depository Inst Reserves: Total, Adj For Reserve Req Chgs (Mil$, SA)
108 FMRNBA	1983:4–2005:2	5	Depository Inst Reserves: Nonborrowed, Adj Res Req Chgs (Mil$, SA)
109 FCLBMC	1983:4–2005:2	1	Wkly Rp Lg Com'l Banks: Net Change Com'l & Indus Loans (Bil$, SAAR)
110 CCINRV	1983:4–2005:2	5	Consumer Credit Outstanding–Nonrevolving (G19)
111 IMFCLNQ	1983:4–2005:2		Commercial & Industrial Loans Outstanding in 1996 Dollars

PRI—Price Indexes

112 PMCP	1983:4–2005:2	1	NAPM Commodity Prices Index (Percent)
113 PWFSA	1983:4–2005:2	5	Producer Price Index: Finished Goods (82 = 100, SA)
114 PWFCSA	1983:4–2005:2	5	Producer Price Index: Finished Consumer Goods (82 = 100, SA)
115 PWIMSA	1983:4–2005:2	5	Producer Price Index: Intermed Mat. Supplies & Components (82 = 100, SA)
116 PWCMSA	1983:4–2005:2	5	Producer Price Index: Crude Materials (82 = 100, SA)
117 PUNEW	1983:4–2005:2	5	CPI-U: All Items (82–84 = 100, SA)
118 PU83	1983:4–2005:2	5	CPI-U: Apparel & Upkeep (82–84 = 100, SA)
119 PU84	1983:4–2005:2	5	CPI-U: Transportation (82–84 = 100, SA)
120 PU85	1983:4–2005:2	5	CPI-U: Medical Care (82–84 = 100, SA)
121 PUC	1983:4–2005:2	5	CPI-U: Commodities (82–84 = 100, SA)
122 PUCD	1983:4–2005:2	5	CPI-U: Durables (82–84 = 100, SA)
123 PUXF	1983:4–2005:2	5	CPI-U: All Items Less Food (82–84 = 100, SA)
124 PUXHS	1983:4–2005:2	5	CPI-U: All Items Less Shelter (82–84 = 100, SA)

125 PUXM	1983:4–2005:2	5	CPI-U: All Items Less Medical Care (82–84 = 100, SA)
126 PSCCOM	1983:4–2005:2	5	Spot Market Price Index: BLS & CRB: All Commodities (1967 = 100)

AHE—Average Hourly Earnings

127 BLS_LEHCC	1983:4–2005:2	5	Construction Average Hourly Earnings of Production Workers (SA)–CES2000000006
128 BLS_LEHM	1983:4–2005:2	5	Manufacturing Average Hourly Earnings of Production Workers (SA)–CES3000000006

OTH—Miscellaneous

129 HHSNTN	1983:4–2005:2	1	U. of Michigan Index of Consumer Expectations (Bcd-83)

2—U.S. Personal Consumption Expenditures (Price Indexes and Nominal Expenditure)

Format is as previously: series number; series; data span (in quarters); transformation code; and series description as appears in the database. The transformation for all data was first difference of logarithms, which is coded as 5. This data set contains 194 monthly price series on Personal Consumption Expenditures with no missing observations, and 194 monthly real consumption series on Personal Consumption Expenditures. Quarterly averages were taken of all series. We describe here the 194 price series. The 194 corresponding real consumption series were ordered and transformed in a similar fashion. Series were downloaded from the underlying tables of the Bureau of Economic Analysis.

1	P1NDCG3	1983:4–2005:2	5	New domestic autos
2	P1NFCG3	1983:4–2005:2	5	New foreign autos
3	P1NETG3	1983:4–2005:2	5	Net transactions in used autos
4	P1MARG3	1983:4–2005:2	5	Net purchases of used autos: Used auto margin
5	P1REEG3	1983:4–2005:2	5	Net purchases of used autos: Employee reimbursement
6	P1TRUG3	1983:4–2005:2	5	Trucks, new and net used
7	P1REVG3	1983:4–2005:2	5	Recreational vehicles
8	P1TATG3	1983:4–2005:2	5	Tires and tubes
9	P1PAAG3	1983:4–2005:2	5	Accessories and parts
10	P1FNRG3	1983:4–2005:2	5	Furniture, including mattresses and bedsprings
11	P1MHAG3	1983:4–2005:2	5	Major household appliances
12	P1SEAG3	1983:4–2005:2	5	Small electric appliances
13	P1CHNG3	1983:4–2005:2	5	China, glassware, tableware, and utensils
14	P1RADG3	1983:4–2005:2	5	Video and audio goods, including musical instruments, and computer goods
15	P1FLRG3	1983:4–2005:2	5	Floor coverings

16	P1CLFG3	1983:4–2005:2	5	Clocks, lamps, and furnishings
17	P1TEXG3	1983:4–2005:2	5	Blinds, rods, and other
18	P1WTRG3	1983:4–2005:2	5	Writing equipment
19	P1HDWG3	1983:4–2005:2	5	Tools, hardware, and supplies
20	P1LWNG3	1983:4–2005:2	5	Outdoor equipment and supplies
21	P1OPTG3	1983:4–2005:2	5	Ophthalmic products and orthopedic appliances
22	P1GUNG3	1983:4–2005:2	5	Guns
23	P1SPTG3	1983:4–2005:2	5	Sporting equipment
24	P1CAMG3	1983:4–2005:2	5	Photographic equipment
25	P1BCYG3	1983:4–2005:2	5	Bicycles
26	P1MCYG3	1983:4–2005:2	5	Motorcycles
27	P1BOAG3	1983:4–2005:2	5	Pleasure boats
28	P1AIRG3	1983:4–2005:2	5	Pleasure aircraft
29	P1JRYG3	1983:4–2005:2	5	Jewelry and watches
30	P1BKSG3	1983:4–2005:2	5	Books and maps
31	P1GRAG3	1983:4–2005:2	5	Cereals
32	P1BAKG3	1983:4–2005:2	5	Bakery products
33	P1BEEG3	1983:4–2005:2	5	Beef and veal
34	P1PORG3	1983:4–2005:2	5	Pork
35	P1MEAG3	1983:4–2005:2	5	Other meats
36	P1POUG3	1983:4–2005:2	5	Poultry
37	P1FISG3	1983:4–2005:2	5	Fish and seafood
38	P1GGSG3	1983:4–2005:2	5	Eggs
39	P1MILG3	1983:4–2005:2	5	Fresh milk and cream
40	P1DAIG3	1983:4–2005:2	5	Processed dairy products
41	P1FRUG3	1983:4–2005:2	5	Fresh fruits
42	P1VEGG3	1983:4–2005:2	5	Fresh vegetables
43	P1PFVG3	1983:4–2005:2	5	Processed fruits and vegetables
44	P1JNBG3	1983:4–2005:2	5	Juices and nonalcoholic drinks
45	P1CTMG3	1983:4–2005:2	5	Coffee, tea, and beverage materials
46	P1FATG3	1983:4–2005:2	5	Fats and oils
47	P1SWEG3	1983:4–2005:2	5	Sugar and sweets
48	P1OFDG3	1983:4–2005:2	5	Other foods
49	P1PEFG3	1983:4–2005:2	5	Pet food
50	P1MLTG3	1983:4–2005:2	5	Beer and ale, at home
51	P1WING3	1983:4–2005:2	5	Wine and brandy, at home
52	P1LIQG3	1983:4–2005:2	5	Distilled spirits, at home
53	P1ESLG3	1983:4–2005:2	5	Elementary and secondary school lunch
54	P1HSLG3	1983:4–2005:2	5	Higher education school lunch
55	P1OPMG3	1983:4–2005:2	5	Other purchased meals
56	P1APMG3	1983:4–2005:2	5	Alcohol in purchased meals
57	P1CFDG3	1983:4–2005:2	5	Food supplied to employees: civilians
58	P1MFDG3	1983:4–2005:2	5	Food supplied to employees: military
59	P1FFDG3	1983:4–2005:2	5	Food produced and consumed on farms
60	P1SHUG3	1983:4–2005:2	5	Shoes
61	P1WGCG3	1983:4–2005:2	5	Clothing for females
62	P1WICG3	1983:4–2005:2	5	Clothing for infants
63	P1WSGG3	1983:4–2005:2	5	Sewing goods for females
64	P1WUGG3	1983:4–2005:2	5	Luggage for females
65	P1MBCG3	1983:4–2005:2	5	Clothing for males
66	P1MSGG3	1983:4–2005:2	5	Sewing goods for males

67	P1MUGG3	1983:4–2005:2	5	Luggage for males
68	P1MICG3	1983:4–2005:2	5	Standard clothing issued to military personnel (n.d.)
69	P1GASG3	1983:4–2005:2	5	Gasoline and other motor fuel
70	P1LUBG3	1983:4–2005:2	5	Lubricants
71	P1OILG3	1983:4–2005:2	5	Fuel oil
72	P1LPGG3	1983:4–2005:2	5	Liquefied petroleum gas and other fuel
73	P1TOBG3	1983:4–2005:2	5	Tobacco products
74	P1SOAG3	1983:4–2005:2	5	Soap
75	P1CSMG3	1983:4–2005:2	5	Cosmetics and perfumes
76	P1OPHG3	1983:4–2005:2	5	Other personal hygiene goods
77	P1SDHG3	1983:4–2005:2	5	Semidurable house furnishings
78	P1CLEG3	1983:4–2005:2	5	Cleaning preparations
79	P1LIGG3	1983:4–2005:2	5	Lighting supplies
80	P1PAPG3	1983:4–2005:2	5	Paper products
81	P1RXDG3	1983:4–2005:2	5	Prescription drugs
82	P1NRXG3	1983:4–2005:2	5	Nonprescription drugs
83	P1MDSG3	1983:4–2005:2	5	Medical supplies
84	P1GYNG3	1983:4–2005:2	5	Gynecological goods
85	P1DOLG3	1983:4–2005:2	5	Toys, dolls, and games
86	P1AMMG3	1983:4–2005:2	5	Sport supplies, including ammunition
87	P1FLMG3	1983:4–2005:2	5	Film and photo supplies
88	P1STSG3	1983:4–2005:2	5	Stationery and school supplies
89	P1GREG3	1983:4–2005:2	5	Greeting cards
90	P1ARTG3	1983:4–2005:2	5	Expenditures abroad by U.S. residents: Government expenditures abroad
91	P1ARSG3	1983:4–2005:2	5	Expenditures abroad by U.S. residents: Other private services
92	P1REMG3	1983:4–2005:2	5	Less: Personal remittances in kind to nonresidents
93	P1MGZG3	1983:4–2005:2	5	Magazines and sheet music
94	P1NWPG3	1983:4–2005:2	5	Newspapers
95	P1FLOG3	1983:4–2005:2	5	Flowers, seeds, and potted plants
96	P1OMHG3	1983:4–2005:2	5	Owner-occupied mobile homes
97	P1OSTG3	1983:4–2005:2	5	Owner-occupied stationary homes
98	P1TMHG3	1983:4–2005:2	5	Tenant-occupied mobile homes
99	P1TSPG3	1983:4–2005:2	5	Tenant-occupied stationary homes
100	P1TLDG3	1983:4–2005:2	5	Tenant landlord durables
101	P1FARG3	1983:4–2005:2	5	Rental value of farm dwellings
102	P1HOTG3	1983:4–2005:2	5	Hotels and motels
103	P1HFRG3	1983:4–2005:2	5	Clubs and fraternity housing
104	P1HHEG3	1983:4–2005:2	5	Higher education housing
105	P1HESG3	1983:4–2005:2	5	Elem. and second. education housing
106	P1TGRG3	1983:4–2005:2	5	Tenant group room and board
107	P1TGLG3	1983:4–2005:2	5	Tenant group employee lodging
108	P1ELCG3	1983:4–2005:2	5	Electricity
109	P1NGSG3	1983:4–2005:2	5	Gas
110	P1WSMG3	1983:4–2005:2	5	Water and sewerage maintenance
111	P1REFG3	1983:4–2005:2	5	Refuse collection
112	P1LOCG3	1983:4–2005:2	5	Local and cellular telephone
113	P1INCG3	1983:4–2005:2	5	Intrastate toll calls
114	P1ITCG3	1983:4–2005:2	5	Interstate toll calls

115	P1DMCG3	1983:4–2005:2	5	Domestic service, cash
116	P1DMIG3	1983:4–2005:2	5	Domestic service, in kind
117	P1MSEG3	1983:4–2005:2	5	Moving and storage
118	P1FIPG3	1983:4–2005:2	5	Household insurance premiums
119	P1FIBG3	1983:4–2005:2	5	Less: Household insurance benefits paid
120	P1RCLG3	1983:4–2005:2	5	Rug and furniture cleaning
121	P1EREG3	1983:4–2005:2	5	Electrical repair
122	P1FREG3	1983:4–2005:2	5	Reupholstery and furniture repair
123	P1PSTG3	1983:4–2005:2	5	Postage
124	P1MHOG3	1983:4–2005:2	5	Household operation services, n.e.c.
125	P1ARPG3	1983:4–2005:2	5	Motor vehicle repair
126	P1RLOG3	1983:4–2005:2	5	Motor vehicle rental, leasing, and other
127	P1TOLG3	1983:4–2005:2	5	Bridge, tunnel, ferry, and road tolls
128	P1AING3	1983:4–2005:2	5	Insurance premiums for user-operated transportation
129	P1IMTG3	1983:4–2005:2	5	Local transportation: Mass transit systems
130	P1TAXG3	1983:4–2005:2	5	Taxicab
131	P1IRRG3	1983:4–2005:2	5	Railway
132	P1IBUG3	1983:4–2005:2	5	Bus
133	P1IAIG3	1983:4–2005:2	5	Airline
134	P1TROG3	1983:4–2005:2	5	Other
135	P1PHYG3	1983:4–2005:2	5	Physicians
136	P1DENG3	1983:4–2005:2	5	Dentists
137	P1OPSG3	1983:4–2005:2	5	Other professional services
138	P1NPHG3	1983:4–2005:2	5	Hospitals: Nonprofit
139	P1FPHG3	1983:4–2005:2	5	Hospitals: Proprietary
140	P1GVHG3	1983:4–2005:2	5	Hospitals: Government
141	P1NRSG3	1983:4–2005:2	5	Nursing homes
142	P1MING3	1983:4–2005:2	5	Health insurance: Medical care and hospitalization
143	P1IING3	1983:4–2005:2	5	Health insurance: Income loss
144	P1PWCG3	1983:4–2005:2	5	Health insurance: Workers' compensation
145	P1MOVG3	1983:4–2005:2	5	Admissions to motion picture theaters
146	P1LEGG3	1983:4–2005:2	5	Admissions to theaters and opera, and entertainments of nonprofit instit. (except athletics)
147	P1SPEG3	1983:4–2005:2	5	Admissions to spectator sports
148	P1RTVG3	1983:4–2005:2	5	Radio and television repair
149	P1CLUG3	1983:4–2005:2	5	Clubs and fraternal organizations
150	P1SIGG3	1983:4–2005:2	5	Sightseeing
151	P1FLYG3	1983:4–2005:2	5	Private flying
152	P1BILG3	1983:4–2005:2	5	Bowling and billiards
153	P1CASG3	1983:4–2005:2	5	Casino gambling
154	P1OPAG3	1983:4–2005:2	5	Other commercial participant amusements
155	P1PARG3	1983:4–2005:2	5	Pari-mutuel net receipts
156	P1REOG3	1983:4–2005:2	5	Other recreation
157	P1SCLG3	1983:4–2005:2	5	Shoe repair
158	P1DRYG3	1983:4–2005:2	5	Drycleaning
159	P1LGRG3	1983:4–2005:2	5	Laundry and garment repair
160	P1BEAG3	1983:4–2005:2	5	Beauty shops, including combination
161	P1BARG3	1983:4–2005:2	5	Barber shops
162	P1WCRG3	1983:4–2005:2	5	Watch, clock, and jewelry repair

163	P1CRPG3	1983:4–2005:2	5	Miscellaneous personal services
164	P1BROG3	1983:4–2005:2	5	Brokerage charges and investment counseling
165	P1BNKG3	1983:4–2005:2	5	Bank service charges, trust services, and safe deposit box rental
166	P1IMCG3	1983:4–2005:2	5	Commercial banks
167	P1IMNG3	1983:4–2005:2	5	Other financial institutions
168	P1LIFG3	1983:4–2005:2	5	Expense of handling life insurance and pension plans
169	P1GALG3	1983:4–2005:2	5	Legal services
170	P1FUNG3	1983:4–2005:2	5	Funeral and burial expenses
171	P1UNSG3	1983:4–2005:2	5	Labor union expenses
172	P1ASSG3	1983:4–2005:2	5	Profession association expenses
173	P1GENG3	1983:4–2005:2	5	Employment agency fees
174	P1AMOG3	1983:4–2005:2	5	Money orders
175	P1CLAG3	1983:4–2005:2	5	Classified ads
176	P1ACCG3	1983:4–2005:2	5	Tax return preparation services
177	P1THEG3	1983:4–2005:2	5	Personal business services, n.e.c.
178	P1PEDG3	1983:4–2005:2	5	Private higher education
179	P1GEDG3	1983:4–2005:2	5	Public higher education
180	P1ESCG3	1983:4–2005:2	5	Elementary and secondary schools
181	P1NSCG3	1983:4–2005:2	5	Nursery schools
182	P1VEDG3	1983:4–2005:2	5	Commercial and vocational schools
183	P1REDG3	1983:4–2005:2	5	Foundations and nonprofit research
184	P1POLG3	1983:4–2005:2	5	Political organizations
185	P1MUSG3	1983:4–2005:2	5	Museums and libraries
186	P1FOUG3	1983:4–2005:2	5	Foundations to religion and welfare
187	P1WELG3	1983:4–2005:2	5	Social welfare
188	P1RELG3	1983:4–2005:2	5	Religion
189	P1FTRG3	1983:4–2005:2	5	Foreign travel by U.S. residents (110)
190	P1EXFG3	1983:4–2005:2	5	Less: Expenditures in the United States by nonresidents (112)
191	P1TDGG3	1983:4–2005:2	5	Durable goods
192	P1TNDG3	1983:4–2005:2	5	Nondurable goods
193	P1TSSG3	1983:4–2005:2	5	Services
194	PPCE	1983:4–2005:2	5	Personal Consumption Expenditures (all items)

3—U.S. Producer Price Indexes

Format is as previously: series number; series mnemonic (NAICS code); data span (in quarters); transformation code; and series description as appears in the database. Quarterly averages were taken of all series. The transformation for all data was first difference of logarithms, which is coded as 5. This data set contains 154 monthly series with no missing observations. All series are downloaded from the website of BLS.

1	311119	1983:4–2005:2	5	Other animal food manufacturing
2	311119p	1983:4–2005:2	5	Other animal food manufacturing (primary products)
3	311211	1983:4–2005:2	5	Flour milling

4	311212	1983:4–2005:2	5	Rice milling
5	311213	1983:4–2005:2	5	Malt mfg.
6	311223a	1983:4–2005:2	5	Other oilseed processing (cottonseed cake and meal and other byproducts)
7	311225p	1983:4–2005:2	5	Fats and oils refining and blending (primary products)
8	311311	1983:4–2005:2	5	Sugarcane mills
9	311313	1983:4–2005:2	5	Beet sugar manufacturing
10	311412	1983:4–2005:2	5	Frozen specialty food manufacturing
11	311520	1983:4–2005:2	5	Ice cream and frozen dessert mfg.
12	311920	1983:4–2005:2	5	Coffee and tea manufacturing
13	312140	1983:4–2005:2	5	Distilleries
14	32211–	1983:4–2005:2	5	Pulp mills
15	32213–	1983:4–2005:2	5	Paperboard mills
16	325620p	1983:4–2005:2	5	Toilet preparation mfg. (primary products)
17	325920	1983:4–2005:2	5	Explosives manufacturing
18	32731–	1983:4–2005:2	5	Cement mfg.
19	327320	1983:4–2005:2	5	Ready mixed concrete mfg. and dist.
20	327410	1983:4–2005:2	5	Lime
21	327420	1983:4–2005:2	5	Gypsum building products manufacturing
22	327910	1983:4–2005:2	5	Abrasive product manufacturing
23	331210	1983:4–2005:2	5	Iron steel pipe & tube mfg. from purch. steel
24	333210	1983:4–2005:2	5	Sawmill & woodworking machinery mfg.
25	334310	1983:4–2005:2	5	Audio & video equipment mfg.
26	335110	1983:4–2005:2	5	Electric lamp bulb & part mfg.
27	336370	1983:4–2005:2	5	Motor vehicle metal stamping
28	337910	1983:4–2005:2	5	Mattress mfg.
29	311421	1983:4–2005:2	5	Fruit and vegetable canning
30	311423	1983:4–2005:2	5	Dried and dehydrated food manufacturing
31	311513	1983:4–2005:2	5	Cheese manufacturing
32	311611	1983:4–2005:2	5	Animal except poultry slaughtering
33	311612	1983:4–2005:2	5	Meat processed from carcasses
34	311613	1983:4–2005:2	5	Rendering and meat byproduct processing
35	311711	1983:4–2005:2	5	Seafood canning
36	311712	1983:4–2005:2	5	Fresh & frozen seafood processing
37	311813p	1983:4–2005:2	5	Frozen cakes, pies, & other pastries mfg. (primary products)
38	3118233	1983:4–2005:2	5	Dry pasta manufacturing (macaroni, spaghetti, vermicelli, and noodles)
39	312111p	1983:4–2005:2	5	Soft drinks manufacturing (primary products)
40	312221	1983:4–2005:2	5	Cigarettes
41	3122291	1983:4–2005:2	5	Other tobacco product mfg. (cigars)
42	313111	1983:4–2005:2	5	Yarn spinning mills
43	3133111	1983:4–2005:2	5	Broadwoven fabric finishing mills (finished cotton broadwoven fabrics not finished in weaving mills)
44	315111	1983:4–2005:2	5	Sheer hosiery mills
45	315191	1983:4–2005:2	5	Outerwear knitting mills
46	315223	1983:4–2005:2	5	Men's boy's cut & sew shirt excl. work mfg.

47	315224	1983:4–2005:2	5	Men's boy's cut & sew trouser, slack, jean mfg.
48	315993	1983:4–2005:2	5	Men's and boys' neckwear mfg.
49	316211	1983:4–2005:2	5	Rubber and plastic footwear manufacturing
50	316213	1983:4–2005:2	5	Men's footwear excl. athletic mfg.
51	316214	1983:4–2005:2	5	Women's footwear excl. athletic mfg.
52	316992	1983:4–2005:2	5	Women's handbag & purse mfg.
53	321212	1983:4–2005:2	5	Softwood veneer or plywood mfg.
54	3212191	1983:4–2005:2	5	Reconstituted wood product mfg. (particleboard produced at this location)
55	3219181	1983:4–2005:2	5	Other millwork including flooring (wood moldings except prefinished moldings made from purchased moldings)
56	321991	1983:4–2005:2	5	Manufactured homes mobile homes mfg.
57	3221211	1983:4–2005:2	5	Paper except newsprint mills (clay coated printing and converting paper)
58	322214	1983:4–2005:2	5	Fiber can, tube, drum, & other products mfg.
59	324121	1983:4–2005:2	5	Asphalt paving mixture & block mfg.
60	324122	1983:4–2005:2	5	Asphalt shingle & coating materials mfg.
61	324191p	1983:4–2005:2	5	Petroleum lubricating oils and greases (primary products)
62	325181	1983:4–2005:2	5	Alkalies and chlorine
63	3251881	1983:4–2005:2	5	All other basic inorganic chemical manufacturing (sulfuric acid gross new and fortified)
64	3251921	1983:4–2005:2	5	Cyclic crude and intermediate manufacturing (cyclic coal tar intermediates)
65	325212	1983:4–2005:2	5	Synthetic rubber manufacturing
66	325222	1983:4–2005:2	5	Manufactured noncellulosic fibers
67	325314	1983:4–2005:2	5	Fertilizer mixing only manufacturing
68	3254111	1983:4–2005:2	5	Medicinal & botanical mfg. (synthetic organic medicinal chemicals in bulk)
69	3261131	1983:4–2005:2	5	Unsupported plastics film sheet excluding packaging manufacturing
70	326192	1983:4–2005:2	5	Resilient floor covering manufacturing
71	326211	1983:4–2005:2	5	Tire manufacturing except retreading
72	327111	1983:4–2005:2	5	Vitreous plumbing fixtures access ftg. mfg.
73	327121	1983:4–2005:2	5	Brick and structural clay tile
74	327122	1983:4–2005:2	5	Ceramic wall and floor tile
75	327124	1983:4–2005:2	5	Clay refractories
76	327125	1983:4–2005:2	5	Nonclay refractory manufacturing
77	327211	1983:4–2005:2	5	Flat glass manufacturing
78	327213	1983:4–2005:2	5	Glass container manufacturing
79	327331	1983:4–2005:2	5	Concrete block and brick manufacturing
80	3279931	1983:4–2005:2	5	Mineral wool manufacturing
81	331111	1983:4–2005:2	5	Iron and steel mills
82	331112	1983:4–2005:2	5	Electrometallurgical ferroalloy product mfg.
83	331221	1983:4–2005:2	5	Rolled steel shape manufacturing
84	331312	1983:4–2005:2	5	Primary aluminum production

85	331315	1983:4–2005:2	5	Aluminum sheet, plate, & foil mfg.
86	331316	1983:4–2005:2	5	Aluminum extruded products
87	331421	1983:4–2005:2	5	Copper rolling, drawing, & extruding
88	3314913	1983:4–2005:2	5	Other nonferrous metal roll draw extruding (titanium and titanium base alloy mill shapes excluding wire)
89	3314923	1983:4–2005:2	5	Other nonferrous secondary smelt refine alloying (secondary lead)
90	331511	1983:4–2005:2	5	Iron foundries
91	3322121	1983:4–2005:2	5	Hand and edge tools except machine tools and handsaws (mechanics' hand service tools)
92	332213	1983:4–2005:2	5	Saw blade & handsaw mfg.
93	3323111	1983:4–2005:2	5	Prefabricated metal building and component manufacturing (prefabricated metal building systems excluding farm service bldgs. & residential buildings)
94	332321	1983:4–2005:2	5	Metal window and door manufacturing
95	332431	1983:4–2005:2	5	Metal can mfg.
96	324393	1983:4–2005:2	5	Other metal container manufacturing (steel shipping barrels & drums excl. beer barrels more than 12 gallon capacity)
97	332611	1983:4–2005:2	5	Spring heavy gauge mfg.
98	3326122	1983:4–2005:2	5	Spring light gauge mfg. (precision mechanical springs)
99	3327224	1983:4–2005:2	5	Bolt, nut, screw, rivet, & washer mfg. (externally threaded metal fasteners except aircraft)
100	332913	1983:4–2005:2	5	Plumbing fixture fitting & trim mfg.
101	332991	1983:4–2005:2	5	Ball and roller bearings
102	332992	1983:4–2005:2	5	Small arms ammunition mfg.
103	332996	1983:4–2005:2	5	Fabricated pipe & pipe fitting mfg.
104	332998	1983:4–2005:2	5	Enameled iron & metal sanitary ware mfg.
105	333111	1983:4–2005:2	5	Farm machinery & equipment mfg.
106	333131	1983:4–2005:2	5	Mining machinery & equipment mfg.
107	333132	1983:4–2005:2	5	Oil and gas field machinery and equipment mfg.
108	333292	1983:4–2005:2	5	Textile machinery
109	333293	1983:4–2005:2	5	Printing machinery & equipment mfg.
110	3332941	1983:4–2005:2	5	Food products machinery mfg. (dairy and milk products plant machinery)
111	3332981	1983:4–2005:2	5	All other industrial machinery mfg. (chemical manufacturing machinery equip. and parts)
112	3333111	1983:4–2005:2	5	Automatic vending machine mfg. (automatic merchandising machines coin operated excluding parts)
113	333512	1983:4–2005:2	5	Machine tool metal cutting types mfg.
114	333513	1983:4–2005:2	5	Machine tool metal forming types mfg.
115	3335151	1983:4–2005:2	5	Cutting tool & machine tool accessory mfg. (small cutting tools for machine tools and metalworking machinery)

116	333612	1983:4–2005:2	5	Speed changer industrial high speed drive & gear mfg.
117	333618	1983:4–2005:2	5	Other engine equipment mfg.
118	3339111	1983:4–2005:2	5	Pump & pumping equipment mfg. (indus. pumps except hydraulic fluid power pumps)
119	333922	1983:4–2005:2	5	Conveyor & conveying equipment mfg.
120	3339233	1983:4–2005:2	5	Overhead crane hoist & monorail system mfg. (overhead traveling cranes and monorail systems)
121	3339241	1983:4–2005:2	5	Industrial truck, tractor, trailer, stacker, machinery mfg. (industrial trucks and tractors motorized and hand powered)
122	333992	1983:4–2005:2	5	Welding & soldering equipment mfg. (welding & soldering equipment mfg.)
123	333997	1983:4–2005:2	5	Scale & balance except laboratory mfg.
124	334411	1983:4–2005:2	5	Electron tube mfg.
125	334414	1983:4–2005:2	5	Electronic capacitor mfg.
126	334415	1983:4–2005:2	5	Electronic resistor mfg.
127	334417	1983:4–2005:2	5	Electronic connector mfg.
128	3345153	1983:4–2005:2	5	Electricity measuring testing instrument mfg. (test equipment for testing electrical radio & communication circuits & motors)
129	334517p	1983:4–2005:2	5	Irradiation apparatus manufacturing (primary products)
130	3351211	1983:4–2005:2	5	Residential electric lighting fixture mfg. (residential electric lighting fixtures except portable & parts)
131	335122	1983:4–2005:2	5	Commercial electric lighting fixture mfg.
132	335129	1983:4–2005:2	5	Other lighting equipment mfg.
133	335212	1983:4–2005:2	5	Household vacuum cleaner mfg.
134	335221	1983:4–2005:2	5	Household cooking appliance mfg.
135	335311	1983:4–2005:2	5	Power distribution specialty transformer mfg.
136	335312	1983:4–2005:2	5	Motor & generator mfg.
137	335314p	1983:4–2005:2	5	Relay & industrial control mfg. (primary products)
138	335911	1983:4–2005:2	5	Storage battery mfg.
139	3359291	1983:4–2005:2	5	Other communication and energy wire mfg. (power wire and cable made in plants that draw wire)
140	335932	1983:4–2005:2	5	Noncurrent carrying wiring device mfg.
141	335991p	1983:4–2005:2	5	Carbon & graphite product mfg. (primary products)
142	336321p	1983:4–2005:2	5	Vehicular lighting equipment mfg. (primary products)
143	337121	1983:4–2005:2	5	Upholstered household furniture mfg.
144	337122	1983:4–2005:2	5	Wood household furniture except upholstered
145	337124	1983:4–2005:2	5	Metal household furniture
146	337211	1983:4–2005:2	5	Wood office furniture mfg.
147	3372141	1983:4–2005:2	5	Nonwood office furniture (office seating including upholstered nonwood)

148 3399111	1983:4–2005:2	5	Jewelry except costume mfg. (jewelry made of solid platinum metals and solid karat gold)
149 3399123	1983:4–2005:2	5	Silverware & hollowware mfg. (flatware and carving sets made wholly of metal)
150 339931	1983:4–2005:2	5	Doll & stuffed toy mfg.
151 339932	1983:4–2005:2	5	Game toy & children's vehicle mfg.
152 339944	1983:4–2005:2	5	Carbon paper & inked ribbon mfg.
153 3399931	1983:4–2005:2	5	Fastener, button, needle, & pin mfg. (Buttons and parts except for precious or semiprecious metals and stones)
154 3399945	1983:4–2005:2	5	Broom, brush, & mop mfg. (other brushes)

4—International Data

Format is as previously: contains series number; series mnemonic; data span (in quarters); transformation code; and series description as appears in the database. The transformation codes are: 1—no transformation; 2—first difference; 4—logarithm; 5—first difference of logarithm. Our international data set contains fifty quarterly series. The series were taken mainly from Data Insight's International Monetary Fund (IMF) (International Financial Statistics [IFS]), OECD (Main Economic Indictators [MEI]) databases. Some series were obtained from national statistics agencies (NatS), Global Insight (GI), and the European Central Bank (ECB).

America

Brazil				
1 NatS	SCN4_PIBPMAS4	1983:4–2005:2	5	Real Gross Domestic Product, SA (average 1990 = 100)
2 IFS	L64A@C223.M	1983:4–2005:2	5	Consumer Price Index
3 IFS	L60B@C223.Q	1983:4–2005:2	1	Interest Rate, Money Market Rate
Canada				
4 GI	CANSIM 3800002	1983:4–2005:2	5	Real Gross Domestic Product (GDP), Chained $1,997, SAAR
5 IFS	L64@C156.M	1983:4–2005:2	5	Consumer Price Index
6 IFS	L60C@C156.Q	1983:4–2005:2	1	Interest Rate, Treasury Bill Rate
7 IFS	L61@C156.Q	1983:4–2005:2	1	Interest Rate, Govt. Bond Yield, Long Term > 10 years
Mexico				
8 NatS		1983:4–2005:2	5	Real Gross Domestic Product, MIL. 1993 Mexican Pesos
9 IFS	L64@C273.M	1983:4–2005:2	5	Consumer Price Index
10 IFS	L60C@C273.Q	1983:4–2005:2	1	Interest Rate, Treasury Bill Rate

Europe

France				
11 ECB	ESA.Q.FR.Y.0000. B1QG00.1000. TTTT.Q.N.A	1983:4–2005:2	5	Real Gross Domestic Product

12	IFS	L64@C132.M	1983:4–2005:2	5	Consumer Price Index
13	IFS	L60C@C132.Q	1983:4–2005:2	1	Interest Rate, Treasury Bill Rate, 3 months
14	IFS	L61@C132.Q	1983:4–2005:2	1	Interest Rate, Govt. Bond Yield, Long Term
Germany					
15	GI	L99BV&R@C134.Q	1983:4–2005:2	5	Real Gross Domestic Product, Index (2000 = 100)
16	IFS	L64D@C134.M	1983:4–2005:2	5	Consumer Price Index (combined with L64@C134.M)
17	IFS	L60C@C134.Q	1983:4–2005:2	1	Interest Rate, Treasury Bill Rate
18	IFS	L61@C134.Q	1983:4–2005:2	1	Interest Rate, Govt. Bond Yield, Long Term
Italy					
19	ECB	ESA.Q.IT.Y.0000. B1QG00.1000. TTTT.L.N.A	1983:4–2005:2	5	Real Gross Domestic Product, chain linked
20	IFS	L64@C136.M	1983:4–2005:2	5	Consumer Price Index
21	IFS	L60C@C136.Q	1983:4–2005:2	1	Interest Rate, Treasury Bill Rate
22	IFS	L61@C136.Q	1983:4–2005:2	1	Interest Rate, Govt. Bond Yield, Long Term
Netherlands					
23	ECB	ESA.Q.NL.Y.0000. B1QG00.1000. TTTT.Q.N.A	1983:4–2005:2	5	Real Gross Domestic Product, constant prices
24	IFS	L64@C138.M	1983:4–2005:2	5	Consumer Price Index
25	IFS	L61@C138.Q	1983:4–2005:2	1	Interest Rate, Govt. Bond Yield
					United Kingdom
26	ECB	ESA.Q.GB.Y.0000. B1QG00.1000. TTTT.Q.N.A	1983:4–2005:2	5	Real Gross Domestic Product, constant prices
27	IFS	L64@C112.M	1983:4–2005:2	5	Consumer Price Index
28	IFS	L60C@C112.Q	1983:4–2005:2	1	Interest Rate, Treasury Bill Rate
29	IFS	L61@C112.Q	1983:4–2005:2	1	Interest Rate, Govt. Bond Yield, Long Term
Asia					
China[14]					
30	DRI	JGDPRZNS@ CH.Q		*	Real Gross Domestic Product, constant prices
31	IFS	L60L@C924.Q	1983:4–2005:2	1	Interest Rate, Deposit Rate
Hong Kong					
32	IFS	L99B&P&W@ C532.Q	1983:4–2005:2	5	Real Gross Domestic Product, 2000 prices
33	IFS	L64@C532.M	1983:4–2005:2	5	Consumer Price Index
34	DRI	RMIB3S@HK.M	1983:4–2005:2	1	Interest Rate, Interbank Offered Rate

14. For China, real GDP numbers are based on GDP growth numbers from declarative referential integrity (DRI) database and estimates of the level of GDP from Abeysinghe and Gulasekaran (2004). Consumer Price Index: no series starting in 1984 found.

Japan				
35 IFS	L99BV&R@C158.Q	1983:4–2005:2	5	Real Gross Domestic Product, 2000 prices
36 IFS	L64@C158.M	1983:4–2005:2	5	Consumer Price Index
37 MEI	JPN.IR3TCD01.ST	1983:4–2005:2	1	Interest Rate, 3-months' rates on CDs
38 IFS	L61@C158.Q	1983:4–2005:2	1	Interest Rate, Govt. Bond Yield, Long Term
Korea				
39 GI	GDPR@KO.Q	1983:4–2005:2	5	Real Gross Domestic Product, 2000 prices
40 IFS	L64@C542.M	1983:4–2005:2	5	Consumer Price Index
41 IFS	L61@C542.Q	1983:4–2005:2	1	Interest Rate Yield on National Housing Bond
Malaysia				
42 IFS	L99BV&P@C548.Q	1983:4–2005:2	5	Real Gross Domestic Product, 2000 prices
43 IFS	L60C@C548.Q	1983:4–2005:2	1	Interest Rate, Treasury Bill Rate, 3 months
Singapore				
44 GI	GDPR@SI.Q	1983:4–2005:2	5	Real Gross Domestic Product, 2000 prices
45 IFS	L64@C576.M	1983:4–2005:2	5	Consumer Price Index
46 IFS	L60C@C576.Q	1983:4–2005:2	1	Interest Rate, Treasury Bill Rate
Taiwan				
47 NatS		1983:4–2005:2	5	Real Gross Domestic Product, 2001 prices
48 DRI	CPI@TA.M	1983:4–2005:2	5	Consumer Price Index
49 DRI	RMCP180S@TA.Q	1983:4–2005:2	1	Interest Rate, Commercial Papers, 3–6 months, sec. mkt.

References

Abeysinghe, T., and R. Gulasekaran. 2004. Quarterly real GDP estimates for China and ASEAN4 with a forecast evaluation. *Journal of Forecasting* 23 (6): 431–47.

Andrews, D. W. K. 1993. Tests for parameter instability and structural change with unknown change point. *Econometrica* 61 (4): 821–56.

Backus, D. K., P. J. Kehoe, and F. E. Kydland. 1995. International business cycles: Theory and evidence. In *Frontiers of business cycle research,* ed. Thomas F. Cooley, 331–57. Princeton, NJ: Princeton University Press.

Bai, J., and S. Ng. 2006. Confidence intervals for diffusion index forecasts and inference for factor augmented regressions. *Econometrica* 74 (4): 1133–50.

Baxter, M. 1995. International trade and business cycles. In *Handbook of international economics,* vol. 3, ed. G. M. Grossman and K. Rogoff, 1801–64. Amsterdam: North-Holland.

Benigno, G., and B. Pierpaolo. 2001. Monetary policy rules and the exchange rate. Center for Economic Policy Research (CEPR) Discussion Paper no. 2807.

Bergman, U. M., M. D. Bordo, and L. Jonung. 1998. Historical evidence on business cycles: The international experience. In *Beyond shocks: What causes business cycles?* ed. J. C. Fuhrer and S. Schuh, 65–113. Boston, MA: Federal Reserve Bank of Boston, Federal Reserve Bank of Boston Conference Series no. 42.

Bernanke, B. S. 2005. The global saving glut and the U.S. current account deficit. Remarks at the Homer Jones Lecture. 14 April, St. Louis, Missouri.

———. 2007. Globalization and monetary policy. Remarks at the Fourth Economic Summit, Stanford Institute for Economic Policy Research. March Stanford, California.

Bernanke, B. S., J. Boivin, and P. Eliasz. 2005. Measuring monetary policy: A factor augmented vector autoregressive (FAVAR) approach. *Quarterly Journal of Economics* 120 (1): 387–422.

Blanchard, O., and J. Simon. 2001. The long and large decline in U.S. output volatility. *Brookings Papers on Economic Activity* 1: 135–64. Washington, DC: Brookings Institution.

Boivin, J. 2006. Has U.S. monetary policy changed? Evidence from drifting coefficients and real-time data. *Journal of Money, Credit, and Banking* 38 (5): 1149–73.

Boivin, J., and M. P. Giannoni. 2002. Assessing changes in the monetary transmission mechanism: A VAR approach. Federal Reserve Bank of New York, *Economic Policy Review* 8 (1): 97–112.

———. 2006a. DSGE models in a data-rich environment. NBER Working Paper no. 12772. Cambridge, MA: National Bureau of Economic Research, December.

———. 2006b. Has monetary policy become more effective? *Review of Economics and Statistics* 88 (3): 445–62.

Boivin, J., M. P. Giannoni, and I. Mihov. 2009. Sticky prices and monetary policy: Evidence from disaggregated U.S. data. *American Economic Review* 99 (1): 350–84.

Borio, C., and A. Filardo. 2006. Globalisation and inflation: New cross-country evidence on the global determinants of domestic inflation. Bank for International Settlements (BIS), Basel, Switzerland. Working Paper no. 227.

Canova, F., M. Ciccarelli, and E. Ortega. 2003. Similarities and convergence in G-7 cycles. University of Pompeu Fabra. Working Paper.

Ciccarelli, M., and B. Mojon. 2005. Global inflation. European Central Bank (ECB) Working Paper Series no. 537.

Clarida, R., J. Galí, and M. Gertler. 2000. Monetary policy rules and macroeconomic stability: Evidence and some theory. *Quarterly Journal of Economics* 115 (1): 147–80.

———. 2002. A simple framework for international monetary policy analysis. *Journal of Monetary Economics* 49 (5): 879–904.

Clark, T. E., and K. Shin. 2000. The sources of fluctuations within and across countries. In *Intranational macroeconomics,* ed. Gregory Hess and Eric van Wincoop, 189–220. Boston, MA: Cambridge University Press.

Cogley, T., and T. J. Sargent. 2002. Evolving post-World War II U.S. inflation dynamics. In *NBER macroeconomics annual 2001,* vol. 16, ed. B. S. Bernanke and K. S. Rogoff, 331–73. Cambridge, MA: MIT Press.

———. 2005. Drifts and volatilities: Monetary policies and outcomes in the post WWII U.S. *Review of Economic Dynamics* 8 (2): 262–302.

Cushman, D. O., and T. Zha. 1997. Identifying monetary policy in a small open economy under flexible exchange rates. *Journal of Monetary Economics* 39 (3): 433–48.

Doyle, B. M., and J. Faust. 2005. Breaks in the variability and comovement of G-7 economic growth. *Review of Economics and Statistics* 87 (4): 721–40.

The Economist 2005. A foreign affair: Inflation is increasingly determined by global rather than local economic forces. *Economic Focus,* October 20.

Ehrmann, M., M. Fratzscher, and R. Rigobon. 2005. Stocks, bonds, money markets and exchange rates: Measuring international financial transmission. ECB Working Paper Series no. 452.

Eichenbaum, M., and C. L. Evans. 1995. Some empirical evidence on the effects of shocks to monetary policy on exchange rates. *The Quarterly Journal of Economics* 110 (4): 975–1009.

Faust, J., J. H. Rogers, S.-Y. B. Wang, and J. Wright. 2007. The high-frequency response of exchange rates and interest rates to macroeconomic announcements. *Journal of Monetary Economics* 54 (4): 1051–68.

Fernández-Villaverde, J., J. F. Rubio-Ramírez, T. J. Sargent, and M. W. Watson. 2007. ABCs (and Ds) of understanding VARs. *American Economic Review* 97 (3): 1021–26.

Fisher, R. W., and W. M. Cox. 2007. The new inflation equation. *Wall Street Journal,* Opinion. April 6.

Forni, M., M. Hallin, M. Lippi, and L. Reichlin. 2000. The generalized dynamic factor model: Identification and estimation. *Review of Economics and Statistics* 82 (4): 540–54.

Gerlach, S. 1988. World business cycles under fixed and flexible exchange rates. *Journal of Money, Credit, and Banking* 20 (4): 621–32.

Gregory, A. W., A. C. Head, and J. Raynauld. 1997. Measuring world business cycles. *International Economic Review* 38 (3): 677–702.

Grilli, V., and N. Roubini. 1995. Liquidity and exchange rates: Puzzling evidence from the G-7 countries. New York University, Leonard N. Stern School of Business, Department of Economics Working Paper no. 95–17.

———. 1996. Liquidity models in open economies: Theory and empirical evidence. *European Economic Review* 40 (3–5): 847–59.

Hausman, J. A., and W. E. Taylor. 1983. Identification in linear simultaneous equations models with covariance restrictions: An instrumental variables interpretation. *Econometrica* 51 (5): 1527–49.

Heathcote, J., and F. Perri. 2004. Financial globalization and real regionalization. *Journal of Economic Theory* 119 (1): 207–43.

Helbling, T. F., and T. A. Bayoumi. 2003. Are they all in the same boat? The 2000–2001 growth slowdown and the G-7 business cycle linkages. Manuscript, International Monetary Fund. Washington, DC: IMF.

Ihrig, J., S. Kamin, D. Lindner, and J. Marquez. 2007. Some simple tests of the globalization and inflation hypothesis. Board of Governors of the Federal Reserve System, International Finance Discussion Paper no. 891.

Justiniano, A. 2004. Sources and propagation mechanisms of foreign disturbances in small open economies: A dynamic factor analysis. Board of Governors of the Federal Reserve System. Unpublished Manuscript.

Justiniano, A., and G. E. Primiceri. 2008. The time varying volatility of macroeconomic fluctuations. *American Economic Review* 98 (3): 604–41.

Kamin, S. B., M. Marazzi, and J. W. Schindler. 2006. The impact of Chinese exports on global import prices. *Review of International Economics* 14 (2): 179–201.

Kilian, L. 1998. Small-sample confidence intervals for impulse response functions. *Review of Economics and Statistics* 80 (2): 218–30.

Kim, S., and N. Roubini. 2000. Exchange rate anomalies in the industrial countries: A solution with a structural VAR approach. *Journal of Monetary Economics* 45 (3): 561–86.

Kose, M. A., C. Otrok, and C. H. Whiteman. 2003. International business cycles: World, region, and country specific factors. *American Economic Review* 93 (4): 1216–39.

———. 2005. Understanding the evolution of world business cycles. IMF Working Paper no. 05-211. Washington, DC: International Monetary Fund.

Kose, M. A., E. S. Prasad, and M. E. Terrones. 2003. How does globalization affect the synchronization of business cycles? *American Economic Review Papers and Proceedings* 93 (2): 57–62.

Lane, P., and G. M. Milesi-Ferretti. 2006. The external wealth of nations mark II: Revised and extended estimates of foreign assets and liabilities, 1970–2004. IMF Working Paper no. 06-69. Washington, DC: International Monetary Fund.

Lubik, T., and F. Schorfheide. 2006. A Bayesian look at new open economy macroeconomics. In *NBER macroeconomics annual 2005,* ed. M. Gertler and K. Rogoff, 313–66. Cambridge, MA: MIT Press.

Lumsdaine, R. L., and E. S. Prasad. 2003. Identifying the common component in international economic fluctuations. *Economic Journal* 113 (484): 101–27.

McConnell, M. M., and G. Perez-Quiros. 2000. Output fluctuations in the United States: What has changed since the early 1980s? *American Economic Review* 90 (5): 1464–76.

Monfort, A., J.-P. Renne, R. Rüffer, and G. Vitale. 2003. Is economic activity in the G7 synchronized? Common shocks vs. spillover effects. CEPR Discussion Paper no. 4119.

Rogoff, K. 2003. Globalization and global disinflation. Paper presented at the Federal Reserve Bank of Kansas City conference, Monetary Policy and Uncertainty: Adapting to a Changing Economy. 29 August, Jackson Hole, WY.

Scholl, A., and H. Uhlig. 2006. New evidence on the puzzles: Monetary policy and exchange rates. Society for Computational Economics. Computing in Economics and Finance. Working Paper no. 5.

Sims, C. A., and T. Zha. 2006. Were there regime switches in U.S. monetary policy? *American Economic Review* 96 (1): 54–81.

Smets, F., and R. Wouters. 2007. Shocks and frictions in U.S. business cycles: A Bayesian DSGE approach. *American Economic Review* 97 (3): 586–606.

Stock, J. H., and M. W. Watson. 1999. Forecasting inflation. *Journal of Monetary Economics* 44 (2): 293–335.

———. 2002. Macroeconomic forecasting using diffusion indexes. *Journal of Business Economics and Statistics* 20 (2): 147–62.

———. 2003. Has the business cycle changed and why? In *NBER macroeconomics annual 2002,* ed. M. Gertler and K. S. Rogoff, 159–218. Cambridge, MA: MIT Press.

———. 2005. Understanding changes in international business cycle dynamics. *Journal of the European Economic Association* 3 (5): 968–1006.

Comment Lucrezia Reichlin

Domestic and International Factors

The chapter addresses the difficult, but very topical question of whether globalization has affected the transmission mechanism of U.S. monetary policy and, in particular, whether it has made it less effective.

Lucrezia Reichlin is a professor of economics at London Business School.

The chapter relies partly on data analysis and partly on a counterfactual Vector Auto Regression (VAR) exercise. In both cases the authors exploit information from two large data sets, one containing U.S. data (the domestic panel) and the other providing data on the rest of the world (the foreign panel).

A distinctive feature of the analysis is that the authors rely on factor analysis techniques in order to exploit information from the large data sets. The authors extract common domestic factors (denoted by Ct) from the domestic panel and common foreign factors (denoted by C_t^*) from the foreign panel via principal components. They then study the impact of foreign factors on domestic variables from a variety of perspectives.

The particular questions analyzed in the chapter are the following:

1. How much of the variance of key U.S. economic time series is captured by C_t and how much by C_t^* (exercise 1)?
2. Has the importance of C_t^* increased over time (exercise 2)?
3. Do common foreign factors C_t^* Granger-cause domestic factors C_t and is the Granger causality relationship stable over time (exercise 3)?
4. Do global forces mitigate the effects of U.S. monetary policy more than they used to do? This analysis is carried out by mean of a structural VAR on the factors (a factor-augmented vector autoregression [FAVAR] in the spirit of Bernanke, Boivin, and Eliasz [2005])(exercise 4).

My discussion raises a fundamental conceptual problem in the methodology proposed by the chapter. I will show two examples, one where national and foreign factors are perfectly correlated and the other where they are not. The examples show that the proportion of the variance of observable domestic variables explained by foreign factors is not interpretable even when controlling for the correlation between domestic and foreign factors. My examples also imply that Granger causality tests, as those proposed in exercise 3, are not informative on the role of global forces in national dynamics. By the same reasoning, neither is the VAR exercise proposed in exercise 4.

Does Globalization Matter? The Econometric Strategy of the Chapter

Let us summarize the steps of the authors' methodology.

Step 1: Extract the Factors

The $K \times 1$ vector of the U.S. factors is extracted from the $N \times 1$ vector of the U.S. data assuming that the data follow the process:

$$X_t = \Lambda C_t + e_t.$$

Similarly, the $K^* \times 1$ vector of the foreign factors C_t^* can be extracted from the $N^* \times 1$ vector of foreign variables assuming:

$$X_t^* = \Lambda^* C_t^* + e_t^*.$$

Exercises 1 and 2 are based on step 1 and consist of computing the proportion of the variance of observable variables X_t to be attributed to C_t^* and C_t.

Step 2: VAR on the Factors

The relationship between foreign and domestic factors is estimated via the following VAR:

$$\begin{pmatrix} C_t^* \\ C_t \end{pmatrix} = \begin{pmatrix} \Psi_{11}(L) & \Psi_{12}(L) \\ \Psi_{21}(L) & \Psi_{22}(L) \end{pmatrix} \begin{pmatrix} C_{t-1}^* \\ C_{t-1} \end{pmatrix} + \begin{pmatrix} u_t^* \\ u_t \end{pmatrix}.$$

They are interested in studying Granger causality of past C_t^* on C_t (exercise 3) and in computing the effect of the identified domestic monetary policy shock on the basis of an unrestricted VAR in which past foreign factors are allowed to affect domestic factors and a restricted VAR in which that effect is set to zero (exercise 4).

In particular, exercise 3 consists of testing the hypothesis that $\Psi_{21}(L) = 0$. If it were to prove impossible to reject the hypothesis, we would conclude that foreign factors did not help in forecasting domestic factors. In exercise 4 the restricted VAR is constrained so as $\Psi_{21}(L) = 0$. The idea of the experiment is that, if results based on the restricted VAR were significantly different than those based on the restricted specification, one would conclude that globalization had affected the transmission mechanism of the monetary policy shock. Vice-versa, if results were the same, we would conclude that globalization did not matter.

The next sections will review critically the methodology.

Example 1: Autarky and Globalization

Consider a simple barter economy with two geographical areas: the United States (domestic economy) and the rest of the world, with the variables of the latter being indicated by a star superscript. Let us denote the difference in the log of real consumption per capita as Δy_t and the real interest rate as r_t. The equilibrium conditions in this barter economy are given by the following Euler equations:

$$E_t \Delta y_{t+1}^* = \gamma^* r_t^*,$$

where E_t is the expectation operator at time t and γ is the elasticity of intertemporal substitution.

Under autarky, the rate r_t that clears the U.S. capital market is determined at the U.S. level and the United States can be considered an island in the economic sense.

Under globalization, the rate r_t that clears the world capital market is determined at the world level so as to fulfill the equilibrium condition:

$$\frac{E_t \Delta y^*_{t+1}}{\gamma^*} = \frac{E_t \Delta y_{t+1}}{\gamma}.$$

At equilibrium, we will have $r_t = r^*_t = r^W_t$ and from the Euler equations expected domestic consumption is:

$$E_t \Delta y_{t+1} = \gamma r^W_t.$$

This expression shows that domestic variables reflect information on foreign variables since the domestic interest rate equals the world interest rate. In general, any domestic macroeconomic variables reflecting expected consumption must contain information on the world interest rate and therefore have a global component.

The point can also be understood from the budget constraint, which is derived from the intertemporal theory of the current account. There, the current account ca_t is the discounted sum of future expected net output no_t and the future discounted sum of world interest rates:

$$ca_t = -\sum_{j=1}^{\infty} \beta^j E_t \Delta no_{t+j} + \gamma \sum_{j=0}^{\infty} \beta^j E_t r^W_{t+j}.$$

The expression implies that the information on the world interest rate is already contained in the current account data. The U.S. panel used by the authors, for example, contains current account data and the domestic factors must therefore be correlated with national factors as in fact they are.

Let us now examine the VAR implied by our simple example.[1]

Assume that the world interest rate follows an exogenous AR(1) process:

$$r^W_t = \rho r^W_{t-1} + u_t,$$

where u_t is an exogenous shock that may depend on domestic and foreign shocks. The VAR representation of the solution to the model is:

$$\begin{pmatrix} y^*_t \\ y_t \end{pmatrix} = \begin{pmatrix} \rho & 0 \\ 0 & \rho \end{pmatrix} \begin{pmatrix} y^*_{t-1} \\ y_{t-1} \end{pmatrix} + \begin{pmatrix} -\gamma/(1-\rho) \\ -\gamma^*/(1-\rho) \end{pmatrix} u_t.$$

This is a case in which Ψ_{21} in the authors' VAR is equal to zero at all lags and consumption in the rest of the world does not statistically affect U.S. consumption (foreign variables/factors do not Granger-cause domestic variables/factors). The procedure proposed by the authors would lead to the conclusion that the rest of the world consumption has no impact on domestic consumption.

However, as we have seen, this conclusion is clearly wrong: when the foreign interest rate moves, foreign consumption moves as well and the world interest rate changes in order to restore the world equilibrium, therefore

1. I thank Boivin and Giannoni for making the relationship of my example and their VAR explicit in correspondence related to the discussion of their chapter.

affecting domestic consumption. Notice that, since the restricted model is the same as the unrestricted model, the inclusion of foreign variables will not alter the transmission mechanism, although the structure of the model implies that under autarky, unlike under globalization, foreign factors do not affect domestic factors. Granger-causality will be rejected statistically because expected consumption already incorporates information on the world interest rate and, as a consequence, foreign factors have no additional marginal forecasting power.

It is clear that in this case, the coefficients $\Psi_{21}(L)$ provide no information on the effect of international factors on domestic variables.

The general problem is that observed domestic variables are the result of a general equilibrium process that reflects changes in both domestic and foreign forces. Domestic dynamic, therefore, incorporates the effect of foreign forces. The only way to disentangle domestic and foreign forces is to identify domestic and foreign shocks or to estimate the deep parameters of a structural model. From estimates of the effect of foreign variables (or foreign factors) on domestic variables (or domestic factors) there is nothing to learn.

The same point can be explained from the statistical point of view.

Let us go back to the VAR on factors estimated by the authors and described here in this section. Notice that the coefficients $\Psi_{ij}(L)$ have the same interpretation as partial correlation coefficients: $\Psi_{21}(L)$ reveals the dynamic effect of the past of C_t^* on C_t once we have netted out the effect of the past values of C_t.

In the limit case in which C_t and C_t^* are entirely driven by a global component, as in the previous example, this coefficient would be zero and we would be led to the wrong conclusion that international factors have no effect on domestic factors. If, on the other hand, the correlation were not perfect, the estimates of the coefficients would reveal the effect of foreign-specific forces on domestic factors, rather than the effect of foreign factors (global and foreign-specific) on domestic factors.

Notice that the fact that we cannot identify the effect of global forces on the transmission mechanism of monetary policy has nothing to do with whether the coefficients of the VAR are identified (rank condition discussed by the authors in the text). This is simply the consequence of the fact that the factors, as the variables themselves, contain both global and region-specific components.

Obviously, this discussion applies whether we are focusing on a VAR on observed domestic and foreign variables or on a VAR on unobserved factors as done by the authors.

Example 2: Sectoral Output

To provide more intuition for my point, let me propose a different example.

Suppose that output $y_{k,t}$ in each of K sectors of the U.S. economy evolves according to

$$y_{k,t} = A_k(L)y_{k,t-1} + B_k(L)x_{k,t} + u_{k,t},$$

where $x_{k,t}$ denotes exports of sector k (to all countries), and $u_{k,t}$ is a domestic demand disturbance specific to sector k. Suppose also that foreign country j's imports of goods produced by sector k of the U.S. economy are equal to

$$x^j_{k,t} = \theta^j \gamma_k Y^*_{j,t},$$

where $Y^*_{j,t}$ is the national income of country j in period t, θ^j is the marginal propensity to import U.S. goods of country j, and k is the fraction of imports from the United States that are purchased from sector k (assumed to be the same for each of the foreign countries). Total exports of a given U.S. sector are then equal to

$$x^j_{k,t} = \sum_{J=1}^{J} x^j_{k,t}.$$

Finally, suppose, for simplicity, that the evolution of the variables $Y^*_{j,t}$ is driven purely by "foreign" disturbances, unrelated to developments in the United States.

It follows that the evolution of each of the sectors of the U.S. economy can be written as

$$y_{k,t} = A_k(L)y_{k,t-1} + \gamma_k B_k(L)X_t + u_{k,t},$$

where

$$X_t = \sum_{j=1}^{J} \theta^j Y^*_{j,t}.$$

Suppose that the "domestic" data set consists of the sectoral outputs $\{y_{k,t}\}$ for each of the K sectors of the U.S. economy, while the "foreign" data set consists of the levels of national income $\{Y^*_{j,t}\}$ for some K^* of the J foreign countries. On the assumption that there are not too many important common factors among the domestic demand disturbances $\{u_{k,t}\}$, the authors' procedure would identify the variable X_t as one of the "domestic" common factors. At the same time, X_t may not be among, or even too closely correlated with, the few largest "foreign" common factors. While our assumptions imply that X_t is purely a function of "foreign" disturbances, it need not be well explained by the several most important factors extracted from the foreign data set. For, while those factors are constructed so as to explain as much as possible of the variation in the variables in the foreign data set as a whole, they need not explain a great deal of the variation in any individual variable in the foreign data set. The fact that the particular linear combination of foreign variables represented by X_t happens to be important for the U.S. economy is no reason for the variables that best explain it to have been selected among the small number of leading "foreign factors." Indeed, X_t need not even be part of the foreign data set, if that data set happens not to include all the important importers of U.S. products, or if it happens to aggregate regions with different marginal propensities to import from the United States as single foreign national income series.

This simple example shows that the mere fact that factors are extracted from a set of U.S. time series need not mean that the variables in question are not substantially affected by foreign disturbances; in the example, X_t is one of the "domestic factors," but 100 percent of the variation in this variable is due to foreign disturbances. Moreover, one cannot control for this problem simply by checking to what extent the "domestic factors" are correlated with the small number of leading "foreign factors" identified through the authors' procedure; one could find that X_t is little explained by variation in those few foreign factors, even though it is actually entirely a function of foreign disturbances. In this example, no foreign variables other than the history of X_t are of any relevance whatsoever to forecasting any of the variables in the "domestic" data set. Thus, if X_t is among the "domestic factors," one should not find any role for the identified "foreign factors" in improving forecasts of the domestic factors, after already conditioning on the past history of X_t and the other domestic factors themselves (we would reject Granger causality). Yet this would not imply that foreign developments have little effect on the evolution of the U.S. economy. It would be quite possible that a large fraction of the variation in every sector of the U.S. economy is due to variations in X_t, and hence ultimately to foreign disturbances, despite the finding that $\Psi_{21}(L) = 0$.

Reference

Bernanke, B., J. Boivin, and P. Eliasz. 2005. Measuring the effects of monetary policy: A factor augmented vector autoregressive (FAVAR) approach. *Quarterly Journal of Economics* 120 (1): 387–422.

Rejoinder Jean Boivin and Marc P. Giannoni

Our discussant criticizes the chapter on the grounds that "all exercises performed are difficult to interpret" because domestic factors C_t are affected jointly by domestic and foreign shocks.[1] She takes issue with our interpretation of "VAR based results with international variables" and concludes, on the basis of two simple polar examples, that "[i]n order to estimate the effect of global forces, we need to identify global shocks and their propagation."

Given that the discussant argues that her main critique of the chapter

1. This addendum constitutes a response to the main issues raised by our discussant, Lucrezia Reichlin, in her written discussion dated October 30, 2007.

"applies whether we are focusing on a VAR on observed domestic and foreign variables or a VAR on unobserved factors," we focus here on issues raised in the context of our conventional VAR. These issues are both about econometric identification and economic interpretation. A more detailed discussion of these points as well as a discussion of issues referring to the estimation of factors from large data sets are left in a separate note (posted on the authors' websites).

Discussion's Examples, Stochastic Singularity, and VARs

The discussion is essentially about the fact that when the correlation among macroeconomic variables is too high, it might not be possible to identify quantities of interest. To illustrate this point, the discussant provides *two examples* in which this correlation is so high in fact that the systems suffer from stochastic singularity. As the discussion mentions, the two proposed examples have the property that the foreign factors C_t^* *do not Granger cause* the domestic factors C_t, after controlling for past domestic variables. The discussant argues that the effects of foreign factors on domestic factors cannot be interpreted in these examples, and concludes from this that our results cannot be interpreted.

We fully agree with our discussant that *if* foreign factors *did not* Granger cause domestic factors, as is assumed in both examples, it would be difficult to identify and interpret our results (see sections 8.2.3, 8.3.3 and 8.4.1 of chapter). It is well known that VARs may be inadequate in such situations. Fortunately, this problem can be detected empirically, and it turns out that the data that we consider reject the hypothesis of stochastic singularity. Our chapter reports and discusses test results showing that foreign factors C_t^* *do Granger cause* the domestic factors C_t, after controlling for past domestic variables. As argued in the chapter, Granger causality from foreign factors to domestic factors in our empirical setup implies that the effect of foreign factors on domestic factors *can be properly identified* by the empirical strategy that we adopted. So, as interesting as the examples presented in the discussion might be, and despite their elegance, our findings suggest that they are not relevant in practice.

Can We Estimate the VAR Coefficients?

Aside from the issue just addressed, the discussion suggests that our empirical procedure might not identify the true effect of foreign variables on domestic variables. It is alleged that our VAR parameters are inconsistently estimated depending on whether the VAR residuals involve global (i.e., worldwide common shocks) or merely region-specific shocks. While this issue arises in multiple parts of the discussion, it appears most clearly in the section, "A Simple Statistical Point." That section refers to our general formulation of the VAR for the factors C_t^* and C_t. To simplify the notation, and without loss of generality, let us reduce this system to a VAR(1) in the scalar variables C_t^*, C_t:

$$\begin{bmatrix} C_t^* \\ C_t \end{bmatrix} = \begin{bmatrix} \psi_{11} & \psi_{12} \\ \psi_{21} & \psi_{22} \end{bmatrix} \begin{bmatrix} C_{t-1}^* \\ C_{t-1} \end{bmatrix} + \begin{bmatrix} u_t^* \\ u_t \end{bmatrix}. \tag{1}$$

The reduced-form shocks u_t^* and u_t (assumed to be i.i.d. over time) may be driven both by a global (or "worldwide" common) shock g_t, and by region-specific shocks ε_t^*, ε_t (assumed to be uncorrelated across regions), say, in the following way:

$$\begin{bmatrix} u_t^* \\ u_t \end{bmatrix} = Fg_t + \begin{bmatrix} \varepsilon_t^* \\ \varepsilon_t \end{bmatrix}. \tag{2}$$

The coefficient ψ_{21} reveals the dynamic effect of the past foreign factor C_{t-1}^* on the domestic factor C_t, controlling for the past value of C_t.

The discussant claims that "in the limit case in which C_t and C_t^* are entirely driven by a global component [g_t, the coefficient ψ_{21}] will be zero and we would wrongly conclude that international factors have no effect on domestic factors." This raises issues of economic interpretation, which we discuss in the following section on economic interpretation, as well as econometric issues. The discussant furthermore argues that "[i]f the correlation [between C_t^* and C_t] is not perfect, the estimates of the coefficients will reveal the effect of foreign-specific forces on domestic factors, but not the effect of foreign factors (global plus foreign specific) on domestic factors." This is a claim that ordinary least squares (OLS) estimation of VAR parameters is not consistent. However, standard econometric results show that VAR coefficients, ψ_{ij}, can in general be consistently estimated and do not depend on the mixture of common (g_t) versus variable-specific shocks (ε_t^*, ε_t). In the detailed note mentioned previously, we show, using a simple simulated example, that our empirical procedure generally recovers the true coefficients.

Do We Need to Identify All Shocks?

The discussant criticizes our so-called exercise 4, in which we attempt to determine whether global forces mitigate the effects of U.S. monetary policy more than they used to. The discussant interprets this exercise as an attempt to identify how *worldwide common shocks* might have mitigated the effect of U.S. monetary policy. The discussant's main point is to argue that our strategy does not identify worldwide exogenous shocks, and hence, that it cannot shed light on the question.

This interpretation of our exercise and of our results is, however, inappropriate. As we emphasized in the chapter, the goal of our exercise 4 is *not* to determine the role of such worldwide shocks, but instead to determine to what extent the transmission of U.S. monetary policy shocks on the U.S. economy depends on the subsequent adjustment of foreign variables, which we summarize by *endogenous* foreign factors (C_t^*).

To determine the effect of foreign variables on the transmission of U.S. monetary policy, we merely need to identify one shock: a monetary policy shock. This is done in our chapter by adopting a common recursive identification assumption. Clearly the validity of such an assumption is debatable, but once one accepts it, the exercise performed is well defined and entirely conventional in the VAR literature. As is common in the literature, *we do not need to identify all of the other exogenous shocks* to determine the effect of monetary policy shocks under this identifying assumption. We then perform a simple counterfactual experiment that involves shutting down the feedback effect of foreign endogenous variables on domestic variables. Clearly, as we recognize at the end of section 8.4.4, such an exercise is potentially subject to the Lucas critique, but this is not the object of the discussant's complaints.

In our setup, as is the case in the examples proposed by the discussant, worldwide common *shocks* are by construction orthogonal to the U.S. monetary policy shocks, and hence, do not contribute to the object of our interest (i.e., the transmission of U.S. monetary policy). While identifying worldwide shocks might be interesting for other exercises, it is not necessary to do so for the question in which we are interested.

It is important to note that there is nothing special about the international aspect of our VAR. Our exercise 4 is completely analogous to the exercises performed by many researchers using closed economy VARs to investigate the effect of systematic monetary policy. In such a context, the variables of the VAR are typically believed to be driven by common shocks such as productivity shocks. Yet again, in order to characterize the effects of monetary policy, it is not necessary to identify all shocks.

Economic Interpretation

Finally, the discussion claims that the coefficients ψ_{21} measuring the effect of foreign factors (C^*) on domestic factors (C), even if they could be perfectly estimated, do not provide any relevant information. For instance, in example 2 of the discussion, the true value of ψ_{21} is 0. The discussant thus concludes on this basis that "[t]he procedure proposed by the authors would assess that the rest of the world consumption has no impact on domestic consumption. However [. . .] this conclusion is clearly wrong [. . .] The coefficients [ψ_{21}] do not tell us anything about the effects of international factors on national variables."

The critique is unfortunately misguided. Nowhere in our chapter have we suggested that the rest of the world would, in such an example, have no effect on the domestic economy. In fact we do not assess the importance of foreign factors for domestic factors on the basis of ψ_{21}. Instead, we do so by looking at R^2 statistics. Contrary to the discussant's claim, if the model of example 2 in the discussion were true, we would find that much of the variance of domestic consumption is strongly correlated with foreign consumption; in the case that the domestic and foreign elasticities of intertemporal substitution are equal ($\gamma = \gamma^*$), the R^2 statistics reported in table 8.1 of our chapter would be precisely 1 in this example, suggesting considerable comovement of foreign and domestic variables.

Does the coefficient ψ_{21} then provide any relevant information in that case? Certainly. Again, if the model of example 2 were true, the true value of ψ_{21} would be 0. This coefficient is used in the context of our exercise 4, for the characterization of the effect of foreign variables on the transmission of monetary policy. Having the coefficient ψ_{21} equal to 0 in this example simply reflects the fact that in response to a monetary policy shock, unexpectedly raising the domestic (and world) real interest rate by a given amount results in the *same* response of domestic consumption in the open economy as in the case of complete autarky (i.e., if there were no interaction with the rest of the world). This is precisely what the theoretical model proposed in example 2 of the discussion predicts, and it is also what our empirical procedure would conclude.

Our empirical strategy would thus have delivered the right answers in this example. As we argue in the more detailed note (posted on our website), our approach would also generally provide the right answer in example 1 of the discussion. The discussion's conclusion that "[t]he coefficients [ψ_{21}] do not tell us anything about the effects of international factors on national variables" is therefore inaccurate.

9

Monetary Policy in Europe versus the United States
What Explains the Difference?

Harald Uhlig

9.1 Introduction

Interest rate paths during the last decade or so have been remarkably different in the United States and in Europe (see figure 9.1). What explains the difference?

The analysis of this chapter leads to the conclusion that the difference is due to surprises in productivity as well as surprises in wage demands—moving interest rates in opposite directions in Europe and the United States—but not due to a more sluggish response in Europe to the same shocks or to different monetary policy surprises. To obtain these conclusions, I have specified and estimated a hybrid new-Keynesian dynamic stochastic general equilibrium (DSGE) model and have used it to investigate three potential interpretations for the U.S.-European monetary union (EMU) difference.

The first interpretation is to argue that monetary policy is simply different. A number of observers have argued that the difference in policy shows the difference between an established central bank in the United States (which knows what it is doing and acts decisively, if need be), versus a new central bank in Europe, run by a committee that is too timid and too inertial to anything in time, following the U.S. example with too much caution and delay. A

Harald Uhlig is a professor of economics at the University of Chicago, a research associate of the National Bureau of Economic Research, and a research fellow of the CEPR.

This research was started when the author was professor at Humboldt Universität zu Berlin and there supported by the Deutsche Forschungsgemeinschaft through the SFB 649 "Economic Risk." I am grateful to Andreas Hornstein for a very useful conversation, and to Andy Levin for an excellent discussion and for pointing out an algebraic mistake (now corrected). I am grateful to participants at the Barcelona meeting for many additionally useful remarks. I apologize that I must keep most of these excellent comments and appropriate criticisms as inspiration for future work.

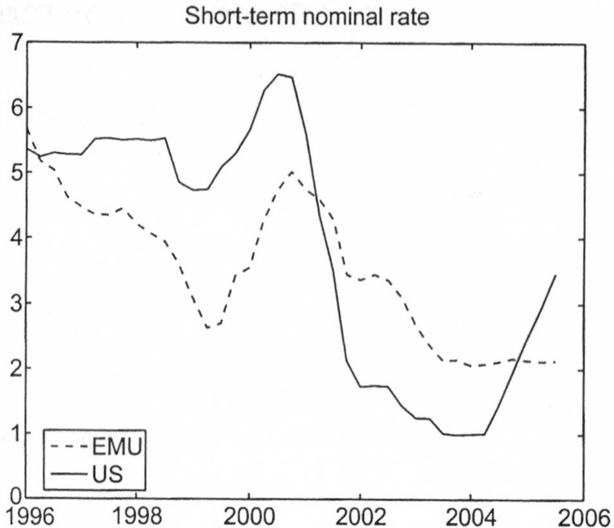

Fig. 9.1 Central bank rates in the EMU and in the United States

more benign interpretation—recently put forth by European Central Bank (ECB) president Trichet in a speech, "Activism and alertness in monetary policy," in Madrid 2006—argues that instead it is the ECB holding the steering wheel steady, while the monetary policy pursued by the Fed is just erratic.

The second interpretation is that the shocks simply have been different. For example, growth in the United States was considerably higher in the second half of the 1990s, giving rise to fear of "overheating" there and thereby possibly necessitating policy interventions, which then needed to be reversed, as the U.S. economy spun into a recession. While the decline in growth rates in EMU may have been similarly large between 2000 and 2002, the growth rate only briefly achieved U.S. levels in 2000 (see figure 9.2).

The third interpretation is that the structure of the economies are simply different. There are three striking differences in particular:

1. Labor markets are more rigid in Europe than in the United States. While one can point to some measures, the evidence here comes more from a variety of sources and qualitative measures, starting with labor market regulations and government interference in the labor market to union memberships and the role of unions in economic policy and the governance of firms.

2. The share of government is larger in Europe than it is in the United States. For the period from 1985 to 2005, mean government consumption to gross domestic product (GDP) was 16 percent in the United States and 20 percent in Europe. For government expenditure, the contrast was even more

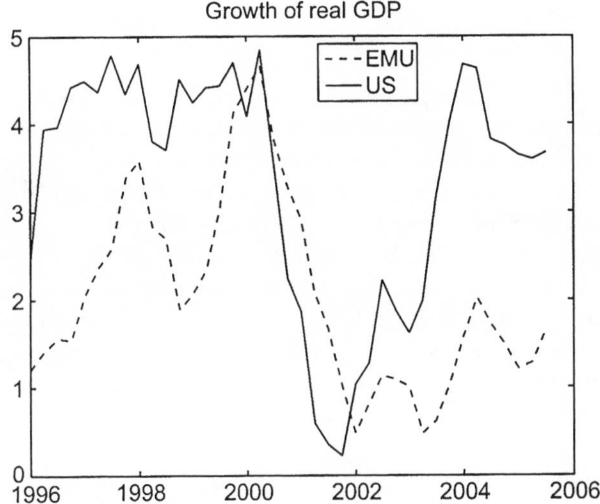

Fig. 9.2 Real GDP growth in the United States and EMU

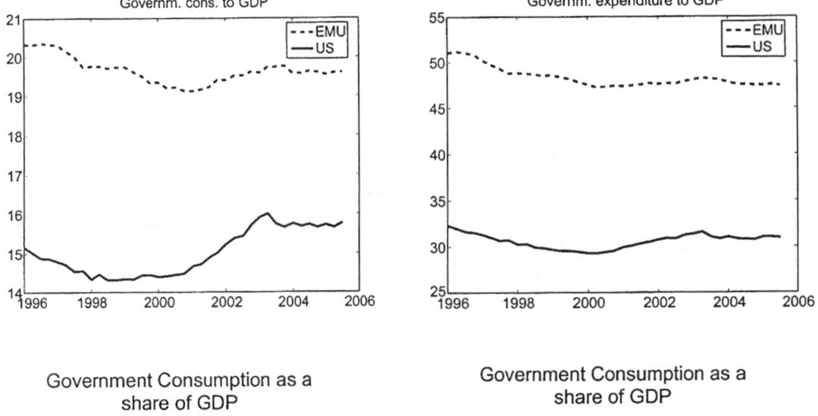

Fig. 9.3 Government consumption and government expenditure

striking, with 32 percent in the United States versus 50 percent in Europe (see also figure 9.3). Furthermore, fiscal policy is arguably more decentralized in Europe, with Brussels playing a minor role vis-à-vis the nation states in Europe compared to the federal government vis-à-vis state and local governments in the United States.

3. A much larger share of business is bank-financed rather than market-financed in EMU, compared to the United States. For example, de Fiore and Uhlig (2006) document that the ratio of debt-to-equity is .41 in the United States and .61 in Europe. Furthermore, the ratio of bank-to-bond

finance is 7.3 in the EMU and thus ten times as high as 0.74, the value for the United States.

It seems a priori plausible that these differences play a significant factor in the explanations for monetary policy. For example, government spending tends to be rather smooth and acyclical: a larger share of government spending might therefore lessen the role of price rigidities for the private economy.

Recent advances in the modeling of dynamic stochastic general equilibrium models—for example, Smets and Wouters (2003), Christiano, Eichenbaum, and Evans (2005) and related work—in particular have made it possible in principle to impose the key structural differences of the economy, estimate monetary policy reaction functions, and quantitatively account for the movements in key variables by a decomposition into the model-specific structural shocks. This avenue is therefore well-suited for answering the question at hand.

These models are built on recent advances in investigating the role of sticky prices for the economy and the new-Keynesian paradigm (see, in particular, Clarida, Galí, and Gertler [1999] and Woodford [2003]). Applying them directly to the task at hand poses three challenges, however.

1. Most of these models emphasize the role of sticky prices and the output gap in driving inflation rates. Frictions from the interaction between financial intermediation and monetary policy typically play no role or a role only insofar as they influence the output gap. This makes it challenging to address the third of the three key differences mentioned previously.

2. The distortionary role of nonmonetary economic policy typically plays a minor role. This makes it hard to address the first and the second of the aforementioned key differences.

3. In quantitative applications and estimations, many observable time series are used. An equivalent number of shocks is then used in order to generate a regular one-step ahead variance-covariance matrix of the prediction errors. This makes it challenging to avoid pushing key dynamic features of the economy into "measurement errors" instead, which then receive a structural interpretation.

There is an earlier literature, emphasizing financial frictions and the reallocational role of monetary injections. For example, Lucas and Stokey (1987) emphasize the role of cash for some of the transactions, while Bernanke, Gertler, and Gilchrist (1999) emphasize credit contracts arising in the presence of asymmetric information. While the new-Keynesian approach in focusing on sticky prices may be appealing for a number of reasons, it is useful for the task at hand to bring lessons of that earlier literature into this framework.

There are important contributions in the literature on which I can draw for this task. In their seminal paper, Christiano, Eichenbaum, and Evans (2005) (henceforth, CEE) impose a cash-in-advance constraint for firms to pay their wage bill. Firms borrow these funds from financial intermediaries who in turn obtain funds from household deposits as well as central bank cash injection. While this feature of their paper seems there mostly to create some sort of money demand, it opens the possibility of studying financial frictions further. Schmitt-Grohe and Uribe (2004) and Altig et al. (2004) assume an additional cost for purchasing consumption goods, which depends on the velocity of the household's cash balances. Christiano, Motto, and Rostagno (2003) introduce a fairly rich banking sector, allowing for various monetary aggregates such as bank reserves and demand deposits, to study the role of money in the Great Depression.

To keep the model tractable, yet allow for some potentially important avenues, I largely follow the lead of CEE. I additionally allow for a cash-in-advance constraint on consumption good purchases in order to judge the relative importance of private transactions to firm borrowing. I allow for the possibility that not all cash injections are permanent, but instead are taken out of the system again at the end of the period (which one might think of as a one-off reverse transaction). Finally, I explicitly account for the cost of borrowing in the profit maximization problem and price setting problem of the firm, giving rise to an interest rate cost channel (see also Barth and Ramey [2001] and Secchi and Gaiotti [2006]). This is a modest contribution to solving the first of the three challenges listed previously.

I will explicitly allow for distortionary taxation of labor income, used to finance a stock of government as well as a certain level of government expenditure. I view this as a beginning to make progress on the second challenge. Certainly, several—although not all—monetary policy models of recent vintage have allowed for such influence of nonmonetary policy: this model is in the same tradition. In particular, Schmitt-Grohe and Uribe (2006) add distortionary income taxation to CEE.

For the third challenge, I use Dynare and thus off-the-shelves estimation techniques, and discuss some issues arising from mapping the dynamics into the dynamics for few observable series only, employing the "ABCD" framework of Fernandez-Villaverde, Rubio-Ramirez, and Sargent (2007). In particular, I will focus on a small set of observable variables, judiciously chosen, and allow for as many shocks as there are variables. It will turn out that one needs to be careful. It is not just enough to insure an invertible mapping from the shocks to the innovations of the variables, but furthermore, it is important to check invertibility of the Value at Risk (VAR) representation itself. We do this by "visually" inspecting the VAR coefficients in the derived representation (see section 9.4).

In sum, the model can perhaps best be described as a variant of the CEE model, with the following deviations:

1. The costs of adjusting the capital stock arise from the investment-to-capital ratio, not the investment-to-previous-investment ratio.
2. There is a cash-in-advance constraint for household consumption purchases.
3. Only a fraction of the cash injections, which "liquify" the loan market for firms, may permanently increase the money supply.
4. The interest rate costs for borrowing part of the input bill explicitly arises in the objective function of the intermediate good firms.
5. Capital utilization is constant.
6. There is a distortionary tax on wage income and firm profits. There is government debt.
7. There is no indexation.
8. There is real wage sluggishness, following Blanchard and Galí (2005).
9. Monetary policy is assumed to follow a Taylor rule.
10. There are six shocks: a productivity shock, an investment-specific shock, a wage setting shock, a monetary policy shock and two fiscal policy shocks, a tax rate shock, and a spending shock. For estimation, I only "turn on" the tax rate shock.
11. Estimation is in terms of five variables, inverting for the shocks per the recursive law of motion.

The approach of this chapter (as well as the results) share many similarities with the two slightly earlier papers by Sahuc and Smets (2008) and Christiano, Motto, and Rostagno (2007).

Sahuc and Smets (2008, 507) likewise come to the "overall conclusion [. . .] that differences in the size and the persistence of the shocks hitting the two economies is the main driving force behind the different interest rate behaviour." Their model differs from mine in several dimensions. Most notably, perhaps, there is no role for fiscal policy and hardly a role for differences in the financial structure in their paper.

Christiano, Motto, and Rostagno (2007) also share the view with this chapter that "the U.S. economy was aided during the most severe phase of the [2001] recession by favourable productivity shocks, which [. . .] helped keep inflation in check. By contrast, the slowdown in the Euro Area was exacerbated by negative productivity forces which also prevented inflation from ebbing" (5). These authors furthermore emphasize the greater persistence of ECB policy compared to Fed policy. This is in some contrast to our findings: while, for example, monetary policy shocks are more persistent in the EMU than the United States according to our findings, interest rates are not.

The model by Christiano, Motto, and Rostagno (2007) features a much more detailed entrepreneurial sector as well as more details on the banking sector, and therefore makes more progress than this chapter in its ability to address the differences in financial structure between the United States and

Europe. There is no role for fiscal policy in their paper, though. Their model is driven by fifteen shocks, whereas my model features only five. The costs of adjusting capital in their model are determined by the change in investment, whereas it is determined (more classically) by the ratio of investment to capital here.

These two papers therefore complement the investigation here. Despite a number of modeling differences they come to fairly similar conclusions, which ought to provide additional trust in the conclusions drawn.

Section 9.2 explains the model. A technical appendix provides the details for the analysis of the model. Section 9.3 explains the estimation strategy and lists the parameters used for the comparison. Section 9.4 is devoted to the invertibility issue. Section 9.5 provides results. Section 9.6 discusses these results and offers some tentative conclusions.

9.2 The Model

The model is a combination of a cash-in-advance model and a Calvo sticky-price model, amended with a role for a government.

Time is discrete. There are identical households, who supply labor and enjoy final consumption. They own all firms. They use cash for parts of their transactions. There is a competitive sector of final goods producing firms. There is a unit interval of monopolistic intermediate good firms, using labor to produce output and setting sticky prices. They need to borrow a fraction of their input bill from commercial banks. Commercial banks take deposits from households and receive cash injections from the central bank. They lend to intermediate goods firms. The central bank injects cash and thereby sets the nominal interest rate. The government taxes wage income and uses it to finance government purchases as well as debt repayments. Nominal wages are sluggish on the aggregate level.

A period has four parts:

1. Shocks are realized. The new nominal wage for the period is set. The central bank injects cash Ψ_t to banks.

2. A fraction of intermediate good firms is chosen to reset its price. Intermediate good firms "guess" demand and produce accordingly, hiring labor at the market wage. They are assumed to be required to borrow a fixed fraction of the input bill from banks.

3. Households shop, using cash at hand as well. Government shops, using tax receipts as well as a short-term credit line from the central bank.

4. Financial markets open. Firms pay capital rental payments and wages to households. Firms pay interest to banks. They pay profits to households. Households pay taxes to the government. The government issues new bonds and repays old bonds. The household splits the remaining cash into deposits with banks and cash-at-hand for the next period.

9.2.1 Households

Households enjoy final consumption c_t and dislike labor n_t according to

$$U = E\left[\sum_{t=0}^{\infty} \beta^t (\log(c_t - \chi c_{t-1}) - An_t^{1+\sigma})\right], \tag{1}$$

where $0 \leq \chi < 1$ is a habit parameter and $1/\sigma > 0$ is the Frisch elasticity of labor supply. Households enter period t, holding deposits D_{t-1} at financial intermediaries and cash-at-hand H_{t-1}. In the second part of the period, they supply labor n_t according to demand at the market wage W_t. In the third part, they use cash-at-hand to shop for a fraction η of consumption,

$$H_{t,res} + \eta P_t c_t = H_{t-1}, \tag{2}$$

holding residual cash $H_{t,res} \geq 0$. I essentially assume that there are cash goods and credit goods as in Lucas and Stokey (1987), but that these cash and credit goods are purchased in fixed proportion for consumption, and that investment goods are always credit goods.[1] The latter would be implied by a Leontieff specification for the preferences in cash and credit goods. In principle, the household may spend less cash than available. However, I shall assume that shocks and parameters are such that the constraint on residual cash is binding, $H_{t,res} = 0$.

In the fourth part of the period, households receive after-tax nominal wages and trade all contingent claims, as well as firm shares and government bonds, and pay for the remaining $(1 - \eta)$ share of their purchases ("credit goods"). Netting out all household-to-household trades, the financial market budget constraint is

$$\begin{aligned} H_t + D_t + q_t B_t + (1 - \eta)P_t c_t + P_t x_t &= \\ (1 - \tau_t)W_t n_t + (1 + i_t)D_{t-1} + P_t r_t K_{t-1} &+ (1 - \tau_V)V_t + B_{t-1} + H_{t,res}, \end{aligned} \tag{3}$$

where H_t is cash-at-hand for the next period, D_t is deposited with banks, q_t is the discount price for government bonds B_t, $1 + i_t$ is the return paid by banks on deposits D_{t-1}, $P_t r_t$ is the nominal rental rate for capital, V_t is the value added of intermediate good firms, and B_{t-1} are the debt repayments by the government.

One can extend this budget constraint with between-household trades. In particular, let $\Lambda_{t,t+k}$ be the discount price on the financial market at t for an extra unit of cash on the financial market at date $t + k$.

Also, households produce new capital subject according to

$$k_t = \left(1 - \delta + \varphi\left((1 + u_{x,t})\frac{x_t}{k_{t-1}}\right)\right)k_{t-1}, \tag{4}$$

1. A key reason for introducing the cash-in-advance constraint on only a fraction of the goods is that otherwise the money stock becomes quantitatively large in this model, implying that seignorage is a substantial fraction of the government budget constraint.

where the adjustment cost function $\varphi(\cdot)$ satisfies

$$\varphi(\delta) = \delta,\ \varphi'(\delta) = 1,\ \delta\varphi''(\delta) = -\frac{1}{\varpi}$$

for some $\varpi > 0$ (see Jermann [1998]), and where $u_{x,t}$ is a possibly persistent investment-specific disturbance,

$$u_{x,t} = \rho_x u_{x,t-1} + \varepsilon_{x,t}, \tag{5}$$

following Fisher (2006).

9.2.2 Final Good Firms

Final good firms take inputs $y_{t,j}$ to produce a final good y_t according to the production function

$$y_t = \left(\int_0^1 y_{t,j}^{1/(1+\mu)} dj\right)^{1+\mu}. \tag{6}$$

They purchase intermediate goods at price $P_{t,i}$ per unit and sell the final good at price P_t.

9.2.3 Intermediate Good Firms

Given a current intermediate goods price $P_{t,j}$, intermediate good firms "guess" their demand $y_{t,j}$ resulting from the demand of final good firms, see equation (62). They thus hire labor $n_{t,j}$ at nominal wages W_t and rent capital $k_{t,j}$ at nominal rental rates $P_t r_t$ to produce output according to

$$y_{t,j} = \begin{cases} \gamma_t k_{t,j}^{\theta} n_{t,j}^{1-\theta} - \Phi & \text{if } \gamma_t n_{t,j} > \Phi \\ 0 & \text{otherwise,} \end{cases} \tag{7}$$

where γ_t is an exogenous process for the change in technology and Φ is a parameter of the production function and might be thought of as a fixed cost of production. Let $\hat{\gamma}_t = \log(\gamma_t) - \log(\bar{\gamma})$ for some appropriate $\bar{\gamma}$, and assume

$$\hat{\gamma}_t = \rho_{\gamma,L}\hat{\gamma}_{t-1} + u_{\gamma,t} \tag{8}$$

$$u_{\gamma,t} = \rho_{\gamma,u} u_{\gamma,t-1} + \varepsilon_{\gamma,t}.$$

I assume that the firm needs to obtain a loan $L_{t,j}$ for a fraction ξ_t of the input bill, on which a nominal market interest rate i_t needs to be paid. The rest of the input bill is paid for per trade credit (or more efficient market instruments) to be settled at the end of the period, on which no interest needs to be paid. That is, let MC_t be the nominal marginal costs of producing an extra unit of output, excluding the additional costs of borrowing (see equation [54]). Then,

$$L_{t,j} = \xi \text{MC}_t y_{t,j}$$

and the value added of this firm (or, equivalently, end-of-period profits) are

$$V_{t,j} = (P_{t,j} - (1 + \xi i_t)\mathrm{MC}_t)y_{t,j}. \tag{9}$$

Firms get to reoptimize prices with probability $1 - \alpha$, independently of their past. If they cannot reoptimize prices, they will be adjusted at the average inflation rate; that is,

$$P_{t,j} = \overline{\pi} P_{t-1,j}. \tag{10}$$

When given a chance to reoptimize prices, they will choose it so as to maximize discounted value added along the no-optimization-of-prices path[2]

$$\mathrm{NPV}_{t,j} = E\left[\sum_{k=0}^{\infty} \alpha^k \Lambda_{t,t+k} V_{t,j}\right], \tag{11}$$

where $\Lambda_{t,t+k}$ is the market price at date t for an extra unit of cash at date $t + k$ on the financial markets in part four of the period.

9.2.4 Commercial Banks

Banks compete for deposits from households and can borrow from the central bank. They then compete for giving loans to firms. Banks collect the returns on their loans in the fourth part of the period, and then repay households as well as the central bank. In equilibrium, banks make zero profits. Thus, there will be a market nominal rate of return i_t on loans, deposits, and central bank money.

9.2.5 The Central Bank

The central bank provides cash Ψ_t into the economy via providing loans to the commercial banks at the nominal interest rate i_t. It may be best to think of this as open market operations. The interest earnings on this open market operation constitute seignorage. Additionally, the central bank declares a fraction ν of the cash injection to be seignorage, not to be taken out of the system after repayment by the commercial banks. Thus, the government receives a central bank profit transfer of $(\nu + i_t)\Psi_t$ in part four of the period.

Note that only $\nu\Psi_t$, but not the interest earnings on the cash injection (or even the entire cash injection) constitute an increase in the money supply,

$$M_t = M_{t-1} + \nu\Psi_t. \tag{12}$$

The parameter ν allows the distinction between a short-run liquidity injection and a long-run increase in money supply. If $\nu = 0$, liquidity is provided only temporarily, and taken out of the economy after the injection. Seignorage is then given only by the interest earned on the short-term injection. By

2. Note that I assume that value added or profits are taxed at rate τ_V. Because I hold this rate constant, maximizing the net present value of before-tax value added is equivalent to maximizing the net present value of after-tax value added, which would be the more appropriate objective.

contrast, $\nu = 1$ means that any short-term injection also increases money supply in the long run.

Recall that the output gap is defined as the difference between actual output and the output that would emerge in the absence of sticky prices and absence of stickiness in wages; that is, for $\alpha = 0$ and $\omega = 1$, but keeping the friction of borrowing from banks. In an economy without sticky prices and sticky wages and without the need to borrow from banks, real marginal costs will be constant. The percent deviation of actual real marginal costs

$$\text{mc}_t = \frac{\text{MC}_t}{P_t} \tag{13}$$

from its steady-state level can therefore serve as a proxy for the output gap.

I therefore assume that the central bank follows a Taylor rule in setting interest rates, using this ratio that

$$i_t = \bar{i} + \rho_{i,L} i_{t-1} + (1 - \rho_{i,L})\left(\zeta_\pi\left(\frac{\pi_t}{\bar{\pi}} - 1\right) + \zeta_x\left(\frac{\text{mc}_t}{\overline{\text{mc}}} - 1\right) + u_{i,t}\right), \tag{14}$$

where

$$\pi_t = \frac{P_t}{P_{t-1}} \tag{15}$$

is inflation, where π is the inflation target, $\bar{i}$ is the steady-state nominal rate, ζ_π and ζ_x are coefficients of the policy rule, and where

$$u_{i,t} = \rho_{i,u} u_{i,t-1} + \varepsilon_{i,t} \tag{16}$$

is a possibly persistent distortion to the Taylor rule, driven by the monetary policy shock $\varepsilon_{i,t}$.

9.2.6 The Government

The budget constraint of the government at the end of the period is given by

$$q_t B_t = B_{t-1} + P_t g_t - \tau_t W_t n_t - \tau_V V_t - (\nu + i_t)\Psi_t. \tag{17}$$

The government does not carry cash from one period to the next. However, the government is assumed to finance its purchases within the period via a short-term credit from the central bank. Thus, government spending $P_t g_t$ is akin to a short-term cash injection on the demand side. This is consistent with the view that the central bank acts as the "checking account" bank to the government. Note that I do not allow the government to borrow from the central bank in the long term.

Define real debt

$$b_t = \frac{B_t}{P_t}, \tag{18}$$

real seignorage

$$\psi_t = \frac{\Psi_t}{P_t}, \tag{19}$$

real value added

$$v_t = \frac{V_t}{P_t}, \tag{20}$$

as well as real wages

$$w_t = \frac{W_t}{P_t}. \tag{21}$$

I assume that the government aims at some steady-state debt-to-GDP ratio $\bar{b}/\bar{y}$, as well as some steady-state level government-spending-to-GDP ratio $\bar{g}/\bar{y}$. Given all other parameters, let $\bar{\tau}$ be the steady-state tax rate on wage income consistent with these targets.

I assume that the government follows the policy rule of adjusting future tax and spending plans, if the current debt level b_t deviates from its target level $\bar{b}$,

$$\tau_t - \bar{\tau} = \zeta_\tau \left(\frac{b_{t-1} - \bar{b}}{\bar{y}} - 1 \right) + u_{\tau,t} \tag{22}$$

$$\frac{g_t}{\bar{y}} = \zeta_g \left(\frac{b_{t-1} - \bar{b}}{\bar{y}} - 1 \right) + u_{g,t}, \tag{23}$$

where $\zeta_\tau \geq 0$ and $\zeta_g \leq 0$ such that the dynamics of government debt remains stable, and where both equations are driven by possibly persistent distortions

$$u_{\tau,t} = \rho_\tau u_{\tau,t-1} + \varepsilon_{\tau,t} \tag{24}$$

$$u_{g,t} = \rho_g u_{g,t-1} + \varepsilon_{g,t}, \tag{25}$$

driven by the fiscal tax shock $\varepsilon_{\tau,t}$ and the fiscal spending shock $\varepsilon_{g,t}$.

9.2.7 Labor Markets and Wage Setting

I assume that wages move sluggishly on the aggregate level. A common form to generate nominal wage sluggishness is to assume Calvo wage stickiness for wage setters (see Erceg, Henderson, and Levin [2000]). A different literature has emphasized frictions or sluggishness stemming from bargaining as the route cause (see Shimer [2005] or Hall [2005]), giving direct rise to real wage sluggishness. The form I use here has been adapted from Blanchard and Galí (2005) and has been used, for example, in Uhlig (2007).

More specifically, let $W_{t,f}$ be the wage emerging from the first-order condition of the households' maximization problem. I assume that

$$W_t = ((1 - \omega)\pi_t W_{t-1} + \omega \Upsilon W_{t,f})(1 + u_{w,t}) \tag{26}$$

for some $\Upsilon > 1$ and a possibly persistent stochastic distortion

$$u_{w,t} = \rho_w u_{w,t-1} + \varepsilon_{w,t}. \tag{27}$$

An alternative interpretation of the distortion $u_{w,t}$ is to view it as being driven by fluctuations in the preference parameter A, manifested in stochastic fluctuations of the market-clearing wage $W_{t,f}$. This perspective may be a reasonable shortcut in order to account for the fluctuations in female labor supply, for example.

Assuming moderate-size fluctuations, actual wages will exceed the wage stemming from the first-order condition, $W_t > W_{t,f}$, and thus, labor markets will be demand constrained. That is, I assume that households always supply labor at the going wage. Note that (26) can be rewritten in terms of real wages as

$$w_t = ((1 - \omega)w_{t-1} + \omega \Upsilon w_{t,f})(1 + u_{w,t}), \tag{28}$$

where $w_{t,f} = W_{t,f}/P_t$.

9.2.8 Aggregation and Market Clearing

1. Money market: Post-injection money supply equals end-of-period money demand. This is given by

$$M_t = D_t + H_t. \tag{29}$$

2. Final goods market:

$$g_t + c_t + x_t = y_t. \tag{30}$$

3. Labor market:

$$n_t = \int_0^1 n_{t,j} dj. \tag{31}$$

4. Capital market:

$$k_{t-1} = \int_0^1 k_{t-1,j} dj. \tag{32}$$

5. Loan market:

$$D_{t-1} + \Psi_t = L_t = \int_0^1 L_{t,j} dj. \tag{33}$$

9.2.9 Equilibrium and Solution

An equilibrium is an allocation, policy parameters and prices (including returns and profits) such that

1. The allocation solves the problem of the representative household, given prices and policy parameters.

2. The allocation solves the firms maximization problems, given prices and policy parameters.
3. The constraints for the government and the central bank hold.
4. Markets clear.

To solve for the equilibrium, I characterize the first-order conditions, explicitly solve for the steady state, and characterize the dynamics per log-linearization around the steady state. I then compute the recursive law of motion solving these log-linearized equations. Details are available in a technical appendix.

9.3 Data and Estimation

I assume that $u_{g,t} \equiv 0$; that is, I assume that there are no fiscal spending shocks. This is reasonable in light of the smoothness[3] in figure 9.3.

There are five shocks in the model: I therefore need observations on five time series to solve for these shocks:

1. Inflation, π_t. I calculate it using the GDP deflator, since I am using real GDP in some other measures. A popular alternative is to use the consumer price index (CPI).
2. The central bank interest rate or short rate, i_t.
3. Labor productivity, y_t/n_t. For y_t, I use real GDP. For n_t, I use employment rather than hours worked. In a boom, more part-time labor will be hired, but also, more "uncounted" hours are worked by employees: thus, it may be that employment rather than hours is a more reasonable variable to measure fluctuations in labor input. It was also the series that was more easily available.
4. The consumption-to-GDP ratio, c_t/y_t. Cochrane (1994) in particular has shown that this ratio has predictive power for GDP growth and a number of other variables. Theory implies that this statistic indeed provides key information, so it is included here.
5. The debt-to-GDP ratio, b_t/y_t.

For the EMU, the data has been obtained from the ECB, and is in use for the area-wide model. For the United States, the data has been obtained from the Federal Reserve Bank of St. Louis. For debt, I have used the series GFDEBTN; that is, debt on the federal level.

I have used quarterly data from 1985 to 2005, striking a compromise between getting a reasonably long time span for data and relying on a reasonably stable monetary policy environment. While EMU only exists since

3. It also appeared to be initially sensible for the invertibility issue discussed in the next section, when doing an exploration of the model properties with freely chosen parameters. That issue seemed to disappear with the estimated parameters, though.

1999, one might argue that the Bundesbank has effectively played the role of a European central bank in the time before.

I am comparing the model in its log-linearized version—that is, in terms of log-deviations from the steady state—to the data. I therefore take logs of all variables, and removed the means. The resulting five time series used in estimation can therefore be seen in figure 9.4. In particular, I have linearly

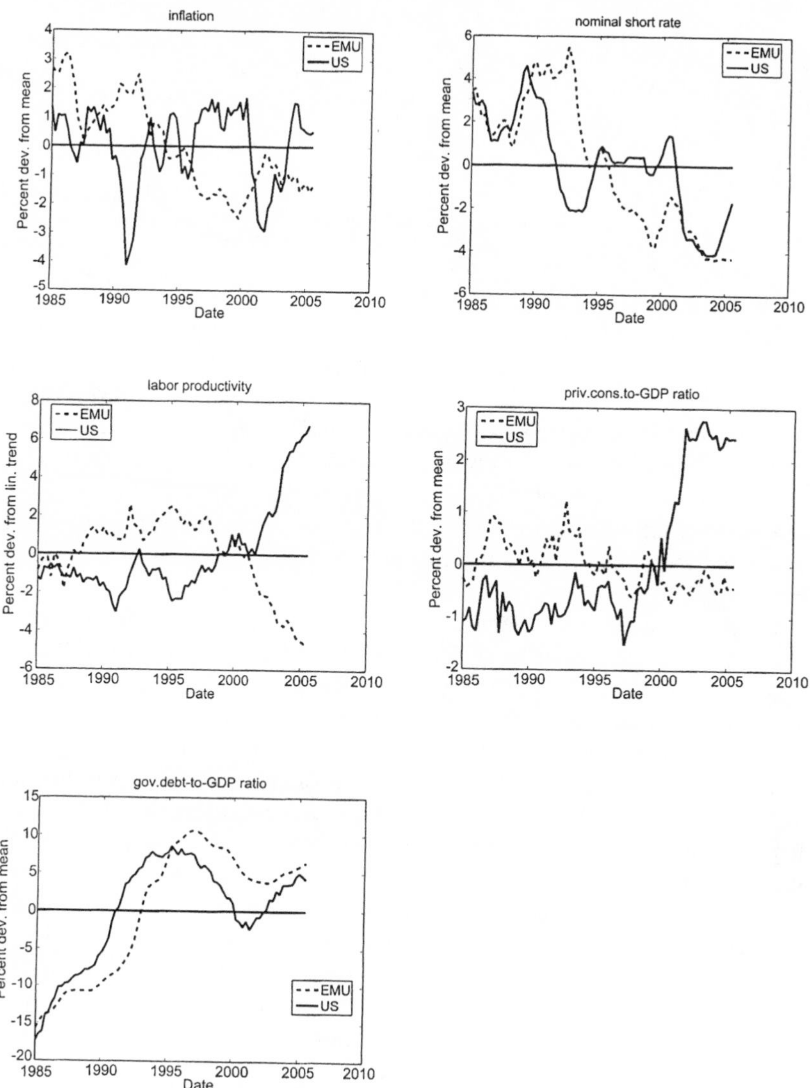

Fig. 9.4 Data used for estimation

Table 9.1 List of parameters fixed a priori

Parameter	U.S.	EMU, if different	Interpretation
γ	1		Productivity
β	0.99		Discount factor
θ	0.36		Capital share
δ	0.02		Depreciation rate
σ	1		Inverse Frisch elasticity
Φ	$0.8 \cdot$ markup		Fixed cost
μ	0.5		Markup
ϖ	2		Cost of adjustment of capital
Υ	1.1		Wage markup
ξ	0.1	0.5	Bank financing share
g/y	0.15	0.2	Gov. spending to GDP
b/y	0.62		Debt-to-GDP ratio
π	1.033		Inflation
τ_V	0.2		Profit or value added tax

detrended labor productivity. If there is a constant time trend in γ_t, it is fairly straightforward to correct all equations for it: essentially, this amounts to a slight correction in the discount rate. If the time trend is stochastic, the correction would imply a different set of equations, comparing everything to the current level of productivity. Since I log-linearized the model around a steady state with constant productivity, the linear detrending method is therefore more compatible with the theory.

The linearized model has been estimated using Dynare. In so doing, I have fixed a number of parameters, and estimated others. A list is given in tables 9.1 and 9.2.

For the parameters fixed a priori, I have set $\overline{n} = 1$, backing out the preference parameter A, rather than vice versa. In order to capture the different importance of banking in Europe versus the United States, I have fixed $\xi = 0.5$ for Europe, and $\xi = 0.1$ for the United States. A good calibration for these numbers would be sensible: the results here instead should be taken as indicative for what would happen for reasonable, although perhaps not sufficiently carefully calibrated, values for these parameters. The factor five was chosen to roughly reflect the approximately fivefold financing of firms through banks (rather than capital market instruments and stocks) in Europe compared to the United States. I have used 1 for the inverse Frisch elasticity σ of labor supply. All the other parameters are fairly standard.

For the estimated parameters, I have chosen rather uninformative priors. For parameters that should sensibly be in the unit interval, I used a uniform distribution, or, equivalently, a beta distribution with mean 0.5 and a standard deviation of $1/\sqrt{12} = 0.29$. For parameters that ought to be positive, I have used an inverted gamma distribution with infinite variance. I have used

Table 9.2 **List of estimated parameters**

Parameter	Distribution	Mean	Standard deviation	Interpretation
η	beta	0.5	0.29	Cash-in-advance share
ν	beta	0.5	0.29	Permanent liquidity
α	beta	0.5	0.29	Calvo prob. of stickiness
χ	beta	0.5	0.29	Habit share
ω	beta	0.5	0.29	Wage sluggishness
ρ_w	beta	0.5	0.29	Autocorr. wage disturb.
$\rho_{\gamma,L}$	beta	0.5	0.29	Autoregr. techn.
$\rho_{\gamma,u}$	beta	0.5	0.29	Autocorr. techn. disturb.
ρ_x	beta	0.5	0.29	Autocorr. inv disturb.
$\rho_{i,L}$	beta	0.5	0.29	Autoregr. int. rate
$\rho_{i,u}$	beta	0.5	0.29	Autocorr. int. rate disturb.
ρ_τ	beta	0.5	0.29	Autocorr. tax disturb.
ζ_τ	inv.gamma	0.5	∞	Tax rule
ζ_g	normal	–0.2	1	Spending rule
ζ_π	inv.gamma	1.5	∞	Taylor rule: on inflation
ζ_x	inv.gamma	0.5	∞	Taylor rule: on markup
stderr(ε_γ)	inv.gamma	0.2	∞	Std. err techn.
stderr(ε_i)	inv.gamma	0.2	∞	Std. err int. rate
stderr(ε_τ)	inv.gamma	0.2	∞	Std. err tax rate
stderr(ε_x)	inv.gamma	0.2	∞	Std. err inv. shock
stderr(ε_w)	inv.gamma	0.2	∞	Std. err wage shock

Note: std. err. = standard error.

a normal distribution centered at zero and a standard deviation of 1 for ζ_g, which is certainly wide.

9.4 A, B, C, and D's of VARs

When estimating a model with just a subset of variables, the issue of invertibility may be of concern. Invertibility may matter even more for recovering the sequence of shocks explaining the observations. I use the ABCD framework of Fernandez-Villaverde, Rubio-Ramirez, and Sargent (2007) to investigate the issue: the name of their paper has inspired the choice of the title for this subsection.

Let x_t be the list of log-deviations from steady state for all variables in the economy, including the exogenous disturbances $u_{i,t}$, and so forth. Let y_t be a list of observable variables, and let ε_t be the vector of i.i.d. shocks driving the system. Solving the linearized model with, for example, the methods exposited in Uhlig (1999), provides a recursive law of motion

(34) $$x_t = Ax_{t-1} + B\varepsilon_t$$

(35) $$y_t = Cx_{t-1} + D\varepsilon_t.$$

Assume that D is square and invertible, and that the eigenvalues of $(A - BD^{-1}C)$ are strictly less than one in modulus. Fernandez-Villaverde, Rubio-Ramirez, and Sargent (2007) show that

$$y_t = C\sum_{j=0}^{\infty}(A - BD^{-1}C)^{-j}y_{t-j-1} + D\varepsilon_t \tag{36}$$

is an (infinite-order) vector autoregression for y_t, and that $D\varepsilon_t$ are the one-step ahead forecasts for y_t.

Let

$$y_t = C\sum_{j=0}^{k}(A - BD^{-1}C)^{-1}y_{t-j-1} + D\varepsilon_t + \vartheta_{k,t}, \tag{37}$$

be a finite-order approximation to the infinite-order VAR in (36), defining the approximation error $\vartheta_{k,t}$. Given a recursive law of motion as in (34) and (35), and assuming D to be square and invertible, it is always possible to calculate the finite-order approximation (37). In practice, one would drop $\vartheta_{k,t}$ from this equation, hoping that it is small. Equation (37) then provides for a convenient procedure to recover the residuals ε_t driving the data.

But $\vartheta_{k,t}$ may not be small, either, because the eigenvalues of $(A - BD^{-1}C)$ are not strictly less than one in modulus, or because they are only just below one, with the coefficients in (36) only gradually dying out with increasing lag length. The latter is the problem emphasized by Chari, Kehoe, and McGrattan (2005).

It may thus be useful to examine how fast the coefficients in (37) die out at a specific parameterization of the model. Grouping the coefficients together according to lag length, I do this in figure 9.5 for the coefficient specifications

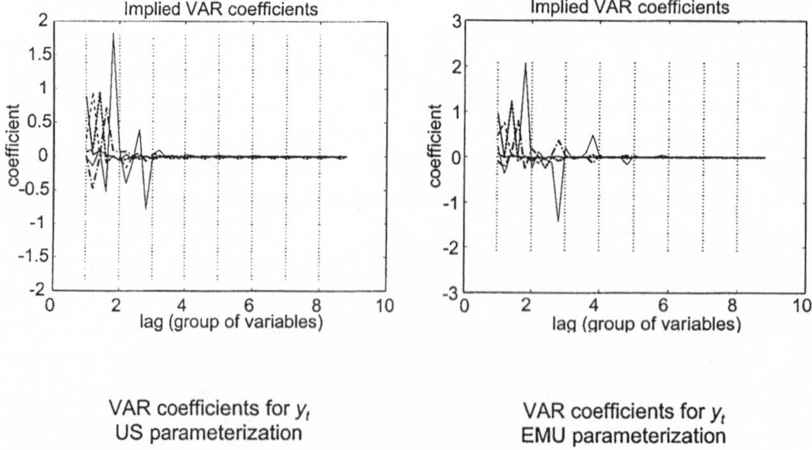

VAR coefficients for y_t
US parameterization

VAR coefficients for y_t
EMU parameterization

Fig. 9.5 Coefficients in the derived VAR representation for y_t

following for the United States and EMU. Note that the VAR coefficients die out quite fast.

9.5 Results

9.5.1 Estimates

The results of the estimation are provided in table 9.3. The results are taken directly from Dynare, using standard settings. While some of the confidence intervals are perhaps too tight—most likely pointing to yet insufficient sampling—the estimates all appear to be reasonable.

Taking these estimates at face value, there are some interesting differences as well as similarities in the comparison of the United States to EMU. Surprisingly, according to these estimates, wages actually appear to be more flexible and less sluggish in the EMU rather than the United States, with $\omega = 0.18$ and $\rho_w = 0.88$ there, as opposed to $\omega = 0.06$ and $\rho_w = 0.686$ in the EMU. Less surprisingly, prices appear to be more sticky in EMU with $\alpha = 0.778$ than the United States, with $\alpha = 0.668$. Productivity (or, for the United

Table 9.3 **Estimation results**

	U.S.		EMU	
Parameter	Mean	Conf. interval	Mean	Conf. interval
η	0.57	[0.23, 0.90]	0.38	[0.16, 0.60]
ν	0.27	[0.00, 0.68]	0.981	[0.974, 0.995]
α	0.668	[0.667, 0.676]	0.778	[0.769, 0.793]
χ	0.64	[0.64, 0.65]	0.35	[0.30, 0.42]
ω	0.18	[0.17, 0.18]	0.061	[0.055, 0.078]
ρ_w	0.88	[0.88, 0.89]	0.686	[0.682, 0.685]
$\rho_{\gamma,L}$	0.00	[0.00, 0.00]	0.979	[0.978, 0.980]
$\rho_{\gamma,u}$	0.93	[0.93, 0.96]	0.266	[0.248, 0.262]
ρ_x	1	[1, 1]	0.962	[0.958, 0.964]
$\rho_{i,L}$	0.73	[0.73, 0.74]	0.289	[0.285, 0.290]
$\rho_{i,u}$	0.24	[0.22, 0.24]	0.496	[0.495, 0.498]
ρ_τ	0.99	[0.99, 0.99]	0.985	[0.982, 0.984]
ζ_τ	0.18	[0.18, 0.18]	0.356	[0.352, 0.355]
ζ_g	–0.058	[–0.058, –0.058]	0.079	[0.078, 0.079]
ζ_π	1.07	[1.07, 1.07]	1.192	[1.192, 1.193]
ζ_x	0.35	[0.35, 0.35]	0.211	[0.210, 0.211]
std. err.(ε_γ)	0.26	[0.24, 0.26]	0.30	[0.29, 0.33]
std. err.(ε_i)	2.38	[2.38, 2.55]	1.08	[1.05, 1.24]
std. err.(ε_τ)	1.56	[1.58, 1.64]	0.52	[0.49, 0.58]
std. err.(ε_x)	2.15	[2.07, 2.25]	1.95	[1.81, 2.16]
std. err.(ε_w)	0.84	[0.80, 0.87]	0.49	[0.45, 0.56]

Note: std. err. = standard error.

States, the productivity disturbance), tax disturbances, and investment-specific disturbances are all essentially random walks.

The fraction η of cash required for consumption transactions is about one-third in EMU and about one-half in the United States. Monetary injections seem to be temporary in the United States, $\nu = 0.27$, but permanent in Europe, $\nu = 0.981$. Interest rates show a persistence of $\rho_{i,L} = 0.289$: one-third in EMU and about three-quarters in the United States: if anything, interest rate choices appear to be more sluggish in the United States. The Taylor rule coefficients are about 1.2 on inflation and 0.2 on markup in the EMU, which is reasonable. They are slightly lower for inflation and slightly higher on markup for the United States.

The feedback coefficients for fiscal policy differ in an interesting way. In response to a higher debt burden, the United States moderately raises taxes, $\zeta_\tau = 0.18$, and cuts spending, $\zeta_g = -0.058$, while the Europeans actually increase spending, $\zeta_g = 0.079$, and finance it by raising taxes even more, $\zeta_\tau = 0.356$.

Monetary policy shocks, tax shocks, and wage shocks show considerably larger standard deviations in the United States than in EMU.

As a postscriptum, the estimation results and therefore the conclusions based on them should be viewed with a considerable degree of caution. Note that the parameters are estimated rather indirectly: identification is achieved through their impact on the dynamics of the whole system, rather than some more direct consequence. It is likely that misspecification of the model can easily thwart the attempt to draw reasonable inference here: investigating that issue is beyond the scope of this chapter.

Even with the route taken here, it turns out that the model and its estimation appear to be quite sensitive, in particular with respect to the parameters ξ, as well as the fiscal policy parameters $\bar{g}/\bar{y}$, ζ_τ, ζ_g. For example, it is fairly easy to find parameter combinations where Dynare delivers nonsensical results or complains about violations of the Blanchard-Kahn condition for the prior, while it is still possible to calculate solutions with my "toolkit": as an example, take $\xi = 1$, $\bar{g}/\bar{y} = 0.35$, $\zeta_\tau = 1$, $\zeta_g = 0$, and otherwise taking prior means for all other variables. For some other parameter settings, one obtains warnings about badly scaled matrices and difficulties in starting the Markov chain. It is also not unusual that the posterior maximization procedure encounters a cliff shortly before it declare the maximum to be reached. This is true in particular for the estimation of the U.S. model, possibly explaining the unplausibly tight confidence bands for several parameters. The estimation results can also depend quite substantially on $\bar{g}/\bar{y}$ and ξ, which have been fixed a priori. In sum, either the model or the estimation procedure is ill-behaved in certain aspects. Exploring these sensitivities and the reasons further would be interesting, but beyond the scope of this chapter.

9.5.2 Impulse Responses

To understand the properties of the model, I have calculated the impulse responses to shocks 1 percent in size, with the estimated parameters set at the posterior means rounded to two digits. Figure 9.6 shows the impulse response of the nominal interest rate. Figure 9.7 shows the response of out-

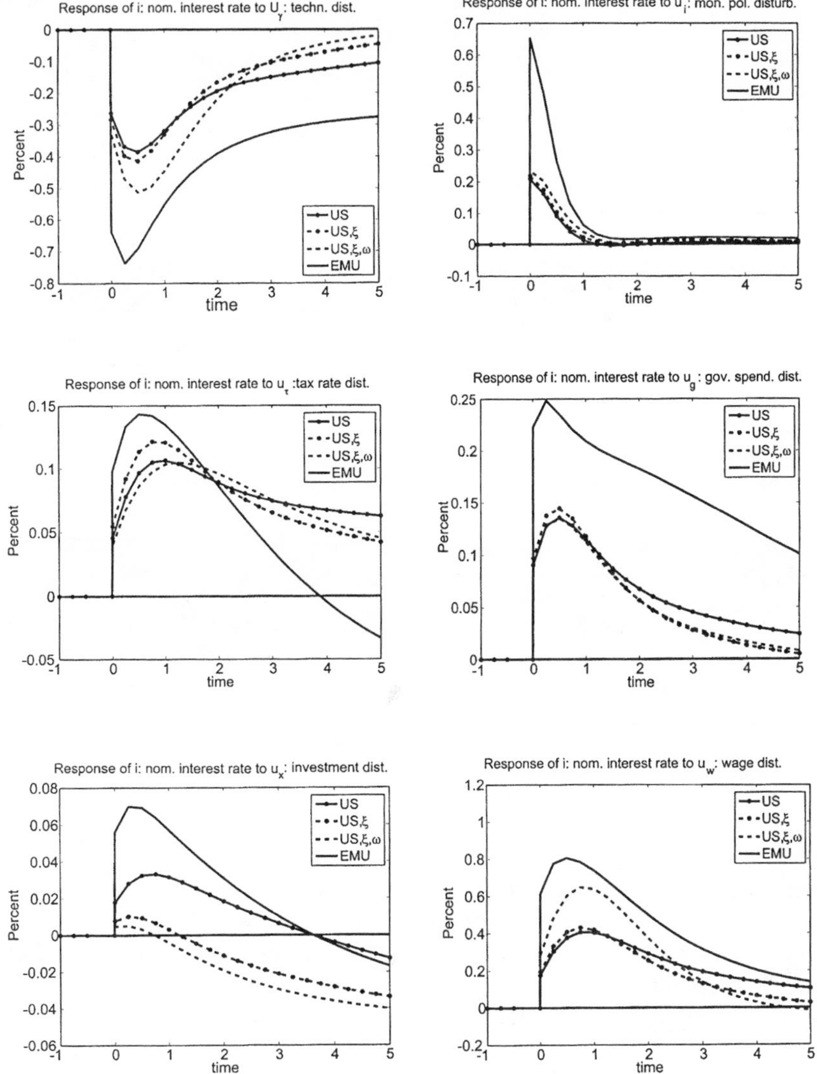

Fig. 9.6 Impulse responses of interest rates

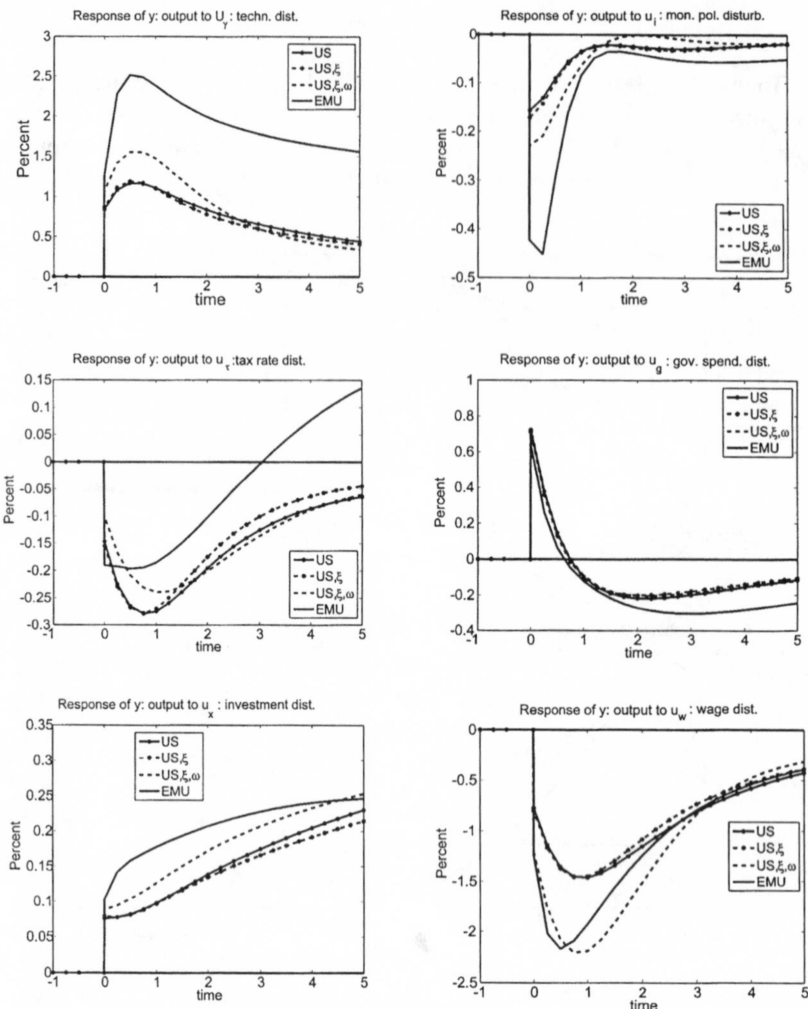

Fig. 9.7 Impulse responses of interest rates

put and figure 9.8 shows the response of inflation. A technical appendix also shows the impulse responses of the remaining variables used for estimating the model; that is, labor productivity, the consumption-to-output ratio, and the debt-to-output ratio.

In these figures, I have also considered two "intermediate" parameterizations to judge the contribution of two features in particular: the higher (assumed) requirement for bank lending in the EMU parameterization, and the parameterization of the labor market with ω and ρ_w. Starting from the U.S. parameterization, I have first only changed the parameter ξ from 0.2

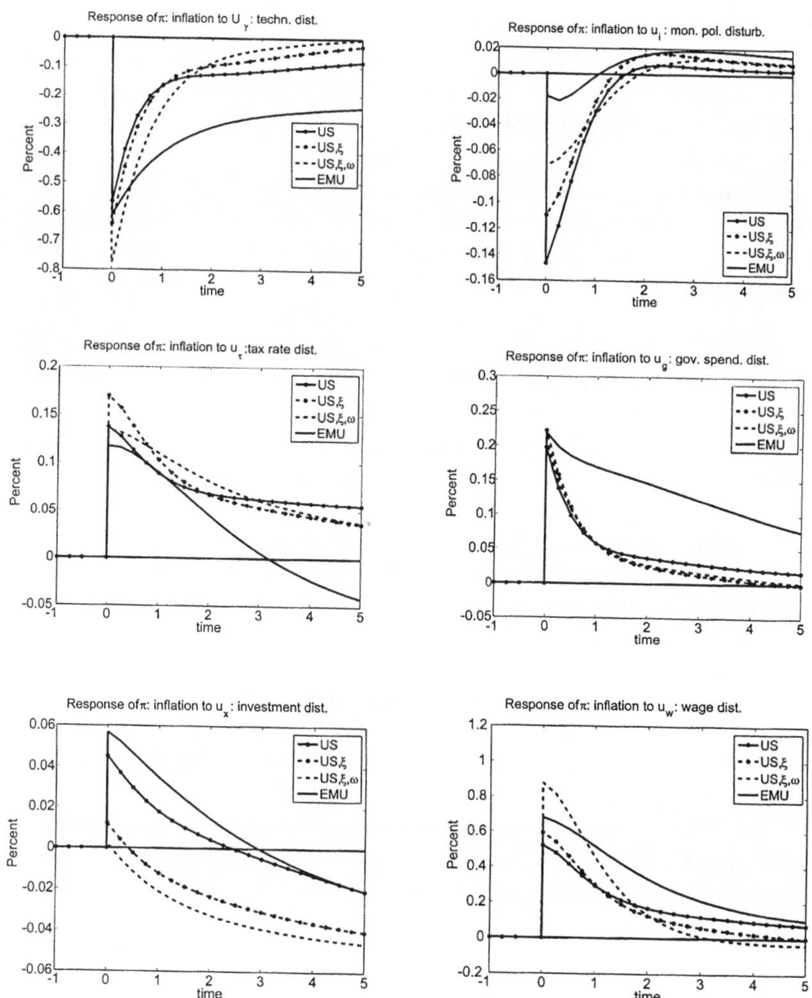

Fig. 9.8 Impulse responses of interest rates

to 1. Next I also have changed the parameters for the labor market to the EMU estimates.

It turns out that the banking requirement ξ matters only for a few key responses and variables. For example, the response of nominal interest rates as well as inflation to investment disturbances moves sizably, when changing ξ. The change in labor market parameters matters in particular in the response of inflation to monetary policy shocks—which becomes less pronounced in the United States, if using EMU labor market parameters—as well as the reaction to wage disturbances of all three variables.

Note also that the difference in the monetary policy reaction function in

EMU compared to the United States shows, if anything, a more pronounced reaction to shocks one standard deviation in size, which then is counterbalanced by the fact that these shocks appear to be smaller. The shape and thus the speed of the reaction looks similar across both regions. That is, by and large, the EMU monetary policy reaction function looks like the U.S. monetary policy reaction function, scaled up a bit, perhaps by a factor of two. This is inconsistent with the view that monetary policy in EMU is sklerotic or that it is indecisive decision-making by a committee of monetary policy makers in Europe.

9.5.3 Answering the Question

Equipped with these tools, I can finally provide an answer to the question with which this chapter started out. The answer is provided[4] graphically in figure 9.9. Note that all figures there have been drawn on the same scale for comparison. This figure decomposes the surprise movements in the United States and the EMU into the five shocks, and adds up their contributions to the cumulative forecast error, compared to the no-shock prediction in 1998. That is, the sequence of shocks, shown in figure 9.10, give rise to impulse responses of the short-term interest rate or central bank interest rate: these impulse responses are cumulated at each point in time, for all present and past shocks (back to 1998) shown.

It turns out that three main sources of the movements come from technology shocks, from monetary policy shocks, and finally, from wage shocks. Interestingly, the monetary policy shocks provide a fairly similar pattern for both Europe and the United States. The top right-hand plot in figure 9.9 shows that monetary policy was tighter in both the United States and EMU in 2000, but considerably looser in 2004, than can be explained by all other variables and historical experience. If one views these shocks as policy mistakes, one would conclude that pretty much the same mistakes have been made in both regions, and that, if anything, the Fed seemed to follow the ECB rather than the other way around.

Surprise movements in productivity provide for a key difference between the United States and EMU. Note that movements in labor productivity in the new millenium were sharply different in the United States and in EMU, as evidenced by the left figure in the second row of figure 9.4. Figure 9.6 shows that monetary policy reacts to surprise rises in productivity and thus the surprise fall in marginal costs by lowering interest rates, see the top left panel. The central bank can afford to do so, since inflation is falling anyhow, as a result, see the top left panel in figure 9.8. Together, it then may no longer surprise that the productivity movements in this millenium led to a consid-

4. It would be even better to provide standard errors in these graphs, based on the posterior distribution for the previously given parameters.

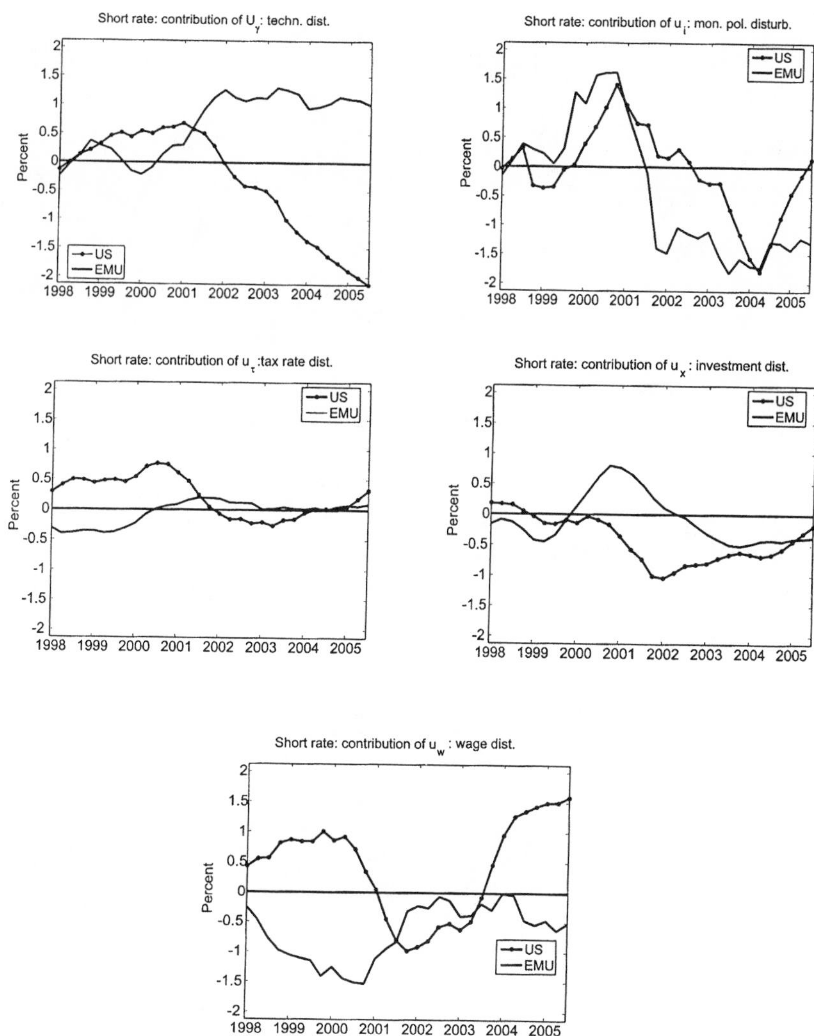

Fig. 9.9 Contribution of each shock to the cumulative forecast error, compared to the no-shock prediction starting in 1996

erable downward drift of interest rates in the United States, but upward pressure in the EMU (see the top left panel in figure 9.9).

The main additional difference then arises due to surprise wage movements. In the United States, they have contributed to raising interest rates before 2000 and after 2004, with the opposite movements in the EMU (see the bottom panel in figure 9.9).

While the reaction function of U.S. and EMU monetary policy to both

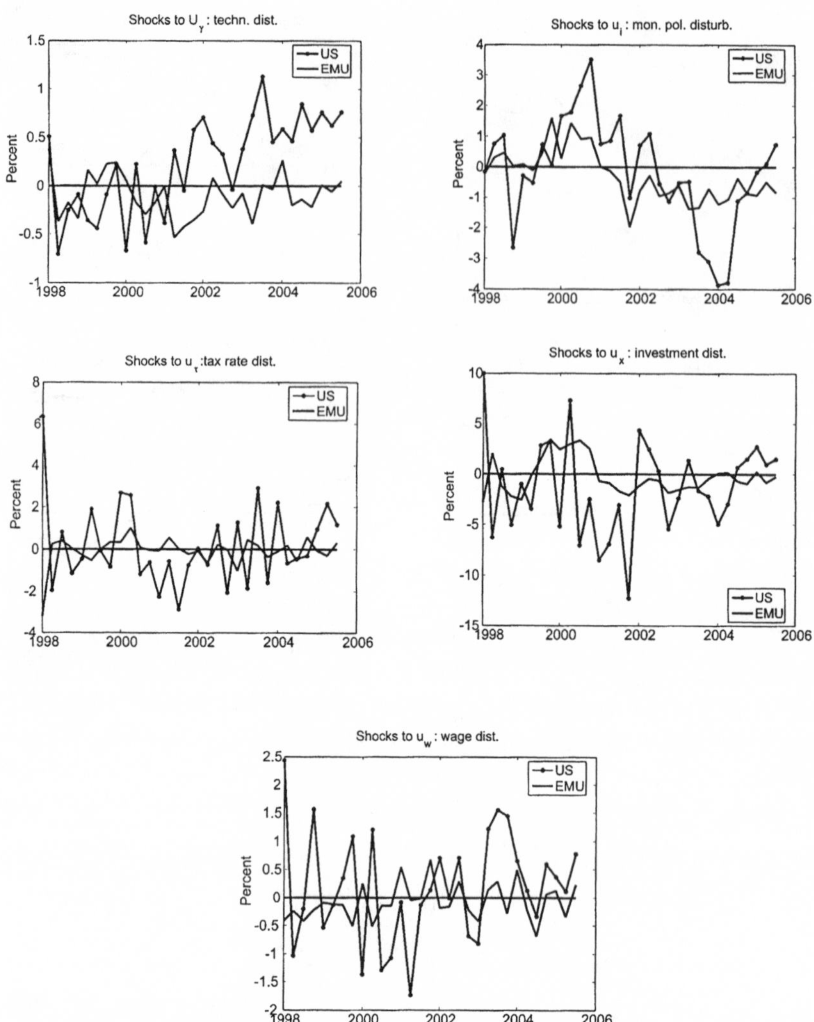

Fig. 9.10 Sequence of shocks

wage shocks and productivity shocks differ quantitatively (see figure 9.6), they do not differ qualitatively. The differences in the interest rate movements in figure 9.9 arises due to different shocks, actually almost moving in oppositive direction for both variables.

In sum, it appears that the difference between the two monetary policies seen in figure 9.1 is due to both surprises in productivity as well as surprises in wage demands, moving interest rates in opposite directions in Europe and the United States, but not due to a more sluggish response in Europe to the same shocks or to different monetary policy surprises.

9.6 Discussion and Conclusion

The conclusion from this quantitative exercise appears to be that the difference between the two monetary policies seen in figure 9.1 is due to both surprises in productivity as well as surprises in wage demands, moving interest rates in opposite directions in Europe and the United States, but not due to a more sluggish response in Europe to the same shocks or to different monetary policy surprises. If anything, it appears that monetary policy in EMU reacts more strongly to shocks, when they appear.

But a number of words of caution are in order. First, these conclusions hinge on a particular choice of shocks propagating in the economy. There is a trade-off between missing an important disturbance as explanation versus adding spurious shocks and thus risking to misinterpret important economic dynamics as movements in these spurious disturbances instead.

Second, the conclusions hinge on the particular model chosen. Is there any sense that they are correct across a wide range of models or approaches? The model may be faulty in a number of crucial features, or improve on these features compared to other models. How are we to judge this? Acknowledging misspecification of the theory and seeking robust approaches to answer the key question may be a way to proceed further (see, e.g., Hansen and Sargent 2001).

Third, while the chapter has provided an accounting method for explaining the different interest paths in the United States and the EMU, it has not asked whether this difference is, in fact, optimal or what the optimal reaction function should have been. That is, it may be the case that U.S. monetary policy has behaved badly and EMU monetary policy has done the right thing, or the other way around. The previous analysis has not addressed this issue all. The tools for pursuing this question are provided in, for example, Schmitt-Grohe and Uribe (2004, 2005) or Levin et al. (2006). One could even combine the perspective of optimality with the acknowledgment of misspecification and a desire for robustness (see, e.g., Levin and Williams 2003).

At the end of the day, there appears to be little else than delivering quantitative answers, based on thoughtfully chosen assumptions. This chapter hopes to make a contribution to that end. Along its novel features it has provided a possibility for considering traditional lending channels of monetary policy alongside the sticky-price perspective pursued by the more recent new-Keynesian literature. To that end, a hybrid new-Keynesian cash in advance model has been provided, estimated, and used to quantitatively answer the question at hand.

Some progress has been made. But much more needs to be done.

Technical Appendix

Analysis

First-Order Conditions

Households

Households solve

$$\max_{c_t,b_t,d_t,h_t} E\left[\sum_{t=0}^{\infty} \beta^t(\log(c_t - \chi c_{t-1}) - An_t^{1+\sigma})\right] \tag{38}$$

$$s.t.\ \eta c_t = \frac{h_{t-1}}{\pi_t}$$

$$h_t + d_t + q_t b_t + (1-\eta)c_t + x_t = (1-\tau_t)w_t n_t + \frac{1+i_t}{\pi_t}d_{t-1} + r_t k_{t-1} + (1-\tau_V)v_t + \frac{b_{t-1}}{\pi_t} \tag{39}$$

$$k_t = \left(1 - \delta + \varphi\left((1+u_{x,t})\frac{x_t}{k_{t-1}}\right)\right)k_{t-1}. \tag{40}$$

Let ϱ_t be the Lagrange multiplier on the first constraint (38), λ_t on the second constraint (39), and ς_t the Lagrange multiplier on the third constraint (40). Note that

$$\Lambda_t = \frac{\lambda_t}{P_t} \tag{41}$$

would therefore be the Lagrange multiplier on the second constraint written in nominal terms. Therefore,

$$\Lambda_{t,t+k} = \beta^k \frac{\Lambda_{t+k}}{\Lambda_t} = \frac{\lambda_{t+k}P_t}{\lambda_t P_{t+k}}. \tag{42}$$

The first-order conditions are

$$\frac{\partial L}{\partial c_t}: \eta\varrho_t + (1-\eta)\lambda_t = \frac{1}{c_t - \chi c_{t-1}} - \beta\chi E_t\left[\frac{1}{c_{t+1} - \chi c_t}\right] \tag{43}$$

$$\frac{\partial L}{\partial h_t}: \lambda_t = \beta E_t\left[\frac{\varrho_{t+1}}{\pi_{t+1}}\right] \tag{44}$$

$$\frac{\partial L}{\partial d_t}: \lambda_t = \beta E_t\left[\lambda_{t+1}\frac{1+i_{t+1}}{\pi_{t+1}}\right] \tag{45}$$

$$\frac{\partial L}{\partial b_t}: \lambda_t q_t = \beta E_t\left[\frac{\lambda_{t+1}}{\pi_{t+1}}\right] \tag{46}$$

$$\frac{\partial L}{\partial x_t}: \lambda_t = (1+u_{x,t})\varphi'\left((1+u_{x,t})\frac{x_t}{k_{t-1}}\right)\varsigma_t \tag{47}$$

$$\text{(48)} \quad \frac{\partial L}{\partial k_t}: \varsigma_t = \beta E_t[\lambda_{t+1} r_{t+1}]$$
$$+\beta E_t\left[\varsigma_{t+1}\left(1 - \delta + \varphi\left((1 + u_{x,t+1})\frac{x_{t+1}}{k_t}\right)\right)\right]$$
$$-\beta E_t\left[\varsigma_{t+1}\left((1 + u_{x,t+1})\varphi'\left((1 + u_{x,t+1})\frac{x_{t+1}}{k_t}\right)\frac{x_{t+1}}{k_t}\right)\right].$$

Also note that the first-order condition with respect to labor determines the target real wage $w_{t,f}$,

$$\text{(49)} \quad \frac{\partial L}{\partial n_t}: \lambda_t(1 - \tau_t)w_{t,f} = (1 + \sigma)An_t^{\sigma}.$$

Final Good Firms

Maximizing profits

$$P_t y_t - \int_0^1 P_{t,j} y_{t,j} dj,$$

subject to the production function (6) results in the demand function

$$\text{(50)} \quad y_{t,j} = \left(\frac{P_t}{P_{t,j}}\right)^{(1+\mu)/\mu} y_t$$

and the price aggregation

$$\text{(51)} \quad P_t = \left(\int_0^1 P_{t,j}^{-1/\mu} dj\right)^{-\mu}$$

$$\text{(52)} \quad = ((1 - \alpha)(P_t^*)^{-1/\mu} + \alpha(\overline{\pi} P_{t-1})^{-1/\mu})^{-\mu}.$$

Intermediate Good Firms

Cost minimization leads to the nominal marginal costs of producing an extra unit of output,

$$\text{(53)} \quad \text{MC}_t = P_t \theta^{-\theta}(1 - \theta)^{\theta-1}\gamma_t^{-1} r_t^{\theta} w_t^{1-\theta},$$

and therefore to the real marginal costs

$$\text{(54)} \quad \text{mc}_t = \theta^{-\theta}(1 - \theta)^{\theta-1}\gamma_t^{-1} r_t^{\theta} w_t^{1-\theta},$$

excluding the costs of borrowing from bank.

Cost minimization also implies that

$$\text{(55)} \quad r_t k_{t,j} = \theta \text{mc}_t \gamma_t k_{t,j}^{\theta} n_{t,j}^{1-\theta}$$

$$\text{(56)} \quad w_t n_{t,j} = (1 - \theta)\text{mc}_t \gamma_t k_{t,j}^{\theta} n_{t,j}^{1-\theta}.$$

Therefore, the capital-labor ratio $k_{t,j}/n_{t,j}$ is the same across all firms, and equal to the aggregate ratio k_{t-1}/n_t. Aggregating (55) and (56) across all firms yields

$$(57) \qquad r_t k_{t-1} = \theta \mathrm{mc}_t \gamma_t k_{t-1}^{\theta} n_t^{1-\theta}$$
$$w_t n_t = (1-\theta)\mathrm{mc}_t \gamma_t k_{t-1}^{\theta} n_t^{1-\theta}.$$

Note that (57) follows from (57) with (54) or vice-versa. I will therefore drop (57) when collecting all equations following. Alternatively, observe that (57) and (54) imply the more intuitive equation

$$(58) \qquad \frac{1}{\theta} r_t k_{t-1} = \frac{1}{1-\theta} w_t n_t.$$

To calculate the aggregate production function, observe that

$$\gamma_t k_{t-1}^{\theta} n_t^{1-\theta} = \int_0^1 (y_{t,j} + \Phi) dj = \left(\int_0^1 \left(\frac{P_t}{P_{t,j}} \right)^{(1+\mu)/\mu} dj \right) y_t + \Phi,$$

so that

$$(59) \qquad y_t = \left(\frac{S_t}{P_t} \right)^{1+\mu/\mu} (\gamma_t k_{t-1}^{\theta} n_t^{1-\theta} - \Phi),$$

where

$$(60) \qquad S_t = \left(\int_0^1 P_{t,j}^{-(1+\mu)/\mu} dj \right)^{-\mu/(1+\mu)}$$
$$= ((1-\alpha)(P_t^*)^{-(1+\mu)/\mu} + \alpha(\overline{\pi} S_{t-1})^{-(1+\mu)/\mu})^{-\mu/(1+\mu)},$$

and where $(S_t/P_t)^{(1+\mu)/\mu}$ can be thought of as a correction of the Solow residual due to sticky prices. This correction is known to disappear in a first-order log-linear approximation (see also [123]), but it may be relevant in higher-order approximations.

When a firm can reoptimize its price $P_t^* = P_{t,j}$, it seeks to maximize the objective (11), taking into account the dependence of demand on its chosen price in future dates, if prices cannot be reoptimized, and taking into account the costs of borrowing from banks,

$$(61) \qquad y_t(P_{t-k}^*) = \left(\frac{P_t}{\overline{\pi}^k P_{t-k}^*} \right)^{(1+\mu)/\mu} y_t.$$

This problem can be rewritten as

$$(62) \qquad \max_{P_t^*} E\left[\sum_{k=0}^{\infty} \alpha^k \Lambda_{t,t+k} y_{t+k}(P_t^*)(P_t^* - P_{t+k}(1 + \xi i_{t+k})\mathrm{mc}_{t+k}) \right].$$

The first-order condition becomes—as usual (or with some calculation)—

$$(63) \qquad P_t^* E_t\left[\sum_{k=0}^{\infty} \alpha^k \Lambda_{t,t+k} \overline{\pi}^k y_{t+k}(P_t^*) \right] =$$
$$(1+\mu) E_t\left[\sum_{k=0}^{\infty} \alpha^k \Lambda_{t,t+k} y_{t+k}(P_t^*) P_{t+k}(1 + \xi i_{t+k})\mathrm{mc}_{t+k} \right],$$

which essentially says that P^* is a markup of μ over nominal marginal costs inclusive of the costs of borrowing,

$$P_{t+k}(1 + \xi i_{t+k})\mathrm{mc}_{t+k},$$

appropriately discounted.

Aggregating (9) across all firms delivers

$$v_t = y_t - (1 + \xi i_t)\mathrm{mc}_t \gamma_t k_{t-1}^{\theta} n_t^{1-\theta}. \tag{64}$$

Banks

Note that the required loan quantity per intermediate good firms is

$$L_{t,j} = \xi \mathrm{MC}_t(y_{t,j} + \Phi). \tag{65}$$

Aggregating, and equalizing to available funds yields in real terms

$$\frac{d_{t-1}}{\pi_t} + \Psi_t = \xi \mathrm{mc}_t \gamma_t k_{t-1}^{\theta} n_t^{1-\theta}, \tag{66}$$

which I shall use instead of (33).

Parameters

The fundamental parameters are

$$A, \beta, \chi, \sigma, \theta, \delta, \Phi, \mu, \overline{\gamma}, \rho_{\gamma,L}, \rho_{\gamma,u}, \rho_x, \varpi,$$

and the variance of the technology shock and investment-specific shock. The parameters for prices, wages, and credit markets are

$$\Upsilon, \alpha, \omega, \xi, \rho_w, \eta,$$

and the variance of the wage shock. The policy parameters are

$$\overline{g}, \overline{b}, \overline{\pi}, \nu, \tau_V,$$

as well as the feedback coefficients

$$\zeta_\tau, \zeta_g, \zeta_\pi, \zeta_x, \rho_{i,L}, \rho_{i,u}, \rho_\tau, \rho_g,$$

and variances of the policy shocks.

Collecting the Equations

The equations characterizing the equilibrium are (HH: "household"; "FG": final good firms; "IG": intermediate good firms; "CB": central bank; "GOV": government; "MC": labor market and market clearing):

$$\text{HH: } 0 = -\eta c_t + \frac{h_{t-1}}{\pi_t} \tag{67}$$

$$\text{HH: } 0 = -h_t - d_t - q_t b_t - (1-\eta)c_t - x_t + (1-\tau_t)w_t n_t + r_t k_{t-1} + \frac{1+i_t}{\pi_t} d_{t-1} + (1-\tau_V)v_t + \frac{b_{t-1}}{\pi_t} \tag{68}$$

$$\text{(69)}\quad \text{HH: } 0 = -k_t + \left(1 - \delta + \varphi\left(\frac{x_t}{k_{t-1}}\right)\right)k_{t-1}$$

$$\text{(70)}\quad \text{HH: } 0 = -\eta\varrho_t - (1-\eta)\lambda_t + \frac{1}{c_t - \chi c_{t-1}} - \beta\chi E_t\left[\frac{1}{c_{t+1} - \chi c_t}\right]$$

$$\text{(71)}\quad \text{HH: } 0 = -\lambda_t + \beta E_t\left[\frac{\varrho_{t+1}}{\pi_{t+1}}\right]$$

$$\text{(72)}\quad \text{HH: } 0 = -\lambda_t + \beta E_t\left[\lambda_{t+1}\frac{1 + i_{t+1}}{\pi_{t+1}}\right]$$

$$\text{(73)}\quad \text{HH: } 0 = -\lambda_t q_t + \beta E_t\left[\frac{\lambda_{t+1}}{\pi_{t+1}}\right]$$

$$\text{(74)}\quad \text{HH: } 0 = -\lambda_t + (1 + u_{x,t})\varphi'\left((1 + u_{x,t})\frac{x_t}{k_{t-1}}\right)\varsigma_t$$

$$\text{(75)}\quad \text{HH: } 0 = -\varsigma_t + \beta E_t[\lambda_{t+1} r_{t+1}]$$
$$+\beta E_t\left[\varsigma_{t+1}\left(1 - \delta + \varphi\left((1 + u_{x,t+1})\frac{x_{t+1}}{k_t}\right)\right)\right]$$
$$-\beta E_t\left[\varsigma_{t+1}\left((1 + u_{x,t+1})\varphi'\left((1 + u_{x,t+1})\frac{x_{t+1}}{k_t}\right)\frac{x_{t+1}}{k_t}\right)\right]$$

$$\text{(76)}\quad \text{HH: } 0 = -\lambda_t(1 - \tau_t)w_{t,f} + (1 + \sigma)An_t^{\sigma}$$

$$\text{(77)}\quad \text{FG: } 0 = -y_t(P_{t-k}^*) + \left(\frac{P_t}{\overline{\pi}^k P_{t-k}^*}\right)^{(1+\mu)/\mu} y_t$$

$$\text{(78)}\quad \text{FG: } 0 = -P_t + ((1-\alpha)(P_t^*)^{-1/\mu} + \alpha(\overline{\pi}P_{t-1})^{-1/\mu})^{-\mu}$$

$$\text{(79)}\quad \text{IG: } 0 = -S_t + ((1-\alpha)(P_t^*)^{-(1+\mu)/\mu}$$
$$+ \alpha(\overline{\pi}S_{t-1})^{-(1+\mu)/\mu})^{-\mu/(1+\mu)}$$

$$\text{(80)}\quad \text{IG: } 0 = -y_t + \left(\frac{S_t}{P_t}\right)^{(1+\mu)/\mu}(\gamma_t k_{t-1}^{\theta} n_t^{1-\theta} - \Phi)$$

$$\text{(81)}\quad \text{IG: } 0 = -\text{mc}_t + \theta^{-\theta}(1-\theta)^{\theta-1}\gamma_t^{-1} r_t^{\theta} w_t^{1-\theta}$$

$$\text{(82)}\quad \text{IG: } 0 = -r_t k_{t-1} + \theta\,\text{mc}_t\gamma_t k_{t-1}^{\theta} n_t^{1-\theta}$$

$$\text{(83)}\quad \text{IG: } 0 = -P_t^* E_t\left[\sum_{k=0}^{\infty}(\alpha\beta)^k \frac{\lambda_{t+k}P_t}{\lambda_t P_{t+k}}\overline{\pi}^k y_{t+k}(P_t^*)\right]$$
$$+(1+\mu)E_t\left[\sum_{k=0}^{\infty}(\alpha\beta)^k \frac{\lambda_{t+k}P_t}{\lambda_t P_{t+k}} y_{t+k}(P_t^*)P_{t+k}(1 + \xi i_{t+k})\text{mc}_{t+k}\right]$$

$$\text{(84)}\quad \text{IG: } 0 = v_t - y_t + (1 + \xi i_t)\text{mc}_t\gamma_t k_{t-1}^{\theta} n_t^{1-\theta}$$

(85) $$\text{CB: } 0 = -i_t + \bar{i} + \rho_{i,L} i_{t-1} + (1 - \rho_{i,L})\left(\zeta_\pi\left(\frac{\pi_t}{\bar{\pi}} - 1\right) + \zeta_x\left(\frac{\text{mc}_t}{\overline{\text{mc}}} - 1\right) + u_{i,t}\right)$$

(86) $$\text{CB: } 0 = -m_t + \frac{m_{t-1}}{\pi_t} + \nu\Psi_t$$

(87) $$\text{GOV: } 0 = -q_t b_t + \frac{b_{t-1}}{\pi_t} + g_t - \tau_t w_t n_t - \tau_V v_t - (\nu + i_t)\Psi_t$$

(88) $$\text{GOV: } 0 = -\tau_t + \bar{\tau} + \zeta_\tau\left(\frac{b_{t-1} - \bar{b}}{\bar{y}} - 1\right) + u_{\tau,t}$$

(89) $$\text{GOV: } 0 = -\frac{g_t}{\bar{y}} + \zeta_g\left(\frac{b_{t-1} - \bar{b}}{\bar{b}} - 1\right) + u_{g,t}$$

(90) $$\text{MC: } 0 = -w_t + ((1 - \omega)w_{t-1} + \omega\Upsilon w_{t,f})(1 + u_{w,t})$$

(91) $$\text{MC: } 0 = -m_t + d_t + h_t$$

(92) $$\text{MC: } 0 = -y_t + g_t + c_t + x_t$$

(93) $$\text{MC: } 0 = -\frac{d_{t-1}}{\pi_t} - \Psi_t + \xi \text{mc}_t \gamma_t k_{t-1}^{\theta} n_t^{1-\theta}$$

(94) $$\text{MC: } 0 = -\pi_t + \frac{P_t}{P_{t-1}}$$

together with the specification for the exogenous processes

(95) $$\text{techn.: } \hat{\gamma}_t = \rho_{\gamma,L}\hat{\gamma}_{t-1} + \varepsilon_{\gamma,t}$$

(96) $$\text{mon.pol: } u_{i,t} = \rho_{i,u} u_{i,t-1} + \varepsilon_{i,t}$$

(97) $$\text{taxes: } u_{\tau,t} = \rho_\tau u_{\tau,t-1} + \varepsilon_{\tau,t}$$

(98) $$\text{gov.spend.: } u_{g,t} = \rho_g u_{g,t-1} + \varepsilon_{g,t}$$

(99) $$\text{investment: } u_{x,t} = \rho_x u_{x,t-1} + \varepsilon_{x,t}$$

(100) $$\text{wages: } u_{w,t} = \rho_w u_{w,t-1} + \varepsilon_{w,t}.$$

The previous equations determine the quantities

$$b_t, c_t, g_t, n_t, v_t, y_t, \text{mc}_t, k_t, x_t, r_t,$$

the demand function

$$y_t(P^*_{t-k}),$$

real money balances

$$d_t, h_t, m_t, \Psi_t,$$

multipliers

$$\varrho_t, \lambda_t, \varsigma_t,$$

prices and tax rate

$$i_t, P_t, P_t^*, q_t, S_t, w_t, w_{t,f}, \pi_t, \tau_t,$$

as well as the exogenous processes

$$\gamma_t, u_{i,t}, u_{r,t}, u_{g,t}, u_{x,t}, u_{w,t}.$$

Note that these are 34 equations for 33 variables. One may drop either the household budget constraint, the government budget constraint, or one of the market-clearing conditions, due to Walras' law.

Steady State

Household

To calculate the steady state, and since my focus is not on a steady-state comparison across various parameters, I assume a value for $\bar{n}$ and instead back out the compatible preference parameter A. The capital accumulation equation (69) implies

$$\bar{x} = \delta \bar{k}. \tag{101}$$

The first-order conditions (71) and (74) of the households imply

$$\bar{\varrho} = \frac{\bar{\pi}}{\beta} \bar{\lambda} \tag{102}$$

$$\bar{\varsigma} = \bar{\lambda}. \tag{103}$$

For the rental rate of capital, the first-order condition (75) implies

$$\bar{r} = \frac{1}{\beta} - 1 + \delta. \tag{104}$$

The first-order conditions (72) and (73) imply

$$1 + \bar{i} = \frac{1}{\bar{q}} = \frac{\bar{\pi}}{\beta}. \tag{105}$$

Firms

We shall assume that the parameters imply $\bar{v} > 0$. Equations (78), (79), and (94) deliver

$$\bar{P}_t^* = \bar{S}_t = \bar{P}_t = \bar{\pi} \bar{P}_{t-1}.$$

With equation (77),

$$y(\overline{P}^*_{t-k}) = \overline{y}.$$

The markup equation (83) for the intermediate good implies

$$\overline{\text{mc}} = \frac{1}{(1+\mu)(1+\xi\overline{\iota})}. \tag{106}$$

This and equation (82) imply

$$\overline{r}\overline{k} = \theta\overline{\text{mc}}\,\overline{\gamma}\overline{k}^{\theta}\overline{n}^{1-\theta},$$

or

$$\overline{k} = \left(\frac{\theta\overline{\text{mc}}\,\overline{\gamma}}{\overline{r}}\right)^{1/(1-\theta)}\overline{n}. \tag{107}$$

From this and (81) or, equivalently, (57), obtain

$$\overline{w} = (1-\theta)\overline{\text{mc}}\,\overline{\gamma}\left(\frac{\overline{k}}{\overline{n}}\right)^{\theta} = (1-\theta)\theta^{\theta/(1-\theta)}(\overline{\text{mc}}\,\overline{\gamma})^{1/(1-\theta)}\overline{r}^{-\theta/(1-\theta)}. \tag{108}$$

With this as well as equations (80, 92, 70, 90, 84)

$$\overline{y} = \overline{\gamma}\overline{k}^{\theta}\overline{n}^{1-\theta} - \Phi \tag{109}$$

$$\overline{c} = \overline{y} - \overline{g} - \delta\overline{k} \tag{110}$$

$$\overline{\lambda} = \left(\eta\frac{\overline{\pi}}{\beta} + 1 - \eta\right)^{-1}\frac{1-\beta\chi}{1-\chi}\frac{1}{\overline{c}} \tag{111}$$

$$\overline{w}_f = \frac{\overline{w}}{\Upsilon} \tag{112}$$

$$\overline{v} = \overline{y} - (1+\xi\overline{\iota})\overline{\text{mc}}\,\overline{\gamma}\overline{k}^{\theta}\overline{n}^{1-\theta} \tag{113}$$

$$= \frac{\mu}{1+\mu}\overline{\gamma}\overline{k}^{\theta}\overline{n}^{1-\theta} - \Phi \tag{114}$$

$$= \overline{y} - \frac{1}{1+\mu}(\overline{y} + \Phi), \tag{115}$$

which now allows to solve for the steady-state values of the Lagrange multipliers in (102).

Monetary Quantities

Cash demand is given by (67) or

$$\overline{h} = \eta\overline{\pi}\overline{c}.$$

To calculate the other monetary quantities, combine the three steady-state relationships of (86, 91, 93),

$$\nu\overline{\psi} = \overline{m}\left(1 - \frac{1}{\overline{\pi}}\right)$$

$$\overline{m} = \overline{d} + \overline{h}$$

$$\xi\overline{mc}(\overline{y} - \Phi) = \frac{\overline{d}}{\overline{\pi}} + \overline{\psi},$$

to obtain

$$\overline{m} = \frac{\overline{\pi}\nu}{\overline{\pi} + \nu - 1}\left(\xi\overline{mc}(\overline{y} - \Phi) + \frac{\overline{h}}{\overline{\pi}}\right) \tag{116}$$

$$\overline{\psi} = \frac{\overline{\pi} - 1}{\overline{\pi}\nu}\overline{m} \tag{117}$$

$$\overline{d} = \overline{m} - \overline{h}. \tag{118}$$

Note that the fraction appearing in the equation for $\overline{m}$ equals 1, if either $\overline{\pi} = 1$ or $\nu = 1$. For technical reasons, one must set $\nu \neq 0$. Note that $\overline{\pi} = 1$ implies $\overline{\psi} = 0$.

Remaining Equations

The steady-state government budget constraint (88)

$$\overline{\tau}\overline{w}\overline{n} = \frac{1 - \beta}{\overline{\pi}}\overline{b} + \overline{g} - \tau_V\overline{v} - (\nu + \overline{\iota})\overline{\psi}, \tag{119}$$

can be solved for the steady-state level of taxes $\overline{\tau}$. With this and (76), calculate the preference parameter A per

$$A = \frac{\overline{\lambda}(1 - \overline{\tau})}{1 + \sigma}\overline{n}^{-\sigma}\overline{w}_f. \tag{120}$$

Note finally that (95) to (98) deliver

$$\overline{z} = \overline{a} = \overline{f}_\tau = \overline{f}_g = 0.$$

Log-Linearization

Let hat on variables denote the logarithmic deviation from steady-state values; for example, $\hat{c}_t = \log(c_t) - \log(\overline{c})$. For nominal quantities, in particular prices, I use, likewise, $\hat{P}_t = \log(P_t) - \log(\overline{P}_t)$, where I note that $\overline{P}_t = \overline{\pi}^k\overline{P}_0$, starting from some initial level $\overline{P}_0$. I make the following exceptions for the notation, so as to allow zero values in steady state or to obtain meaningful quantities:

$$r_t = \overline{r} + \hat{r}_t$$

$$i_t = \overline{\iota} + \hat{\iota}_t$$

$$\tau_t = \bar{\tau} + \hat{\tau}_t$$
$$g_t = \bar{g} + \hat{g}_t\bar{y}$$
$$b_t = \bar{b} + \hat{b}_t\bar{y}$$
$$\psi_t = \bar{\psi} + \bar{m}\hat{\psi}_t.$$

Hence, $\hat{r}_t$, $\hat{\tau}_t$, and $\hat{\imath}_t$ are in percent, $\hat{g}_t$ and $\hat{b}_t$ are in percent of steady-state output, and $\hat{\psi}_t$ is in percent of the steady-state money supply. Most equations can be log-linearized in a straightforward manner, but some equations require a bit more thought. They are explained now.

Pricing Decisions

The following derivation is standard in the literature on new-Keynesian models and is replicated here for completeness.

Equations (78) and (79) log-linearize to

$$\text{(121)} \qquad \hat{P}_t = (1-\alpha)\hat{P}^*_t + \alpha\hat{P}_{t-1}$$
$$\hat{S}_t = (1-\alpha)\hat{P}^*_t + \alpha\hat{S}_{t-1}$$

and thus

$$\text{(122)} \qquad \hat{S}_t = \hat{P}_t.$$

This substantiates the claim that the correction to the Solow residual in (59) vanishes in a first-order approximation.

The first-order condition (83) of the intermediate good firms log-linearizes to

$$\text{(123)} \qquad \hat{P}^*_t = (1-\alpha\beta)E_t\left[\sum_{k=0}^{\infty}(\alpha\beta)^k\left(\frac{\xi}{1+\xi\bar{\imath}}\hat{\imath}_{t+k} + \widehat{\mathrm{mc}}_{t+k} + \hat{P}_{t+k}\right)\right].$$

A rather "pedestrian" but fail-safe way to see this is to indeed replace all variables, say x_{t+k}, with their log-linearized counterpart $x(1+\hat{x}_{t+k})$, drop all products of hat-variables as "higher order" (or better, do not write them down—there are many). Simplify the constants, employing equation (106). A slightly more sophisticated approach is to immediately log-linearize products, say $x_t y_t z_t$ to $xyz(1+\hat{x}_t+\hat{y}_t+\hat{z}_t)$.

The previous equation can be rewritten as

$$\text{(124)} \qquad \hat{P}^*_t = (1-\alpha\beta)\left(\frac{\xi}{1+\xi\bar{\imath}}\hat{\imath}_t + \widehat{\mathrm{mc}}_t + \hat{P}_t\right) + \alpha\beta E_t[\hat{P}^*_{t+1}].$$

From equation (122), substitute $\hat{P}^*_t$ and $\hat{P}^*_{t+1}$ per

$$\hat{P}^*_t = \frac{1}{1-\alpha}(\hat{P}_t - \alpha\hat{P}_{t-1}).$$

Combine terms to obtain the new-Keynesian Phillips curve

$$(125)\qquad \hat{\pi}_t = \beta E_t[\hat{\pi}_{t+1}] + \kappa\left(\frac{\xi}{1+\xi\bar{\imath}}\hat{\imath}_t + \widehat{\text{mc}}_t\right),$$

where

$$(126)\qquad \kappa = \frac{(1-\alpha)(1-\alpha\beta)}{\alpha}.$$

One may view the driving term

$$\frac{\xi}{1+\xi\bar{\imath}}\hat{\imath}_t + \widehat{\text{mc}}_t$$

either as reflecting marginal costs inclusive of the costs of borrowing or as a correction to net marginal cost by an interest rate cost channel, as emphasized by Christiano et al. (2003).

Collecting Log-Linearized Equations Without Expectations

We shall drop the budget constraint of the household—appealing to Walras' law—as well as equations from pricing decisions and demand, which are no longer needed. All remaining equations without expectations are, in log-linearized form:

$$(127)\qquad \text{HH}: 0 = -\hat{c}_t + \hat{h}_{t-1} - \hat{\pi}_t$$

$$(128)\qquad \text{HH}: 0 = -\hat{k}_t + \delta\hat{x}_t + (1-\delta)\hat{k}_{t-1} + \delta u_{x,t}$$

$$(129)\qquad \text{HH}: 0 = -\hat{\varsigma}_t + \hat{\lambda}_t + \frac{1}{\varpi}(\hat{x}_t - \hat{k}_{t-1}) - \left(1 - \frac{1}{\varpi}\right)u_{x,t}$$

$$(130)\qquad \text{HH}: 0 = -\hat{\lambda}_t + \frac{\hat{\tau}_t}{1-\bar{\tau}} - \hat{w}_{t,f} + \sigma\hat{n}_t$$

$$(131)\qquad \text{IG}: 0 = -\frac{\bar{y}}{\bar{y}+\Phi}\hat{y}_t + \hat{\gamma}_t + \theta\hat{k}_{t-1} + (1-\theta)\hat{n}_t$$

$$(132)\qquad \text{IG}: 0 = -\widehat{\text{mc}}_t + \theta\frac{\hat{r}_t}{\bar{r}} + (1-\theta)\hat{w}_t - \hat{\gamma}_t$$

$$(133)\qquad \text{IG}: 0 = -\frac{\hat{r}_t}{\bar{r}} + \widehat{\text{mc}}_t + \gamma_t + (1-\theta)(\hat{n}_t - \hat{k}_{t-1})$$

$$(134)\qquad \text{IG}: 0 = \frac{\bar{v}}{\bar{y}-\bar{v}}\hat{v}_t - \frac{\bar{y}}{\bar{y}-\bar{v}}\hat{y}_t + \frac{\xi}{1+\xi\bar{\imath}}\hat{\imath}_t + \widehat{\text{mc}}_t + \hat{\gamma}_t + \theta\hat{k}_{t-1} + (1-\theta)n_t$$

$$(135)\qquad \text{CB}: 0 = -\hat{\imath}_t + \rho_{i,L}\hat{\imath}_{t-1} + (1-\rho_{i,L})(\zeta_\pi\hat{\pi}_t + \zeta_x\widehat{\text{mc}}_t + u_{i,t}).$$

$$(136) \quad \text{CB: } 0 = -\hat{m}_t + \frac{1}{\overline{\pi}}(\hat{m}_{t-1} - \hat{\pi}_t) + \nu\hat{\psi}_t$$

$$(137) \quad \text{GOV: } 0 = -\overline{q}(\overline{b}\hat{q}_t + \overline{y}\hat{b}_t) + \frac{1}{\overline{\pi}}(\overline{y}\hat{b}_{t-1} - \overline{b}\hat{\pi}_t) + \overline{y}\hat{g}_t$$

$$-\overline{w}\,\overline{n}\hat{\tau}_t - \overline{\tau}\,\overline{w}\,\overline{n}(\hat{w}_t + \hat{n}_t) - \tau_V\overline{v}\hat{v}_t - (\nu + \overline{\imath})\overline{m}\hat{\psi}_t - \overline{\psi}\hat{\imath}_t$$

$$(138) \quad \text{GOV: } 0 = -\hat{\tau}_t + \zeta_\tau\hat{b}_{t-1} + u_{\tau,t}$$

$$(139) \quad \text{GOV: } 0 = -\hat{g}_t + \zeta_g\hat{b}_{t-1} + u_{g,t}$$

$$(140) \quad \text{MC: } 0 = -\hat{w}_t + (1 - \omega)\hat{w}_{t-1} + \omega\hat{w}_{t,f} + u_{w,t}$$

$$(141) \quad \text{MC: } 0 = -\overline{m}\hat{m}_t + \overline{d}\hat{d}_t + \overline{h}\hat{h}_t$$

$$(142) \quad \text{MC: } 0 = -\overline{y}\hat{y}_t + \overline{y}\hat{g}_t + \overline{c}\hat{c}_t + \overline{x}\hat{x}_t$$

$$(143) \quad \text{MC: } 0 = \frac{\overline{d}}{\overline{d} + \overline{\pi}\,\overline{\psi}}(\hat{d}_{t-1} - \hat{\pi}_t) + \frac{\overline{\pi}\,\overline{m}}{\overline{d} + \overline{\pi}\,\overline{\psi}}\hat{\psi}_t$$

$$+ \widehat{\text{mc}}_t + \hat{\gamma}_t + \theta\hat{k}_{t-1} + (1 - \theta)\hat{n}_t$$

together with the specification for the exogenous processes

$$(144) \quad \text{techn.: } \hat{\gamma}_t = \rho_{\gamma,L}\hat{\gamma}_{t-1} + u_{\gamma,t}$$

$$(145) \quad u_{\gamma,t} = \rho_{\gamma,u}u_{\gamma,t-1} + \varepsilon_{\gamma,t}$$

$$(146) \quad \text{mon.pol: } u_{i,t} = \rho_{i,u}u_{i,t-1} + \varepsilon_{i,t}$$

$$(147) \quad \text{taxes: } u_{\tau,t} = \rho_\tau u_{\tau,t-1} + \varepsilon_{\tau,t}$$

$$(148) \quad \text{gov.spend.: } u_{g,t} = \rho_g u_{g,t-1} + \varepsilon_{g,t}$$

$$(149) \quad \text{investment: } u_{x,t} = \rho_x u_{x,t-1} + \varepsilon_{x,t}$$

$$(150) \quad \text{wages: } u_{w,t} = \rho_w u_{w,t-1} + \varepsilon_{w,t}.$$

Collecting Log-Linearized Equations with Expectations

All equations with expectations in log-linearized form are:

$$(151) \quad \text{HH: } 0 = -\frac{(1 - \beta\chi)(1 - \chi)}{\eta(\overline{\pi}/\beta) + 1 - \eta}\left(\eta\frac{\overline{\pi}}{\beta}\hat{\varrho}_t + (1 - \eta)\hat{\lambda}_t\right)$$

$$+\chi\hat{c}_{t-1} - (1 + \beta\chi^2)\hat{c}_t + \beta\chi E_t[\hat{c}_{t+1}]$$

$$(152) \quad \text{HH: } 0 = -\hat{\lambda}_t + E_t[\hat{\varrho}_{t+1} - \hat{\pi}_{t+1}]$$

$$(153) \quad \text{HH: } 0 = -\hat{\lambda}_t + E_t[\hat{\lambda}_{t+1} + \frac{\hat{\imath}_{t+1}}{1 + \overline{\imath}} - \hat{\pi}_{t+1}]$$

$$(154) \quad \text{HH: } 0 = -\hat{\lambda}_t - \hat{q}_t + E_t[\hat{\lambda}_{t+1} - \hat{\pi}_{t+1}]$$

$$(155) \qquad \text{HH: } 0 = -\hat{\varsigma}_t + \beta E_t[\bar{r}\hat{\lambda}_{t+1} + \hat{r}_{t+1}] + \beta E_t[(1-\delta)\hat{\varsigma}_{t+1} + \frac{\delta}{\varpi}(\hat{x}_{t+1} - \hat{k}_t + u_{x,t+1})]$$

$$(156) \quad \text{FG, IG: } 0 = -\hat{\pi}_t + \beta E_t[\hat{\pi}_{t+1}] + \kappa\left(\frac{\xi}{1+\xi\bar{\imath}}\hat{\imath}_t + \widehat{\mathrm{mc}}_t\right).$$

These equations and the equations without expectations determine the evolution of the log-deviations for the quantities

$$\hat{b}_t, \hat{c}_t, \hat{g}_t, \hat{n}_t, \hat{v}_t, \hat{y}_t, \widehat{\mathrm{mc}}_t, \hat{k}_t, \hat{x}_t, \hat{r}_t,$$

real money balances

$$\hat{d}_t, \hat{h}_t, \hat{m}_t, \hat{\psi}_t,$$

multipliers

$$\hat{\varrho}_t, \hat{\lambda}_t, \hat{\varsigma}_t,$$

prices and tax rate

$$\hat{\imath}_t, \hat{q}_t, \hat{w}_t, \hat{w}_{t,f}, \hat{\pi}_t, \hat{\tau}_t.$$

Note that there are twenty-three equations for twenty-three variables, plus the equations for the exogenous processes.

Note that q_t is the inverse of the one-period risk free return $R_{t,f}$ from period t to $t + 1$. Hence

$$\hat{R}_{t,f} = -\hat{q}_t.$$

Note that generally $\hat{\imath}_t \neq \hat{R}_{t-1,f}$, since $\hat{\imath}_t$ can react to shocks within period t.

Define

$$(157) \qquad \hat{r}_t^* = \hat{r}_t + \frac{1}{\varpi}(\hat{x}_t - \hat{k}_{t-1}) - \left(1 - \delta - \frac{1}{\varpi}\right)u_{x,t} - \frac{1}{\beta\varpi}(\hat{x}_{t-1} - \hat{k}_{t-2}) + \frac{1}{\beta}\left(1 - \frac{1}{\varpi}\right)u_{x,t-1}.$$

One may interpret this as the log-deviation of the return to capital, taking into account the cost of adjustment and the additional discounting due to the extra period of being able to spend the rental rate on consumption. With this definition and the help of equation (130), one can rewrite (155) as

$$(158) \qquad 0 = -\hat{\lambda}_t + \eta(\hat{\lambda}_t - \hat{\varrho}_t) + E_t[\lambda_{t+1} + \beta\eta(1-\delta)(\hat{\varrho}_{t+1} - \hat{\lambda}_{t+1}) + \beta\hat{r}^*_{t+1}],$$

which may be a more intuitive or familiar expression.

Figures

Shown here are the impulse responses of the three variables used for estimating the model, not shown in the body of the chapter.

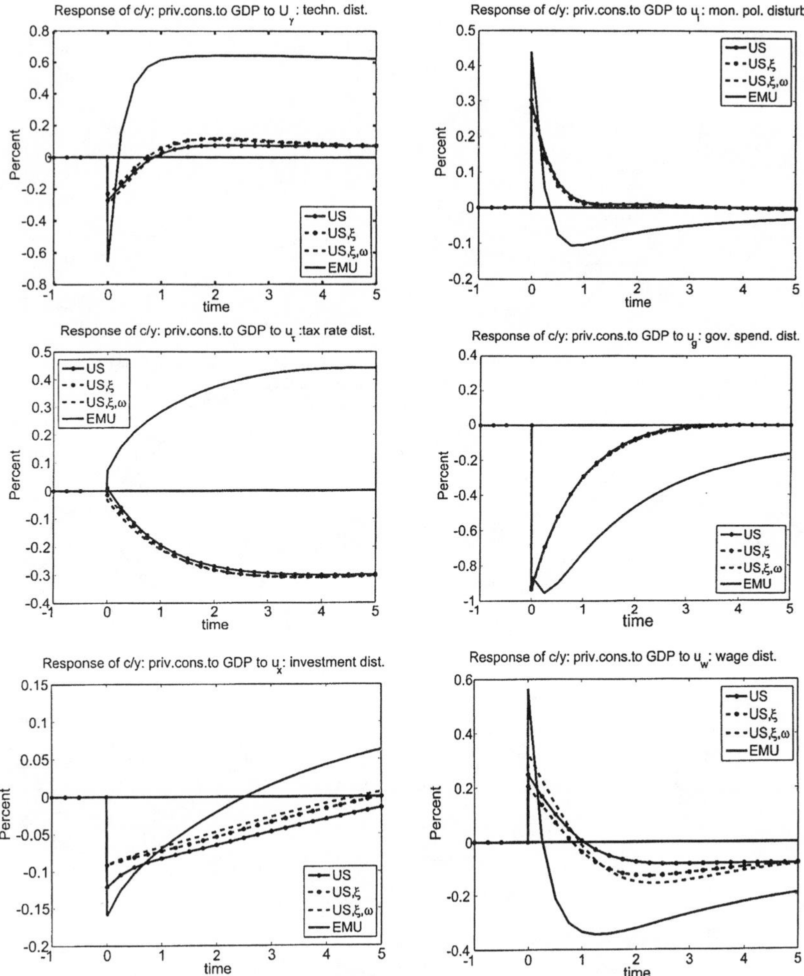

Fig. 9A.1 Impulse response of the log consumption-output ratio to six shocks, each providing a comparison of three model specifications for the United States and one specification for the EMU

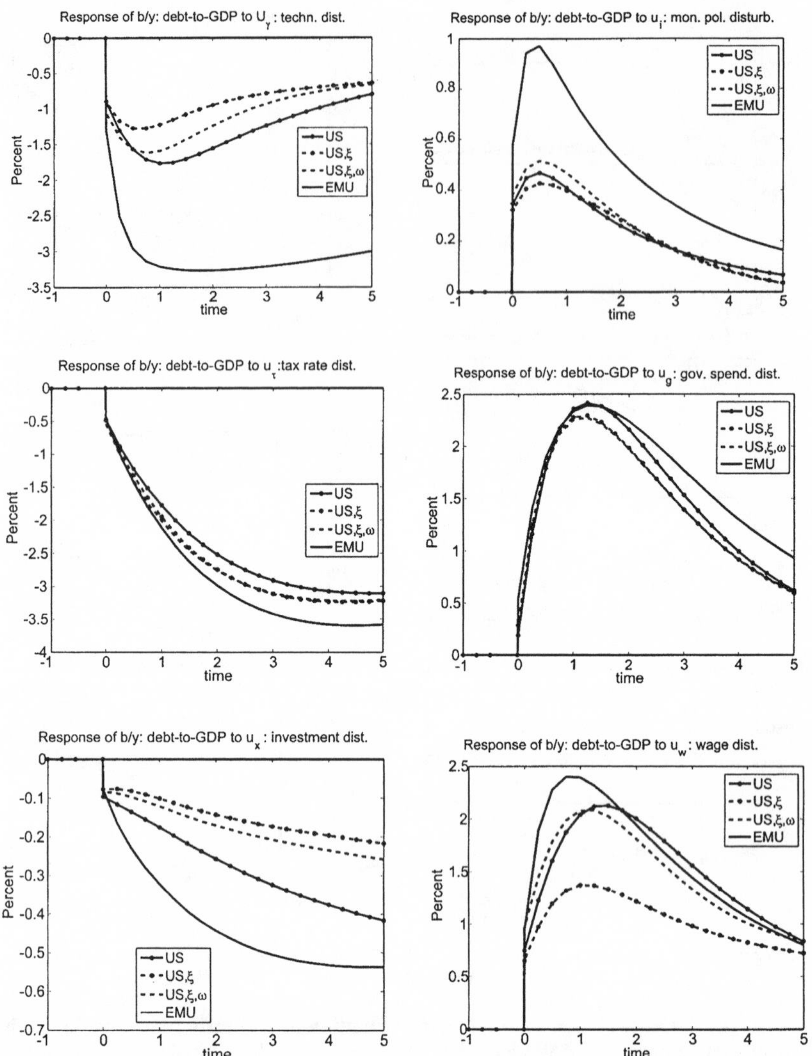

Fig. 9A.2 Impulse response of the debt-output ratio to six shocks, each providing a comparison of three model specifications for the United States and one specification for the EMU

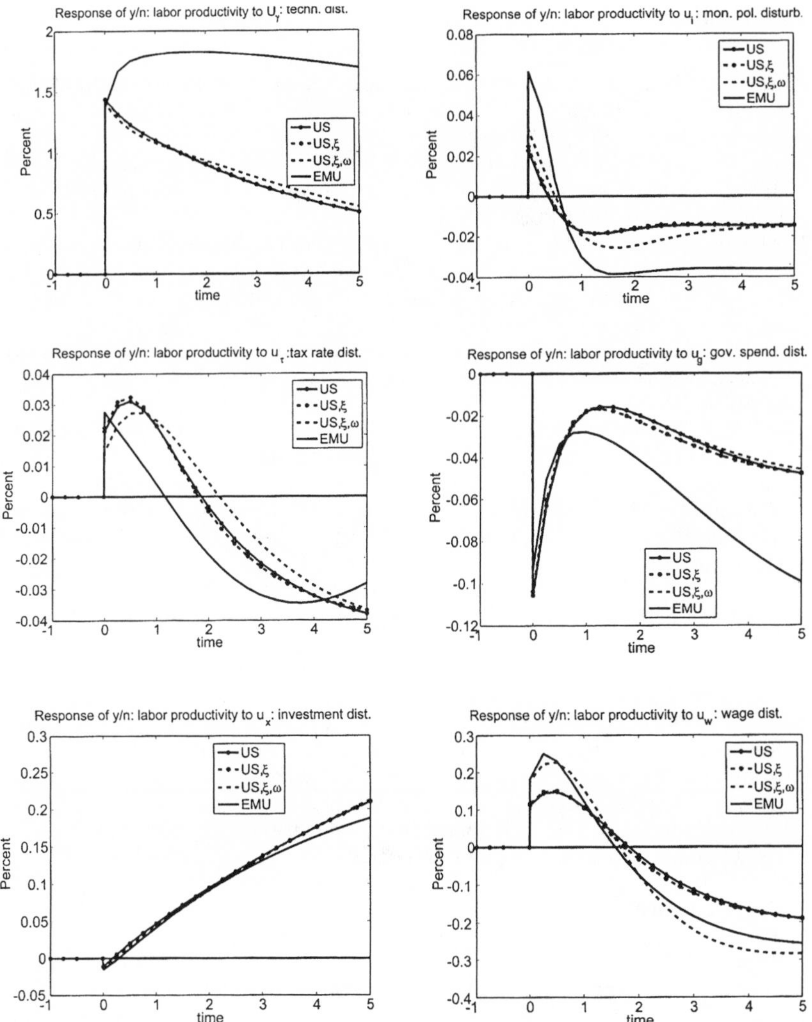

Fig. 9A.3 Impulse response of the log output-labor ratio (i.e., the log labor productivity) to six shocks, each providing a comparison of three model specifications for the United States and one specification for the EMU

References

Altig, D., L. J. Christiano, M. Eichenbaum, and J. Linde. 2004. Firm-specific capital, nominal rigidities, and the business cycle. Sveriges Riksbank (Central Bank of Sweden), Working Paper Series no. 176.

Barth, M., and V. Ramey. 2001. The cost channel of monetary transmission. *NBER Macroeconomics Annual 2001,* ed. B. S. Bernanke and K. S. Rogoff, 1991–240. Cambridge, MA: MIT Press.

Bernanke, B. S., M. Gertler, and S. Gilchrist. 1999. The financial accelerator in a quantitative business cycle framework. In *Handbook of macroeconomics, Volume 1C. Handbooks in economics, vol. 15,* ed. J. B. Taylor, and M. Woodford, 1341–93. Amsterdam: Elsevier Science, North-Holland.

Blanchard, O., and J. Galí. 2005. Real wage rigidities and the new Keynesian model. Massachusetts Institute of Technology, Department of Economics Working Paper no. 05-27.

Chari, V. V., P. J. Kehoe, and E. R. McGrattan. 2005. A critique of structural VARs using real business cycle theory. Federal Reserve Bank of Minneapolis, Working Paper no. 631.

Christiano, L., M. Eichenbaum, and C. Evans. 2005. Nominal rigidities and the dynamic effects of a shock to monetary policy. *Journal of Political Economy* 113 (1): 1–45.

Christiano, L., R. Motto, and M. Rostagno. 2003. The Great Depression and the Friedman-Schwartz hypothesis. Federal Reserve Bank of Cleveland Working Paper.

———. 2007. Shocks, structures or monetary policies? European Central Bank (ECB) Working Paper no. 774, July.

Clarida, R., J. Galí, and M. Gertler. 1999. The science of monetary policy: A new Keynesian perspective. *Journal of Economic Literature* 37 (4): 1661–1707.

Cochrane, J. 1994. Permanent and transitory components of GNP and stock prices. *Quarterly Journal of Economics* 109 (February): 241–66.

de Fiore, F., and H. Uhlig. 2006. Bank finance versus bond finance: What explains the differences between U.S. and Europe? ECB Working Paper no. 547.

Erceg, C. J., D. W. Henderson, and A. T. Levin. 2000. Optimal monetary policy with staggered wage and price contracts. *Journal of Monetary Economics* 46 (2): 281–313.

Fernandez-Villaverde, J., J. F. Rubio-Ramirez, and T. J. Sargent. 2007. A,B,C's (and D's) for understanding VARS. *American Economic Review* 97 (3): 1021–26.

Fisher, J. D. M. 2006. The dynamic effects of neutral and investment-specific technology shocks. *Journal of Political Economy* 114 (3): 413–51.

Hall, R. E. 2005. Employment fluctuations with equilibrium wage stickiness. *American Economic Review* 95 (1): 50–65.

Hansen, L. P., and T. J. Sargent. 2001. Acknowledging misspecification in macroeconomic theory. *Review of Economic Dynamics* 4 (3): 519–35.

Jermann, U. J. 1998. Asset pricing in production economies. *Journal of Monetary Economics* 41 (2): 257–75.

Levin, A., A. Onatski, J. Williams, and N. Williams. 2006. Monetary policy under uncertainty in micro-founded macroeconometric models. In *NBER macroeconomics annual 2005,* ed. M. Gertler and K. Rogoff, 229–87. Cambridge, MA: MIT Press.

Levin, A., and J. Williams. 2003. Robust monetary policy rules with competing reference models. *Journal of Monetary Economics* 50:945–75.

Lucas, R. E., Jr., and N. L. Stokey. 1987. Money and interest in a cash-in-advance economy. *Econometrica* 55 (3): 491–513.

Sahuc, J.-G., and F. Smets. 2008. Differences in interest rate policy at the ECB and the Fed: An investigation with a medium-scale DSGE model. *Journal of Money, Credit and Banking* 40 (2–3): 505–21.

Schmitt-Grohe, S., and M. Uribe. 2004. Optimal fiscal and monetary policy under sticky prices. *Journal of Economic Theory* 114 (2): 198–230.

———. 2005. Optimal fiscal and monetary policy in a medium-scale macroeconomic model. In *NBER macroeconomic annual 2005,* ed. M. Gertler and K. Rogoff, 383–425. Cambridge, MA: MIT Press.

Secchi, A., and E. Gaiotti. 2006. Is there a cost channel of monetary policy transmission? An investigation into the pricing behavior of 2,000 firms. *Journal of Money, Credit, and Banking* 38 (8): 2013–37.

Shimer, R. 2005. The cyclical behavior of equilibrium unemployment and vacancies. *American Economic Review* 95 (1): 25–49.

Smets, F., and R. Wouters. 2003. An estimated dynamic stochastic general equilibrium model of the Euro area. *Journal of the European Economic Association* 1 (5): 1123–75.

Uhlig, H. 1999. A toolkit for analysing nonlinear dynamic stochastic models easily. In *Computational methods for the study of dynamic economies,* ed. R. Marimon and A. Scott, 30–61. New York: Oxford University Press.

———. 2007. Explaining asset prices with external habits and wage rigidities in a DSGE model. *American Economic Review Papers and Proceedings* 97 (2): 239–43.

Woodford, M. 2003. *Interest and prices: Foundations of a theory of monetary policy.* Princeton, NJ: Princeton University Press.

Comment Andrew Levin

Over the past decade or so, researchers at academic institutions and central banks have been active in specifying and estimating dynamic stochastic general equilibrium (DSGE) models that can be used for the analysis of monetary policy.[1] While the first generation models were relatively small and stylized, more recent models typically embed a much more elaborate dynamic structure aimed at capturing key aspects of the aggregate data.[2] Indeed, a number of central banks are now employing DSGE models in the forecasting process and in formulating and communicating policy strategies.

Andrew Levin is associate director of the Division of Monetary Affairs at the Federal Reserve Board.

The views expressed in this comment are solely those of the author, and should not be interpreted as representing the views of the Board of Governors of the Federal Reserve System nor of anyone else associated with the Federal Reserve System.

1. Pioneering early studies include King and Wolman (1996, 1999); Goodfriend and King (1997); Rotemberg and Woodford (1997, 1999); Clarida, Galí, and Gertler (1999); and McCallum and Nelson (1999).

2. See Christiano, Eichenbaum, and Evans (2005); Smets and Wouters (2003); Levin et al. (2006); and Schmitt-Gröhe and Uribe (2006).

However, a crucial ongoing issue in conducting such analysis is to determine the extent to which the policy implications may be sensitive to the particular specification of the behavioral equations, the incidence of the exogenous shocks, and the econometric methodology used to estimate the model.

Harald's chapter follows this approach in addressing an interesting and highly relevant topic: he uses a medium-scale DSGE model to provide an accounting of the differences in monetary policy paths that have been observed in the euro area and the United States over the past decade. While this topic has been considered in two other recent studies—Christiano, Motto, and Rostagno (2008) and Sahuc and Smets (2008), henceforth referred to as CMR and SS, respectively—Harald's analysis involves distinct choices with respect to the model specification and the empirical approach. Thus, the fact that his analysis yields fairly similar results—namely, that the differences in policy paths are largely attributable to the specific shocks that have influenced each economy—provides important confirmation regarding the robustness of that conclusion.

In the remainder of this comment, I will highlight some of the model specification issues and then discuss the estimation results for the parameters related to monetary policy. Finally, I will take a somewhat broader perspective in considering several key factors that have influenced the evolution of the U.S. economy over the past decade and the extent to which further work is needed to incorporate these influences, perhaps in the next generation of DSGE models.

Model Specification

With twenty-three endogenous variables, Harald's model is a bit smaller than the CMR model (which has twenty-nine variables) and substantially larger than the SS model (which has "only" nine variables). Of course, a number of judgmental choices inevitably arise in specifying a model of this scale; here I would like to point out four particularly interesting modeling issues:

1. Harald's analysis follows the classical q-theory approach in assuming that *capital accumulation* is subject to adjustment costs that are proportional to the squared level of investment, whereas CMR and SS assumed that these adjustment costs are proportional to the squared growth rate of investment. As emphasized by Christiano, Eichenbaum, and Evans (2005), the latter specification has the advantage of being able to generate a hump-shaped response of aggregate investment in response to a monetary policy shock, consistent with the implications of structural vector autoregressions. Furthermore, while the formal microeconomic foundations of higher-order adjustment costs were initially somewhat opaque, Basu and Kimball (2003) have shown that this mechanism may be viewed as providing a reduced-form representation of an underlying framework with planning delays in investment.

2. In motivating his study, Harald emphasizes the contrasting patterns of *corporate finance* in the euro area and the United States; namely, business investment in Europe is much more likely to be financed by bank loans rather than publicly traded bonds. Nevertheless, credit market frictions are absent from Harald's model, whereas CMR incorporate the debt-contracting framework of Bernanke, Gertler, and Gilchrist (1999), henceforth denoted as BGG. From an empirical standpoint, the BGG framework could provide a means of gauging whether cross-country differences in corporate finance are associated with systematic differences in the steady-state magnitude of the external finance premium. Furthermore, the BGG framework implies endogenous variation in the external finance premium in response to the equity-to-debt ratio—a mechanism that could be particularly important in interpreting the evolution of the U.S. economy over a decade of relatively large swings in equity prices.

3. Harald's study is also motivated by the contrasting structure of *labor markets* in the euro area and the United States; for example, differences in unionization rates, unemployment compensation, and various other aspects of labor market regulation and tax policies. In light of these considerations, Harald's model allows for sluggishness in real wage adjustment, following the formulation of Blanchard and Galí (2006). In contrast to CMR and SS, however, Harald rules out any role for nominal wage inertia in influencing the evolution of the macroeconomy.

4. One other aspect of Harald's model specification is also worth noting; namely, his formulation of the *monetary policy rule*. As in the enormous literature on Taylor-style rules, he assumes that the short-term interest rate responds to the lagged interest rate as well as to deviations of inflation from target; however, he departs from that literature (and from CMR and SS) in assuming that policy responds to movements in real marginal cost instead of movements in the output gap. Because he assumes that nominal wages are completely flexible, this distinction is irrelevant in his model; that is, the output gap is proportional to the deviation of real marginal cost from steady state. In the data, however, there is a much weaker correlation between real marginal cost (as measured by the inverse of the labor share) and the Hodrick-Prescott (HP)-filtered output gap; hence, compared with more conventional specifications, Harald's approach might yield very different empirical implications about the extent to which movements in the stance of monetary policy should be attributed to systematic versus idiosyncratic components.

Specification of Exogenous Disturbances

Harald's empirical approach involves five exogenous disturbances—namely, shocks to the level of total factor productivity (TFP), the level of investment efficiency, the wage markup, the labor tax rate, and the monetary policy rule. The number of disturbances is a bit smaller than in the SS model (seven shocks) and noticeably more parsimonious than the CMR model (fifteen shocks). Of course, the choice of shocks is nontrivial in seeking to provide a meaningful accounting for the evolution of macroeconomic outcomes in the euro area and the United States over the past decade. For example, one could imagine the desirability of including persistent shocks to the *growth rates* of TFP and investment efficiency that might enable the model to match the "new economy" experience of the United States more closely. Similarly, as discussed further following, the model might need to allow for exogenous time variation in government spending and in the public debt target in order to capture the evolution of U.S. fiscal policy. Finally, a number of observers have used the term "opportunistic disinflation" to characterize U.S. monetary policy from the late 1980s through the late 1990s, suggesting that the model might also need to allow for gradual time variation in the implicit inflation goal, as in the CMR and SS models.

Specification of Observed Variables

The number of observed time series in Harald's chapter matches the number of exogenous disturbances (as in SS and CMR), thereby facilitating inference about the actual incidence of shocks hitting each economy during the sample period. Thus, with only five shocks, Harald evidently faced some fairly difficult choices in picking a specific set of five observed variables: the consumption share of gross domestic product (GDP); labor productivity (that is, output per worker); the inflation rate of the GDP price deflator; the short-term nominal interest rate; and the ratio of government debt to GDP. A few comments are worth noting regarding this selection of observed variables:

1. In stark contrast to SS and CMR, Harald's empirical specification does not employ any direct measure of real GDP growth or HP-filtered levels of output or employment. Thus, the interpretation of some key macroeconomic fluctuations (such as the downturn in U.S. economic activity in 2001) is based on inferences from movements in labor productivity and the consumption share.
2. Given Harald's objective of analyzing the role of credit market imperfections in the evolution of the macroeconomy, it might have been ideal if the empirical analysis could have included some measure(s) of domestic credit and/or risk premiums on corporate debt.
3. Harald's analysis follows the bulk of the empirical DSGE literature in measuring inflation in terms of the GDP price deflator, which reflects value added rather than the actual prices charged for goods and services. However, it should be noted that oil import price shocks can have a perverse impact on this measure of inflation, because a value added deflator puts positive weight on output price changes and *negative* weight on input price changes.

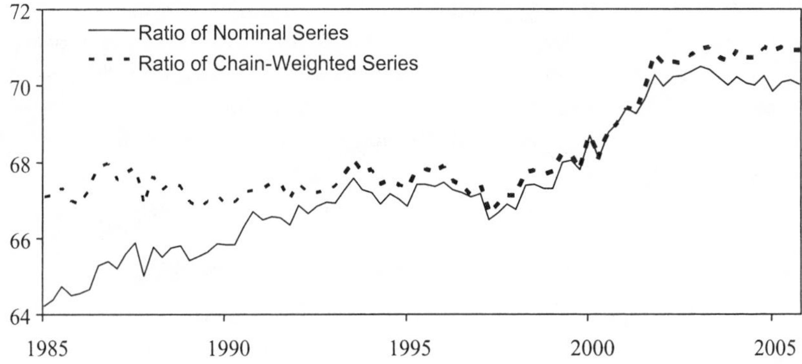

Fig. 9C.1 The evolution of the U.S. consumption share of GDP

4. Finally, while the consumption share of GDP may be reasonably viewed as stationary for the Euro Area, this series is clearly *not* stationary for the United States; that is, the savings rate exhibits a stochastic trend over the two decades of the sample period, and hence the series should presumably be HP-filtered rather than simply demeaned. Moreover, a stochastic trend is present in the relative price of consumption goods versus investment goods; hence, as shown in figure 9C.1 of this comment, the ratio of chain-weighted real consumption to chain-weighted real GDP (the measure used in Harald's analysis) is systematically different from the nominal consumption share of nominal GDP, with potentially important implications for the estimation results and the interpretation of recent macroeconomic developments.[3]

Estimated Parameters

Although it would be interesting to discuss the entire set of parameter estimates, in light of the space constraints I will simply make a few remarks about the inferences regarding the parameters of the monetary policy rule:

$$i_t = \zeta_{iL} i_{t-1} + (1 - \zeta_{iL})[\zeta_{\pi}\hat{\pi}_t + \zeta_x \widehat{\text{mc}}_t + u_{it}].$$

As previously noted, the policy rate i_t is adjusted in response to its own lagged value as well as to the current inflation rate $\hat{\pi}_t$ and to real marginal cost $\widehat{\text{mc}}_t$, where each variable is expressed in percentage points, and the hat indicates that the variable is measured as a deviation from steady state.

For both the euro area and the United States, the parameter estimates

3. With nonstationary relative prices, the ratio of chain-weighted real consumption to chain-weighted real GDP does not have any clear economic interpretation; for further discussion, see Whelan (2000); Edge, Laubach, and Williams (2004); and Smets and Wouters (2007).

for ζ_π are only slightly larger than unity, implying that monetary policy in each economy has responded only weakly to inflation over the past two decades, and indeed has barely even satisfied the Taylor principle. However, this finding contrasts sharply with conventional wisdom and with most previous empirical studies. For example, Smets and Wouters (2003) employed the following specification of the monetary policy rule in their analysis of euro area data:

$$i_t = \gamma_{iL} i_{t-1} + (1 - \gamma_{iL})[\hat{\pi}_{t-1} + \gamma_\pi(\hat{\pi}_{t-1} - \pi^*_{t-1}) + \gamma_y \hat{y}_{t-1}]$$
$$+ \gamma_{\Delta\pi}\Delta\hat{\pi}_t + \gamma_{\Delta y}\Delta\hat{y}_{t-1} + \varepsilon_{it},$$

and obtained a posterior mean of 1.7 for γ_π, while Levin et al. (2006) used the same policy rule specification in analyzing U.S. data and obtained a posterior mean of 2.7 for ζ_π; using Harald's notation, these estimates would imply that ζ_π has a value of about 3 for the euro area and about 4 for the United States.

Several factors may be relevant in explaining these contrasting results. First, as already noted, Harald's specification assumes that monetary policy responds to movements in real marginal cost, whereas the policy rule specification in most other studies involves some explicit measure of the output gap. Second, Harald's formulation explains any remaining higher-order dynamics of monetary policy in terms of serially correlated disturbances to the policy rule, whereas other recent studies find that policy responds significantly not only to levels but also to *changes* in the inflation rate and the output gap. Finally, Harald's specification assumes a constant inflation target, whereas other recent studies have allowed the central bank's inflation objective to vary over time. This assumption could have significant consequences for characterizing the evolution of monetary policy in each economy, because the average inflation rate for the synthetic euro area exhibited a gradual decline in conjunction with the approach to European Monetary Union, while the U.S. inflation rate exhibited a significant downward shift in the early 1990s that some observers have described as *opportunistic disinflation.*[4]

Interpreting the Evolution of the U.S. Economy

Now I would like to take a somewhat broader perspective in discussing several factors that have had important influences on the evolution of the U.S. economy over the past decade. I hope that these comments will be useful in highlighting some significant issues with respect to the specification of the behavioral equations and the disturbances in empirical DSGE models.

4. Levin and Piger (2004) report evidence of downward shifts in euro area and U.S. inflation rates in the early 1990s, while Orphanides and Wilcox (2002) discuss the characteristics of opportunistic disinflation.

1. The U.S. economy experienced a remarkably large swing in productivity growth over the past decade. The upward part of this swing has often been referred to as the "new economy" era, but fewer commentators seem to have emphasized that this era has apparently now drawn to a close. Thus, while Harald's model—as in a number of other empirical DSGE studies—is specified in terms of shocks to the *level* of productivity, it seems that allowing for persistent shocks to the *growth rate* of productivity would be important in accounting for the recent evolution of the macroeconomy. Furthermore, Harald's analysis—like most other studies—assumes that every shock to the economy can be immediately observed by private agents and policymakers, whereas the reality is that even professional forecasters face a substantial *real-time* challenge in distinguishing persistent swings in productivity growth from the more common variety of transitory fluctuations. For example, Tetlow and Ironside (2007) have recently documented the magnitude of the revisions in FRB/US model-based assessments of the path of U.S. potential GDP growth. For illustrative purposes, figure 9C.2 of this comment depicts five vintages of these FRB/US assessments and underscores the extent to which the characteristics of the initial upward swing in productivity growth were not obvious at its onset in the mid-1990s, while the more recent downturn in potential output growth was not apparent in the real-time assessments that were constructed in early 2001 and mid-2003. Given this pattern of revisions, it seems clear that the next generation of DSGE models needs to incorporate real-time data filtering as well as other forms of learning about the structure and state of the economy.

2. The U.S. fiscal outlook has also been subject to dramatic swings over the past decade. For example, at a Congressional hearing in early 2001, Chairman Greenspan summarized the fiscal outlook at that juncture: "Indeed,

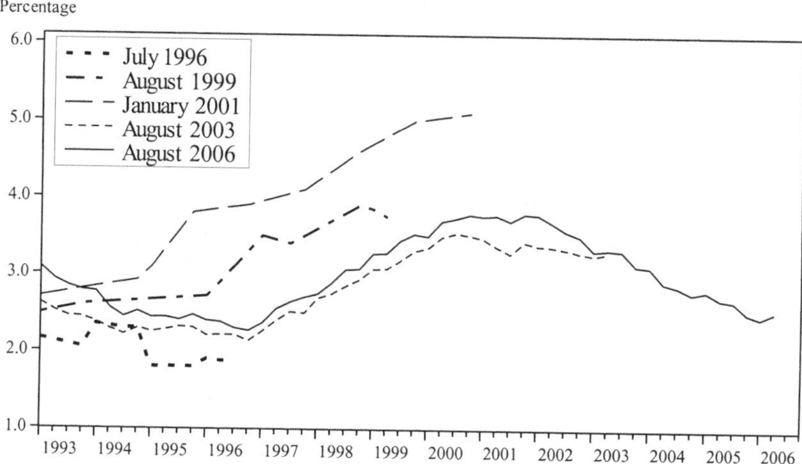

Fig. 9C.2 Real-time assessments of U.S. potential GDP growth

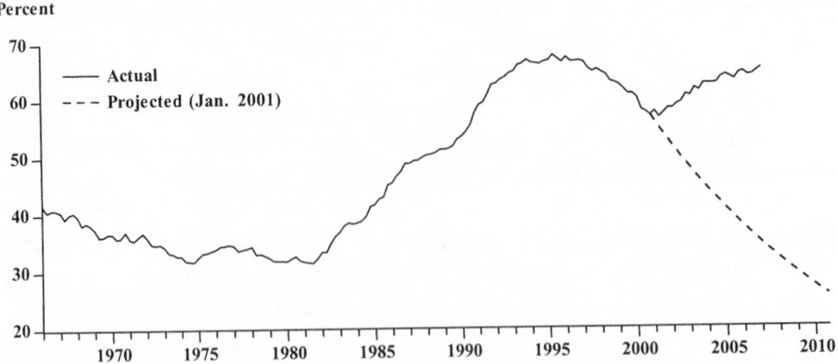

Fig. 9C.3 The evolution of the U.S. government debt/GDP ratio

in almost any credible baseline scenario, short of a major and prolonged economic contraction, the full benefits of debt reduction are now achieved before the end of this decade[. . .]The time has come, in my judgment, to consider a budgetary strategy that is consistent with a preemptive smoothing of the glide path to zero federal debt or, more realistically, to the level of federal debt that is an effective irreducible minimum" (Greenspan 2001).

Nevertheless, as shown in figure 9C.3 of this comment, the ratio of U.S. government debt to GDP has not declined toward zero as projected, but in fact has increased noticeably over the past half-decade or so. This outcome reflects the combined influences of the tax reduction measures that were adopted in early 2001 (partly in response to rosy fiscal projections) and the increased government expenditures that have occurred in the wake of the 9/11 terrorist attacks. The shock to U.S. real government consumption spending is also visible in the left panel of figure 9.3 of Harald's chapter; however, his empirical specification only involves shocks to the tax rate, not to government spending. Figure 9C.3 of this comment also highlights the extent to which the U.S. government debt/GDP ratio does *not* appear to be mean stationary, at least not over the four decades from 1965 to 2005. Thus, to provide a reasonable empirical accounting for the evolution of government debt in a DSGE framework, one might need to incorporate some combination of shocks to the debt target or perhaps some form of nonlinear error correction mechanisms in the determination of government spending and taxes.

3. As noted previously, the BGG framework provides a means of gauging the evolution of credit market frictions over the past decade. In particular, while the wedge between the cost of external and internal finance is not directly observable, the cross-section and time-series behavior of this premium have recently been estimated by Levin, Natalucci, and Zakrajsek (2004), using a novel panel data set that includes balance sheet information,

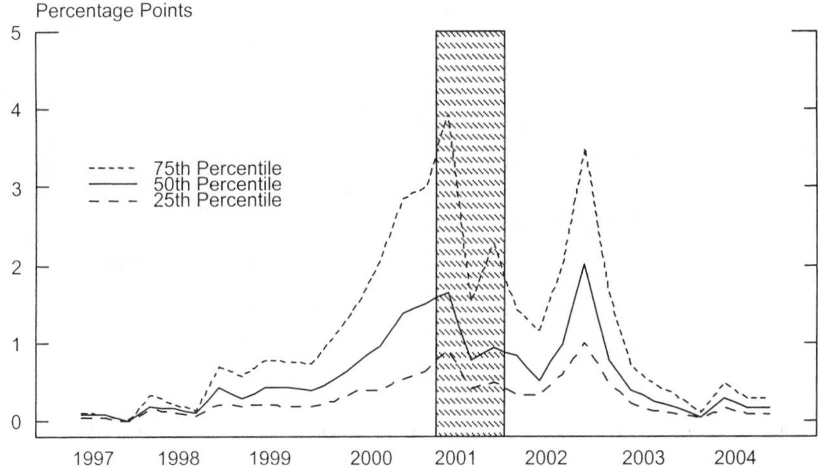

Fig. 9C.4 The evolution of the U.S. external finance premium

measures of expected default risk, and credit spreads on publicly-traded debt for about 800 U.S. firms.

As shown in figure 9C.4 of this comment, the external finance premium for the sales-weighted median firm in this sample was negligible during the expansionary periods of 1997 to 1999 and 2003 to 2004, but increased markedly in mid-2000 (prior to the onset of the 2001 recession) and remained elevated until the end of 2002. Indeed, the cost of external finance rose even more sharply for the upper seventy-fifth percentile of the cross-sectional distribution; that is, for firms in the sample representing one-fourth of total sales. Given that these estimates are based on financial data for relatively large firms with publicly traded equity and debt, one may well presume that smaller firms would tend to face even larger swings in the external finance premium or perhaps face credit rationing due to collateral constraints—a mechanism not incorporated in the BGG framework. Thus, incorporating credit market frictions into empirical DSGE models (such as CMR) should be a priority for further research.

4. Over the past few years, there have also been substantial swings in the U.S. inflation outlook. For example, in early 2004, Chairman Greenspan gave an address to the American Economic Association in which he stated, "A two-decade long decline in inflation . . . eventually brought us to the current state of price stability[. . .]Our goal of price stability was achieved by most analysts' definition by mid-2003. Unstinting and largely preemptive efforts over two decades had finally paid off" (Greenspan 2004).

As shown in figure 9C.5, real-time data at that point in time indicated that core inflation—as measured by the annual average inflation rate for personal consumption expenditures (PCE), excluding food and energy—had fallen

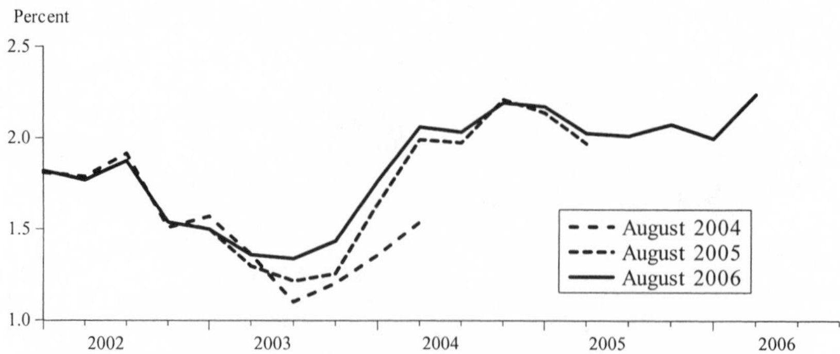

Fig. 9C.5 The real-time evolution of the U.S. core PCE inflation rate

to around 1 percent as of mid-2003. Thus, assuming that this measure of inflation exhibits an upward bias of about 50 basis points or more due to unobserved improvements in the quality of goods and services, it would certainly be reasonable to infer that the true underlying rate of consumer inflation was quite close to zero; that is, "price stability." In contrast, more recent vintages of data have led to a markedly different inflation outlook, partly because the core PCE inflation rates for 2003 and 2004 were subsequently revised upwards by nearly 75 basis points, and partly because the post-2001 decline in core inflation turned out to be largely transitory. These developments highlight the extent to which the implications of real-time data—and the subsequent revision process—need to be incorporated into the next generation of empirical DSGE models.

5. Finally, it should be noted that Harald's analysis (like most other recent studies) assumes that the central bank's inflation goal is completely transparent and credible to the private sector. This assumption might be reasonable in some empirical contexts; for example, from 1976 through 1998, the Deutsche Bundesbank regularly communicated to the public regarding its medium-term inflation objective, and expectations regarding the German inflation outlook appear to have been firmly anchored over this period.[5] However, evidence from financial market data and surveys of professional forecasters suggests that in recent years U.S. long-run inflation expectations have not been as firmly anchored as in other economies—such as the euro area, Sweden, and the United Kingdom—where the central bank has a more explicit inflation objective.[6]

For example, as shown in figure 9C.6 of this comment, the cross-sectional dispersion of professional forecasters' long-run inflation expectations has

5. See Coenen, Levin, and Christoffel (2007).

6. See Levin, Natalucci, and Piger (2004); Gürkaynak, Levin, and Swanson (2007); and Beechey, Johannsen, and Levin (2007).

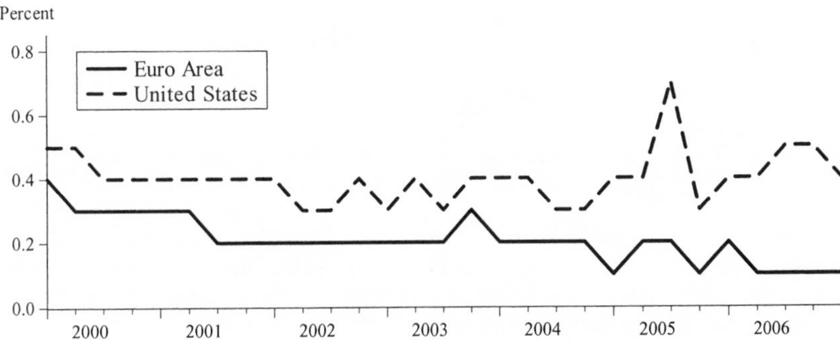

Fig. 9C.6 Dispersion in professional forecasters' long-run inflation expectations

been noticeably greater in the United States than in the euro area; indeed, in late 2006, the standard deviation across forecasters was only 0.1 percent for the Euro Area and 0.4 to 0.5 percent for the United States.[7] In this light, it is worth noting that the Federal Reserve has recently implemented significant enhancements to its communication strategy, including the regular publication of Federal Open Market Committee (FOMC) members' forecasts for consumer inflation three years ahead—a horizon that provides further information about each member's assessment of the inflation rate that best promotes the Federal Reserve's dual mandate of price stability and maximum sustainable employment.[8]

References

Basu, S., and M. Kimball. 2003. Investment planning costs and the effects of fiscal and monetary policy. University of Michigan. Unpublished Manuscript.

Beechey, M., B. Johannsen, and A. Levin. 2007. Are long-run inflation expectations more firmly anchored in the euro area than in the United States? Centre for Economic Policy Research (CEPR) Discussion Paper no. 6536.

Bernanke, B. 2007. Federal Reserve communications. Speech delivered at the Cato Institute 25th Annual Monetary Conference. 14 November, Washington, DC. Available at: http://www.federalreserve.gov/newsevents/speech/bernanke20071114a.htm.

Bernanke, B., M. Gertler, and S. Gilchrist. 1999. The financial accelerator in a quantitative business cycle framework. In *Handbook of macroeconomics,* ed. J. Taylor, and M. Woodford, 1341–93. Amsterdam: Elsevier Press.

Blanchard, O., and J. Galí. 2006. Real wage rigidities and the new Keynesian model.

7. These series are taken from the European Central Bank (ECB) Survey of Professional Forecasters and the Federal Reserve Bank of Philadelphia Survey of Professional Forecasters, respectively. Dispersion is calculated as the cross-sectional standard deviation of responses to the respective survey questions. Forecasts for the Euro Area pertain to five-year-ahead inflation in the euro area harmonized index of consumer prices (HICP). Forecasts for the United States pertain to the inflation rate for the consumer price index (CPI) over the coming ten years.

8. See Bernanke (2007) and Mishkin (2007).

Massachusetts Institute of Technology, Department of Economics Working Paper no. 05-27.
Christiano, L., M. Eichenbaum, and C. Evans. 2005. Nominal rigidities and the dynamic effects of a shock to monetary policy. *Journal of Political Economy* 113 (1): 1–45.
Christiano, L., R. Motto, and M. Rostagno. 2008. Shocks, structures or monetary policies? The euro area and U.S. after 2001. *Journal of Economic Dynamics and Control* 32 (8): 2476–2506.
Clarida, R., J. Galí, and M. Gertler. 1999. The science of monetary policy: A new Keynesian perspective. *Journal of Economic Literature* 37 (4): 1661–1707.
Coenen, G., A. Levin, and K. Christoffel. 2007. Identifying nominal and real rigidities in aggregate price-setting behavior. *Journal of Monetary Economics* 54 (8): 2439–66.
Edge, R., T. Laubach, and J. Williams. 2004. Learning and shifts in long-run productivity growth. Finance and Economics Discussion Series no. 2004-21, Board of Governors of the Federal Reserve System.
Goodfriend, M., and R. King. 1997. The new neoclassical synthesis and the role of monetary policy. *NBER macroeconomics annual 1997,* ed. B. Bernanke and J. J. Rotemberg, 231–96. Cambridge, MA: MIT Press.
Greenspan, A. 2001. Testimony to U.S. Senate Committee on the budget. 25 January, Washington, DC.
———. 2004. Risk and uncertainty in monetary policy. Speech delivered at the annual meetings of the American Economic Association. 3 January, San Diego, CA.
Gürkaynak, R., E. Swanson, and A. Levin. 2007. Does inflation targeting anchor long-run inflation expectations? Evidence from long-term bond yields in the U.S., U.K., and Sweden. CEPR Discussion Paper Series no. 5808.
King, R., and A. Wolman. 1996. Inflation targeting in a St. Louis model of the 21st century. *Federal Reserve Bank of St. Louis Economic Review* 78 (May): 83–107.
———. 1999. What should the monetary authority do when prices are sticky? In *Monetary policy rules,* ed. J. B. Taylor, 349–98. Chicago: University of Chicago Press.
Levin, A., and J. Piger. 2004. Is inflation persistence intrinsic in industrial economies? European Central Bank (ECB) Working Paper no. 334.
Levin, A., F. Natalucci, and J. Piger. 2004. The macroeconomic effects of inflation targeting. *Federal Reserve Bank of St. Louis Economic Review* 86 (July): 51–80.
Levin, A., F. Natalucci, and E. Zakrajsek. 2004. The magnitude and cyclical behavior of financial market frictions. Finance and Economics Discussion Series no. 2004-70, Board of Governors of the Federal Reserve System.
Levin, A., A. Onatski, J. Williams, and N. Williams. 2006. Monetary policy under uncertainty in micro-founded macroeconometric models. In *NBER macroeconomics annual 2005,* ed. M. Gertler, and K. Rogoff, 229–87. Cambridge, MA: MIT Press.
McCallum, B. T., and E. Nelson. 1999. Performance of operational policy rules in an estimated semi-classical structural model. In *Monetary policy rules,* ed. J. B. Taylor, 15–45. Chicago: University of Chicago Press.
Mishkin, R. 2007. The Federal Reserve's enhanced communication strategy and the science of monetary policy. Speech delivered to the Undergraduate Economics Association, Massachusetts Institute of Technology. 29 November, Cambridge, MA. Available at: http://www.federalreserve.gov/newsevents/speech/mishkin 20071129a.htm.
Orphanides, A., and D. Wilcox. 2002. The opportunistic approach to disinflation. *International Finance* 5 (1): 47–71.

Rotemberg, J. J., and M. Woodford. 1997. An optimization-based econometric framework for the evaluation of monetary policy. *NBER Macroeconomics Annual 1997,* ed. B. Bernanke and J. J. Rotemberg, 297–346. Cambridge, MA: MIT Press.

———. 1999. Interest rate rules in an estimated sticky-price model. In *Monetary policy rules,* ed. J. B. Taylor, 57–119. Chicago: University of Chicago Press.

Sahuc, J., and F. Smets. 2008. Differences in interest rate policy at the ECB and the Fed: An investigation with a medium-scale DSGE model. *Journal of Money, Credit, and Banking* 40 (2): 505–21.

Schmitt-Gröhe, S., and M. Uribe. 2006. Optimal fiscal and monetary policy in a medium-scale macroeconomic model. In *NBER macroeconomics annual 2005,* ed. M. Gertler, and K. Rogoff, 383–425. Cambridge, MA: MIT Press.

Smets, F., and R. Wouters. 2003. An estimated dynamic stochastic general equilibrium model of the euro area. *Journal of the European Economic Association* 1 (5): 1123–75.

Smets, F., and R. Wouters. 2007. Shocks and frictions in U.S. business cycles: A Bayesian DSGE approach. *American Economic Review* 97 (3): 586–606.

Tetlow, R., and B. Ironside. 2007. Real-time model uncertainty in the United States: The Fed, 1996–2003. *Journal of Money, Credit, and Banking* 39 (7): 1533–61.

Whelan, K. 2000. A guide to the use of chain aggregated NIPA data. *Finance and Economics Discussion Series* no. 2000-35. Board of Governors of the Federal Reserve System.

10 Globalization and Inflation Dynamics
The Impact of Increased Competition

Argia M. Sbordone

10.1 Introduction

The policy debate about the macroeconomic effects of globalization has centered on two main themes: that globalization has contributed to bring down U.S. inflation, and that it has affected the sensitivity of inflation to output fluctuations. Several recent policymakers' speeches have addressed the issue of whether more intense competition, generated by the increase in trade experienced since the 1990s, has changed the role of domestic factors in shaping the inflation process. Chairman Bernanke (2006), for example, has underlined how the dependence of factor markets on economic conditions abroad might have reduced the market power of domestic sellers, how the pricing power of domestic producers might have declined, and how lower import prices both of final and intermediate goods might have contributed to maintain overall inflation at low levels. Similarly, President Yellen (2006) and Governor Kohn (2006) have discussed several direct and indirect impacts of more global markets on U.S. inflation.

In this chapter I explore how globalization might have impacted U.S. inflation by using the analytical framework of the new-Keynesian model of inflation dynamics. Within this framework, I focus in particular on the effects that an increase in market competition generated by an increase in trade might have on the sensitivity of inflation to real marginal costs of production.

Argia M. Sbordone is Assistant Vice President of the Federal Reserve Bank of New York.

Prepared for the NBER conference on International Dimensions of Monetary Policy held in Girona, Spain, on June 11–13, 2007. I thank Mike Woodford for inspiration and for long conversations, my discussant Tommaso Monacelli and all the conference participants for their comments, and Krishna Rao for excellent research assistance. The views expressed in this chapter do not necessarily reflect the position of the Federal Reserve Bank of New York or the Federal Reserve System.

The relationship between inflation and marginal cost is a key determinant of the overall "slope" of the new-Keynesian Phillips curve (NKPC), which links the dynamics of inflation to the level of economic activity. In the price setting model most often used to derive the NKPC (the one based on the contribution by Calvo [1983]), this relationship depends primarily on the frequency of price changes, but it is also affected by strategic complementarity in price setting. It is this last mechanism that provides a way of formalizing the "globalization" argument, according to which the increase in the openness of the economy has affected the sensitivity of inflation to output variations.

I depart here from the assumption of constant elasticity of substitution among differentiated goods, which is typically made in the Calvo model, and adopt instead a specification where the elasticity is function of the firm's relative market share. This modification implies that changes in the importance of trade that affect relative market shares affect in turn the elasticity of demand faced by firms, hence their desired markups. Through this channel they may ultimately have an impact on the elasticity of aggregate inflation to real marginal costs and on the slope of the Phillips curve.

To preview my results: I find that an increase in the number of goods traded is indeed able to generate the sort of real rigidities that may lead to a change in the slope of the Phillips curve. The sign of the change, however, depends on how fast the elasticity of substitution among goods increases; hence, different assumptions about the curvature of the demand function may lead to different answers. For large enough increases in the number of goods traded, the slope of the Phillips curve is in general declining. However, the evidence on U.S. trade patterns so far provides little ground to assume that we are yet in the declining portion of the curve.

There are a number of caveats to these results. In particular, the elasticity of inflation to marginal cost is only one of the determinants of the slope of the Phillips curve—the overall response of inflation to output (or output gap)—and its increase or decline does not necessarily imply that the change in the overall response has the same sign. However, the elasticity of inflation to marginal cost is arguably the component most affected by variations in the degree of market competition and it is the one brought up in policy discussions of the effects of global competition on the "pricing power" of domestic firms. Hence a study of implications of global competition should be centered on this elasticity. I return to this point in the conclusion.

The chapter is organized as follows. Section 10.2 overviews existing evidence about the change in the slope of the Phillips curve and discusses the ensued debate. Section 10.3 analyzes the channels through which the increase in trade that characterizes globalization may affect the dynamics of inflation. Section 10.4 introduces the analytical framework that is used to pin down these effects, and section 10.5 adapts the framework to analyze the effects of firms' entry on the dynamics of price adjustments. Section

10.6 evaluates the quantitative impact of trade increase on the marginal cost slope of the Phillips curve, and section 10.7 concludes.

10.2 Has the Slope of the Phillips Curve Changed?

The policymakers' concerns over a change in the slope of the Phillips curve in recent years derive from its role in assessing the cost of disinflation. A flatter Phillips curve carries the implication that, for a given degree of inflation persistence, reducing inflation involves a higher "sacrifice ratio" than otherwise; namely, it requires enduring a longer period of unemployment above the natural rate for every desired percentage point of reduction in inflation. On the other hand, as noted by Mishkin (2007), a flatter Phillips curve also implies that an overheated economy will tend to generate a smaller increase in inflation.

Most of the empirical analyses supporting the policymakers' concerns address the issue of the flattening of the Phillips curve in the context of traditional "accelerationist" Phillips curves. Roberts (2006) and Williams (2006), for example, estimate smaller Phillips curves' slopes in samples covering the post-1984 period. Williams in particular analyzes samples with moving starting points—from 1980:1 to 1999:4, but with a fix end point (2006:4)—and finds evidence of a flatter curve and a higher sacrifice ratio in the samples that start in the 1990s relative to those estimated in the full sample. However, he also finds that in the more recent samples the unit sum restriction on the lag coefficients, which defines the accelerationist curve, is violated. Furthermore, when in these samples the lag coefficients are left unconstrained, the estimate of the slope coefficient indeed increases.

An alternative source of evidence that the slope of the Phillips curve has declined in more recent samples is provided by estimates in the context of general equilibrium models. Boivin and Giannoni (2006), for example, estimate that the coefficient of marginal cost in a new-Keynesian Phillips curve declines from .011 to .008 in the post-1984 period; Smets and Wouters (2007), in a similar general equilibrium model, report that the estimated interval between price changes is higher in the 1984 to 2004 sample relative to the 1966 to 1979 period, which implies that the slope declined in the more recent period.

While the just-cited studies aim at relating the change in the inflation-output trade-off to the change in monetary policy that took place in the early 1980s, in a recent Bank for International Settlements (BIS) study Borio and Filardo (2007) link instead variations in the slope of the Phillips curve to globalization. Specifically, they estimate a traditional Phillips curve for many countries over the two periods 1980 to 1992 and 1993 to 2005, and document that in the more recent period there has been both a decline in the autoregressive coefficient—hence a decline in inflation persistence—and a decline in the slope, hence a drop in the sensitivity of inflation to domestic output gap. For the United States, in particular, the authors report a decline in the estimated coefficient of lagged inflation from .92 to .82 across the two samples, and a decline in the elasticity of inflation to output gap from .13 to .09. They take this evidence as the starting point of an investigation of a "global slack" hypothesis, according to which the decline in the sensitivity of inflation to domestic measures of output gap is explained by the fact that global measures of demand pressure have become in the later period the main driving force of inflation dynamics.

A successor study (Ihrig et al. 2007) finds that the purported support for the global slack hypothesis is not robust to the specification of the measures of global slack. For example, the study finds that variables such as domestic output time the ratio of trade to gross domestic product (GDP), and import prices time the ratio of imports to GDP do not have statistically significant coefficients. The study, however, does not dispute the evidence that the Phillips curve appears to have flattened since the 1990s; it contests the interpretation that this is indeed an effect of globalization. Overall, the authors in fact conclude that the estimated effect of foreign output gaps is in general insignificant, and that there is no evidence that the trend decline in the sensitivity of inflation to domestic output is due to globalization; moreover, they find no increase in the sensitivity of inflation to import prices.

An International Monetary Fund (IMF) study (2006) also estimates traditional inflation regressions where the coefficient on the slack variable interacts with measures of central bank credibility and openness of the economy. The study estimates a negative coefficient on the interaction term between domestic output gap and trade openness, measured by the share of non-oil imports in GDP, and interprets this result as evidence that the increase in trade has contributed to the decline of the slope of the Phillips curve. The study, however, examines the group of advanced economies as a whole, and does not present results for the United States alone. Finally, in the context of a similar traditional Phillips curve estimated for the United States, Ball (2006) allows interaction of the output coefficient with trade, and finds only a modest effect.

In this chapter I do not estimate the slope of the Phillips curve, but propose instead a simple theoretical framework to analyze the quantitative importance of globalization effects on such a slope. Specifically, I modify the well-known new-Keynesian model of inflation dynamics to identify the channels through which an increase in market competition can generate a flattening of the Phillips curve.

10.3 Channels of Globalization Effects on Inflation

The basic channel emphasized both in policy debates and empirical studies as a potential carrier of globalization effects on inflation dynamics is trade integration, which—especially when accompanied by policy incentives—would bolster competition. Increased competition, the argument goes, creates two effects: a direct effect of containment of costs, by restraining increases in workers' compensations and reducing real import prices, and a second, indirect effect of creating pressure to innovate, which contributes to increasing productivity. Higher productivity in turn further lowers production costs: if markups are constant, lower production costs reduce the pressure on prices. But the margins that firms are willing to charge over their costs might be reduced as well, moderating the extent of price increases.

To understand how these effects work, it is useful to decompose the relation between consumer price inflation and domestic output (the one typically analyzed in empirical studies) in three distinct parts. First, there is the relation between consumer price index (CPI) inflation and domestic inflation. In an open economy, consumer price inflation reflects the price dynamics of goods produced both domestically and abroad that are consumed at home. Second, there is the relation between domestic inflation and the marginal cost of production, and finally, the relationship between the marginal cost of production and domestic output.

The central relationship that describes how variations in marginal cost translate into fluctuations in domestic prices is the one most likely affected by an increase in competition.

When analyzed through the lens of the new-Keynesian approach to the construction of a Phillips curve, the strength of this relationship depends on a number of factors. The first is the frequency of price revisions: the longer prices are kept fixed, the more nominal disturbances translate into real effects, rather than aggregate inflation. This is referred to as the nominal rigidity component. The second component is the sensitivity of the desired firms' price to marginal costs versus other prices. If price setters take into account other firms' prices when they set their own price, then the presence of even a small number of firms that do not change their price induces flexible-price firms to change their price by a lesser amount. A third component is the sensitivity of marginal costs to the output of the firm (versus its sensitivity to the average marginal cost): when marginal costs of the price setter are increasing in its own output, the desired price increase is smaller because the firm takes into account the decline in marginal cost due to the loss in demand incurred for the price increase. Finally, the pricing decisions are affected by the sensitivity of the firm's own output to its relative price; namely, by how elastic is the demand curve of the individual producer. The last three components are commonly referred to as "strategic complementarity" or "real rigidity" channels.[1]

Both nominal and real rigidities are known to be important in assessing the size of the "slope" of the new-Keynesian Phillips curve with respect to marginal costs. They have been analyzed in theoretical works and explored

1. See the discussion of those terms in Woodford (2003 chap. 3).

in empirical studies aiming at reconciling estimated "slopes" with reasonable degrees of nominal rigidity.[2]

In this chapter, I focus on the real rigidity component and analyze how it can be affected by the openness of the economy through the increase in competitiveness generated by an increase in the number of goods traded in the economy.

To do this I borrow from the new trade literature, and in particular from a recent contribution by Melitz and Ottaviano (2008), who present a model of trade with monopolistic competition and firm heterogeneity to study the effect of trade liberalization on productivity and markups. The authors show that import competition induces a downward shift in the distribution of markups across firms. A key element of their model is the dependence of the elasticity of demand upon the relative size of the market. This setting has been used in general equilibrium models by Bilbiie, Ghironi, and Melitz (2006a, 2006b) to study endogenous entry as a propagation of business cycles and efficiency properties of these models, adopting a framework of flexible prices.

Here I study instead a model of staggered prices. I consider a monopolistically competitive market where there is a fixed entry cost and a given distribution of firms. A reduction in individual firms' production costs moves up the firms' distribution curve, making it profitable for more firms to enter the market. The resulting increase in the variety of goods traded increases the overall degree of competition: this is captured in the model by making the demand elasticity, and hence, the markup, vary with the number of goods that are traded. Variable markups in turn impact the price setting process and the dynamics of the relationship between inflation and marginal cost.

My focus is specifically on how the process of new entries and the interaction of firms in the price setting process affect the relationship between aggregate inflation and marginal costs. I will not discuss the other two components of the CPI inflation-domestic output relationship that I described—the relation between domestic and CPI inflation and the relation between marginal cost and domestic output. These relationships obviously matter for the assessment of the overall effect of openness on the Phillips curve's slope, and an explicit modeling of the Phillips curve in open economy may as well illustrate that its slope is lower than that of the closed economy.[3] Nevertheless, understanding the channels through which market entry changes the degree of real rigidity, and how that may emphasize or reduce the inflation-output trade-off, is of primary importance.

Similarly, I will not discuss effects of globalization on inflation of the kind

2. See literature cited later.

3. Several aspects of the difference between open and closed economy are discussed by Woodford (chapter 1 in this volume).

argued by Rogoff (2003, 2006)—that in a global environment central banks have less incentive to inflate the economy. Although this lower incentive is another effect of the increased competitiveness of the economy, it is related to central banks' incentives,[4] rather than to the market mechanisms to which I am interested in here.

10.4 A Structural Framework

The Calvo model of staggered prices provides a useful framework to disentangle the various theoretical channels that compose the inflation-marginal cost relationship. Because the baseline model is well known, here I only summarize its main features to set the stage for the generalizations that I discuss next.

The model has a continuum of monopolistic firms, indexed by i, which produce differentiated goods, also indexed by i, over which consumers' preferences are defined. Firms produce with a constant returns to scale technology and have access to economy-wide factor markets. The optimal consumption allocation determines the demand for each differentiated good, $c_t(i)$, as

$$c_t(i) = C_t\left(\frac{p_t(i)}{P_t}\right)^{-\theta}, \tag{1}$$

for $\theta > 1$; here $p_t(i)$ is the individual good i price, and C_t indicates aggregate consumption, defined by the constant elasticity of substitution aggregator of Dixit and Stiglitz:

$$C_t = [\int c_t(i)^{(\theta-1)/\theta}\, di]^{\theta/(\theta-1)}, \tag{2}$$

and P_t is the corresponding aggregate price (the minimum cost to buy a unit of the aggregate good C_t): $P_t = [\int p_t(i)^{1-\theta} di]^{1/(1-\theta)}$. The model further assumes random intervals between price changes: in every period, only a fraction $(1 - \alpha)$ of the firms can set a new price, independently of the past history of price changes, which will then be kept fixed until the next time the firm is drawn to change prices again. By letting α vary between 0 and 1, the model nests assumptions about the degree of price stickiness from perfect flexibility $(\alpha = 0)$ to complete price rigidity (the limit as $\alpha \to 1$). The expected time between price changes is then $1/(1 - \alpha)$.

The pricing problem of a firm that revises its price in period t is to choose the price $p_t(i)$ that maximizes its expected stream of profits

$$E_t\left\{\sum_{j=0}^{\infty} Q_{t,t+j}\mathsf{P}_{t+j}(i)\right\}, \tag{3}$$

4. The increase in competitiveness on one hand reduces the monopoly wedge that determines the inflation bias of the central bank, and on the other makes prices and wages more flexible, reducing the real effects of unanticipated monetary policy, hence the gain from inflating.

where time t profits $\mathsf{P}_t(i)$ are a function $\mathsf{P}(p_t(i), P_t, y_t(i), Y_t; \Gamma_t)$; $y_t(i)$ is firm's output, defined by (1), $Q_{t,t+j}$ is a stochastic discount factor, and the variable Γ_t stands for all other aggregate variables. The first-order condition for the optimal price is

$$E_t\left\{\sum_{j=0}^{\infty} Q_{t,t+j}\mathsf{P}_1(p_t^*, P_{t+j}, y_{t+j}(i), Y_{t+j}; \Gamma_{t+j})\right\} = 0, \tag{4}$$

where the evolution of aggregate prices is

$$P_t = [(1-\alpha)p_t^{*1-\theta} + \alpha P_{t-1}^{1-\theta}]^{1/(1-\theta)}. \tag{5}$$

Log-linearizing these two equilibrium conditions around a steady state with zero inflation, with usual manipulations, one obtains the familiar form of inflation dynamics as function of expected inflation and real marginal costs s_t

$$\pi_t = \zeta\hat{s}_t + \beta E_t\pi_{t+1}, \tag{6}$$

where a hat indicates the log-deviation from a nonstochastic steady state, β is the steady-state value of the discount factor, and the "slope" is defined as[5]

$$\zeta = \frac{(1-\alpha\beta)(1-\alpha)}{\alpha}. \tag{7}$$

In this baseline framework, the extent of the nominal rigidity determines how marginal costs translate into inflation fluctuations. In order to introduce potential channels of transmission of marginal cost pressures of the kind discussed previously the model needs to be generalized.

10.4.1 The Inflation/Marginal Cost Relation: Some Generalizations

Generalizations of the baseline model can lead to changes in the nominal rigidity component of the slope or introduce some form of real rigidity of the kind discussed previously by adding new terms to expression (7).

One instance in which the nominal rigidity term is modified, despite maintaining an exogenous probability of changing prices, occurs when one allows for a nonzero steady-state inflation. In this case the expression for inflation dynamics is derived as a (log)-linear approximation of the model equilibrium conditions (4) and (5) around a steady state characterized by positive, rather than zero inflation, as is the case in the baseline model. Such an approximation modifies the terms in the discount and the rigidity coefficient in the slope (9). As first shown by Ascari (2004), in such a case the slope coefficient would be:

$$\zeta = \frac{(1-\alpha\beta\overline{\Pi}^{\theta})(1-\alpha\overline{\Pi}^{\theta-1})}{\alpha\overline{\Pi}^{\theta-1}}, \tag{8}$$

5. Throughout the chapter I will use the term "slope" to indicate the elasticity of inflation to marginal cost, rather than to output.

where $\overline{\Pi}$ denotes the gross trend inflation rate. The slope in this case depends not only upon the primitives of the Calvo model, the probability of changing prices $1 - \alpha$, and the elasticity of demand, but also upon the steady-state level of inflation. In this case the NKPC has also a richer dynamic, because it includes additional forward-looking terms, unless particular forms of indexation are postulated.[6]

A further modification of the nominal rigidity component is obtained by replacing the assumption of a constant probability of price reoptimization with a state-dependent probability (see Dotsey, King, and Wolman 1999).

The generalizations that provide a more direct channel through which the competitive effect of more global markets integration can alter the Phillips curve's slope are those that introduce real rigidity factors in the slope coefficient. Such modifications were at first introduced with the purpose of reconciling empirical estimates of the slope with a degree of nominal rigidity more in line with that documented in firms' surveys.[7] In fact, for any given degree of nominal rigidity, the existence of strategic complementarity lowers the slope or, alternatively, a given empirical estimate of the slope is consistent with a lower degree of nominal rigidity.

Assuming, for example, that some or all factor markets are firm-specific implies that the marginal cost of supplying goods to the market is not equal for all goods at any specific point in time. In such cases firms' marginal costs depend not only on economy-wide factors, but also on the firm's own output[8] and, for any given increase in marginal cost, this dependence makes the desired price increase smaller. Returning to a baseline case with zero steady-state inflation, the slope ζ in these cases becomes

$$\zeta = \frac{(1 - \alpha\beta)(1 - \alpha)}{\alpha} \frac{1}{1 + \theta s_y}, \tag{9}$$

where the strategic complementarity term $1/(1 + \theta s_y)$ depends upon the demand elasticity θ, which measures the sensitivity of the own output of the firm to its relative price, and the sensitivity of the firm's marginal cost to its own output, s_y. The parameter s_y in turn depends on other model

6. If one assumes that nonreoptimized prices are indexed at least partly to trend inflation, this additional dynamic is eliminated and the slope is unaffected by the steady-state inflation $\overline{\Pi}$. Models with positive trend inflation can be generalized to the case of time varying steady-state inflation; in this case the model describes the dynamics of inflation deviations from a time varying trend: $\hat{\pi}_t = \ln(\Pi_t/\overline{\Pi}_t)$. Cogley-Sbordone (2008) estimate a NKPC with time varying trend inflation. Ireland (2007) and Smets and Wouters (2003), among others, estimate general equilibrium models in the new-Keynesian literature, allowing for a time varying trend inflation; their assumptions, however, deliver a time-invariant slope.

7. For evidence from survey data see, for example, Blinder et al. (1998).

8. Sbordone (2002) discusses this case. A more sophisticated model assumes that capital is endogenously determined, and its limited reallocation is due to the existence of adjustment costs. Woodford (2005) discusses this model, and concludes that the hypothesis of a fixed capital is a good enough approximation. For another empirical application, see Eichenbaum and Fisher (2007).

assumptions: for example, when labor is traded in an economy-wide labor market but capital is firm specific and therefore cannot be instantaneously reallocated across firms, a constant returns to scale production function implies that s_y is equal to the ratio of the output elasticities with respect to capital and labor.[9] In a more general case where labor markets as well are firm-specific, the parameter s_y is a composite parameter that includes also the elasticity of the marginal disutility of work with respect to output increases (Woodford 2003).

Another extension is the case in which each firm's desired markup over its marginal cost depends upon the prices of other firms. Because the desired markup depends on the firm's elasticity of demand, a variable desired markup can be obtained by assuming a variable demand elasticity. Modeling this case thus requires departing from the standard Dixit-Stiglitz aggregator. For example, the aggregator proposed in the macro literature by Kimball (1995) allows for the elasticity of substitution between differentiated goods to be a function of their relative market share.

Kimball was interested in a variable elasticity of demand to generate countercyclical movements in the firm's desired markup, and sufficient real rigidity to make a model of sticky prices plausible (i.e., without having to assume too large a percentage of firms keeping prices constant for long periods of time). His objective was to generate more flexible demand functions, particularly "quasi-kinked" demand functions, characterized by the property that for the firm at its normal market share, it is easier to lose customers by increasing its relative price than to gain customers by lowering its relative price. By making the elasticity of demand depend upon the firm's relative sales, Kimball's preferences generate another kind of strategic complementarity that amplifies the effect of nominal disturbances and, everything else equal, reduces the size of the Phillips curve's slope.[10] Such property has spurred new research on various implications of the assumption of a nonconstant elasticity of demand. Dotsey and King (2005) use a specific functional form for the Kimball aggregator in a calibrated DSGE model to study the dynamic response of inflation and output to monetary shocks in the context of a state-dependent pricing model. Levin, Lopez-Salido, and Yun (2006) adopt the Kimball specification to analyze the interaction of strategic complementarity and steady-state inflation. In empirical work, Eichenbaum and Fisher (2007) use the same specification to pin down a realistic estimate of the frequency of price reoptimization in the Calvo model. Finally, in the context of an open economy model, Gust, Leduc, and Vigfusson (2007) extend these preferences to the demand of home produced and imported goods, to show that with strategic complementarity

9. For example, with a Cobb-Douglas production technology $s_y = a/(1-a)$, where $1-a$ is the output elasticity with respect to labor.

10. See the discussion of these preferences in the context of models with price rigidities in Woodford (2003).

lower trade costs reduce the pass-through of exchange rate movements to import prices.

Departing from the constant demand elasticity assumption along the lines of Kimball, the consumption aggregate in (2) is replaced by an aggregate C_t, implicitly defined by

$$\int_{\Omega} \psi\left(\frac{c_t(i)}{C_t}\right) di = 1, \tag{10}$$

where $\psi(\cdot)$ is an increasing, strictly concave function, and Ω is the set of all potential goods produced (a real line). With this notation the Dixit-Stiglitz aggregator corresponds to the case where $\psi\,(c_t\,(i)/C_t) = (c_t\,(i)/C_t)^{(\theta-1)/\theta}$ for some $\theta > 1$. With an aggregator function of the form (10) one can show[11] that the Calvo model implies an inflation dynamics of the baseline form, where the slope (considering again for simplicity the case of an approximation around a steady state with zero inflation) becomes

$$\zeta = \frac{(1-\alpha\beta)(1-\alpha)}{\alpha}\,\frac{1}{1+\overline{\theta}(\overline{s}_y+\overline{\varepsilon}_{\mu})}. \tag{11}$$

Here $\overline{\theta}$ is the steady-state value of the firm's elasticity of demand, which is now a function $\theta(x)$ of the firm's relative sales (denoted by x); $\overline{\varepsilon}_{\mu}$ is the steady-state value of the function $\varepsilon_{\mu}(x)$ that represents the elasticity of the markup function $\mu(x)$, which also depends on the firm's relative sales, and $\overline{s}_y$ is the steady-state value of the elasticity of the firm's marginal cost with respect to its own sales. The interactions of the new variables in the strategic complementarity term $1/1 + \overline{\theta}(\overline{s}_y + \overline{\varepsilon}_{\mu})$ determines to what extent the slope ζ differs from that of the baseline case.

Expression (11) formalizes all the channels through which globalization may affect the strength of the relationship between inflation and marginal costs that I discussed in section 10.3. It shows that the slope coefficient depends upon a number of variables: (a) the frequency of price revisions, represented by the coefficient α: less frequent price revisions (a higher value of α) correspond to lower ζ; (b) the sensitivity of the desired firm's price to marginal cost versus other prices, the term $\overline{\varepsilon}_{\mu}$; (c) the sensitivity of marginal cost to the firm's own output, the term $\overline{s}_y$; and (d) the sensitivity of the firm's own output to the relative price, $\overline{\theta}$.[12] The higher these sensitivities, the lower the slope (ζ).

The Calvo model enriched with these modifications is now a suitable framework for discussing the effects of globalization: the task is to relate the factors that drive the value of the slope to the increase in trade openness, that is one of the characteristics of a more global environment. This is what

11. See the later derivation for the specific parametrization considered.

12. In addition, in approximations that allow for positive steady-state inflation, the slope is possibly affected by the level of trend inflation, which may interact with the demand elasticity, as in (8).

I consider next. Leaving aside the issue of whether globalization affects the frequency of price adjustments, and more generally the nominal rigidity term, in the next section I focus on the effects of an increase in trade on the strategic complementarity term.

10.5 The Effect of Firms' Entry

10.5.1 Kimball Preferences with a Variable Number of Goods

I extend Kimball's (1995) model to an environment where the number of traded goods is variable. The model implies that the elasticity of demand depends on the firm's relative output share: by relating this share to the number of goods traded, the steady-state elasticity of demand becomes a function of the number of traded goods in steady state. This implies that the degree of strategic complementarity varies with the number of traded goods; hence, so does the slope of the inflation-marginal cost curve.

I assume that households' utility is defined over an aggregate C_t of differentiated goods $c_t(i)$, defined implicitly by (10), where $\psi(.)$ is an increasing, strictly concave function, and I also assume that $\psi(0) = 0$. If the set of goods that happen to be sold is $[0, N]$, then $c_t(i) = 0$ for all $i > N$; and C_t satisfies[13]

(12) $$\int_0^N \psi\left(\frac{c_t(i)}{C_t}\right) di = 1.$$

The elasticity of demand, in this setup, is defined as a function

(13) $$\theta(x) = -\frac{\psi'(x)}{x\psi''(x)},$$

where x indicates the relative market share of the differentiated goods. In Kimball's formulation the elasticity of demand is lower for those goods that sell more because their relative price is lower. Accordingly, the desired markup pricing over costs is as well a function of the market share:

(14) $$\mu(x) = \frac{\theta(x)}{\theta(x) - 1}.$$

The optimal consumption allocation across goods is the solution to the following problem:

$$\min_{\{c_t(i)\}} \int_0^N p_t(i)c_t(i)di \quad \text{s.t.} \quad \int_0^N \psi\left(\frac{c_t(i)}{C_t}\right) di = 1.$$

13. Note that under this assumption changes in the number of goods available for sale involve no change in preferences as the utility function is independent of N. This contrasts with Benassy's (1996) generalization of the Dixit-Stiglitz preferences, that depend on the value N.

The first-order conditions for this problem are

$$p_t(i) = \frac{1}{\Lambda_t C_t}\psi'\left(\frac{c_t(i)}{C_t}\right), \tag{15}$$

for each $i \in [0, N]$, where Λ_t is the Lagrange multiplier for the constraint. The solution to this minimization problem gives the demand for each good i as

$$c_t(i) = C_t\psi'^{-1}(p_t(i)\Lambda_t C_t), \tag{16}$$

where Λ_t is implicitly defined by the requirement that

$$\int_0^N \psi(\psi'^{-1}(p_t(i)\Lambda_t C_t))\, di = 1. \tag{17}$$

Expression (17) defines a price index $\tilde{P}_t \equiv 1/\Lambda_t C_t$ for any set of prices $\{p_t(i)\}$, independent of C_t. We can then write the demand curve for good i as

$$y_t(i) = Y_t\psi'^{-1}\left(\frac{p_t(i)}{\tilde{P}_t}\right). \tag{18}$$

Note that the aggregate "price" $\tilde{P}_t$ is not in general the same as the conventional price index, which here is defined, as in the case of Dixit-Stiglitz preferences, as the cost of a unit of the composite good; that is,

$$P_t = \frac{1}{C_t}\int_0^N p_t(i)c_t(i)di = \int_0^N p_t(i)\psi'^{-1}\left(\frac{p_t(i)}{\tilde{P}_t}\right)di, \tag{19}$$

where the second equality follows from (18). Both P_t and $\tilde{P}_t$, however, are homogeneous of degree one functions in $\{p_t(i)\}$.

10.5.2 Steady State with Symmetric Prices

I am interested in the properties of the demand curve in a steady state with symmetric prices $p_t(i) = p_t$ for all i. In this case, it follows from (12) that the relative demand $c_t(i)/C_t$ is equal to

$$\frac{c_t(i)}{C_t} = \psi^{-1}\left(\frac{1}{N}\right), \tag{20}$$

for all i, and from (15):

$$\tilde{P}_t = \frac{p_t}{\psi'(\psi^{-1}(1/N))}. \tag{21}$$

From the definition of P_t in (19) it also follows that

$$P_t = p_t\left[N\psi^{-1}\left(\frac{1}{N}\right)\right]. \tag{22}$$

The elasticity of demand in such a steady state, denoted by θ, is

$$\bar{\theta} = -\frac{\psi'(x)}{x\psi''(x)}, \tag{23}$$

where $x = \psi^{-1}(1/N)$ denotes the relative share in the symmetric steady state. Note how this elasticity differs from the case of the Dixit-Stiglitz aggregator, where the elasticity of demand is a constant $\theta(x) = \theta$ for all x. Here the demand elasticity depends upon the relative market share of the good, and its value in steady state, $\bar{\theta}$, is a function of the number of goods traded in steady state, N. I am interested in seeing *how* this steady state elasticity $\bar{\theta}$ varies with N. The extent of this variation depends on how the elasticity function $\theta(x)$ varies with x.[14]

The assumptions made so far do not have implications for the sign of $\theta'(x)$. However, if we assume, as Kimball (1995) does, that the function $\theta(x)$ is decreasing in x, since $\psi^{-1}(1/N)$ is decreasing in N, it follows that $\bar{\theta}$ is *increasing* in N. This is in line with the general intuition that the more goods are traded in a market, the more likely it is for the demand to decrease more in response to a small increase in prices.

As $\bar{\theta}$ varies with the number of goods traded, so does the desired markup of prices over costs, evaluated in steady state. I define the steady-state desired markup as $\bar{\mu} \equiv \bar{\theta}/(\bar{\theta} - 1)$: if $\bar{\theta}$ is increasing in N, then the steady-state desired markup is decreasing in N. For what it is discussed later, it is also important to evaluate the extent to which the markup itself, as defined in (14), varies with the relative sales, and therefore with the number of traded goods.

The elasticity of the mark-up function to the firm's market share is

$$\varepsilon_{\mu}(x) = \frac{\partial \log \mu(x)}{\partial \log x} = \frac{x\mu'(x)}{\mu(x)}, \tag{24}$$

which, evaluated at $x = \psi^{-1}(1/N)$, is denoted as[15]

$$\bar{\varepsilon}_{\mu} = \frac{x\mu'(x)}{\mu(x)}.$$

The elasticity $\bar{\varepsilon}_{\mu}$ determines how much $\bar{\mu}$ varies for a small variation in N.[16] Since

$$\frac{\partial \log \mu}{\partial \log N} = \frac{\partial \log \mu}{\partial \log x} \bullet \frac{\partial \log x}{\partial \log N} = \bar{\varepsilon}_{\mu} \cdot \frac{\partial \log x}{\partial \log N},$$

14. The function $\theta(\bullet)$ could also be expressed as a function of the relative price, rather than the market share, as in Gust, Leduc, and Vigfusson (2007).

15. Note that this elasticity could alternatively be defined as $\varepsilon_{\mu}(x) = -\varepsilon_{\theta}(x)/[\theta(x) - 1]$, where $\varepsilon_{\theta}(x) = (\partial \log \theta(x))/(\partial \log x)$.

16. The value of $\bar{\varepsilon}_{\mu}$ is important to determine the degree of strategic complementarity in price setting, for small departures from the uniform-price steady state (see Woodford 2003).

and since $1/N = \psi(x)$,

$$\frac{\partial \log N}{\partial \log x} = -\frac{x\psi'(x)}{\psi(x)} = -N\psi^{-1}\left(\frac{1}{N}\right)\psi'\left(\psi^{-1}\left(\frac{1}{N}\right)\right),$$

we have that

$$\frac{\partial \log \mu}{\partial \log N} = \frac{-\bar{\varepsilon}_{\mu}}{N\psi^{-1}(1/N)\,\psi'(\psi^{-1}(1/N))}.$$

The elasticity of μ with respect to N has therefore the opposite sign of the elasticity $\bar{\varepsilon}_{\mu}$. In turn, we can determine how $\bar{\varepsilon}_{\mu}$ must vary with N by considering how $\varepsilon_{\mu}(x)$ varies with x. Because we can argue that $\log \mu$ is a convex function of $\log x$,[17] it follows from definition (24) that $\varepsilon_{\mu}(x)$ is an increasing function of x: we can then conclude that $\bar{\varepsilon}_{\mu}$ is a *decreasing* function of N.

Finally, it can be shown that the steady-state sensitivity of the firm's marginal cost to its own output, $\bar{s}_y$, is also a function of N. This elasticity depends upon assumptions about the form of the production function and about consumer preferences, which I have not spelled out yet. The nature of the dependence of $\bar{s}_y$ on N, however, can be illustrated by way of some simple assumptions. Let the production function of firm i be

$$y_t(i) = h_t(i)^{1-a} - \Phi, \tag{26}$$

where $h(i)$ is labor hours and Φ is a fixed cost. This leads to a labor demand function

$$h_t(i) = (y_t(i) + \Phi)^{1/(1-a)}. \tag{27}$$

Assuming an economy-wide labor market, with nominal wage W_t, the total cost of production of firm i is $W_t h_t(i)$, and its real marginal cost is

$$s_t(i) = \frac{MC_t}{P_t}(y_t(i);\Gamma_t) = \frac{1}{1-a}\frac{W_t}{P_t}(y_t(i) + \Phi)^{a/(1-a)}, \tag{28}$$

where Γ_t indicates aggregate variables that enter into the determination of firms' marginal costs. The elasticity of the marginal cost to firm's own output is then

$$s_y(y_t(i);\Gamma_t) = \frac{a}{1-a}\left[\frac{y_t(i)}{y_t(i) + \Phi}\right].$$

Evaluating this elasticity at a steady state with symmetric prices gives

17. This follows from the hypothesis that $\theta'(x) < 0$, so that $\mu(x)$ is an increasing function of x. In this case it is not possible for $\log \mu$ to be a concave function of $\log x$, because this would require $\log \mu$ to be negative for positive and small enough x. But this cannot happen, no matter how large $\theta(x)$ gets for small x. If $\log \mu$ must be convex, at least for small values of x, it is convenient to assume that it is a globally convex function of $\log x$.

(29) $$\bar{s}_y = \frac{a}{1-a}\left[\frac{xY}{xY+\Phi}\right] = \frac{a}{1-a}\left[\frac{x}{x+\Phi/Y}\right],$$

where again $x = \psi^{-1}(1/N)$ and Y denotes the steady state of aggregate output. Since both x and Y are functions of N, so is $\bar{s}_y$: whether it increases or decreases with N depends upon whether x or $1/Y$ decreases more sharply with N. I discuss this point with some detail in the appendix.

We have thus established that the steady-state elasticity of demand $\bar{\theta}$ is *increasing* in N, while the elasticity of the desired markup evaluated in steady-state $\bar{\varepsilon}_\mu$ is *decreasing* in N; how the elasticity of the marginal cost to firm's own output $\bar{s}_y$ depends on N is established numerically in the quantitative exercise that I conduct in section 10.6. The overall role of N in the price/marginal cost relationship is examined next.

10.5.3 The Price Setting Problem

The firms' pricing problem in this setup generalizes the problem considered in section 10.4. Price setting firms at t choose their price $p_t(i)$ to maximize the following expected string of profits over the life of the set price:

$$E_t\left\{\sum_{j=0}^{\infty}\alpha^j Q_{t,t+j}\left[p_t(i)Y_{t+j}\psi'^{-1}\left(\frac{p_t(i)}{\tilde{P}_{t+j}}\right) - \mathsf{C}\left(Y_{t+j}\psi'^{-1}\left(\frac{p_t(i)}{\tilde{P}_{t+j}}\right);\Gamma_{t+j}\right)\right]\right\},$$

where $\mathsf{C}(\cdot)$ is the firm's cost function; generalizing (4), the first-order condition (FOC) for this problem are

$$E_t\sum_{j=0}^{\infty}\left(\alpha^j Q_{t,t+j}P_{t+j}Y_{t+j}x\left(\frac{p_t(i)}{\tilde{P}_{t+j}}\right)\left[\theta\left(x\left(\frac{p_t(i)}{\tilde{P}_{t+j}}\right)\right)-1\right]\right.$$
$$\left.\times\left[\frac{p_t(i)}{P_{t+j}} - \mu\left(x\left(\frac{p_t(i)}{\tilde{P}_{t+j}}\right)\right)s\left(Y_{t+j}\psi'^{-1}\left(\frac{p_t(i)}{\tilde{P}_{t+j}}\right);\Gamma_{t+j}\right)\right]\right) = 0,$$

where the relative share is $x(P/\tilde{P}) \equiv \psi'^{-1}(P/\tilde{P})$. The elasticity of demand $\theta(x)$ and the markup function $\mu(x)$ are defined in (13) and (14), and $s(y_t(i);\Gamma_t)$ is the real marginal cost of producing quantity $y_t(i)$ in period t, given aggregate state Γ_t, which is unaffected by the pricing decision of firm i.[18]

Log-linearizing the FOC around a steady state with zero inflation one obtains:

(30) $$E_t\sum_{j=0}^{\infty}(\alpha\beta)^j\left[\left(\hat{p}_t^* - \sum_{k=1}^{j}\pi_{t+k}\right) + \bar{\varepsilon}_\mu\bar{\theta}\left(\hat{p}_t^* - \sum_{k=1}^{j}\tilde{\pi}_{t+k} + \log\left(\frac{P_t}{\tilde{P}_t}\right) - K\right)\right.$$
$$\left. + \bar{s}_y\bar{\theta}\left(\hat{p}_t^* - \sum_{k=1}^{j}\tilde{\pi}_{t+k} + \log\left(\frac{P_t}{\tilde{P}_t}\right) - K\right) - \hat{s}_{t+j}\right] = 0,$$

18. Note that the real marginal cost is defined as the ratio $MC_t(i)/P_t$, not the ratio $MC_t(i)/\tilde{P}_t$.

where p^* denotes the optimal price and $\hat{p}_t^* = \log(p_t^*/P_t) - \log(p/P)\,|_{ss}$; $\pi_t \equiv \Delta \log P_t$, $\tilde{\pi}_t \equiv \Delta \log \tilde{P}_t$; $K \equiv \log(P/\tilde{P})\,|_{ss}$; $\bar{s}_y = (\partial \log s_t(i))/(\partial \log y_t(i))\,|_{ss}$, $\hat{s}_t = \log s(Y_t;\Gamma_t) - \log s(Y;\Gamma)\,|_{ss}$, and the steady-state values follow from previous calculations. In particular, from (22)

$$\log\left(\frac{p^*}{P}\right)|_{ss} = -\log\left[N\psi^{-1}\left(\frac{1}{N}\right)\right];$$

from (22) and (21)

$$\log\left(\frac{P}{\tilde{P}}\right)|_{ss} = \log\left[N\psi^{-1}\left(\frac{1}{N}\right)\psi'\left(\psi^{-1}\left(\frac{1}{N}\right)\right)\right],$$

and, since $\log s \equiv \log[(MC/p)(p/P)]$ it follows that:

$$\log s(Y;\Gamma)\,|_{ss} = -\log\bar{\mu} - \log\left[N\psi^{-1}\left(\frac{1}{N}\right)\right]. \tag{31}$$

Log-linearizing the dynamics of the price indices, one gets, for $\tilde{P}_t$

$$\int_0^N\left(\log p_t(i) - \log\tilde{P}_t - \log\left[\psi'\left(\psi^{-1}\left(\frac{1}{N}\right)\right)\right]\right)di = 0,$$

which, to a first-order approximation, gives

$$\log\tilde{P}_t = \frac{1}{N}\int_0^N \log p_t(i)di - \log\left[\psi'\left(\psi^{-1}\left(\frac{1}{N}\right)\right)\right].$$

For P_t, as defined in (19), we have

$$\int_0^N\Bigg\{\log p_t(i) - \log P_t + \log\left[N\psi^{-1}\left(\frac{1}{N}\right)\right]$$
$$+\frac{\psi'(x)}{x\psi''(x)}\left(\log p_t(i) - \log\tilde{P}_t - \log\left(\frac{p(i)}{\tilde{P}}\right)|_{ss}\right)\Bigg\}di = 0,$$

which, to a first-order approximation, implies

$$\log P_t = \frac{1}{N}\int_0^N \log p_t(i)di + \log\left[N\psi^{-1}\left(\frac{1}{N}\right)\right]. \tag{32}$$

Therefore, to a first-order approximation,

$$\log\left(\frac{P_t}{\tilde{P}_t}\right) = \log\left[N\psi^{-1}\left(\frac{1}{N}\right)\right] + \log\left[\psi'\left(\psi^{-1}\left(\frac{1}{N}\right)\right)\right] \equiv K,$$

and therefore

$$\tilde{\pi} = \pi_t.$$

Under the assumption of Calvo staggered prices, we can also write the expression for the general price level (32) as

$$\log P_t = \frac{1}{N}\left(\alpha \int_0^N \log p_{t-1}(i)di\right) + (1-\alpha)\log p_t^* + \log\left[N\psi^{-1}\left(\frac{1}{N}\right)\right]$$

$$= \alpha \log P_{t-1} + (1-\alpha)\left\{\log p_t^* + \log\left[N\psi^{-1}\left(\frac{1}{N}\right)\right]\right\}$$

$$= \alpha \log P_{t-1} + (1-\alpha)(\hat{p}_t^* + \log P_t),$$

where the last equality follows from the definition of $\hat{p}_t^*$. We then have

$$\alpha \log P_t = \alpha \log P_{t-1} + (1-\alpha)\hat{p}_t^*. \tag{33}$$

10.5.4 The Slope of the NKPC

The log-linearized equilibrium conditions (30) and (33) can now be expressed, respectively, as

$$E_t \sum_{j=0}^{\infty}(\alpha\beta)^j\left[\left(1 + \bar{\theta}(\bar{\varepsilon}_\mu + \bar{s}_y)\left(\hat{p}_t^* - \sum_{k=1}^{j}\pi_{t+k}\right) - \hat{s}_{t+j}\right)\right] = 0 \tag{34}$$

and

$$\pi_t = \frac{1-\alpha}{\alpha}\hat{p}_t^*. \tag{35}$$

With typical transformations, (34) and (35) imply again an expression for inflation of the form

$$\pi_t = \zeta\hat{s}_t + \beta E_t\pi_{t+1},$$

where, however, the slope is now defined as in (11) and, more explicitly, as

$$\zeta = \frac{(1-\alpha\beta)(1-\alpha)}{\alpha}\,\frac{1}{1 + \bar{\theta}(N)\,[\bar{\varepsilon}_\mu(N) + \bar{s}_y(N)]}. \tag{36}$$

Through the functions $\bar{\varepsilon}_\mu$, $\bar{s}_y$, and $\bar{\theta}$ the slope ζ depends upon the number of goods traded in steady state.[19] As previously discussed, $\bar{\theta}$ is increasing in N while $\bar{\varepsilon}_\mu$ is decreasing in N, and the elasticity $\bar{s}_y$ will be shown to be decreasing in N as well. Thus, the net effect of a change in the steady-state value of traded goods on the slope depends on the relative size of the response of all these variables. This is what I analyze next.

19. It should also be observed that N has an additional effect on inflation dynamics that can be seen by rewriting (6) as

$$\pi_t = \zeta(\log s_t - \log \bar{s}) + \beta E_t\pi_{t+1}.$$

The steady-state value of the marginal cost is a function of the steady-state markup $\bar{\mu}$ and the steady-state relative price p/P, which are both functions of N: $\log \bar{s}(N) = -\log \bar{\mu}(N) - \log[N\psi^{-1}(1/N)]$.

10.6 Quantitative Effect of Trade Increase on the Phillips Curve Slope

In order to evaluate the quantitative impact of the trade increase on the slope ζ, I need to parametrize the function $\psi(x)$. First, I choose a functional form along the lines of Dotsey and King (2005), setting:

$$\psi(x) = \frac{1}{(1+\eta)\gamma}[(1+\eta)x - \eta]^{\gamma} - \frac{1}{(1+\eta)\gamma}(-\eta)^{\gamma},$$

where the constant term is chosen to satisfy the condition $\psi(0) = 0$ stated before.

For this specification of $\psi(x)$ the demand function (16) is

$$\frac{c_t(i)}{C_t} = \frac{1}{1+\eta}\left[\left(\frac{p_t(i)}{\tilde{P}_t}\right)^{1/(\gamma-1)} + \eta\right],$$

a sum of a constant and a Dixit-Stiglitz term, where the parameters γ and η control the elasticity and the curvature of the function. I discuss later the calibration of the parameters γ and η for the quantitative exercise.

Using the derivations of the previous section, I can now write explicit expressions for the variables that enter the slope of the Phillips curve and show how they depend on N in a steady state with symmetric prices. The steady-state relative share x in (20) is

$$(37) \qquad x \equiv \psi^{-1}\left(\frac{1}{N}\right) = \frac{1}{1+\eta}\left\{\left[\frac{(1+\eta)\gamma}{N} + (-\eta)^{\gamma}\right]^{1/\gamma} + \eta\right\};$$

the steady-state elasticity (23) is

$$(38) \qquad \bar{\theta} = \frac{\eta - (1+\eta)\psi^{-1}(1/N)}{(\gamma-1)(1+\eta)\psi^{-1}(1/N)},$$

and the elasticity of markup (25) is the following function of N:

$$\bar{\varepsilon}_{\mu} = \frac{\eta(\gamma-1)(1+\eta)\psi^{-1}(1/N)}{[\eta - (1+\eta)\psi^{-1}(1/N)][\eta - \gamma(1+\eta)\psi^{-1}(1/N)]}.$$

Finally, the steady-state markup is

$$\bar{\mu} = \frac{\eta - (1+\eta)\psi^{-1}(1/N)}{\eta - \gamma(1+\eta)\psi^{-1}(1/N)}.$$

Plugging numerical values for the parameters η and γ in these expressions allows us to determine the quantitative effect of an increase in N on the slope of the inflation-marginal cost function.

Unfortunately, the literature does not offer much guidance for what are the most plausible values for η and γ. One possibility is to choose a combination of these two parameters that guarantees a desired value for the markup (hence, for the demand elasticity) in a steady state where the relative share x is equal to 1. Dotsey and King (2005), for example, set $\gamma = 1.02$, and determine η so that $\bar{\theta}(1) = 10$ (or a markup of 11 percent), which gives $\eta = -6$.[20] Levin, Lopez-Salido, and Yun (2006), in order to have a markup of 16 percent in their baseline case, choose instead a lower value of 7 for the elasticity $\bar{\theta}(1)$, and set $\eta = -2$. In an open economy model Gust, Leduc, and Vigfusson (2007) choose η to match their model's implications for the volatility of output, and then select γ to give a 20 percent markup pricing in steady state (and $\bar{\theta}(1) = 6$). This implies setting $\gamma = 1.15$ and $\eta = -1.87$. The larger is η in absolute value, the more concave is the demand function. This is shown in figure 10.1 for the case in which $\bar{\theta}(1) = 7$, and in figure 10.2 for the case of $\bar{\theta}(1) = 10$. In each figure the line with circles corresponds to $\eta = 0$, which is the Dixit-Stiglitz case of constant elasticity. The other two lines are Kimball's demand functions with different curvatures. The value of the parameters η and γ are indicated in the figures.

I start the quantitative exercise by considering the parametrization of Levin, Lopez-Salido, and Yun (2006), and then evaluate the case of a lower initial markup (higher demand elasticity), according to the parametrization of Dotsey and King (2005). The steady-state elasticity $\bar{\theta}(1)$ assumed in these studies is relatively in line with estimates of the Dixit-Stiglitz elasticity obtained from macro data.[21] In micro data, however, estimates of the elasticity of substitution are very sensitive to the level of aggregation. Broda and Weinstein (2006), for example, estimate elasticities for a large number of goods at three different levels of aggregation, and find higher elasticities for more disaggregated sectors. That means that varieties are closer substitutes when disaggregation is higher. Although their estimated elasticities cover a wide range of values, the median elasticity for the period 1972 to 1988 ranges from 2.5 to 3.7, depending on the aggregation level.[22] This suggests to investigate as well the effects of parametrizations of the aggregator function based on a much lower value of the demand elasticity in the initial steady state. Identifying this state with the period 1972 to 1988, which represents a preglobalization period, I consider parameter values for η and γ that satisfy $\bar{\theta}(1) = 3$. Figure 10.3 shows the demand functions for this case, in a manner analogous to figures 10.1 and 10.2.[23]

20. It follows from (23) that for $x = 1$: $\bar{\theta} = -1/((\gamma - 1)(1 + \eta))$.

21. For example, in Cogley-Sbordone (2008) we estimate a Calvo model with a Dixit-Stiglitz specification and time varying inflation trend. Using aggregate data on inflation, unit labor costs, output, and interest rates we estimate an elasticity of about 10.

22. It is also interesting to note that their estimated elasticities across each disaggregation group appear to slightly decrease, rather than increase, in the 1990 to 2001 period versus the 1972 to 1988. Their interpretation is that imported goods have become more differentiated over time.

23. Whatever the assumed values of $\bar{\theta}(1)$, I choose for η only two alternative values, -3 and -2, as reported in the figures: more negative values would make the demand curve too kinked. Given η, a value for γ follows from expression (23) evaluated at $x = 1$.

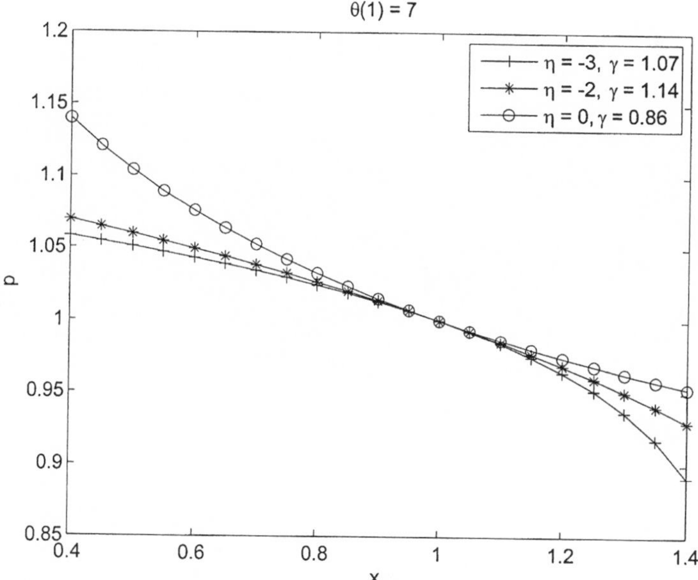

Fig. 10.1 Demand functions for various parametrizations; $\overline{\theta}(x) = 7$ at $x = 1$

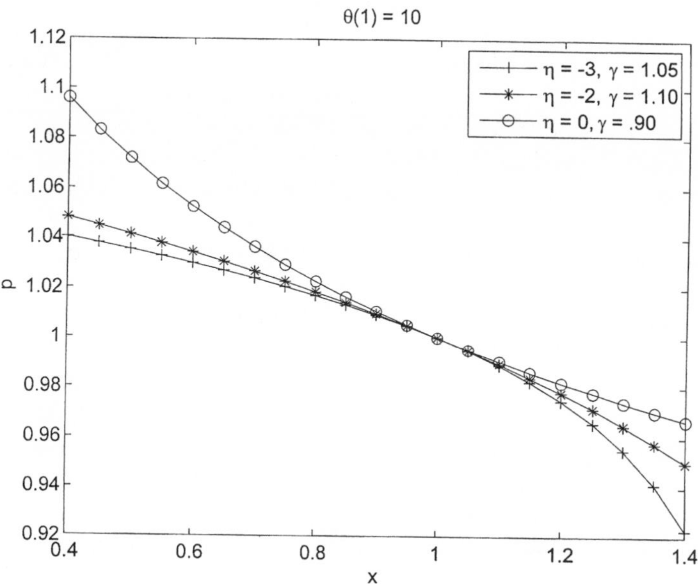

Fig. 10.2 Demand functions for various parametrizations; $\overline{\theta}(x) = 10$ at $x = 1$

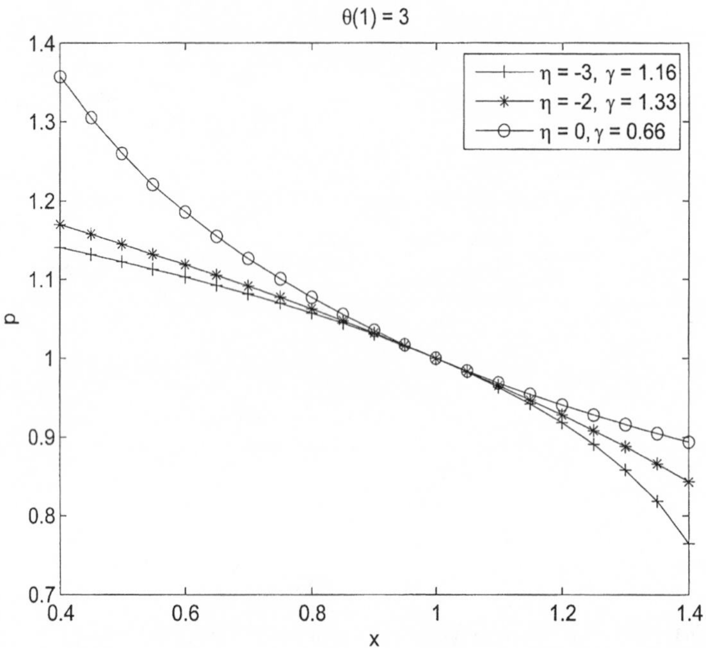

Fig. 10.3 Demand functions for various parametrizations; $\overline{\theta}(x) = 3$ at $x = 1$

The behavior of the various components of the "strategic complementarity" term of the slope, and the slope itself,[24] computed with the parametrization of Levin, Lopez-Salido, and Yun (2006)[25] is shown in figure 10.4. These functions are all evaluated at the market share $x = \psi^{-1}(1/N)$, thus they are a function of the number of goods traded in steady-state N, which is reported on the horizontal axis. The graphs on the top row show the steady-state market share x and the demand elasticity $\overline{\theta}$, those on the second row show the markup $\overline{\mu}$ and the markup elasticity $\overline{\varepsilon}_{\mu}$, and the last row reports the elasticity of the marginal cost to output $\overline{s}_y$ and the Phillips curve slope ζ.

In each graph the curves with crosses depict the case of a more concave demand ($\eta = -3$ and $\gamma = 1.07$) while the curves with stars correspond to a less concave demand function ($\eta = -2$ and $\gamma = 1.14$). Note how the decline in the desired markup is consistent with the evidence that an increase in trade is making the economy more competitive, as documented, for example, by Chen, Imbs, and Scott (2006) for European countries.

The behavior of the strategic complementarity term depends on the rela-

24. The slope is computed for a given nominal rigidity term. This term is defined as $((1 - \alpha)(1 - \alpha\beta))/\alpha$ and does not depend on N. By calibrating $\beta = .99$ and $\alpha = .7$, the assumed nominal rigidity corresponds to an average interval of nine to ten months between price changes.

25. That is, the combinations of the parameters η and γ are such that the demand elasticity in a steady state with unit market share is equal to 7.

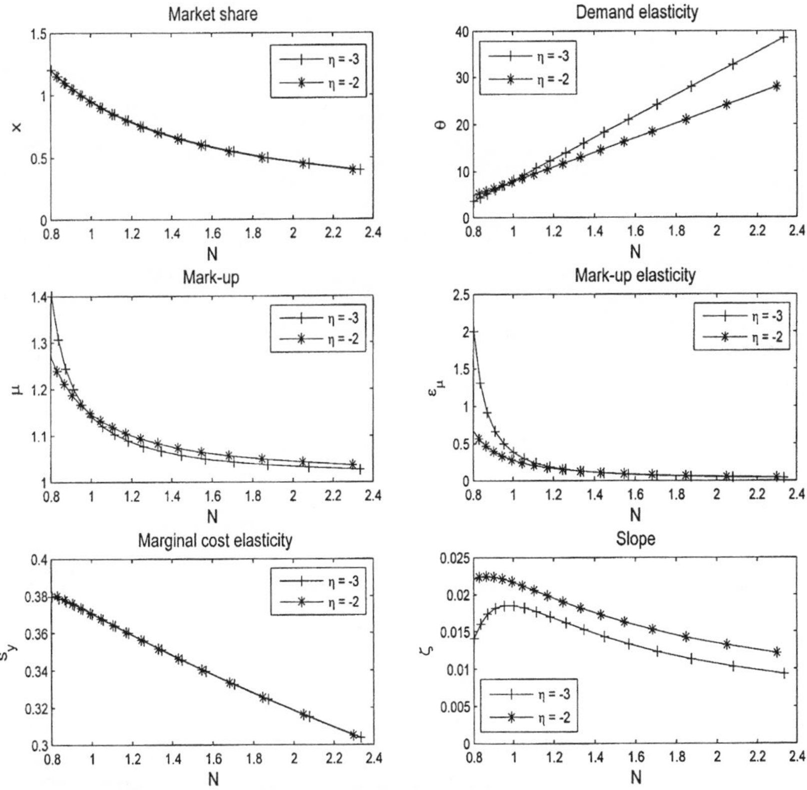

Fig. 10.4 Parametrizations: $\eta = -2$, $\gamma = 1.14$, and $\eta = -3$, $\gamma = 1.07$

tive response of the two terms on the denominator of expression (36), $\bar{\theta}(N)$ and $(\bar{\varepsilon}_{\mu}(N) + \bar{s}_y(N))$, to changes in the number of traded goods N. For both parametrizations reported in the figure, the demand elasticity $\bar{\theta}$ (graph on the top right corner) increases almost linearly in N; the elasticity $\bar{s}_y$ (graph on the bottom left of the figure) and the markup elasticity $\bar{\varepsilon}_{\mu}$ decline with N. The markup elasticity, in particular, which is a convex function of N, declines very rapidly as N starts to increase, more so when the demand function is more concave—the case depicted by the crossed curves in the figure. This sharp decline in $\bar{\varepsilon}_{\mu}$ causes the decline in the term $(\bar{\varepsilon}_{\mu} + \bar{s}_y)$ to dominate the increase in the elasticity $\bar{\theta}$, thus generating a moderate increase in the slope of the Phillips curve for these values. In the case of a less concave function, as the starred lines show, the changes in the two terms $\bar{\theta}$ and $(\bar{\varepsilon}_{\mu} + \bar{s}_y)$ offset one another at low values of N so that the slope is essentially unchanged, and then it declines monotonically when N increases further. For large enough values of traded goods, however, the slope declines regardless of the concavity of the demand function.

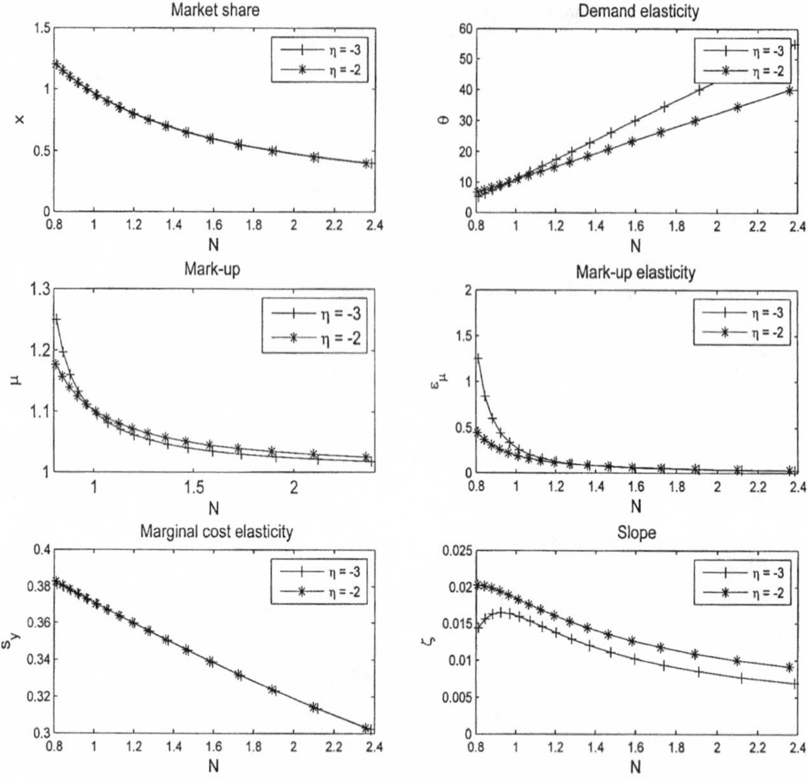

Fig. 10.5 Parametrizations: $\eta = -2$, $\gamma = 1.10$, and $\eta = -3$, $\gamma = 1.05$

To evaluate the sensitivity of the outcome depicted in figure 10.4 to different calibrations of the parameters of the aggregator function, the next two figures plot the behavior of the same variables for the two alternative parametrizations found in the literature.

Figure 10.5 is obtained by choosing parameters as in Dotsey and King (2005). Both combinations of the parameters η and γ indicated in the figure deliver a steady-state demand elasticity $\overline{\theta}(1) = 10$, which is higher than the case presented in figure 10.4. As the figure shows, this case is relatively similar to the previous one, except that the function $\overline{\varepsilon}_\mu$ has a less steep path. As a consequence, the extent of the increase in the slope when N increases near the low initial level is reduced.

One observes, instead, larger differences for the case where the aggregator function is parametrized in line with the empirical estimates of demand elasticity from microdata (e.g., Broda and Weinstein 2006). In this case the demand elasticity in the steady state with unit market share is set to a smaller value than in the baseline case: $\overline{\theta}(1) = 3$. This case is reported in figure 10.6.

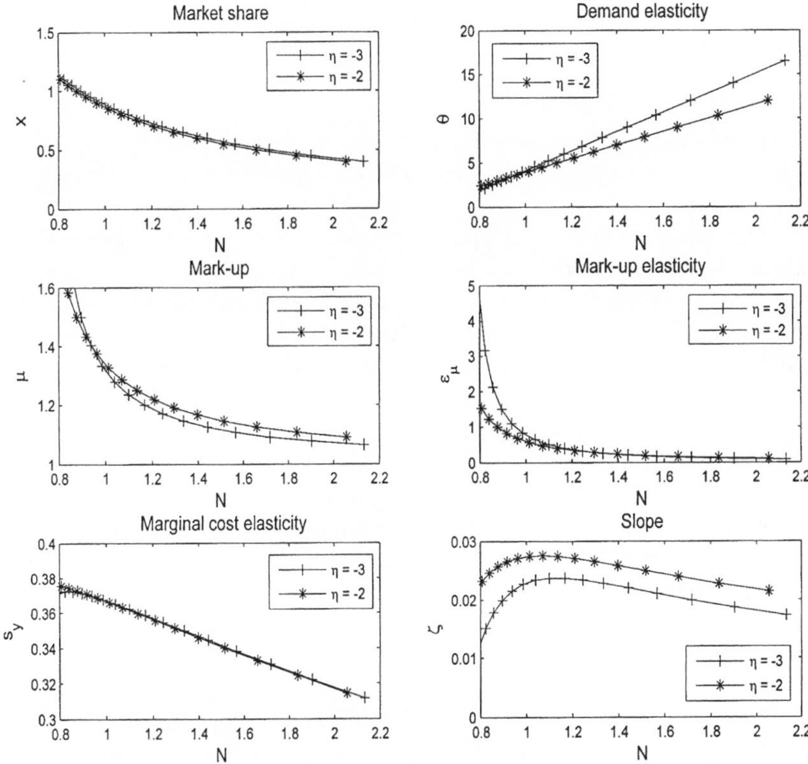

Fig. 10.6 Parametrizations: $\eta = -2$, $\gamma = 1.33$, and $\eta = -3$, $\gamma = 1.16$

The assumption of a smaller elasticity in the initial steady state implies less curvature of the demand function when the relative price increases (see previous figure 10.3). As a consequence, the elasticity of demand increases at a slower pace when the number of traded goods increases, while the desired markup, which starts from more elevated values because of a lower initial elasticity, declines rapidly. The markup elasticity, very high in the initial steady state, declines sharply, making the term $\bar{\varepsilon}_{\mu}$ dominate the behavior of the slope. As the graph on the lower right corner shows, in this case the slope of the Phillips curve indeed increases for a larger range of values of N for both parametrizations in the figure, and more markedly so the more concave is the demand function. Furthermore, although as N grows the slope eventually declines, it remains always above its initial value for the range of increases in traded goods considered in the figure.

Overall, the message of those graphs is that an increase in competition, in this model, does not necessarily have the effect of reducing the slope of the Phillips curve. While it is true that competition increases the elasticity of demand faced by the producers, it also determines a decline in the desired markup pricing of the firms, and it is the way in which these two effects play out that ultimately determines the effect of more competition on the Phillips curve trade-off.

10.6.1 Measuring the Trade Increase

The previous figures illustrate how moving from a steady state with low N to a steady state with high N can affect the slope of the new-Keynesian Phillips curve. However, they also show that the magnitude of the change in the slope is sensitive to the parametrization of the demand curve. And within each parametrization, it matters how big the change is in the number of traded goods going from one steady state to another, because of the non-monotonicity of the slope function ζ. Hence, in order to make a quantitative assessment of the impact of the increase in market competition on the new-Keynesian Phillips curve trade-off, one would need to measure the size of the increase in trade associated with the globalization of the 1990s in a way appropriate to represent the variable N of the model.

The U.S. goods imports increased significantly in the 1960 to 2006 period. Figure 10.7 shows that the share of goods imports on GDP went from a little more than 4 percent in 1960 to about 22 percent by the end of 2006, with an increase from about 12 to 22 percent since 1989. For this latest period, however, the increase in import share, excluding oil products, is more modest, going from about 8 to 12 percent.

The model, however, associates the increase in competition with an increase in the number of goods traded in the economy. For this purpose a more appropriate measure can be provided by the change in the number of varieties, as reported in the study by Broda and Weinstein (2006), which addresses the issue of the effect of globalization on trade.

Broda and Weinstein study the period 1972 to 2001, which they divide in two subperiods, 1972 to 1988 and 1990 to 2001. For each of them they report the number of varieties traded.[26] They register an increase in the total varieties of goods available to consumers of about 42 percent from 1990 to 2001: the number of varieties went from approximately 182,000 to about 259,000 (table I of the paper). They observe, though, that a large number of varieties have a very small market share: to correct for a possible bias, they also provide a measure of value-weighted varieties. Under this measure, the increase in varieties is much smaller, of the order of 5 percent.[27] In the following calculations I take these two numbers as rough measures of the increase in the number of goods N, and evaluate the effect of increases of this magnitude on the slope of the Phillips curve.

26. They define a variety as "import of a particular good from a particular country" (Broda and Weinstein 2006, 550) and use two different sources for each subperiod (data on 1989 are not included because of the unification of Germany in that year, which makes the data not comparable with those of the following years).

27. This measurement is obtained from the reported λ ratio in table VII of Broda and Weinstein (2006). The gross increase in varieties is computed as the inverse of the (median) λ ratio reported for the corrected count and for the one in table I.

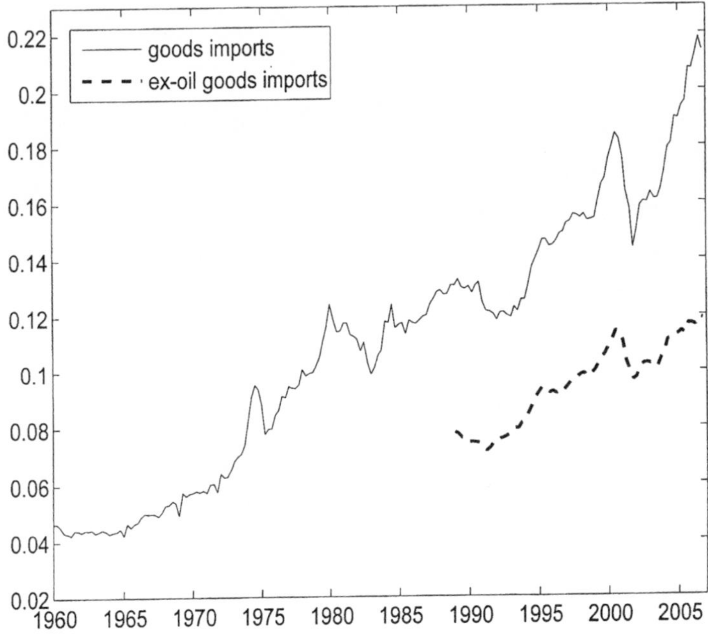

Fig. 10.7 Goods imports/GDP ratios, 1960–2006

Figure 10.8 reproduces four of the slope functions reported in previous graphs. The first row of the figure reproduces the two slopes obtained under the parametrizations of the aggregator function reported in figure 10.4. These parametrizations, to recall, assume a demand elasticity of 7 in a steady state with unit market shares, but differ about the curvature of the demand function around that point. The left graph corresponds to a more concave demand function ($\eta = -3$), the one on the right to a less concave demand ($\eta = -2$). Consider the left graph first: in the initial steady state the number of goods traded is approximately $N = 1/\psi(x) = 0.96$, while by construction the elasticity of demand at that point is $\overline{\theta}(1) = 7$. As discussed, the increase in the quantity of traded goods documented by Broda and Weinstein (2006) is of the order of 5 percent in terms of their value-weighted measure, but of about 42 percent when unweighted. The shaded area between the first two vertical lines (from left to right) indicates the effect of moving from the initial steady state to a new steady state, where the number of traded goods is 5 percent higher. The vertical line farther to the right indicates a new steady state where the number of traded goods is instead 42 percent higher than the initial value. As the graph shows, a 5 percent increase in N is too small a change to affect the size of the slope: the decline in the two functions $\overline{\varepsilon}_{\mu}$ and $\overline{s}_{y}$ is almost entirely offset by the increase in the elasticity $\overline{\theta}$, so that the slope is essentially unchanged, at a value of about 0.018. A 42 percent

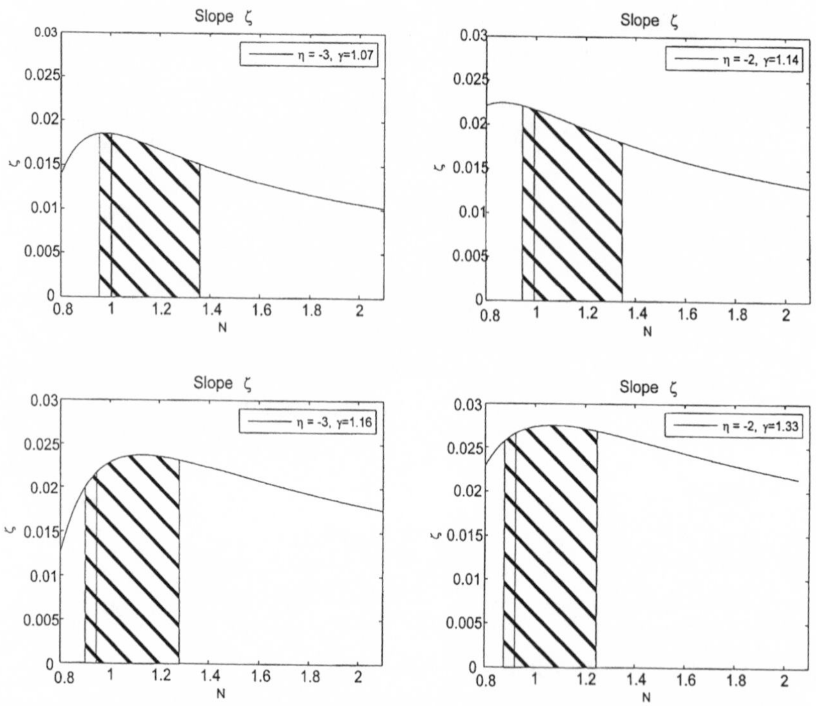

Fig. 10.8 Effect of *N* on the slope ζ

increase, on the other hand, generates an overall increase in the term $(\bar{\varepsilon}_\mu + \bar{s}_y)\,\bar{\theta}$, because the decline in the component $(\bar{\varepsilon}_\mu + \bar{s}_y)$ is more than offset by the increase in $\bar{\theta}$. Thus, the slope declines from about 0.018 to 0.015. In the case of a less concave demand function (graph on the upper right) even a small increase in the steady-state value of *N* has the effect of lowering the value of the slope. In this case, in fact, the increase in the elasticity dominates the "real rigidity" component of the slope, making ζ smaller for any value of *N* larger than its initial value.

The quantitative assessment that emerges from the second row of figure 10.8 is quite different. Here I report the Phillips curve slope as a function of the number of traded goods in the two parametrizations considered in figure 10.6. Relative to the previous case, these parametrizations assume that $\bar{\theta}(1) = 3$. As in the row above, the slope in the left graph is obtained under the assumption of a more concave demand function relative to the one on the right. In both cases, as discussed in the previous section, the slope tends to increase with *N* for a larger range of values. In the initial steady state the slope is about 0.019; in a steady state where the number of traded goods is only 5 percent higher, the slope rises to 0.021, and in a steady state where

N is almost twice as large the slope is 0.023. This result is robust to the assumption of a less concave demand function (graph on the lower right of the figure), although the value of the slope in this case is higher for all values of N.

Overall, according to the model presented, it would be difficult to argue that the increase in trade observed in the 1990s in the United States should have generated an increase in competition leading to a decline in the slope of the inflation/marginal cost relation. It is indeed quite possible that the increased competition has instead resulted in an increase in the slope. Moreover, this conclusion is obtained without allowing for any increase in the frequency of price adjustment in a more competitive environment, of the kind hypothesized by Rogoff (2003). Note, however, that since one is comparing two different steady states, the results depend very critically on the curvature of the demand function in the initial steady state, and on how far the new steady state is from the initial one.

10.7 Conclusion

In this chapter I discuss whether globalization, by generating an increase in market competition, has the potential of reducing the inflation output trade-off; namely, whether it is responsible for the flattening of the Phillips curve that many empirical analyses suggest occurred in the past twenty years or so.

I use the Calvo model of inflation dynamics to disentangle the components of this trade-off, and focus on the relationship between inflation and marginal costs. To analyze how this relationship, which I call the relevant "slope" of the curve, is affected by trade and market competition I depart from the model's traditional assumption of constant elasticity of demand, making this elasticity depend instead on the relative market share of the differentiated goods. When trade moves the economy from a steady state with low trade to one with higher trade, the elasticity of demand facing the firms increases, but the elasticity of the desired markup declines. The balance of these two forces is the key element determining how the degree of strategic complementarity, and with it the inflation-marginal costs component of the Phillips curve slope, vary.

I argue that it is not clear that the trade increase observed in the globalization period is strong enough to have generated a decline in this component of the slope. When marginal cost is related to output, there is a further effect of the trade increase on the overall slope, since in the model the elasticity of marginal cost to aggregate output comprises the elasticity $\bar{s}_y$, which is indeed a decreasing function of number of traded goods. This effect is, however, quantitatively small, as the figures show.

A proper analysis of all the effects of a more integrated economy on the inflation-output trade-off would require to move more clearly to an open economy setup, which would allow one to account for the price dynamics of goods produced abroad and consumed, as final or intermediate goods, in the domestic economy. As it has been shown (see, e.g., Razin and Yuen 2002) the open economy Phillips curve is flatter than the curve of a closed economy, even in the presence of a constant elasticity of marginal cost to output, because the overall slope is declining in a trade openness parameter. My analysis could be interpreted as an analysis of the effects of increase in competition—for a given degree of openness of the economy—when an increase in the actual trade takes place.

That said, it does not necessarily mean that globalization had no effect on inflation dynamics. Throughout my analysis I maintain that the nominal rigidity component of the slope is unchanged. This is not because the frequency of price changes is unaffected by a more global environment. It is simply because it is reasonable to assume that it is not the amount of trade per se that should induce a more frequent adjustment of prices. Price stickiness is instead typically motivated by reoptimization costs, which are essentially driven by the cost of gathering information.

Moreover, the claims that globalization affects the frequency of price adjustment go both ways. On one hand, Rogoff (2003) argues that globalization has led to greater price flexibility—in the model this translates in a lower α, hence in a steepening of the curve. On the other hand, if globalization has brought an overall lower level of inflation, as argued by many, then there is less incentive to revise prices often, because the cost of price misalignment is lower. Endogenizing the frequency of price adjustment is indeed an active area of research.

Appendix

This appendix explains how I compute the elasticity of marginal cost defined in expression (29) as a function of the number of traded goods N. This computation involves quantifying how aggregate output Y varies with N, and calibrating the fixed costs Φ. From expression (28), one derives the steady-state real marginal cost as

$$s = \frac{1}{1-a} w\,(xY + \Phi)^{a/(1-a)}, \tag{39}$$

where w denotes the steady-state real wage. Assuming a fairly standard preference specification: $u(C, h) = \log C - [1/(1 + v)]h^{1+v}$, the desired real wage is $w_t = H_t^v C_t$. Aggregate hours H_t are

$$H_t = \int_0^N h_t(i)\, di = \int_0^N (y_t(i) + \Phi)^{1/(1-a)} di,$$

where I used the definition of hours in (27). Steady-state aggregate hours are then

$$H = N(xY + \Phi)^{1/(1-a)}.$$

Substituting H in the expression for the equilibrium real wage allows us to rewrite (39) as

$$s = \frac{1}{1-a} N^{\nu}(xY + \Phi)^{(\nu+a)/(1-a)} Y. \quad (40)$$

From expression (31) in the text the steady-state real marginal cost is $s = 1/(N\bar{\mu}x)$. Combining this expression with (40) I obtain that

$$xY + \Phi = \left(\frac{1-a}{\bar{\mu}xYN^{1+\nu}} \right)^{(1-a)/(\nu+a)}. \quad (41)$$

This expression defines a concave, increasing function $Y = Y(N)$. For a given calibration of the parameters a, ν, and Φ, each value of N determines a value of Y, which together with the value of x allows us to compute a value for the elasticity $\bar{s}_y$. I set the parameter ν to be equal to 2, which corresponds to a Frisch elasticity of labor supply of .5, the high end of the range typically found in micro studies, and I set $1 - a = .68$, to roughly match the average observed labor share for the United States. To calibrate the fixed cost of production Φ I first use the entry condition to establish a zero-profit upper bound to it, which I denote as Φ^u:

$$\Phi^u = \frac{1}{N^{1-a}} \left(1 - \frac{1-a}{\mu} \right).$$

Then I set Φ sufficiently close but strictly lower than Φ^u to allow entry of new firms with positive profits, and choose $\Phi = .2$. The results are not very sensitive to the range of values chosen for these parameters, since they have mostly a scale effect on $\bar{s}_y$, and hence on ζ, without affecting its curvature.

References

Ball, L. M. 2006. Has globalization changed inflation? NBER working paper no. 12687. Cambridge, MA: National Bureau of Economic Research, November.

Benassy, J.-P. 1996. Taste for variety and optimum production patterns in monopolistic competition. *Economics Letters* 52 (1): 41–47.

Bernanke, B. 2006. Globalization and monetary policy. Speech at the Fourth Economic Summit, Stanford Institute for Economic Policy Research. March, Stanford, CA.

Bilbiie, F. O., F. Ghironi, and M. J. Melitz. 2006a. Endogenous entry, product variety, and business cycle. Unpublished Manuscript.

———. 2006b. Monopoly power and endogenous variety in dynamic stochastic general equilibrium: Distortions and remedies. Unpublished Manuscript.

Blinder, A. S., E. R. D. Canetti, D. E. Lebow, and J. B. Rudd. 1998. *Asking about prices: A new approach to understanding price stickiness.* New York: Russell Sage Foundation.

Borio, C., and A. Filardo. 2007. Globalization and inflation: New cross-country evidence on the global determinants of domestic inflation. Bank for International Settlements. BIS Working Paper no. 227.

Boivin, J., and M. P. Giannoni. 2006. Has monetary policy become more effective? *Review of Economics and Statistics* 88 (3): 445–62.

Broda, C., and D. E. Weinstein. 2006. Globalization and the gains from variety. *Quarterly Journal of Economics* 121 (2): 541–85.

Calvo, G. A. 1983. Staggered prices in a utility-maximizing framework. *Journal of Monetary Economics* 12 (3): 383–98.

Chen, N., J. Imbs, and A. Scott. 2006. Competition, globalization and the decline of inflation. Center for Economic Policy Research (CEPR) Discussion Paper no. 4695.

Cogley, T., and A. M. Sbordone. 2008. Trend inflation, indexation, and inflation persistence in the New Keynesian Phillips curve. *American Economic Review* 98 (5): 2101–26.

Eichenbaum, M., and J. Fisher. 2007. Estimating the frequency of price reoptimization in Calvo-style models. *Journal of Monetary Economics* 54 (7): 2032–47.

Dotsey, M., and R. G. King. 2005. Implications of state-dependent pricing for dynamic macroeconomic models. *Journal of Monetary Economics* 52 (1): 213–42.

Dotsey, M., R. G. King, and A. Wolman. 1999. State-dependent pricing and the general equilibrium dynamics of money and output. *Quarterly Journal of Economics* 114 (3): 655–90.

Gust, C., S. Leduc, and R. J. Vigfusson. 2007. Trade integration, competition, and the decline in exchange-rate pass-through. Board of Governors of the Federal Reserve System. International Finance Discussion Paper no. 864.

Ihrig, J., S. B. Kamin, D. Lindner, and J. Marquez. 2007. Some simple tests of the globalization and inflation hypothesis. Board of Governors of the Federal Reserve System. International Finance Discussion Paper no. 891.

International Monetary Fund. 2006. How has globalization affected inflation? In *World Economic Outlook, April 2006,* ed. IMF, Chapter III, 97–134. Washington, DC: IMF.

Ireland, P. 2007. Changes in the Federal Reserve's inflation target: Causes and consequences. *Journal of Money, Credit and Banking* 39 (8): 1851–82.

Kimball, M. S. 1995. The quantitative analytics of the basic neomonetarist model. *Journal of Money, Credit, and Banking* 27 (4): 1241–77.

Kohn, D. L. 2006. The effects of globalization on inflation and their implications for monetary policy. Remarks at the Federal Reserve Bank of Boston's 51st Economic Conference. 16 June, Chatham, MA.

Levin, A., D. Lopez-Salido, and T. Yun. 2006. Strategic complementarities and optimal monetary policy. Kiel Institute for the World Economy. Kiel Working Paper no. 1355.

Melitz, M. J., and G. I. P. Ottaviano. 2008. Market size, trade and productivity. *Review of Economic Studies* 75 (1): 295–316.
Mishkin, F. S., 2007. Inflation dynamics. NBER Working Paper no. 13147. Cambridge, MA: National Bureau of Economic Research, June.
Razin, A., and C.-W. Yuen. 2002. The "New Keynesian" Phillips curve: Closed economy vs. open economy. *Economics Letters* 75 (1): 1–9.
Roberts, J. M. 2006. Monetary policy and inflation dynamics. *International Journal of Central Banking* 2: 193–230.
Rogoff, K. S. 2003. Globalization and global disinflation. Paper presented at the Federal Reserve Bank of Kansas City Conference on Monetary Policy and Uncertainty: Adapting to a Changing Economy. 28–30 August, Jackson Hole, WY.
———. 2006. Impact of globalization on monetary policy. Paper presented at the Federal Reserve Bank of Kansas City conference on the New Economic Geography: Effects and Policy Implications. 24–26 August, Jackson Hole, WY.
Sbordone, A. M. 2002. Prices and unit labor costs: A new test of price stickiness. *Journal of Monetary Economics* 49 (2): 265–92.
Smets, F., and R. Wouters. 2003. An estimated dynamic stochastic general equilibrium model of the euro area. *Journal of the European Economic Association* 1 (5): 1123–75.
Williams, J. C. 2006. The Phillips curve in an era of well-anchored inflation expectations. Federal Reserve Bank of San Francisco. Unpublished Working Paper.
Woodford, M. 2003. *Interest and prices: Foundations of a theory of monetary policy.* Princeton, NJ: Princeton University Press.
———. 2005. Firm-specific capital and the new Keynesian Phillips curve. *International Journal of Central Banking* 1 (2): 1–46.
Yellen, J. 2006. Monetary policy in a global environment. Speech at the Conference "The Euro and the Dollar in a Globalized Economy." May, University of California at Santa Cruz.

Comment Tommaso Monacelli

Introduction

Does globalization affect inflation? This issue has attracted considerable interest recently, especially among monetary policymakers. Much of the attention has focused on the role of globalization in the form of increased trade integration. Yet if the link between globalization and inflation seems suggestive, it is not clear whether it pertains to the *level* as opposed to the *volatility* of inflation (or both). For instance, Rogoff (2006) argues that globalization strengthens the degree of competition and therefore dampens the inflationary bias temptation of the monetary authority, thereby leading to lower *average* inflation. Somewhat differently, Bernanke (2006) argues that the link between globalization and inflation may work via two complementary channels: a direct (*terms of trade*) effect due to lower import prices,

Tommaso Monacelli is an associate professor of economics at Università Bocconi.

and an indirect (*pro-competitive*) effect due to competitive pressures, lower markups, and strategic complementarity (reduced pricing power of domestic firms).

Sbordone's approach aims at exploring the latter pro-competitive effect in detail. Her chapter is an example of how far the rigor of microfoundations can take us in the structural evaluation of inflation dynamics.[1] Her precise question is: does increased trade integration, by boosting the degree of competition in the economy, feature any sizable effect on the *slope* of the Phillips curve? In particular, can higher trade intensity be conducive to a *flattening* of the Phillips curve? Clearly, through this channel, any variation in the real marginal cost and/or output gap would lead (ceteris paribus) to a lower *variability* in inflation.[2]

In a nutshell, Sbordone's chapter interprets trade integration as a source of *real rigidity*, where the relevant definition of real rigidity is whatever structural factor reduces the elasticity of inflation to the real marginal cost. This "primary" link between marginal cost and inflation is a key dimension in the empirical literature on the new-Keynesian Phillips curve (NKPC henceforth).[3]

The conclusion is as honest as any endeavor in rigorous thinking can be: although in principle increased trade can entail a flattening of the Phillips curve, the sign and the strength of this effect depends on the second derivative of the (steady-state) price elasticity of demand to the number of consumed varieties. The sign of this derivative can lead, under certain conditions, even to a steepening of the Phillips curve.

In my comments I will argue that, although impeccable, Sbordone's reasoning on the topic is far from being exhaustive. I will make two points in particular. First, the link between increased trade and the competitive conditions of the economy should account for a more genuine dimension of openness: namely, the degree of *substitutability* of goods. If increased trade is synonymous with a wider spectrum of consumed varieties, the extent to which the same new varieties are close substitutes of the domestically produced ones bears crucial implications. Second, alternative sources of real rigidity may stem from other features of openness that are not modeled in Sbordone's framework. Such features include: (a) the share of imported inputs in production, and (b) the degree of pass-through of exchange rate movements to import prices. This will lead me to more general considerations on how "to build" an *open economy* version of the NKPC.

1. See Woodford (2003) for a summa of the extensive ramifications of this approach.

2. Recently Mishkin (2007) has argued that a flattening of the Phillips curve has been the result of an increased credibility of monetary policy leading to lower inflation. For this channel to be at work, though, one can only resort to a *state-dependent* pricing framework, thereby lower inflation reduces the frequency of price adjustment and hence, reduces the slope of the Phillips curve.

3. Galí and Gertler (1999); Sbordone (2002).

Pro-competitive Effects, Strategic Complementarity, and the Phillips Curve

In Sbordone's chapter, the link between trade and the slope of the NKPC works via variations in the *price elasticity* of demand, which in turn induce variations in the desired level of the markup. In a standard new-Keynesian model based on Dixit-Stiglitz constant elasticity of substitution (CES) preferences, the price elasticity of demand is a constant exogenous parameter. Sbordone introduces Kimball (1995) preferences over differentiated varieties, a feature that makes the price elasticity of demand a function of the quantity produced, thereby leading to a kinked demand function for any individual variety. Thus, increased trade leads to more varieties, and therefore, possibly to a lowered price elasticity of demand and to a flatter Phillips curve. In this vein, trade is conducive to the pro-competitive effect emphasized by Bernanke (2006).

Sbordone's model is, however, isomorphic to a closed economy model enriched with two nonstandard features: (a) a nonconstant CES aggregator à la Kimball; (b) the presence of a finite number of varieties. The latter is treated as an exogenous extensive margin, since firms' entry and exit decisions are not analyzed. In the absence of these features, the model would nest the standard Calvo-Yun sticky-price model.

In particular, the aggregate consumption index can be written:

$$\int_0^N \psi\left(\frac{c(i)}{C}\right) di = 1,$$

where N is the steady-state number of varieties, which is a free parameter, and $\psi(\cdot)$ is an increasing strictly concave function. Notice that the number varieties do not exert any effect on preferences, not even a basic "love for variety" effect à la Dixit-Stiglitz-Spence.

To simplify, let me abstract from the presence of firm-specific inputs, which can constitute per se an alternative and complementary source of real rigidity. Sbordone shows that the elasticity of (domestically produced goods price) inflation to the real marginal cost can be written:

$$\zeta = \kappa_C\left[\frac{1}{1 + \theta(N)\varepsilon_\mu(N)}\right]. \tag{1}$$

In the previous expression, κ_C denotes the elasticity of inflation to the real marginal cost in the standard Calvo-Yun model, $\theta(N)$ is the steady-state value of the price elasticity of demand (which in turn depends on the number of varieties N), and $\varepsilon_\mu(N) > 0$ is the steady-state elasticity of the markup function to the number of varieties. Notice that, in the spirit of the aforementioned "pro-competitive effect," we have $\theta'(N) > 0$. The elasticity $\varepsilon_\mu(N)$ captures the sensitivity of the desired (equilibrium) markup to other firms' prices, and hence a "strategic-complementarity motive" in price setting.

It is clear that the effect on the slope ζ of an increase in the number of varieties N depends on the sign of the first derivative of $\varepsilon_\mu(N)$ with respect to N. Sbordone shows that $\varepsilon'_\mu(N) < 0$, so an increase in N can have an ambiguous effect on ζ. In addition, Sbordone shows under what conditions the pro-competitive effect (via a variation in $\theta[N]$) prevails over the strategic complementarity effect (via a variation in $\varepsilon_\mu[N]$) in lowering the elasticity ζ of the marginal cost function (and therefore in inducing an increased real rigidity effect). Under certain calibrations, however, a rise in N can even lead to a higher value of the elasticity ζ.

An Open Economy Model with Strategic Complementarity

In this section I argue that accounting for *openness* can substantially alter the strength of the strategic-complementarity effect working via the markup elasticity $\varepsilon_\mu(N)$. What this argument requires is opening the economy to trade and distinguishing the role of imported goods as potentially *imperfect substitutes* of domestically produced goods.

In the following, I sketch a model of a small open economy in which imports enter the consumption basket via a Kimball aggregator, as in Gust, Leduc, and Vigfusson (2006). Prices are assumed to be flexible throughout.

The consumption aggregator of domestic households is defined as the function:

$$G\left(\frac{C_{H,t}(i)}{C_t}, \frac{C_{F,t}(i)}{C_t}\right) = [(1 - N^*)C_{H,t}^{1/\rho} + N^* C_{F,t}^{1/\rho}]^\rho - \frac{1}{(1+\eta)\gamma} + 1,$$

where $C_H(i)$ and $C_F(i)$ denote consumption of domestically produced and imported variety i, respectively, N^* is the *share* of *imported* goods in consumption, $\eta \neq 0$ is a parameter that governs the curvature of the demand function (with $\eta = 0$ implying a typical CES demand function for variety i), ρ is a parameter that governs the elasticity of substitution between domestic and imported goods, and $\gamma > 1$.

The bundle of foreign imported goods reads:

$$(2) \qquad C_{F,t} = \frac{1}{N^*}\int_0^{N^*} \frac{(1-N^*)}{(1+\eta)\gamma}\left[\left(\frac{1+\eta}{1-N^*}\right)\frac{C_{F,t}(i)}{C} - \eta\right]^\gamma di,$$

with $C_{H,t}$ having a similar expression.

Optimal demand for the individual domestic variety reads:

$$(3) \qquad C_{H,t}(i) = (1 - N^*) \left[\frac{1}{(1+\eta)}\left(\frac{P_{H,t}(i)}{\tilde{P}_t}\right)^{1/(\gamma-1)}\left(\frac{P_{H,t}}{\tilde{P}_t}\right)^{\gamma(\gamma-\rho)}\right],$$

where $P_{H,t}(i)$ is the price of domestic variety i, $P_{H,t}$ is the utility-based price of the bundle $C_{H,t}$ of domestic goods, and $\tilde{P}_t$ is an aggregate price index that depends on both the price of the domestic consumption bundle and on the price of the imported bundle:

$$\tilde{P}_t = [(1 - N^*)\, P_{H,t}^{\gamma/(\gamma-\rho)} + N^*\, P_{F,t}^{\gamma/(\gamma-\rho)}]^{(\gamma-\rho)/\gamma}. \tag{4}$$

Notice that $\tilde{P}$ differs from the utility-based aggregate consumer price index (CPI) but is still a homogeneous of degree one function.

In this context, the optimal *desired* markup for the domestic firms reads:

$$\mu_{H,t} = \left[\gamma + \eta(\gamma - 1)\left(\frac{P_H}{\tilde{P}}\right)^{\rho/(\rho-\gamma)}\right]^{-1}. \tag{5}$$

Notice that $\eta = 0$ implies $\mu_{H,t} = \mu_H$ for all t, which is the standard CES case of constant desired markup. With $\eta \neq 0$ the desired markup features an additional time varying endogenous term $\eta(\gamma - 1)\,(P_H/\tilde{P})^{\rho/(\rho-\gamma)}$, which we could think of as a *strategic-complementarity factor.*

By using (4) and defining the terms of trade $S_t = P_{F,t}/P_{H,t}$ as the relative price of imported goods, the desired markup can be expressed as a function of the terms of trade

$$\mu_{H,t} = h(\gamma, \eta, \rho, N^*, S_t). \tag{6}$$

We can, in turn, define $\varepsilon_{\mu_H}(N^*)$ as the *elasticity* of the desired markup to the terms of trade; that is, the open economy analog to $\varepsilon_{\mu}(N)$ in Sbordone's model. We notice that a *terms-of-trade* induced strategic-complementarity effect requires $\varepsilon_{\mu_H}(N^*)$ to be *positive.* Consider, in fact, a terms-of-trade appreciation (a fall in S_t), in the form of a fall in the relative price of imported goods. For a strategic-complementarity effect to be at work, this should lead, via (6), to a *fall* in the desired markup of domestic firms $\mu_{H,t}$, which should in turn generate an incentive for domestic firms to also *reduce* their prices.

Furthermore, we notice that (6) allows us to evaluate the effect on the elasticity $\varepsilon_{\mu_H}(N^*)$ of an increase in the number of *imported* varieties, as opposed to an increase in the *overall* number of varieties as analyzed in Sbordone's chapter. The latter aspect is important, for an increase in trade genuinely corresponds to an increase in the share of varieties imported *relative* to the share of varieties produced domestically. This relative effect naturally suggests that the elasticity of substitution between imported and domestic varieties may play a crucial role in the analysis. A first pass on the data reminds us that both S_t and the markup are countercyclical in the United States (see, e.g., Backus, Kehoe, and Kydland 1994), so the unconditional correlation between $\mu_{H,t}$ and S_t is likely to be positive.

In the following, I systematically evaluate the sign of the elasticity $\varepsilon_{\mu_H}(N^*)$

and how the magnitude of the same elasticity varies with the share of imported varieties N^*. Log-linearizing (5) and (4) around a steady-state with $S = 1$, and combining, one can write the following expression for ε_{μ_H}:

$$\varepsilon_{\mu_H} = \frac{\eta(\gamma - 1)\,\rho\,N^*}{[\gamma + \eta(\gamma - 1)]^2\,(\rho - \gamma)} > 0.$$

Hence, we see that: (a) ε_{μ_H} is increasing in N^* (suggesting that indeed the degree of strategic complementarity is strengthened by stronger trade integration); (b) the sign of ε_{μ_H} depends on the values of γ, η, ρ.

Parameters γ, η, ρ feature in the expression for the (trade) *elasticity of substitution* between domestic and imported varieties, which reads:

$$\rho^T \equiv \frac{\rho}{(\rho - \gamma)(1 + \eta)}.$$

The calibrated values of γ, η, ρ will in turn depend on which value for ρ^T can be considered realistic. The literature is, however, far from unanimous on the likely empirical magnitude of the trade elasticity. Macroeconomists think it is low, in a range between 1.2 and 2, whereas the micro/trade literature typically believes that such elasticity is very high.[4] For instance, Bernard et al. (2003) set $\rho^T = 4$, Heathcote and Perri (2002) estimate $\rho^T = 0.9$. Estimates from open economy dynamic stochastic general equilibrium (DSGE) models such as Justiniano and Preston (2006), De Walque, Smets, and Wouters (2006), and Rabanal and Tuesta (2005) estimate values around $\rho^T = 1.5$. Adolfson et al. (2007) is the first DSGE study that estimates a value for ρ^T in the high range, and in particular equal to 5. At the other end of the spectrum, however, Corsetti, Dedola, and Leduc (2008) set $\rho^T = 0.5$.

When using the Kimball aggregator, a typical source of uncertainty concerns the curvature of the demand function governed by η. Here the range varies from the value $\eta = -2$ chosen by Levin, Lopez-Salido, and Yun (2007) to the value $\eta = -6$ chosen by Dotsey and King (2005) (DK henceforth), with higher values of η (in absolute value) corresponding to a more pronounced curvature of the demand function (i.e., to a more pronounced smoothed kink).

Figure 10C.1 plots the value of ε_{μ_H} as a function of N^* conditional on $\eta = -2$ but for alternative values of the trade elasticity ρ^T. At the high end of the spectrum I choose the value $\rho^T = 4$ calibrated in Bernard et al., whereas at the low end I choose the value $\rho^T = 0.5$ as in Corsetti, Dedola, and Leduc (2008).[5]

Two aspects are worth emphasizing. First, the elasticity of the markup function to the terms of trade is *positive* and *increasing* in N^*. This con-

4. See Ruhl (2008) for an argument trying to reconcile both views.

5. In particular I choose $\gamma = 1.1$ as in Gust, Leduc, and Vigfusson (2006), so that the chosen value for ρ^T implies residually a value for ρ. Notice that $\gamma = 1$ generates the standard CES case.

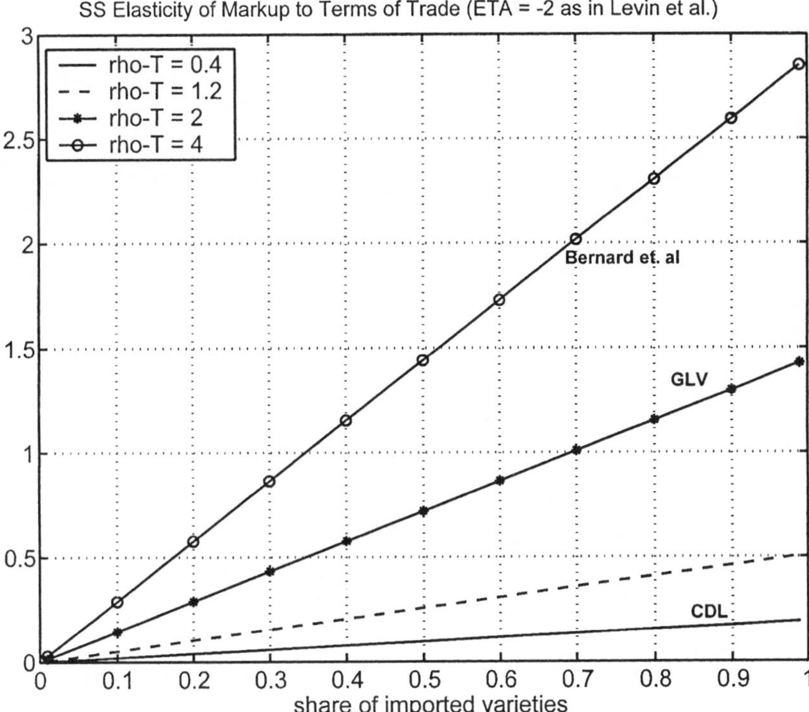

Fig. 10C.1 Effect of varying the share of imported varieties on the steady-state elasticity of the markup to the terms of trade, case $\eta = -2$

Notes: GLV stands for Gust, Leduc, and Vigfusson (2006), CDL for Corsetti, Dedola, and Leduc (2006).

firms that an open economy pro-competitive effect acting via the terms of trade is at work, and is increasing in the share of imported varieties in the economy. Second, and most importantly, the partial derivative of $\varepsilon_{\mu H}$ is strongly affected by the value of the trade elasticity of substitution. The larger the elasticity ρ^T the stronger the effect on $\varepsilon_{\mu H}$ of any given increase in N^*, and therefore the stronger the induced "strategic-complementarity" effect. Intuitively, if increased trade amounts to a larger share of *imported* varieties, any variation in the price of those varieties will exert a stronger competitive effect on the prices of *domestic* varieties, the more closely substitutable the same imported varieties are relative to the domestically produced ones.

Figure 10C.2 displays the results of a similar exercise, but now conditional on a value of $\eta = -6$ as in Dotsey and King (2005). Hence we see that the curvature of the demand function also matters, with a more pronounced curvature leading to an even stronger effect of the number of varieties on the markup elasticity. However, the intensity of this partial effect is of an

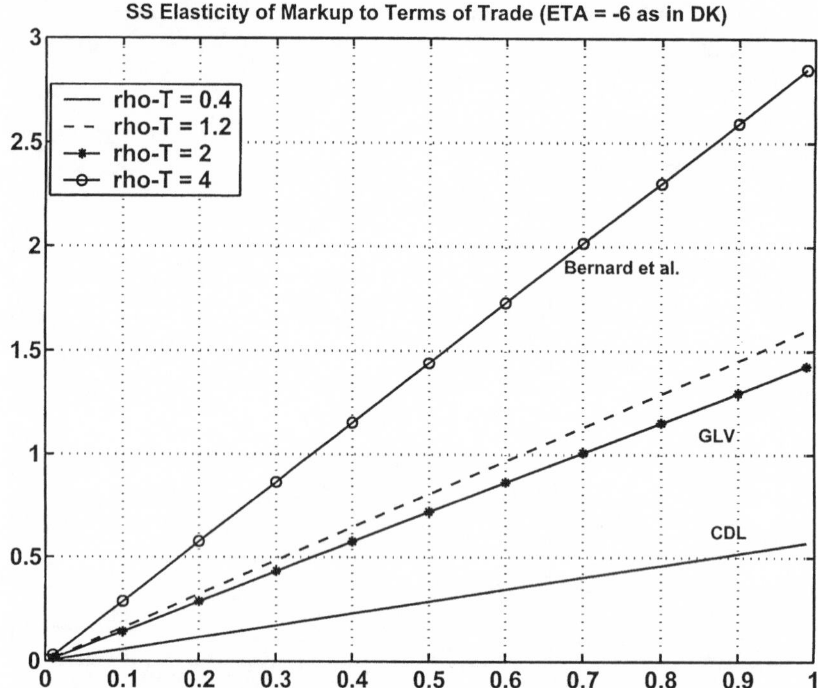

Fig. 10C.2 Effect of varying the share of imported varieties on the steady-state elasticity of the markup to the terms of trade, case $\eta = -6$

Notes: GLV stands for Gust, Leduc, and Vigfusson (2006), CDL for Corsetti, Dedola, and Leduc (2006).

order of magnitude smaller than the partial effect induced by the choice of alternative values of ρ^T.

Building an Open Economy NKPC

The openness dimension may be conducive to channels of real rigidity that are independent of any source of strategic complementarity in price setting. Consider, to start with, the *primary* form of the NKPC (the inflation and real marginal cost relationship analyzed by Sbordone) derived in the open economy model of Galí and Monacelli (2005):

$$\pi_{H,t} = \beta E_t \{\pi_{H,t+1}\} + \kappa_H mc_t, \tag{7}$$

where the slope $\kappa_H \equiv (1 - \theta\beta)(1 - \theta)/\theta$, as typical in the Calvo-Yun framework, depends on the discount factor β and on the probability θ of not being able to reset the price optimally. Notice that in (7) there is no role of openness as a real rigidity factor. Two key assumptions are responsible for this result. First, complete exchange rate pass-through on import prices. Second, imports are final *consumption* goods only.

This does not imply, however, that openness does not exert any influence on inflation. In fact, the form of the primary NKPC for *CPI inflation* π_t reads:

$$\pi_t = \beta E_t\{\pi_{t+1}\} + \kappa_H mc_t + \frac{\alpha}{1-\alpha}\tilde{q}_t,$$

where α is the share of imported goods in consumption (a measure of the degree of openness), and $\tilde{q}_t \equiv [\Delta q_t - \beta\Delta E\{q_{t+1}\}]$ is a composite term capturing leads and lags of the real exchange rate q_t (all in percentage deviations from steady state). The composite term $\tilde{q}_t$ summarizes the role of open economy factors, but once again the latter do not exert any effect on the elasticity of inflation to the real marginal cost, which still coincides with κ_H.

Introducing Imports as Intermediate Production Inputs

Suppose now that imports are modeled both as final consumption goods and intermediate *production inputs.* Let δ be the share of intermediate imports over total imports and ω be the share of intermediate imports in total production inputs. The production function for variety *i* therefore reads $Y(i) = H^{1-\phi}(i)\, M^{\phi}(i)$, where H is labor hours, M is an imported production input, and $\phi \equiv \omega\delta$. In this case, the expression for the (log) real marginal cost becomes $mc_t = (1-\phi)(w_t - p_{H,t}) + \phi z_t$, where z_t is the relative price of imported inputs, w_t is the nominal wage rate, and $p_{H,t}$ is the price of domestically produced goods (all in logs).

The implied CPI-NKPC becomes:

$$\pi_t = \beta E_t\{\pi_{t+1}\} + (1-\phi)\kappa_H lsh_t + \xi_t, \tag{8}$$

where $lsh_t \equiv (w_t + n_t - p_{H,t}) - y_t$ is the time varying *labor income share,* $\lambda \equiv \alpha(1-\delta)$, and $\xi_t \equiv [\lambda/(1-\lambda)]\tilde{q}_t + \kappa_H\phi z_t$ is a composite term in the relative prices $\tilde{q}_t$ and z_t.

Hence, in this case the elasticity of inflation to the labor share $(1-\phi)\kappa_H$ depends on the share of imported inputs ϕ, with a higher share leading to a smaller elasticity. Notice, however, that it is trade openness in *production* inputs that acts as a real rigidity factor, whereas the elasticity of inflation to the labor share is not affected by openness in *consumption* imports.

Sticky Import Prices

Suppose, next, that along with domestic consumption prices import prices are also sticky. For simplicity we assume that only imported consumption goods prices are sticky in local currency, whereas the prices of imported inputs remain flexible.[6] The main implication of import price stickiness is that it leads to deviations from the law of one price (or, alternatively, imperfect exchange rate pass-through). Both domestic and imported goods

6. Recent evidence in Gopinath and Rigobon (2007) finds pervasive evidence of price stickiness for import prices at the dock.

inflation are now driven by a NKPC-type equation (see, e.g., Monacelli 2005):

$$\pi_{H,t} = \beta E_t \{\pi_{H,t+1}\} + \kappa_H mc_t$$

$$\pi_{F,t} = \beta E_t \{\pi_{F,t+1}\} + \kappa_F \psi_{F,t},$$

where $\psi_{F,t}$ is a term that captures log deviations from the law of one price (which in turn act as variations in the real marginal cost for local importers). Combining the two previous equations one obtains the following CPI-NKPC equation:

$$\pi_t = \beta E_t \{\pi_{t+1}\} + (1 - \lambda)(1 - \phi)\kappa_H lsh_t + \chi_t, \quad (9)$$

where $\chi_t \equiv (1 - \lambda)\phi\kappa_H z_t + \lambda\kappa_F[\psi_{F,t} + (\lambda - \alpha)s_t]$ is a new composite term in the relative prices z_t and s_t (the log terms of trade), and in the "law-of-one-price gap" $\psi_{F,t}$.

Hence, the main implication of introducing import price stickiness (imperfect pass-through) is that the elasticity of inflation to the labor share depends now on the degree of openness in *both* consumption and production imports, λ and ϕ, respectively. In both cases, a higher degree of openness decreases the elasticity of inflation to the labor share, contributing to an increase in real rigidity.

In order to assess the quantitative importance of openness in consumption goods relative to openness in production inputs as a real rigidity factor, we look at some numbers. We set the share of imported inputs over *total imports* in the United States to $\delta = 0.38$, as from estimates in Bardhan and Jaffee (2004). We set the share of imported goods in consumption equal to $\alpha = 0.25$, and the share of imported inputs in *total inputs* in the United States to $\omega = 0.082$, as from Campa and Goldberg (2006). With these numbers at hand we can compute values for λ and ϕ. Finally, we set $\beta = 0.99$ and the Calvo probability of not resetting prices $\theta = 0.75$ (a typical value in the literature).

In the benchmark closed economy model the value for the marginal cost elasticity is:

$$\kappa_H \equiv \frac{(1 - \theta\beta)(1 - \theta)}{\theta} = 0.0858.$$

In the case in which imports are both consumption goods and intermediate production inputs (see equation [8]) the elasticity of inflation to the labor share reduces to

$$(1 - \phi)\kappa_H = 0.0832.$$

Notice that the reduction in the labor share elasticity is, however, not quantitatively important.

Finally, in the case in which I introduce both imports as production inputs *and* deviations from the law of one price (as a result of stickiness in import consumption prices), I obtain a value for the labor share elasticity (see equation [9]):

$$(1 - \lambda)(1 - \phi)\kappa_H = 0.0632.$$

Hence, we see that import price stickiness may in principle act as a quantitatively more important real rigidity factor relative to openness in production inputs.

Conclusions

Sbordone's chapter is clear, rigorous, and intriguing. The issue of how trade globalization may exert an impact on inflation dynamics is, however, far from being exhausted here. In particular, I have argued that openness can potentially act as an important *real rigidity* factor if we properly account for: (a) the degree of substitutability between imported and domestically produced goods; (b) the role of imports as intermediate production inputs; and (c) incomplete exchange rate pass-through as a result of price stickiness in import consumption prices. Accounting for all these features may contribute to better shape the debate on the role of trade integration in affecting the form of the Phillips curve, and therefore on the likely *quantitative* effects of globalization on inflation dynamics.

References

Adolfson, M., S. Laséen, J. Lindé, and M. Villani. 2007. Bayesian estimation of an open economy DSGE model with incomplete pass-through. *Journal of International Economics* 72: 481–511.

Backus, D., P. K. Kehoe, and F. E. Kydland. 1994. Dynamics of the trade balance and the terms of trade: The J-curve? *American Economic Review* 84 (1): 84–103.

Bardhan, A. D., and D. Jaffee. 2004. On intra-firm trade and multinationals: Foreign outsourcing and offshoring in manufacturing. University of California at Berkeley. Working Paper.

Bernanke, B. 2006. Globalization and monetary policy. Speech given at the Fourth Economic Summit, Stanford Institute for Economic Policy Research. March, Stanford, CA.

Bernard, A., J. Bradford, J. Eaton, and S. Kortum. 2003. Plants and productivity in international trade. *American Economic Review* 93 (4): 1268–90.

Campa, J. M., and L. S. Goldberg. 2006. Distribution margins, imported inputs, and the sensitivity of the CPI to exchange rates. NBER Working Paper no. 12121. Cambridge, MA: National Bureau of Economic Research, March.

Corsetti, G., L. Dedola, and S. Leduc. 2008. International risk sharing and the transmission of productivity shocks. *Review of Economic Studies* 75 (2): 443–73.

De Walque, G., F. Smets and R. Wouters. 2006. An open economy DSGE model linking the euro area and the U.S. economy. Paper presented at Bank of Canada Workshop, "Commodity Price Issues." 10–11 July.

Dotsey, M., and R. King. 2005. Implications of state dependent pricing for dynamic macroeconomic modeling. *Journal of Monetary Economics* 52 (1): 213–42.

Galí, J., and M. Gertler. 1999. Inflation dynamics: A structural econometric analysis. *Journal of Monetary Economics* 44 (2): 195–222.

Galí, J., and T. Monacelli. 2005. Monetary policy and exchange rate volatility in a small open economy. *Review of Economic Studies* 72 (3): 707–34.

Gopinath, G., and R. Rigobon. 2008. Sticky borders. *Quarterly Journal of Economics* 123 (2): 531–75.

Gust, C., S. Leduc, and R. J. Vigfusson. 2006. Trade integration, competition, and the decline in exchange-rate pass-through. Board of Governors of the Federal Reserve System. International Finance Discussion Papers no. 864.

Heathcote, J., and F. Perri. 2002. Financial autarky and international real business cycles. *Journal of Monetary Economics* 49 (3): 601–27.

Justiniano, A., and B. Preston. 2006. Can structural small open economy models account for the influence of foreign shocks? Columbia University. Unpublished Manuscript.

Kimball, M. S. 1995. The quantitative analytics of the basic neomonetarist model. *Journal of Money, Credit, and Banking* 27 (2): 1241–77.

Levin, A., D. Lopez-Salido, and T. Yun. 2007. Strategic complementarities and optimal monetary policy. Kiel Institute for the World Economy. Kiel Working Paper no. 1355.

Mishkin, F. S. 2007. Globalization, macroeconomic performance, and monetary policy. Speech delivered at the Domestic Prices in an Integrated World Economy Conference, Board of Governors of the Federal Reserve System. 27 September, Washington, DC.

Monacelli, T. 2005. Monetary policy in a low pass-through environment. *Journal of Money, Credit, and Banking* 37 (6): 1047–66.

Rabanal, P., and V. Tuesta. 2006. Euro-dollar real exchange rate dynamics in an estimated two-country model: What is important and what is not. IMF Working Paper no. 06/177. Washington, DC: International Monetary Fund.

Ruhl, K. J. 2008. The international elasticity puzzle. University of Texas at Austin. Working Paper.

Rogoff, K. 2006. Impact of globalization on monetary policy. Paper presented for symposium sponsored by the Federal Reserve Bank of Kansas City, "The New Economic Geography: Effects and Policy Implications." 24–26 August, Jackson Hole, WY.

Sbordone, A. 2002. Prices and unit labor costs: A new test of price stickiness. *Journal of Monetary Economics* 49 (2): 265–92.

Woodford, M. 2003. *Interest and prices.* Princeton, NJ: Princeton University Press.

IV
General Observations

11

The Effects of Globalization on Inflation, Liquidity, and Monetary Policy

Lucas Papademos

11.1 Introduction

My chapter focuses on the effects of globalization on inflation, liquidity, and monetary policy. This subject has received increasing attention among academic economists and policymakers over the past two years. Indeed, a number of distinguished participants in this conference have contributed to the ongoing analysis and public debate on this topic. I have observed, however, that relatively less emphasis has been given so far to the impact of globalization on liquidity and the related implications for monetary policy and financial stability. For this reason, I will also devote some time to these aspects.

It might be interesting to recall that a number of pertinent issues, which I will also address, were already very topical more than 400 years ago, in sixteenth-century Spain. As a consequence of what, undoubtedly, was one of the first and most impressive periods of globalization—benefiting Catalonia, however, only 200 years later[1]—significant effects on inflation were observed. Of course, I refer to the Spanish discovery of the Americas and the large influx of gold and silver from the New World. The resulting rise in inflation in Spain quickly spread to Western Europe as a whole.[2] One is thus tempted to talk about the first evidence of global excess liquidity driving global inflation trends. Economic historians have labeled that

Lucas Papademos is Vice-President of the European Central Bank.

1. In 1778, Catalonia was allowed to trade with the Americas by decree of Charles III.

2. Adam Smith estimated that "the discovery of the abundant mines of America reduced, in the sixteenth century, the value of gold and silver in Europe to about a third of what it had been before." See Smith (1776).

inflationary period a "price revolution."[3] Then, as now, there was academic debate, beginning as early as the sixteenth century, on whether inflation was due to excess liquidity or rather diminishing domestic economic slack linked to urbanization and income growth.[4] And, I am sure, it was no coincidence that the quantity theory of money was invented by scholars of the School of Salamanca, who were inspired by the price revolution period in sixteenth-century Spain.[5]

Even the potential links between globalization, the flattening of the Phillips-curve, and the growing importance of global economic slack were issues already debated at that time. Historians tell us that urbanization also contributed to increased trade between Europe's regions, which made prices more responsive to distant changes in demand. Another topical issue I will elaborate on—the link between global excess liquidity and financial stability—also has its roots in sixteenth-century Spain. Rising inflation and the dependency on gold and silver imports are mentioned as causes of multiple bankruptcies and economic crashes.[6]

Following the agenda set by the sixteenth-century globalization episode, this chapter is divided into two main parts. The first part deals with the effects of globalization on inflation dynamics and price stability from a monetary policy perspective. I will elaborate on the likely impact on product and labor markets as well as the impact on monetary aggregates and financial markets. In the second part, I will reflect on the link between globalization and financial stability, again focusing on the role of central banks. In this context, I will point to the risks associated with global imbalances and asset price boom and bust cycles. I will conclude by addressing two pertinent questions: namely, (a) whether central banks need to adapt their monetary policy strategies in order to cope with the challenges of globalization; and (b) whether monetary policy has become less effective as a consequence of globalization.

As I have already mentioned the term globalization a number of times, and many more references will follow, let me briefly define it in fairly broad terms: it is the process of rapidly increasing global economic integration. Over the past decade, this process involved, and is evidenced by, the unprecedented and pervasive growth in the cross-border trade of goods and services as well as of financial and real assets, but it also involved the swift transfer of technologies, information, and ideas.

3. Hamilton (1934), 186–94, 195–210.

4. Bernholz and Kugler (2007).

5. Navarro, one of the most famous scholars of the School of Salamanca, wrote in 1566 that "Other things being equal, in countries where there is a great scarcity of money, all other saleable goods, and even the hands and labour of men, are given for less money than where it is abundant." Martin de Azpilcueta Navarro, "Comentario Resolutorio de Usuras y Cambios" (Salamanca, 1556).

6. See, for example, Munro (1994).

11.2 Globalization, Price Stability, and Monetary Policy

11.2.1 Impact of Globalization on Product and Labor Markets

Let me start by briefly reviewing both the theoretical arguments and the empirical evidence pertaining to the effects of globalization on product and labor markets. It would be too easy to dismiss any inflationary effects stemming from globalization with the argument that its impact will essentially and ultimately result in a change in relative prices and that, ceteris paribus, the overall rate of inflation should not be affected. First, integration is not a one-off event. Steadily rising integration could potentially lead to steadily falling unit labor costs and, ceteris paribus, to protracted periods of lower inflation. Second, a higher degree of openness (and thus increased competition) could lead to permanently higher productivity growth and, again other things being equal, to lower inflation. Third, globalization could affect other aspects of the inflation process and the conduct of monetary policy: the slope of the Phillips-curve, the wedge between the "socially optimal" and the "natural" or "potential" output level, the "natural rate of unemployment" or the non-accelerating inflation rate of unemployment (NAIRU) and even the relative emphasis placed on preserving price stability by the central bank when formulating monetary policy. Thus, globalization could eventually affect the inflationary impact of supply shocks and, more generally, inflation dynamics and the size of the "inflation bias" in the economy.[7]

Many economists and policymakers have examined the effects of globalization on one or several of these factors and processes, partly in order to better understand or explain the recent period of low inflation. Interestingly, sometimes the theoretical arguments and empirical findings point in opposite directions: some have argued that increasing global competition will tend to impinge on domestic monopolistic structures and reduce economic distortions.[8] Furthermore, the slope of the short-term Phillips curve would increase in the short run as national economies would become more flexible. These two propositions and implied parameter changes in models imply a permanent reduction in the inflation bias. Others have argued instead that the short-term Phillips curve should become flatter.[9] This reasoning is based on a variety of potential channels: an increased degree of openness reduces the responsiveness of inflation to domestic slack, as profit margins adjust more under increasing competitive pressure and wage setting is

7. "Inflation bias" in this context refers to the component of inflation that results from the implementation of time-inconsistent policies when nominal rigidities create an incentive for policymakers to reduce unemployment by exploiting the short-run trade-off between inflation and unemployment.

8. Rogoff (2004, 2006). See Romer (1993) for a similar argument related to openness as a factor that leads to increasing the costs of an inflationary monetary policy due to fears of capital outflows.

9. See, for example, Bean (2006a, 2006b).

influenced by the threat of outsourcing jobs and labor immigration. There are other factors, however, which potentially could flatten the short-term Phillips curve—the underlying, structural slope or the estimated, effectively observed slope—and that are not necessarily linked to globalization: for example, inflation expectations that are well-anchored to price stability, and less frequent price updates of firms in a low inflation environment.

Alternative or complementary propositions have also been advanced. It has been argued that the whole debate about the slope of the short-term Phillips curve is not particularly relevant, if at all.[10] In a highly globalized economic environment, lower inflation could simply be due to a decline in the "natural rate of unemployment" or the NAIRU. Importantly, Assaf Razin, among others, has recently shown how the degree of trade and financial integration might both flatten the slope of the short-term Phillips curve and raise the optimal weight to be placed on the central bank's inflation objective, when monetary policy maximizes consumer preferences.[11] This would lead to the conduct of a more aggressive (optimal) monetary policy in the presence of supply shocks.[12]

Not surprisingly, this debate has triggered a series of empirical studies trying to shed more light on the issue. I will focus on evidence for the euro area. In a recent and often-cited Bank for International Settlements (BIS) paper, Claudio Borio and Andrew Filardo[13] argue that short-term Phillips curves have become flatter across countries and that measures of global economic slack have become more important than of domestic slack in explaining domestic inflation. Their own results, however, show that this is not the case in the euro area. Moreover, research at the European Central Bank (ECB) does not reveal any statistically significant structural breaks with respect to the slope of the short-term Phillips curve in the euro area or any decline in the estimated value of the slope over time. Other evidence regarding a possible change in the slope of the short-term Phillips curve in the euro area is also very mixed, especially with regard to the potential effect of increased openness on the slope.[14] The failure to capture econometrically significant globalization effects could, of course, be due to the relatively recent nature of certain aspects of this phenomenon and the impact of other factors that might have had relatively greater influence on inflation dynamics during the past ten years. For this reason, the potential effects of globalization on inflation dynamics, through their influence on behavioral or structural features of the labor and product markets, deserve close monitoring and further analysis.

10. Frankel (2006).

11. Razin and Binyamini (2007).

12. It would also reduce the "inflation bias," as the effect on the bias of a larger weight on the inflation objective dominates that of a flatter Phillips curve in this model.

13. Borio and Filardo (2007).

14. Gnan and Valderrama (2006); Ihrig et al. (2007); IMF (2007); Bean (2005); see also Ciccarelli and Mojon (2005), who find that global factors have greater explanatory power in determining domestic inflation.

The policy relevance of this debate is further complicated by the fact that even if future empirical studies would confirm a significant drop in the responsiveness of inflation to domestic slack in Phillips curve equations, it is not at all clear whether this should be interpreted as a flattening of the aggregate supply curve in the short term. Such "reduced form" evidence can be observationally equivalent to the evidence that could result from an unchanged structural relationship in an economy where the central bank has been successful in reducing inflation and output volatility, which would correspondingly reduce or could even eliminate the empirical correlation between inflation and the output gap.[15] For this reason, economists and policymakers have to be particularly careful when using simple reduced form estimated Phillips curve equations to calculate the NAIRU and then employ the estimated value as a benchmark for assessing inflationary pressure.

There are two lessons I derive from this review of theory and evidence. First, there is no consensus at a theoretical level on the relative importance of the various potential effects of globalization on the inflation process through this channel. Second, the available empirical results provide no clear message either, except that, so far, there is not much evidence to support the view that globalization has resulted in a flatter short-term Phillips curve, particularly in the euro area. This situation is, of course, not very comforting for a central banker. The good news is that all studies point toward a lower inflation bias, although for different reasons.

Another related issue is whether, and to what extent, globalization has affected prices and wages more directly in the euro area product and labor markets in the short-to-medium term. Estimates obtained at the Organization for Economic Cooperation and Development (OECD)[16] employing an accounting framework suggest that the more direct effect of globalization (captured by measures of economic openness) on average annual consumer price inflation is within the range of 0.0 to –0.3 percentage points over the period 2000 to 2005. The average size of the estimated impact is not overwhelming, but at least the upper limit of this range is not negligible either. An internal ECB study finds a comparable negative effect ranging between 0.1 and 0.2 percentage point over the period 1995 to 2004. The net direct impact of globalization on harmonized index of consumer prices (HICP) inflation is the result of two components: an inflation-dampening effect from noncommodity import prices and an inflation-augmenting effect from commodity import prices, including oil prices. The two effects are, of course, linked and may largely offset each other as the economic success of emerging market economies is largely responsible for higher world commodity prices. Moreover, the interpretation of such estimated effects is not straightforward. The domestic economy's response to the emergence of new international

15. Boivin and Giannoni (2006) and Bean (2005).
16. Pain, Koske, and Sollie (2006).

low-cost competitors is not captured by these estimates. Furthermore, it is not clear to what extent and for how long these effects should be expected to persist.

The empirical evidence on the direct impact of globalization on labor markets is also mixed. Indeed, it seems that the findings are getting less rather than more robust and it may be difficult to disentangle the effects of globalization from those resulting from technological advances. In theory, it could be expected that the increased openness of economies may affect the demand for labor by firms in advanced economies directly, as a result of intensified international competition and, indirectly, by raising the real wage elasticity of labor demand. There is some evidence confirming these theoretical propositions.[17] The quadrupling of the effective global labor force over the last twenty years has led to a fall in the labor share of unskilled workers' sectors in advanced economies and to a more moderate rise in the labor share of skilled workers' sectors. In the euro area, shifts in labor demand are predominantly resulting in changes in employment rather than in wages. The International Monetary Fund (IMF) concludes, however, that technological advances had an even bigger impact on the labor share of unskilled workers' sectors than globalization as such.

11.2.2 Impact on Monetary Aggregates and Financial Markets

As you are aware, the ECB's monetary policy strategy attributes a prominent role to the analysis of monetary aggregates and their counterparts in the assessment of risks to price stability over the medium to longer run. Two processes associated with globalization have made the analysis of monetary aggregates for the purpose of extracting information for assessing future risks to price stability more complex.[18]

The first process is the growing size of international capital flows. The sum of the stocks of foreign assets and foreign liabilities of the total economy as a percentage of gross domestic product (GDP)—the most frequently used measure of financial globalization—increased threefold in advanced economies between the early 1990s and 2004.[19] In the euro area alone, the sum of outstanding foreign assets and liabilities increased from 190 percent of GDP in 1999 to 280 percent in 2005.[20] With larger stocks of foreign assets and liabilities, the probability of occasionally large and volatile net flows has risen. When euro area residents sell securities to non-euro area residents or when they borrow abroad, the net external assets of monetary financial institutions (MFIs) in the euro area rise and the stock of

17. International Monetary Fund (2007).

18. See ECB (2007a, 2007b); Ferrero, Nobili, and Passiglia (2007); von Landesberger (2007).

19. Ferguson et al. (2007).

20. Over the same horizon, the net foreign liability position of the euro area only increased from 6.5 percent to 10 percent of GDP.

broad money (M3) expands, if the settlement of these transactions involves domestic and foreign banks. Cross-border mergers and acquisitions (M&A) activity of nonfinancial corporations can also account for a parallel change in net foreign assets and money. Both cross-border portfolio investments and M&A activity are genuine elements of the process of globalization. Unfortunately, simply accounting for the external sources of money growth and then mechanically correcting for cross-border portfolio flows or M&A activity, on the presumption of their likely remote direct effects on consumer prices, is not an advisable option. Rather, these transactions have to be analyzed with respect to their information content concerning their potential wealth effects on residents' income and on asset prices.[21] Depending on the outcome of this analysis, the policy implications could be far from negligible.

The second process is financial innovation. The increasingly global nature of financial markets and the low level of world interest rates in recent years have fostered financial innovation. These developments, in turn, have contributed to the rapid growth of the activities of Other Financial Intermediaries (OFIs), which include investment funds and financial vehicle corporations, as well as dealers in securities and derivative products. While the overall share of OFIs' money holdings in M3 is only about 10 percent in the euro area so far and households hold about 50 percent of the stock of broad money, OFIs have contributed significantly to the annual growth of euro area M3 since 2005, adding up to 2 percentage points in some months, mainly due to the emergence and expansion of loan securitization. The motives of OFIs for holding money balances are likely to be of a fundamentally different nature than those of households or nonfinancial corporations. Moreover, the process of securitization of loans itself positively affects the capacity of banks (of MFIs, to be precise), to issue new loans and thus it could have an indirect expansionary effect on M3 growth. How can we deal with the influence of these factors on money creation and their potential effects on the medium and long-term inflation outlook? In general, the same answer applies with regard to changes in net external assets. Given that the OFIs' money holdings and investment activities could have indirect effects on consumer price developments via asset prices, it would be premature to automatically exclude, without further analysis, the money balances held by OFIs from the monetary aggregates when assessing the risks to price stability.[22]

The general conclusion that emerges from these considerations is that monetary analysis has become more challenging in the global economy as it has to explicitly take account of changes in domestic money and credit markets induced by, or accompanying, financial globalization. To address this challenge, the Eurosystem is currently stepping up its analytical efforts

21. See, for example, the description of the link between M&A activity and asset prices in Pepper (2006).

22. ECB Monthly Bulletin (2007b).

to deepen its understanding of several aspects of these processes and their implications for the assessment of medium- to longer-term risks to price stability.

11.3 Globalization, Financial Stability, and the Role of Central Banks

A second set of important issues I would like to address concerns the potential effects of globalization on financial stability. The safeguarding of financial stability is an objective embedded, to varying degrees, in central bank statutes, reflecting national or area-wide institutional arrangements. But in all cases, a sufficient degree of financial stability is a necessary condition for the preservation of price stability by central banks. Globalization could have implications for financial stability through various channels. I will focus on its potential implications through its effects on global imbalances and asset price cycles.

11.3.1 Risks Associated with an Abrupt Unwinding of Global Financial Imbalances

Incomplete financial globalization,[23] reflecting the low level of financial market development in otherwise fast-growing emerging market economies, combined with the "savings glut" hypothesis, can partly account for the current level and evolution of global net foreign asset and liability positions. This explanation notwithstanding, the possibility of a disorderly unwinding of global imbalances cannot be excluded for several reasons. First, the structural factors underlying the large financial flows from Asia and oil-exporting countries into the United States cannot persist forever. Second, economic policies that have been causing, or have thus far failed to address, a variety of market distortions and inefficiencies, have also been contributing to existing financial imbalances. Financial market participants may eventually question the sustainability of some of these policies and change their behavior in anticipation of their ultimate consequences. There is no doubt that financial globalization fosters international risk-sharing, promotes economic growth, and reduces macroeconomic volatility. Nevertheless, the size of and the particular asymmetry in net foreign asset positions observed since the late 1990s involves potential medium to longer term risks to financial stability. Major and abrupt asset price adjustments, associated with a disorderly unwinding of global financial imbalances, could be the main propagation mechanism of a financial turbulence. I would like to add, however, that currently the probability of such a disorderly unwinding scenario seems very low, as economic policies are shifting in the right direction, although clearly more needs to be done. Furthermore, as shown by ECB research, historically, the necessary rebalancing of global demand in periods of current account

23. Bini Smaghi (2007).

adjustment was usually achieved in an orderly fashion and involved domestic demand and supply reallocations and did not require major asset price movements.[24]

The potential role of monetary policy with regard to global imbalances has been examined but the conclusions are not clear. Research at the ECB has shown how the combined effects of domestic monetary policy, fiscal policy, and productivity developments could influence current account positions.[25] Related exchange rate movements could lead to additional valuation effects with implications for gross foreign asset and liability positions. One interesting question to explore is whether the conduct of symmetric monetary policies—for example, in two countries linked by a fixed exchange rate regime—could affect the relative current account position between these countries. Such an outcome could reflect asymmetries in the interest elasticities of saving and different wealth effects related to heterogeneous financial market development and capitalization. But these issues, though theoretically interesting, are very much unchartered policy territory.[26]

11.3.2 Impact through Asset Price Boom and Bust Cycles

Let me now turn to the potential impact of financial globalization on financial stability through the effects on asset prices and risk premia. As colleagues at the BIS were first to emphasize, a potential interaction between globalization and monetary policy may inadvertently contribute to the creation of global excess liquidity, which could later play a role in the development of asset price boom and bust cycles. The benign effects of global competition and low-cost imports on consumer prices might lead to an underestimation of the stimulative effects of monetary policy that is consistent with the preservation of price stability over the medium term, but which can be characterized as accommodative as evidenced by buoyant credit and money growth over a prolonged period. A strong and persistent expansion of monetary liquidity could fuel or even trigger an asset price boom. During the bust phase of the asset price cycle, the associated credit crunch might lead to an economic downturn and a negative deviation from the objective of consumer price stability, and possibly even to deflation, which would exacerbate the financial crisis.

The channel through which monetary liquidity could affect the dynamics of asset prices could be "purely monetarist" or reflect the influence of other factors as more recently explained with reference to behavioral finance. An environment of high monetary liquidity could affect the risk-taking behavior of financial intermediaries and other financial market participants. High

24. Bems and Dedola (2006); Algieri and Bracke (2007); Engler, Fidora, and Thimann (2007); Fratzscher, Juvenal, and Sarno (2007).

25. Bems, Dedola, and Smets (2007).

26. See Dedola (2006) for a discussion of this hypothesis.

monetary liquidity and financial market liquidity[27] could be signs of arbitrage strategies such as carry trades and "liquidity seeking" behavior, which could temporarily distort the pricing of risk.[28] In fact, ECB research shows that there is evidence that monetary liquidity shocks have played a role in driving asset prices, particularly housing prices across OECD countries, during the boom phase of asset price cycles, and that they have also contributed to explaining the negative effects on economic activity during the subsequent bust phase.[29] Other Eurosystem research has identified effects of an accommodative monetary policy on housing prices in the euro area and in the United States.[30] The intriguing aspect of this hypothesis and of the associated empirical findings is that the monetary policy stance might be perfectly appropriate for and consistent with the preservation of price stability over a short-to-medium term horizon. Nevertheless, the potential implications for asset price boom and bust cycles could signal that the monetary policy stance could prove too accommodative for maintaining price stability in the long run.

11.4 Implications for Policy

11.4.1 Do Monetary Policy Strategies Have to Be Adapted?

I would like to conclude by addressing the two questions that I raised at the beginning that concern the potential implications of globalization for the strategy and effectiveness of monetary policy. More specifically, the first question is whether monetary policy strategies have to be adapted in order to cope with the rapidly increasing global economic integration. In providing an answer, I will concentrate on and highlight the ECB's monetary policy strategy.

A monetary policy strategy comprises two main elements: the policy objective, including the time horizon for its attainment, and the analytical framework, which relates policy instruments and goals and provides the basis for assessing the prospects for attaining the policy objective and the associated risks. The ECB's strategy includes a quantitative definition of its primary objective of preserving price stability and has a medium-term orientation in achieving this goal. Globalization has no fundamental bearing on this element of the strategy, but it has some implications: it does underscore the relative importance of price stability as a central bank goal and the need to formulate and conduct monetary policy so as to preserve price stability

27. See ECB Financial Stability Review (2007a, box 9) for a discussion of the concepts of monetary and financial market liquidity.

28. Rajan (2005, 2006).

29. Adalid and Detken (2007); and Detken (2006), with regard to the link between liquidity and low bond yields.

30. Greiber and Setzer (2007).

over a medium-to-longer term horizon. As I noted earlier, recent research has stressed that increased openness to trade and financial interdependence should reinforce the central bank's emphasis on the objective of price stability relative to minimizing output volatility.[31] Such a result can also be derived in a model with endogenous portfolio choices, while focusing on the risk-sharing properties of cross-border trade in nominal bonds.[32] Moreover, in an environment of price stability but persistent rapid money growth and rising leverage, financial liberalization and integration could lead to the accumulation of financial imbalances over a number of years, increasing the probability of a boom and bust cycle in financial markets with repercussions on price stability over the longer term. This possibility implies that monetary policy should place increased emphasis on the preservation of price stability over a longer time horizon, extending beyond the medium term.

With regard to the analytical framework, globalization can, in principle, affect market structures, agent behavior, and inflation dynamics, thus requiring close monitoring and careful assessment of its effects. The economic analysis employed by the ECB to assess the short-to-medium term risks to price stability could be subject to greater parameter or model uncertainty as well as increased measurement error associated with unobservable variables, such as potential output, which underlie the assessment of real activity and inflation pressure. However, the econometric evidence in the euro area has not yet identified significant indirect effects, reflecting structural or behavioral influence of globalization on inflation dynamics. Nevertheless, the complexity of economic analysis has increased and its task has become more challenging, and there is clearly a need to better understand and measure the impact of globalization.

In a period of potentially significant structural change in the product and labor markets, cross-checking the assessment of risks based on economic analysis by monetary analysis becomes more important. This proposition is conceptually correct. Unfortunately, the influences of financial globalization on money and credit growth imply that, in practice, monetary analysis is also becoming more challenging and requires increased sophistication. It is necessary to rely on a wide range of analytical tools and models in order to identify the underlying trend in monetary developments and to assess its implications for price stability. At the same time, as I already stressed, in an environment of increased global financial integration, a deeper and broader analysis of developments in monetary liquidity can enhance our understanding of potential risks to financial stability, which, if they materialize, can have repercussions for output volatility and price stability over the longer term. For these reasons, pertinent research at the ECB will be further strengthened, including the analysis of the interactions between financial

31. Razin and Binyamini (2007).
32. Devereux and Sutherland (2007).

globalization and innovation on the one hand, and monetary and market liquidity on the other, as well as their potential implications for monetary policy and financial stability.

All in all, there is no reason to change in any fundamental way the analytical framework we employ for assessing the prospects for and the risks to price stability in response to globalization. On the contrary, I conclude that the ECB's strategy, with its medium-to-longer term orientation and the prominence it assigns to the analysis of monetary developments and liquidity conditions for cross-checking the outcome of economic analysis, is well placed to address some of the implications of globalization for inflation dynamics and long-term financial and price stability. Nevertheless, an improved understanding of the influence of globalization on the monetary policy transmission mechanism will enhance the analysis underlying our decisions. This brings me to the second and last question on policy effectiveness.

11.4.2 Has Monetary Policy Effectiveness Been Reduced?

Has monetary policy become less effective as a consequence of increased financial integration? More specifically, has the associated comovement of long-term interest rates impaired the functioning of one of the channels of the monetary policy transmission mechanism? Or, alternatively, has monetary policy gained effectiveness in times of almost perfect capital mobility and floating exchange rates, in line with the standard macroeconomic (IS/LM) paradigm, as recently stressed by central bank colleagues?[33]

Indeed, it is theoretically plausible to argue that certain features of globalization have influenced to varying degrees some of the key determinants of long-term interest rates, such as the global riskless real rate of interest and the real risk premium.[34] In addition, expected inflation and the inflation risk premium may have been diminished to some degree by forces of globalization, though successful monetary policy across the globe has certainly been the main factor. There is some empirical evidence that in the euro area, as well as in a broader sample of OECD countries, long-term rates are reacting less to changes in short-term rates than they used to.[35] Global factors seem to be increasingly important for the determination of national real bond yields.[36] Furthermore, the comovement of U.S., German, and Japanese bond yields has been exceptionally high over the last three years.[37] My

33. See Yellen (2006) and Weber (2007).

34. Wu (2006). Wu's article is also available at http://www.dallasfed.org; see especially the box "Determining Bond Yields: A Primer."

35. Reichlin (2006).

36. Giannone, Lenza, and Reichlin (2007). Interestingly, already Barro and Sala-i-Martín, in their classic 1990 article, found that real interest rates for seven of the nine OECD countries they investigated mainly depended on world factors for the period 1958 to 1989.

37. Ferguson et al. (2007).

interpretation of these findings is that, although there is little doubt that global forces have played an important role in the determination of domestic long-term interest rates, they do not provide sufficient and convincing evidence to conclude that the effectiveness of monetary policy in controlling inflation has been reduced. The increased significance of global factors identified by empirical analysis is likely to reflect common trends as well as the similar orientation of monetary policies and their success in containing inflationary pressures. But nothing prevents national monetary policies from diverging from such a common orientation, which itself has been fostered by increasing competition between currencies.[38] A central bank is still able to preserve price stability, or choose and achieve a long-term inflation objective under floating exchange rates. However, the relative importance of the different channels of transmission of the effects of monetary policy might be affected by the ongoing global economic integration. This underscores the importance of the central bank's credible commitment to its objectives and of effective and consistent communication.[39]

11.5 Concluding Remarks

To sum up, the effects of globalization on product, labor, and financial markets can be potentially far-reaching. However, the implications for monetary policy are overall fairly contained. The phenomenon of globalization neither calls for any fundamental change in the monetary policy strategy nor does it affect in any material way the general effectiveness of monetary policy. Globalization implies a greater emphasis on the price stability objective over a medium-to longer-term horizon. It also implies that monetary analysis has become more challenging but at the same time relatively more important for assessing long-term risks to price stability and financial stability. Moreover, globalization can affect the relative significance and the functioning of some channels of the monetary policy transmission mechanism, but the available empirical evidence for the euro area suggests that such effects are limited so far. In this context, I would favor the approach of the German writer, philosopher, and engineer Novalis, who mentioned that "hypotheses are like nets; only those who throw nets will catch fish." Clearly, more research is essential. We need close monitoring and careful analysis of the empirical evidence as well as an improved understanding of the influence of globalization on the monetary policy transmission mechanism. This will help improve the quality and robustness of the analysis underlying our ability to continue to fulfill our mandate to maintain price stability and to contribute to the safeguarding of financial stability.

38. See Kroszner (2007).
39. See Papademos (2006).

References

Adalid, R., and C. Detken. 2007. Liquidity shocks and asset price boom/bust cycles. European Central Bank (ECB) Working Paper Series no. 732.

Algieri, B., and T. Bracke. 2007. Patterns of current account adjustment: Insights from past experience. ECB Working Paper Series no. 762.

Barro, R. J., and X. Sala-i-Martín. 1990. World real interest rates. In *NBER Macroeconomics Annual 1990,* ed. O. J. Blanchard and S. Fischer, 15–61. Cambridge, MA: MIT Press.

Bean, C. 2005. Monetary policy in an uncertain world. Oxonia Distinguished Speakers Seminar, the Oxford Institute of Economic Policy. 22 February. Oxford, England.

———. 2006a. Comments on Kenneth Rogoff: Impact of globalization on monetary policy. Paper presented at the Federal Reserve Bank of Kansas City 30th Annual Economic Symposium. 26 August, Jackson Hole, WY.

———. 2006b. Globalisation and inflation, Speech to the LSE economics society. London School of Economics. 24 October, London.

Bems, R., and L. Dedola. 2006. Current account reversals and capital markets integration: The adjustment of the U.S. external position revisited. ECB Working Paper Series no. 719.

Bems, R., L. Dedola, and F. Smets. 2007. U.S. imbalances: The role of technology and policy. ECB Working Paper no. 719.

Bernholz, P., and P. Kugler. 2007. The price revolution in the 16th century: Empirical results from a structural vectorautoregression model. University of Basle. Working Paper.

Bini Smaghi, L. 2007. Global capital and national monetary policies. Speech at the European Economic and Financial Centre. 18 January, London.

Borio, C., and A. Filardo. 2007. Globalisation and inflation: New cross-country evidence on the global determinants of domestic inflation. Bank for International Settlements (BIS) Working Paper no. 227.

Boivin, J., and M. P. Giannoni. 2006. Has monetary policy become more effective? *The Review of Economics and Statistics* 88 (3): 445–62.

Ciccarelli, M., and B. Mojon. 2005. Global inflation. ECB Working paper series no. 537.

Dedola, L. 2006. Global imbalances and "excess liquidity": Is there a link? ECB, Directorate General Research, Research Bulletin no. 4.

Detken, C. 2006. Comment on "the bond yield 'conundrum' from a macro-finance perspective." *Monetary and Economic Studies* 24 (S-1): 109–19. Institute for Monetary and Economic Studies, Bank of Japan.

Devereux, M. B., and A. Sutherland. 2007. Financial globalization and monetary policy. International Macroeconomics, Centre for Economic Policy Research (CEPR) Discussion Paper Series no. 6147.

Engler, P., M. Fidora, and C. Thimann. 2007. External imbalances and the U.S. current account: Do Supply-side changes lessen the exchange rate adjustment? ECB Working Paper Series no. 761.

European Central Bank. 2007a. *Financial Stability Review.* Frankfurt ECB, December.

European Central Bank. 2007b. Interpreting monetary developments since mid-2004. *Monthly Bulletin,* July.

Ferguson, R., P. Hartmann, F. Panetta, and R. Portes. 2007. International financial stability. Draft Report prepared for the International Center for Monetary and Banking Studies (ICMB) Conference. 3–4 May, Geneva.

Ferrero, G., A. Nobili, and P. Passiglia. 2007. The sectoral distribution of money supply in the euro area. Temi di discussione, Banca d'Italia.

Frankel, J. 2006. What do economists mean by globalization? Implications for inflation and monetary policy. Written for Academic Consultants Meeting, Board of Governors of the Federal Reserve System.
Fratzscher, M., L. Juvenal, and L. Sarno. 2007. Asset prices, exchange rates and the current account. ECB Working Paper Series no. 790.
Giannone, D., M. Lenza, and L. Reichlin. 2007. The equilibrium level of the world real interest rate. Paper presented at the First Annual Risk Management Institute Research Conference, "Capital Flows and Asset Price: The International Dimension of Risk." 6–7 July, Singapore.
Gnan, E., and M. T. Valderrama. 2006. Globalization, inflation and monetary policy. *Monetary Policy and the Economy* 4 (January): 37–54.
Greiber, C., and R. Setzer. 2007. Money and housing: Evidence for the euro area and the U.S. Deutsche Bundesbank, Economics Department. Discussion Paper Series 1: Economic Studies, no. 2007, 12.
Hamilton, E. 1934. *American treasure and the price revolution in Spain, 1501–1650.* Cambridge, MA: Harvard University Press.
Ihrig, J., S. B. Kamin, D. Lindner, and J. Marques. 2007. Some simple tests of the globalization and inflation hypothesis. Board of Governors of the Federal Reserve System, International Finance Discussion Paper no. 891.
International Monetary Fund (IMF). 2007. The globalization of labor, *World economic outlook: Spillovers and cycles in the global economy,* ed. IMF, 161–92, chapter 5. Washington, DC: IMF.
Kroszner, R. S. 2007. Globalization and capital markets: Implications for inflation and the yield curve. Remarks at the Center for Financial Stability (CEF). 16 May, Buenos Aires, Argentina.
Munro, J. 1994. Patterns of trade, money, and credit. In *Handbook of European history 1400–1600: The late Middle Ages, Renaissance and Reformation,* ed. J. Tracy, T. Brady, and H. Oberman, 175. Leiden: E. J. Brill.
Pain, N., I. Koske, and M. Sollie. 2006. Globalisation and inflation in the OECD economies. OECD Economics Department Working Papers no. 524.
Papademos, L. 2006. Monetary policy in a changing world: Commitment, strategy and credibility. Speech at the Fourth Conference of the International Research Forum on Monetary Policy. 1 December, Washington, D.C.
Pepper, G., with M. Olivier. 2006. *The liquidity theory of asset prices.* New York: Wiley Finance.
Rajan, R. 2005. Has financial development made the world riskier? NBER Working Paper no. 11728. Cambridge, MA: National Bureau of Economic Research, November.
———. 2006. Monetary policy and incentives. Paper presented at the Bank of Spain Conference on Central banks in the 21st century. 8 June, Madrid.
Razin, A., and A. Binyamini. 2007. Flattening of the short-run trade-off between inflation and domestic activity. Paper presented at the Symposium on "The Phillips Curve and the Natural Rate of Unemployment," 3–4 June, Kiel Institute of World Economy.
Reichlin, L. 2006. Panel remarks at the Thirteenth International Conference, "Financial Markets and the Real Economy in a Low Interest Rate Environment." Bank of Japan, 1–2 June, 2006, Tokyo.
Rogoff, K. 2004. Globalization and global disinflation. International Monetary Fund paper prepared for the Federal Reserve Bank of Kansas City Symposium on "Monetary Policy and Uncertainty: Adapting to a Changing Economy." 28–30 August, 2003, Jackson Hole, WY.
———. 2006. Impact of globalization on monetary policy. Harvard University paper prepared for the symposium sponsored by the Federal Reserve Bank of Kansas

City Symposium on "The New Economic Geography: Effects and Policy Implications." 24–26 August, Jackson Hole, WY.

Romer, D. 1993. Openness and inflation: Theory and evidence. *Quarterly Journal of Economics* 108 (4): 869–903.

Smith, A. 1776. *An inquiry into the nature and causes of the wealth of nations, vol. X,* the Harvard Classics, ed. C. J. Bullock. New York: P. F. Collier & Son.

von Landesberger, J. 2007. Sectoral money demand models for the euro area based on a common set of determinants. ECB Working Paper no. 741.

Weber, A. 2007. Challenges posed by (financial) globalisation. Lecture at the University of Pune. 15 March, Pune, India.

Wu, T. 2006. Globalization's effect on interest rates and the yield curve. *Economic Letter—Insights from the Federal Reserve Bank of Dallas* 1 (9).

Yellen, J. L. 2006. Monetary policy in a global environment. Speech at the Conference on "The Euro and the Dollar in a Globalized Economy," U.C. Santa Cruz. 27 May, University of California Santa Cruz, CA.

12

Globalization and Monetary Policy
Missions Impossible

John B. Taylor

Globalization is not a new issue in monetary economics. Indeed, for at least three decades the forces of globalization have been presenting challenges for both monetary policy and the theory that underlies it. The challenges never seem easy. When I look back on the history of this period and consider the challenges faced, I am reminded of the theme from Mission Impossible: in one episode after another, people pursued a seemingly impossible mission and in the end the mission was, amazingly, accomplished.

In this chapter, I examine three such missions impossible in the area of globalization and monetary policy. The first—*M:i:I*—begins thirty years ago, the second—*M:i:II*—begins ten years ago, and the third—*M:i:III*—takes place today. For each mission, I discuss: (a) the theory, or the ideas developed to accomplish the mission; (b) the policy, or the implementation of these ideas; and (c) the results. Unlike the movies, the connection between the theory, the policy, and the results is not obvious, but speculating about the connection is intriguing.

12.1 Mission Impossible I

Go back thirty years to the mid- to late-1970s. Inflation in the United States was into double digits and had been rising for a decade. The volatility of inflation was also high: consumer price index (CPI) inflation reached 12

John B. Taylor is Professor of Economics and Senior Fellow, Stanford University and the Hoover Institution.

This is a written version of a poolside talk given at the conference, "The International Dimensions of Monetary Policy," Girona, Spain, June 2007, sponsored by the National Bureau of Economic Research. I wish to thank Andrew Levin and Josephine Smith for useful comments and assistance.

percent in 1975, fell to 5 percent in 1977, and then increased to 15 percent before the decade was over. Like inflation, the volatility of real gross domestic product (GDP) was very high: the standard deviation of real GDP growth was about 3 percent, recessions came frequently, and expansions were short-lived. According to NBER dating, there were recessions in 1969 and 1970, 1973 to 1975, 1980, and 1981 and 1982; and some had chronicled another recession in 1977 and 1978—a growth recession. So there was a recession about every three or four years. There seemed to be a connection between the fluctuations in real GDP and inflation; each time inflation rose and reached a new peak it was followed by a recession, in boom-bust cycle fashion.

There was also a global connection. The Bretton Woods fixed exchange rate system had broken down in the early 1970s. Hence, central banks around the world were groping to find an alternative to the fixed exchange rate that had guided so many of them in the past. The lack of a workable framework for monetary policy, fluctuations in the velocity of money, and an incomplete understanding of the inflation-output trade-off created similar instabilities in inflation and output around the world. The standard deviation of real GDP growth in the other G7 countries was comparable to that in the United States.

12.1.1 The Objective Function and the Mission

It was also during the 1970s that economists—especially macroeconomists and monetary economists—began to focus explicitly on finding policies that could improve this economic performance. Given the dismal macroeconomic conditions at the time, this intense policy focus was not surprising. It was at this time that researchers began to use an explicit objective function in their research papers. The objective was simply to reduce the volatility of inflation and real GDP. Soon it was hard to find a paper in which the policy objective was not stated. It was usually written down algebraically in the form of a quadratic objective function

$$\lambda \mathrm{Var}(y) + (1-\lambda)\mathrm{Var}(\pi), \tag{1}$$

where y represented real GDP relative to normal levels, π represented the inflation rate, and Var represented the variance, or expected squared deviation of inflation or real GDP from a target. The weight λ described the relative importance of each variable and for most of the models there was a trade-off between these two variances. See, for example, Sargent and Wallace (1975), Kydland-Prescott (1977), and Taylor (1979). The purpose of the research was to find a policy to minimize the objective function, or more simply put, to increase output and price stability. The form of the policy to accomplish this was either a policy rule for the monetary instruments, or alternatively, a dynamic time path for these instruments.

Because the actual $\mathrm{Var}(\pi)$ and $\mathrm{Var}(y)$ were large at the time, the research seemed highly relevant and important. But it also seemed difficult, if not impossible, and hence the analogy with the dramatic opening of a mission impossible episode: "*Your mission, should you choose to accept it, is to reduce inflation and output volatility around the world.*" The "you" in this analogy—the Impossible Mission Force (IMF)—was the community of researchers and policy makers interested in monetary policy and theory—monetary economists both inside and outside central banks. Focused on the mission, they went about their research, bringing a vast array of new ideas to bear on the problem. They introduced rational expectations into the macro models, devised new theories of price and wage rigidities, estimated parameters with new econometric techniques, solved more and more complex models, and optimized with stochastic control theory and dynamic programming. Many of the new research ideas—including the application of rational expectations, the Lucas (1976) critique, and the time inconsistency problem—led to a greater focus on formulating the policy decisions as a policy rule rather than as a onetime path for the instruments.

Looking back, the huge amount of research output was amazing. But much more amazing was that the mission was actually accomplished. The variance of inflation and the variance of real GDP did come down, and by a very large amount. Compared to the recession-prone economy of the past, the United States went into a period where recessions occurred only once every nine or ten years on average, far less frequent than once every three or four years. Only two recessions occurred in the twenty-five years between the end of the 1981 to 1982 recession in the United States and 2007, and these two recessions have been very short and mild by historical comparison. The standard deviation of real GDP growth was cut in half to 1.5 percent. Though this improvement began in the United States in the early 1980s, it was not until the 1990s that people began to document and study the decline in volatility of real GDP, a phenomenon that is now called the Great Moderation or the Long Boom. The improvement did not only occur in the United States. Similar improvements were seen in countries around the world. The G7 countries as a whole, for example, also cut the standard deviation of real GDP in half.

There is a debate about the reasons for the improvements. I have argued (Taylor 1998) that they were caused mainly by changes in monetary policy, implying that the mission was accomplished through more than luck alone. There is also a debate about whether the research influenced the changes in monetary policy—about whether these ideas had actual consequences. Although causality and influences are complex and difficult to prove, there is certainly a close relationship in time between the monetary research, the monetary policy, and the improvement in economic stability. This close intertemporal relationship has been nicely captured by Cecchetti et al. (2007). Figure 12.1 is drawn directly from the Cecchetti et al. paper. It takes the Taylor rule as representative of the type of policy recommendation that emerged from the research, and shows that the improvement in economic

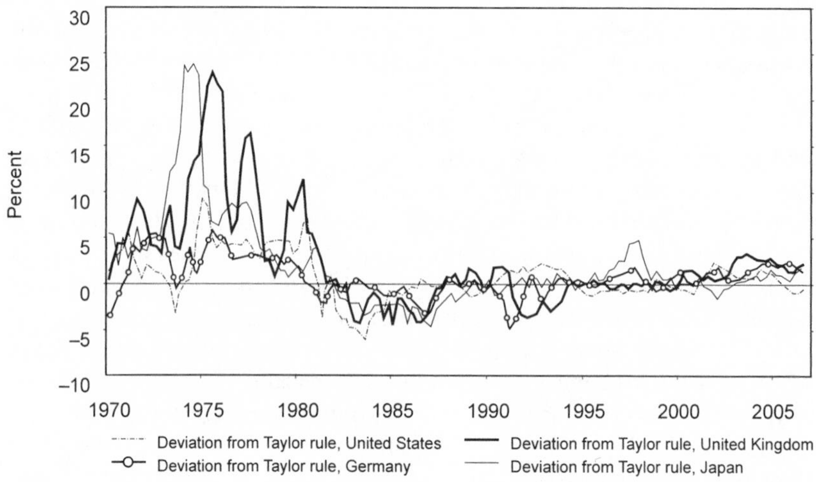

Fig. 12.1 Empirical evidence of monetary policy regime shifts from deviations from a policy rule

Source: Cecchetti et al. (2007).

performance occurred at about the same time that monetary policy began to follow that kind of recommendation. Again this does not prove causation, and indeed the timing is so close that two-way causation may be involved, although it is clear that the monetary policy rules were meant to be normative recommendations rather than simply descriptions of actual policy.

Figure 12.1 also illustrates the global nature of these changes: the close correlation and timing between the greater adherence of actual policy to recommended policy rules and the better economic performance can be seen in other countries, not only the United States. The connection between the ideas, the policies, and the results are a global phenomenon that spread quickly around the world—certainly another manifestation of globalization.

12.1.2 Out of Global Models Came Simple Rules

Although the rational expectations models that were first used to find optimal monetary policy rules in the 1970s were closed economy models, by the early 1980s monetary policy evaluation was moving rapidly in a global direction, and ultimately the recommended policy rules for the interest rate, like the one plotted in figure 12.1, emerged from new multicountry models with rational expectations. Examples include the modeling efforts at the Federal Reserve Board, the International Monetary Fund (IMF), and Stanford (Taylor 1993)—all participants in the Brookings project on monetary policy regimes (Bryant, Hooper, and Mann 1993). This evolution of models in an international direction was motivated by the policy mission. These *M:i:I* models were the first multicountry policy evaluation models with rational expectations, staggered price and wage setting, and a focus on evaluating monetary policy as a policy rule with a specific objective function. They also usually assumed perfect capital mobility, interdependence of capital and foreign exchange markets, expectations theories of the term structure of interest rates, uncovered interest rate parity, and direct price setting links between different countries. Designed so that they could address questions about exchange rate regimes—fixed versus flexible—the models focused on finding monetary policy rules to minimize objective functions like (1) for many countries.

12.1.3 Zero Response to the Exchange Rate

The exchange rate played a significant role in these models. Its expected rate of change affected relative rates of return from holding one currency versus another, as capital could move around the globe to obtain the best return. Its level affected the relative price of goods in different countries and thus affected exports and imports. Its past rate of change affected inflation through the pass-through mechanism.

With such a significant role for the exchange rate in the models, it was surprising to everyone that they called for monetary policy rules in which the interest rate settings by the central bank should not react directly to the exchange rate. Rather, optimal policy decisions should respond primarily to inflation and real GDP. More technically, to minimize the objective function, the central bank's policy rule for the interest rate rule should include inflation (as a deviation from the target rate of inflation) and real GDP (relative to potential GDP), but not the level or rate of change in the exchange rate. To be sure, more recent work on small open economy models (e.g., Ball 1999) shows that reacting to the exchange rate can improve economic performance, but the gains are small and do not hold up across all models. Nevertheless, as I describe in my following discussion of Mission Impossible III, there is now a generation of *M:i:III* multicountry rational expectations models with staggered price setting. These models might yield different policy results. However, since the *M:i:I* models assumed perfect capital mobility, it is hard to see why more globalization of financial markets alone would change the results.

There are two explanations for the minimal role for the exchange rate (Taylor 2001). First, exchange rates are volatile compared with real GDP and inflation, so reacting to them could cause the interest rate to be too volatile, which would have harmful effects on the economy. Second, responding to inflation automatically provides a response to the exchange rate. A depreciation of the exchange rate, to some degree, passes through to inflation. Thus, raising the interest rate as inflation rises is in part a response to a depreciation of the exchange rate.

12.1.4 Not to Worry about Coordination in the Design of Policy Rules

Given that the international monetary models had strong links between different countries, it was natural to ask whether a central bank in one country should react directly to events in another country. For example, a recession abroad will tend to lower inflation at home through the impact of import prices and other channels; thus, an optimal response to a foreign recession might be to lower the interest rate to keep the inflation rate on target. The formal way to address this question is to consider the possibility of coordinating the *design* of monetary policy rules across countries (Taylor 1985). Using game theory terminology, the Cournot-Nash solution represents the noncooperative case; it occurs when policymakers in one country take as given policy reactions in the other countries—as if the Fed staff takes the policy rules of other central banks as given when it does alternative policy simulations—and that the Fed reacts optimally given those foreign policy rules. The Cournot-Nash solution assumes that other central banks do the same thing, and that there is an equilibrium where the rule that every central bank takes as given for other central banks is actually optimal for those other central banks. In contrast, the coordinated or cooperative solution is where all central banks jointly maximize a global objective function that incorporates objective functions like (1) for all countries.

The results of the research were that the cooperative solution entailed a smaller response of the interest rate to an inflation rate increase than the Cournot-Nash solution. When a central bank raises its interest rate in response to an increase in inflation rate at home, the exchange rate tends to appreciate in that country and to depreciate in the other countries. The depreciation abroad tends to be inflationary abroad and requires that the central banks in the other countries tighten. It is also optimal to react to inflation developments in other countries, but the response is different in the cooperative versus the noncooperative case. In the cooperative case, the interest rate is cut when inflation rises in the other countries; this provides an appreciation of the currency in the other country and mitigates the inflation rise abroad and the output effects at home. However, according to the estimated models the effects were very small quantitatively, and as a practical matter the policy recommendations could ignore these international effects (Carlozzi and Taylor 1985).

12.2 Mission Impossible II

For our second example we go back to another period of dismal economic performance: the period of emerging market crises in the 1990s, or more precisely from 1994 to 2002. Table 12.1 lists the large number of crises that occurred around the world during this period—starting with the Mexican crisis in 1994 and the associated Tequilla contagion, continuing onto the Asian crisis and its contagion, the Russian crisis and its contagion, and ending with Uruguay in 2002. Guillermo Calvo (2005) aptly characterized the crises during this period in his Graham Lecture at Princeton University, saying, “Their frequency and global spread set them apart from anything else that we have seen—at least since World War II." The frequency and spread was so great and unusual that the period is better described as one "eight-year financial crisis" rather than eight years of financial crises.

Thousands of research papers have been written about this crisis period, many with the goal of better understanding and ultimately bringing an end to the crisis period. Hence, again we have the analogy with the dramatic opening of a mission impossible episode: "*Your mission, should you choose to accept it, is to reduce the frequency and global spread of financial crises.*" The "you" in Mission Impossible II is the international community of monetary and finance experts both inside and outside of governments and central banks, with the IMF and its staff playing a much bigger role than in Mission Impossible I. Examples include the participants in the NBER project on crises in emerging markets under the direction of Jeffrey Frankel, Sebastian Edwards, and Michael Dooley; this project alone resulted in thirteen conferences and eight books during the crisis period (see www.nber.org/crisis/).

12.2.1 The End of the Eight-Year Crisis

Remarkably, and similarly with Mission Impossible I, this impossible mission also seems to have become a mission accomplished. As table 12.1 shows, we have not had a financial crisis or contagion of the kind we experienced regularly during the crisis period anywhere on the globe since 2002. And while we will certainly have financial crises in the future, the eight-year crisis period has come to an end. Figure 12.2 plots the spread between the interest rates on sovereign debt in emerging market countries and interest rates on U.S. Treasuries. It shows how much risk levels have declined since the crisis period; even allowing for some overshooting there has been a dramatic change.

The debate about why this crisis period ended has just begun, and only a few papers have been written about it, is in contrast to the debate about what caused the Great Moderation, which has been going on for a decade. In my view, changes in economic policy, motivated in part by new economic ideas, played a big role in ending the crisis period; there were changes both in individual policies in the emerging market countries and in international monetary policy conducted by the International Monetary Fund and its major shareholders. Because comparatively little has been written to explain the improved performance since 2002—it is only the five-year anniversary—it is more difficult to trace causality than in the case of Mission Impossible I, though the correlation and the timing between the ideas, the policies, and the results are equally clear.

One of the most valuable recommendations that came out of the research on financial crises is that individual emerging market countries could take steps to prevent or at least significantly reduce the likelihood of crises. Models of financial crises developed in the 1990s and the actual experiences of policymakers with crises in the 1990s showed that currency

Table 12.1 Eight years of crises or one eight-year crisis?

Tequila effect
Mexico: 1994–1995
Argentina: 1995–1996
Asian crisis contagion
Thailand 1997–1998
Indonesia 1997–1998
Malaysia 1997–1998
Korea 1997–1998
Russian contagion
Russia: 1998
Brazil: 1998–2002
Romania: 1998–1999
Ecuador: 1998–1999
Argentina: 1999–2001
Turkey: 2000–2001
Uruguay: 2002
No major crises or contagion: 2002–present

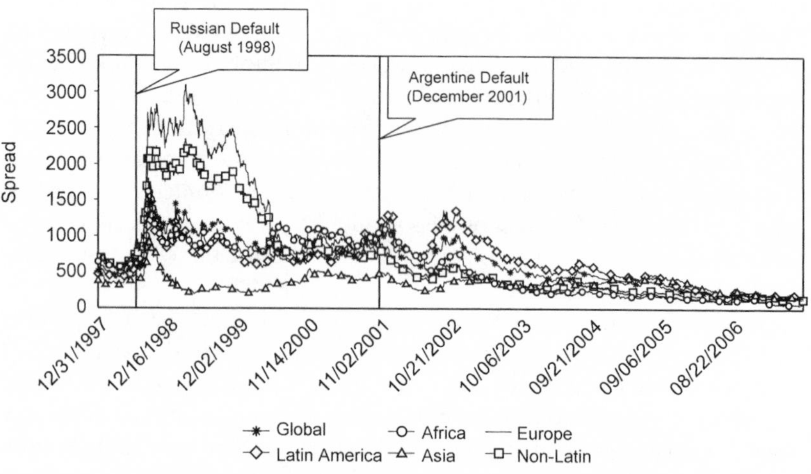

Fig. 12.2 Emerging Markets Bond Index (EMBI) 1 spread by region

mismatches—including large stocks of debt denominated in foreign currencies—could convert a currency depreciation into a major debt crisis (Goldstein and Turner 2004). They also showed that overly expansionary monetary policies under a fixed exchange rate could lead to a sudden and sharp depreciation, once investors realized that reserves would be insufficient to maintain the increasingly overvalued exchange rate.

The policy implications of this research were clear: avoid currency mismatches, get inflation down and keep it down, adopt a more flexible exchange rate policy, keep the debt to GDP ratio sustainable, and accumulate more foreign reserves. Many emerging market countries have learned such lessons and have moved toward these sensible policies. Certainly reserves are higher and inflation is lower than during the eight-year crisis period. And, just as predicted by the theory and hoped by the theorists, the number of crises has declined.

In addition the contagion of the crises has declined sharply, which has itself reduced the likelihood of crises. To see this, compare the global contagion that occurred following the Russian financial crisis in 1998 with the complete absence of contagion following the Argentine crisis just three years later in 2001 (Taylor 2007a, chapter 3). More recently, flare ups in Thailand or Turkey seemed to have little impact abroad, unlike the 1990s. I believe that policy changes in the operation of the international financial system have been largely responsible for this decline in contagion, and that these changes were also motivated by theory.

12.2.2 Predictability and the Exceptional Access Framework of the IMF

The most important international monetary policy lesson learned from the crisis period was the need for the IMF to change the way it responds to financial crises—most importantly, to be more deliberative and "predictable" about when it would exceed normal lending limits and provide large-scale assistance. In my view, this lack of predictability was a factor in the contagion of crises. According to most economics theories of contagion, in which uninformed traders tend to follow informed traders, surprise changes in policy are much more likely to cause contagion than predicted or anticipated changes in policy. Of course, the idea that anticipated policy changes have a smaller impact than unanticipated changes goes back to the early days of rational expectations modeling.

The lack of predictability was most evident in the case of Russia, where the IMF increased support in July 1998 and then one month later (in August 1998) indicated that it would remove support. This surprise was a reason for the global contagion at the time. There was also a lack of predictability of IMF responses in other crises. The Asian countries still feel that the IMF was not as responsive to their crises as it was in the case of Mexico. The initial refusal to provide additional funds to Uruguay in 2002 which, if not reversed, would have severely disrupted the payments system was another example (Taylor 2007b). This assessment is not meant to be critical of individual people at the IMF. Indeed, the lack of predictability was due to a lack of a clear framework about how the IMF should operate in such situations; it reflected considerable disagreement among the shareholders about the role of the IMF.

Fortunately, the shareholders of the IMF have come into much closer agreement on this issue, and they did so at about the same time the crisis period ended. They asked that the IMF introduce a more predictable decision framework into its operations, and the IMF has done so. Called the *exceptional access framework* (EAF), it was put in place at the IMF in early 2003. The EAF represents a significant change in policy for the IMF, and it reflected a change in position by the G7 countries, and in particular by the United States. In an action plan in April 2002 the G7 said "we are prepared to limit official sector lending to normal access levels except when circumstances justify an exception. . . . Limiting official sector lending and developing private sector lending are essential parts of our Action Plan." The EAF stated exactly what the exceptions were. It lists a set of principles or rules that determine whether IMF support will be provided. Its aim, again in the words of the G7, was "to increase predictability and reduce uncertainty about official policy actions in the emerging markets."

12.2.3 Time Inconsistency and More Predictable Restructurings of Sovereign Debt

One of the barriers to adopting the EAF was the lack of a reliable framework for countries to engage with their private sector creditors if and when sovereign debt had to be restructured. Without such a framework it would be very difficult for the IMF to adhere to any limits or rules. In typical time inconsistency fashion, the IMF and their shareholders could say they were adopting limits, but then, when the crisis occurred, would be expected to abandon those limits. To deal with this time inconsistency problem, a new mechanism was proposed for the bond contracts. This mechanism—called collective action clauses (CACs)—allowed bond holders to agree with their sovereign debtors to restructure debt if need be. Hence, a feasible and understandable plan B would be available to countries, allowing the IMF to say no if the limits were exceeded.

After a year of intense discussions in the international community, Mexico issued bonds in New York with collective action clauses (CACs) for the first time in February 2003. Many other countries then followed. These clauses represent a great improvement in the process of restructuring debt. In fact, they go hand-in-hand with the EAF: the reason why the EAF was acceptable to IMF shareholders, management, and staff was that there was a procedure (the CACs) that countries could use to restructure their debt without large-scale borrowing from the IMF. In technical terms, the CACs solved the time inconsistency problem.

12.3 Mission Impossible III

The third example of globalization and monetary policy takes place in the present, and it flows naturally from the first two examples: *"Your mission, should you choose to accept it, is to prevent the forces of globalization from reversing the missions already accomplished."* The "you" for Mission Impossible III is again the international community of monetary experts inside and outside central banks, including, of course, those who presented papers at the conference (included in this volume) and many others doing research on the global dimensions of monetary policy: Fisher (2006); Helbling, Jaumotte, and Sommer (2006); Kohn (2006); and Rogoff (2006) are recent examples. In deciding whether or not to accept this mission, you might ask, "Do we really need a mission?" Well, why else do this research; why publish another NBER conference volume? Or you might question the mission: "Is this mission really ambitious enough? Shouldn't we try to do more with Mission I and II?" Well, it is hard to see how macroeconomic conditions around the world could get much better than they have been for the past two plus decades. Preventing them from deteriorating so that the world economy can grow smoothly is difficult enough. Indeed, it may be the most challenging of the three missions impossible I describe here.

12.3.1 Do Not Switch Regimes without a Very Good Reason

In some ways the chapters in this conference volume are already pursuing this mission by building and simulating multicountry rational expectations models to evaluate monetary policy rules. For example, the paper presented in this conference volume by Nicoletta Batini (chapter 5), finds that not responding to the exchange rate in the monetary policy rule is nearly optimal, similar to the research described in Mission Impossible I. Another example is the paper presented by Frank Smets (chapter 3, this volume), which investigated the gains from monetary policy coordination among countries; they find that these gains are small, much as the research I described under Mission Impossible I, though as Chris Sims argued in his comments on that paper, there is still a need to consider coordination in the design of interest rate rules.

There is an important difference in the papers used in Mission Impossible III compared with those in Mission Impossible I, however: the recent *M:i:III* models are based on a more thorough set of microfoundations and employ a welfare analysis based on individual utility rather than on the objective of reducing the fluctuations in real GDP and inflation (see Woodford 2003). Therefore, they may be better able to deal with sudden changes in the global economy for which we have little empirical experience.

Nevertheless, the results of very recent research suggest that the forces of globalization should not change the way monetary policy has operated in the United States and other countries during the past two decades. But is the world changing more rapidly than models? Are there changes that central banks should be on the lookout for as the globalization process continues?

12.3.2 Be on the Lookout for These Changes

How could the forces of globalization lead to a deterioration of monetary policy? One of the most notable structural changes in the global economy in recent years is the sharp reduction in exchange rate pass-through. Some have attributed this decline to globalization and the increased foreign competition; others see it as due to the greater focus on monetary policy on price stability (Taylor 2000). Whatever the reason, the reduction in exchange rate pass-through due to a more inflation-focused monetary policy has reduced further the need to coordinate policy in the game theory sense that I discussed previously. Hence, while the forces of globalization might suggest the need for more coordination, the reality could be just the opposite.

Another important change is the reduction in the slope of the short-run Phillips curve (Roberts 2006). Some have argued that this change has been due to globalization (Rogoff 2003) with greater competition reducing prices, though this is inconsistent with inflation being a monetary phenomenon, unless one can show that the greater competition affects monetary policy decisions. Another possibility is that the lower slope of the Phillips curve is due to a greater impact of inflation in other countries. If so, then the lower coefficient on output in the inflation equation would be offset by higher coefficients in other countries' inflation equations, but Ihrig et al. (2007) show that this is not the case. Another possibility is that direct linkages between wages in different countries have strengthened due to off-shoring, though there is still little evidence of an increased wage-to-wage connection. Another explanation is due to Roberts (2006), who argues that the slope has gotten flatter because monetary policy has become more responsive—the coefficients in the central bank's policy rule have increased. In other words, it is not changes in the global economy that have caused the Phillips curve to flatten, but rather successful monetary policy. If so, adjusting policy to be more accommodative to inflation—which might be called for if this were a structural change—would lead to a return to suboptimal performance.

Another example of how globalization can adversely affect monetary policy decisions may have already begun, though much more study is needed. When thinking about monetary policy in an international setting, it is often stated that central banks need to consider the interest rate set by other central banks. If there is concern about exchange rate fluctuations, then moving the interest rate too far or too rapidly away from prevailing international interest rates could cause the currency to appreciate or depreciate, something that the central bank might want to avoid. Many central bankers, even those with flexible exchange rate policies, watch the U.S. federal funds rate set by the Federal Reserve when making policy decisions. In principle, the Fed could also take foreign interest rates into account, especially interest rate decisions of large trading partners such as the eurozone or Japan.

Consider the case of a two-country model; it could apply to Europe and the United States. Suppose that interest rates at the Fed and the European Central Bank (ECB) are set according to the following policy rules:

$$(2) \qquad i = \alpha i^* + 1.5\pi + .5y$$

$$i^* = \alpha^* i + 1.5\pi^* + .5y^*,$$

where the asterisk represents the ECB and i is the short-term policy interest rate, π is the inflation rate, and y is the deviation of real GDP from trend growth. It is reasonable to assume that $0 \leq \alpha < 1$ and $0 \leq \alpha^* < 1$. Without the foreign interest rate terms ($\alpha = \alpha^* = 0$), these equations would be two Taylor rules, which for the sake of this argument we take as optimal. (Assuming that another rule is optimal will lead to similar results.) Solving these two equations for the interest rates results in:

$$(3) \qquad i = \frac{1}{1 - \alpha\alpha^*}[1.5\pi + .5y + \alpha(1.5\pi^* + .5y^*)],$$

with an analogous equation for Europe. In other words, the inflation and output response coefficients in the optimal rule are multiplied by one over one minus the product of the two interest rate response coefficients. For reasonably large responses to the foreign interest rate in both countries, the results could be a significant departure from what would otherwise be an optimal policy for each country. Unless it is offset by changes in other parameters, large foreign interest rate reactions could lead to a policy mistake.

How plausible is this kind of mistake? How large could it be? Some estimated values for the response coefficients are suggestive. For the eurozone, consider the sample from 2000.1 to 2006.4. For this period, I measured inflation as the four-quarter rate of change in the harmonized index of consumer prices and the real GDP gap as the deviation of log real GDP from its Hodrick-Prescott trend. I first computed the residual from a Taylor rule. I then regressed this residual on a constant and on the federal funds rate. The estimated coefficient on the federal funds rate is .21 and statistically significant with a standard error of .056. The plot of the actual and fitted values from this regression is shown in figure 12.3. A good part, but not all of the negative residual (where the ECB policy rate is below the rule) is "explained" by the federal funds rate being lower than normal. If one simply adds the federal funds rate to an estimated policy rule (with a constant term) in the eurozone during this period—rather than use the residuals from the Taylor rule—the estimated coefficient is .11.

For the United States, I also measured inflation as the four-quarter rate of change in the consumer price index and the real GDP gap as the deviation of log real GDP from its Hodrick-Prescott trend. Using the same procedure as before with the foreign interest rate given by a Special Drawing Rights (SDR)-weighted interest rate (excluding the United States and reweighting), the coefficient on the foreign interest rate is .93 with a standard error of 0.15. For the period from 2000.1 to 2006.3 the actual and fitted values from the regression estimated over that period are shown in figure 12.4. Again, a substantial part of the gap between the actual policy and the policy rule is "explained" by the foreign interest rate.

These strong foreign interest rate effects are not unusual, and are found

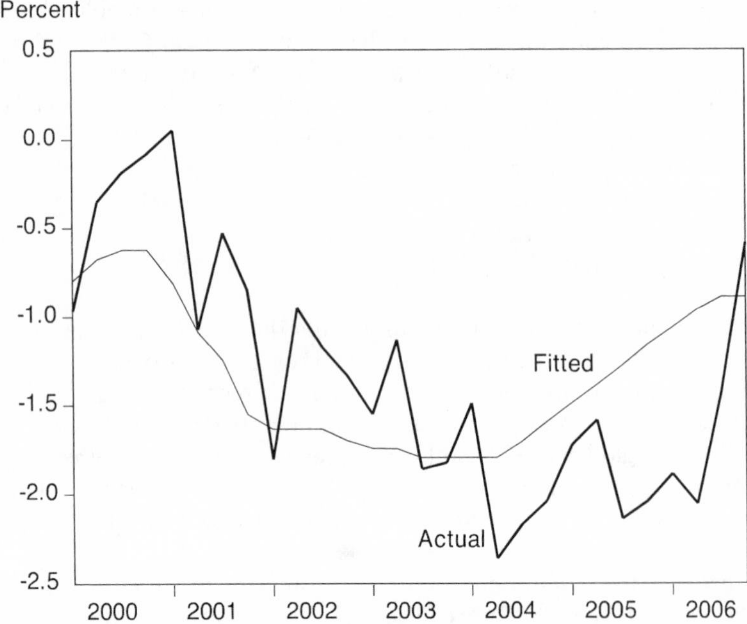

Fig. 12.3 Residual from eurozone policy rule (1.5, 0.5)

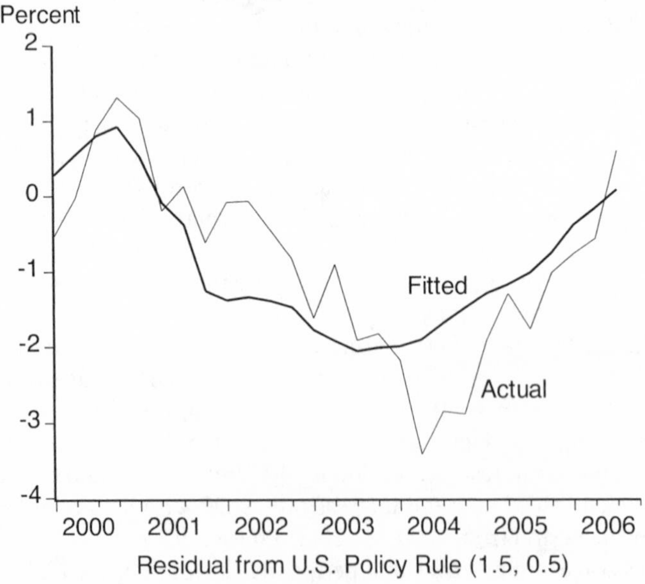

Fig. 12.4 Residual from U.S. policy rule (1.5, 0.5)

in estimates of policy rules at other central banks. They could, of course, be spurious. During this sample period the Federal Reserve apparently was worried about the risks of deflation and therefore may have cut the interest rate below what it otherwise would be.

Nevertheless, if Mission Impossible III is to be achieved, it is necessary for researchers inside and outside central banks to be on the lookout for the type of problem illustrated by this and my other examples.

References

Ball, L. 1999. Policy rules in open economies. In *Monetary policy rules,* ed. J. B. Taylor, 127–56. Chicago: University of Chicago Press.

Bryant, R. C., P. Hooper, and C. L. Mann. 1993. *Evaluating policy regimes: New research in empirical macroeconomics.* Washington, DC: Brookings Institution.

Calvo, G. 2005. Crises in emerging market countries: A global perspective. Graham Lecture, Princeton University.

Carlozzi, N., and J. B. Taylor. 1985. International capital mobility and the coordination of monetary rules. In *Exchange rate management under uncertainty,* ed. J. S. Bhandari, 186–211. Cambridge, MA: MIT Press.

Cecchetti, S. G., P. Hooper, B. C. Kasman, K. L. Schoenholtz, and M. W. Watson. 2007. Understanding the evolving inflation process. Paper presented at the U.S. Monetary Policy Forum 2007. 9 March, Washington, DC.

Fisher, R. 2006. Coping with globalization's impact on monetary policy. Remarks at the National Association for Business Economics Panel Discussion at the 2006 Allied Social Science Associations Meeting. 6 January, Boston, MA.

Goldstein, M., and P. Turner. 2004. *Controlling currency mismatches in emerging markets.* Washington, DC: Peterson Institute of International Economics.

Helbling, T., F. Jaumotte, and M. Sommer. 2006. How has globalization affected inflation. In *World economic outlook,* ed. International Monetary Fund, chapter 3. Washington, DC: IMF.

Ihrig, J. E., S. B. Kamin, D. Linder, and J. Marquez. 2007. Some simple tests of the globalization and inflation hypothesis. Board of Governors of the Federal Reserve System. International Finance Discussion Paper no. 891.

Kydland, F. E., and E. C. Prescott. 1977. Rules rather than discretion: The inconsistency of optimal policy. *The Journal of Political Economy* 85 (3): 473–92.

Kohn, D. L. 2006. The effects of globalization on inflation and their implications for monetary policy. Speech given at the Federal Reserve Bank of Boston's 51st Economic Conference. 16 June, Chatham, MA.

Lucas, R. E. 1976. Econometric policy evaluation: A critique. *Carnegie-Rochester Conference Series on Public Policy* 1: 19–46.

Roberts, J. 2006. Monetary policy and inflation dynamics. *International Journal of Central Banking* 2 (3): 193–230.

Rogoff, K. 2003. Globalization and global disinflation. Paper presented at Monetary Policy and Uncertainty: Adapting to a Changing Economy, a Symposium sponsored by the Federal Reserve Bank of Kansas City. 28–30 August, Jackson Hole, WY.

———. 2006. Impact of globalization on monetary policy. Paper presented at The New Economic Geography: Effects and Policy Implications, a Symposium sponsored by the Federal Reserve Bank of Kansas City. 24–26 August, Jackson Hole, WY.

Sargent, T. J., and N. Wallace. 1975. "Rational" expectations, the optimal monetary instrument, and the optimal money supply rule. *Journal of Political Economy* 83 (2): 241–54.

Taylor, J. B. 1979. Estimation and control of an econometric model with rational expectations. *Econometrica* 47 (5): 1267–86.

———. 1985. International coordination in the design of macroeconomic policy rules. *European Economic Review* 28 (1–2): 53–81.

———. 1993. *Macroeconomic policy in a world economy: From econometric design to practical operation.* New York: W. W. Norton.

———. 1998. Monetary policy and the long boom. *Review,* Federal Reserve Bank of St. Louis (November/December): 3–12.

———. 2000. Low inflation, pass-through, and the pricing power of firms. *European Economic Review* 44 (7): 1389–1408.

———. 2001. The role of exchange rates in monetary policy rules. *American Economic Review, Papers and Proceedings* 91 (2): 263–67.

———. 2007a. *Global financial warriors: The untold story of international finance in the post 9/11 world.* New York: W. W. Norton.

———. 2007b. The 2002 Uruguayan financial crisis: Five years later. Paper presented at the Conference on the 2002 Uruguayan Financial Crisis and its Aftermath. 29 May, Montevideo.

Woodford, M. 2003. *Interest and prices: Foundations of a theory of monetary policy.* Princeton, NJ: Princeton University Press.

Panel Remarks

Donald L. Kohn

The global economic landscape has been transformed in recent decades by the increasing international integration of markets for goods and services, factors of production, and finance. That process has been spurred by several developments, among the most notable being the opening of previously closed economies; the reduction of tariff and regulatory barriers in open economies; declines in the cost of transporting goods, services, and information; greater mobility of capital and labor; and the creation of new ways to package and trade risk on financial markets. The closer integration across national borders has increased the exposure of economies to changing conditions abroad—including economic shocks and changes in the pricing and trading of financial assets. In addition, relationships among interest rates, exchange rates, spending propensities, resource utilization, and price-level pressures have evolved as economies have opened up.

Nonetheless, I agree with the thrust of the chapters in this conference volume—if there is a surprise, it is in the apparently gradual and limited effects of those transformations on domestic economic activity and inflation. The basic structure and relationships of the domestic economy as they bear on monetary policymaking remain intact. Policymakers must judge the actual and expected relationships between aggregate demand and potential domestic supply and, using that judgment, assess the likely course of inflation; they are able then to adjust the short-term policy interest rate to keep prices stable and the economy operating near its potential. Although for-

Donald L. Kohn is Vice Chairman of the Board of Governors of the Federal Reserve System.

eign developments have come to play a larger role in these judgments, most key relationships have changed only gradually and in predictable directions. Given that exchange rates fluctuate freely, monetary policymakers continue to exercise control over key variables and should be held accountable for results in their respective economies.

However, despite the gradual evolution, global integration has had some potentially important implications for policymaking that we need to study further. As I have already noted, greater integration opens economies to shocks originating abroad or on global markets. As risks become more broadly shared in more-complete markets, and as investors and borrowers increasingly operate in many markets at the same time, the financial arena becomes an important channel for the international transmittal of economic developments. Also, the greater integration of global flows of goods and services means that a demand or supply shock in one country or region will affect prices and quantities elsewhere to a greater degree than previously. Vulnerabilities encompass not only standard supply and demand shocks but also changes in attitudes and expectations that can be transmitted rapidly to multiple markets and currencies. For example, although businesses have been operating increasingly integrated supply chains for at least a decade, many countries at the outset of the U.S. crash in dot-com equities saw themselves as largely isolated from it. But they quickly found themselves subject to changing attitudes in equity markets around the world and vulnerable to shifts in demand that moved through long, integrated supply chains in ways that might not have been obvious before the event.

Moreover, the conduct of monetary policy may come to face different, and in some respects greater, sources of uncertainty as economies continue to integrate. Exchange rates, for example, are more important for policy, but they seem to be among the less well understood asset prices, rarely responding as models predict they should to changes in actual or expected interest rates. For example, in 2001, the Federal Reserve reduced its policy rate aggressively—more so than other currency areas—to combat recession, but the dollar rose, blunting the effect of the easing. In addition, exchange rates appear to respond to financial capital flows—to demands for financial assets and financial claims on real assets—as well as to the current account and trade balance determinants so prominent in our models.

More generally, the behavior of many asset prices appears to have evolved as markets have become more complete and integrated. Interest rates and equity prices seem to be more correlated across markets. Some of this greater correlation may be related to the greater openness to common shocks. But some of the rise in correlation undoubtedly also reflects the increased ability of market participants to arbitrage across larger numbers of disparate markets.

Although the coefficients in our models are mostly shifting slowly, the pace and degree of evolution are not always easy to predict. Major developments—such as the extraordinary decreases in the cost of transmitting data and the opening up of Eastern Europe, China, and India—are reshaping trade flows and the domestic influence of international developments in ways that may surprise us.

Indeed, a global dimension seems to be part of some of the more puzzling macroeconomic developments over the past several years: the growth and persistence of the U.S. current account deficit; the restraint on labor compensation and increase in business profits in so many locations; the damped global demand from businesses for capital goods despite high profitability; and the long period of low long-term interest rates, damped volatility, and low risk spreads in most financial markets. Many of these developments occurred simultaneously in a number of regions of the world and were unexpected or difficult to explain using purely domestic factors. Many involved cross-border flows of goods, services, labor, physical investment, and financial capital in ways that probably would not have been feasible ten or twenty years ago.

But as I suggested at the outset, these puzzling or unprecedented elements of globalization have not revolutionized the conduct of monetary policy. The changes have mostly been gradual, with modestly evolving effects on the needed policy settings. And none of these developments mean that monetary policymakers cannot still be held accountable for the stability of prices and output in their local economies. But as the puzzles suggest, we do need to recognize that the pace of global integration has picked up and that our understanding of its implications is far from complete. As policymakers and as economists, we need to keep working on enhancing our knowledge and our abilities to integrate shifting international influences into the conduct of monetary policy.

Rakesh Mohan

Introduction

In these panel remarks I will try and present the key dilemmas we are facing in India, but that I believe almost all the developing countries in Asia are also facing. The result is that none of us are really following what seem to be well accepted principles of monetary policymaking. And yet we have collectively exhibited the highest growth in the world in the last twenty-five years and over, while also experiencing generally low inflation.

In recent years, the growing integration of goods and financial markets has transformed the environment in which monetary policy operates. While monetary policy has been successful in keeping inflation low in many countries since the early 1990s, some are arguing that its ability to do so in the

Rakesh Mohan was at the time of this conference Deputy Governor of the Reserve Bank of India.

future can be questioned. Domestic inflation may no longer be a function of domestic slack; rather, it is the global output gaps that perhaps matter for domestic inflation. On the one hand, the integration of China, India, and other EMEs has helped to enhance global supply, but on the other hand their impact on global demand for commodities is leading to inflationary pressures. Similarly, long-term interest rates are increasingly influenced by trends in the global savings-investment gap and, as has been discussed in this workshop, are bearing a weaker relationship with short-term policy rates. There is also some disconnect between current account balances and exchange rate movements on the one hand and between exchange rates and prices on the other hand. This raises some questions over the efficacy of the exchange rate channel. Furthermore, risk premia remain close to record lows, even as global imbalances and the threat of disorderly adjustment persist. Finally, despite the glut of global liquidity, consumer price inflation remains relatively benign, notwithstanding some hardening over the past year. The question that arises is whether the glut will eventually lead to higher goods and services inflation or to that in asset prices. Indeed, interestingly the price and output stability witnessed in major economies in the last two decades has not been accompanied by stability in asset prices and exchange rates. These monetary policy puzzles raise a number of issues on the conduct of monetary policy in open economies: the conclusion of this conference is perhaps that these are really not puzzles—at least in Europe and the United States (Mohan 2005).

Concerns and Dilemmas

Against this backdrop let me set out the concerns and dilemmas facing authorities in the emerging market economies (EMEs), particularly in Asia, in the conduct of monetary policy in a globalized world.

In view of the rising trade openness, economies are more vulnerable to external demand and exchange rate shocks. This can necessitate significant changes in trade and other current account flows in a short span of time, as was reflected in the aftermath of the Asian financial crisis when a number of economies in this region had to make substantial adjustments in their current accounts. Central banks are required to take into cognizance such eventualities in the conduct of monetary policy.

Currently, the more serious challenge to the conduct of monetary policy, however, emerges from capital flows in view of significantly higher volatility in such flows as well as the fact that capital flows in gross terms are much higher than those in net terms. Swings in capital flows can have a significant impact on exchange rates, domestic monetary and liquidity conditions, and overall macroeconomic and financial stability.

Global capital flows reflect not only the domestic economy's growth prospects but also reflect the relative interest rate differentials. Reflecting the fairly low interest rates in major advanced economies, the search for yield has led to a large volume of capital inflows to emerging economies, vastly in excess of current account deficits, and, in many cases, such capital flows are in addition to continuing surpluses on current accounts. In fact, according to the World Bank's *Global Development Finance 2007,* reserve accretion of all EMEs put together is roughly equal to total net private flows to them. Large capital flows can render domestic currencies overvalued and can get intermediated to speculative activities such as real estate/stock markets. In their efforts to maintain external competitiveness and financial stability, the central banks in EMEs have absorbed the forex surpluses. Further, in view of the price stability objective, these central banks have sterilized the monetary impact of their foreign exchange intervention operations through open market operations (OMOs), issuances of central banks bills, treasury bills and bonds, further liberalization and, more recently, greater flexibility in exchange rates. Given the large volume of capital flows, central banks in the past year have also been forced to resort to unorthodox methods, such as raising reserve requirements of banks in order to manage the liquidity situation. And, in the case of Thailand, controls on inflows—including the use of unremunerated reserve requirement—have also been imposed.

Furthermore, external borrowings of many emerging market economies are usually denominated in foreign currency. Large devaluations not only lead to inflation but can also cause serious currency mismatches with adverse impact on balance sheets of borrowers (banks as well as corporates), as has been discussed. A financial accelerator mechanism can exacerbate these effects and threaten financial stability.

The experience of living with capital flows since the 1990s has fundamentally altered the context of development finance, while also bringing about a drastic revision in the manner in which monetary policy is conducted. The importance of capital flows in determining the exchange rate movements has increased considerably, rendering some of the earlier guideposts of monetary policy formulation possibly anachronistic. On a day-to-day basis, it is capital flows that influence the exchange rate and interest rate arithmetic of the financial markets. Instead of the real factors underlying trade competitiveness, it is expectations and reactions to news that drive capital flows and exchange rates, often out of alignment with fundamentals. Capital flows have been observed to cause overshooting of exchange rates as market participants act in concert while pricing information.

In the fiercely competitive trading environment where exporters seek to expand market shares aggressively by paring down margins, even a small change in exchange rates can develop into significant and persistent real effects. A key point is that for the majority of developing countries, which are labor-intensive exporters, exchange rate volatility can, therefore, have significant employment, output, and distributional consequences. Moreover, if large segments of economic agents lack adequate resilience to withstand volatility in currency and money markets, the option of exchange rate adjustments may not be available, partially or fully. Therefore, the central bank may need to carry out foreign exchange operations for stabilizing the market. On the other hand, in the case of advanced economies, the mature and well-developed financial markets can absorb the risks associated with large exchange rate fluctuations with negligible spillover on to real activity. Consequently, the central banks in such economies do not have to take care of these risks through their monetary policy operations.

The experience with capital flows has important lessons for the choice of the exchange rate regime. The advocacy for corner solutions is distinctly on the decline. The weight of experience seems to be tilting in favor of intermediate regimes with country-specific features, without targets for the level of the exchange rate, the conduct of exchange market interventions to ensure orderly rate movements, and a combination of interest rates and exchange rate interventions to fight extreme market turbulence. In general, emerging market economies have accumulated massive foreign exchange reserves as a circuit breaker for situations where unidirectional expectations become self-fulfilling. It is a combination of these strategies that will guide monetary authorities through the impossible trinity of a fixed exchange rate, open capital account, and an independent monetary policy.

For developing countries, considerations relating to maximizing output and employment weigh equally upon monetary authorities as price stability. Accordingly, it is difficult to design future monetary policy frameworks with only inflation as a single-minded objective. Thus, the operation of monetary policy has to take into account the risks that greater interest rate or exchange rate volatility entails for a wide range of participants in the economy. Both the fiscal and monetary authorities inevitably bear these risks. The choice of the exchange rate regimes in some developing countries, therefore, reveals a preference for flexible exchange rates along with interventions to ensure orderly market activity, but without targeting any level of the exchange rate. There is interest in maintaining adequate international reserves and a readiness to move interest rates flexibly in the event of disorderly market conditions.

Indian Specifics

Like other EMEs, the conduct of monetary policy is increasingly influenced by the evolving dynamics of capital flows. In this context, a brief discussion of a few relevant stylized facts of the Indian economy would be useful. First, real gross domestic product (GDP) growth has recorded strong growth since 2003–4, averaging 8.6 percent per annum over the four-year period ending 2006–7. This growth is significantly higher than world economic growth. This would suggest that equilibrium real interest rates for a country like India would be higher than world interest rates. Second, inflation in India has averaged between 4.5 and 5.0 percent, which remains higher than that in major advanced economies. These growth and inflation differentials taken together would lead to nominal interest rates being relatively higher in a growing economy such as India. Moreover, the growth in India has been achieved in an environment of macroeconomic stability. Thus, both push factors and pull factors have made India as an attractive destination of global capital flows. Third, since the early 1990s, India has witnessed a progressive opening up of the economy to external flows. There has been a sustained increase in capital flows and capital flows have remained significantly in excess of the current financing need. Fourth, it is pertinent to note that, unlike many other economies running surpluses on their current account, India has been running a deficit (except for three years) on the current account. The current account deficit has averaged close to 1 percent of GDP since the early 1990s and this would suggest that the exchange rate in India has been fairly valued.

Fifth, the challenges for monetary policy with an open capital account get exacerbated if domestic inflation firms up. In the event of demand pressures building up, increases in interest rates might be advocated to sustain growth in a noninflationary manner, but such action increases the possibility of further capital inflows if a significant part of these flows is interest sensitive and explicit policies to moderate flows are not undertaken. These flows could potentially reduce the efficacy of monetary policy tightening by enhancing liquidity. Such dilemmas complicate the conduct of monetary policy in India if inflation exceeds the indicative projections. During 2006–7, as domestic interest rates hardened on the back of withdrawal of monetary accommodation, external foreign currency borrowings by domestic corporates witnessed a significant jump in India, leading to even higher flows. In case there are no restrictions on overseas borrowings by banks and financial institutions, such entities could also annul the efforts of domestic monetary tightening.

In this environment, leaving the exchange rate to be fully determined by capital flows can, as noted earlier, pose serious setbacks to exports and, over time, external sector viability. Indeed, as the Asian financial crisis showed, real appreciation can lead to future vulnerability and avoidable volatility in the economy. Thus, like other central banks grappling with the impossible trinity, the Reserve Bank has been operating in an intermediate regime. The Indian rupee exhibits substantial two-way movements and the Reserve Bank intervenes in the foreign exchange market to smoothen out volatility. A multipronged approach has been followed to manage the external flows to ensure domestic economic and financial stability. The key features of the package of measures include: liberalization of policies in regard to capital account outflows; encouraging prepayment of external borrowings; alignment of interest rates on nonresident deposits; and greater flexibility in the exchange rate. These measures have been supplemented with sterilization operations to minimize the inflationary impact of the flows and to ensure domestic financial stability. Operations involving sterilization are undertaken in the context of a policy response, which has to be viewed as a package encompassing exchange rate policy, level of reserves, interest rate policy along with considerations related to domestic liquidity, financial market conditions as a whole, and degree of openness of the economy.

Sustained and large capital flows and their sterilization through open market operations, however, led to a dwindling stock of government securities with the Reserve Bank by early 2004. Given the provisions of the Reserve Bank Act, a market stabilization scheme (MSS) was introduced in 2004 to provide the Reserve Bank greater flexibility in its monetary and liquidity operations.[1] As noted earlier, large capital flows to EMEs, including India, in the past few years are partly the reflection of extended monetary accommodation by G-3 central banks. In case monetary conditions were to tighten further in the major advanced economies, the flow of capital to the EMEs could reduce vastly. Similarly, the possibility of increased risk aversion by foreign investors cannot be ruled out and this could be associated with large and sudden withdrawal from the EMEs as was evidenced in May and June 2006 and March 2007. Thus, authorities in the EMEs should be fully prepared for large and unanticipated withdrawal of funds by foreign investors. In such a scenario, a scheme like the MSS—absorption at times of heavy inflows and unwinding of balances at times of reversal/lower inflows—can smooth domestic liquidity conditions. Thus, the MSS, as operated in India, can be viewed as a truly market-based stabilization scheme.

In recognition of the cumulative and lagged effects of monetary policy, the preemptive monetary tightening measures that were initiated in September 2004 continued during 2006–7 and 2007–8. Between September 2004 and June 2008, the repo rate and the reverse repo rate were increased by 175 and 150 basis points, respectively, while the cash reserve ratio (CRR) has been raised by 200 basis points. In view of the need to maintain asset quality against the backdrop of strong and sustained growth in

1. In early 2004, it was recognized that the finite stock of government paper with the Reserve Bank could potentially circumscribe the scope of outright open market operations for sterilizing capital flows. The Reserve Bank cannot issue its own paper under the extant provisions of the Reserve Bank of India Act, 1934, and such an option has generally not been favored in India. Central bank bills/bonds would impose the entire cost of sterilization on the Reserve Bank's balance sheet. Besides, the existence of two sets of risk-free paper—gilts and central bank securities—tends to fragment the market. Accordingly, the liquidity adjustment facility (LAF), which operates through repos of government paper to create a corridor for overnight interest rates and thereby functions as an instrument of day-to-day liquidity management, had to be relied upon for sterilization as well. Under these circumstances, the Market Stabilization Scheme (MSS) was introduced in April 2004 to provide the monetary authority an additional instrument of liquidity management and sterilization. Under the MSS, the government issues Treasury bills and dated government securities to mop up domestic liquidity and parks the proceeds in a ring-fenced deposit account with the Reserve Bank of India (RBI). The funds can be appropriated only for redemption and/or buyback of paper issued under the MSS. The ceiling for the MSS is decided in consultation with the Government; on October 4, 2007, the ceiling was raised to Rs. 2,000 billion.

credit, monetary measures were reinforced by tightening of provisioning norms and risk weights. In the context of large capital inflows and implications for liquidity and monetary management, the interest rate ceilings on nonresident deposits have been reduced by 75 to 100 basis points since January 2007.

Concluding Observations

This is a brief snapshot of some of the issues facing Asian EMEs, and India in particular. In general, our monetary policies are not following conventional rules, but it would certainly be true to say that we do all emphasize low inflation and price stability, but in the context of financial stability as an equally important objective.

Globalization has clearly affected what we do. Globalization has transformed the environment in which monetary policy operates, leading to progressive loss of discretion in the conduct of monetary policy. Much of the discussion in this conference has, however, concluded that for the United States and European Union, globalization has little relevance for monetary policy making. This reminds me of a comment that T.N. Srinivasan made at a presentation I made in 1977 in my PhD thesis on a dynamic computable general equilibrium (CGE) model of India. I had concluded that my model exhibited the same quality of robustness that the Indian economy did: that nothing much happened to the model despite significant shocks to the system. His comment was: "Your model is so robust that you can throw it off the Empire State Building and nothing will happen to it!" Perhaps looking for the effects of globalization on U.S. monetary policy has the same problem. As the largest economy in the world whose currency is the key reserve currency, should we expect the same effects of globalization on monetary policy as we would on smaller economies?

With the opening up of the economies and greater integration, monetary authorities in EMEs are no longer concerned with mere price stability. Financial stability has emerged as a key objective of monetary policy, especially in emerging economies. The adverse implications of excess volatility leading to financial crises are more severe for low-income countries. They can ill afford the downside risks inherent in a financial sector collapse. Central banks need to take into account, among others, developments in the global economic situation, the international inflationary situation, interest rate situation, exchange rate movements, and capital movements while formulating monetary policy. At the same time, central banks in the EMEs would need to take initiatives to further widen and deepen their financial markets that can increasingly shift the burden of risk mitigation and costs from the authorities to the markets.

Several countries in Asia have followed a relatively flexible exchange rate policy to ensure smooth adjustment along with corrections in the world economy. Such flexibility has served these countries well. However, the world has to guard against any new risks arising out of any large corrections in the exchange rates of the world's major currencies accompanied by rising inflation and interest rates. First, the protectionist tendencies need to be curbed in keeping with the multilateral spirit of trade negotiations. Second, we need to work collectively toward developing a sound international financial architecture, the lack of which, it may be recalled, has led to excessive caution on the part of developing countries in building large reserves. Third, given the need for financial stability alongside monetary stability, central banks need to be cautious before joining the recent trend of separating the monetary and supervisory authorities, particularly in view of the muted responses to the pricing channels of monetary policy.

José Viñals

I will focus my comments on the challenges posed by globalization to central banks of advanced countries and emerging markets in their pursuit of both *price stability* and *financial stability.*

Starting with the facts, the recent wave of globalization we have experienced over the past ten to fifteen years has coincided with a very favorable macroeconomic performance. Inflation has come down and been kept low, global growth has been high, and financial markets have performed quite well. Consequently, prima facie there is nothing that should lead us into thinking that globalization has made the life of central bankers more difficult. If anything, one might suspect that it may have on the whole made it easier.

Nevertheless, we should delve further into the issue to ascertain whether this impression is in fact correct. In this regard, I think it is useful to take into account the impact of globalization through both the economic (e.g., trade, competition) and financial (e.g., capital flows) channels on both advanced economies and emerging markets.

As concerns the *economic channel,* the available evidence suggests that globalization has provided a favorable backdrop for the conduct of monetary policies aimed at achieving or maintaining price stability. In advanced economies globalization has led both to lower low-skilled manufacturing import prices and to higher commodity import prices. These two opposing forces have, on balance, exerted a modest disinflationary effect in advanced countries in recent years. Although it is clear that such changes in relative prices cannot lead to any permanent consequences for the rate of inflation over the medium term (as this is chosen by the central bank), they have reduced measured inflation on a temporary basis. Moreover, as such changes in relative prices have been over a prolonged period, the downward

José Viñals is Deputy Governor of the Banco de España.

impact on the actual rate of inflation has also been prolonged, even if not permanent.

Interestingly, the consequences for emerging markets have been quite different, particularly in those economies that are net exporters of low-skilled manufactures and/or commodities. As is well known, in recent years many of these countries have run large trade surpluses and accumulated foreign reserves that have contributed to domestic monetary expansions and resulted in internal inflation pressures. However, in my opinion, this has not been so much because of globalization but because of the pegged exchange rate or managed floating policies pursued in many cases. Indeed, floating exchange rate policies would have avoided the foreign reserves accumulation processes that have been at the origin of inflation pressures.

The next question to ask is whether economic globalization has had more permanent effects on inflation by enhancing domestic wage and price discipline through intensified external competition and offshoring. Indeed, there is some evidence that suggests that estimated short-term Phillips curves are now flatter in a number of countries. While this evidence is not uncontroversial, it is nevertheless useful to think about what this would imply were it to be confirmed by subsequent analyses.

The answer, as we might suspect, very much depends on why there is such a flattening. Those who strongly believe that globalization is the main factor behind it will conclude that this allows for more relaxed monetary policies in the presence of a more favorable short-term trade-off. On the contrary, those who believe that it is not so much globalization but rather the anti-inflationary credibility of central banks that is responsible for the flattening of the curve through better anchoring of inflationary expectations, draw very different implications. Specifically, they point to the dangers of unwarrantedly relaxing monetary policies, as this would deanchor inflationary expectations and lead to an upward shift in the now flatter curve with the resulting increases in inflation. As you may imagine, being a central banker I tend to side with the second view and thus believe that preemptive monetary policy is as important as ever even if the short-term trade-off appears to be more favorable nowadays.

As concerns the impact of globalization through the *financial channel,* I think that the consequences for central banks are more important. On the one hand, the conduct of domestic monetary policy is becoming more complex insofar as long-term real interest rates are increasingly being determined at the global level and, particularly, because in recent years it has become more difficult to understand why long-term real interest rates are so low worldwide. In practice, this "conundrum" leaves central bankers with higher margins of uncertainty regarding the level of the "neutral" equilibrium real rate against which to gauge the stance of monetary policy.

On the other hand, financial globalization poses considerable challenges for central banks as concerns the preservation of financial stability. In recent years, financial globalization has led to a new global financial landscape as a result of several developments: (a) the trend toward bank disintermediation, exemplified by the surge of new players such as hedge funds, private equity firms, and special investment vehicles; (b) the appearance of new, increasingly complex and hard-to-value structured products; and (c) the rapid integration of national financial markets in a global environment of increasingly unconstrained capital flows.

While it is true that the new financial landscape contributes to the completion of financial markets and allows for a better dispersion of risks, it is also the case that an increasing part of the global financial system is operating through unregulated entities, where transparency is rather weak. As a result, it is now more difficult for the authorities in charge of financial stability to know how much risk there is in the financial system, who is ultimately bearing it, and whether there are pockets of vulnerability where risk is being concentrated.

Admittedly, the new financial system has shown significant resilience in recent years when faced with a number of adverse shocks (e.g., the bursting of the dot-com bubble, September 11, corporate scandals, downgrading of General Motors and Ford bonds, Amaranth fall), which points to the value of risk diversification. However, doubts exist about whether the new system will prove so resilient when faced by larger shocks in the future, in particular given the pockets of vulnerability to which I referred.

All of these uncertainties linked to financial globalization pose considerable challenges for central banks in preserving financial stability. Moreover, they can complicate the task of monetary policy in preserving price stability insofar as there is a need to know how the new financial landscape affects the monetary transmission mechanism. These complexities are likely to increase over time.

In spite of the aforementioned uncertainties and challenges, there is no doubt that financial globalization has been a very beneficial development for the global economy and not just for advanced economies. Indeed, emerging markets have also greatly benefited from the freedom of capital flows, which has provided external discipline on central banks and increased the penalties—in the form of sudden stops and capital flow reversals—for not following low inflation policies. Moreover, financial globalization has also helped financial stability in these economies by providing a favorable backdrop for the development of domestic capital markets. As is known, in emerging markets the development of bond markets in local currency allows for the dedollarization of the economy and makes the domestic financial system more resilient.

To conclude, the process of globalization does not seem to have diminished the ability of central banks to run monetary policies that effectively pursue price stability. Nevertheless, it has to be acknowledged that interactions within the global economy have to be increasingly taken into account when setting policy. Moreover, going forward it is the financial dimension of globalization that is likely to be most challenging for central banks, both for the conduct monetary policy and particularly for the maintenance of financial stability. This is where I feel that more research is needed.

References

Mohan, R. 2005. Some apparent puzzles for contemporary monetary policy. Reserve Bank of India Bulletin, December.

World Bank. 2007. *Global development finance 2007: The globalization of corporate finance in developing countries.* Washington, DC: World Bank Publications.

Contributors

Malin Adolfson
Research Department
Sveriges Riksbank
SE-103 37 Stockholm, Sweden

Philippe Bacchetta
Department of Economics
Université de Lausanne
Extranef, 1015 Lausanne Switzerland

Nicoletta Batini
International Monetary Fund
Western Hemisphere Department
Washington, DC 20431

Olivier J. Blanchard
Department of Economics, E52-357
Massachusetts Institute of Technology
50 Memorial Drive
Cambridge, MA 02142-1347

Jean Boivin
HEC Montréal
3000, chemin de la Côte-Sainte-Catherine
Montréal, Québec
Canada H3T 2A7

Günter Coenen
European Central Bank
Kaiserstrasse 29
D-60311 Frankfurt am Main Germany

Giancarlo Corsetti
Economics Department
European University Institute
Villa San Paolo
Via della Piazzuola 43
50133 Florence, Italy

Luca Dedola
European Central Bank
66-68 Neue Mainzer St.
D-60311 Frankfurt Germany

Christopher Erceg
Division of International Finance
Board of Governors of the Federal Reserve
20th and C Streets NW
Washington, DC 20551

Andrea Ferrero
Macroeconomic and Monetary Studies Function
Federal Reserve Bank of New York
33 Liberty Street, 3rd floor
New York, NY 10045

Jordi Galí
Centre de Recerca en Economia Internacional (CREI)
Ramon Trias Fargas 25
08005 Barcelona Spain

Mark Gertler
Department of Economics
New York University
269 Mercer Street, 7th Floor
New York, NY 10003

Marc P. Giannoni
Columbia Business School
824 Uris Hall
3022 Broadway
New York, NY 10027-6902

Christopher Gust
Division of International Finance
Board of Governors of the Federal Reserve
20th Street and Constitution Avenue, NW
Washington, DC 20551

Donald L. Kohn
Board of Governors of the Federal Reserve
20th Street and Constitution Avenue, NW
Washington, DC 20551

Sylvain Leduc
Division of International Finance
Board of Governors of the Federal Reserve
20th and C Streets NW, Stop 43
Washington, DC 20551

Andrew Levin
Division of Monetary Affairs
Board of Governors of the Federal Reserve
20th Street and Constitution Avenue, NW
Washington, DC 20551

Paul Levine
Department of Economics
University of Surrey
Guildford, Surrey
GU2 7XH, England

Giovanni Lombardo
European Central Bank
Kaiserstrasse, 29
60311 Frankfurt am Main, Germany

David López-Salido
Division of Monetary Affairs
Board of Governors of the Federal Reserve
20th Street and Constitution Avenue, NW
Washington, DC 20551

Frederic S. Mishkin
Columbia Business School
3022 Broadway, Uris Hall 619
New York, NY 10027

Rakesh Mohan
Deputy Governor
Reserve Bank of India
Central Office
Mumbai—400 001 India

Tommaso Monacelli
Università Bocconi and Igier
Via Roentgen 1
20136 Milan Italy

Lucas Papademos
European Central Bank
Kaiserstrasse 29
D-60311 Frankfurt am Main Germany

Joseph Pearlman
Department of Economics, Finance, and International Business
London Metropolitan University
31 Jewry Street
London EC3N 2EY England

Paolo Pesenti
Federal Reserve Bank of New York
33 Liberty Street
New York, NY 10045

Lucrezia Reichlin
London Business School
Regent's Park
London NW1 4SA England

David Romer
Department of Economics
549 Evans Hall
University of California
Berkeley, CA 94720-3880

Julio J. Rotemberg
Graduate School of Business
Harvard University, Morgan Hall
Soldiers Field
Boston, MA 02163

Argia M. Sbordone
Macroeconomic and Monetary Studies Function
Federal Reserve Bank of New York
33 Liberty Street
New York, NY 10045

Christopher A. Sims
Department of Economics
Princeton University
104 Fisher Hall
Princeton, NJ 08544

Frank Smets
European Central Bank
Kaiserstrasse, 29
60311 Frankfurt am Main, Germany

Roland Straub
European Central Bank
Kaiserstrasse, 29
60311 Frankfurt am Main, Germany

Lars E. O. Svensson
Sveriges Riksbank
SE-103 37 Stockholm
Sweden

John B. Taylor
Herbert Hoover Memorial Building
Stanford University
Stanford, CA 94305-6010

Harald Uhlig
Department of Economics
University of Chicago
1126 East 59th Street
Chicago, IL 60637

José Viñals
Bank of Spain
C/Alcalá, 48
28014 Madrid Spain

Michael Woodford
Department of Economics
Columbia University
420 W. 118th Street
New York, NY 10027

Author Index

Subject Index